The Ford
Presidency

The Ford Presidency

A History

ANDREW DOWNER CRAIN

McFarland & Company, Inc., Publishers

Jefferson, North Carolina, and London

LIBRARY OF CONGRESS ONLINE CATALOG

Crain, Andrew Downer.
The Ford presidency : a history / Andrew Downer Crain.
p.   cm.
Includes bibliographical references and index.

ISBN 978-0-7864-4145-7
softcover : 50# alkaline paper ∞

1. Ford, Gerald R., 1913–2006.
2. United States — Politics and government —1974–1977.   I. Title.
E865.C73 2009   973.925092 — dc22   2008053223

British Library cataloguing data are available

On the cover: *upper* Ford reads a proclamation on September 8, 1974,
granting Richard Nixon "a full, free and absolute pardon" for all
"offenses against the United States" (AP Photo);
lower, left to right at work in the Oval Office January 27, 1976;
Gerald and Betty Ford with dog Liberty; Ford presents his
inflation-fighting program to Republican candidates in Indianapolis
on October 16, 1974 (photograph by David Hume Kennerly).
All courtesy Gerald R. Ford Presidential Library and Museum.

Manufactured in the United States of America

McFarland & Company, Inc., Publishers
Box 611, Jefferson, North Carolina 28640
www.mcfarlandpub.com

To my wife Laura,
who has been incredibly understanding as I spent
six years of our free time working on this book.
Thank you for your love and support.

Table of Contents

Preface   1

1. The Fall of Spiro Agnew   3
2. The Fall of Richard Nixon   17
3. Beginning   36
4. Pardon   55
5. Inflation, Public Enemy Number 1   72
6. Reform   82
7. Vladivostok   91
8. Recession, Public Enemy Number 1   103
9. CIA Scandal   115
10. Sinai II Agreement   131
11. The Fall of South Vietnam and Cambodia   146
12. Helsinki   169
13. Portugal and Spain   178
14. Cities in Crisis   186
15. Halloween Massacre and the End of SALT   194
16. Deregulation   202
17. Angola   210
18. China and East Timor   232
19. Primary Campaign   243
20. Kissinger For/Against Human Rights   264
21. General Election   270

Chapter Notes   283
Bibliography   319
Index   327

Preface

During the last six years, I have come to share the admiration that is readily apparent among Gerald Ford's former colleagues when they talk about him. They describe a man without pretense who set out to create a White House that was as open and forthright as he was. I have also come to agree with the historical consensus that Ford's honesty and decency helped restore public trust after Watergate. To explain why, I spend the first two chapters of this book chronicling the events that led to Ford taking office. It is a story that has been told before, but I think it is important to remember just how sordid Watergate was, in order to understand what Ford accomplished. As Ford's friend Melvin Laird told me, people need to understand that the country went through something.

Many of the issues that Gerald Ford faced still resonate today: how to respond to an exponential increase in oil prices; how to promote peace in the Middle East; whether to limit the activities of the CIA; how to restrict the influence of money in politics; and how to unify the nation after an unpopular war. But this book is not about how nothing has changed during the last thirty years. I try to avoid the trap of pointing to the similarities between past and current events as evidence that we have learned nothing from history and are doomed to repeat it.

Some things are different today because of the successes of the Ford administration. Peace in the Middle East continues to be elusive, but Israel is no longer subject to regular invasions by neighboring countries, thanks in large part to Henry Kissinger's shuttle diplomacy between Israel and Egypt. The Cold War is over, thanks in part to Ford's decision to sign the Helsinki Accords. These successes are not Ford's alone. They are examples of the continuity between administrations that is often overlooked in American history. The effort to mediate a peace agreement between Israel and Egypt began under Nixon and culminated during the Carter administration, while the fall of the Soviet Union was facilitated by forty years of consistent American foreign policy. In domestic affairs, the deregulation program begun by Ford led to some of the most significant accomplishments of the Carter administration.

Some things are different today because American leaders have learned from the mistakes made by Ford and his colleagues. Ford struggled to fight double-digit inflation, which at the time appeared to be the inevitable result of skyrocketing oil and food prices. But the country has weathered similar oil and food price shocks in recent years without experiencing overall inflation. To explain why, I diverge from most histories of the Ford administration and focus on monetary policy. The economic chapters of this book explain that Fed chairman Arthur Burns allowed the oil and food price shocks to divert his attention from the need to slow money growth to tame inflation, while his successors have avoided that mistake.

I cannot report that our leaders have learned the right lessons in all cases. After working in the most open White House in modern history, Richard Cheney and Donald Rumsfeld have not followed Ford's example. For Rumsfeld, it was never in his nature to emulate his former boss. He may have approved of Ford's openness, but Rumsfeld needed total control, and he chafed under the loose atmosphere in the Ford White House. Richard Cheney is a different matter, and the Cheney you will see in these pages is quite different from the picture we have of him today. By all reports he was friendly with the staff, candid with reporters, open to political opponents, and receptive to a wide variety of ideas. Either he has consciously decided to change the way he operates, or we are receiving a two-dimensional picture of him today. I suspect it is a little of both.

Cheney and Rumsfeld apparently learned the wrong lesson from the intelligence investigations of 1975. The CIA scandal that broke while Ford was in office should serve as a caution that, one way or another, the secrets of the CIA will see the light of day, and the nation will pay a price for violating basic principles of international law and decency. But Bush administration leaders have apparently concluded that the agency's powers were unacceptably weakened during the investigations, so they have gone out of the way to remove all restrictions on CIA activities. The result has been the rendition program and the use of coercive interrogation techniques, which have damaged the country's standing in the world and undermined the American effort in Iraq.

This preface is the only place you will read about current events in this book. Historians are not particularly good at commenting on current events — we are just as subject to political and ideological passions as anyone else — so I will let you draw your own parallels to today's news. Of course, current events shape my analysis, as do recent advances in scholarship. For example, in the chapter on Angola, I have incorporated the extraordinary research of Piero Gleijeses, who has used Cuban documents to demonstrate the fundamental flaws in the assumptions that led the Ford administration to intervene in the Angolan civil war.

<hr>

Gleijeses is just one of the scholars to whom I owe an enormous debt. In particular, the works of John Robert Greene, Yanek Mieczkowski, James Cannon, Michael Turner, and James Reichley have been invaluable. Other works cited in this book are listed in the bibliography, but the list is not exhaustive of the materials that proved helpful.

Several collections listed in the bibliography deserve special mention. The oral history collection of the Association for Diplomatic Studies and Training includes first-hand accounts of all foreign policy matters discussed in this book; the National Security Archive at George Washington University has compiled all declassified documents in a searchable database; and the American Presidency Project has created an online database of all public statements, orders, speeches, and press conferences of each president.

I want to thank everyone who agreed to interviews for this book. In particular, Melvin Laird and William Seidman went beyond the call of duty and devoted substantial time to respond to my questions.

I owe the greatest debt to Stacy Davis and the rest of the staff at the Gerald R. Ford Presidential Library, who are always helpful, responsive, and professional. I urge anyone who is interested in the time period to visit the library in Ann Arbor, Michigan. You will be warmly welcomed. If you are interested in domestic issues, the records of the Economic Policy Board are a good place to start. For each significant issue, William Seidman prepared a summary for Ford that included the differing opinions within the administration, and the president's decisions are documented in follow-up memos. In foreign policy, the transcripts of Ford's meetings with Kissinger and Scowcroft are fascinating. (Scowcroft took verbatim notes of the meetings in longhand.) The primary source material that the United States government makes available is astounding, and the people of the Presidential Library System and the National Archives are always willing to help you find what you need.

1

The Fall of Spiro Agnew

During the summer of 1973, Spiro Agnew looked like a sure bet to become president of the United States. His rise to within a hair's-breadth of the most powerful office in the world had been astonishing. When Nixon surprised the political world by choosing him for his running mate in 1968, Agnew had been governor of Maryland for only two years, and he was virtually unknown outside of his home state. The *Washington Post* called Agnew's nomination "perhaps the most eccentric political appointment since the Roman emperor Caligula named his horse a consul."[1] Now, five years later, Nixon was facing impeachment, and Agnew was the heir apparent. At the same time, Gerald Ford looked destined to retire as minority leader of the House of Representatives. The presidency was the furthest thing from his mind; as a twenty-five-year veteran of the House, Ford had one professional goal — to become Speaker.[2] But the last few elections had convinced him that the Republicans would not take control of the House anytime soon, and he told his wife Betty that he would retire after one more term.

They were a study in contrasts, the man who looked to become president and the man who actually would succeed to the office. Agnew was all flash and no substance, sporting expensive suits and tripping around the world to glad-hand foreign dictators. Ford was all substance and zero flash — he was an expert in arcane subjects like the federal budget, and he had an unfortunate affinity for plaid. Agnew was known for his gregarious articulation, Ford for his down-home, plain-spoken style. Agnew could be a rousing speaker, while Ford was dry as toast on the stump. Agnew would lash out at his political enemies — Hubert Humphrey called him the "brass knuckles of the administration"[3] — while Ford was known for treating political opponents with dignity and respect. Most importantly, they were exact opposites in terms of personal integrity. Agnew would resign after being caught taking bribes in the White House, while Ford was that supposedly mythical creature: an honest politician.

Ford's friends and colleagues invariably used two words to describe him: "honest" and "decent." His former speechwriter, David Gergen, called him "the most decent man I have known in the presidency," adding that "Ford's honesty also reminds us of what we want our leaders to be."[4] George H. W. Bush said of him, "simply put, one of the most decent and capable men I ever met."[5] Jimmy Carter said that Ford was "one of the most admirable public servants and human beings I have ever known."[6] Eighteen years of service in the House taught Democrat Martha Griffiths that Ford's honesty was genuine. "In all the years I sat in the House, I never knew Mr. Ford to make a dishonest statement nor a statement part-true and part-false. He never attempted to shade a statement, and I never heard him utter an unkind word."[7] Politicians inured to the cutthroat ways of Washington often gushed sentimentality when they talked about him. When asked about his former boss, Brent Scowcroft reflexively blurted out that he was "a wonderful man."[8] California representative Pete McCloskey was

3

even sappier: "I can get tears in my eyes when I think about Jerry Ford. We love him."[9] New York representative Barber Conable added that "nobody could stay very mad at Jerry Ford for long."[10]

At any other time, the fact that a corrupt vice president was replaced with an honest one would have been a historical curiosity, but in the context of Watergate, Ford's unimpeachable character was critical. The differences between Ford and Nixon were as striking as his differences with Agnew. Nixon hated his political opponents with a passionate intensity, while Ford considered them friends; Nixon treated political battles as assaults on his integrity, while Ford never took things personally; and Nixon was obsessed with never letting the other side fight dirtier than him, while Ford played the political game with integrity.

It was Ford's ability to treat opponents as friends that made him truly unique. He had countless opportunities to make enemies as he climbed the ladder in the House, and as he fought tenaciously for his conservative views; yet, after a quarter century of political battles, he claimed "many adversaries, but no enemies."[11] Michigan senator Robert Griffin agreed: "The nicest thing about Jerry Ford is that he just doesn't have enemies."[12] He had no enemies because, in the words of columnist Jack Germond, he "had the great quality of understanding the difference between an enemy and an adversary."[13] He treated members on the other side of the aisle with dignity, and they repaid him with respect.

It was these traits — honesty, decency and a willingness to treat opponents with respect — that allowed Ford to restore the nation's trust after Nixon's resignation. To understand why restoring confidence was so vital, we have to remember what Watergate was about; or for those who are too young to remember it, we need to understand the enormity of the scandal. Three things come to mind when we think about Watergate: it started with a break-in, there was a cover-up, and it ended when Nixon was caught in a lie. But we forget the heart of the matter, because the crime of breaking into the Democratic National Committee headquarters was far less important than the obstruction of the investigation that followed. And the term "cover-up" does not adequately capture the wholesale subversion of the justice system that was involved, including bribing witnesses, suborning perjury, and destroying evidence; and it also fails to convey the administration's disdain for the law, because it doesn't encompass wiretapping journalists, using the IRS to attack political opponents, extracting illegal campaign contributions from corporations, and selling federal offices. Lies were part and parcel of these activities, but the fact that Nixon was caught in a lie was less important than the subject of the lie — the important thing was that the tapes proved that he had obstructed justice. We remember the lie because of the reaction of Nixon's supporters, who had defended him for months based on his assurances that he had not been involved. They were devastated when they realized he was lying, and it is their disappointment that we remember, such as the unforgettable words of William Safire: "Those who invested their lives in the causes he shared will never forget that Nixon failed, not while daring greatly, but while lying meanly."[14]

After all the lies, the crimes, and the manifest disdain for the law, Ford's honesty and decency were exactly what was needed to restore the trust and faith of the American people. Ford has been called the "accidental president," and it was an accident that Agnew's corruption was exposed before Nixon resigned. But it was no accident that Nixon picked Ford to succeed him — the choice was compelled by Ford's congressional colleagues, who knew that he was the leader that the nation so desperately needed. To understand how that happened, and to appreciate the enormity of Watergate, we have to return to the time when Agnew was on top of the world.

During the summer of '73, Watergate was an all-consuming obsession for most Americans. Nearly every household — 87 percent — tuned in for all or part of the televised Senate Watergate hearings, which were chaired in a home-spun but purposeful manner by 76-year-old Sam Ervin from North Carolina. The hearings dramatically portrayed the scandal which had been the focus of extensive newspaper reporting for months. Nixon had already been forced to dismiss most of his top aides, including Chief of Staff Robert Haldeman, Assistant to the President John Ehrlichman, Attorney General Richard Kleindienst, former attorney general John Mitchell, Counsel to the President Charles Colson, and FBI director L. Patrick Gray. During his presidency, Nixon had spent almost all of his time with Haldeman, Ehrlichman, Colson, and Secretary of State Henry Kissinger. Only Kissinger survived the scandal.[15]

The hearings were great political theater, as administration officials admitted that they had committed burglaries, paid hundreds of thousands of dollars to the Watergate defendants, offered executive clemency to the defendants, perjured themselves before a grand jury, destroyed documents, wiretapped journalists, and attempted to use the CIA to subvert the criminal investigation. The hearings revealed a Nixon White House which was secretive and obsessed with leaks. Administration officials told the Ervin Committee that they first tried to trace leaks by wiretapping respected journalists such as William Beecher and Hedrick Smith of the *New York Times*, Henry Brandon of the *London Sunday Times*, and Marvin Kalb of CBS, along with members of the White House staff, like Deputy White House Counsel John Sears, speechwriter William Safire, and Kissinger aides Morton Halperin and Helmut Sonnenfeldt. When that didn't work, Ehrlichman set up a White House unit named the Plumbers to find and plug leaks. Three of the Watergate defendants had been Plumbers: James McCord, the security director of the Nixon campaign; G. Gordon Liddy, the general counsel of the campaign; and a former CIA agent named Howard Hunt. Ehrlichman told the Ervin Committee that he approved a Plumbers operation to discredit Daniel Ellsberg, a defense analyst who had leaked the Pentagon Papers. The Plumbers broke into the office of Ellsberg's psychiatrist but could not find his files.[16]

During the 1972 election, Liddy, Hunt and McCord were transferred to perform political intelligence for Nixon's campaign, where they bungled the break-in at the Watergate hotel. Immediately after the burglars were arrested, some of the highest-ranking members of the United States government destroyed evidence. Haldeman told his aide Gordon Strachan to "make sure our files are clean."[17] Mitchell suggested to Magruder that "it might be good if he had a fire."[18] White House Counsel John Dean told the committee that Ehrlichman asked him to shred documents from a safe in Hunt's White House office, and to "deep six" a briefcase from the safe by throwing it into the Potomac River. According to Dean, he was uncomfortable with the suggestion, so he and Ehrlichman gave the documents to acting FBI director L. Patrick Gray and told him that the documents should never see the light of day. Gray burned the documents along with his Christmas trash.[19]

The next attempt to subvert the investigation did not seem significant at the time, but it would prove decisive in the end. Former CIA director Richard Helms and CIA deputy director general Vernon Walters testified that Ehrlichman had asked them to tell the FBI to drop its Watergate investigation on the spurious grounds that it might compromise CIA operations in Mexico. They refused.[20] The attempt to use the CIA to undermine the investigation would eventually be Nixon's undoing, but at the time it was overshadowed by other revelations.

The most astonishing revelation was that administration officials had paid the Watergate burglars $462,000 to keep quiet. Three employees of Nixon's 1968 campaign, including finance chairman Herbert Kalmbach, told bizarre stories about skulking around Washington at night and leaving bags of cash for Howard Hunt's wife, who then distributed it to the other defendants.[21] And the White House promised that the graft would continue. Magruder told the Ervin Committee that he lied to the grand jury after he received "assurances about income and being taken care of from the standpoint of my family and a job afterwards and also that there would be good opportunity for executive clemency."[22] James McCord testified that former White House plumber John Caulfield called him before the trial and promised that if he remained silent, he would receive financial aid, executive clemency, and a job.[23]

Only one witness testified that Nixon knew about the subversion of the legal system: White House Counsel John Dean. The slightly-built 45-year-old with round glasses did not look like the kind of man who could take down a president, but he had a memory for details and he told a convincing story. Dean testified that he first asked to meet with the president when the burglars demanded more money while they were awaiting sentencing. Like many of Nixon's supporters, he thought that if he could just get to Nixon and tell him what was going on, the president would put a stop to it, but he experienced a rude awakening. Dean told the committee that he tried to shock the president by telling him that that another $1 million would be required to insure the continued silence of the burglars, but Nixon was unfazed — he said that raising the money wouldn't be a problem.[24]

According to Dean, when the burglars kept asking for more, he asked for another meeting with Nixon, and he poured out his concerns after telling Nixon that Watergate was "a cancer on the presidency":

> I then proceeded to tell him some of the highlights that had occurred during the cover-up. I told him that Kalmbach had been used to raise funds to pay these seven individuals for their silence at the instructions of Ehrlichman, Haldeman, and Mitchell.... I told him that ... I had assisted Magruder in preparing his false story for presentation to the grand jury. I told him that cash that had been at the White House had been funneled back to the re-election committee for the purpose of paying the seven individuals to remain silent.[25]

It was damning stuff, but Dean stood alone, because there was no other evidence supporting him. It was the word of the president against the testimony of a disgraced aide, and many Americans were inclined to believe their president — only 22 percent of Americans thought that he should step down. Americans weren't convinced that Nixon had to go, but his approval ratings fell from 68 percent in January to 31 percent at the end of the hearings.[26] Then the committee discovered evidence that would prove who was telling the truth. On July 16, Deputy Assistant to the President Alexander Butterfield testified that Nixon had installed a system to tape all conversations in the Oval Office. If Dean was telling the truth, the conversations he described would be on the tapes, but Nixon refused to produce the tapes, even after he received subpoenas from the committee and the special prosecutor. The issue was sent to the courts, where Nixon fought to save his presidency. At the same time, Congress began deliberating his fate after Representative Robert Drinan introduced an impeachment resolution.[27]

With Nixon fighting to keep his office, attention turned to his putative successor. The American people had not seen much evidence that Spiro Agnew was up to the job — he was known only for occasionally blurting out outrageous statements. Nixon was first drawn to Agnew by the lack of restraint the governor of Maryland showed when lashing out at protesters. When African American students at Bowie State protested against Maryland's racially-segregated university system, Agnew shut down the college, telling the press that "scroungy student dissenters" should be treated "like the naughty children they are."[28] After the riots that followed the assassination of Martin Luther King, Agnew accused the African American leaders of Baltimore (who had risked bodily injury trying to stop the riots) of pandering to "caterwauling, riot-inciting, burn-America-down type of leaders."[29]

Agnew's associates claim that there was more to him than tough talk. William Safire maintains that Agnew was "a man of ideas and articulation," and Agnew's political assistant David Keene called him "a politician who was interested in ideas."[30] If Agnew really was a man of ideas, he never expressed them publicly, and Nixon never showed that he valued them. The only prominent role Nixon ever gave him was administration attack dog. When the press criticized the administration's Vietnam strategy in 1970, Nixon sent Agnew on the road to fight back, and he played his part with relish — House Speaker Carl Albert said that he "revealed a surprising talent for invective."[31] It must have been great fun for the two young speechwriters Nixon sent along, Patrick Buchanan and William Safire. They were brilliant, zealous and precocious, and Agnew made no attempt to restrain their youthful enthusiasm. Whatever they wrote, the vice president said. Agnew called intellectuals an "effete corps of impudent snobs"; he accused liberals of "pusillanimous pussyfooting"; he referred to the press as "nattering nabobs of negativism"; and he called Nixon's critics "hopeless, hysterical hypochondriacs of history." The only lasting impression the public had of their vice president was of a man who rattled off phrases like "when you've seen one city slum, you've seen them all" and "a society which comes to fear its children is effete."[32]

Then, on August 7, 1973, Americans got to see a whole new side of Agnew: his crooked side. Papers across the country reported that United States Attorney George Beall had been collecting sworn statements from Baltimore construction contractors who had bribed the vice president.[33] The night before the story broke, Attorney General Elliott Richardson told Nixon that the evidence of Agnew's guilt was irrefutable. "There's no mistake. They've got him — credible witnesses, documents, heaven knows what else. In all my years as a prosecutor, I have never seen such an open-and-shut case."[34] The contractors admitted that they had paid Agnew a cut of the fees from contracts that had been awarded when Agnew was county executive and governor, and that Agnew continued to take the bribes after he became vice president. An engineer testified that he had delivered an envelope containing $10,000 to Agnew in his White House office, and another claimed to have made fourteen payments of $2,000 to Agnew in the Vice Presidential Office in the Executive Office Building and his Washington apartment.

Agnew claimed that the allegations against him were "false and scurrilous and malicious.... The charges against me are, if you'll pardon the expression, damned lies."[35] But Nixon wasn't convinced, and he decided that the last thing he needed while he was fighting off impeachment was a vice president who was fighting his own impeachment battle. Attorney General Richardson also concluded that Agnew would have to resign, but not because he wanted to help Nixon's impeachment case. Richardson was a proper Bostonian with a squeaky-clean reputation whom Nixon had appointed to restore credibility after his previous two attorneys general had been forced to resign. Richardson decided that the last thing the nation needed was concurrent impeachment proceedings, one against the president and one against the vice president, with the presidential succession depending on which impeachment proceeding concluded first. In Richardson's opinion, it was imperative that Agnew resign so that a new vice president could be confirmed before the impeachment process against Nixon was too far along.[36]

Al Haig had the same concern — he was "preoccupied, not to say terrified" of "the growing likelihood of the simultaneous impeachment of the president and the vice president."[37] He turned to Ford for advice, because of the minority leader's reputation for probity, and Ford told him that the vice president had "no other alternative but to resign."[38] During his time of tribulation, Agnew received surprising spiritual support from another politician with a squeaky-clean reputation. Georgia governor Jimmy Carter called to tell the vice president that he was in his prayers. "I felt he needed to hear a friendly voice."[39]

Ford played a minor role in Agnew's last-ditch gambit to save his job. It was no secret that Nixon would try to block any criminal investigation by arguing that a sitting president cannot be criminally charged until after he is removed from office, and Agnew tried to invoke the same principle even though it had never been applied to the vice president.[40] To bolster his case, Agnew asked the House of Representatives to begin impeachment proceedings against him so that he could ask a court to stay the criminal investigation until Congress completed its work. Agnew believed that he could win a political showdown in the House, or, if he lost there, that he could win the one-third of votes in the Senate necessary to block his removal from office.

On September 26, Ford accompanied Agnew to a meeting with Speaker Carl Albert and other House leaders, where Agnew presented a letter asking for impeachment proceedings. Albert was the son of a coal miner from Bug Tussle, Oklahoma, a graduate of Oxford, and a student of the history of the House who spent much of his free time researching congressional history in the Library of Congress. He was sympathetic to Agnew's plight, but his primary consideration was the proper role of the House, and his discussions with other Democratic leaders reaffirmed his initial conclusion that the House should not intervene. "I knew instantly that the House must not involve itself in a nearly completed criminal investigation before the federal courts."[41] The next day, Albert announced that the House would refuse Agnew's request. "The vice president's letter relates to matters before the courts. In view of that fact, I, as Speaker, will not take any action on the letter at this time."[42]

Agnew had no more luck when he asked the United States District Court in Maryland to stay the grand jury proceedings. After Solicitor General Robert Bork opposed the petition, the court turned down Agnew's request.[43] The decision ended the vice president's last hope of forestalling the prosecution. He was left with a painful choice — either resign or face criminal indictment followed by almost-certain conviction and jail. Despite his earlier protestations that he would fight until the end, he chose to resign. Judge Walter Hoffman mediated the negotiations between Agnew's lawyers and the federal prosecutors. The parties agreed that: Agnew would resign and plead no contest to one count of tax evasion; Attorney General Richardson would recommend that Agnew serve no jail time; and Judge Hoffman would give the attorney general's recommendation "great weight."[44]

At 2:00 in the afternoon of October 10, Judge Hoffman's courtroom in the United States Courthouse in Baltimore was packed with reporters who thought they were about to witness government attorneys present Agnew's indictment. The vice president was not expected to appear, so the reporters were taken by surprise when Agnew walked in and took his place alongside his three attorneys. One of his attorneys, Judah Best, walked to the Judge's chambers, where he called an associate waiting outside Kissinger's office and instructed him to deliver Agnew's letter of resignation to the secretary of state. Best returned and whispered to Agnew, "Your letter of resignation has been delivered to the secretary of state as you directed."[45]

Agnew's resignation became effective at 2:05, and he sat in the courtroom not as vice president but as any other citizen of the United States.

Judge Hoffman entered and ordered the observers to keep quiet. "You will not be permitted to leave at any time during the course of the proceeding, and there will be no disturbances or outcries of any kind from anyone. If so, the marshals have received instructions to take you into custody." As the reporters watched dumbfounded, Agnew's attorneys informed the court that he had resigned as vice president and that he was pleading no contest to a single count of tax evasion. Judge Hoffman gave Agnew a three-year suspended sentence and a $10,000 fine.[46] The hearing was over, and so was Agnew's political career. Just three months earlier he looked like a sure bet to become president, and now he was the first vice president to resign in disgrace.

Agnew's resignation was the seventeenth time in American history that the country was without a vice president, each prior instance because either the president or the vice president had died. The first sixteen times the office remained vacant until the next election. This time would be different, because Nixon was empowered to appoint a new vice president by the Twenty-Fifth Amendment, which had been enacted in response to the assassination of President Kennedy. When the Senate Judiciary Subcommittee on Constitutional Amendments was drafting the amendment in 1967, Nixon told the committee that the president's choice of a new vice president should not be subject to congressional approval. Congress disagreed, and the Twenty-Fifth Amendment required approval by both houses of Congress.[47]

Having failed to win his case in 1967, Nixon now needed to find a nominee who would be approved by a Democratic Congress which was in the process of impeaching him. He had already been rebuffed regarding his first choice, former Texas governor John Connally, who Nixon held in unusually-high esteem. According to Kissinger, Connelly was "the only person about whom I never heard Nixon make a denigrating comment."[48] Democrats in Congress did not agree with Nixon's assessment of Connally — they considered him a traitor because he had switched allegiances to the Republican Party earlier that year. Democratic dislike for Connally was reinforced by allegations that he had been involved in the administration's fundraising scandals.[49]

During the week before Agnew's resignation, Nixon told White House counselors Mel Laird and Bryce Harlow that he had offered the job to Connally. The choice dismayed Laird and Harlow, and they told the president that Connally wouldn't be confirmed. Nixon stuck to his guns, but they finally convinced him to let them make preliminary inquiries about Connally's chances of confirmation. As they predicted, the responses were uniformly negative. Deputy Senate Majority Leader Robert Byrd said, "Tell my friend Dick Nixon that if he sends Connally's name to the Senate, blood will be running out from under that Senate door."[50] Republican representative Silvio Conte said, "I will accept anyone the president sends up except Connally."[51] House Majority Leader Tip O'Neill told the press that there was one person who he would not vote for, John Connelly.[52] Laird summed it up for Nixon: "Mr. President, we cannot get Connally confirmed. It will be a disaster."[53] Nixon gave in, and he had Haig call Connally to break the bad news. Laird then began to lobby for his friend Jerry Ford, who he considered the best possible choice for the country at the time. Laird began arranging meetings for congressional leaders to let Nixon know that Ford was their choice.[54]

Nixon was meeting with Ford while Agnew was announcing his resignation. They had been good friends ever since they were young members of the House in the late '40s, and Ford had publicly supported his friend during the dark days of his career: when other Republicans tried to convince Eisenhower to dump Nixon as his running mate; after Nixon lost a presidential race to Kennedy; and after Nixon lost an election for governor of California. When Ford arrived at the president's office in the Executive Office Building, he found Nixon smoking a pipe in a big leather chair and looking "about as relaxed as I'd ever seen him." Nixon told Ford about Agnew's resignation, and he said that the vice president had "acted like many public officials in Maryland. That's the way things are done there." The president then got to the reason for the meeting — he asked the minority leader to poll his membership and send him a list of their first, second and third choices for a successor by the next day. Following his meeting with Ford, Nixon called GOP national chairman George Bush and Senate Minority Leader Hugh Scott and asked them to poll their organizations.[55]

Nixon also met with the two top Democrats in Congress, Senate Majority Leader Mike Mansfield and Speaker of the House Carl Albert, and asked them to suggest successors to Agnew. Mansfield tried to steer him toward someone who would not be a viable candidate in the next presidential election, such as former senator John Sherman Cooper of Kentucky or former secretary of state William Rogers, and he warned, "There is one fellow we're going to go over with a fine-tooth comb if his name is sent up." He did not mention Connally by name, but it was clear who he meant. Albert was not planning to offer any suggestions, but after Mansfield made his, Albert said that he had one. Nixon asked, "Who is it? Jerry Ford?" And Albert responded, "Yes sir. He would be the easiest man that I know of to confirm in the House of Representatives."[56] Later that day, Nixon heard the same thing from Tip O'Neill. "If you want easy sledding, the guy you should have is Jerry Ford. He will get through for you without any problems."[57]

Nixon asked Laird — who called Ford "my closest friend" — whether the minority leader would accept the nomination if asked. Laird had not talked to Ford about the idea, but he went out on a limb and said, "I know it." As soon as he left the meeting, he called Ford and said, "I don't want any hemming and hawing. I want you to say yes." He didn't get an immediate answer because Ford said that he needed to discuss the issue with his wife. When Betty encouraged him to accept — despite the fact that he had promised to retire in 1977 — Ford called back and said he and Betty agreed that being vice president would be "a nice way for 3½ years to end their political service."[58]

The next day, Nixon retired to Camp David to make his decision. According to Nixon, he had four criteria. He wanted a candidate who was qualified to be president, who he agreed with ideologically, who was a loyal Republican, and who was likely to be confirmed. Before the trip he had already narrowed his choices to four: Connally, Ford, former governor of New York Nelson Rockefeller, and California governor Ronald Reagan. The results of his poll confirmed that Nixon's top choices were also the top choices of the party leadership. Rockefeller and Reagan were in a virtual tie for first, Connally came in third, and Ford finished fourth; but Ford led by a wide margin among members of Congress.[59]

Nixon already knew that Connally had no chance of confirmation, and he decided against Rockefeller and Reagan because they were both divisive figures with other Republicans. Rockefeller was the standard-bearer of the moderate wing of the party, and conservatives hated him after an acrimonious primary race against Barry Goldwater in 1964. Reagan was the heir to Goldwater as the favorite of the right wing, but he was anathema to Republican moderates. Nixon concluded that nominating either Rockefeller or Reagan would "split the Republican Party down the middle and result in a bitter partisan fight."[60]

Nixon then considered the fourth name on the list, Gerald Ford. He was the all–American boy — a football star and war veteran who had returned home to run for Congress. After playing center for a University of Michigan football team that won two national championships, Ford turned down offers from the Green Bay Packers and the Detroit Lions, choosing instead to go to Yale Law School. After Pearl Harbor, he served in the navy in the Pacific, where he became an ardent internationalist and supporter of a strong defense. After the war, his newfound internationalism led him to run for the House because he objected to the isolationist views of the incumbent Republican from Grand Rapids, Barney Jonkman. For the next twenty-five years Ford worked in the House, earning the respect of friends and foes alike.

Ford met all of Nixon's criteria — Nixon considered him qualified to be president, he was an old friend and consistent supporter, and, as a "moderate in domestic affairs, conservative in fiscal affairs, and dyed-in-the-wool internationalist in foreign affairs,"[61] he shared Nixon's ideological beliefs. He was an old-fashioned fiscal conservative, one of the last of a dying breed. According to Library of Congress historian Dr. Joseph Gorman, Ford voted for reducing spending and balancing the budget "virtually without deviation."[62] He voted for more spending in only one area, national defense, which he considered to be the government's top priority. On social issues he was a moderate, favoring abortion rights and steering Republicans in the House away from their traditional practice of joining with Southern Democrats to defeat civil rights legislation.[63] It was the last factor, confirmability, which put Ford over the top. He was beloved by his congressional brethren, so confirmation was not an issue, and that was the thing that convinced Nixon that he was the right choice.

> He was my oldest and closest friend of the four finalists, that he shared my views on domestic as well as foreign policy issues, that he was willing to step up to making tough decisions on unpopular issues, and that he above all could always be counted upon to be a team player. Some of the others among the final four met most of these tests, but Ford's confirmability gave him an edge which the others could not match and was the decisive factor in my final decision — a decision I think was right at the time and have not regretted since that time.[64]

Nixon made the right choice. During the height of the Watergate crisis the country needed a leader who could reestablish American's trust in its leaders and who could unite a divided nation. Ford was uniquely qualified to meet that need, while the other candidates Nixon had considered for the vice presidency were not. Agnew and Connally could not have reestablished America's trust. Even before Agnew had been caught receiving envelopes full of money at the White House, he had been known only for his furious and divisive attacks on administration critics. Connally had been indicted the week before Ford took office for his alleged role in a fund-raising scandal. Although he was later acquitted, Connally never had a reputation for integrity. And Rockefeller and Reagan could not have united the country because each was hated by his political opponents. Only Ford had the attributes needed at the time: unquestioned integrity, the ability to treat political opponents with respect, and the respect and affection of his political opponents.

On Friday October 12, Haig called Ford and asked him to join Senate minority leader Hugh Scott for a meeting at the Oval Office. The request was not unusual; Nixon often met with Ford and Scott about legislative matters. When Ford and Scott arrived, Haig asked Ford to wait while Scott met with the president. Ford stewed until Scott left, but he didn't have to wait long after he was invited in. Nixon came right to the point and asked Ford to be vice president. Nixon was relieved when Ford accepted, and he was just as happy when he said that he planned to retire in January 1977. "Well, that's good, because John Connally is my choice for 1976."[65]

That afternoon, White House Press Secretary Ron Ziegler told the press that Nixon would call the nominee at 7:00 and announce his decision two hours later. When Ford arrived home he didn't tell his family the news. Typical of Ford—who would remain emotionally steady throughout the events of the next few years—he did not allow the excitement of the moment to disrupt his healthy routine. He took his nightly swim and was ready when Nixon called. Ford had Betty join the call, and the president officially offered him the job.[66]

At 9:00, Nixon stood before congressional and cabinet leaders in the East Room of the White House for his televised announcement. For the first time in a long time, the nation saw its president smile. He knew that Ford was the first choice of the assembled congressional leaders, and he tailored his announcement to play to their hopes. Playing the moment for all it was worth, he signaled that his choice would be Ford. "He is a man who has served for twenty-five years in the House of Representatives with great distinction." The room erupted. One congressman yelled, "Beautiful! Beautiful!" Another shouted, "Oh baby, that's great! That's just great!" Nixon continued to work the crowd. "Ladies and gentlemen, please don't be premature. There are several here who have served twenty-five years in the House of Representatives." Then he finally made his formal announcement. "Our distinguished guests and my fellow Americans, I proudly present to you the man whose name I will submit to the Congress of the United States for confirmation as the vice president of the United States, Congressman Gerald Ford of Michigan." The crowd erupted again. Ford, who had been sitting between Carl Albert and Tip O'Neill, walked to the podium and put his arm around Nixon's shoulder. Nixon turned to Ford and said, "They like you," and Ford answered, "I have a couple of friends out there."[67]

In the midst of the Watergate scandal, reporters were in a puritanical mood, and they refused to see the reaction of congressional leaders for what it was, relief and joy that Nixon was nominating a man they knew to be the honest and decent leader that America desperately needed. Anthony Lewis of the *New York Times* called the announcement the "most repellent American public ceremony in memory." Theodore H. White called it "a ceremony marked by a tasteless cheerfulness."[68]

Ford's congressional colleagues—liberal, moderate and conservative—uniformly praised Nixon's choice. Senator Strom Thurmond of South Carolina—perhaps the most conservative member of Congress—said he was "extremely pleased." On the other end of the political spectrum, Minnesota Democratic senator Walter Mondale said, "The President is to be congratulated." Fellow Minnesota senator Hubert Humphrey, an old friend of Ford's, called to congratulate him. Those not chosen by Nixon responded with grace, but it was hard for their spouses not to express disappointment. Reagan said that Nixon had chosen "wisely." Nelson Rockefeller offered his "heartiest congratulations," but his wife Happy said that her husband had not been chosen because "weakness never turns to strength."[69]

─────

The next day, Nixon formally sent the nomination to Congress for advice and consent pursuant to the Twenty-Fifth Amendment. Although the vast majority of congressional members supported the choice of Ford, a small number of Democrats tried to torpedo the nomination because they saw no reason to change the current order of succession—with Agnew gone, Democrat Speaker Albert was next in line for the presidency. The most public proponent of delaying Ford's nomination was Bella Abzug, who told Albert, "Get off your goddamned ass, and we can take this presidency."[70] In the *New York Times*, Abzug gave a more honorable explanation for her opposition. "Under the Succession Act of 1947, we already have an elected official designated to replace the president in the absence of a vice president. The Speaker of the House is just as well qualified to stand around and wait as is House Minority Leader Ford."[71] In a meeting of Democratic members of the House Judiciary Committee, John

Conyers led the charge against a quick confirmation. "I think it's absolutely ludicrous for us to even be talking about going ahead with Ford when the president who made this nomination is subject to impeachment." Robert Drinan chose bombast over reason. "If we go ahead with this nomination and don't move on impeachment, I'm going to blow the whistle on the committee. I'll call it what it is, a cover-up!"[72]

The Democrats who wanted to table the Ford nomination were motivated by genuine abhorrence of the crimes of the Nixon administration, but they allowed partisan passion to cloud their judgment regarding the best interests of the nation. Had Congress refused to act on the Ford nomination, the movement to impeach Nixon would have been seen as nothing more than a partisan effort to reverse the results of the 1972 election, and it would have been virtually impossible for any Republican to support impeachment. To the nation's good fortune, Democratic congressional leaders rose above partisanship for the good of the country. While Bella Abzug, Robert Drinan, and John Conyers could not rise to the occasion, Carl Albert, Mike Mansfield, Tip O'Neill, and Peter Rodino did. Albert had no interest in becoming president — he "thought that was nonsense"[73] — and the House Judiciary and Senate Rules Committees proceeded expeditiously to confirm Ford.

One week later the Ford nomination was almost derailed by the "Saturday Night Massacre," when Nixon fired Special Prosecutor Archibald Cox for not cooperating in his fight to keep the tapes secret. On the same day that Nixon announced his nomination of Ford, the United States Circuit Court in Washington ordered him to produce nine tapes to Cox and the Ervin Committee. Nixon was faced with a painful choice: turn over the tapes or appeal to the Supreme Court. In desperation, he invented a third option, offering to provide summaries of the tapes and allow conservative Democratic senator John Stennis to listen to the tapes and verify that the summaries were accurate. Nixon met with Sam Ervin and Howard Baker, the senior Democratic and Republican members of the Ervin Committee, and they agreed to the compromise. But Cox rejected the compromise and insisted on receiving the actual tapes.

Nixon was livid, but he could not fire Cox himself— only the attorney general had the authority to fire a special prosecutor — so on Friday, October 19, he told Attorney General Richardson to fire him. Richardson agreed at first, but his staff threatened to quit if he did. He told Haig the next day that he would resign rather than execute the order, as did Deputy Attorney General William Ruckelshaus, who was the legal successor to Richardson. Solicitor General Robert Bork was next in line, and the formal succession ended with him. Bork met with Richardson and Ruckelshaus earlier that day to consider Nixon's directive, and he said that he would execute the order because it would not be in the country's interest for all three of the officials in the Justice Department succession to resign. As Bork explained at the time, "If I don't carry out the president's order after Richardson and Ruckelshaus have refused to do so, no other official in the Justice Department will carry out the order either. That can't be good for the country."[74] "If you really are determined to get rid of Cox," Ruckelshaus told Nixon, "I think Bork may be your man." Nixon told Bork to fire Cox, and Bork complied.[75]

Nixon did not anticipate the storm of protest that followed. He was particularly surprised by the strong reaction from Republicans, including the House leaders who delivered a message to the White House declaring that they would no longer defend against impeachment unless Nixon turned over the tapes. Nixon did not lose the support of Barry Goldwater, but he did not escape his wrath. Goldwater issued a statement asserting that Nixon's credibility "has reached an all-time low from which he may not be able to recover." Two weeks later he gave the president his grudging support when he said that he still believed that Nixon was "not guilty of anything, and we're going to have to live with him."[76] The intense reaction to the Saturday Night Massacre foiled Nixon's plan to keep the tapes secret, and he was left with no choice but to turn over the six tapes. And he did not escape the harassment from special prosecutors. Bork hired a new special prosecutor, Leon Jaworski, a conservative Democrat from Texas and the former president of the American Bar Association. Connally knew Jaworski, and he vouched for him to Nixon, so the president concurred with Bork's decision.[77]

During the week following the Saturday Night Massacre, House members submitted twenty-one impeachment resolutions. There were no established procedures for impeachment, and some of his colleagues urged Speaker Albert to set up a partisan special committee to prosecute Nixon. As usual, Albert's primary consideration was the integrity of the House, and he wanted the procedure to be above question. He met with Ford — who remained minority leader while he was awaiting confirmation — to work out the details, and they agreed that the least-partisan forum was the House Judiciary Committee, chaired by Peter Rodino. Albert promised to stop any effort to create a partisan special committee, and Ford promised that the Republican leadership would support the choice of the Judiciary Committee. "Whatever the committee decision," Albert later explained, "no one could claim it had been rigged."[78]

—◦◦◦—

The Saturday Night Massacre provided new ammunition for the Democrats who wanted to forestall Ford's confirmation. Eleven House Democrats submitted a resolution demanding that Ford's nomination be tabled "until such time as the President has complied with the final decision of the court system as it regards the White House tapes."[79] But the party leaders had no interest in delay, and Albert told the press that the House "should not hold the nomination of the vice president designate hostage."[80]

The Senate Committee of Rules and Administration requested an FBI background investigation of Ford, and the bureau detailed more than 350 agents to research every aspect of his life. Ford told his staff to hold nothing back, and the FBI issued a report which found nothing of significance. The IRS audited Ford's tax returns and found only one item about which there was any dispute, a deduction for clothing the Fords wore to a Republican convention, and the Fords paid the tax due on $871.44 in additional income.[81]

The Senate Rules Committee hearings began on November 1, 1973, and the House Judiciary Committee hearings followed two weeks later. In his opening statement to the Senate committee, Ford emphasized the importance of honesty. "Truth is the glue that holds government together, and not government but civilization itself." He followed with a statement that would be echoed by Jimmy Carter two years later. "I do not think a President under any circumstances that I can envision ought to lie to the American people." The committee was pleased when Ford said an impeachment inquiry was "the way to clear the air," and their fears were allayed when he said that no person is above the law, and that if the Supreme Court ruled that Nixon must turn over the tapes, he would have no question but to obey. One answer would come back to haunt him, and it came in response to an ambiguous compound question. When he was asked whether a president succeeding Nixon should "prevent or terminate any investigation or criminal prosecution charges" against him, Ford said, "I don't think the public would stand for it."[82] It was a poorly-worded question, primarily focused on whether a president should stop an investigation into Watergate, but it would later be remembered as Ford promising not to pardon Nixon.

Much of the questioning related to Ford's role in shutting down an early investigation into Watergate by the Wright Patman's House Banking Committee. Patman was hardly the ideal person to lead the Watergate inquiry; he was churlish and had a reputation for using committee investigations for partisan purposes. One month before the 1972 election, Patman's request for subpoena power was denied when six Democrats joined the Republicans in voting against it. During his testimony, Ford admitted that he had urged Republican committee members to vote against expanding the investigation, but he insisted that he had not been acting at the direction of the White House.[83] In retrospect, it is hard to see the relevance of this issue. There is nothing improper or unusual about a congressman opposing a patently partisan investigation during an election year, even if the allegations being investigated turn out to be true. An investigation by a known Democratic partisan during the campaign would have been viewed as nothing more than an attempt to influence the election. The Ervin Committee hearings and the House Judiciary Committee investigation were viewed as fair because they took place after the election and because they were conducted by leaders who were viewed as impartial. The fair and nonpartisan process encouraged the American people to accept the evidence and allowed Republican leaders to break with Nixon.

Ford's nomination passed the Senate Rules Committee without dissent, and the Senate confirmed him on November 27 in a 92 to 3 vote. During the vote, Democrat after Democrat took the floor to explain that, while they had serious reservations about Ford's conservative views, they were voting for him because of his honesty and integrity. Ford's old friend Senator Edward Kennedy was one of them:

> On a wide range of crucial issues of national importance, on civil rights, on bussing, on social concerns, and on civil liberties, I have consistently supported positions that the nominee has opposed.... The record of the hearings before the Senate Rules Committee and thus far before the House Judiciary Committee shows Mr. Ford as an honest man, a man of integrity, a man who accepts the limitations on the power of the executive written into the Constitution nearly 200 years ago.... Finally, what stands out from his responses to questions and from the testimony of his colleagues is a record free of the political corruption that has stained too much of our political institutions.[84]

When the House Judiciary Committee began its hearings on November 15, Ford opened his testimony by again stressing the importance of honesty. "I think people ought to tell the truth. Especially politicians." Ever loyal, Ford told the committee that he would continue to support Nixon.

> Of course I support the president. He is my friend of a quarter-century. His political philosophy is very close to my own.... To be honest, I imagine that as a vice president you do your presidential criticizing a little more privately than publicly. But those of you who know me know that I am my own man and that the only pledge by which I have bound myself in accepting the president's trust and confidence is that by which we are all bound before God and under the Constitution, to do our best for America.[85]

The House hearings covered one issue not addressed before the Senate, Ford's unsuccessful attempt in 1970 to impeach Supreme Court Justice William O. Douglas. After two of Nixon's Supreme Court nominees failed to win confirmation, Ford had delivered an impassioned plea to the House to appoint a special committee to investigate whether Douglas had violated federal laws prohibiting judges from making money from outside sources, but the majority Democrats killed the request. The hearings took a strange turn when Ford revealed that he had been driven by his innate prudishness. He found it unforgivable that Douglas had published an article in the *Evergreen*, a magazine that included pictures of naked women, or as Ford called it, "a pornographic magazine with a portfolio of obscene photography." During the hearings, Jerome Waldie goaded Ford into a breach of decorum — Ford pulled the magazine out of his briefcase, held it up, and displayed the nude photographs to the committee.[86]

On November 29, the committee voted to approve Ford's nomination 29 to 8, with all seventeen Republicans and twelve Democrats voting yes, and the full House followed with a 387-to-35 vote to confirm on December 6. Before the vote, Rodino called Ford to tell him that his nomination would be approved, but he himself would vote no. Rodino had been a supporter of Douglas, and he was offended by Ford showing the nude photographs to the committee. "I was a liberal. I believed that Justice Douglas was a great jurist. And there was something about Ford showing those nude pictures to the television cameras that just did not sit well with me."[87]

Like their Senate colleagues, House Democrats declared that they were voting for Ford because of his character, notwithstanding their major ideological differences. David Obey of Wisconsin declared that, even though he disagreed with Ford "on the vast majority of major issues," he would vote to confirm because he held Ford's "integrity in high respect. I sincerely believe him to be an honest man, and I think we all believe that above everything else right now the country needs in the vice-presidency an individual whose honesty and integrity is not questioned." Andrew Young of Georgia explained that he was "casting a vote of faith and hope that he will be a uniting and stabilizing force in a nation beset by division and crisis."[88]

On the evening of December 6, Betty Ford stood smiling on the podium in the House chamber at the Capitol as she held a Bible between her husband and Chief Justice Warren Burger. Nixon looked on from several feet to the right as Warren administered the oath that made Ford the nation's 40th vice president. Nixon wanted to hold the ceremony in the White House, but Ford insisted that it take place in his place of work for the last quarter century. After he took the oath, Ford gave a short address in his normal flat tone, which seemed reassuringly calm on that day. "Together we have made history here today.... In exactly eight weeks, we have demonstrated to the world that our great republic stands solid, stands strong upon the bedrock of the Constitution." He added a signature line. "I am a Ford, not a Lincoln. My addresses will never be as eloquent as Mr. Lincoln's. But I will do my very best to equal his brevity and his plain speaking." At the end of the speech his former colleagues beamed as Ford said, "To you, Mr. Speaker, and to all of my friends here, however you voted an hour ago, I say a very fond goodbye."[89]

When Ford's nomination was first announced, many national commentators blasted Nixon's choice. The *New York Times* called him a "routine partisan of narrow views"; the *Washington Post* wrote that Nixon should have chosen a nominee of "genuine fitness and distinction," and declared that "Gerald Ford is not such a man"; and the *Wall Street Journal* said that his nomination reflected poorly on Congress: "The nomination of Mr. Ford caters to all the worst instincts on Capitol Hill—the clubbiness that made him the choice of Congress, the partisanship that threatened a bruising fight if a prominent Republican presidential contender were named, the small-mindedness that thinks in terms of those who should be rewarded rather than who could best fill the job."[90] The reviews were more favorable after Ford was publicly examined by the Senate and the House. The *Wall Street Journal* admitted that, although Ford would not have been their top choice, "it is a comfort to see him sworn in as Vice President." The editors acknowledged that the confirmation hearings demonstrated that Ford was a man of honesty, and "much of the criticism of him has been far overdone."[91] On the day of Ford's swearing-in, Columnist William Greider of the *Washington Post*, one of those who reacted negatively to the Ford announcement, explained why he and so many others had had a change of heart. "The more they thought about Jerry Ford, the more they thought of him."[92]

2

The Fall of Richard Nixon

Most vice presidents spend their time staring out from the Executive Office Building, wistfully wondering how to get involved in the big doings over in the West Wing. They wonder what happened to the promises of partnership from the campaign trail, as they are shut out by staff members who have known the president for years and by the president himself, who prefers to rely on aides whom he can fire if they disappoint him. Like most vice presidents, Ford was excluded from the day-to-day operation of the Nixon administration, but that didn't bother him in the least.

Even if the Nixon people had been inclined to involve Ford in the administration, there would not have been much to bring him into, because the White House was barely functioning. With his presidency crumbling and his enemies closing in, Nixon's paranoia overcame his ability to function, and he withdrew from the world. According to speechwriter David Gergen, Nixon "crept into a shell so that few of us saw him for more than a glimpse at a time," and Laird says that he and Harlow had to "break down the door" to see the president.[1] Press Secretary Ziegler continued his impassioned defense of Nixon, bickering with hostile reporters in daily press briefings, but everyone else was hunkered down waiting for the end. Nixon's lawyers, Fred Buzhardt, Leonard Garment and James St. Clair, were working frantically on what they knew was a losing effort, and they were ethically torn as they were forced to explain why evidence was disappearing and defend previous administration lies.

No sane person would have wished to be more involved in that White House, and Ford was nothing if not sane. He remained in the Executive Office Building, surrounded by his small staff, which was nominally led by Chief of Staff Robert Hartmann, a former Los Angeles Times bureau chief who had worked in Ford's House office. Everyone who knew the stocky former reporter agreed on two things: he was a heavy drinker and he was ill-tempered. Richard Reeves called him "nasty, vindictive and loud — and that was when he was sober."[2] White House staffer Michael Raoul-Duval said that he was "just a very difficult to get along with human being."[3] Hartmann jokingly referred to himself as "S.O.B.," or "Sweet Ol' Bob."[4] He wasn't always pleasant, but as a speechwriter Hartmann could turn a phrase, and Ford valued his frank, if somewhat paranoid, advice.

Ford quickly learned that Hartmann had no management skills, so he brought in William Seidman to bring order to the chaos. Seidman was the former managing partner of Seidman and Seidman, a national accounting firm based in Michigan. He was energetic and organized, and he would serve Ford well over the next few years. Ford also brought in Assistant Secretary of Defense Jack Marsh to handle national security issues. Marsh was a country lawyer from Strasburg, Virginia, who became friends with Ford when he was elected to the House in 1962.

Hartmann suggested that he travel as much as possible, so Ford accepted every offer to take a trip out of town. In his eight months in office, Vice President Ford gave more than 500 speeches.[5] Most people in his position would have shied away from discussing Watergate, but ducking questions went against Ford's nature, and he held a press conference at every stop of his travels. But he could not be completely candid about the scandal because he felt obligated as a member of the administration to defend Nixon, and because, as the president's presumptive successor, he did not want to appear to be trying to undermine his boss. Juggling these concerns, Ford publicly criticized Nixon's aides but not the president himself. It was an easy position for him to take because it is what he believed — at least at first. Like many other stalwart Nixon defenders, Ford's first instinct was to accept that the president was telling the truth. "He's been my friend for twenty-five years. He is my friend. I believe he is innocent of any charges."[6] Ford attributed Watergate solely to the actions of the people around him. Hartmann recognized how hard it was for the vice president to renounce his old friend. "Richard Nixon still seemed to be his hero, more sinned against than sinning."[7]

It took a while for Ford to find the right balance. He immediately broke the promise he made during his confirmation hearings. "I can't imagine me going out and attacking the press."[8] He got caught up trying to prove his chest-pounding bona fides to the administration, and he told Nixon's speechwriters that he wanted "a real tough speech" to give to the American Farm Bureau Federation in Atlantic City on January 16.[9] A tough speech is what they wrote, and a tough speech is what he gave, showing none of his famous judgment and restraint. In his speech, Ford said that Nixon was being attacked by "a few extreme partisans ... bent on stretching out the ordeal of Watergate for their own purposes." He proclaimed that they were trying to take over the country. "If they can crush the president and his philosophy, they are convinced that they can then dominate the Congress and, through it, the nation."[10]

The speech disappointed Ford's old friends, who reined him in. After the speech, he went to Grand Rapids for "Jerry Ford Day," where his former constituents told him that they felt let down by the speech, and he heard the same thing from his golfing partners when he returned to Washington. Ford decided that he would not become another Agnew, simply spouting the angry rhetoric penned by Nixon's speechwriters. Hartmann wrote all of his speeches after that.

———— ◈◈◈ ————

Defending Nixon became much more difficult when the White House released the transcripts of 48 conversations on April 30. It was another of Nixon's desperate attempts to avoid turning over the tapes, and the transcripts had been heavily edited to remove "expletives" and material "clearly unrelated to the Watergate matter." Nixon had made many of the deletions himself, trying in vain to get rid of embarrassing material, but even the heavily-edited transcripts showed the sordid side of Nixon. There was something to offend everyone: his conservative Christian backers were taken aback by his constant swearing; minority groups were appalled by his frequent use of ethnic epithets; his political opponents were terrified by his threats to use federal agencies against them; and virtually everyone was horrified by his encouraging witnesses to lie and contemplating paying off the Watergate defendants. Even with the profanity removed, Nixon's language was memorable: he praised Dean for "putting your fingers in the leaks"; he suggested a "stonewall"; he said that his aides had to "keep the cap on the bottle"; and he suggested that they "pick the boil and take the heat."[11]

The transcripts provided plenty of ammunition for Nixon's critics, but they were ambiguous enough for his supporters to argue that there was no evidence directly tying him to criminal activities. The most damning transcript confirmed Dean's version of his March 21, 1973, meeting with Nixon. Just as Dean told the Ervin Committee, Nixon said that he could get another $1 million to keep the defendants silent. "On the money, if you need the money you could get that. You could get a million dollars. You could get it in cash. I know where it could be gotten. It is not easy, but it could be done." Nixon was saved by the fact that he did not actually order the payment of hush money — he and Dean just kept talking about whether to pay the defendants or come clean, which Nixon dubbed the "hangout route."[12]

Although not fatal to his case, the transcripts were bad enough to convince most Americans that Nixon had to go; for the first time, a majority of Americans favored impeachment.[13] The *Chicago Tribune* echoed the reaction of most of the nation: "We saw the public man in his first administration, and we were impressed. Now in about 300,000 words we have seen the private man, and we are appalled."[14] Ford, on the other hand, kept defending his boss: "The president, in my opinion, is completely innocent."[15]

To Nixon's dismay, the release of the transcripts did not end the battle for the tapes. The Judiciary Committee ruled that the transcripts did not comply with its subpoena, and Special Prosecutor Jaworski subpoenaed 64 more tapes. On June 10, Nixon sent a letter to the Judiciary Committee declaring that he would "draw a line" and not provide any further evidence, and the battle for the tapes went back to the courts.[16]

———〜〜〜———

The transcripts were just a piece of the evidence piling up against Nixon. In July the House Judiciary Committee issued the evidence from its impeachment hearings in sixteen volumes, and the Ervin Committee issued its final report. Some of the activities described in the reports were repugnant but arguably legal, including the administration's dropping of an antitrust suit against ITT after the company agreed to finance the 1972 Republican Convention, and Nixon's agreement to raise price supports for milk products after dairy cooperatives made large donations to his campaign. But there were plenty of indisputable crimes. The reports showed how the Nixon reelection campaign had wantonly ignored federal campaign financing laws. The campaign accepted illegal contributions from some of the most recognized names in American business, such as Ashland Oil ($100,000), Gulf Oil ($100,000), Phillips Petroleum ($100,000), American Airlines ($55,000), Braniff Airways ($50,000), Northrop Corporation ($150,000), Goodyear Tire ($40,000), and 3M ($30,000). Those weren't the donations that sent Nixon's chief fund-raiser, Herbert Kalmbach, to jail; it was the ambassadorships he traded for donations after receiving approval through "Haldeman's office." Some of the money Nixon collected ended up in slush funds rather than the campaign coffers, such as the $100,000 Howard Hughes gave to the president's friend Bebe Rebozo, who never forwarded it to the campaign committee. Rebozo claimed that the money had remained untouched in a safety deposit box the whole time, but Kalmbach testified that he once admitted loaning some of the money to Nixon's brothers and his secretary Rose Mary Woods. After the donation became public, Rebozo returned the $100,000 to Hughes, but the money he returned included five $100 bills that had been printed after Hughes made his contribution.[17]

The Ervin Committee got a glimpse of just how malevolent Nixon's people could be when Dean revealed that the administration kept an "enemies list," which he explained was "rather extensive and continually being updated."[18] In 1972 Dean sent a list to the top officials in the government, with proposals about "how we can use the available federal machinery to screw our political enemies."[19] The transcripts showed that he was clearly acting at the president's direction. When Haldeman told Nixon that Dean was working with the IRS and "moving ruthlessly on the investigation of McGovern people," Nixon encouraged Dean to continue using federal agencies against his enemies:

I want the most comprehensive notes on all those who tried to do us in.... They are asking for it and they are going to get it. We have not used the power in this first four years as you know. We have never used it. We have not used the Bureau and we have not used the Justice Department but things are going to change now.[20]

Nixon's only defense was that the IRS was more scrupulous than he was. When the White House sent the enemies lists to IRS commissioners Randolph Thrower and Johnnie Walters, they both threatened to resign rather than follow up on them, and the Congressional Joint Committee on Internal Revenue Taxation concluded that the IRS did not treat people on the lists differently from other citizens. But the agency was not completely unresponsive to administration requests — it sent Nixon's aides a report of tax investigations of George Wallace for them to use to stop a potential third-party Wallace campaign in 1972. Three weeks before Wallace's Alabama primary gubernatorial election, columnist Jack Anderson published excerpts from the report.[21]

Wallace wasn't the only candidate they attacked. Employees of the Nixon campaign followed members of Democratic candidates' families, paid journalists for information on Democratic campaigns, planted spies in Democratic campaigns, forged letters under the letterheads of Democratic candidates, leaked false items to the press, sabotaged campaign schedules, and pilfered confidential campaign files. For example, campaign aide Donald Segretti admitted that during the Florida primary he had distributed literature on Muskie campaign stationary alleging sexual misconduct by Democratic candidates Hubert Humphrey and Scoop Jackson.[22] The Muskie campaign was also the target of the administration's "national security" wiretaps. The administration had maintained wiretaps on two National Security Agency employees after they left government service and began working for the Muskie campaign. In fact, one of the taps had been ordered after the employee announced that he was leaving government service. The administration also had ordered taps on aides who did not have access to national security information, including speechwriter William Safire and an aide to domestic advisor John Ehrlichman.[23]

Several full volumes dealt with how the administration had tampered with the evidence itself, and in particular the tapes. Nixon had promised Senator Ervin that the tapes would remain "under my sole personal control," and he kept that promise, not allowing even his lawyers to listen to them. Nevertheless, some tapes went missing, and others had missing sections. The most famous was an 18½-minute gap in a conversation between Nixon and Haldeman on June 20, 1972, three days after the break-in. While the meeting covered several subjects, Haldeman's notes showed that the only part missing from the tape was the discussion of Watergate. The White House claimed that Nixon's secretary, Rose Mary Woods, mistakenly erased the tape, but the explanation was highly improbable. A panel of experts appointed by Judge Johm Sirica concluded that the gap could not have been made by Woods' typewriter or foot pedal — it was made by someone erasing and rerecording over the tape at least five times. If Woods did not erase the tape, the only alternative was Nixon. White House records showed that the tape had remained in the tape vault until it was delivered to Woods on September 28, 1973, and after that date only Woods and Nixon had access to the tape.[24]

Nixon's personal finances were also under scrutiny. At issue was the deduction he claimed for donating his pre-presidential papers to the National Archives, the problem being that he didn't make the donation before Congress eliminated the deduction on July 25, 1969. The documents attached to Nixon's tax returns were backdated to make the deduction appear legal. The White House issued statements claiming that Nixon had not been involved in the details of the preparation of his tax returns, but his accountant Arthur Blech and attorney

Frank DeMarco publicly stated that the president had been aware of the details of his returns. The IRS announced that Nixon owed $432,787 in back taxes.[25]

Faced with all of this evidence against his old friend, Ford still couldn't bring himself to admit that Nixon was guilty—he even claimed that the committee reports proved the president's innocence.[26] Until this point, Ford had avoided reviewing the actual evidence, but he acquiesced to administration pleas after the Judiciary Committee issued a report of omissions and distortions in the transcripts. After the discrepancies were published in July, Ford listened to two tapes and told the press that it was "very understandable how there could be different interpretations of the words that were spoken." The event was stage-managed by Nixon's staff, but they must have been distraught when his honesty showed through. When he was asked which version of the transcripts were more accurate, all he could say was "I think you could read it either way." He also urged the White House to release the actual tapes and all other evidence. In the end, he said the tapes could lead to "honest differences."[27]

But the differences appeared to be anything but honest. The White House transcript of a March 22, 1973, meeting had Nixon saying that Mitchell was proposing that they "get off the cover-up line," while the Judiciary Committee had Nixon saying "get on with the cover-up plan."[28] The most damning thing the White House left out was Nixon's statement on March 22, 1973:

> I don't give a shit what happens. I want you all to stonewall it, let them plead the Fifth Amendment, cover-up or anything else, if it'll save it—save the plan. That's the whole point.[29]

Even with all this damning evidence, Chairman Rodino was unsure whether any of the Republicans on the Judiciary Committee would vote against Nixon; and without a significant number of Republicans, impeachment would be seen as nothing more than an attempt by the Democrats to reverse the results of the 1972 election. He knew that three southern Democrats and a handful of Republicans were leaning toward impeachment, so he met with Republican William Cohen and Democrat Walter Flowers and asked them to try to forge a consensus among the wavering members. On the morning of July 23, Cohen and Flowers met with Democrats Raymond Thornton and James Mahn, and Republicans Lawrence Hogan, Thomas Railsback, and Robert McClory. Each of them reported that he had already decided to vote for impeachment. After the meeting, Timmons called Nixon to tell him the result. Nixon thought that all was lost, but Haig convinced him to call Alabama governor George Wallace to see if he could change Flowers' mind. When the governor said that he could not sway Flowers, Nixon hung up the phone and said, "Well, there goes the presidency."[30]

Harold Donohue opened the Judiciary Committee deliberations on the evening of July 24 by formally moving for Nixon's impeachment. During the ensuing ten-hour debate it was apparent that a significant number of Republicans would vote against Nixon. Hamilton Fish said that he would vote to impeach "with deep reluctance" because he believed that Nixon had violated the core of the conservative principle of law and order.[31] Caldwell Butler explained his vote to impeach by saying, "It is a sad chapter in American history, but I cannot condone what I have heard, I cannot excuse it and I cannot and will not stand for it."[32] The Republicans who argued the president's case argued that there was no concrete evidence of Nixon's involvement. Charles Sandman of New Jersey said, "Find me clear and direct evidence involving the president of the United States in an impeachable offense, and I will vote for impeachment."[33] He would get that clear and direct evidence within two weeks.

More than 35 million Americans watched on television the next day as the committee voted 27–11 to approve Article 1, which alleged that Nixon had engaged in obstruction of justice. Six Republicans voted for impeachment, and neither they nor the Democrats celebrated. Flowers acknowledged that he let down Nixon supporters. "I probably have enough pain for both them and me." Barbara Jordan, normally loquacious, could only say, "I don't want to talk to anybody." Republican Tom Railsback said, "I don't feel very good about it." The sentiment was echoed by Rodino, who said, "I'm not happy."[34] After the vote, Rodino broke down and cried, and he called his wife. "Pray that we did the right thing. I hoped it didn't have to be this way."[35]

Over the next two days the committee approved Articles 2 and 3, charging Nixon with violating the constitutional rights of citizens and failing to produce documents and tapes. Two articles failed: Article 4, which charged Nixon with failing to pay his taxes, and Article 5, based on the failure of the administration to obtain a declaration of war before bombing Cambodia.

———

Nixon's defenders weren't giving up. Republican David Dennis of Indiana said, "It's only Round One. There'll be a good scramble in the House."[36] Minority leader John Rhodes predicted that Nixon would win the vote before the House as a whole, but he admitted that the situation was volatile. The Democrats gave different odds. Majority leader Tip O'Neill predicted that the House would vote to impeach by a 50-vote margin. Privately, Nixon's aides agreed with O'Neill, predicting that he would lose the vote in the House.[37]

Nixon's chances were better in the Senate, where he was counting on conservative southern Democrats joining with Republicans to prevent his removal from office. The *Washington Post* predicted that the vote would be 60 to 40, seven votes short of the two-thirds necessary to remove him from office, but Nixon's support in the Senate was wavering. Some of Nixon's oldest supporters were having second thoughts, including Bob Dole, who had been Nixon's most pugnacious defender. During the 1972 campaign, Dole gave a series of speeches calling Watergate "a barrage of unfounded and unsubstantiated allegations by George McGovern and his partner-in-mud-slinging, the *Washington Post*." As it became clear that the president's aides had been involved, Dole had the same response as many other Nixon supporters — he believed that Nixon himself was innocent but those around him were not. He told the press that Haldeman and Ehrlichman should resign, and "the credibility of the administration is zilch, zero." But now he was wondering whether Nixon himself was to blame, which was bad news, because Dole was very influential with his fellow Senate Republicans.[38]

———

At first blush it seems that Dole, Ford, and other Nixon partisans must have been blind to all of the evidence that was piling up against the president. In reality, they weren't ignoring the evidence; they just accepted that the president was telling the truth. Looking back, it is hard to believe the number of times they accepted that the president was telling the truth, but the human tendency to believe the best about the people we respect and admire is profound. Nixon's supporters accepted Nixon's statements that he had not been involved in the details of the preparation of his taxes, despite the fact that his attorney and his accountant publicly stated that he had taken an interest in the minutia of his returns. They accepted that he had been unaware of the $100,000 in cash that Howard Hughes had given to Bebe Rebozo, even in light of Kalmbach's testimony that Rebozo loaned some of the money to Nixon's secretary and brothers. Nixon's supporters accepted that he had not been aware that eleven corporations had made more than $1 million in illegal contributions to his 1972 campaign. They accepted his statement that "ambassadorships have not been for sale to my knowledge," even in light of Kalmbach's testimony that the deal with Symington had been approved through "Haldeman's office," and the fact that the president had followed through on the promises.[39]

Nixon's supporters accepted that he was unaware of the sabotage conducted by his campaign. His supporters accepted his protestations that the 1969–71 wiretaps had been instituted for legitimate national security purposes, despite the tenuous connection between many of the wiretaps and national security. They accepted that he was telling the truth when he said that he did not know about the break-in at the offices of Ellsberg's psychiatrist, even though he told Ehrlichman to do whatever was necessary to obtain psychological information about Ellsberg.[40]

Nixon's supporters accepted that he did not know about the break-in at the Watergate hotel, and, more importantly, they believed him when he said that he did not try to obstruct the investigation that followed. "I took no part in, nor was I aware of, any subsequent efforts that may have been made to cover up Watergate."[41] They needed to believe him, because Nixon conceded that "the crime of obstruction of justice is a serious crime and would be an impeachable offense."[42] Nixon's supporters accepted that he was telling the truth when he said, "I did not know, until the time of my own investigation, of any effort to provide the Watergate defendant with funds," and, "At no time did I authorize any offer of executive clemency for the Watergate defendants, nor did I know of any such offer."[43] They believed that he had honestly concluded that the materials he deleted from the transcripts were "clearly unrelated to the Watergate matter," even though many of the omitted passages were patently relevant. They also believed him when he said that he had not tampered with the tapes. They even accepted his implausible explanation that Rose Mary Woods was responsible for the 18½-minute gap.

Finally, Nixon's supporters accepted his statements that he had not used government agencies to impede the Watergate investigation. They believed him when he said, "At no time did I attempt, or authorize others to attempt, to implicate the CIA in the Watergate matter."[44]

———

On August 5, 1974, the remaining Nixon supporters learned that they had been fools to accept his word. Twelve days earlier he had lost the final round of his fight to keep the tapes secret when a unanimous Supreme Court ruled against him.[45] When he received the news, Nixon called the lawyer most involved in his defense, Fred Buzhardt, and said, "There might be a problem with the June 23 tape."[46] During the defense of Watergate, Buzhardt had been in an impossible position, trying to maintain his integrity and follow Nixon's orders at the same time. Maybe that is what made him so morose, avoiding the light-hearted banter the White House staff used to relieve the tension. Until the court ruling, Nixon did not let him listen to the tapes, and when Buzhardt finally listened to Nixon's meeting with Haldeman on June 23, 1972, he realized it was more than a problem—it was fatal to the president's case. The tape, which became known as the "smoking gun," proved that Nixon was lying when he said that he had not tried to use the CIA to block the Watergate investigation.

> All right, fine.... You call them in.... Don't, don't lie to them to the extent to say there is no involvement, but just say this is sort of a comedy of errors, bizarre, without getting into it, "the President believes that it is going to open the whole Bay of Pigs thing up again. And, ah because these people are plugging for, for keeps and that they should call the FBI in and say that we wish for the country, don't go any further into this case," period.[47]

It was the final nail in Nixon's coffin—undeniable proof of obstruction of justice, which he had admitted was an impeachable offense.

———

The Supreme Court ruling began the end game of Nixon's presidency, which was to last for sixteen more days. Since Nixon was withdrawn from the world, the final moves were orchestrated by Haig. The four-star general had been chief of staff for just over a year — he had been Kissinger's chief of staff before Nixon asked him to replace Haldeman. He was a hard-working, no-nonsense military officer, but he would occasionally break his stony demeanor to crack jokes or imitate Kissinger. In Gergen's words, Haig was "a rock of stability, keeping the government on course during a time of constitutional crisis, steadying the president and the staff, and pushing toward a just resolution."[48] Kissinger said the same thing with typical hubris. "Al Haig is keeping the country together, and I am keeping the world together."[49]

Nixon finally sat down to consider his options on July 31, one week after the Supreme Court ruling. The president had a practice of sketching out his thoughts on yellow legal pads, and this time he wrote down three options: resign now, wait for a House vote to impeach and then resign, or fight through a Senate trial. It didn't take him long to realize that resignation was the only viable option. His decision was confirmed the next day when he met with Haig in the presidential office in the Executive Office Building. The chief of staff explained that he had reviewed the transcript with the lawyers defending Watergate, James St. Clair, Leonard Garment, and Fred Buzhardt, and each thought that the tape would have a "terminal effect" on his defense. Nixon understood the gravity of the situation, and he had decided to resign. He asked Haig to meet with Ford and to tell him to be ready to take over, but to caution him to keep absolute secrecy and to remind him that the president reserved his right to change his mind. "He's a good and decent man, and the country needs that now."[50]

When Haig returned to his office, he found Buzhardt waiting for him. Haig knew Buzhardt from West Point, and he had trusted his advice throughout his career. Buzhardt was there to explain Nixon's options, and it is not clear if he was acting at the president's direction, whether Haig had asked for the analysis, or if Buzhardt was acting on his own initiative. Buzhardt listed Nixon's options:

1. Nixon could temporarily step aside while he defended himself before the Senate, with Ford becoming acting president until the impeachment question was settled.
2. Nixon could delay his resignation, hoping for some turn of events that might save his presidency.
3. Nixon could try to persuade the House to settle for a vote of censure instead of impeachment.
4. Nixon could pardon himself and then resign.
5. Nixon could pardon some or all of the Watergate defendants, pardon himself, and then resign.

At some point, one more option was added:

6. Nixon could resign and hope that his successor would pardon him.[51]

According to Buzhardt, he gave Haig a list of five items, and option 6 was added later without his knowledge. Haig claims that Buzhardt included the pardon option in the list and emphasized the option by handing Haig a draft pardon and a memo explaining that a president could pardon someone who had not yet been charged with a crime.[52] Ford's advisors would assume that the idea was Nixon's because they were certain that every move was being orchestrated by the president, but they did not realize how withdrawn he had become, and they did not understand that Haig had decided to orchestrate an end of the crisis for the sake of the nation. Nixon was certainly capable of ordering Haig to see if Ford would agree to pardon him, and Haig was capable of doing it on his own. Haig and Kissinger had floated the idea months before at a staff meeting, but Laird told them to "stay away from Ford."[53]

Whatever the genesis of the sixth option, it must have been added to determine if Ford would agree to pardon Nixon. In the next few days Ford would avoid accepting any deal, but only because he was steered in the right direction by the people around him.

—◦◦◦—

It was not yet nine in the morning when Haig called Ford and asked to meet as soon as possible. When Ford told his chief of staff about the meeting, Hartmann was immediately suspicious of Haig's intentions, and he suggested that either he or fellow aide Jack Marsh attend the meeting as a witness. Ford asked Hartmann to stay. When Haig arrived and found Hartmann in attendance, he wasn't pleased. Marsh would have been a better choice, because he was a friend and had Haig's trust. Hartmann did not; Haig considered him to be "caustic, aggressive, rude."[54] He wasn't Haig's type of guy, and their mutual distrust would continue after Ford became president.

Haig opened the meeting bluntly. "Things are deteriorating. The whole ball game may be over." Because he didn't trust Hartmann, Haig did not say what was on the smoking gun tape—all he said was that turning it over would be fatal to Nixon's defense. "When that happens, it is the consensus of the president's lawyers and advisers, and my own opinion as well, that the president's chances of avoiding impeachment in the House or winning acquittal in the Senate will disappear." Because Hartmann was there, Haig didn't give Ford the list of options. All he did was prepare him for Nixon's decision. "Mr. Vice President, I think you should prepare yourself for changes in your life. I can't predict what will happen, or when, but I think you should hold yourself in readiness."[55]

Haig decided that he needed to meet with the vice president alone, and early that afternoon he called Ford at his Senate office and asked to meet without Hartmann. When Ford agreed, Hartmann told Ford not to meet with Haig alone, but all Ford said was, "Never mind. I'll fill you in."[56] When Haig arrived at Ford's office at the Executive Office Building, he described the June 23 tape and said that Nixon intended to step down. "Are you ready, Mr. Vice President, to assume the presidency in a short period of time?" Ford responded, "If it happens, Al, I am prepared." Haig listed Nixon's six options, but he explained that he was not recommending any of them. Other than mentioning the pardon option, Haig did not make any comment on it, and Ford did not express any opinion about any option. He told Haig that he needed time to think and consult with his wife and White House Counsel St. Clair. They each agreed to be available to discuss developments at any time day or night. As Haig was walking out of the office, Ford put his arm around his shoulders and thanked him for the way he was handling the crisis.[57]

After his meeting with Haig, Ford asked Hartmann to set up a meeting with St. Clair for the next morning. In the waning days of the Nixon administration, suspicion was in the air, and no one was more suspicious than Hartmann. When Ford described the pardon option, he blew his top. "That last option Haig mentioned, that Nixon resign in return for an agreement that he receive a pardon from the new president. I don't like that at all." When Ford explained that Haig had not pushed for any of the options, Hartmann was not mollified.

I know, I know. But Haig didn't come over here to go away empty-handed. And he didn't discuss this delicate matter without Nixon's knowing about it. And he mentioned the pardon option, and you sat there listening to him. Well, silence implies assent. He probably went back to the White House and told Nixon that he'd mentioned the idea and that you weren't uncomfortable with it. It was extremely improper for him to bring the subject up.... I think you should have taken Haig by the scruff of the neck and the seat of the pants and thrown him the hell out of your office, and then you should have called an immediate press conference and told the world why.

Ford told Hartmann that he was overreacting.[58] He was, but he was right to remind Ford to avoid even the appearance that he was making a deal for the presidency.

———～———

When Haig returned to the White House he met with Nixon and reported on his discussion with Ford. The meeting was short, and Nixon said nothing when Haig told him that Ford did not respond to the six options.[59] Haig then began a series of meetings with Nixon's top aides to let them know about the June 23 tape. He told Kissinger that the tape was the "smoking gun."[60] Haig also showed the transcript to Nixon's most ardent supporters, speechwriter Patrick Buchanan and press secretary Ronald Zeigler, and they agreed that the tape was the end of the presidency. Buchanan reluctantly admitted that the fight was over. "He has to resign."[61]

On the afternoon of August 1, Nixon met with Ziegler and told him about his decision to resign. Nixon said that Ford was "a decent man, and the country needs that now." Zeigler was devastated, but he told Nixon that he would support his decision. When Nixon told him that he wanted to announce the resignation on Friday, August 2, Zeigler convinced him that they needed more time to prepare, and Nixon postponed the announcement to the following Monday.[62]

That evening, while Ford was getting ready to go to a formal dinner, Hartmann tried again to convince him to explicitly reject the pardon option. Hartmann made a better case than he had earlier by focusing on Ford's need to avoid any implication that he had a role in Nixon's resignation:

> Boss, you just can't get involved with this thing in any way. Whatever the president decides, whatever Haig and his lawyers tell him, the vice president must not have any part of it. And you ought not even be thinking about pardons.... You are going to be president. But you won't be able to run the country if you have anything at all to do with the way Nixon leaves office. You can't advocate resignation any more than you can advocate impeachment. Somebody else has to push him over the cliff, or he has to jump himself.

Ford said that he needed to think it over. "Well, I'm going to sleep on it."[63] When he told Betty about his meeting with Haig over a glass of bourbon after dinner, her first reaction was understandable. "My God, this is going to change our whole life." When she heard about Haig's list of options, she had the same reaction as Hartmann. "You can't do that, Jerry." Ford's response was a glimpse into his thinking. "This just has to stop. It's tearing the country to pieces."[64] In other words, his first instinct was to offer Nixon a pardon — not because he wanted to cut a deal to become president, but because he had already concluded that a pardon was in the nation's interest.

After 1:00 that morning, Ford had a short phone call with Haig. There are two versions of what happened. Hartmann remembers that the day after the call Ford told him that he called Haig and told him to "do whatever they decided to do; it was all right with me."[65] Both Ford and Haig remember the call differently. They both have written that Haig called Ford as he and Betty were going upstairs to bed. Haig said, "Nothing has changed. The situation is as fluid as ever." Ford responded, "Well, I've talked with Betty, and we're prepared, but we can't get involved in the White House decision-making process." And Haig replied, "I understand. I'll be in touch with you tomorrow."[66] According to Haig, he was surprised that Ford thought that he had asked him to become involved in Nixon's decision-making process, so he called Buzhardt and rudely woke him. "Goddamnit, what did you do to me?" Buzhardt explained, "I didn't do anything to you. Al, that's all we did was give the options."[67]

The different recollections could be important because if Ford told Haig to "do whatever they decided to do, it was alright with me," he may have signaled his acceptance of the pardon option. In the version from Haig's and Ford's memoirs there could be no such implication, and the discussion between Haig and Buzhardt is more consistent with that version. Even if Ford did signal his acceptance of option 6, he undid the damage the next day.

That night Nixon had dinner with his friend Bebe Rebozo on the presidential yacht *Sequoia*. When Rebozo tried to talk him out of resigning, Nixon held firm. The president had a hard time with uncomfortable situations, and he asked his old friend to break the news to his family. When Nixon returned to the White House his daughter Tricia joined him in his study, and Nixon told her about his decision to resign. She walked across the room, put her arms around her father, kissed his forehead and said, "You're the most decent man I've ever known." Nixon said, "Well, I just hope I haven't let you down." But he knew he had.[68]

————

At 8:00 the next morning Ford met with St. Clair in the Executive Office Building. At Ford's request, St. Clair gave his assessment of the smoking gun tape. "Probably the same as yours. Unquestionably, this will lead the House to impeach the president. It'll lead the Senate to convict him. The only question now is: What does he do? Resign or fight it through?" When Ford asked St. Clair about the list of options Haig had given him, it was clear that the White House counsel had not seen it, and St. Clair added that he had not given any advice regarding the ability of the president to pardon someone who had not yet been convicted.[69]

When St. Clair left at 9:00, Hartmann brought in Marsh in another attempt to convince Ford to tell Haig that he would not agree to a pardon. The 47-year-old Marsh was a former country lawyer from Strasburg, Virginia, and possessed a gentlemanly manner. As a Democratic representative from Virginia, Marsh had been a colleague of Ford in the House for eight years, and Ford trusted his advice, which was more level-headed than Hartmann's.[70] Marsh later explained that he was trying to prevent a situation where Ford had "agreed to a pardon and there would be an appearance of a quid pro quo."[71] When the vice president described his discussions with Haig, Marsh warned him that the fact that he did not reject the pardon option could be construed as a signal that he was open to it. Ford again focused on whether a pardon ultimately would be the right thing for the country. "You could make a strong case for a pardon, that it would be in the national interest." Marsh explained that the issue was not whether a pardon was justified, but whether Ford could offer it in return for Nixon's resignation. Even though Marsh was more restrained than Hartmann, Ford was taken aback by how strongly he seemed to feel, and he promised to think it over.[72]

At Hartmann's suggestion, Ford also agreed to solicit the opinion of his old friend Bryce Harlow. Harlow was considered a Republican elder statesman, and Ford trusted his advice. Harlow had been an advisor to Eisenhower and Nixon, and he was, in the words of William Safire, "the courtliest short person in Washington since James Madison."[73] When they met in the Executive Office Building after lunch, Ford described the events of the past two days and asked, "What do you think, Bryce?" Harlow agreed with Hartmann and Marsh:

> You are going to be president for nearly three and hopefully seven years. Whether Nixon resigns or is convicted, the probability is that the question of a pardon will come before you sometime before you leave office.... There must not be any cause for anyone to cry "deal" if you have to make that decision, or any mystery about your position now that you know what Haig and St. Clair have told you. But the most urgent thing, Mr. Vice President, is to tell Al Haig, straight out and

unequivocally, that whatever discussions you and he had yesterday and last night were purely hypothetical and conversational, that you will in no manner, affirmatively or negatively, advise him or the president as to his future course, and nothing you may have said is to be represented to the president, or to anyone else, to the contrary.[74]

Ford was finally convinced, and he and Marsh wrote out a script for the call with Haig. It took a few minutes to reach Haig, who was meeting with the president, but when they finally connected, Ford got right to the point. "I want you to understand that I have no intention of recommending what the president should do about resigning or not resigning and that nothing we talked about yesterday afternoon should be given any consideration in whatever decision the president may wish to make." All Haig said in response was: "You're right." After the call, Hartmann, Harlow, and Marsh went for a drink to celebrate "a good day's work."[75]

That was the end of any pardon discussion. Before the call, Ford's advisors had been concerned that he may have tacitly agreed to a pardon because he did not reject the idea out of hand. They rightly wanted the vice president to be above reproach, and they rightly encouraged him to avoid any possible implication that there was a deal. But in retrospect, Ford's failure to immediately reject the pardon option cannot reasonably be interpreted as acceptance. At most, he signaled to Nixon and Haig that a pardon was an option that he would consider. He made no promises or offers to Nixon, tacitly or otherwise, and in case there was any doubt, Ford's call to Haig made clear that there was no promise of a pardon.[76] Nixon would have to make his decision to resign on his own.

———— ∿∿∿ ————

After his call with Haig, Ford went to Capitol Hill for a meeting with Senate majority leader Mike Mansfield and minority leader Hugh Scott to discuss the rules for Nixon's impeachment trial. As presiding officer of the Senate, Ford was entitled to preside over the trial, but as Nixon's successor he thought he should have no role in it, and he explained that he would not even exercise his right to vote to break a tie. After Mansfield left the meeting, Scott told Ford that he and Goldwater estimated that Nixon had 34 potential votes in the Senate, exactly the number needed to prevent his removal, but eleven of those votes were soft. Scott concluded the meeting with tearful thanks to Ford. "You're all we've got now, and I mean the country, not the party."[77]

That night, Nixon told his family about his decision to resign — Pat Nixon had learned of her husband's decision from Rebozo earlier that day. She and their daughters convinced him to reconsider, and he decided to release the tape transcripts and see what reaction ensued. If the reaction was as expected, he would follow through on his decision to resign. If the reaction was muted, he would continue to fight. He called Haig and told him to stop working on the resignation speech and to begin work on a statement to accompany the transcript.[78]

The next day, Saturday, August 3, Ford left for a trip to Mississippi and Louisiana. He was faced with a conundrum. At every stop in his travels the vice president had been declaring that he knew of no evidence directly linking Nixon to the cover-up, but he could no longer truthfully say that, and if he omitted it, reporters would notice. On the way to Mississippi, Hartmann tried to convince Ford to put a statement in his speech reiterating his earlier comments. Ford demurred, hoping beyond hope that reporters wouldn't ask. Ford's hopes were dashed by the first question when he landed in Hattiesburg. "Does the vice president now think Nixon will be impeached?" Ford responded that "unless there is some change, he will be," but he added, "I still believe the president is innocent of any impeachable offense."[79] Ford later explained that he was afraid that a change in his public stance, or a refusal to answer, "would lead the press to conclusions that I now wanted to see the president resign to avoid an impeachment vote in the House and probably conviction in the Senate."[80]

———— ∽∾∽ ————

On Monday, August 5, Nixon released the transcript of the June 23 tape, but first Haig met with members of the White House staff to give them advance notice of what was coming. He started with a graphic military expression. "Gentlemen, are your sphincters tight?" And he concluded by saying that Nixon was "guilty as hell."[81] The news was devastating to the young members of the staff. Theodore White reported the thoughts of one young staffer lying on his couch after the meeting with Haig. "Oh, those bastards, those sons of bitches out there who've been saying all these things about the president all year — those bastards I hated, they were right."[82]

Nixon lost his last defenders when he released the transcript of the June 23 meeting. When he read the transcript, Republican National Committee chairman George Bush was convinced that Nixon had to go:

> Shortly before the president's second inauguration, I still firmly believed that President Nixon had nothing to do with the unfolding scandal that became known simply as Watergate.... The "smoking gun" tape ... was proof the president had been involved, at least in the cover-up. This was proof the president had lied. After this, I lost faith in Nixon. I could not forgive him this lie.[83]

Nixon's remaining support in the House evaporated. Minority Leader Rhodes announced that he would vote for impeachment; and when he was asked whether there was anything Nixon could do to save himself, Rhodes replied, "I suppose there might be, but I can't think what it is."[84] Before the transcript was released, Haig showed it to Representative Charles Wiggins, who held Nixon's old seat and who had been Nixon's most ardent supporter on the Judiciary Committee. Wiggins' reaction was typical. "Holy smoke! It's all over.... It's all over. The minute this tape comes out, he'll lose all but a few Republicans. He may even lose me." Wiggins tearfully told the press that he had reached the "painful conclusion" that it was in the national interest for Nixon to resign.[85] Nixon also lost the support of the other nine Republicans on the Judiciary Committee who had voted against impeachment. They announced their change in position on August 6 and gave their reasons in a thoughtful statement that accompanied the committee's final report. The former Nixon defenders asserted that impeachment was justified only for "serious misconduct dangerous to the system of government established by the constitution," and they concluded that Nixon had admitted to committing such a crime. "We believe that the charges of conspiracy to obstruct justice, in essence, if not in terms, may be taken as substantially confessed by Mr. Nixon on August 5, 1974, and corroborated by ample other evidence in the record." The statement should have ended forever any thought that Nixon had been hounded from office.

> We know that it has been said, and perhaps some will continue to say, that Richard Nixon was "hounded from office" by his political opponents and media critics. We feel constrained to point out, however, that it was Richard Nixon who impeded the FBI's investigation of the Watergate affair by wrongfully attempting to implicate the Central Intelligence Agency; it was Richard Nixon, who created and preserved the evidence of that transgression and who, knowing that it had been subpoenaed by this committee and the Special Prosecutor, concealed its terrible import, even from his own counsel, until he could do so no longer.[86]

The situation was just as bad in the Senate. When the transcript was released, Barry Goldwater and Hugh Scott were meeting to tally Nixon's support. Their poll — which was taken before the transcript was released — showed that 36 senators might vote for Nixon, just two more than necessary to prevent his removal from office. The two men agreed that enough senators were having second thoughts that he was likely to lose. Goldwater told Scott that he was one of those senators, and then he said, "The president is gone.... The vice president is the only hope for unifying the country."[87] After the meeting with Scott, Goldwater read the transcript. "I was mad. I was goddamned mad when I got to the office."[88] When he received a call from Bush, Goldwater told him that Nixon's support in the Senate was gone. "I don't think the president can get fifteen votes in the Senate, and I'm not going to protect him anymore."[89] Robert Dole and John Tower agreed with Goldwater's assessment — Dole said that the number of senators supporting Nixon had fallen from forty to twenty. "I just think he loses. I just think everything is downhill."[90]

Ford landed at Andrews Air Force Base just as the White House was releasing the transcript. When he got to his office in the Executive Office Building, Haig joined him, and Ford was struck by how haggard and exhausted he looked. Haig explained that Nixon had still not decided whether to resign.[91] Although the reaction to the June 23 tape was as bad as he had feared, Nixon wavered all day, with his aides telling him it was over and his family urging him to fight. Nixon finally relented in the afternoon, and at dinner with his family aboard the *Sequoia* he declared that his decision was final.

But Nixon still wavered, and at a cabinet meeting the next morning he announced that he would not resign; he would let the legal process take its course. After the announcement, the meeting was tense — Bush later described the atmosphere as "unreal." In a breach of protocol, Ford got up and read a statement pledging continued support of the administration's policies but declaring that he would no longer profess Nixon's innocence. "I wish to emphasize that had I known and had it been disclosed to me what has been disclosed in reference to the Watergate affair in the last twenty-four hours, I would not have made a number of the statements that I have made, either as minority leader or as vice president of the United States." Bush rose and said, "Mr. President, it is my considered judgment that you should now resign." Attorney General Saxbe couldn't control himself when Nixon suggested an inflation summit. "Mr. President, I don't think we ought to have a summit conference. We ought to be sure you have the ability to govern." Kissinger brought the meeting back to earth. "We are here to do the nation's business."[92]

After the Cabinet meeting, Ford went to a lunch with Republican senators, where the mood was ugly. Goldwater told Ford, "He ought to resign now." Peter Dominick agreed. "Does the president know how we feel? The list of potential charges against him is incredible. His case is insupportable. He ought to get out now and not be forced out by the Congress." Edward Brooke also predicted that Congress would force Nixon out of office. "If he chooses to go through the impeachment process, he will lose decisively." And Norris Cotton suggested that a delegation of Nixon's former supporters in the Senate visit the president to break the bad news about his lack of support. Ford, uncomfortable playing any role in Nixon's removal from office, left the meeting. After Ford left, Goldwater vented his anger. "There are only so many lies you can take, and now there has been one too many. Nixon should get his ass out of the White House — today!"[93]

That afternoon, Nixon summoned Haig and Zeigler to his office at the Executive Office Building and told them that he had decided to resign effective noon on Friday, August 9, with a televised announcement the night before. "Things are moving very fast now, so I think it should be sooner than later. I have decided on Thursday night. I will do it with no rancor and no loss of dignity. I will do it gracefully." When he left the meeting, Haig called Ford and told him that it would all be over within seventy-two hours.[94]

At eight o'clock the next morning, Haig sat on the sofa in Ford's office and told him the same thing. "Mr. Vice President, I am here on the president's instructions to tell you that you should prepare yourself to assume the presidency at noon on Friday." He again cautioned that Nixon had the right to change his mind until the actual resignation. When Haig asked whether the White House staff could assist him in any way, Ford had only one request: "Look after the president, Al."[95]

Early that evening Nixon met in the Oval Office with Senate Republican Leader Scott, Senator Goldwater, and House Republican Leader Rhodes. When he learned about the meeting, Haig was afraid that if the congressional leaders told Nixon to resign, he would get his back up and refuse. Haig met with Goldwater at noon and told him that Nixon's decision to resign had to be his own, both because of Nixon's likely reaction and because the office of the presidency would be impaired if a group of senators could insist that the president step down. Goldwater understood. "You're right on every count. Don't worry, Al. We won't say a word about resignation to Nixon or anyone else." Goldwater was true to his word — the congressional leaders told Nixon that he would lose in the Senate, but they did not suggest that he resign. After less than half an hour, the meeting was over, and Scott explained to the waiting reporters that he told the president the situation was gloomy. "He asked me, 'Damn gloomy?' I said, 'Yes, sir.'"[96]

That night, Tricia Nixon and her husband Edward Cox tried one last time to convince her father not to resign. Cox said that the prosecutors would never let up if he resigned. "I know these people. They are smart and ruthless; they hate you. They will harass you and hound you in civil and criminal actions across this country for the rest of your life if you resign." This time, Nixon did not waver.[97]

———————

On Thursday morning crowds gathered in front of the White House, waiting in the rain to catch a glimpse of history. At 11:00 a somber and silent Ford entered the Oval Office for a meeting with the president. It was awkward at first, until Nixon broke the silence by telling Ford that he planned to announce his resignation that evening. He thought to himself how the presidency magnified its occupant's strengths and weaknesses, and he concluded that Ford would hold up well. After declaring, "Jerry, I know you'll do a good job," the president relaxed and gave some advice to his successor. Nixon suggested keeping Haig for the transition period, and he told Ford that Kissinger would be indispensable. Ford explained that he had already decided to ask the secretary of state to stay, and Nixon explained how to handle him. "Henry is a genius, but you don't have to accept everything he recommends. He can be invaluable, and he'll be very loyal, but you can't let him have a totally free hand." Nixon also had several policy suggestions: keep a lid on spending, work closely with Fed chairman Arthur Burns, follow a strong policy in Vietnam and Cambodia, and avoid wage and price controls. Finally, Nixon told Ford that it would be important for him to have a strong vice president and recommended Nelson Rockefeller. He closed with a story about what President Eisenhower told him on the day before the 1969 inaugural. "You know, I have only one regret on this great day. This is the last time I can ever call you Dick, Mr. President." Nixon said, "Jerry, this is the last time I'll call you Jerry, Mr. President." Tears came to Ford's eyes, and he said goodbye in commonplace, but heartfelt, language. "I'll see you tomorrow. Give Pat and the family my best." Nixon concluded in the same vein. "You and Betty will enjoy living in the mansion. We'll see you tomorrow."[98]

After he left Nixon, Ford called Kissinger and asked him to stay on, adding that he would like to announce his decision that night. Kissinger agreed. "You can count on me, Mr. Vice President."[99] Ford trusted and respected Kissinger, and he knew that the announcement would be popular because the secretary of state's approval ratings were at a record high of 85 percent. Just two months before, the cover of *Newsweek* had a drawing of Kissinger in a superman cape with the headline "It's Super K." He was the winner of the Nobel Peace Prize; he had negotiated the end to the Vietnam War; he had opened China to the West; and he had successfully negotiated an arms control agreement with the Soviets. His staff thought that America's greatest foreign policy asset was his mind and its greatest liability was his ego.[100] Winston Lord called Kissinger "the most brilliant person that I've ever met."[101] As Ford would learn, resentment toward Kissinger was growing on the right and the left, but he would never regret keeping him.

At noon that day, Special Prosecutor Jaworski went to Haig's home for a private meeting. The two men had established a good working relationship over the past months, and Haig had a favor to ask. When Jaworski arrived, Haig told him that Nixon would announce his resignation later that night, and he asked the special prosecutor for a statement that there had been no deal in exchange for the resignation. Jaworski readily agreed. Haig said that the decision to resign had been hard on Nixon and that the president would invoke his Fifth Amendment rights if prosecuted. Jaworski said that he sympathized with Nixon's plight, but he made no comment on any future prosecutions. Haig also explained that Nixon was "going to be taking his tapes and papers with him, Leon. There's no hanky-panky involved. Your office will have access to them if you need them. He's going to San Clemente tomorrow and the tapes and papers will be shipped out later." Jaworski cautioned that his office would demand access to the documents.[102]

At the same time, Nixon was meeting with Buzhardt in the Presidential Office in the Executive Office Building. Nixon explained that he did not expect a pardon, and he asked whether he would be prosecuted, but Buzhardt could not give him any consolation. Nixon, clearly worried, tried to make light of a possible jail sentence by remarking that some of the best political writing of the century had been written in jail by men like Gandhi and Lenin. Halfway through the meeting they were joined by Ziegler and Haig, who had just returned from his meeting with Jaworski. Haig told Nixon that there had been no negotiations with Jaworski, but the special prosecutor did not appear to bear hostile feelings. Based on his experience with Jaworski, Haig predicted that the president had "nothing to fear," but Nixon took no solace. "Considering the way his office has acted in the past, I have little reason to feel assured."[103] Ziegler left the meeting and went to the press room, where he was visibly upset as he read a statement. "Tonight, at 9 o'clock, Eastern Daylight Time, the President of the United States will address the nation on radio and television from his Oval Office."[104]

At 7:30 that evening Nixon walked alone from the White House to the Executive Office Building, while the crowd outside the fence sang "America the Beautiful" and waved flags. At the Executive Office Building Nixon met for half an hour with Senate president pro tem James Eastland, Senate majority leader Mansfield, Senate minority leader Scott, Speaker of the House Albert and House minority leader Rhodes. Nixon told the congressional leaders that it was his inclination to stay and fight, but he knew that the nation would be torn apart if he did, so he had decided to resign. Nixon then walked back to the White House, where he met with forty-six congressional supporters in the Cabinet Room. After Nixon told them he would resign and thanked them for their support, he lost control and left the meeting. Barry Goldwater later described the scene for the press. "He just told us that the country couldn't operate with a half-time president. Then he broke down and cried and he had to leave the room. Then the rest of us broke down and cried."[105]

At 9:01 on the evening of August 8, 1974, Nixon addressed the nation from the Oval Office. He announced his resignation in a disjointed speech which barely touched on the scandal that was forcing him from office, focusing instead on how resigning went against his temperament. "I have never been a quitter. To leave office before my term is completed is abhorrent to every instinct in my body." He explained that he was resigning because he had concluded that continuing to fight was not in the nation's interest. He apologized for the pain the fight had caused, but not for the actions that led to the fight in the first place. "I regret deeply any injuries that may have been done in the course of the events that led to this decision. I would say only that if some of my judgments were wrong — and some were wrong — they were made in what I believed at the time to be the best interests of the nation." He closed by wrapping himself in the mantle of Teddy Roosevelt:

> I have fought for what I believed in. I have tried, to the best of my ability, to discharge those duties and meet those responsibilities that were entrusted to me. Sometimes I have succeeded; and sometimes I have failed. But always I have taken heart from what Theodore Roosevelt said about the man in the arena whose face is marred by dust and sweat and blood, who strives valiantly, who errs and comes short again and again because there is no effort without error and shortcoming, but who does actually strive to do the deed, who knows the great enthusiasms, the great devotions, who spends himself in a worthy cause, who at the best knows in the end the triumphs of high achievements and who at the worst, if he fails, at least fails while daring greatly.[106]

After Nixon's address, Jaworski followed through on his promise to Haig by issuing a statement. "There has been no agreement or understanding of any sort between the president or his representatives and the special prosecutor relating in any way to the president's resignation."[107] In the light rain in front of his home in Alexandria, Ford followed Nixon's address with a short statement:

> This is one of the most difficult and very saddest periods, and one of the saddest incidents I've ever witnessed. Let me say that I think the president has made one of the greatest personal sacrifices for the country, and one of the finest personal decisions on behalf of all of us.... I pledge to you tonight, as I will pledge tomorrow and in the future, my best efforts and cooperation, leadership and dedication that is good for America and good for the world.[108]

———————

At 9:36 the next morning, Nixon gave an emotional farewell speech to the White House staff in the East Room. Nixon was never comfortable delivering extemporaneous remarks, and the stress of the occasion caused him to ramble. He spoke about his father's lemon ranch, and he called his mother "a saint." The president spoke from the heart when he thanked the members of the White House staff for their support. "And so I say to you on this occasion, as we leave, we leave proud of the people who have stood by us and worked for us and served this country. We want you to be proud of what you have done. We want you to continue to serve in government, if that is your wish." He continued with strangely-inappropriate fatherly advice. "Always give your best, never get discouraged, never be petty." In closing, the president who had destroyed himself by hating those who hated him said without any apparent sense of irony: "Always remember, others may hate you, but those who hate you don't win unless you hate them, and then you destroy yourself."[109]

At 11:35, Nixon became an ordinary citizen when Secretary of State Kissinger received a short letter. "I hereby resign as President of the United States."[110] After his speech to the White House staff, Nixon and his wife Pat went to the Diplomatic Reception Room where they met Gerald and Betty Ford. Nixon shook Ford's hand. "Good luck, Mr. President. As I told you

Gerald and Betty Ford escort Richard and Pat Nixon to the helicopter after Nixon resigned and before Ford is sworn in as president, August 9, 1974. (Photograph by Oliver F. Atkins; courtesy of Nixon Presidential Materials Project, National Archives and Records Administration.)

when I named you, I know the country is going to be in good hands with you in the Oval Office." As the Fords walked the Nixons to the helicopter on the White House lawn, the four old friends exchanged pleasantries. Pat Nixon said, "My heavens, they've even rolled out the red carpet for us. Well, Betty, you'll see many of these red carpets, and you'll get so you hate 'em." When they reached the helicopter door, Betty Ford said, "Have a nice trip, Dick." Ford recalled the moment. "The president grabbed my elbow and held it for a split second longer than necessary, as if to say 'Good luck.'" Nixon and Ford shook hands. Nixon said, "Goodbye, Mr. President," and Ford replied, "Goodbye, Mr. President."[111] Nixon boarded the helicopter, leaving the presidency to his old friend.

3

Beginning

It was just after noon on August 9, 1974, when Gerald and Betty Ford walked back to the East Room of the White House for the ceremony that would make him president. As they entered the room they were greeted with thunderous applause from the assembled crowd, which included the White House staff, the Cabinet, the Joint Chiefs of Staff, the Supreme Court, and selected members of Congress. Ford smiled as he walked across the room to join Chief Justice Warren Burger on a small platform between portraits of George and Martha Washington. Burger didn't bother with a lengthy introduction before beginning the ceremony. "Mr. Vice President, are you prepared to take the oath of office as President of the United States?" "I am, sir," Ford declared, as he placed his hand on his family Bible opened to one of his favorite passages:

> Trust in the Lord with all thine heart; and lean not unto thine own understanding. In all thy ways acknowledge him, and he shall direct thy paths.[1]

After Ford recited the oath of office, the chief justice said, "Congratulations, Mr. President." The audience responded with another standing ovation, and the new president kissed his wife on the cheek. Ford turned to the television cameras and delivered a short and appropriate speech, which he called "just a little straight talk among friends." Hartmann had written the speech in the preceding two days, and Ford did not change a word. The speech was perfect for the occasion, and it may have been the most salutary service Hartmann ever performed for his boss.

In his address, Ford acknowledged the infamy of the events that had forced Nixon to resign, calling the occasion "an hour of history that troubles our minds and hurts our hearts." After assuring that he had not "gained office by any secret promises," he proclaimed a new atmosphere of openness and honesty in the White House:

> I believe that truth is the glue that holds government together, not only our government but civilization itself. That bond, though strained, is unbroken at home and abroad. In all my public and private acts as your president, I expect to follow my instincts of openness and candor with full confidence that honesty is always the best policy in the end.

Then Ford added the speech's signature line: "My fellow Americans, our long national nightmare is over. Our Constitution works; our great Republic is a government of laws and not of men. Here the people rule." The new president fought back tears as he asked, "May our former president, who brought peace to millions, find it for himself," and he closed by reaffirming his oath of office:

> I now solemnly reaffirm my promise I made to you last December 6: to uphold the Constitution, to do what is right as God gives me to see the right, and to do the very best I can for America. God helping me, I will not let you down.[2]

In that short ceremony Ford became the leader of a disillusioned and exhausted country. Watergate was not the only thing that had troubled Americans' minds and hurt their hearts. In the preceding fifteen years the country had suffered through urban riots, protests against the Vietnam War, assassinations of national leaders, Watergate, and sweeping social changes. The process of societal change had been divisive, but the result was that Americans were far freer than ever before — they could marry people of different races, use contraception, and get divorced. The expansion of liberty for women and African Americans was even more striking — they were being educated in large numbers for the first time, they could pursue the careers of their choosing for the first time, and African Americans were finally allowed to vote. The result of the social changes, a wholesale expansion of liberty, was obviously a good thing, but the fights for freedom had taken a toll.

Social turmoil overshadowed the fact that the country's 212 million residents were more safe and prosperous than any in history. When Ford took office, the United States was at peace for the first time in a decade, and the country had experienced uninterrupted economic growth and prosperity since World War II.[3] Yet the American people didn't feel secure. They thought of the United States as weak, and they were uncertain about the future. The biggest threat to prosperity was inflation, which hit an annual rate of 15.6 percent the month Ford took office. Oil prices had spiked after the Organization of Petroleum Exporting Countries cut back on production during the Yom Kippur War of 1973. At the same time, the Arab nations embargoed oil shipments to the United States — which should have had little impact on consumers, as the American oil companies shifted their purchases to countries not participating in the embargo. But Nixon mismanaged the crisis with a complicated system of price controls on oil products, causing shortages of gasoline, heating oil, and natural gas in various parts of the country. As lines formed at gas stations, the American people felt vulnerable to the whims of foreign leaders.

The country remained strong, and its democratic institutions had operated effectively during Watergate, but its people were worn out. And they were divided between disillusioned, defeated, and bitter conservatives and mistrustful, alienated, and confrontational liberals. Watergate contributed to the new cynicism, but faith in government had already been eroded by the antiwar protests and social tumult of the '60s. The number of citizens who trusted the government to do the right thing had fallen from three quarters in the early '60s to just over a third at the time Ford took office.[4] Ford's primary goal was to unite the nation and restore faith in American institutions. He would succeed admirably, ushering in a period of relative tranquility that would last for the remainder of the millennium.

The inauguration began Ford's honeymoon period. Americans embraced their new president and his family, who seemed to epitomize the new informal atmosphere in the country. Betty's fun-loving nature was instantly apparent, and, if anything, she stood on ceremony less than her husband. She did not naturally enjoy public entertaining, but she made everyone feel comfortable, and she had an infectious sense of humor. She was also every bit as candid with the press as her husband, which occasionally caused him political problems. The prime example was an interview she gave to *60 Minutes* in the summer of 1975, when she honestly answered any and all of Morley Safer's questions, no matter how personally intrusive they were. She recognized the possibility that her daughter Susan might have an affair. "I think she's a perfectly normal human being like all young girls." She said that her children had probably tried marijuana, and she called the *Roe v. Wade* decision "the best thing in the world, a great, great decision."[5] For the rest of her husband's presidency she continued to work for women's rights, traveling the country lobbying for the Equal Rights Amendment. She also used her office to raise funds for underprivileged and handicapped children.

Of the Fords' four children, only 17-year-old Susan moved into the White House. She was attending a private high school in Bethesda, and she would start college at Mount Vernon College the next year. Steven was a year older than Susan, and he was spending a year working on a ranch in Utah before starting at Duke. Twenty-two-year-old John had just graduated from Washington State University, and he was working that summer as a forest ranger in Yellowstone National Park. The oldest son, Michael, and his wife Gayle lived in Massachusetts, where he attended Cromwall Theological Seminary. The Fords were a casual, friendly, photogenic family, and the nation found it easy to like them.

But what Americans found most refreshing was that Ford was the exact opposite of his predecessor — Alan Greenspan says they were "as different as day and night."[6] Nixon was a bundle of neuroses, while Ford called himself "disgustingly sane."[7] Nixon was hostile to the press, while Ford joked with reporters.[8] Nixon assumed the worst about everyone, while Ford believed that everyone was as honest as he was. Many of Ford's aides urged him to be more suspicious, including Hartmann, whose paranoia rivaled Nixon's, and who told his boss, "You don't suspect ill motives of anyone until you're kicked in the balls three times. As a human being, that's a virtue. But as a president, it's a weakness."[9] Representative Charles Goodell said that Ford was "genuinely naïve, and he has no instinct for power, for manipulation."[10] Ford's old friend Melvin Laird, whose instinct for manipulation was second to none, agreed with Goodell's assessment. "Jerry doesn't catch on as rapidly as he should to the political significance of an event or an issue."[11]

Ford's lack of guile led people to question his intelligence, and the media didn't hesitate to reinforce that perception. In a statement that was anything but fair, Richard Reeves wrote, "It is fair to say that Ford is slow."[12] Reporters repeated insults that presidents Nixon and Johnson had made about Ford. They reported a story about the ever-insecure Nixon asking Nelson Rockefeller: "Can you imagine Jerry Ford sitting in this chair?"[13] Even more-colorful quotes came from Johnson, who vented his frustration when Ford criticized his handling of the Vietnam War. Johnson told aides, "That's what happens when you play football without a helmet," and "Jerry Ford is so dumb he can't fart and chew gum at the same time."[14] Ford was hardly the only target of barbs from his two predecessors. Johnson called Senator William Fulbright "half-bright" after he criticized the Vietnam War.[15] Nixon denigrated almost everyone. Kissinger could think of only one person who he never disparaged, John Connally.[16]

Johnson's true feelings about Ford were better reflected in his actions rather than the comments he made during fits of pique. He worked well with Ford over the years and chose him to serve on the Warren Commission. Like Johnson, Nixon's opinions of Ford were better reflected by his actions rather than his words. After all, Nixon would not have chosen Ford to be his vice president had he not respected his abilities. But at the time, even that was cited as evidence that Nixon had no respect for Ford. During Ford's first week as president, *Time Magazine* retold the story that he was not Nixon's first choice for vice president.[17] Nixon's first choice was Agnew, and it should not have been a criticism of Ford to say, "He's no Spiro Agnew." Nevertheless, the press passed along rumors that Nixon chose Ford to make impeachment less palatable.

Part of the problem was that Ford was an inept public speaker, but he was emotionally secure enough to admit this shortcoming to Kissinger. "I am not one of those oratorical geniuses. There is no point in my trying to be one. I just have to be myself."[18] Kissinger agreed that Ford "was not then articulate, but that doesn't mean he wasn't highly intelligent."[19] Ford had no problem projecting his intelligence in informal discussions. Speechwriter David Gergen found himself dealing with a leader who was "more intelligent and more physically graceful than the press said."[20] Fed chairman Arthur Burns said that he had "no problem talking economics with Ford. He had a better grasp of economics than any other president I served."[21] Alan Greenspan agrees that Ford "had a sophisticated and consistent outlook on economic policy."[22] Ford's congressional colleagues agreed. Democratic senator William Proxmire, who played football with Ford at Yale, said that he had "a good mind, a first-rate mind."[23]

The new president was decisive to the point of stubbornness — John Osborne called Ford "a stubborn cuss."[24] As president, his decisiveness would usually serve him well, and he would be committed to do what was right regardless of political fallout. But on several important occasions — when he pardoned Nixon, when he fired several key aides at the end of 1975, and when he said that Eastern Europe was not dominated by the Soviet Union — his stubbornness prevented him from understanding how his actions would be interpreted and from making a real effort to explain his reasons to the public.

Ford liked to compare himself to Harry Truman, and he shared Truman's stubbornness, his plain-spoken manner, and his willingness to make unpopular decisions. Like Ford, Truman was beset by suggestions that he wasn't smart enough to hold the office; and they weren't alone in American history. Even some of the founding fathers had their intelligence questioned. A century ago, Henry Adams wrote a description of James Monroe that could have been written of Ford:

> Of all the great names in American history, that of Monroe seems to the keen eyes of critics to stand on the smallest intellectual foundation ... but ... he enjoyed general respect as a man whose personal honesty was above dispute, and whose motives were sincerely pure.[25]

—◦◦◦—

In August 1974 the questions about the new president's intelligence didn't affect his popularity — all that mattered was that he wasn't Nixon. Many of Ford's advisors were urging Ford to dramatically demonstrate a break with the previous administration by firing the entire Nixon staff, and two of his old friends made that pitch even before he left for the White House on his first day in office. At 8:00 that morning he met, at his suburban Virginia home, with his former law partner, Philip Buchen, and former Wisconsin congressman John Byrnes. Buchen had been a close confidante of the new president since college. One of Buchen's legs had been crippled by polio in his childhood, but he never became bitter. He was good-natured, unflappable, and judicious, and he would give Ford sound advice during the next two and a half years.

Burns and Buchen came to Ford's house that morning to brief him on the recommendations of an informal team that had been planning for the transition to his administration. The informal transition team had been established — originally without Ford's knowledge — by Buchen three months earlier when he recruited four friends, his former assistant Brian Lamb, former head of the Office of Telecommunications Policy Clay Whitehead, former Kissinger aide Larry Lynn, and Jonathan Moore, a former aide to New York governor Nelson Rockefeller and Elliott Richardson. The team worked in secret until three days before Nixon resigned, when Buchen was having dinner with Ford and told him about the transition team. Ford suggested that they add members with more stature and experience, such as Byrnes, Michigan senator Robert Griffin, Interior Secretary Rogers Morton, Pennsylvania governor William Scranton, former Nixon aide Bryce Harlow, and U.S. Steel lobbyist William Whyte. All were friends of Ford, and all had his respect.[26]

The first recommendation that Buchen and Byrnes passed on from the transition team was a new structure for the White House staff— a "spokes-and-wheel" framework with numerous people reporting directly to Ford and no formal chief of staff directing White House operations. Ford liked the suggestion, because he shared the transition team's belief that a too-powerful chief of staff was a cause of Watergate — he believed the scandal was the result of "a strong chief of staff and ambitious White House aides who were more powerful than members of the Cabinet but who had little or no practical political experience or judgment."[27] Ford would later conclude that the spokes-and-wheel structure "simply didn't work."[28] He learned that a chief of staff was essential for the efficient operation of the White House. "You need a filter, a person that you have total confidence in who works so closely with you that in effect his is almost an alter ego. I just can't imagine a president not having an effective chief of staff."[29] The fundamental problem was that the spokes-and-wheel structure didn't suit the new president. One of Ford's primary strengths was his honesty and openness, so a spokes-and-wheel structure was not necessary to promote an open atmosphere, and he needed a strong chief of staff to offset his informal management style.

Byrnes and Buchen also had suggestions for a formal transition team, and Ford accepted all but one. He agreed to Secretary of the Interior Rogers Morton, his Yale classmate Pennsylvania governor William Scranton, and John Marsh from his vice presidential staff. But he vetoed the recommendation of HEW Undersecretary Frank Carlucci as transition team leader. Ford crossed out Carlucci's name and wrote in "Rumsfeld." U.S. Ambassador to NATO Donald Rumsfeld was an old friend of Ford's from the House — he had been one of the young Republicans who engineered Ford's rise to power — and Ford had already sent a message to Europe requesting that he return to manage the transition. Rumsfeld was vacationing with his wife on the French Riviera when he received the message. He immediately flew to Washington, where he was met at the airport by his former assistant, Richard Cheney.[30]

Rumsfeld and Cheney would run the White House for most of Ford's term, and both would be frustrated by its loose atmosphere. Rumsfeld would outmaneuver all his rivals, but he would be openly irritated by his inability to exert control. According to John Osborne, Rumsfeld wanted more explicit authority "with a passion bordering on ferocity."[31] In the end, Cheney agreed that more structured lines of authority would have been preferable, but his calm demeanor allowed him to thrive without them. During the administration he believed that the open atmosphere led to good policy:

> There's less tight control and while it may produce better policy, I don't know whether it does or not. It's certainly a much more enjoyable way to work. And the reason people come to town to participate in an administration is to have a piece of the action and access to the president and to be able to influence the course of public affairs. And certainly a great many more people have that sense now than was true in the Nixon years. It would be hard. I'd be hard put to say that it leads to better policy. I think it does, but I can't prove it.[32]

After Ford decided on the members of the formal transition team, Buchen and Byrnes came to the final recommendation of the informal team, which was to fire the entire White House staff and all Cabinet members except for Kissinger. It would be a drastic measure, and Ford refused to accept that it was necessary. The transition team believed that replacing the entire staff would signal a clean break from the former administration, but Ford recognized that Nixon had recruited many talented individuals, and he saw no reason to get rid of good people in a symbolic gesture. Rumsfeld later summarized Ford's dilemma:

> The president was subject to two tugs. On the one hand, he recognized that these people were overwhelmingly fine, decent human beings. Most of them had never thought of doing anything wrong.... On the other hand, executive authority under Nixon had come to appear, both exter-

nally and internally, illegitimate. Things had reached a state in the government where if someone would say, "Good morning," others would think, "What does he really mean by that?"[33]

Ford had already decided against a purge, and he announced his decision to the top White House staffers in his introductory meeting that afternoon. He asked the assembled leaders to let their subordinates know that there would not be wholesale firings, but he warned that some changes would take place over time. For the time being, he would replace only a few people who had been closely connected to the defense of Watergate, such as Press Secretary Ziegler. He had already called Jerald terHorst, a Grand Rapids native who worked for the *Detroit News*, and asked him to take over as press secretary.

───〰〰〰───

Ford's meeting with the staff leaders was just one of a whirlwind of meetings he was subjected to on his first day in office. His first meeting was in the Red Room with congressional leaders, who agreed to his request to address a joint session of Congress on the following Monday, August 12. Ford then walked to the Roosevelt Room, where he and Kissinger met with the ambassadors from NATO countries. Kissinger had arranged for him to meet with sixty ambassadors that first day, most in group meetings with ambassadors from Latin America, Europe, and Asia. Ford met individually with the ambassadors of China, the Soviet Union, Israel, South Vietnam and several Arab nations.[34]

In the meeting with the South Vietnamese ambassador, Ford gave him a letter for President Nguyen Van Thieu. Ford tried to assure the South Vietnamese that he would enforce the peace agreement negotiated by his predecessor. "The existing commitments this nation has made in the past are still valid and will be fully honored in my administration."[35] But both Ford and Thieu were fully aware that it was Congress that controlled how much aid would be sent to South Vietnam, and Congress was not in a giving mood. One of Nixon's last acts as president was to sign into law a $1 billion limit on American assistance to Vietnam for fiscal year 1975, cutting the administration's request by more than a third.[36]

Following his meetings with the ambassadors, Ford went down the hall to the Cabinet Room to meet with his economic advisors, including Fed chairman Arthur Burns, Secretary of the Treasury William Simon, and Alan Greenspan, who had recently been nominated by Nixon to be chairman of the Council of Economic Advisers. Greenspan was the rising star in the group, and Rumsfeld had already told Ford to heed his advice. "This is a wonderful situation. It's an absolute homerun ball. You couldn't pick a better person."[37] In time, Greenspan would have more influence on Ford than any other economic advisor. In the meeting, Ford laid out his two primary economic goals: taming inflation and reducing the size of the federal budget, and he asked each of the economists to submit a policy proposal.

At just after 1:00 that afternoon, Ford introduced Press Secretary terHorst at a news conference, where he again promised an open administration: "We will have an open, we will have a candid administration. I can't change my nature after 61 years."[38] His relations with the press had been friendly over the years — he had been an open source of information in the House, and as vice president Ford frequently spent hours, martini in hand, chatting with reporters in the press cabin of Air Force Two. CBS reporter Phil Jones described the new president's relations with the media: "He's proud that he has lots of adversaries in Congress but no enemies. The same goes for the press."[39]

At 5:40 on that evening, Ford met in the Cabinet Room with his transition team. The crowd was big. It included the official transition team — Rumsfeld, Morton, Scranton, and Marsh; the informal transition team — Whitehead, Byrnes, Buchen, Harlow, Griffin, Whyte, and Leon Parma; and key staff members Haig, terHorst, and Hartmann. Ford wanted to give some of his trusted advisors significant roles in his administration, but there were no vacant posts for him to fill, so he announced that he had named several "counselors to the president" with Cabinet rank, including Hartmann, Marsh, Buchen, and Seidman. At first the responsibilities of the counselors were only vaguely defined, but each took over specific areas during the following weeks. Seidman became counselor for economic affairs, Hartmann took over the White House speechwriting office, and Buchen became White House counsel. At the meeting on his first day, Ford announced that Marsh would be counselor for national security and international affairs, but Marsh protested that giving him responsibility for international affairs might undermine Kissinger's authority. The president agreed, and Marsh became responsible for relations with Congress.[40]

That night the Fords hosted a celebration at their Alexandria home for a small group of friends. Laird described the scene:

> We were out at his home, just a few of us. We were all sitting on the floor with the kids, and Jerry was serving a light supper, and I'll never forget what a wonderful thing it was to watch him because he was answering all the questions from his children about what it meant to them and how their lives were going to change somewhat.[41]

As the guests left, Ford asked photographer David Kennerly to stay behind. Kennerly had won a Pulitzer Prize in Vietnam, and he was the *Time Magazine* photographer assigned to cover Ford as vice president. Kennerly quickly accepted when Ford asked him to become the official White House photographer. Kennerly would become a symbol of the administration's laid-back atmosphere, wearing blue jeans, sporting a beard, and cracking jokes.[42]

—∿∿∿—

Ford spent the first week of his presidency commuting from his home in Alexandria, because the Nixons had not yet moved their belongings out of the White House. To the delight of the nation, Ford did not change his normal routine. On his second day in office he opened his front door to retrieve the morning paper wearing light blue pajamas, only to find spectators and reporters. Unfazed, Ford talked with the assembled crowd and signed autographs. For the next few days he stopped and chatted with the crowd every morning and evening.[43]

Haig was waiting for Ford when he arrived at work at 8:30 on Saturday, his second day in office. Haig was there to issue a demand to stay on as chief of staff. "I have certain authorities as chief of staff, and one of these authorities is hiring and firing. And the first guy to go will be Hartmann." Ford had no intention of giving Haig that kind of power, and was not about to let go a trusted aide, so he told Haig, "Bob Hartmann is someone I will handle."[44] The meeting sealed Haig's fate. He could not stand disrespect — it went against everything he learned in the military — and Hartmann would show him plenty of it over the next few weeks. It was a situation doomed to failure, and Haig would leave within two months.

At his first Cabinet meeting at 10:00 that Saturday morning, Ford asked everyone to remain. "I think we have a fine team here, and I am looking forward to working with each and all of you." He told the Cabinet secretaries to be open with the press, and he expressed his admiration for the way they had handled the final days of the Nixon presidency. Ever solicitous, Kissinger rose and spoke on behalf of the entire Cabinet, promising "unflagging support and total loyalty to you."[45]

After the Cabinet meeting, Ford met with Kissinger in the Oval Office and told him that he had no intention of running in 1976. Kissinger told the president that he was making

During his first week as president, Ford leaves his Alexandria home for his commute to the White House. Photograph taken between August 9 and 16, 1974. (Photograph by David Hume Kennerly; courtesy Gerald R. Ford Library.)

"a very serious mistake," because other nations "would know they were dealing with a lame-duck President, and therefore our foreign policy initiatives would be in a stalemate." Kissinger's response was typical overreaction. Although he was expert at understanding the long-term interests of the United States in relation to other countries, he rarely assumed that his counterparts in other countries could understand their interests in relation to the most powerful country in the world, and he assumed that other countries acted solely on their assessment of particular American leaders. Nevertheless, Ford was convinced, and he told Kissinger that he would not make any announcement about his plans for the 1976 election.[46]

Benton Becker was also at the White House that weekend, researching Ford's options with regard to the records of the Nixon administration, which included 42 million pages and 880 reels of tapes. From the beginning of the republic, the United States has followed the curious practice of allowing constitutional officers — presidents, members of Congress, and justices of the Supreme Court — to keep the papers of their offices when their terms ended. Starting with George Washington, Congress approved the practice by appropriating funds for the purchase of the papers, and the practice was formally recognized by the Presidential Libraries Act of 1955. In Nixon's case, the applicability of this precedent was complicated by the fact that the Ford administration had received several subpoenas for the documents, which included the Watergate tapes, and by evidence that Nixon had tampered with the tapes.[47]

The day before he resigned, Nixon put in motion the process of having his documents delivered to him. He changed his deed of gift to the National Archives, giving himself sole access to the documents until January 1, 1985, and he told Sergeant William Gulley, the administrator of the White House military affairs office, to start packing up the documents and sending them to San Clemente. Gulley started work that day, and one of the first things Nixon did after arriving in San Clemente was to call Haig and ask about his papers. Ford became aware of the plan to remove the papers when one of his aides, William Casselman, was given a memo to Nixon staffers instructing them to pack up their documents, copy any needed by the Ford administration, and send the originals to San Clemente. The memo acknowledged that some documents would have to remain at the White House for legal reasons. Ford called in Becker, an attorney who had worked on his confirmation hearings, to investigate and advise him. As they discussed the issues, Ford, Buchen, Casselman, and Becker agreed that the memorandum's definition of the scope of documents that needed to stay at the White House was too narrow.[48]

On Saturday evening, Becker saw a line of Air Force trucks parked at the West Wing entrance of the White House being loaded with Nixon's documents and personal effects to be airlifted to San Clemente. Becker ordered the Secret Service to stop the operation, and the Air Force men unloaded the records. At his order, the Nixon administration documents were boxed up and stored on the fourth floor of the Executive Office Building until Ford decided what to do with them.[49]

Ford's first full week in office started when Egyptian foreign minister Ismail Fahmy landed in Washington on Sunday. Fahmy had an important message to deliver: Anwar Sadat wanted to begin peace talks with Israel. It was an idea that Sadat had floated to Nixon during the last weeks of his presidency — building on the disengagement agreement that ended the Yom Kippur War to negotiate a more permanent agreement. It was a courageous and far-sighted plan, and he found willing partners in Ford and Kissinger.

Ford asked if they should first try to negotiate a resolution of the Palestinian problem by brokering an agreement between Israel and Jordan, but Fahmy confirmed what Ford and Kissinger already knew, that the Arab world no longer viewed Jordan as a representative of the Palestinian people. Jordan and the Palestinian Liberation Organization had become enemies in 1970 when the PLO, which was then based in Jordan, tried to assassinate King Hussein. The Jordanians expelled the PLO from the country, but the Arab nations would never again support Jordan's claim to represent the Palestinians. Ford and Kissinger also knew that the most Israel would be willing to give up in the West Bank was six kilometers. Ford and Kissinger recognized that Fahmy was right, and they agreed that the next step in the Middle East peace process would be bilateral negotiations between Israel and Egypt. For the next two and a half years Kissinger would spend his considerable talents trying to broker a peace agreement.[50]

At 5:45 P.M. on Monday, August 12, Ford walked through the entrance of the House chamber for his address to a joint session of Congress. The legislators gave the new president a rousing standing ovation, cheering him as an old friend and as the leader they hoped would restore America's faith in government. The applause went on so long that Ford turned to Speaker Albert and said, "You're wasting good TV time."[51]

Ford's speech was not memorable, but it struck the right tone. He wanted to focus the nation's efforts on fighting inflation, which was running at a 15 percent annual rate, so he proclaimed that inflation was "domestic enemy number one," and he announced that he would personally preside over a summit conference on inflation. In foreign policy, Ford said that he would stay the course set by Nixon. "I have fully supported the outstanding foreign policy of President Nixon. This policy I intend to continue." In particular, he promised to continue détente. "To the Soviet Union, I pledge continuity in our commitment to the course of the past 3 years." As for Southeast Asia, Ford promised that he would be "determined to see the observance of the Paris agreement" by North Vietnam, and he predicted an "early compromise settlement" in Cambodia.[52] He would not be able to follow through on his commitment to force Hanoi to comply with the peace agreement, and his prediction of peace in Cambodia would be far off the mark, to the great sorrow of the Cambodian people.

In his address, Ford gave a glimpse into his idiosyncratic ideas about how to fight inflation. "It does no good to blame the public for spending too much when the government is spending too much." He believed that if he could convince the American people and Congress to spend less, inflation would subside. Earlier that day he demonstrated with tangible action that he intended to fight the war on inflation by trying to influence the daily decisions of two hundred million American citizens, as well as every corporation in the country. That morning he issued a statement that he was "very disappointed" with General Motors for raising the prices of its cars by 9.5 percent.[53]

Nobody bothered to tell GM about the press release; company executives learned about Ford's disapproval from press reports. They were dumfounded because they had given the federal government advance notice of the price increase in a meeting with chairman of the Council of Economic Advisers Herbert Stein and Economic Counselor to the President Kenneth Rush. Neither Stein nor Rush objected because the price increases appeared to be reasonable. GM was one of the large companies that had been subject to Nixon's price controls, and as a result its cars were priced below the market. After Ford's statement, former GM chairman James Roche called Rush and reiterated that the price increases were justified by increases in labor and material costs, but Rush asked the company to make some accommodation to the new president. Ford also called GM chairman Dick Gerstenberg and told him that the price hike was not in the best interest of the country. The company announced that it would reduce its price increase by $64 a car — the increase would be 8.5 percent rather than 9.5 percent.[54]

Ford considered it a significant psychological victory. It wasn't. His strong-arming the company would have no impact on inflation, and it certainly did nothing to address its underlying cause, which was that Fed chairman Arthur Burns had allowed the money supply to grow at an unprecedented rate during the previous four years. For the rest of his administration, Ford would fight inflation by trying to influence individual decisions of buyers and sellers, and he would ignore the continuing growth of the money supply, leaving the underlying problem for his successor.

━━━━━

When he was preparing for his speech, Ford demonstrated that he had no illusions about the peace in Southeast Asia. In their draft, his speechwriters had called the peace agreement "a settlement which made it possible for us to remove our forces with honor," but Ford crossed out the words "with honor."[55] Even though he was pessimistic about the peace, Ford believed that the United States should do what it could to support its allies. In his speech, Ford made a plea for more aid to South Vietnam than the $700 million that the House Appropriations Committee had just approved for fiscal year 1975. Ford's pleas had no effect. Four days after the speech the Senate Committee on Appropriations recommended that only $700 million be appropriated for South Vietnam.[56]

On the same day as the Senate Committee vote, the government of South Vietnam made a decision that would lead to its rapid demise. The American defense attaché in Vietnam, General John Murray, met with top South Vietnamese military leaders, and he presented a bleak prognosis. He predicted that the South Vietnamese would lose quickly if they tried to defend their entire territory, and he suggested that they cede some territory and defend a smaller area. The Vietnamese leaders agreed that his proposal was the right thing to do militarily, but they explained that it was out of the question politically. General Murray left the meeting convinced that the decision doomed the South Vietnamese.[57]

━━━━━

The first foreign policy crisis of the administration began two days after Ford's speech to Congress. On Wednesday, August 14, Ford was awakened by a call from Kissinger to inform him that Turkey had broken a cease-fire agreement on the island of Cyprus. The crisis had been brewing for several months, since the power-sharing arrangement between the Greek and Turkish Cypriots was undermined earlier that summer by the military dictatorship that ruled Greece. The head of the Greek junta, Brigadier General Dimitrios Ioannides, was committed to incorporating Cyprus into Greece (which the Greeks called *enosis*). On July 15, Ioannides had orchestrated a putsch against the president of Cyprus, Archbishop Makarios III, and replaced him with a terrorist thug named Nicos Sampson. Ioannides claimed he was not trying to engineer *enosis* between Greece and Cyprus, but his protestations were not believed by anyone — with the possible exception of Kissinger.[58]

The Nixon administration was surprised by the coup. While they did nothing to actively support the junta's actions, Nixon and Kissinger did nothing real in response to the coup. British foreign secretary James Callaghan suggested that the only way to avert a Turkish invasion was for the U.S. to "exert very great pressure" on Greece, and Defense Secretary James Schlesinger proposed that the administration cut off all military aid, but Kissinger refused to put any real pressure on the Greek government. Turkey was governed by a former student of Kissinger's at Harvard, Socialist prime minister Bulent Ecevit. To forestall an invasion, Kissinger had Nixon write a strong letter to Ecevit warning Turkey not to invade, but the letter was never delivered. When Ambassador William Macomber and his assistant James Spain went to meet with Ecevit, they had to wait outside the prime minister's office while he finished a telephone call. As they entered his office, they heard Ecevit on the phone saying, "Yes, I understand. Of course, I know you must tell us not to, Henry, but I am glad you understand our position." It was clear that he was talking to Kissinger, and as Ecevit hung up the phone he told the American diplomats, "Well, as I was just telling Henry, we are going tomorrow morning, but you Americans have no reason to worry about it."[59] The Turks invaded on June 20, and they quickly achieved their goal of establishing a beachhead on the northern coast with a corridor to the capital, Nicosia. Consequently, the Greeks agreed to a cease-fire.

The Greek junta was humiliated, which became a blessing for the people. On the day after the cease-fire, the Greek military withdrew its support for the Ioannides dictatorship, and the junta ceded power to a civilian unity government. The country exploded with joy, with people flooding the streets of Athens. The next day, the last democratically-elected leader of Greece, Constantine Karamanlis, returned from exile in France and became the new premier. American ambassador Henry Tasca had been closely associated with the junta, so Kissinger replaced him with Assistant Secretary of State Jack Kubisch, who had good relations with Karamanlis. One of Ford's first acts was to approve the appointment, and he met with Kubisch and Kissinger on his first day in office. Ford also invited the new Greek prime minister to Washington for a discussion of Cyprus, but Karamanlis declined the offer.[60]

The day after Ford took office a peace conference opened in Geneva, but neither Greece nor Turkey was willing to make any significant concessions. At the start of the conference, British foreign secretary Callaghan told the American negotiators, Robert Oakley and Arthur Hartman, that he had received intelligence reports that the Turks would break the cease-fire in five days. The British wanted to land a squadron of F-4 Phantom jets on Cyprus to deter an attack. The negotiating team cabled the information to Washington, but American intelligence disagreed with the British assessment, so Kissinger did not agree to the British plan. Foreign Secretary Callahan asked Kissinger to jointly send a message to Turkey that British troops on the island would resist any Turkish military action. Kissinger refused — he thought that threatening force would prod the Turks into an attack. The most forceful action he was willing to take was to call Ecevit and threaten "a major diplomatic effort" if Turkey attacked.[61]

The Turks forced a showdown on August 13, the day the British had predicted. The Turkish representative at the peace talks demanded that the Greeks accept a partition of the island, and the Greek representative asked for 36 hours to consult with his government. The Turks refused to give the additional time, and the Greek representative had no choice but to refuse. Turkey attacked one hour later. Turkey's foreign minister, Turan Günes, made no apologies. "Now is the time to settle the Cyprus problem once and for all, and that's what we are doing. Let public opinion embrace the Greeks and cuss us out. We don't care."[62] When Kissinger woke Ford that morning, he asked the new president for approval to turn down a British proposal for NATO to threaten air strikes against Turkey. "We should not twist their arm." With Ford's agreement, Kissinger refused to support retaliation or any form of sanctions against Turkey.[63] Neither Ford nor Kissinger spoke out against the Turkish assault.

The Turkish army gained control of the northeastern third of the island in two days and called a unilateral truce, but the Greeks were furious. For a time it looked like Greece and

Turkey would be drawn into a full-scale war, and a conflict was only averted when Karamanlis made the politically-unpopular decision to back down. He was more concerned about fortifying the fragile new democracy than pursuing Greece's jingoistic aims in Cyprus. The Greek Cabinet met the day after Turkey resumed the offensive, and only Karamanlis opposed a declaration of war. He convinced his cabinet to ask for a NATO response, under the principal that an attack on one is an attack on all, but the alliance was not willing to take military action against one of its members. Karamanlis massed Greek troops on the Turkish border, but he was probably using the crisis as a pretext to get the army out of Athens, preempting any possible coup. Karamanlis pulled Greece from the brink of war at the last minute, and he explained his actions in a nationally-televised speech.

The people of Cyprus paid a dear price during the war, which was fought with brutality on both sides. The war was the final act of the separation of Greek and Turkish populations throughout the Mediterranean. After the fall of the Ottoman Empire at the start of the 20th century, the governments of Greece and Turkey decided that the Greeks and Turks — who had lived together through the centuries — had to live apart. The result was untold misery, as Greeks were forced out of Anatolia, and Turks were compelled to leave Greece. The misery continued in Cyprus, where nearly half of the people became refugees. Before the 1974 war, villages across Cyprus had both Greek and Turkish sectors, but after the Turkish invasion hundreds of thousands of refugee Turks traveled north, and Greeks fled southward from the Turkish army.[64]

Having suffered a humiliating defeat, the Greek public turned its anger on the United States. The Greeks resented America's support of the military dictatorship, and they thought that the U.S. should have restrained the junta from the Cyprus coup, preventing the ensuing catastrophe. Throughout the rest of the year, hundreds of thousands of Greeks regularly took to the streets to march on the American embassy. Bowing to popular pressure, Karamanlis withdrew Greece from NATO's integrated command — but not from the alliance itself — and he announced that he would insist on renegotiation of American bases in the country. Privately, Karamanlis told Ambassador Kubisch that he would not insist on closing the bases, and he promised to keep his country in NATO. He asked the Americans to trust him to handle the situation.[65]

The Greek Cypriots also blamed the United States for the disaster that befell them, and they took vengeance on Americans on the island. On August 19, American ambassador Roger Davies was killed when Greek Cypriots marched on the embassy in Nicosia. When the protestors threw rocks, set cars on fire, and climbed the fence, Davies refused to leave; he was killed when they fired automatic weapons into the building. Ford took the news hard — for the first time he felt the burden of having someone who worked for him killed on the job. Premier Karamanlis reacted to "this sad event" by promising to suppress any further violence with "merciless severity."[66]

At the beginning of the civil war, the American public sided with Turkey because they objected to the Greek junta's orchestration of the coup and its transparent attempt to incorporate Cyprus into Greece. But after August 14, public opinion swung strongly against the Turks and in favor of the newly-democratic Greek government. Kissinger was baffled at what he viewed as a fickle public, but in actuality the American people were consistent in their expectations.[67] The public expected the administration to pressure its allies against aggression — first against Greece's overt aggression against the Cyprus government, and then against Turkey's overt violation of the cease-fire.

Kissinger fell short of those expectations. Throughout his time in office he was unwilling to pressure America's allies, or even publicly criticize them. It was one of his greatest failings as a statesman. Even when countries like Greece and Turkey—and later Indonesia—overtly violated the sovereignty of other nations, Kissinger caused the U.S. to remain mute in response. Each time, Kissinger justified his inaction by claiming that the Americans could not have prevented their allies from acting. Maybe he was right, but the reputation of the United States suffered from his failure to try. Maybe America could not have prevented Greece from toppling the Cyprus government or Turkey from invading, but at least the U.S. would have been on the record as opposing aggression. At least it would have been apparent to the world that America expected its allies—and not just its enemies—to follow international law. In the absence of any meaningful response by the executive branch, Congress decided to act, and the administration would fight a losing battle against sanctions on Turkey.

———〰———

On the same day the Cyprus crisis broke, Wednesday, September 14, the issue of who owned Nixon's documents became public when the press learned about Becker stopping the Air Force trucks that weekend. When reporters asked Press Secretary terHorst about the incident, he said that "the tapes are in the protective custody of the Secret Service, but they have been ruled to be the personal property of former president Nixon," and he volunteered that the special prosecutor's office agreed. The press secretary was repeating what Buzhardt had told him that afternoon, but, after the press conference, Attorney General William Saxbe and Special Prosecutor Leon Jaworski undercut him by denying that they had been consulted. TerHorst complained to Ford that Buzhardt had not been straight with him, and the president concluded that Buzhardt and St. Clair were too closely tied to the defense of Watergate to remain. Their resignations were announced the next day, and Ford appointed Buchen as White House counsel. Haig was furious about Buzhardt's firing, and he screamed at terHorst after the announcement. "Do you feel good, executing a sick man?" It was the last straw for the chief of staff, and he decided to resign, but he told his aid Jerry Jones that he would stay "long enough to get Nixon the pardon."[68]

After terHorst's press conference, Buzhardt decided that he should send the tapes to Nixon while he still could, and he told Jerry Jones to "go box all the tapes." Jones did as he was told. "It was hotter than hell—an August afternoon in an office that had no air-conditioning. As I put the tapes into cardboard boxes, I made an inventory for each box. For hours I was there, and I was just finishing up when Fred came in. I looked at him. He was ashen." Buzhardt had changed his mind. "Jerry, we just can't do this. If we let these tapes out of here, all hell is going to break loose. You and I may go to jail.... Lock them back up."[69] The tapes stayed with the rest of the documents, waiting for Ford to decide what to do with them.

The press reports about the Air Force trucks spurred the office of the special prosecutor into action. Jaworski asked for a meeting with the White House, and on August 15, Buzhardt, Becker, and Buchen met with representatives of the special prosecutor's office. Buchen diffused the situation by promising that the documents would not be sent to California until their legal status was resolved, and the White House followed with a statement agreeing that the documents would not be moved pending further discussions. Jaworski said that he was "satisfied with these arrangements," and terHorst told the press that the White House had not changed its determination that the documents were Nixon's property.[70]

At Ford's request, Attorney General Saxbe provided a memorandum—written by future Supreme Court Justice Antonin Scalia—with the official Justice Department conclusion that the documents belonged to Nixon. "To conclude that such materials are not the property of former president Nixon would be to reverse what has apparently been the almost unvaried understanding of all three branches of the government since the beginning of the Republic, and to call into question the practices of our presidents since the earliest times." The memo qualified this opinion by recognizing that Nixon's ownership rights were limited by public interest rights and by the fact that the documents were subject to court orders and subpoenas.[71] When he received the memo, Ford met with Buchen, Hartmann, and Becker to decide what to do, and Becker convinced him not to send the documents to Nixon. "If those records are put on an airplane and sent to Richard Nixon, history will record this as the final act of cover-up — there will be one helluva bonfire in San Clemente." Ford was swayed by Becker's impassioned speech, and he restricted shipments to San Clemente to the former president's personal items.[72]

On that same Wednesday, Ford had his first substantive discussions with Soviet ambassador Anatoly Dobrynin, who had returned from a vacation for the meeting. The two men already knew each other, and their discussion was comfortable and informal. Dobrynin was an extraordinary man for a Soviet diplomat — he tried to establish friendly personal relations with American officials, and he and Kissinger regularly discussed matters outside of the usual diplomatic channels.

Ford started the discussion by promising to continue détente, and he suggested a summit meeting in the Soviet port city of Vladivostok. After promising to pass the request on to Brezhnev, Dobrynin turned to the sensitive subject of Jewish emigration from the Soviet Union. Congress was considering granting the Soviet Union most favored nation trade status, but Washington senator Scoop Jackson was pushing an amendment that would make the USSR's trade status contingent on the Russians allowing 100,000 Jews to emigrate to Israel each year. When Ford told Dobrynin that some form of the Jackson-Vanik Amendment would pass, the Soviet ambassador offered informal assurances that 55,000 Jews would be allowed to emigrate each year, but he said that the Russians would not put the commitment in writing. Ford promised to consider the offer.[73]

The next morning Ford had breakfast in the Oval Office with Senator Jackson, Democratic senator Abraham Ribicoff, and Republican senator Jacob Javits. Ford explained the Soviet offer on Jewish emigration, and he explained that the agreement could not be in writing or the Russians would back out. Ribicoff and Javits favored accepting the offer, but Jackson was adamantly opposed, and he accused Ford of not being tough enough. All Jackson was willing to do was reduce the requirement for annual Jewish emigration from 100,000 to 75,000.[74]

Ford ended his first full week in office with a meeting with King Hussein of Jordan, who arrived with his wife, Queen Alia, on Friday. Their discussions were cordial and not particularly substantive, but the party that followed was memorable. That night the Fords hosted a party at the White House for the king and queen. Many of the guests had not been allowed in the White House for years, including liberal Republican senator Mark Hatfield, World Bank president Robert McNamara, and representatives of the *Washington Post*. Breaking with the protocol of the Nixon administration, the Fords stayed to dance after the entertainment ended, because, as the new president explained, "We love to dance." The guests were jubilant, and they celebrated the new open atmosphere in the White House. As she left, Queen Alia said that it had been "a swinging party," and toward the end of the evening Hatfield yelled out, "Happy New Year!"[75]

The party was a small display of the new open atmosphere, but the new president was looking for a more substantive way of demonstrating the differences between his administration and Nixon's. When he took office, Ford asked his advisors to suggest ways for him to demonstrate that he really was starting a new administration, and Secretary of Defense Schlesinger suggested that Ford make some accommodation for the fifty-thousand men who had evaded the draft by fleeing the country, which Nixon had adamantly refused to consider. Ford conferred with his old friend Melvin Laird, who thought it was a fine idea and told Ford that he had already prepared a plan for an amnesty when he was Nixon's secretary of defense. When Ford discussed the idea with Hartmann, Marsh, Haig, and Buchen, they convinced him that a blanket amnesty was not appropriate, and they suggested a process to allow draft dodgers to "earn" amnesty. Ford dubbed it "earned re-entry," and he decided to announce the proposal at the national convention of the Veterans of Foreign Wars, most of whom opposed any form of amnesty.[76]

In Congress and as vice president, Ford had opposed amnesty for draft dodgers, declaring that "if they want to return to the United States now, I feel that they must also be willing to be tried in our courts."[77] So it was a surprise when he announced a draft clemency in Chicago on August 19. In his statement, Ford explained his change of heart by mixing quotes from Truman and Lincoln:

> Like President Truman and President Lincoln before him, I found on my desk, where the buck stops, the urgent problem of how to bind up the nation's wounds. And I intend to do that.... So, I am throwing the weight of my presidency into the scales of justice on the side of leniency. I foresee their earned re-entry — earned re-entry — into a new atmosphere of hope, hard work, and mutual trust. I will act promptly, fairly, and very firmly in the same spirit that guided Abraham Lincoln and Harry Truman. As I reject amnesty, so I reject revenge.[78]

Ford had taken a risk by announcing his clemency program to an audience that was almost uniformly hostile to the idea. He could have been booed off the stage, but Ford believed that the veterans deserved to hear the news from him personally. Despite the fact that most of the audience hated the idea, there were no boos or grumblings. The crowd gave him a standing ovation.[79]

———— ✺ ————

The next day, Ford demonstrated that he was not afraid of being overshadowed by talented subordinates by announcing that he would nominate Nelson Rockefeller to be vice president. Rockefeller had been urged on him by Nixon, Haig and Laird, all of whom told him to pick a strong VP.[80]

Ford began to consider his options in earnest on the day he took office by asking John Rhodes and Hugh Scott to solicit suggestions from Republican members of Congress. He also asked members of the Cabinet and the White House staff for their recommendations. He tapped Laird and Harlow to help him narrow down the candidates; Laird had already taken himself out of the running, telling Ford that he needed to pick a leader of great stature. "I have an idea that Nixon picked Agnew because he was insecure and didn't want anyone who would overshadow him. Don't you do anything like that. When you're president, you don't have to worry about being overshadowed by anyone."[81] Laird "made as strong a plea for Rockefeller as I could. I felt that it would be the best ticket for 1976. I figured it was a winner."[82]

When the votes came in, George Bush and Nelson Rockefeller were the top two candidates. Bush received 255 total votes to Rockefeller's 181, and no one else was close. Donald Rumsfeld — one of Ford's first choices — tied for fifteenth with eight votes.[83] Harlow prepared a list of the candidates, assigning points to each for national stature, executive experience and political benefits. Bush came in first with 42 points, but only seven points separated him and the fifth-place Rockefeller. Harlow called Bush "strongest across the board"; and Bush had been contacting friends and supporters, asking them to promote his candidacy. Rockefeller came in fifth with 35 points, but Harlow said that he was "professionally the best qualified by far." Harlow concluded that there were only two real choices. "In sum, it would appear that the choice narrows to Bush and Rockefeller."[84] Ford added one name to the short list — Donald Rumsfeld. He first signaled his preferences on Friday, August 16, by asking FBI director Clarence Kelley for background checks on Rockefeller, Bush and Rumsfeld.[85]

On Saturday, Ford secluded himself in the Oval Office to make his choice. He knew each candidate personally, and he carefully weighed the advice he had received. In the end he chose Rockefeller because of his executive experience. He called Haig into the Oval Office and told him to locate Rockefeller. When Haig reached Rockefeller at his summer home in Seal Harbor, Maine, Ford joined the call and offered him the job. Rockefeller said that he was "honored. This is a great thrill." Ford told Rockefeller that he would have a more substantive role than most vice presidents. In addition to attending meetings of the Cabinet and the National Security Council, Ford wanted Rockefeller to head the Domestic Council and supervise domestic policy. "I want you on the domestic and Henry on the foreign, and then we can move these things." Rockefeller was skeptical. "I was a little bit from Missouri about this — they'd have to show me." Ford, knowing that Rockefeller was thinking of running for president in 1976, said that he would expect his support. "I will run, Nelson, and your loyalty is important." Rockefeller said that he needed to discuss the offer with his wife and family.[86]

Rockefeller had never aspired to be vice president, and he turned down Nixon's offer to be his running mate in 1960, refusing to be "standby equipment." But he certainly wanted to be president. He had run unsuccessfully for the Republican nomination in 1960, 1964, and 1968, and he recently had resigned as governor of New York, an office he had held since 1958, to make one more run. The '64 campaign was a hard-fought battle against Goldwater, which earned Rockefeller the hatred of conservatives who fundamentally disagreed with his advocacy for an activist government. Even though he had no desire to be vice president, Rockefeller called Ford the next day and accepted out of a sense of duty to the country in its time of need. He was also swayed by his respect for Ford — he "loved the guy."[87]

Ford made the announcement from the Oval Office on the morning of August 20 after first calling Bush to break the news that he had not been chosen. Ford also called Nixon, who approved of the choice. As Ford recalled the conversation, Nixon predicted that "the extreme right wing ... would be very upset, but I shouldn't worry because I couldn't please them anyway."[88] In his televised announcement, Ford praised Rockefeller as "a person dedicated to the free enterprise system, a person who is recognized abroad for his talents, for his dedication to making this a peaceful world."[89] When Ford finished his short announcement, Rockefeller graciously accepted the nomination:

> You, Mr. President, through your dedication and your openness have already reawakened faith and hope, and under your leadership, we as a people and we as a nation have the will, the determination, and the capability to overcome the hard realities of our times. I am optimistic about the long-term future. Thank you, sir.[90]

In the press conference that followed, Rockefeller predicted that Ford would run for president in 1976. That was news, because Ford had never repudiated his confirmation hearing testimony that he had no intention of running for a full term. Later that day, Press Secretary terHorst found Ford in the Rose Garden and asked about Rockefeller's comments. Ford explained that he had changed his mind. "I didn't think I would run. Now I probably will run." When terHorst asked whether he could make an official announcement, Ford gave his approval. "I don't see why not. Why should we pretend?"[91]

—⁊∾∾—

As Rockefeller noted during the ceremony announcing his appointment, Ford's "dedication and ... openness have already reawakened faith and hope."[92] The openness of his administration was a refreshing change from the aura of secrecy that had surrounded its predecessor. The Nixon White House had been a miserable place, with an "atmosphere of intimidation ... that demanded the total loyalty of its underlings."[93] What struck Nixon staffer Jerry Jones was the total lack of humor:

> They tended to lose their sense of humor.... Any organization has that kind of built-in intentional stress which the Nixon White House had, you got a lot of people working like hell, a little dour, a little frightened.[94]

It was an atmosphere that made immorality seem normal.[95] Woodward and Bernstein quoted "a well-placed" official who remarked, "If there was an honest and a dishonest way to do something, and if both ways would get the same results, we picked the dishonest way."[96]

When Ford took over, the change in atmosphere was marked. In the words of Jules Witcover, "It was as though the presidency suddenly had been given back to the people."[97] Tip O'Neill agreed. "The transition from Nixon's administration to Ford's was a thing of awe and dignity."[98] Hugh Sidey thought that the new openness reflected the basic nature of the country. "The transformation is doing so well not from mystique but from candor, not from majesty but from humility, not from complexity but from plainness.... Ford's first days look like genius because they are so ordinary, so like the rest of America."[99]

To White House aides used to dealing with Nixon, Ford was a breath of fresh air. William Hyland said that Ford was "gracious and supportive from the beginning.[100] Ford joked with reporters and staff members in a way that Nixon had never deigned to do.[101] Deputy director of OMB Paul O'Neill noticed the new atmosphere. "People are smiling. It's been a long time since I've seen anyone smile in the White House."[102] Kissinger knew that the atmosphere had changed during his first meeting with Ford. "Starting with that first meeting, I never encountered a hidden agenda. He was sufficiently self-assured to disagree openly, and he did not engage in elaborate maneuvers about who should receive credit."[103] A Nixon aide told Ron Nessen that the staff's job was easier under Ford. "With Nixon, you had to try to save him from his worst instincts. With Ford, you have to try to save him from his best instincts."[104]

Ford expected his aides to follow his lead. "The code of ethics that will be followed will be the example that I set.... I will be as candid and as forthright as I possibly can. I will expect any individuals in my administration to be exactly the same."[105] According to Gergen, the staff happily followed suit:

> In my experience over the past thirty years, every White House — save one — has on occasion willfully misled or lied to the press.... The exception to the rule was, of course, the Ford White House. More than one of our modern presidents has been a congenital liar; Jerry Ford was a congenital truth-teller. And his staff took their cues from him.... I cannot remember a single conversation in which Ford's aides connived to put together a statement for him or the press secretary that would intentionally mislead. It just didn't occur to people.[106]

The American people appreciated the new openness, and Ford was riding a wave of goodwill — at the close of his first month in office, media reports were almost uniformly favorable, and Ford's approval ratings exceeded 70 percent.[107] One aide recalled fondly the reception that Ford received from the public. "I can remember what it was like to travel with Ford outside the Beltway during those first few weeks. His reception was one of tumultuous popularity."[108] But it was not to last. Ford's support would take a precipitous fall in a matter of weeks. He would intentionally lose significant support with a far-sighted and courageous decision to pardon his predecessor, and he would inadvertently lose more support with an unconvincing program to control inflation.

4

Pardon

One month after he took office, Gerald Ford was riding high. He had demonstrated his forthright character by instilling a new open environment at the White House; he had proven that he could take decisive action in the face of political opposition when he chose Nelson Rockefeller as his vice president; he had shown his forgiving nature by announcing a clemency program for draft dodgers; and the public liked what they saw — his approval ratings were above 70 percent. Then, exactly one month after taking office, Ford dissipated his public favor with another forthright and decisive act of forgiveness — his pardon of Richard Nixon. History would vindicate the pardon, but it cost him dearly at the time.

Ford pardoned Nixon because he was able to see the big picture better than almost everyone else at the time. The rest of the nation focused on whether Nixon deserved to be pardoned, and to them the answer was easy: there was no way he deserved one more than other criminal defendants, and he certainly did not deserve a pardon any more than his aides who had been convicted of Watergate-related crimes. Democratic senator Lloyd Bentsen reluctantly favored prosecution. "The possibility of a president — a former president — behind bars is personally repugnant to me, but I'm also caught with the proposition that no man should be above the law."[1] The American Bar Association passed a resolution declaring that the law must be applied impartially, "regardless of the position or status of any individual alleged to have violated the law."[2] Even Ford's son Mike told reporters that Nixon owed the American people a "total confession." Ford responded as a supportive father, not a politician. "All my children have spoken for themselves since they first learned to speak, and not always with my advance approval. I expect that to continue."[3] It wasn't just the pardon opponents who focused on the fairness issue; proponents did too. Senator Hugh Scott lamented Nixon's suffering, as did Nelson Rockefeller, who said, "Let him go — he's suffered enough."[4] They made a weak case because there really was no good argument that Nixon deserved a pardon when others had to stand trial.

Almost alone, Ford looked past the fairness issue and considered the big picture, which was whether a pardon was in the national interest, and he realized that the American people would be better off if he helped end the divisions of Watergate with a pardon. Ford started looking at the big picture even before he took office — in the days before Nixon's resignation, he told Marsh and Hartmann, "You could make a strong case for a pardon, that it would be in the national interest."[5] He said the same thing when he talked to Betty about his discussions with Haig. "This just has to stop. It's tearing the country to pieces."[6]

It is hard to comprehend in retrospect the extent of the country's obsession with Watergate. In 1974 the nation entered uncharted territory — no president had ever been impeached or forced to resign. Looking back, it is clear that the American democratic institutions were capable of handling the situation, but at the time the prevailing view was that the country was enduring a "constitutional crisis." The uncertainty was exacerbated by the political passions involved. Democrats hated Nixon, and they found their suspicions of him confirmed over and over again. Republicans were furious because they thought that the Democrats were trying to reverse the results of the last two elections, but later they turned their anger against Nixon as they realized how much he had let them down.

From the moment Nixon boarded the helicopter for his trip to San Clemente, the press started speculating about whether he would be criminally charged and whether Ford would pardon him. They asked terHorst about the possibility during his first press conference, and he responded by misquoting Ford's testimony during his confirmation hearings: "I do not think the public would stand for it."[7] Ford made the statement in response to a compound question focused primarily on whether a president "should prevent an investigation into Watergate."[8] Ford was careful in his testimony — as he was in all of his public statements — never to rule out the option of a pardon, but his numerous pledges to establish an open administration caused most people vaguely to recall that he had promised not to pardon his predecessor. Apparently terHorst shared this confusion.

In San Clemente, Nixon did not expect a pardon. He was terrified of going to jail, and he asked anyone who called him whether he would be prosecuted. He called Congressman Dan Kuykendall and asked whether Jaworski would "want to pick the carcass."[9] Jaworski's public comments should have given Nixon some solace — he said that he had "no interest whatsoever in trying the President of the United States in open court." Haig had convinced the special prosecutor that Nixon was on death's door, and Jaworski was also convinced that Nixon could not get a fair trial. His staff disagreed, and they were working hard to convince him to indict the former president. To get Jaworski past his belief that Nixon had suffered enough, they explained that the former president's agony was not his concern, but a factor for Ford to take into consideration in deciding whether to issue a pardon.[10]

———— ⁓⁓ ————

Ford didn't need prodding to pardon Nixon, but he got it anyway from many of the remaining Nixon aides. Kissinger privately pushed for a pardon, while Haig gave the pros and cons without overtly advocating either side — he kept telling the president, "It's your decision, sir" — but Ford was well aware that the general wanted him to issue a pardon.[11] The best advice came from one of his military aides, Bob Barrett. "We're all Watergate junkies. Some of us are mainlining, some are sniffing, some are lacing it with something else, but all of us are addicted. This will go on and on unless someone steps in and says that we, as a nation, must go cold turkey. Otherwise, we'll die of an overdose."[12]

It was the questions at Ford's first press conference on August 28 that convinced him to act immediately. He expected that most questions would be about the economy and foreign affairs, even though during his prep session Hartmann and Assistant Press Secretary Paul Miltich told him that the media cared only about Nixon. In actuality, the press asked as many questions about economic issues and foreign affairs as about Watergate, but Ford was shocked at the number of questions about Watergate, and it was those questions that he remembered five years later. "The first question — from Helen Thomas of United Press International — dealt with whether or not I thought Nixon should have immunity from prosecution. Others that followed were variations on the theme. Was I considering pardoning Nixon?"[13] Ford thought he had not been adequately prepared, and his off-the-cuff answers were ambiguous. "Until any legal process has been undertaken, I think it unwise and untimely for me to make any commitments." Again, he was careful not to reject a pardon out of hand. "I am not ruling it out. It is an option and a proper option for any president."[14]

As he listened to the questions, Ford thought, "Goddamn it, I am not going to put up with this."[15] The press conference convinced him that the Watergate obsession would continue unless he pardoned Nixon. As an old friend, Ford was sympathetic to Nixon's agony, but that was not what drove him to issue the pardon. More than anything, he thought that as president he needed to focus on issues other than Watergate. In particular, he was frustrated by the amount of time he spent listening to "lawyers' endless arguments about Nixon's tapes and documents."[16]

> I was called upon to spend 25 percent of my time in the Oval Office listening to the Department of Justice and my White House Counsel as to what I should do with Mr. Nixon's tapes and papers. I finally decided the only way to spend 100 percent of my time on the serious problems of the Federal Government and 30 million citizens was to get rid of the time spent on Mr. Nixon's tapes and papers. To do that, I pardoned Mr. Nixon, got his problems off my White House desk, so I could spend all of my time on the nation's problems at home and abroad.[17]

Two days after the press conference, Ford met in the Oval Office with Haig, Buchen, Hartmann and Marsh. The president started the meeting by lighting his pipe and declaring that he would issue a pardon as soon as he was certain that he had the legal authority to do so. Hartmann was dismayed by Ford's pronouncement, but he tried the argument least likely to change the president's mind — he cited polls that showed that a majority of the public opposed a pardon — and he should not have been surprised with Ford's response. "Damn it, I don't need the polls to tell me whether I'm right or wrong." When Buchen said that he agreed with a pardon but said it was too early to issue one, Ford got peevish. "Will there ever be a right time?"[18] Another concern ate at Marsh until the next day when he tracked down Ford eating ice cream in the study next to the Oval Office. Marsh started by saying, "You may want to throw me out of this office." He reminded Ford that his discussions with Haig in the days before Nixon resigned could be construed as Haig offering a resignation in return for a pardon, but Ford stopped eating and dismissed Marsh's concerns. "Maybe they will, but we both know the facts."[19]

Ford had already asked Buchen to research whether he could pardon someone who had not been indicted or convicted, and he asked him to sound out Jaworski about the charges the special prosecutor was considering and how much time would elapse between indictment and trial. On the following Tuesday, Buchen met with Ford to read out the results of his research. He told Ford that the president had the authority to issue a pardon before Nixon was indicted, and he added a detail that Ford considered important; a 1915 Supreme Court case, *Burdick v. United States*, held that accepting a pardon "carries an imputation of guilt, acceptance, a confession of it."[20] Ford had all the information he needed, and he was determined to pardon his predecessor, but Buchen asked Ford to let him use the pardon as leverage to settle once and for all the issue of the papers and tapes. Ford agreed, but with a reservation. "I don't intend to condition the pardon on his making an agreement on the papers and tapes."[21]

Buchen had been in a quandary about what to do with the Nixon papers since he received Saxbe's opinion that the former president owned the documents. He asked the attorney general whether the administration could file a lawsuit asking a court to determine who should have access to the documents, but Saxbe said that a court was unlikely to take the case. Benton Becker was struggling with the same issue, and he even passed word to Jaworski that he would welcome a subpoena, but one never came. Becker met with Sirica and suggested that he take custody of the papers, but the judge said, "No thank you."[22] Buchen finally saw a way out when Nixon hired Washington criminal defense lawyer Herbert Miller, which opened a channel of communication for a possible settlement. Miller had worked with Ford and Becker as an attorney for the Warren Commission. After his meeting with Ford, Buchen called Miller and invited him to meet in the apartment that Buchen had rented in the Jefferson Hotel.

When Miller arrived at the hotel later that day, he angrily demanded that the papers be sent to Nixon, but he calmed down when Buchen explained that Ford wanted to work out a reasonable resolution to get the documents to Nixon that took into consideration the subpoenas and court orders. Miller thought they could work out a solution, and he offered to draft an agreement to address the issue. Buchen wrapped up the meeting with the good news that Ford was considering a pardon, but he cautioned that a final decision had not been made. After he left, Miller arranged another meeting in the Jefferson Hotel, this time with Jaworski. Miller was worried that if Nixon accepted a pardon, he would be embarrassed by opposition from the special prosecutor's office. To Miller's surprise, Jaworski promised to support the pardon.

Miller returned to the Jefferson Hotel two days later with a draft agreement which proposed that the documents be held by the General Services Administration for three years. The draft was silent on what would happen then, but Buchen presumed the documents would then be given to Nixon. The tapes would be destroyed after five years if Nixon so directed, but in any circumstances they would be destroyed after ten years. The three men discussed the draft and reached a tentative agreement under which the documents would be sent to a federal facility near San Clemente for three years. Two keys would be needed to access the documents, one held by Nixon and the other by the GSA. Buchen told Miller that Ford had tentatively decided to issue a pardon, and he explained that the president would like a statement of contrition from Nixon. He made clear that such a statement was not a precondition of a pardon, but he urged Miller to get one. Recognizing that Ford wanted to act quickly, Miller suggested that a representative of the White House accompany him to San Clemente to work out the final details of the agreement and a statement.[23]

After the meeting, Buchen and Becker met with Ford and Haig. Ford asked Becker to accompany Miller, and Haig arranged for an Air Force plane to fly the two attorneys to San Clemente that night. Ford was happy to hear that the parties had made progress, but in an earlier meeting Kissinger had convinced him that the tapes could be embarrassing to people in Washington, so Ford asked that the tapes be held confidential for 50 years. It was not Ford's finest moment — potential embarrassment is not a valid reason to keep information about governmental activities from the public — but he mitigated his mistake by telling Becker that the new term was not a condition of reaching an agreement. Ford also told Becker to try to get a statement of contrition, but he again said that a statement was not a precondition of a pardon. Haig thought there was no way Nixon would make a statement. "You will never get it." As Becker left the meeting, Ford put his hand on his shoulder and said, "I will never, ever give up those records. They belong to the American people. You let President Nixon know that I feel very strongly about this."[24] In other words, Nixon could get a pardon without agreeing to a deal to keep the documents safe, but he would not get his papers without one.

Becker took a risk and violated his instructions immediately upon arriving in San Clemente. He and Miller landed at El Toro Marine Air Base in California at midnight, and they were taken directly to Nixon's compound. Zeigler was there to meet them, and he started the discussion by declaring that "President Nixon will make *no* statement of admission or complicity in return for a pardon from Jerry Ford." Becker was put off by Zeigler's bluster, so he bluffed. "Mr. Zeigler, I've never been to San Clemente before and for that matter I don't work for the government, so ... I'm a bit confused. Can you tell me how to reach the Air Force pilot that brought me here, so that I could instruct him to take me back to Washington? I'll also need a car and driver to take me back to El Toro." For once in his life, Zeigler was at a loss for words, but Miller diffused the situation by suggesting that, since they were all tired, they should take up the issue in the morning. Both Becker and Zeigler mellowed, and they spent the next hour and a half discussing the problem of the documents and tapes. At 2:00 in the morning Becker and Miller checked into a nearby hotel.[25]

———*∞∞∞*———

While Becker was on his way to California, Ford decided to announce the pardon as soon as possible. The impetus was Buchen's report of his meeting with the special prosecutor. Jaworski expected the grand jury to indict Nixon any day, and he gave Buchen a letter which predicted that "a period from nine months to a year, and perhaps even longer" would elapse between indictment and trial.[26] Jaworski also gave Buchen a memorandum from Deputy Special Prosecutor Henry Ruth, which listed ten areas that Jaworski's office was pursuing, but also made clear that Nixon's conviction was anything but certain. "None of these matters at the moment rises to the level of our ability to prove even a probable criminal violation by Mr. Nixon." In another memo, which was not passed on to Buchen, Ruth explained that a pardon was a reasonable option. "One can make a strong argument for leniency, and if President Ford is so inclined, I think he ought to do it early rather than late."[27]

Ford was horrified by the thought that the nation would be obsessed with Watergate for another year as Nixon awaited trial, so he decided that he needed to act:

> I was very sure of what would happen if I let the charges against Nixon run their legal course. Months were sure to elapse between an indictment and trial. The entire process would no doubt require years: a minimum of two, a maximum of six.... The story would overshadow everything else. No other issue could compete with the drama of a former President trying to stay out of jail. It would be virtually impossible for me to direct public attention to anything else. Passions on both sides would be aroused. A period of such prolonged vituperation and recrimination would be disastrous for the nation. America needed recovery, not revenge. The hate had to be drained and the healing begun.[28]

Ford wanted to issue the pardon before the grand jury indicted Nixon, which could happen any day. So he met with Haig, Buchen, Hartmann, and Marsh and told them that he intended to announce the pardon the next morning. They convinced him to wait until Becker returned, which would be, at the latest, on Saturday. Ford agreed, but he declared that he would not wait "one day later than Sunday."[29]

———*∞∞∞*———

After sleeping three hours, Becker woke up at 5:30 the next morning and called Buchen, who told him that Ford planned to announce the pardon on Sunday afternoon. When he got dressed following the call, Becker noticed that his wife had forgotten to pack cuff links, so he used paper clips to hold his sleeves together for his meeting with the former president.

When Becker and Miller arrived at the Nixon compound they were again joined by Zeigler, and the three men spent the morning going over the draft agreement line by line, with Miller and Zeigler retiring to Nixon's study from time to time to discuss the issues with the former president. At noon Zeigler gave Becker a draft statement from Nixon that did not remotely resemble a statement of contrition — the most the former president was willing to say was that the demands of the office caused him to rely too much on his staff. Becker told Zeigler that the draft was worse than no statement at all, but he again explained that a statement was not a precondition of a pardon. Miller and Zeigler called in a speechwriter and asked for a new draft, which was ready at 3:00. The draft still contained no statement of contrition, but it did contain an acknowledgement by Nixon of poor judgment. Becker again said that the new draft was still worse than no statement at all, and he suggested that Nixon acknowledge that he had not acted properly when the Watergate investigation was before the courts. The speechwriter generated a new draft that said, "I was wrong in not dealing with Watergate more forthrightly and directly, particularly when it reached a judicial stage." Becker called Buchen and explained the terms of the agreement and read him the statement. Buchen told Ford that the language was the best they could expect, and the president approved the deal.

By then it was 5:00 on Friday night, and Becker asked to meet with Nixon to explain the implications of accepting the pardon. When he was escorted into the former president's office, Becker was shocked by Nixon's appearance:

> My first impression and the one that continues with me to this day was, unhappily, one of freakish grotesqueness. His arms and body were so thin and frail as to project an image of a head size disproportionate to a body.... I met a man whom I might more reasonably expect to meet in an octogenarian nursing home. He was old. Had I never known of the man before and met him for the first time, I would have estimated his age to be 85.

Nixon was alert for most of the discussion, but he drifted at times. Becker recalled that "the former president spoke to me then in the most pathetic, sad frame of mind that I believe I have ever seen anyone in my life." When Becker explained that the law construed acceptance of a pardon as an admission of guilt, Nixon said that he understood. As Becker was getting up to leave, Nixon asked him to wait:

> Mr. Becker, wait a moment, please. You have been so fair and thoughtful that I want to give you something. But I don't have anything any more. They took it all from me. Everything I had is gone. I tried to get you a presidential tie pin with my name on it, but I don't even have them any more. There's nothing left from my presidency. I asked Pat to get these.

Nixon opened a desk drawer and gave Becker two small white boxes. "From my personal jewelry box. There aren't any more of these in the world; you have got the last one." Becker took the boxes, which contained a presidential tie pin and two presidential cuff links.[30]

———

Becker arrived at Andrews Air Force Base at 5:00 on the morning of September 7 and went home for a short nap before returning to the White House to meet Ford. Haig and Buchen joined the meeting as Becker explained the agreement and Nixon's proposed statement. When Haig saw the language where Nixon admitted that he had been "wrong in not dealing with Watergate more forthrightly and directly," he asked Becker if he had put a gun to the former president's head. Ford was saddened when Becker described Nixon's condition. "I'm not a medical doctor, but I really have serious questions in my mind whether that man is going to be alive at the time of the election." Ford said, "Well, 1976 is a long time away." But Becker replied, "I don't mean 1976. I mean 1974."[31]

In San Clemente, Nixon was having second thoughts. He called Miller and said that he was considering rejecting the pardon because it would be construed as an admission of guilt. "I'd just as soon go through the agony of a trial, so we can scrape away at least all the false charges, and fight it out on those where there may be a doubt." Miller urged Nixon to accept the pardon, and he told the president that he was unlikely to get a fair trial. An hour later Nixon called Miller and said that he would accept the pardon. "I'll sign it. I'm not sure it's the right thing to do ... but I'll do it." Once he became resigned to a pardon, Nixon spent the next two days worrying that Ford would change his mind at the last minute. A slight complication arose when Becker called San Clemente and learned that Zeigler had watered down Nixon's statement. Ford refused to consider the new statement. "We can't tolerate any weakened statement. Call Ziegler back and tell him that." Zeigler backed down, and the statement remained unchanged.[32]

When he left the meeting with Ford, Becker met with Arthur Sampson, the administrator of the General Services Administration, who signed the agreement on behalf of the GSA. Under the agreement, Nixon retained "all legal and equitable title" to the documents, but agreed that they should be deposited temporarily in a federal facility near San Clemente, "within secure storage areas to which access can be gained only by use of two keys," one given to Nixon and the other given to the Archivist of the United States. After three years, Nixon had the right to take possession of the documents. The tapes would remain in deposit until September 1, 1979, and after that date Nixon could direct that they be destroyed. In any event, the tapes would be destroyed upon Nixon's death or on September 1, 1984, whichever came first.[33]

—◆◆◆—

With the pardon announcement less than a day away, Ford's aides decided to bring ter-Horst into the loop — the press secretary had no idea that Ford was considering a pardon until Hartmann gave him a copy of the draft announcement that Saturday afternoon. The press secretary was furious that Ford would even consider pardoning Nixon, and he threw the draft back at Hartmann. "You know what this means? Jerry Ford is throwing away his presidency to do a favor for Richard Nixon.... You guys walked into it. Well, that's fine. But I'm not sticking around."[34] Like most Americans at the time, terHorst was thinking about whether Nixon deserved the pardon, and he could not understand how Ford could grant Nixon a full pardon, but only partial clemency to draft resisters. The press secretary decided to resign because he believed that the pardon "flew in the face of my own understanding of the Constitution and its credo of equal justice for rich and poor, strong and weak."[35] He also could not understand how Ford could issue a pardon without a clear statement of guilt. "I had been reared in the belief that forgiveness can be extended only after admission of wrongdoing."[36]

The press secretary delivered his letter of resignation the next morning.[37] To replace ter-Horst, rather than considering all the top reporters, Ford decided to pick someone he knew. Hartmann suggested that Ford replace terHorst with Ron Nessen, who had covered Ford's vice presidency for NBC. It wasn't an inspired choice. Between Hartmann and Nessen, the public relations staff at the White House was without a seasoned professional at the top, and the two would make things worse by continually fighting for control.

—◆◆◆—

As usual, Ford played golf with Laird that weekend. Without prompting, Laird told Ford that he was trying to drum up support for a pardon, but Ford surprised him by saying that he had decided to issue one the next day. Laird told Ford that issuing a pardon so early would be political disaster, and, given some advance notice, he would have both Republicans and Democrats "begging him to do it." But Ford refused to wait.[38] Before he announced the pardon, Ford gave a heads-up to congressional leaders. None of the leaders objected, but Tip O'Neill's response was pithy. "Jesus, don't you think it's kind of early?"[39]

From the Oval Office on September 8, 1974, Ford announces his pardon of Richard Nixon. (Photograph by David Hume Kennerly; courtesy Gerald R. Ford Library.)

At 11:05 on the morning of Sunday, September 8, Ford announced the pardon from behind his desk in the Oval Office. "I have come to a decision which I felt I should tell you and all of my fellow American citizens, as soon as I was certain in my own mind and in my own conscience that it is the right thing to do." Unfortunately, the speech Hartmann had prepared stressed Nixon's suffering, rather than the true reasons behind the president's decision. "It is common knowledge that serious allegations and accusations hang like a sword over our former president's head, threatening his health as he tries to reshape his life, a great part of which was spent in the service of this country and by the mandate of its people." It was not until the end of the speech that Ford gave the real reason he was issuing the pardon — to put Watergate behind the nation:

> My concern is the immediate future of this great country.... As President, my primary concern must always be the greatest good of all the people of the United States whose servant I am. As a man, my first consideration is to be true to my own convictions and my own conscience. My conscience tells me clearly and certainly that I cannot prolong the bad dreams that continue to reopen a chapter that is closed. My conscience tells me that only I, as president, have the constitutional power to firmly shut and seal this book. My conscience tells me it is my duty, not merely to proclaim domestic tranquility but to use every means that I have to insure it.

It was a good passage — particularly the words "it is my duty, not merely to proclaim domestic tranquility but to use every means that I have to insure it" — but it was lost in all the talk about relieving Nixon's agony, which Ford returned to at the end of his speech. "Finally, I feel that Richard Nixon and his loved ones have suffered enough and will continue to suffer, no matter what I do, no matter what we, as a great and good nation, can do together to make his goal of peace come true." Ford then looked down and read the pardon, Proclamation 4311, executing the proclamation as he read it:

Now, THEREFORE, I, GERALD R. FORD, President of the United States, pursuant to the pardon power conferred upon me by Article II, Section 2, of the Constitution, have granted and by these presents do grant a full, free, and absolute pardon unto Richard Nixon for all offenses against the United States which he, Richard Nixon, has committed or may have committed or taken part in during the period from January 20, 1969, through August 9, 1974.[40]

—◆◆◆—

Ford made the right decision in granting the pardon, but his administration botched the announcement, as he later recognized. "I have to confess that my televised talk failed to emphasize adequately that I wanted to give my full attention to grave economic and foreign policy matters."[41] His aides made the same mistake. In speaking to the media after the pardon announcement, both Buchen and terHorst called the pardon "an act of mercy."[42] If Ford and his aides had stressed that his primary reason for the pardon was that it was in the nation's interest to put Watergate in the past, the argument would not have convinced everyone, but the public would have understood that Ford had one overriding consideration in granting the pardon, the welfare of the American people, and that he did it for them, not as a favor for his old friend.

The precipitous announcement of the pardon was also a mistake. Deputy Press Secretary John Hushen later said that the pardon "was delivered to the country like Pearl Harbor."[43] That does not mean that Ford should have followed the advice of his aides and waited until trial and conviction, which Ford knew was a year away. The country would have fixated on Nixon's prosecution, and Ford would have taken just as much criticism for the pardon at a later date as he did early on. But David Gergen has explained that Ford could have delayed the pardon for a matter of days to prepare the public, giving the people some time to understand the public benefits:

> He could have taken an opportunity in his September press conference to say that Nixon's future was weighing heavily on him, but he had not yet decided what to do. He could then have given three principal reasons why an immediate pardon would serve the nation and two or three arguments the other way. That disclosure would have set off a national debate.[44]

None of Ford's aides suggested such a course, and the professionals responsible for public relations did not develop a plan to counter the criticism they knew was coming. Hartmann tried to talk Ford out of issuing the pardon, and when he was unsuccessful, he wrote a speech which failed to emphasize Ford's true intentions. Ford and his aides decided not to bring terHorst into the loop until the last minute, giving him no time to plan for the negative reaction. When he learned of the pardon, terHorst made no effort to help Ford — his resignation was every bit as abrupt as the pardon.

—◆◆◆—

Ford courageously issued the pardon knowing that it would be unpopular, but he did not anticipate just how unpopular it would be. According to the Gallup poll, Ford's approval rating plummeted from 71 percent to 49 percent just after the pardon, and it kept falling to 32 percent in the next month.[45] Ford thought that the public would be more forgiving. "What I had failed to anticipate was the vehemence of the hostile reaction to my decision.... I thought there would be greater forgiveness. It was one of the greatest disappointments of my presidency that everyone focused on the individual instead of on the problems the nation faced."[46]

When Nixon saw the effect the pardon was having on Ford's popularity, he called to say he was sorry he caused so much trouble, and he offered to "reject pardon if that would help." Ford refused the offer.[47] Nixon's health continued to decline, and at the end of September he was in critical condition as a result of blood clots in his legs from phlebitis. Ford flew to Long Beach, California, to visit Nixon in the hospital. It was his only meeting with his predecessor during his presidency.[48]

Ford's fellow Republicans were split in their views on the pardon. Those in favor lauded it as an act of forgiveness, not as the right thing for the country. Senator Hugh Scott praised Ford for acting "with great humanity to bring an end to an American tragedy." House minority leader John Rhodes said Nixon had paid "a substantial price" and "anything further would be more overkill than justice." Senator Goldwater called the pardon "the only decent and prudent course." Republican comments were not uniformly positive. Senator Lowell Weicker said that the pardon was "neither equal justice nor leadership in a government of laws." Senator Edward Brooke said that a pardon without Nixon's "full confession of his involvement in Watergate is, in my judgment, a serious mistake."[49] Many Republicans were upset that Ford had not waited until after the November elections. Bob Dole called Ford "to thank him for throwing me an anchor with the Nixon pardon."[50]

Democrats were nearly unified in their contempt for the pardon. Rodino called it "a terrible blow to the system of justice as we know it."[51] Senator Kennedy said the pardon looked like "the culmination of the Watergate cover-up."[52] Senate majority Leader Mike Mansfield said that "all men are equal under the law ... includes presidents and plumbers.... What about the 40 or 50 already indicted and some of whom have been sent to prison?"[53] Senator George McGovern questioned its fairness. "It has seemed to me that the central lesson of Watergate should be that no one stands above the rule of law. It is difficult to understand granting immunity to Mr. Nixon while committing his subordinates to prison."[54] A few Democrats raised their lonely voices in praise of Ford's action, including his old friend Hubert Humphrey. "The pardon is right. It is the only decision President Ford could make."[55]

A few editorial pages praised the pardon. The *Winston-Salem Journal* said that the pardon "combines compassion and a desire to serve the best interests of the nation."[56] The *Houston Chronicle* called the pardon "not only an act of compassion but above all, a bold act in the best national interest."[57] But these reasonable editorials were drowned out by extreme denunciations, such as the comments of the ACLU, which were embarrassing in their hyperbole. "If Ford's principle had been the rule in Nuremberg, the Nazi leaders would have been let off and only the people who carried out their schemes would have been tried."[58] The *New York Times* said that Ford "affronted the Constitution and the American system of justice," and called the pardon "a profoundly unwise, divisive and unjust act."[59]

Jaworski told his press spokesman James Doyle that he was "relieved" by the pardon, but he was sickened by the public reaction to it, and he decided to resign. He issued a public statement applauding the pardon, and he responded to critics who said that the pardon denied the public access to information. "It's a mistake to believe there would have been more evidence for the public if Nixon had been tried. If he had been pardoned after indictment, the public would have no new information. If he had gone to trial, we wouldn't have learned any new details."[60]

—◈—

With the pardon out of the way, Haig decided to leave. He couldn't handle the informal atmosphere in the Ford White House, and the lack of respect he was shown by a few new staffers drove him up the wall. Some of Ford's people were suspicious of Haig and the rest of the Nixon holdovers — in the words of David Gergen, they were "like porcupines, prickly to anyone associated with Nixon."[61] Not surprisingly, Hartmann was one of the prickly Ford staffers, and he focused his paranoia on Haig, who responded by demanding total control.

Hartmann challenged Haig's authority at every opportunity, even refusing to attend his staff meetings, telling his assistants, "Fuck Haig. I work for the president."[62] News reports about the conflicts were common, and most of them laid the blame at Haig's feet. Ford recognized that Hartmann was responsible for much of the infighting among his staff, and he suspected that he was behind many of the press stories. Still, he valued his unvarnished advice.[63]

It didn't take long for both Ford and Haig to realize that it would be best if he left, and the president began to discuss the other positions he could offer him. Ford considered appointing him army chief of staff, to replace General Creighton Abrams who had died on September 4, but that would require a Senate confirmation, and Ford heard from key senators that the hearings could be ugly, so he decided to appoint Haig to command NATO forces in Europe. Haig left the White House in the third week of September.[64]

———

Anger about the pardon was fueled by suspicions that it was the result of a deal between Ford and Nixon. Questions about a possible deal arose immediately — on the morning the pardon was announced, Buchen was asked whether it was a result of "secret agreements,"[65] and in the first question of Ford's news conference a week later, Frank Cormier of the Associated Press actually asked whether he had "a secret reason" for issuing the pardon.[66]

Over the next two days, fifteen members of the House submitted resolutions demanding information on the pardon, and the resolutions were referred to the Subcommittee on Criminal Justice of the Judiciary Committee, whose chairman, William Hungate, posed the questions in a letter to the White House. Buchen drafted a terse reply, explaining that the reasons for the pardon were contained in the president's statement, and he attached to the response what Ford later called "a passel of presidential statements, together with the transcripts of my news conferences." Buchen was a political novice, and he did not understand that members of Congress would consider it an affront that Ford had not directly answered the questions. Ford should have known better, but he signed the letter without demanding changes. The response created a storm on Capitol Hill. To diffuse the issue, Marsh asked Hungate to send another set of questions, and the chairman delivered a set of five questions.[67]

When they saw the new questions, Marsh and Hartmann were worried about one which asked whether Ford had discussed "the pardon with any member of the Nixon staff prior to the time you became president," because it required Ford to disclose his meetings with Haig in the days before Nixon's resignation. The difficulty they faced was how to describe the meetings with Haig without raising an endless stream of new questions. Ford immediately understood that the best way to address the issue was to "just go up to Capitol Hill, testify and spell it all out." Marsh and Hartmann agreed, but they were opposed by every other member of the White House staff who uniformly thought it would set a bad precedent. Only twice in American history had presidents testified before Congress, but the exceptions put Ford in good company. Washington testified before Congress more than once, and Lincoln went to the Capitol Building to respond to charges that his wife was a Confederate spy. Ford chose Washington and Lincoln over Fillmore, Buchanan, Nixon, and the rest of his 37 predecessors. He knew that he had to address the suspicions of a deal because they threatened his greatest asset: his reputation for honesty. "I've got nothing to hide. I'm going up there."[68]

When Marsh sounded out congressional leaders, Republican whip Les Arends and House parliamentarian Lew Deschler thought that it was a bad idea, but Senate Majority Leader Mike Mansfield thought that, under the circumstances, Ford should testify. "I think it would be a good thing for him to do.... But tell the president not to make a habit of it." It was the response of Speaker Albert who convinced Ford. "There's nothing more important to this country than the success of Jerry Ford as president. He has a reputation for honesty, and he ought to lay it all out. Some of the things that might have to be disclosed might hurt, but they're not going to hurt that much, and what's to be gained is so much greater." Albert later explained why he was confident Ford would do well. "I knew this man. I knew it was not in Jerry Ford to make a deal with Nixon."[69]

When Marsh met with Hungate to hammer out the rules for Ford's appearance, they decided to get Rodino's concurrence, and they found him exercising in the House gym. While Rodino wiped the sweat from his brow, the three men agreed that Ford would testify for one morning, not under oath, with questioning limited to members of Hungate's subcommittee, Chairman Rodino, and the ranking Republican on the Judiciary Committee.[70]

As they prepared for his testimony, Buchen told Ford that he should lead off with a detailed description of the meetings with Haig, and the president asked him to write the statement. In his first draft, Buchen included the conclusion that Hartmann, Marsh, and Harlow thought at the time — that Haig had offered Nixon's resignation in return for a pardon. It was an accurate statement, but unnecessary, because it related to how Ford's aides interpreted what Haig said rather than just stating the facts.

It was Saturday morning when Buzhardt read the draft, and he immediately called Haig, who had just resigned as chief of staff and was waiting to be confirmed as NATO commander. "Al, I think you'd better come over to the White House. These boys have prepared sworn testimony for the president that could very well result in your indictment." Haig drove to the White House, "angry and bewildered." When he arrived, he demanded to see the draft, and when he saw the conclusion that he had offered Ford the presidency in return for a pardon, he insisted on meeting with Ford immediately. "Whoever wrote this testimony is setting the president up to tell a lie. I won't be a part of it." When Marsh and Buchen refused, Haig broke into a paranoid rant. "I will either see Ford immediately, or I will call a press conference right now, right here in the White House pressroom, and describe the role people around the vice president played in the Grand Rapids group, Bobby Griffin's letter, the appointment of Jenner as minority counsel to the House Judiciary Committee, and a good many other things we all know occurred as part of a secret effort by Ford people to hurry Nixon out of the presidency behind Jerry Ford's back."[71]

Marsh and Buchen knew the only way to mollify Haig was to take him into the Oval Office. Ford had no idea what was happening, and he asked, "Al, what's this about?" Haig blew up. "Did you read the testimony your boys have concocted? They're going to put me in jail for something that's totally wrong." Ford defused the situation by asking what Haig wanted, and the general replied, "The truth. That's all." Ford gave Haig a yellow legal pad and said, "You'll have it, Al. You write that portion as you remember." Haig wrote his version, which concluded that no deal had been offered. Buchen didn't use Haig's version, but he changed the draft to limit it to the facts and not conclusions. The new opening statement related what had been said by Ford and Haig and did not include the contemporaneous interpretations of Ford's advisors. Haig agrees that Ford's testimony, as rewritten, "described what had happened between us with perfect accuracy."[72]

At 9:30 on the morning of October 17, Ford began his testimony in Room 2141 of the Rayburn House Office Building on Capitol Hill. The president opened by explaining that he issued the pardon to "shift our attentions from the pursuit of a fallen president to the pursuit of the urgent needs of a rising nation." He described in great detail the meeting when Haig listed Nixon's six options, including the pardon option, and that Haig "indicated he was not advocating any of the options." Ford told the committee that he did not give Haig any answer at first, because he wanted time to think. Ford then related his call putting the discussion to rest:

> After further thought on the matter, I was determined not to make any recommendations to President Nixon on his resignation. I had not given any advice or recommendations in my conversations with his aides, but I also did not want anyone who might talk to the president to suggest that I had some intention to do so. For that reason I decided I should call General Haig the afternoon of August 2. I did make the call late that afternoon and told him I wanted him to understand that I had no intention of recommending what President Nixon should do about resigning or not resigning, and that nothing we had talked about the previous afternoon should be given any consideration in whatever decision the president might make. General Haig told me he was in full agreement with this position.

Ford concluded by asserting that there was no deal. "In summary, I assure you that there never was at any time any agreement whatsoever concerning a pardon to Mr. Nixon if he were to resign and I were to become president." With one exception, the members of the committee accepted Ford's statement that there was no deal. The exception was Democrat Elizabeth Holtzman, but Ford deftly countered her insinuations. When she expressed her "dismay that the format of this hearing will not be able to provide to the American public the full truth and all of the facts respecting your assurance of a pardon to Richard Nixon," Ford interrupted. "May I comment there? I want to assure you, the members of this subcommittee, the members of the Congress, and the American people, there was no deal, period, under no circumstances."[73]

———《∞》———

Ford's testimony defused the crisis, but he soon learned that he had not put Watergate behind him. "I was confident that I could now proceed without being harassed by Nixon or his problems any more. I thought I could concentrate 100 percent of my time on the overwhelming problems that faced both me and the country. It didn't take me long, however, to discover I was wrong."[74] One issue that wasn't resolved was Nixon's documents and tapes. When the pardon was announced, Jaworski announced that he would not contest it in court, but his office expressed concerns about the agreement on the papers. Jaworski sent deputy special prosecutors Phillip Lacovara and Henry Ruth to meet with Buchen. In a contentious meeting, they tried to convince Buchen to repudiate the agreement with Nixon. Buchen refused, but he did agree to delay sending the documents to California until Jaworski had a chance to convince Congress to act.

When Nixon learned that the administration had agreed to delay sending the documents to California, he filed a lawsuit to enforce the agreement. At the same time, various organizations sued to block sending the documents to San Clemente. On October 21, U.S. District Court Judge Charles Richey issued a temporary restraining order forbidding the transfer of the documents to Nixon. That started three-way negotiations between the White House, Miller, and Jaworski's office. The parties were close to an agreement when Congress acted. The new law, which Ford signed on December 19, did not permanently resolve the issue of ownership of presidential papers — it covered only Nixon's documents and tapes. It ordered the GSA to take possession of the documents, and it established a commission to recommend an ongoing policy of ownership of presidential materials.[75]

Congress finally clarified the ownership of presidential papers with the Presidential

Records Act of 1978. Under the act, the United States government has "ownership, possession, and control" of presidential and vice presidential records, and the National Archives takes control of an administration's records at the end of the administration. The former president has control over access to the documents for twelve years. After that, the records become public, except for documents that are covered by executive privilege or contain national security secrets.

— ◦∿◦ —

Ford was naïve to think that he put all Watergate issues behind him with the pardon, but he was right to see that the pardon was necessary. For a year and a half the country had been obsessed with Watergate, and the obsession would have continued for at least two more years had he not issued the pardon. Jaworski's prediction that nine months would elapse between indictment and trial was almost certainly too short. More than seven months had elapsed between the arrest of the Watergate defendants and trial, and that was a simple burglary case. A complicated obstruction of justice case against a former president would likely have taken at least a year before trial, and appeals would have lasted for at least another year. The pardon caused a firestorm, but the complaints died down a lot more quickly than the Nixon prosecution would have lasted.

Ford's decision to pardon Nixon was courageous because it was made in the face of almost-universal opposition. Over the years the country has learned to appreciate the wisdom of Ford's decision. In 2001 the John F. Kennedy Library foundation gave Ford its Profile in Courage Award for the pardon. During the award ceremony, Senator Ted Kennedy admitted that he was wrong when he lambasted his friend for the pardon:

> Unlike many of us at the time, President Ford recognized that the nation had to move forward, and could not do so if there was a continuing effort to prosecute former president Nixon.... I was one of those who spoke out against his action then. But time has a way of clarifying past events, and now we see that President Ford was right. His courage and dedication to our country made it possible for us to begin the process of healing and put the tragedy of Watergate behind us.[76]

The pardon probably cost Ford the 1976 election, but he never regretted it. In 1988 he told Larry King that he would have done the same thing if he had it all to do over. "I'm more convinced today, Larry, than I was in 1974."[77] Ford had not changed his mind in 2003. "I was right when I made that decision and I'm pleased that the public now seems to agree with me."[78] The pardon decision was Ford at his best. He was uniquely able to focus on the best interests of the country, and he saw that the nation needed to put Watergate in the past. Having decided on the right course, he was not deterred by political considerations. He knew that a pardon would cost him dearly, but he issued it anyway — because he knew it was the right thing to do.

— ◦∿◦ —

When Haig resigned, Ford instantly knew who he wanted to replace him: Donald Rumsfeld.[79] When Rumsfeld returned to the U.S. for his father's funeral, Ford used the opportunity to ask him to replace Haig, and he was named "staff coordinator" on September 30. Haig's resignation did not end the White House infighting because Rumsfeld demanded as much control as Haig did, and because of his overarching ambition. Virtually all members of the White House staff — Nixon holdovers, Michigan men, and new appointees alike — agreed on one thing: Rumsfeld was highly ambitious, and it was apparent that he wanted to be president.[80]

Although Ford refused to name Rumsfeld chief of staff, he was one for all intents and purposes. As Seidman later explained, "Rumsfeld was a chief of staff. You really didn't need to look at the spokes of the wheel diagram to figure that out."[81] The title was less important than the authority Rumsfeld assumed, including control of the Office of the Cabinet Secretary, the Office of the Staff Secretary, the Presidential Personnel Office, and the president's military aides. He put Cheney in direct control of those offices, and the two of them controlled the White House staff and the president's schedule, effectively taking the powers of a chief of staff. They also controlled the paper flow to the president. Rumsfeld and Cheney would develop an options paper for each issue, listing the possible choices and the views of various members of the administration, and Ford would indicate which option he chose. Cheney and Rumsfeld did not change Ford's open-door policy, as Cheney explained at the time. "At least 18 to 20 people on the staff— if they want to see the president would probably have no trouble seeing him at all." Cheney also explained that, at Ford's direction, Cabinet secretaries could call him directly or see him on request. "You've got a standing rule right now that any Cabinet member can see the president whenever he wants to see him, as long as the president, you know, can fit it in. Nobody ever screens out a Cabinet member from seeing the president."[82]

Not everyone was comfortable with Rumsfeld's new authority. Hartmann treated him with the same contempt that he showed Haig, including refusing to show up to staff meetings. News reports about infighting did not abate, and they continued to portray Hartmann as the good guy who was being shut out from the president. But Rumsfeld proved to be a much more adept adversary. Where Haig would fight back in kind, Rumsfeld just put Hartmann in his place. He forced him to circulate speech drafts before they were submitted to Ford, and he made him move out of Rose Mary Wood's old office next to the Oval Office. Hartmann's influence in the administration rapidly declined.[83]

———

Ford's decision not to immediately fire the entire staff when he took over demonstrated a genuine sense of decency, but he miscalculated by not telling the remaining staffers whether they had made the cut. Because Ford did not make his changes immediately, all of the Nixon holdovers felt vulnerable. John Osborne summarized the problem in the *New Republic*:

> Two months after Mr. Ford took over, many veterans of the Nixon time still didn't know whether they were expected to remain or quit. Many who knew that they were expected to leave didn't know when they had to be out.[84]

After Osborne told him that the uncertainty was a problem, Rumsfeld told the remaining Nixon staffers whether they were safe or needed to find a new job.

Ford made a mistake by not making one change right off the bat — he should have replaced Secretary of Defense James Schlesinger. When Ford was vice president he told *New Republic* reporter John Osborne that he would get rid of Schlesinger, but he did not follow through when he took office. Despite the fact that he was a fellow pipe smoker, Ford did not like or respect the secretary of defense. It wasn't Schlesinger's rumpled suits and old-fashioned (for the time) narrow ties that bothered Ford; the problem was that he was far too fond of his brilliance for Ford's taste. Schlesinger fancied himself a student of congressional politics, and his condescending lectures on how to sway Congress infuriated the former House minority leader. Ford was also offended by articles which reported that, during Nixon's final days, Schlesinger had ordered the military not to take orders from the president. Ford was convinced that the articles had been leaked by the secretary of defense, but he denied any involvement when Ford confronted him. After that, Schlesinger did nothing to improve their relationship, and he continually riled Ford by challenging his judgment on congressional matters. Because he allowed Schlesinger to stay, Ford did not have a person he trusted in one of the most important positions in his administration, and he gave the secretary of defense's advice little weight.[85]

As Ford gradually replaced many of the remaining Nixon people, he put together an effective staff, concentrating on choosing quality people rather than on political factors. David Gergen has said that Ford put together "the finest cabinet in the past thirty years."[86] He restored professionalism to the Justice Department after two of Nixon's attorneys general had been implicated in Watergate. As David O'Brien has explained, "Rather than imposing ideological considerations or its own legal-policy goals, Ford's Department of Justice sought high-caliber nominees."[87] When Attorney General Saxbe told Ford that he wanted to finish his career as ambassador to India, and Daniel Patrick Moynihan said he wanted to return to Harvard, Ford sent Saxbe to New Delhi. For a replacement, Rumsfeld suggested University of Chicago president Edward Levi. Levi was a respected legal scholar and former dean of the law school, and he would act with integrity for the next two years.[88]

The way Ford handled the staff was far superior to the way Hartmann acted in his small domain. Hartmann did not follow Ford's lead and evaluate the people he inherited, making distinctions between which people were tainted by scandal and those who were talented, dedicated employees. He fired the entire speechwriting organization, and he didn't even have the decency to do it himself. He hired Paul Theis to lead the office without bothering to tell David Gergen that he had been replaced, and then he told Theis to fire the rest of the speechwriters.[89] Hartmann assumed that the staffers he inherited were arrogant and dedicated to undermining the new administration, but he was wrong. Nixon staff members may have been imperious when the administration was riding high, but after seeing their leaders brought down one by one, the survivors were completely demoralized, and they welcomed Ford's new open style more than anyone. Most Nixon staff members were honorable people, and most stayed to serve the country, not to undermine the new administration. Gergen has explained their thinking: "What to do? To everyone in speechwriting, the answer was obvious: only a rat left a sinking ship. We stayed."[90]

Hartmann's decision to purge the speechwriting office was particularly damaging because he was a poor judge of talent and a lousy administrator. He fired a top-notch speechwriting organization, staffed with people who were to excel in future endeavors, and replaced them with mediocrities he happened to know.[91] Hartmann's deficient speechwriting organization was particularly unfortunate because Ford needed a professional, competent speechwriting organization to offset his ineffective public speaking skills. Rumsfeld periodically asked others to draft alternatives to Hartmann's speeches, often asking David Gergen in the Treasury Department to prepare one. He also demanded that drafts be widely circulated, which resulted in overly-vague language that did not stake out any real positions. Speechwriter Pat Butler explained that the staffing out of speeches had hurt their quality. "From the very first day, I could see what Ford's problem was. His speeches had far too many editors." [92] Staff member Allen Moore commented that the process allowed no emphasis on theme or structure:

> Although Hartmann had the clear responsibility over the process, he really wasn't managing it all that well. I think among his own staff he had — he's got a number of writers and they were all sort of fooling with it. Meanwhile they would scattershot the requests to us, to OMB, to Friedersdorf, and so on. What do you think should be in here? ... There was very little concerted, organized effort to tie the pieces together."[93]

Hartmann insisted that his speechwriters avoid anything that could be considered high-minded or flowery. He believed that his people were writing "like President Ford would write if he had the time."[94] He enforced this rule with a rigidity that did Ford no favors. The president was not allowed to vary from an exaggeratedly-plain style to let his intelligence show and to demonstrate that he had grown during the presidency. Gergen relates that a few months after he left office, Ford asked him to review a draft speech, and Gergen told Ford that it was very good, but he expressed concern that it might be too eloquent for his style. Ford chuckled and told him that he had written it himself in the style he had always wanted to use.[95] That natural eloquence was never allowed to shine through while Ford was president.

5

Inflation, Public Enemy Number 1

One month after he knowingly undercut his popularity with the pardon, Ford torpe-
doed his remaining support with an obviously-ineffective program to fight inflation dubbed
"Whip Inflation Now," or "WIN." The American public was justifiably concerned. Inflation
was in double digits, and the new president was telling them that the way to fix the problem
was to wear WIN buttons, pledge to spend less, and clean their plates.

It seemed that the government had no idea of what it would really take to get the economy back on track. Nixon had taken drastic action, which proved to be completely ineffective. He imposed wage and price controls, putting the government in charge of the prices
companies charged and the wages they paid workers. The controls were singularly ineffective — the inflation rate had doubled in the three years they were in effect — and when Nixon
lifted them, inflation jumped to the double-digit level that Ford inherited.[1] Nixon expanded
the price controls to oil and gasoline in 1973 after OPEC drastically cut back on production,
causing a tripling of oil prices. The complex system of controls caused shortages of gasoline and heating oil, but, at the time, the shortages were wrongly attributed to the Arab oil
embargo.

The solution to the problem proved to be simple but painful — inflation was finally tamed
when the Fed cut back on money growth. Despite the fact that monetary restraint was a traditional remedy for inflation, not many experts understood that it was necessary at the time.
They were diverted by the novelty of the oil price hikes, and some Keynesian economists had
convinced themselves that there was no danger in reducing unemployment by allowing the
money supply to grow at unprecedented rates. Many economists simply didn't want to face
up to the fact that taming inflation would require a period of economic pain. Ford did not
share the belief that monetary growth wasn't dangerous. He thought that the key elements to
an inflation-fighting strategy were fiscal and monetary restraint. But he would be unsuccessful in his attempts to force Congress to cut back spending, and he never understood that the
money supply was growing at unprecedented rates. He also had idiosyncratic beliefs that
inflation could be tamed by trying to make governments, corporations, and individuals spend
less, and it was those beliefs that led him to embrace the WIN program.

Unfortunately, Ford's idiosyncratic views on how to fight inflation were shared by chairman of the Federal Reserve Board Arthur Burns. With his grey hair, dark suits and wire-
rimmed glasses, Burns looked like a traditional conservative economist. He had sterling
credentials — he was one of the nation's foremost experts on business cycles, a former chairman of Eisenhower's Council of Economic Advisers, and a past president of the American
Economics Association and the National Bureau of Economic Research. His demeanor rein-

forced his reputation as a traditional conservative. Burns was a habitual pipe smoker, and he sounded like a professor, with a "slow, didactic style."[2]

Ford had a deep respect for Burns from his days in the House when he regularly sought his advice on economic issues. He believed that Burns was a conservative who ran a tight monetary ship, despite the Fed chairman's regular statements about his lax monetary policy, which Ford thought were designed to divert attention from his tight reign on the economy: "A master at appearing to be flexible, he never lost sight of his fundamental goals."[3] Ford read Burns wrong — it was his conservative appearance that was deceptive, and his statements about his lax monetary policies reflected reality.[4]

Burns wasn't one of the Keynesian economists who maintained that the government should accept a high level of inflation in order to keep unemployment low. He believed that inflation was a grave danger to the economy, and he considered inflation to be "the principal cause of the decline in economic activity in which we now find ourselves."[5] Burns proposed a crusade to "fight inflation with all the energy we can muster,"[6] and he recognized that the fight would necessitate suffering through some bad economic times:

> For a time, we should be prepared to tolerate a slower rate of economic growth and a higher rate of unemployment than any of us would like. A period of slow growth is needed to permit an unwinding of the inflationary processes that have been built into our economy through years of neglect.[7]

While Burns agreed that inflation was a grave danger, he rejected the traditional remedy. It has long been an accepted economic principal that the best way to fight inflation is to cut back on the supply of money, because prices recede when there is less money available to chase goods. Burns thought that monetary policy was an ineffective tool in the modern economy, and he denied that there was "any simple causal relation between monetary expansion and the rate of inflation either during long or short periods."[8] Burns never accepted any responsibility for the inflation that raged during his chairmanship — the most he would admit was that monetary growth could have been a "permissive factor."[9] He believed that the modern economy was inflexible due to "imperfect business competition" and the monopoly power of unions pushing up wages. He proclaimed that monetary policy was not an adequate tool for "dealing with sources of price inflation such as plaguing us now — that is, pressures on costs arising from excessive wage increases."[10] His obsession with unions was odd, because the percentage of the workforce that belonged to unions was declining, and wage increases had not led overall inflation since the '50s.[11]

It wasn't just unions that diverted Burns' attention from monetary policy — he also fixated on one-time increases in food and oil prices, which he called "special factors":

> Prices in the United States have been affected heavily in the past several years by a variety of special factors. Disappointing harvests in 1972 — both here and abroad — caused a sharp run-up of food prices in 1973. Beginning in the fall of last year, the manipulation of petroleum shipments and prices by oil-exporting countries led to huge increases in the price of gasoline, heating oil, and related products.[12]

He was right that oil and food prices had spiked, but the oil and food shocks were not the cause of sustained inflation. Even Burns admitted that only half of the inflation besetting the country was caused by special factors like oil and food increases; and by the time Ford took office, the prices of oil and food were no longer increasing faster than the rate of inflation.[13]

———

From his first Open Market Committee meeting in 1970, Burns allowed the money supply to grow at unprecedented rates — higher than at any time during the '60s — and he continued his overly-expansionary policy into 1973. In 1972 the growth of the most narrow definition of the money supply, M1, hit an unprecedented rate of 9 percent, and the broad index of money stock, M2, grew by double digits for the first time in the post-war period.[14] After three years of unprecedented money growth, the only way to reverse the growth of inflation was to cut back the growth of money and accept the resulting recession. What the economy needed was a good squeeze, but Burns was not willing to take that painful route — the most he would do was to commit to moderation.[15] During the first half of 1974, Burns cut back on monetary growth, but even he admitted that growth was "still too high for stability of average prices over the longer term."[16] To cut back on money growth, the Fed raised interest rates, and when Ford took office the prime rate and the federal funds rate were above 12 percent, with mortgage rates at 9.5 percent. Burns told Ford that "most interest rates in the United States are now at the highest levels in our history."[17]

Inflation was starting to hurt, and average real personal income was declining for the first time in the post-war period. At the same time, Ford's advisors predicted that unemployment would rise. The week before Ford took office, the Labor Department announced that the unemployment had been 5.3 percent in July, only slightly higher than it had been during the first half of the year, but administration economists told Ford that the unemployment rate would increase to between 6 and 6½ percent by the end of the year.[18]

⌒∿∿⌒

In the view of the public, inflation and the stagnant economy seemed to be entirely the result of the oil embargo. There was some truth to this belief, because OPEC's production cutbacks caused a one-time increase in prices and a temporary economic slowdown, but the nation was less vulnerable than it thought. It wasn't readily apparent at the time, but the ability of the cartel to increase prices was limited and wouldn't last forever.

Several factors gave OPEC a unique opportunity to hike prices in the '70s. The first was that American production had peaked in 1970 — the U.S. percentage of world oil production fell from 52 percent in 1950 to 16 percent in 1974.[19] The second was that oil prices had been artificially suppressed in the '50s and '60s because the United States used its dominant position in the world (as the only major power that hadn't been devastated during World War II) to prevent oil-producing companies from raising prices. By the '70s, many of the oil-producing countries had been taken over by radical regimes that nationalized their petroleum industries. Thus, when America's support of Israel during the Yom Kippur War eliminated any reluctance of OPEC to increase prices, the cartel had a rare opportunity to manipulate the market. When the member nations cut back on production, the price of oil jumped to $10 a barrel — from less than $1 per barrel when Nixon took office. While OPEC seemed all-powerful at the time, its control over oil production was being eroded by vast new sources of oil, including Alaska, Mexico, the Arabian Peninsula, and the North Sea. The CIA predicted that the world would be "swimming in oil" by 1980. When Ford took office, Simon told him that the oil crisis was a "short term problem," and Greenspan agreed.[20]

The energy crisis overshadowed the most significant issue, which was that the nation was far too dependent on dirty fuels. Power plants and automobiles were belching toxins into the air, but the perception that the country was running out of energy pushed environmental concerns to the back of the line. Even Jimmy Carter would advocate more use of dirty fuels like coal, and Ford would consistently choose economic factors over environmental concerns.

⌒∿∿⌒

The sensible reaction to OPEC's production cutbacks would have been to increase domestic production, but the Nixon administration did exactly the opposite by limiting the prices oil companies could charge for domestically-produced petroleum products. When domestic production fell after the controls were imposed, Nixon did not respond by lifting them. He lifted limits on oil imports instead, and imports skyrocketed. The price controls contributed to long lines and sold-out gas stations during the oil crisis of 1973-74. Again, the reasonable response would have been to lift the price controls, but Nixon decided to make them more complicated. His Cost of Living Council lifted controls only on "new oil," defined as oil from new wells and oil from old wells above the wells' 1972 volume. Price controls remained on "old oil," that is, oil produced from an existing oil field below the level of production in 1972. Once the oil companies were allowed to charge more for new oil than old, they diverted capital from old oil fields to new fields, and old oil production declined at a rate of 14 percent per year.[21]

Controls on natural gas also caused shortages. Energy companies were forced to charge lower prices for gas that crossed state lines than gas that stayed within a state, so gas producers sold gas in-state rather than shipping it where it was needed. Only one-third of gas was shipped across state lines, and shortages developed in various areas of the country, most notably New England. The shortages were serious; some states found it necessary to cut consumption in half. Faced with the shortages, regulators again chose more complexity rather than the simple solution of lifting the controls. They set up a new system of controls to allocate scarce supplies of gas.[22]

Daniel Yergin and Joseph Stanislaw have called the energy control program "a lasting lesson in the perversities that can ensue when government takes over the marketplace." William Simon, who had run Nixon's oil regulation program, agreed. "The kindest thing I can say about it is that it was a disaster.... All we were actually doing with our so-called bureaucratic efficiency was damaging the existent distribution system."[23] Their very ineffectiveness kept the controls in place. Because energy prices remained high, the controls on oil and natural gas did not expire with the rest of Nixon's price controls, and they were still in place when Ford took office. The price controls were scheduled to expire in June 1975, unless Congress decided to extend them.

Just three days into his presidency, Ford received recommendations about what to do with the controls. John Sawhill, the head of the Federal Energy Administration, suggested making the controls even more complicated. He admitted that it was important to get to "price equalization," that is, making the price of oil the same regardless of where it was produced. The easy way to do that would be to lift the controls and allow the price of old oil to rise to the market price. But he didn't want to do that because of the "windfall profits" that would be made by the shareholders of oil companies. Instead, he recommended a complicated "capacity-based entitlement system" that would achieve "substantial price equalization." Under the proposal, a company would be granted "entitlements" based on the ratio of old to new crude oil that a company was currently refining, and companies could buy and sell the entitlements.[24]

Ford's economists recommended a much more simple solution. The Council of Economic Advisors submitted a memo in favor of immediate deregulation, predicting that price decontrol would result in a one-time rise in the inflation rate of less than 0.4 percent. The rise in inflation would be offset by a 5 percent increase in production, reducing imports by 9 to 16 percent.[25] Ford sided with the CEA in favor of deregulation. On August 28, 1974, he told his domestic advisors to try to get the legislative process started, and he told them to "push hard" for deregulation of natural gas during the pending congressional session.[26]

Ford also disagreed with Sawhill's proposal for a tax on gasoline to discourage consumption. In effect, Sawhill was proposing that the government simultaneously try to reduce and increase the price of gasoline. The sole purpose of price controls was to keep the price of gasoline low, while the sole purpose of Sawhill's gas tax would have been to increase the price. Ford thought that the gas tax had no chance in Congress, and he preferred to let prices increase naturally by lifting controls. But Sawhill would not be deterred, and he went public with a proposal to add a 20-cent-per-gallon tax on October 1, and he followed with an attack on Ford's energy policy in Senate testimony. Ford immediately disowned Sawhill's proposal, declaring that there would not be a new gas tax during his administration. He asked Sawhill to resign and replaced him with associate director of OMB Frank Zarb. Ford also created the Energy Resources Council to handle energy matters, made up of Zarb, Secretary of the Interior Rogers Morton and Treasury Secretary Simon.[27] Zarb and the ERC agreed with Ford's deregulatory inclinations, and they would work efficiently to eliminate the misguided price controls on petroleum products.

The ERC was the counterpart of the Economic Policy Board, which Ford created to handle economic policy. Technically, most of the cabinet was on the EPB, but the key members were Simon, Seidman, and Greenspan. Ford's new OMB director, James Lynn, was a member, but his deputy, Paul O'Neill, ended up having even more influence. Ford learned to rely on O'Neill, who shared his interest in the intricacies of the budget. Simon was the chairman of the board, but Seidman ran the day-to-day operation. He efficiently collected the input from throughout the administration, which he compiled for Ford on all important economic decisions. Because Ford viewed most domestic issues in economic terms, the board would be the most powerful voice on domestic policy within the administration.[28]

The influence of the economists began during Ford's first week in office when they gave the new president their recommendations on economic policy. They all agreed that inflation was the most serious issue facing the country, and the consensus opinion was that the unemployment rate would increase from 5 percent in 1974 to above 6 percent in 1975. Treasury Secretary Simon summed up the situation. "We are faced with an unacceptable rate of inflation and an unacceptable rate of unemployment.... In my view, inflation is the most serious problem, and must be given the highest priority, but it is clear that the unemployment situation cannot be ignored."

The economists were in agreement that reducing federal spending was essential for the fight against inflation, and they proposed cutting $5 to $10 billion from the $305 billion budget for fiscal year '75. Fed Chairman Burns, ever willing to put the responsibility for fighting inflation on someone else, said that the most significant act Ford could take was to reduce federal spending. "No single action could have a more powerful impact on public perception of your sincerity in attacking the causes of inflation than to cut down significantly on this increase." Greenspan called cutting spending "priority Number One in any anti-inflation program." Simon called for a program stressing fiscal restraint, which, "in tandem with monetary policy," would "gradually break the bucking bronco of inflation."

The economists had little to say about monetary policy. The memos had been collected by outgoing chairman of the Council of Economic Advisers Herb Stein, who pointed out this omission in his summary. "Although many economists believe that monetary policy is the single most important determinant of the inflation rate there is little discussion of it in the submissions." Burns was one of the few who did mention monetary policy, but he told Ford that the current policy "relied altogether too much on monetary policy." All of the submissions opposed resumptions of wage and price controls, with the exception of the supposedly-conservative Burns, who proposed a Cost of Living Council with the power to delay wage or price increases by thirty days, along with an embargo on grain exports.[29]

When Ford considered this advice, he decided to implement a "three-pronged strategy to reduce inflation: spending cuts, the maintenance of a prudent monetary policy and, finally, a counseling process whereby administration officials would try to anticipate wage and price increases and urge restraint."[30] Of the three prongs, Ford considered spending cuts to be the most important. "Traditional economic theory says the way to beat inflation is to reduce demand by restraining federal spending."[31] The deficit for 1974 looked like it would be down to just over $3 billion, but it was projected to increase to $9.6 billion in fiscal year '75, and Ford realized that the stagnant economy would cause it to grow to between $25 and $30 billion. Ford recognized that cutting the deficit by $5 billion would not have a significant effect on inflation, and he told the Cabinet that there was a slim chance that Congress would agree to cut spending below $300 billion. Nevertheless, he thought fighting for spending cuts would set the right tone for the rest of his presidency, and that "the importance of that kind of benefit couldn't be underestimated."[32]

———

As he promised in his first speech to Congress, Ford convened a "Summit on Inflation" at the end of September, but first the administration held twelve "mini-summits" with experts in specific fields. The first mini-summit was a televised day-long meeting on September 5 between Ford and twenty-eight economists. Most of the economists agreed with Ford's plans to reduce federal spending, and they urged him to stay the course with the current level of moderate monetary growth. Greenspan told Ford that allowing the money supply to grow at a higher rate "would serve no useful purpose." The most fitting advice came from the father of Monetarism, Milton Friedman, who strongly advised monetary restraint. "There is one and only one cure and we all know it. We have to slow down total spending. Only the federal government can do that and it can do that only by slowing its own spending and slowing monetary growth which will slow private spending." He warned that taming inflation required a period of economic stagnation, and he cautioned Ford not to allow a recession to divert his attention from the fight against inflation:

> We have to reconcile ourselves to the fact that we will not get out of inflation except by going through a temporary but maybe fairly prolonged period of slow economic growth and higher unemployment.... We should not be beguiled on the danger of recession.[33]

The Summit on Inflation took place September 28–29 in the International Ballroom at the Washington Hilton Hotel. Eight hundred people were in attendance, including Ford, despite the fact that his wife Betty had surgery for breast cancer on the first day of the conference. On September 26, doctors discovered the cancer, and she entered the hospital for surgery the next day. In the morning before the conference started, Ford was in the Oval Office with Hartmann when Dr. William Lukash called and reported that the lump was malignant, so he performed a full mastectomy. It would take a week to complete the tests that would show whether the cancer had spread. Ford broke down and cried.[34]

A few days later the tests came back showing that a small amount of the cancer had spread to her lymph nodes, and she was put on drugs for two years. Unlike most women at the time, Betty was open about her surgery, and she urged American women to get tested. As she told the American Cancer Society, her surgery caused her to "realize how many women in the country could be in the same situation.... That realization made me decide to discuss my breast cancer operation openly, because I thought of all the lives in jeopardy.... My illness turned out to have a very special purpose — helping save other lives, and I am grateful for what I was able to do."[35] While Betty was in the hospital, Susan Ford and David Kennerly bought the president and first lady a golden retriever, which Ford named "Liberty." Liberty became a constant companion of Ford during his time in office.[36]

The drugs she was given for her cancer seemed to affect the first lady. Some of the staff noticed that the first lady often withdrew, and she sometimes had difficulty talking. At the time, they attributed it to the medication she was taking after her cancer surgery, but she admitted to being an alcoholic several years after the end of the administration. Again, she used her illness to educate others. She spoke openly about her recovery, and the Fords established the Betty Ford Center, perhaps the preeminent rehabilitation clinic in the country.[37]

—⁓—

At the conference, Burns called for a national crusade against inflation. "Our job is to use all of our energy, all of the ability and knowledge that we can muster, to help protect the jobs of all American workers and the integrity of their money." He asked everyone to take part in the crusade, except himself— he actually announced that the Fed had decided to increase monetary growth.[38]

The big news of the conference came at the end when Ford announced a new voluntary program to fight inflation, which would become Whip Inflation Now. Ford had been sold on the program by Hartmann, who got the idea from speechwriter Paul Theis and William Meyer, the president of Central Automatic Sprinkler Company. Theis and Meyer proposed a program patterned on the Franklin Roosevelt's NRA, called "Inflation Fighters," under which businesses could display an IF emblem if they agreed not to raise prices for one year. Hartmann pitched the idea to Ford, who loved it:

> It didn't take him long to convince me. Once you had 213 million Americans recognizing that inflation was a problem and joining in the effort to do something about it, positive results would have to follow. If both the government and the people tightened their belts voluntarily and spent less than they had before, that would reduce demand, and the inflation rate would start going down.[39]

Most of Ford's economic advisors thought the proposal was harmless but silly; Greenspan remembers being "horrified."[40] Burns was an exception, because it was similar to his proposal for "productivity councils."[41] WIN was also similar to a proposal made by *New York Post* columnist Sylvia Porter at the economic summit. During a break after Porter's presentation, Ford asked if she would be willing to head up his WIN program, and he announced in his closing address that Porter had agreed.[42]

—⁓—

Ten days later Ford made WIN the cornerstone of his first major economic address. Wearing a red and white WIN button, he addressed a joint session of Congress at 4:02 in the afternoon on October 8. The speech began with a patchwork of proposals without a unifying theme. The proposal that drew the most attention was for a one-year five-percent tax surcharge on families making more than $15,000 a year. He then turned to the American people and asked them to join the voluntary program that would symbolize his economic policy:

> A very simple enlistment form will appear in many of tomorrow's newspapers along with the symbol of this new mobilization, which I am wearing on my lapel. It bears the single word WIN. I think that tells it all. I will call upon every American to join in this massive mobilization and stick with it until we do win as a nation and as a people.

Ford presents his inflation-fighting program to Republican candidates in Indianapolis, Indiana, on October 16, 1974. (Photograph by David Hume Kennerly; courtesy Gerald R. Ford Library.)

The program itself was bad enough, but the gratuitous suggestions his speechwriters threw in made the president seem like a kindergarten teacher. "If you cannot spare a penny from your food budget — and I know there are many — surely you can cut the food that you waste by 5 percent." He hit the low point of the speech when he added the classic request of every kindergarten teacher — to share:

> I think there is one final thing that all Americans can do, rich or poor, and that is share with others. We can share burdens as we can share blessings. Sharing is not easy, not easy to measure like mileage and family budgets, but I am sure that 5 percent more is not nearly enough to ask, so I ask you to share everything you can and a little bit more.[43]

Ford considered WIN to be less important than the other elements of his anti-inflation program, but he continued to give it the most prominence, giving a speech solely dedicated to WIN before the Future Farmers of America in Kansas City a week later. The three networks had no desire to televise the speech — they thought that Ford rehashing the WIN proposal wasn't news — but they capitulated when Press Secretary Nessen promised that the speech would contain major substantive announcements.[44]

As it turned out, Ford would have been better off if the networks had ignored what David Gergen has called "a dud, a parody of a fireside chat."[45] The speech was full of awkward metaphors, like when the president compared his inflation proposals to marshmallows. "Now some have said that instead of asking Congress and the nation to bite the bullet, I offered only a marshmallow.... Congress wouldn't even chew that marshmallow." Ford then switched to poultry. "But if they don't like the menu, I may be back with some tough turkey. It is my observation and view that the American people are hungry for some tough stuff to chew on in this crisis." The low point came when Ford told Americans to clean their plates — reporters began to refer derisively to the "clean your plate" speech:

> In the letters that I have received at the White House are thousands of good suggestions; for instance, take all you want, but eat all you take. The first words I can remember in my dad's house were very simple but very direct: Clean up your plate before you get up from the table. And that is still pretty good advice.[46]

Gerald and Betty Ford signed the WIN pledge on November 13 in a ceremony in the Cabinet Room of the White House. More than 200,000 Americans followed Ford's example and sent in signed pledges.[47] That is the kind of number that confuses national politicians — it sounds like a lot until it is compared to the 200 million people in the country. In reality, less than one percent of Americans signed the pledge. It is doubtful that the program would have been effective had most Americans joined, and with just a small fraction of people participating, WIN had no chance. The WIN program was harmless to the economy, but not to Ford. In January 1975, a Harris poll reported that 86 percent of Americans had no confidence in his ability to manage the economy.[48]

It didn't take long for the one percent of Americans who signed the WIN pledge to lose interest. On February 21, 1975, William Baroody, the White House liaison to the WIN committee, wrote to Ford that the program was in bad shape, and he predicted that the Citizen's Action Committee might "elect to vote itself out of business, although such is not the predisposition of its membership."[49] In response to Baroody's memo, most of Ford's advisors unenthusiastically supported the continuance of the WIN program, but Greenspan was not one of them. He wrote to Ford that the program "has not made a perceptible contribution to economic policy or performance in the past, and I am unaware of any reason to expect it to do so in the future." Nessen also supported disbanding the committee. "I suggest the WIN program be allowed to die a quiet and unlamented death."[50] Ford decided to continue the program, but it was eventually quietly disbanded.

On the day of Ford's WIN speech in Kansas City, the Fed increased its targets for money growth. Apparently, the governors of the Fed had not joined the WIN program.[51] As Burns explained to Congress, the Fed followed with a "series of expansive monetary actions."[52] For the first six months of the administration the Fed progressively lowered the target interest rate until it was half the level it was when Nixon resigned.[53] At the end of the year, administration economist William Fellner told Ford that "the Fed has adopted measures usually resulting in rapid growth rates of monetary aggregates."[54] On February 25, Burns told Congress to expect even greater money growth in the months ahead. "Forces have now been set in motion that will, I believe, soon result in a quicker pace of monetary and credit expansion."[55]

WIN wasn't the only misguided economic program that cost Ford politically. He lost support in farm states with a vain attempt to keep food prices down by embargoing grain sales to the Soviet Union. After agricultural secretary Earl Butz predicted that corn production would drop by 12 to 14 percent, Ford thought that grain sales to the Russians "would wreak havoc with our economy and push the inflation rate even higher."[56] In October 1974 he met with two grain companies and convinced them to cancel $500 billion worth of sales to the Soviets, and he followed with temporary embargos on grain sales to the Soviet Union and soybean sales to Japan.[57] The embargos did nothing to reduce inflation because the markets for grain and soybeans were world markets, and the Japanese and the Soviets responded to the embargos by buying from other countries, while the customers from those countries turned to the United States. The world-wide supply of grain was the same, as was the world-wide demand, so the price of world market price for grain remained unchanged. The only substantial effect of the embargo was that it enraged farmers and cost Ford political support.

<hr>

While the WIN program got the most attention, Ford thought that reducing the deficit was the cornerstone of the fight against inflation. "Nothing, in my opinion, was more important than holding the line on federal spending and keeping the budget for fiscal year 1975 at or under $300 billion."[58] Ford kept pushing his five percent tax surcharge through the end of the year, but he knew it had no chance, and he allowed it to die a quiet death. But Ford never stopped trying to restrain spending. On September 20 he used his new power under the Congressional Budget Reform Act of 1974 to ask Congress to defer and withdraw $20.3 billion of previously-mandated spending authority, and he later submitted more than 100 proposed budget cuts. But Congress was not interested. He tried again on November 26 when he sent Congress a proposal for $4.6 billion in budget cuts and $500 million in rescissions and deferrals, but Congress approved only $131 million of the rescissions.[59]

Ford also tried to restrain spending with the veto, which he wielded with gusto. Seidman has explained that Ford considered his veto power "just a part of the bargaining process that he had learned while leading his party in the Congress."[60] Unlike the WIN program, his economic advisors agreed with his veto strategy, with Greenspan leading the cheering.[61] Four days after taking office, Ford vetoed a bill to increase the pay of federal marshals, and he vetoed a bill to fund agricultural research two days later. He continued throughout his presidency, vetoing a total of sixty-six bills — his annual veto rate was higher than all but three other presidents.[62]

Ford was willing to work with Congress after his vetoes, and two-thirds of them were sustained. For example, Ford vetoed the Emergency Employment Appropriation Act, which he estimated would increase the deficit by $2.1 billion. After the veto, Congress pared back the bill, and Ford signed it. The Emergency Housing Act of 1975 followed a similar pattern. Congress passed a bill greater than the one Ford had requested, so he vetoed it, but he signed a more limited version that Congress passed after the veto.[63]

Like in so many other cases, Ford was not swayed by political considerations in his fight to restrain spending. For example, when Defense Secretary Rumsfeld submitted recommendations to close military bases, Ford's congressional liaison, Max Friedersdorf, argued against closing bases in friendly congressional districts; but as Friedersdorf recalled, "President Ford stood absolutely firm. Don Rumsfeld had recommended a list of closings, and the president took the position that it was the right thing to do, and he would not budge."[64]

<hr>

Inflation remained Public Enemy Number 1 only for a short time. While inflation continued at the same pace, the country started to slide into a deep recession. Ford ignored Milton Friedman's admonition to "not be beguiled on the danger of recession." Faced with the recession, Ford would reverse his economic program and propose a tax cut to replace his surcharge.

6

Reform

The '70s were a time of dramatic reform, when American politics, and the government itself, were cleaned up and opened to public scrutiny. For the first time, politicians were forced to follow campaign financing rules, ending an era when most politicians wantonly ignored the law. The result of this wave of reform was that the American political system became far cleaner than it ever had been. But because the remaining abuses were exposed to public view, the American people became more cynical about their government. In some measure, the reformist wave was a reaction to the Watergate scandal, and reform proponents were prominent in the huge class of freshmen Democrats who would sweep into office in the 1974 elections. But the reform movement was not new — it had been going strong for several years.

The movement was kick-started in August 1970 when Common Cause was founded by John Gardner, a progressive Republican who was imbued with an extraordinary sense of public duty. He had resigned as president of the Carnegie Corporation to become Johnson's secretary of HEW, where he implemented the Medicare program and other Great Society initiatives before resigning in opposition to the Vietnam War. He had seen special interest groups functioning in Washington, but he saw no group that represented the people — "everybody's organized but the people" — and he decided to remedy the situation by creating Common Cause. Common Cause became the most prominent proponent of campaign finance reform, and a revolution swept the country in a few years time.[1]

Before the reforms of the early '70s, the federal government and most states had laws on the books to limit the influence of moneyed interests, but the laws were more honored in the breach than the observance. At the federal level, contributions from individuals were limited to $3,000, and all contributions from corporations and unions were illegal; but there was no independent agency to enforce the laws, and they were routinely ignored.[2]

In the House of Representatives, enforcement of campaign financing laws was the domain of the House Administration Committee, which was chaired by Wayne Hays of Ohio. Hays was the prototype of the unscrupulous mossbacks who thrived under the old system. As chairman of the Administration Committee, he controlled his colleagues' staffs, travel budgets, offices, parking, and perks, and he wielded his power effectively, dolling out perks to supporters and sending anyone who opposed him to basement offices. He was also, in the words of California representative Phillip Burton, "the meanest man in Congress."[3] For years Hays wielded his power to stifle any proposed legislation to reform the system.

Enforcement was just as lax in the states. Politicians in states like New York and Florida ignored the campaign finance laws because there was no independent body to enforce them. Pennsylvania had never seen a single prosecution for violation of the laws. In Massachusetts, candidates regularly accepted large cash payments as "walking-around money," while in Indiana, politicians routinely collected kickbacks from political appointees equal to two percent of their salaries — kickbacks added up to 46 percent of the contributions collected by the Indiana Republican Party in 1972. In Ohio, donations by government employees were *de rigueur*, and candidates traditionally avoided disclosure by creating complex webs of campaign committees.[4]

———ⲟⲛⲟ———

Common Cause was remarkably effective when it took aim at these practices. At the federal level and in the states, new laws were passed that made contributions public, limited the amounts individuals could contribute, and made politicians play by the rules. Independent commissions were created to enforce the law, and practices were outlawed that had been commonly used to launder large contributions, such as cash contributions and the use of multiple campaign committees.

The first big step came when Congress passed the Federal Election Campaign Act of 1971, which closed many of the loopholes that had previously allowed politicians to hide where they were getting their money. The law made candidates report contributions over $100 and limited the amount a candidate could contribute to his or her own campaign. At the same time, Congress passed the Revenue Act of 1971, which provided for federal funding of the general election for president, starting in 1976, by a voluntary $1 check-off on tax returns. Any candidate who chose to receive funding had to agree to not accept private contributions.[5]

The reform movement in the states began in 1972 when voters in Colorado and Washington approved campaign financing referenda, and 47 states followed by passing reform laws during the next four years. By 1976, every state but North Dakota required reporting of campaign donations and expenditures, and almost every state outlawed large cash contributions. Thirty-five states limited the amount a candidate could spend on a campaign, and twenty-three states limited the amount any individual could contribute to a campaign. Public financing was less successful, although eleven states established systems for funding campaigns. Most importantly, twenty-five states established independent commissions to enforce the new laws.[6]

———ⲟⲛⲟ———

The new federal campaign financing law had one major flaw — there was no independent commission to enforce the rules. The day before Ford took office, the House passed a bill to remedy the problem and sent it to the conference committee to reconcile the differences with a bill the Senate had passed a year earlier. The bill would languish in the conference committee for two more months because of a fight over public financing of congressional campaigns. The Senate bill included public financing for congressional elections, but when the bill got to the House, it ran into the immovable roadblock to reform, Wayne Hays. Hays held up the bill in his committee for almost a year, and when the Democratic leadership forced him to allow it to move, he stripped all provisions for public financing of congressional campaigns. He also insisted that Congress be given the power to appoint FEC commissioners, which was a deviation from the usual practice of the president appointing commissioners, subject to congressional approval. When the bill was sent to conference committee, Hays refused to budge. The senators finally relented, and the bill that passed in early October provided only for financing of presidential elections.[7]

The bill was the most comprehensive federal campaign financing legislation in American history. It prohibited cash contributions above $100, and each campaign was limited to one central campaign committee, so candidates could no longer hide contributions by setting up complex networks of committees. The law set a $1,000 limit on individual contributions to any campaign, while candidates could spend their own money up to $50,000 for presidential elections, $35,000 for Senate contests, and $25,000 for House races. The law also set the following spending limits for total campaign spending: $10 million in presidential primaries, $20 million in presidential general elections, $100,000 in Senate primaries, $150,000 in Senate general elections, $70,000 in House primaries and $100,000 in House general elections. Federal funding for presidential elections remained voluntary. If a candidate chose to receive funding, the campaign could not accept private contributions. Most importantly, the law finally had some teeth because it created a six-member, bipartisan Federal Election Commission. But the commission would be unique. All other regulatory commissions were appointed by the president, but, at Hays' insistence, Congress had the power to appoint four FEC commissioners, while the president would appoint only two.[8]

Ford signed the bill on October 15, 1974, because "the times demand this legislation," but he expressed doubts about its constitutionality.[9] The law took effect on January 1, 1975, and the FEC was up and running on April 14, 1975, when Ford swore in the first six commissioners, but they would not remain in office for long. The law was appealed immediately, and the Supreme Court ruled on January 30, 1976. In its *Buckley v. Valeo* decision, the court upheld most of the law, including reporting requirements and public financing of presidential campaigns, but not everything passed muster. The court struck down spending limits because "a primary effect of these expenditure limitations is to restrict the quantity of campaign speech by individuals, groups, and candidates." The only spending limits that were allowed to stand were those that a candidate voluntarily accepted in return for federal funds.

The court then turned to whether Congress could limit the amount a candidate spent of his or her own money. Whether these rules passed muster depended on how the court categorized them — were they constitutional limits on donations or unconstitutional limits on expenditures? Without much discussion, the court found that the rules were unconstitutional limits on expenditures. The effect of this decision was that a law designed to curtail the influence of money ended up giving a substantial advantage to wealthy candidates who could easily outspend their opponents.

Not surprisingly, the other thing the court overturned was the unusual method for choosing FEC commissioners. The court held that Congress usurped executive authority when it retained the ability to appoint four commissioners. The court stayed its decision for thirty days to give Congress and the president time to reconstitute the commission in a constitutional manner.[10] It would take Congress longer than that to pass a new law, and Ford was slow in appointing new commissioners, putting the commission in limbo from March 22 to May 21, 1976. During that time the commission was unable to dispense funds, which would impact the presidential primary campaign.

Ford never seriously considered vetoing the Federal Campaign Act Amendments, but the same was not true of the other major piece of reform legislation that hit his desk early in his presidency: amendments to the Freedom of Information Act. A Freedom of Information Act had been on the books since 1966, but the original act had been "crippled and compromised" by reform opponents, in the words of Bill Moyers.[11] The law created no disincentive for agencies to stonewall requests, and the only effective way to get information was to pursue costly litigation. But even litigation was not an option for challenging secrecy classifications because the Supreme Court held that courts did not have the authority to rule on the appropriateness of classifications.

When Ford took office, both the Senate and the House had passed amendments to fix these problems, and the congressional conference committee was working to resolve the differences. The bills required federal agencies to respond to requests within ten days and charge reasonable rates, to be set by the OMB. They gave a reviewing court the authority to conduct an *in camera* review of secret materials to determine if the classification was justified and award attorneys' fees to successful plaintiffs. In its overzealousness, the Senate added provision that allowed a court to order a 60-day suspension of an employee who denied a request "without a reasonable basis in law."[12]

The conference committee decided to give the new president time to weigh in. Three days after he took office, Ford received memos from Roy Ash and Kenneth Cole explaining that the CIA and Department of Defense objected to the short time frames for responding to requests, attorneys' fees for successful plaintiffs, *in camera* review of classified documents by courts, the government having the burden to prove that documents should remain classified, and sanctions on officials who wrongly refused to declassify information. Ford sympathized with the concerns, but he wrote on the memo that a "veto presents problems." Nevertheless, he sent a letter to Congress on August 20 listing the objections.[13]

The conferees addressed some, but not all, of Ford's concerns. On September 23, Senator Kennedy and Representative William Moorhead sent a letter explaining that the burden of proof had been changed to give an agency's classification "substantial weight." The committee changed the law to allow law enforcement agencies to withhold investigatory files if disclosure might interfere with ongoing proceedings, invade any individual's privacy, reveal sources, or endanger law enforcement personnel; and the committee limited personal liability of employees responding to information requests to situations where the employee acted arbitrarily or capriciously. The ten-day time frame for responding to requests remained, as did the ability for courts to award attorneys' fees.[14] The law passed the Senate by a voice vote on October 1, and six days later the House passed it by a 392 to 2 vote.

At first blush, it should have been easy for Ford to sign the bill. He had staked his administration on openness and honesty, and a veto was sure to be overturned. The problem was that by signing the bill Ford would be rejecting the advice of virtually every agency under his purview, including the CIA, the Defense Department, the DOJ, the Civil Service Commission, OMB, the Treasury Department, the Department of Commerce, the State Department, and the Veterans Administration.[15] The reaction of Ford's old friend Buchen was telling. At first he recommended that Ford sign the bill, but when he saw the responses from the rest of the administration, he changed his mind.[16] Ford was faced with the choice of undermining the new administration's reputation for openness by vetoing the law or antagonizing much of the federal government by signing it. Either option would be a symbolic act, because the legislation was certain to become law with or without a veto. Ford decided to demonstrate his support for the people who worked for him, and he vetoed the legislation on October 17.

In his veto message, Ford said that he was "gratified" that the conferees had made changes to meet his concerns, but he was forced to veto the legislation because "significant problems have not been resolved," including allowing courts to conduct *in camera* reviews and subjecting investigatory files to possible disclosure, and he submitted a revised proposal a week later.[17] The proposal got no traction, and the House voted 371 to 31 to override Ford's veto on November 20, and the Senate followed on November 21 by 65 to 27.

As it turned out, the administration was overreacting to perceived problems with the legislation. None of the horrors predicted by the CIA and Department of Defense came to pass. Courts have acted responsibly in reviewing documents, employees have not been routinely subject to sanctions for not responding to requests, and the costs of hiring people to respond to requests have been far outweighed by the benefits to the public. By making the

Freedom of Information Act workable, the 1974 amendments were a landmark in reform. Open government proponents have not been completely happy with the responsiveness of agencies — it is doubtful that they ever will be — but Americans have access to far greater amounts of information about governmental activities than they ever had in the past.

———∽∾∼———

Reform got another big boost from the 1974 congressional elections, which were nearly a clean sweep for the Democrats. Ford crisscrossed the country campaigning for his old colleagues, logging nearly 20,000 miles and visiting fifteen states in October alone. But he couldn't overcome Watergate and the pardon, and the results were even worse than he had feared. In the Senate, the Republican delegation fell from 42 to 37 members. Democrats won four more governorships, increasing their total to 36. The Democrats gained 49 seats in the House, increasing their majority to two-to-one. The election ushered in an unusually large freshman class of 92 new House members, including 75 Democrats. The freshmen Democrats were unusually assertive — they were not willing to accept common wisdom or follow congressional traditions.

Ford was willing to work with the new liberals in Congress. His congressional liaison, Max Friedersdorf, called him "the complete and polar opposite of Nixon in terms of his willingness to approach members of Congress and the ease in which he related to them."[18] His old friend Mel Laird said that Ford "was more willing to compromise with Congress than any recent president that I can remember."[19] But Ford had deep ideological disagreements with the new liberals, who proved to be difficult to work with, to the frustration of Speaker Albert:

> I tried to be the leader of this group that refused to be led. They wanted to build a record, not a policy, and they had the votes to pass bills that I knew Jerry Ford would have to veto.[20]

As soon as they took office, the new freshman class started changing the way things were done. They demanded that control of committee assignments be taken from the hidebound Ways and Means Committee. Ways and Means chairman Wilber Mills was not in a position to put up much of a fight because he was immersed in a scandal. Two months after Ford took office, Mills was pulled over by the Washington police, and a stripper named Fanne Foxe leapt out of his car and jumped in the nearby Tidal Basin. Mills was reelected in the 1974 election, but he resigned a month later after he drunkenly staggered on stage with Foxe's husband at a Boston burlesque club where she was performing. His reign over all tax and spending legislation, as well as all appointments to House committees, was over. Committee assignments were given to the Steering and Policy Committee of the Democratic Caucus, and the freshman class demanded that committee chairs be chosen by a secret vote of the caucus rather than by seniority. In the first vote, three chairmen were deposed: F. Edward Hebert of the Armed Services Committee, John Wright Patman of the Banking, Currency and Housing Committee, and W. R. Poage of the Agriculture Committee.[21]

———∽∾∼———

Reformers in the Congress next took aim at "constituent service funds," kept by 40 percent of members of congress, ostensibly to subsidize their newsletters and travel back home. The Federal Election Commission tried to regulate the funds in July 1975 when it submitted a regulation to Congress to make the funds subject to campaign financing laws. When the Senate vetoed the regulation, the FEC was forced to eliminate its $100 limit on contributions to the funds, and a stripped-down rule that only required reporting of donations and expenditures finally made it through Congress.[22]

In the House, slush fund reform ran into the usual roadblock: Wayne Hays. But his ability to block change ended in spectacular fashion on May 23, 1976, when the *Washington Post* reported that he was keeping his mistress, Elizabeth Ray, on his payroll for a non-existent job. Ray admitted that she received $14,000 per year and that her only job responsibility was to sleep with Hays. "I can't type, I can't file, I can't even answer the phone." At first, Hays denied Ray's allegations. "Hell's fire! I'm a very happily married man."[23] After two days of denials, he admitted the truth. He was forced to give up his chairmanship, and with it the power that he had wielded over the members of the House.

Even after he stepped down from the Administrative Committee, Hays refused to resign from the House, and he fought all efforts of the Ethics Committee to investigate him, but he was faced with a new chairman who refused to back down. When Ethics chairman John Flynt took his post in January 1975, the committee had never disciplined a House member. Flynt changed that, and in 1976 the committee issued its first recommendation of reprimand, directed at Florida democrat Robert Sikes for benefiting from military contracts while chairman of the Military Construction Subcommittee. When the Hays scandal broke, Flynt pushed to hold him accountable, and on August 30 the committee voted to hold public hearings. Hays resigned from the House two days later.[24]

With Hays out of the way, the path was clear for the House leadership to tackle slush funds. Speaker Albert gave Wisconsin representative David Obey the chair of a task force to recommend changes to House ethics rules, and the new eight-member House Commission on Administrative Review recommended abolition of constituent funds. The commission also recommended limits on outside income and honoraria that could be earned by members, and the proposals passed in March 1977. The Senate passed similar rules one month later.[25]

———

The other major reform effort during Ford's presidency involved reigning in American companies that had been bribing foreign governments. Watergate had already revealed that nineteen companies made illegal contributions to the Nixon campaign, and ensuing investigations revealed that SBC, American Airlines, Braniff, 3M, Gulf Oil, Northrop, and Firestone had kept regular slush funds for illegal contributions. As the investigations continued, they revealed that American companies had not only regularly bribed federal and state officials — they bribed foreign officials on a massive scale.

The lead in rooting out foreign bribes was taken by the SEC's chief enforcement officer Stanley Sporkin. The paunchy 43 year old took up the cause with élan. Sporkin saw the world in good-and-evil terms, and he thought that he was battling evil in corporate boardrooms. In normal situations, putting a zealot in a prosecutorial position is dangerous, but in 1975 it took a fanatic to change corporate culture in America. In July 1975 the SEC offered to go easier on companies that came in and disclosed their bribes, and over the next two years more than 300 companies admitted to bribing foreign governments.

Oil companies were among the most egregious violators. Standard Oil of California, Standard Oil of Indiana, Ashland Oil, and Exxon all admitted to making hundreds of thousands of dollars in illegal payments, but they were small-time crooks compared to some of their brethren. Occidental Petroleum made payments of $3 million to a Venezuelan official. Tenneco admitted that it had paid more than $600,000 to state utility commissioners and more than $12 million to foreign consultants to be used as bribes in the preceding five years. Gulf Oil admitted that it had paid more than $12 million in bribes since 1960, more than $5 million of which was funneled to U.S. politicians, while the rest went overseas, including $4 million to the governing party of South Korea.

Military contractors were also flagrant offenders. Northrop paid bribes of more than $30 million to foreign agents in a three-year period, much of it going for bribes to government officials; and its rival, Lockheed, admitted to paying $22 million to foreign officials and political parties. Rockwell admitted to more than half a million dollars in bribes abroad, while Honeywell admitted to $1.8 million of improper foreign payments. Other companies bribed foreign governments to advance their business interests. United Brands paid $2.5 million to the military dictator of Honduras, President Oswaldo Lopez, in return for lower export taxes on bananas. Johnson & Johnson admitted to making payments adding up to $1 million over a four-year period, while Merck admitted to foreign payments of $3.6 million since 1968. ITT admitted to $3.8 million in payments over a five-year period, and GTE admitted that it had paid more than $2 million to foreign officials.

Ford did not push the SEC investigation, but he did nothing to rein in Sporkin. The only time the administration weighed in was when Kissinger was worried that some of America's corrupt allies would be embarrassed if companies were forced to reveal who they had bribed. In late 1975, when the SEC sued Lockheed to force the company to disclose the recipients of bribes, Kissinger filed a letter with the court stating that disclosing the recipients of payments could have "grave consequences" for the interests of the United States. The court ordered Lockheed to provide the information to the SEC, but it required the agency to give the company and the State Department ten days notice before disclosing the information to third parties. It wasn't the administration's finest hour, effectively making the United States government an active participant in concealing the corruption of a foreign government.

The identity of America's corrupt allies did not remain secret for long because the recipients of the bribes were made public by Frank Church's Subcommittee on Multinational Corporations in February 1976. In his testimony, Lockheed president Carl Kotchian admitted that the company had made payments to officials in Germany, Italy, Sweden, and Japan, and to a "high government official in the Netherlands." The name of the official soon leaked — it was Prince Bernhard, who had received $1 million in 1959 to influence the country's decision to buy Lockheed fighter planes. Italy followed with an investigation which revealed that the company had paid Italian officials $2 million to grease the sale of transport planes. Japan's investigation uncovered $12 million worth of bribes to its officials between 1969 and 1975, and the investigation led to the arrest of former prime minister Kakuei Tanaka for taking a $1.7 million payment from Lockheed.[26]

The companies claimed that they had to participate in the corruption in other countries or lose out to foreign companies that did. They had a point — some countries were so corrupt that a company could not do business without bribing officials. Ford bought the argument, and he tried to steer the outcome to allow companies to continue bribing foreign governments. On March 31, 1976, he tried to stem the scandal by setting up a "Cabinet-level" task force, with commerce secretary Elliot Richardson as chairman. After the task force completed its work, Ford issued his recommendations on June 14. He suggested that corporations disclose payments meant to influence foreign officials, and he promised to work for an international agreement to reduce corruption, but he opposed any legislation to make bribing foreign officials a crime.

The point that Ford missed was that American companies were so influential, and the amounts of the bribes were so substantial, that they were doing more than just participating in corruption that already existed — they were actively corrupting foreign countries. Fortunately, members of Congress saw this problem more clearly. In September 1976 the Senate passed legislation submitted by William Proxmire to make bribing foreign officials a crime, but the bill did not pass the House by the time Congress adjourned. The Foreign Corrupt Practices Act finally passed on December 7, 1977, and President Carter signed it the next day.

———◦◦◦———

At the end of Ford's presidency America learned what it was like to have foreign money corrupting its democratic institutions. In October 1976 the *Washington Post* reported that the Justice Department was investigating Korean lobbyist Tongsun Park, who had been paying between $500,000 and $1 million per year to members of Congress. Park was operating on behalf of the South Korean dictator Park Chung Hee, who had given him a monopoly over rice exports to Korea in return for his agreement to use part of the money he made to promote South Korea's interests in Washington.

Park was hardly discrete, handing out cash to members of Congress whenever they needed money. He threw lavish parties and became a regular fixture in the Washington social scene. He had regularly written hundreds of thousands of dollars of checks to cash, and he often had armored cars bring more cash to his residence. On a trip back from Korea he was caught with a list of congressmen with dollar amounts next to their names as he entered the United States through the Anchorage airport. Park was convicted of bribery in 1977.[27]

———◦◦◦———

The reform that seemed most vital at the time proved to be a mistake. After the Saturday Night Massacre there was a strong pressure to make the special prosecutor's office permanent. In 1974 the Senate Subcommittee on the Separation of Powers held four days of hearings to consider a recommendation by the Ervin Committee for a permanent office of the special prosecutor, and proposals by Senator Ervin to give the special prosecutor, attorney general, and solicitor general six year terms, subject to removal only for malfeasance. Most of the witnesses supported the proposals, but several were astute enough to see that a permanent special prosecutor would be a mistake. Senator Alan Cranston asked, "Do we want a special prosecutor on hand all the time — looking for some high official to prosecute?"[28]

Surprisingly, the Watergate special prosecutor weighed in against making its office permanent. In its report, the Watergate Special Prosecution Task Force proposed that special prosecutors be appointed only in special cases, and they perceptively predicted that future independent prosecutors could abuse their power:

> Lack of accountability of an official on a permanent basis carries a potential for abuse of power that far exceeds any enforcement gains that might ensue. An independent prosecutor reports directly on ongoing investigations to no one and could easily abuse his power with little chance of detection.[29]

In 1975 and '76 the Senate Committee on Governmental Operations took up the issue. The committee first proposed a permanent office of the special prosecutor, to be appointed to a five-year term by a panel of three retired appellate court justices. Ford's Justice Department disagreed with the proposal on the grounds that the method of appointing the position was an unconstitutional usurpation of executive power. Ambassador to London Elliot Richardson wrote to the committee that a permanent special prosecutor was "neither necessary nor desirable." The American Bar Association told the committee that a permanent special prosecutor would create the danger of a "runaway special prosecutor." Despite these warnings, the Senate passed a bill in 1976 to permanently establish the office of the special prosecutor, but the bill died in the House.

The special prosecutor law finally passed after Carter took office. It provided for a special prosecutor to be appointed on a finding by the Attorney General, but the prosecutor would be chosen by the D.C. Court of Appeals. Once appointed, the prosecutor had free rein and could be removed by the Attorney General only for "extraordinary impropriety."[30] The idea was that the Court of Appeals would be less partisan than members of the executive or legislative branches, but that expectation would prove to be profoundly mistaken.

———————

The great reform wave of the '70s resulted in "a basic transformation of American politics" by eliminating much of the corruption that had stained American democracy.[31] To the extent the reformers intended to eliminate the role of money in politics, they were disappointed, but to the extent they intended to expose the role of moneyed interests and to make politicians play by the rules, they were successful. Paradoxically, the reforms of the early '70s made Americans more cynical about government. The new disclosure laws helped expose the Watergate scandal, as well as scandals in many states, and increased Americans' natural skepticism about their political leaders. In 1976, David Broder noticed this phenomenon, expressing dismay about "the unpredictability and the seeming arbitrariness of public reaction to financial candor."[32]

7

Vladivostok

When Ford took office, relations between the United States and the Soviet Union were better than at any other time during the Cold War, but the improvement was a matter of degree. American policy toward the Soviet Union had remained remarkably consistent for thirty years, and it would remain consistent for the next fifteen. In the late 1940s, diplomat George Kennan set forth the foreign policy — containment — which would be followed by every president from Truman to Reagan.[1] Presidential candidates promised to change the dynamics of the relationship, but each followed a policy of containment once in office. Each administration engaged in talks with the Soviets to control areas of tension; each administration opposed the expansion of communism in third-world countries; and each administration allowed the Soviet Union a relatively free hand in Eastern Europe.

Within a narrow range, relations between Washington and Moscow became more and less contentious. The early '70s was a time of cordial relations thanks to the opening of contacts championed by West German chancellor Willy Brandt, which he dubbed "Ostpolitik." In the years before Ford took office, trade had burgeoned between Eastern and Western Europe, and citizens of NATO and Warsaw Pact countries were communicating more than they had for decades. Nixon followed Brandt's lead by instituting a policy of "détente," a thaw in relations with the Soviets. By adopting détente, Washington was not abandoning its fight against the expansion of communism; it was establishing lines of communication to prevent conflicts from escalating out of control — a historic achievement, but not a fundamental change in relations.

Relations with Communist China were better than ever, as a result of Nixon's dramatic trip to Beijing in 1972. Nixon and Kissinger had used China as a counterweight against the USSR, and the Soviets were feeling insecure. The Soviets had to keep a great army in Eastern Europe to keep the Warsaw Pact nations in line, and they had another million-man army on their border with China.

———

Ford believed that the improvement in relations was a good thing, and he supported negotiations with the Soviets to limit the nuclear arms race. Nixon and Kissinger had negotiated the first significant arms treaty, known as the Strategic Arms Limitation Treaty, or SALT, which was signed in 1972. Ford wanted to complete a more comprehensive SALT II agreement, as he made clear to the NSC in the first days of his administration. "I think SALT is good for the country. We have the obligation of finding common ground for proper agreement."[2]

Not everyone agreed. The Soviet military leaders hated détente and did everything they could to undermine it.[3] In the United States, opposition to détente was led by neoconservatives, including Norman Podhoretz, Midge Decter, Eugene Rostow, and Irving Kristol. In Congress, the lead détente critic was Democrat Scoop Jackson of Washington, who had once been one of Nixon's primary allies in Congress on defense issues. But when Nixon reached out to China and the USSR, Jackson became his most prominent critic. He was urged on by his aide Richard Perle, who Kissinger called a "son of Mensheviks who thinks all Bolsheviks are evil."[4]

Kissinger brought some of the criticism upon himself— he had done himself no favors by conducting much of Nixon's foreign policy in secret. But fundamentally, the critics of détente did not trust Kissinger's judgment. On both the right and the left, détente critics thought that if the administration had pushed the Soviets harder they could have gotten a better deal. It was an easy argument to make because it was impossible to disprove, and everyone agreed on the ends — who wouldn't want a better deal? In the long run, no administration was able to get a better deal from Brezhnev than Kissinger got. Carter tried, but all he did was to delay the SALT II agreement for several years. Reagan was only able to reach a deal when a new type of leader, Mikhail Gorbachev, took over at the Kremlin.

Another fundamental disagreement was whether the power of the Warsaw Pact was increasing compared to NATO. Containment was premised on the idea that the communist system would ultimately collapse, and until that happened, communist power needed to be contained. Kennan's plan was the flip-side of Churchill's opposition to the appeasement of Hitler. Churchill understood that Germany was growing stronger and needed to be confronted when it was still relatively weak. Kennan understood that the Soviet Union was at the height of its strength in relation to the West when World War II ended, and that time was on the side of the West. Most détente opponents disagreed, and they believed that the military power of the Warsaw Pact was increasing in relation to the West.

A related point of disagreement was whether it was a good idea to trade with the Soviet Union. Détente critics believed that trade would make the Warsaw Pact nations stronger. Theodore Draper argued that by agreeing to trade with the Soviets, the United States was extending the life of the totalitarian regime.[5] Others thought that the United States was giving a lot more than it was getting back. Norman Podhoretz accused Ford of continuing "the Nixon policy of supplying the Soviets with grain and technology in exchange for little more than a smile from Leonid Brezhnev."[6] Midge Decter wrote, "We have negotiated with our enemies what appears to be an exchange of vast wealth from our side for little more than friendly words, or the absence of unfriendly ones, from theirs."[7]

Kissinger disagreed with the idea that it was in America's interest to keep the Soviet Union isolated. He thought that giving the Soviets a stake in a stable international system would be a factor in restraining their actions. It worked, except to the extent that he tried to condition improved relations on the Soviets pulling back from the Third World, which he called "linkage." But linkage never really worked because neither the Soviets nor the Americans ever hesitated to support rebel groups or governments in the Third World for fear of derailing détente.[8] Brezhnev never understood why Kissinger expected the Soviets to restrain their activities in the Third World while the Americans made no effort to reciprocate. Dobrynin has explained that the Soviets treated American complaints dismissively:

> I happened to be present at several meetings of the Politburo dealing with Angola, Somalia, and Ethiopia, and I can report that American complaints were not even seriously considered. The Politburo simply did not see them as a legitimate American concern and not a major factor in our relations with Washington.[9]

Kissinger oversold détente when he claimed that it would induce the Soviets to act more responsibly in the Third World, but détente critics were wrong when they predicted that trade would extend the life of the USSR. In retrospect, it was trade, travel, and communication that led to the fall of communism in Europe. The contacts that developed in the 1970s showed the people of the Soviet Union and Eastern Europe that their lives were far worse than the lives of Westerners, and they began to demand more from their governments. The communist system proved incapable of competing in world markets, and the Soviets took out massive loans to pay for their imports of grain and consumer goods. As the loans came due and their current account deficits exploded, the Soviet leaders felt that they had no choice but to reform the system.

Détente critics played a positive role when they pushed the Nixon and Ford administrations to use the carrot of improved relations and trade concessions to induce the Soviets to respect human rights. Without their pressure, Nixon, Ford, and Kissinger would not have pressed for Jewish emigration and other human rights issues, and the Soviets made concessions as a result. The problem was that détente opponents were never satisfied, and they killed the progress they made by pressing too hard.

The détente critics thought they had allies within the Ford administration, including Defense Secretary Schlesinger and the Joint Chiefs of Staff, but the reality was more complicated. The Joint Chiefs — and in particular Chairman General George Brown — generally supported the SALT process, as did Schlesinger's deputy William Clements. Schlesinger disagreed with some of Kissinger's proposals for arms control negotiations, but he was not a consistent opponent of détente within either the Ford or Nixon administrations, and he was often dismissive of critics of détente. He told Ford that Senator Jackson "has been very inconsistent. He is trying to run with both the hounds and the hares." Nor did Schlesinger support the critics who claimed that the Soviets had violated the SALT I agreement. He and Clements told Ford that an allegation that the Soviets violated the ABM treaty was "a true ambiguity." He told Ford that possible Soviet violations of SALT I provisions on missile silos were not major issues. "Theoretically, it could be a worry, but I do not believe it will turn out to be a problem."[10]

—◦◦◦—

At the time, there was a perception that the Soviets had passed the U.S. militarily, primarily because they had passed American in the number of intercontinental missiles (ICBMs) deployed. Many critics attributed the numerical superiority of the Soviet force to SALT, but the number of Soviet ICBMs peaked in 1971, before the SALT I treaty was signed. Under SALT I, the total number of ICBMs was limited to the number each side had already deployed or had under construction. Because the Soviets had weighted their forces heavily to land-based ballistic missiles — 90 percent of their strategic forces were ICBMs — the treaty appeared unfair to unsophisticated readers. The Soviets were allowed 2,360 missiles to 1,710 for the U.S.

The treaty did not give the Soviets a strategic advantage because the United States still held an overwhelming superiority in bombers and submarines. The U.S. forces were weighted to bombers and submarine missiles — only a third of its strategic forces were ICBMs — and bombers were not limited by the treaty. Furthermore, Soviet ICBMs were larger than American missiles, but the American missiles were more accurate. And the Soviets had numerical superiority in missiles only, not warheads. The Americans had decided to outfit their land-based missiles with multiple warheads (MIRVs) rather than deploying new missiles. Counting MIRVs, the U.S. had three times as many warheads as the USSR. MIRVs were not limited by the treaty, giving the U.S. a significant lead in bombers, submarine missiles, and land-based missile warheads.[11]

The U.S. had not planned to produce more missiles, so the agreement did not limit any of its programs, and both Scowcroft and Kissinger believe that the SALT process helped to get Congress to agree to fund strategic arms programs.[12] But détente critics took the disparity in ICBMs and battered the Nixon and Ford administrations with it. Jackson introduced an amendment requiring that all future arms control agreements be based on "numerical equality."[13]

When Ford took office, the Soviets were in the midst of a program to upgrade their ballistic missiles, which was, in the words of CIA director William Colby, "unprecedented in scope."[14] They were testing four new ballistic missiles, three with MIRVs. The CIA estimated that the Soviets might deploy 1,000 MIRVed missiles by 1980, passing the United States in total ICBM warheads; but when bombers were counted, the U.S. would still have more total warheads by a substantial margin. The Pentagon brass was worried that the new Soviet missiles would make the U.S. ICBM force vulnerable to a first-strike attack, but they admitted that the entire U.S. force was not vulnerable. During the first week of the administration, Colby described the Soviet program for Ford and concluded that "the basis of a mutually deterrent strategic balance is likely to remain essential intact." Kissinger agreed. "With the multiplication of weapons and the explosion of technology, after the next rounds of arms deployments are completed, both sides will still be essentially in strategic equilibrium."[15]

The U.S. was also upgrading its forces. The Air Force was developing a new ballistic missile, the Minuteman III, and America was deploying three major new weapons: the cruise missile, the B-1 strategic bomber, and the Trident submarine. The United States nuclear arsenal increased from 1,700 warheads in 1970 to 7,000 in 1978.[16]

At the same time that many Americans thought their country was becoming weaker in respect to the Soviet Union, the Warsaw Pact leaders were worried that they were falling hopelessly behind NATO. While détente critics focused on the absolute numbers of missiles, tanks, and planes, the Warsaw Pact leaders were taking a more sophisticated view of the quality of their weaponry. They understood that satellite technology gave NATO a tremendous advantage in intelligence; they knew that the Western armies had an advantage in night fighting; and they knew that the Warsaw Pact weapons had much more limited range than NATO weapons. Czechoslovakian general Zachariáš has explained that "it was the quality of equipment and weapons that was crucial."[17] Polish general Wojciech Jaruzelski agreed. "The important thing is not the number, but the quality. NATO had a qualitative advantage."[18] In 1976 the East German defense minister told his counterparts in the Warsaw Pact that the improvement of NATO command and control capabilities was the "most significant modernization since the equipment of NATO forces with nuclear weapons."[19]

———

In reality, the Soviet Union was stagnating. Leonid Brezhnev had run the country since 1964, and the 68-year-old leader seemed as stagnant as his government. Brezhnev and his colleagues, Premier Alexey Kosygin, Defense Minister Andrei Grechko, and Foreign Minister Andrei Gromyko, had all gained power when Stalin killed off their brethren. Having lived through Stalin's purges, they valued stability. Having lived through the horrors of World War II, they valued peace. They were true believers dedicated to advancing communism throughout the world, but they would not chance war with the United States. When Khrushchev appointed Dobrynin ambassador to Washington, he told him to "always bear in mind that war with the United States was inadmissible; this was above all."[20] His instructions were the same under Brezhnev, who told him, "Let there be peace; that's the main thing."[21] In 1976, Brezhnev told his staff that peace was his primary objective. "I really do want peace, and I will not retreat from this position for anything."[22] The Warsaw Pact leaders knew that any invasion of Western Europe would lead to nuclear war, which they viewed as totally unacceptable in any circumstances. Jaruzelski has explained that "the idea of a large-scale conflict became a sort of joke."[23]

In public, Brezhnev was colorless, but he was jovial and full of bluster in person. He looked and acted like an aging Mafia don, wearing a drab suit, collecting expensive American cars, ogling young women, and hanging out with his cronies. Like a Mafia don, he maintained his power by rewarding his allies and undermining his enemies. Like a Mafia don, he spent much of his time mediating conflicts between his subordinates and making sure than none of his henchmen decided that they should take power. Gorbachev later described his mentor's political skills:

> His forte consisted in his ability to split rivals, fanning mutual suspicion and subsequently acting as chief arbiter and peacemaker. In time I discerned another of Brezhnev's characteristics: vindictiveness. He never forgot the slightest disloyalty towards himself, but he was shrewd enough to wait for an appropriate moment to replace the offender. He never resorted to direct confrontation, proceeding cautiously, step by step, until he gained the upper hand.[24]

Brezhnev and his cronies believed that socialism would ultimately prevail over capitalism, but they had ceased to believe that they were building a workers' paradise, and they understood that they would not be able to catch up with the West economically. Dobrynin has summed up Brezhnev's mixed emotions about the United States:

> It was curious that he remained firmly convinced of the necessity of improving our relations with Washington, in part because he actually admired and almost even envied America's living standards and the achievements of its economy, science, and technology. He would tell me about this in private, but he still believed that the future belonged to socialism, which he was certain would ultimately gain the upper hand in the historic competition with capitalism. Even then, he completely excluded any possibility of a war with the United States, for this would amount to "the end of the world."[25]

In foreign policy matters Brezhnev relied almost exclusively on his foreign minister, Andrei Gromyko, except for relations in the Third World, which were controlled by the International Department. Gromyko rigidly followed his instructions from the Kremlin, and the Americans learned that the only purpose in negotiating with him was to deliver messages to the Politburo. In a government filled with stubborn men, he was the most obstinate. Kissinger called him "a heavy road-roller stubbornly moving towards its destination."[26] But behind the scenes at the Kremlin he was a consistent champion of better relations with the U.S.— his primary goal was to avoid a military confrontation with the West.[27]

———

When Ford took office, the Senate was considering whether to approve an agreement Nixon had negotiated for granting most favored nation status to the Soviet Union and allowing the Soviets to obtain loans through the Export-Import Bank, just like its other trading partners. Most favored nation status is the normal relations between nations, in which each treats imports from each other no worse than it treats imports from other nations. In practice, the United States granted most favored nation status to virtually all countries, with the exception of a few rogue states.

The treaty was in danger of being derailed by an amendment submitted by Senator Scoop Jackson and Representative Charles Vanik to condition most favored nation status on the Soviets allowing Jews to emigrate to Israel. At first the threat of the Jackson-Vanik Amendment was successful. It forced Nixon and Kissinger to push the Soviets to allow more Jews to leave the country, and the number they allowed to emigrate rose from 400 in 1968 to 35,000 in 1973. The Soviets considered the focus on Jewish emigration to be interference in their domestic affairs, and they thought that Jackson was trying to create a confrontation for political purposes.[28] They were right that Jackson was motivated by political ambition, but that did not make his dedication to the cause any less real, and it wasn't his political ambitions that would bring Jackson's efforts to naught. He would undo his success over the next few months by not listening when Kissinger and Ford told him that they had pushed the Soviets as far as they would go.

After Jackson rejected Dobrynin's offer to allow 55,000 Jews to emigrate per year in the week after Ford took office, Kissinger asked the senator to consider a complicated settlement to be set forth in exchanges of letters. The Soviets would send the administration a confidential letter committing to allow valid émigrés to leave; the administration would send a letter to the congressional leaders repeating the Soviet promise; and the congressional leaders would respond with a letter that set forth their understanding that the rate of emigration would "rise promptly." Kissinger explained that the deal would fall apart if the number the Soviets committed to was in any of the letters. "We have to distinguish between the objective and what we write down." Jackson said that he understood that the Soviets would not be tied to a quota.[29]

Ford explained the arrangement to Gromyko when he was visiting for the opening of the United Nations in September. Ford arranged to be meeting with Jackson when Gromyko arrived, so the two could meet as Jackson was leaving the Oval Office. After Jackson left, Ford explained the arrangement for the letters. As Kissinger has explained, Gromyko "made a sour face but acquiesced, however reluctantly, provided no target figures were used and no Soviet legal obligations were implied."[30]

The agreement came apart when the letters were exchanged. Ford sent a letter to the senators that indicated that the Soviets would allow emigration to rise above the current level. Despite his acknowledgment at the August 15 meeting that there could be no target number in the letters, Jackson sent back a letter with his understanding that the new level would be 60,000 a year. At first, Ford sent a confirming letter, but he withdrew it in early October when the Soviets objected.

Jackson was angry, but he was being pressured by Jewish groups to reach a deal, so he agreed to work out a new arrangement in an October 8 meeting with Kissinger, Ribicoff, and Javits in the Capitol building. Kissinger proposed an agreement under which the Jackson letter would refer to the 60,000 figure as an "appropriate guideline." Ten days later, Jackson, Vanik, and Javits came to the White House for a meeting with Ford and Kissinger to exchange the letters. Ford had arranged for a press conference on the White House lawn to follow the meeting, which was a mistake, because Jackson killed the deal with his statements. The language of the letters was carefully crafted to avoid any implication that the 60,000 was a quota, but Jackson was not anywhere near that circumspect in his comments. He told the press that he "would consider a benchmark — a minimum standard of initial compliance — to be the issuance of visas at the rate of 60,000 per annum, and we understand the president proposes to use the same benchmark."[31]

The Soviets were angry that Jackson gave the letter to the press. Kissinger claims that he and Jackson had agreed to a "definitive leak" of the letters, but not an official release. Jackson's people disagree. His aide Richard Perle claims that Ford had agreed to release the letters in the October 18 meeting, but Kissinger has the better side of the argument. Perle was not at the meeting, and the minutes of the meeting show that Ford in no way said that the letters could be officially released.[32] Either way, Jackson violated the agreement in his comments to the press. It was Jackson's statement that the 60,000 figure was a "benchmark — a minimum standard of initial compliance" that killed the deal. After the press conference, Dobrynin called Kissinger and complained that Jackson had violated the agreement by claiming that the Soviets had agreed to a yearly quota of 60,000.[33]

The Soviets officially declared the deal dead a week later while Kissinger was in Moscow. At lunch on October 24, Brezhnev objected to the implication that the Soviets had agreed to allow 60,000 Jews to emigrate each year. "These letters are written in clever diplomatic terms — but the undertones are that the Soviet Union has given an undertaking concerning the departure from the USSR of Soviet citizens of Jewish origin — a figure of 60,000! You know that the Soviet Union has not given an obligation in terms of numbers."[34] On the way to the airport, Gromyko made the Soviet position official when he handed Kissinger a letter that said that the USSR "categorically rejected" the letters.[35]

When he left Moscow, Kissinger went to India, Pakistan and Iran, and he followed with a trip to Japan, Korea, China, and Vladivostok. Rather than telling Jackson that the deal was dead, Kissinger sent the letter to Ford that night and proposed that he and Ford meet with the three Senate leaders when he returned from his travels. Kissinger thought that the letter could be read two ways, with "one possible reading of the letter [being] that it does not repudiate our understanding," and he suggested that they try to salvage the deal by treating it that way.[36] It is hard to see how Kissinger could interpret the letter as not repudiating the agreement, but it is understandable that he would try to salvage the agreement with the gambit. If it worked, so much the better. If it failed, the situation was the same as it would have been had they not tried. The problem was that Kissinger did not clear his plan with Jackson. In fact, he never got around to showing the letter to the senators, which he later admitted was a mistake. "I was wrong not to show it to Jackson and others."[37] It was an embarrassing oversight, but it didn't change the outcome. The deal was dead.

Kissinger went to Moscow in an attempt to jumpstart the SALT II negotiations. He was following up on a comment Gromyko made during his September 20 visit to the White House that the Soviets might be more "responsive" in arms control negotiations.[38]

Before Kissinger left, the NSC met several times to develop the American negotiating position. The main question was whether to appease Jackson by demanding "numerical equivalents." All of Ford's advisors agreed that achieving equal numbers of launchers would not be difficult. Under its current plans, the U.S. would reach a total of just under 2,000 launch vehicles, which it could increase to 2,250 if it did not decommission B-52s as planned. The Soviets planned a force of 2,500 missiles and bombers, and it wouldn't be hard to close the 250-warhead gap during negotiations.

In an October 7 NSC meeting, Schlesinger voted for numerical equivalents, because he thought that "unequal numbers would not have much congressional support." Ford was convinced to support numerical equivalents not by Schlesinger's political arguments, but by the military's explanation that it would be consistent with the country's interests. Chairman of the Joint Chiefs Strachley Brown explained that Soviet demands to limit the number of missiles that the U.S. could equip with multiple warheads would have little impact. "Once you get more than about 600 heavy missiles, you have so much overkill that the extra 300 wouldn't make much difference." Schlesinger agreed that limiting MIRVs would not be "strategically important," and he added that "the political perceptions are not so strong on numbers of MIRV missiles." Brown explained that the country already had more reentry vehicles than it needed:

We are putting weapons on target in numbers that, if we didn't have them, wouldn't matter. We are not loading Poseidon all the way up, because we prefer to have the extra range. We have a lot of flexibility in our force, bought and paid for years ago, but frankly, we have more MIRV capacity than we need.[39]

In the second NSC meeting, Schlesinger pushed a new demand — to limit throw weight (the aggregate lifting capacity of a country's missiles) to an equal level on both sides. It wasn't a practical proposal because it would force the Soviets to scrap their large missiles and deploy small missiles, bombers, and submarines. The plan would lead to a more stable system, but the Soviets would be unlikely to agree to completely revamp their strategic forces. Ford rejected Schlesinger's proposal because it had no chance with the Soviets, so he chose to push for equal launchers instead, and he authorized Kissinger to agree to reasonable limits on MIRVs.[40]

When Kissinger arrived in Moscow on October 23 he began the discussions by proposing aggregate limits of 2,200 launchers and 1,320 MIRVs per side. The Soviets readily agreed to the MIRV limit, but they balked at the 2,200 limit on launchers because it would require them to reduce their planned forces by 450 launchers. To get the Soviets to agree to an acceptable aggregate limit, Kissinger offered to stop using the Rota base in Spain to service nuclear submarines. The offer cost nothing because the new Poseidon class subs could cruise all over the world without docking, making the Rota base unnecessary. The administration was also concerned about the impact that the base would have on the development of democracy in Spain. Franco was on his last legs, and his chosen successor, Prince Juan Carlos, appeared to be inclined to open the country's political system. The administration did not want to give the anti-democratic forces on the left a popular issue by continuing to dock nuclear subs at the port.[41]

On October 26, Brezhnev met with the Politburo and convinced them to accept the U.S. proposal of equal aggregates. He opened the discussion with Kissinger that evening by accepting equal aggregates, but at a 2,400 level, and he accepted the American proposal for a 1,320 limit on MIRVs. The increase of 200 launchers was within the mutual limit of 2,500 launchers that Ford had approved, but Brezhnev also threw in details that were unacceptable to the Americans. The U.S. would not be allowed to reach the 2,400 level until the end of the agreement, so for its entire term the Soviets would have an advantage of 200 launchers. The Soviets refused to limit the number of heavy missiles they could MIRV, but they insisted that the U.S. could only build 10 Trident submarines.[42] Kissinger's team believed that these details were the typical Soviet opening negotiating position and that the parties could reach a reasonable solution at a summit.

Later that night Kissinger sent a message to Ford reporting that the Soviet response was a "major step forward toward a SALT agreement." But he asked the president not to tell Schlesinger about the Soviet proposal because he feared that "in its present form, it would be shredded by DOD, leaked to the press and Jackson, and destroyed before we can shape it." Kissinger also related that Brezhnev "demonstrated his rather bizarre sense of occasion" during a meeting that day. The Soviet leader played with a toy artillery piece, pointing it at Kissinger and his aide Helmut Sonnenfeldt, trying to make it fire, without success. After an hour of playing with the cannon, he finally made it go off and danced around the room.[43] Ford was pleased by the report, and he told Kissinger to agree to a summit meeting.

~~~

The summit began on November 23 at Vladivostok, a Soviet city on the Pacific coast of Siberia. But before he left for the summit, Ford met with Dobrynin on the White House lawn. When the Soviet ambassador saw that the president didn't have a hat, he gave him his own beaver fur hat.[44] Ford learned why he needed to dress warm when he landed at the Vladivostok airport, which was covered by deep snow — only one landing strip had been cleared for Air Force One to land. When they stepped off the plane, all the Americans could see was snow, a few buildings, and a small group of men, which turned out to be Brezhnev and his entourage. Brezhnev greeted Ford and led the Americans to a train that would take them ten miles to the resort city of Okeanskaya.

As the train left the station, Brezhnev offered Ford a "cup of tea" and cognac. The discussion was awkward until the two leaders began talking about sports. Kissinger aide William Hyland noted that they bonded over a shared love of sports. "Both were rugged outdoor men of action. They loved sports and good stories."[45] After the discussion, Ford and Brezhnev retired to their compartments. Alone in his berth, Brezhnev had a seizure. He was in the beginning stages of atherosclerosis of the brain, but only his physicians knew it. His doctors controlled the seizure, and they urged him to postpone the negotiations the next day, but Brezhnev refused.[46]

Brezhnev met with Ford at 6:15 that night. The meeting was scheduled to last just over an hour, but it lasted more than six — an amazing demonstration of endurance by Brezhnev after his collapse. During the negotiations in Okeansoaya's small clubhouse, Kissinger took the lead in arguing with Brezhnev and Gromyko, while Ford listened, calmly smoking his pipe. Brezhnev had only limited ability to decide issues, and he spent much of the time on the phone with other members of the Politburo. Ford told Brezhnev that any agreement "must be based on the principle of equivalence," and he insisted that both sides be limited to 2,400 launchers. Brezhnev responded by insisting on limitations on Western European forces and a 2,200 limit on U.S. launchers until the end of the agreement. Ford refused — he needed equality in numbers for political reasons — and it looked like a stalemate.

But then Gromyko hinted at what the Soviets really wanted — he asked about Kissinger's earlier informal promises to stop servicing nuclear subs at the Rota base in Spain. Ford jumped at the suggestion, and he offered to give up the Rota submarine base in 1984 if other Western European forces were not included in the SALT aggregates. Brezhnev responded with a proposal for a mutual limit of 2,400 launchers, with a side letter from the U.S. indicating that they would not build the final 200 launchers until 1985. Kissinger and Ford refused to consider any side letters, but they countered with a proposal that the Soviets would have an advantage in launchers until the end of the agreement, while the U.S. would have an advantage in MIRVs. Brezhnev was intrigued, but he could not agree without the support of the military representative at the meeting, Colonel General Mikhail Kozlov. Brezhnev left the room bellowing, "Kozlov, Kozlov." After some time, Brezhnev and Kozlov returned, and they said that they would accept the first American proposal. Brezhnev proposed that the parties could agree on 2,400 launchers and 1,320 MIRVs each. Each party would be allowed to reach its limit at any time during the agreement. Brezhnev had conceded the most important point at issue.

The Americans were taken aback that Brezhnev had accepted so easily, and they asked for time to caucus. To avoid Soviet listening devices, the delegation met outside in the bitter Siberian cold. Ford was inclined to take the Soviet offer, but Kissinger and his aides convinced him to at least try to get limits on the number of Soviet heavy missiles that could be MIRVed. If agreement could not be reached, then Ford would accept the Soviet offer without such limits. When they reentered the room, Ford and Kissinger indicated that they could accept the proposal, but they asked for a limit on MIRVed heavy missiles. The parties agreed to have dinner and meet again the next day.[47]

When the meetings resumed the next morning, Ford opened by agreeing to count aircraft-launched ballistic missiles with a range of 700 kilometers within the 2,500 limit. Brezhnev said that the Soviets could accept the proposal if aircraft-launched missiles with a range

During the negotiations at Vladivostok, Ford meets with the American negotiation team outside in the bitter Siberian cold to avoid Soviet listening devices. Photograph taken November 23, 1974. (Photograph by David Hume Kennerly; courtesy Gerald R. Ford Library.)

of more than 3,000 kilometers would be banned. Ford replied that the United States could agree only if the Soviets agreed to limit MIRVed heavy missiles to 200. The Soviets took a break and fought over the proposal. Dobrynin was in favor of accepting it, while Gromyko fought hard against limiting MIRVed heavy missiles. Brezhnev decided to push for the solution that the Americans had already decided was their fall-back position. He proposed to Ford that they scrap both the 3,000-kilometer limit on air-launched missiles and the 200 limit on MIRVed heavy missiles, and the issue was settled.[48]

It was a major breakthrough. They had hammered out the framework of a SALT II treaty, but hardliners in both superpowers would derail the agreement during the next two years. After Carter took office, he would try unsuccessfully to get a better deal, but in the end would negotiate a SALT II agreement based on the Vladivostok framework. Congress would refuse to ratify the agreement, but it didn't matter. Until 1986, both countries would live by the terms of the agreement that Ford and Brezhnev developed in Vladivostok.

Ford gained a hat but lost a coat at the summit meeting. At the airport as they were leaving, Ford noticed that Brezhnev was looking covetously at his Alaskan wolf coat, so he gave it to the Soviet leader. On the train back from Vladivostok, Brezhnev suffered a second seizure.[49]

$$\sim\!\!\infty\!\!\sim$$

When they returned home, both Ford and Brezhnev were criticized by hardliners for agreeing to the Vladivostok framework. In Moscow, Defense Minister Gretchko led the opposition to any limit on ICBMs. After a fierce internal battle, the military leaders fell in line and supported the General Secretary.[50]

In Washington, Ford had a harder sell. Jackson immediately went on the attack. As always, he was convinced that the U.S. team could have gotten a better deal. He insisted that the 2,400 limit was too high, and he proposed a limit of 1,700—a pipe dream when the Soviet interests were taken into account. The futility of Jackson's approach was demonstrated when Carter tried it in 1977, getting nowhere.[51] In public, Schlesinger endorsed the agreement, but everyone assumed that he opposed it privately. Jackson and other détente critics would have been shocked to hear Schlesinger's gushing support of the agreement in NSC meetings. "Mr. President, you can win on this—you've got the high ground. This is an equal agreement." As usual, his advice was focused on the political impact of the agreement. "We did better than we expected, but don't say that publicly!" He was dismissive of Scoop Jackson's criticisms. "Mr. President, the attack will probably come from the left, not the right. The Jackson staff has gone haywire on this, and I think Scoop will suffer for it. Jackson has always argued for equal aggregates, and you got that."[52]

―∽∿∾―

After Vladivostok, the trade agreements seemed of lesser importance than SALT, but they would be fatal to the development of détente. When Kissinger testified in support of the trade bill before the Senate Finance Committee on December 3, he did not reveal the existence of the Gromyko letter. He told the committee that the Soviets had not agreed to relax emigration, but that he anticipated that they would if most favored nation status were granted.[53] Whether the senators thought that the letters were still in effect did not matter because they passed the trade bill encumbered by the Jackson-Vanik Amendment. To make matters worse, Congress placed unique restrictions on the Soviets' access to Export-Import Bank loans, limiting credits to $75 million a year without congressional approval. Similar restrictions had not been placed on loans to other countries, including communist nations. After the joint conference committee passed the trade bill, Ford "reluctantly" signed it on January 3 because he was convinced that a veto would be overridden.[54]

On December 18 the Soviets published Gromyko's letter repudiating the arrangement on Jewish emigration. Kissinger learned about the publication when an aide interrupted his breakfast with Dobrynin and gave him a copy of the TASS statement.[55] In July 1975, at a breakfast at Dobrynin's home, Jackson complained about Kissinger's concealment of the letter. He said that members of Congress had convinced themselves that the Soviets would concede on the emigration issue if they kept pressing, and he thought that Kissinger "had outmaneuvered himself."[56] In reality, it was Jackson who had overplayed his hand by refusing to listen to those in the administration who were negotiating with the Russians. They told him that the Soviets had been pushed as far as they would go, and when he refused to accept their advice, the agreement fell apart. Jewish emigration from the USSR fell to almost zero. Jewish emigration would not recover until 1979, after Brezhnev and Carter signed the SALT II agreement. That year, emigration reached a new record of 51,320, but it was a short-lived recovery. When relations deteriorated again after the Soviet invasion of Afghanistan, emigration again fell to fewer than 10,000 per year; emigration stayed at very low levels until Gorbachev took power at the Kremlin.[57]

On December 25, Brezhnev sent a letter to Ford rejecting the requirements of the Jackson-Vanik Amendment, and he called the restrictions on trade and Export-Import loans "fundamentally unacceptable." On January 10 the Soviets notified the administration that they would not seek most favored nation status or comply with the provisions of the trade bill. At the same time the Soviets gave Ford assurances that they wanted to continue good relations on other issues.[58] But, as Dobrynin has explained, the trade bill "effectively blocked the development of trade and economic relations between our countries for a long time."[59]

―∽∿∾―

At the same time, the Vladivostok framework hit new snags. On December 10, Dobrynin and Kissinger exchanged confidential memoranda setting forth the agreements made at the summit. But when staff members began to draft an aide memoir, they could not agree on how to treat cruise missiles. Cruise missiles were new, and the United States had a big lead in their development. When the Ford administration refused to include limits on the missiles, the parties were forced to write around the issue to get the memoir finished.[60] A second weapon soon joined cruise missiles as the issues that held up the SALT II agreement. The weapon was the Soviets' new Backfire bomber. The parties had agreed to count bombers if they were strategic weapons that could be used to attack the other country. The Backfire could reach the U.S. on a one-way mission, but it did not have the range to return, and American intelligence indicated that the Soviets intended the Backfire for "peripheral missions"—it was not intended to be a strategic weapon.

The importance that these two weapons would take on was not justified by strategic factors. In a January meeting, Colby told Ford that, under the Vladivostok agreement, the Soviets would not be able to achieve strategic superiority. "Each side will continue to have many more than enough strategic weapons for assured retaliation after a first strike, or for 'limited option' scenarios.... We do not foresee technological advances which would sharply alter the strategic balance in the USSR's favor during the next ten years." Colby predicted that the Soviets had been pushed as far as they would go. "We do not believe that the Soviets would be willing, in the current round of negotiations, to discuss further reductions."[61]

In the United States, hardliners led by Donald Rumsfeld would use the two weapons to block a SALT II agreement. Hardliners were also ascendant in the USSR because Brezhnev's health continued to deteriorate. He entered the hospital on December 26 and remained there for more than a month. Without strong leadership from the general secretary, hardliners in the Soviet military were able to block reasonable proposals on their side. Both Brezhnev and Ford wanted an agreement, but their ambitions would be thwarted by their aides.

8

Recession, Public Enemy Number 1

While inflation was still chugging along at a double-digit rate in the last quarter of 1974, Ford learned that things would get worse when his administration predicted that the country would soon be in a recession.[1] Greenspan told the president that the recession would be mild, but he would be sorely mistaken. Four months into his presidency, Ford would be faced with the deepest recession in the post-war era, coupled with double-digit inflation. In December the unemployment rate reached 7.2 percent. At the end of the year, the staff of the Fed noted that, while inflation remained at its highest rate since World War II, the recession threatened to be the worst since the war.[2]

Faced with this bad news, Ford promised to convene a meeting of economists over the holidays to come up with a new economic plan. "I intend to keep my experts working over the holidays, translating into specifics a number of new or alternative measures to augment and update the economic package that I will place before the Congress within the next 2 months."[3] The new plan did just what Milton Friedman warned Ford to avoid — he allowed the recession to divert him from the fight against inflation. The new economic plan would help mitigate the recession, but the fundamental problem of inflation would not be addressed. It would take an even deeper recession starting under Ford's successor to put the American economy back on track.

Ford's economic and energy advisors traveled to Vail for meetings at his vacation home on December 27 and 28.[4] The meetings would develop the blueprint for the administration's domestic policy, and the attendance list was telling. Rumsfeld was there, along with Simon, Seidman, Greenspan, and Zarb. Conspicuous in his absence was Vice President Rockefeller, who had taken office the week before. It was the first indication that Rockefeller would not run domestic policy as he had been promised.

Rockefeller planned to control domestic policy by taking over the Domestic Counsel, which Ehrlichman had used to direct domestic policy during the Nixon administration. The new vice president would be partially successful in controlling the counsel, but control of domestic policy eluded him. In the end, it was the economists who would have the president's ear, and the vice president would be out in the cold.

When he joined the administration in December 1974, Rockefeller started his power play by proposing that he be appointed the executive director of the Domestic Counsel and asking Ford to give the counsel authority over the Energy Resources Council and the Economic Policy Board.

Buchen told Ford that he should reject Rockefeller's proposal because the vice president should not be given a staff position. Rumsfeld objected on the same grounds, but he also opposed the proposal because it would take away his authority as the coordinator of issues and the paper flow. Ford agreed and rejected Rockefeller's proposal.[5] The vice president had lost his first battle for control over domestic policy, and now Ford was developing economic and energy policy without Rockefeller in the room.

———◆◆◆———

Before the trip to Vail, Ford told his advisors that he wanted a strategy to combat the recession without increasing spending, which was one of the traditional tools governments had used to reverse economic downturns. As they searched for an alternative, several top administration officials simultaneously came to the conclusion that they should propose a tax cut. It would be a complete reversal of Ford's surcharge proposal, which he had allowed to die when it proved to be very unpopular with his fellow Republicans. After administration economists met to prepare for the Vail meeting, Seidman told Ford that they would propose that the surcharge be replaced with a tax cut. Seidman recognized that recession was "likely to be the most severe since at least 1958, and probably the worst since the 1930s."[6]

Cheney and Rumsfeld became tax-cut proponents in early December when Cheney had drinks at the Washington Hotel with Arthur Laffer, a University of Chicago professor and the former chief economist at OMB. The meeting had been arranged by Jude Wanniski, the associate editor of the *Wall Street Journal*, who was also in attendance.[7] Laffer told Cheney that a tax cut would actually cause revenue to increase and the budget deficit to shrink. In support of his claim, he explained that cutting a tax rate had two offsetting effects. The lower tax rate causes lower revenues, but it also spurs more economic output, which causes tax revenues to increase. There is a point where tax rates are so high that cutting them causes an increase in economic output large enough to offset the revenue loss from the lower tax rate. Laffer grabbed a napkin and drew a graph of the concept. In a 1978 book, Wanniski named the drawing the "Laffer Curve."[8]

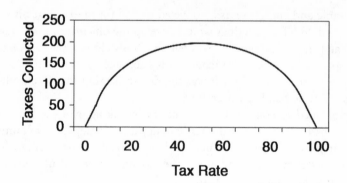

He drew a curve that looked like the one above, where the government collects the maximum amount at a 50 percent tax rate. If tax rate is above 50 percent, a tax cut will result in an increase in revenue. But that doesn't mean that all tax cuts result in lower deficits, as Laffer has admitted. "The Laffer Curve itself does not say whether a tax cut will raise or lower revenues."[9] If the tax rate is below the peak point on the curve (50 percent in the drawing above), cutting taxes will result in lower revenue and higher deficits. For the next thirty years, some Republicans would over-simplify this concept and assume that any tax cut would result in higher tax revenue. They made no effort to determine whether the country's tax structure was to the left of the highest point in the curve (where cutting taxes would result in less revenue) or to the right (where cutting taxes would result in more revenue).

The last half-century has been an age of free-lunch economics. In the '60s and early '70s some Keynesians claimed that the Fed could allow the money supply to grow at unprecedented rates without causing runaway inflation. They were wrong, as the inflation of the '70s proved. But just as free-lunch monetary theories lost popularity, free-lunch fiscal policies gained ascendancy in the form of the Laffer Curve. Adopting the theory proved to be good politics for the Republican Party. It allowed Republicans to abandon their traditional fiscal responsibility and promise tax cuts without the offsetting spending reductions. But the idea that taxes could be cut without increasing deficits proved to be wrong. At the time that Laffer drew his curve, national debt was at a low point in relation to the overall economy. During the post-war era the economy had been growing at a much faster rate than the national debt, so that the debt had dropped from 120 percent of gross domestic product in 1946 to under 34 percent when Ford took office, and it remained between 33 and 36 percent of GDP through the Ford and Carter presidencies. When Laffer's acolytes began cutting taxes in the '80s, that trend was reversed. The growth of the debt began to outpace the growth of the economy — so much so that it is again more than two-thirds of the gross domestic product.[10]

When they got to Vail, Rumsfeld and Cheney found little opposition to their support for tax cuts. Zarb, Seidman, and Greenspan joined them in arguing that by stimulating the economy the tax cut would reduce the deficit. Simon opposed any tax cut, urging Ford not to allow the recession to divert him from the fight against inflation. Ford sided with the tax cut proponents, but he had no illusions — he knew that a tax cut would increase the deficit. It was a difficult decision for him because administration economists were predicting that the recession would cause the deficit to grow to more than $20 billion in fiscal year 1975 and $40 billion in 1976. Ford thought that the nation needed a stimulus in the form of a tax cut, but he told his aides to make sure the proposal was limited, and he tried to mitigate its impact by proposing corresponding spending cuts.[11]

Following the Vail meeting, Ford worked out the details of the tax cut with Rumsfeld, Lynn, O'Neill, Greenspan, and Cheney. The proposal added up to $16 billion in tax cuts, $12 billion of which would go to individuals, with a per-person cap of $1,000. On the spending side, Ford approved a package which included a one-year moratorium on new programs and a 5 percent limit on federal pay increases, social security cost-of-living increases, and increases in federal employee and military retirement payments. Ford's economists estimated that if Congress passed the tax cuts without corresponding spending cuts, the deficit would increase to $33.2 billion in fiscal year 1975 and $46 billion in 76.[12]

At the Vail meeting, Ford and his advisors spent the entire day of the 27th discussing energy issues. The president was given three options: (1) a series of deregulatory legislative proposals, (2) a program of additional governmental controls, and (3) a series of administrative actions to increase the price of domestic oil.[13] His advisors recommended option 1, deregulation. Ford had already decided that deregulation was important because he believed that allowing the price of oil and natural gas to rise was the only way to effectively discourage consumption. "Painful as they are, higher prices do promote conservation."[14] But he did not reject the administrative options, which he considered a valuable tool to force Congress to accept deregulation — by forcing up the price of oil, he could remove the incentive for Congress to keep controls. "I will go forward with a legislative package on using the market mechanism, getting government out of the business of regulating energy, but at the same time, I'll move simultaneously with the administrative options.... And if they don't produce anything, we'll keep the heat on with the administrative package."[15]

Before he left for Vail, Ford had already approved a package to spur domestic energy production that had been put together by his Energy Resources Council. The ERC proposed allowing commercial production at the Naval Petroleum Reserves, which had been created at the turn of the century to provide the military a source of oil during a national emergency. The council proposed leasing for oil production the outer continental shelf and leasing oil shale for development. The ERC also suggested that Ford try to convince the auto industry to improve gas efficiency by 40 percent. The ERC estimated that its proposals would reduce imports by 20 percent in 1975, 30 percent in 1977, and 50 percent by 1985.[16]

Ford decided to announce his new economic and energy proposals in a fireside chat on January 13 and again two days later in his 1975 State of the Union Address. Hartmann's speechwriters took the first stab at the fireside chat. Press Secretary Nessen saw the draft, and he thought it was "awful — ten minutes too long, full of clichés, flowery, with the major points blurred." Nessen told his concerns to Rumsfeld, who convinced him to write an alternative. Neither Hartmann nor Nessen wrote a stirring speech, and Ford made matters worse by taking sections from each draft, cobbling together the final version. Unfortunately, the State of Union Address was prepared the same way. On the morning after the fireside chat, Nessen told Rumsfeld that Hartmann's draft of the State of the Union was "long on hackneyed rhetoric and short on vision or clear statements of policy." For the rest of the day they sat in Rumsfeld's office with Cheney, Greenspan, Seidman, and Zarb and rewrote the speech. Ford met with Hartmann and Rumsfeld's informal team, and he accepted most of Hartmann's draft, inserting several sections of Rumsfeld's.[17]

On the evening of January 13, 1975, Ford addressed the nation from the Lincoln Library at the White House. The program opened with Ford, Rumsfeld, and Nessen talking to each other before a fire. Ford then turned to the camera and began the speech, walking over to take a seat in a chair as he said his first few lines. Ford announced that inflation was no longer public enemy number 1. "The reason is that the situation has changed. You know it, and I know it.... We must shift our emphasis from inflation to recession." To fight the recession, Ford proposed a $16 billion tax cut, and to offset the tax cut, he asked Congress for a moratorium on new federal programs and a 5 percent limit on federal pay increases and cost-of-living increases for federal pensions and social security. To fight energy dependence, Ford proposed deregulation of oil and gas, increases of oil import fees, and the delay of higher pollution standards in return for automobile manufacturers increasing gas efficiency by 40 percent.[18]

Two days later, Ford was forthright when he addressed a joint session of Congress. "I must say to you that the state of the Union is not good. Millions of Americans are out of work. Recession and inflation are eroding the money of millions more." Ford proclaimed that "the emphasis on our economic efforts must now shift from inflation to jobs," and he proposed a "1-year tax reduction of $16 billion," along with corresponding spending cuts. "I will not hesitate to veto any new spending programs adopted by the Congress." The speech included a strange comment about how Fed chairman Burns needed Congress to reduce spending before he could do his job. "Only a reduction in spending can make it possible for the Federal Reserve System to avoid an inflationary growth in the money supply and thus restore balance to our economy."

Ford laid out the energy proposals he approved in Vail. He asked Congress to pass legislation permitting commercial production in the Naval Petroleum Reserves, Alaska, and the outer continental shelf. He also asked Congress to pass legislation to allow conversion of power

Ford giving his 1975 State of the Union Speech, January 16, 1975. (Photograph by David Hume Kennerly; White House photograph courtesy Gerald R. Ford Library.)

plants to coal, along with an investment tax credit for construction of new nuclear power plants. Ford promised to submit legislation to phase out price controls on oil and gas, and then he explained the administrative actions he would take to force Congress to act. He announced that he would increase the price of oil by $1 per barrel on February 1, $2 per barrel on March 1, and $3 per barrel on April 1.[19]

After the speech, Ford was accused of a flip-flop. Three months before, he had proposed a tax increase, and now he wanted to cut taxes. The *New York Times* called the new program a "drastic reversal."[20] From California, Ronald Reagan decried Ford's abandonment of the tax surcharge before inflation had been tamed.[21]

Ford's oil import fee drew the strongest opposition. The week after the speech, Democratic senators Scoop Jackson and Edward Kennedy submitted a resolution to block the increases. The administration and Congress began a cycle that would be repeated all year long, in which Ford would impose price increases on oil; Congress would veto the price increases and extend the expiring price controls; Ford would respond by vetoing the extension and offering a short extension of the controls so a compromise could be worked out; and the cycle would start over. The same week that Jackson and Kennedy submitted their resolution, Ford submitted his omnibus energy bill to Congress, and he ordered the $1 increase in the oil import fee to begin February 1, with $1 increases scheduled for March and April. Congress responded by passing the Jackson-Kennedy resolution voiding the first increase, but Ford vetoed the bill on March 4. Ford included an olive branch with his veto — he announced that he would delay the next increases of the import fee and the deregulation of domestic oil by 60 days, giving Congress time to present a compromise, and the veto was sustained.[22]

On February 4, Ford submitted his fiscal year 1976 budget, including $16 billion in tax cuts. The budget projected that the budget deficit would grow to $52 billion, up from $34.7 billion in fiscal year 1975 and only $3.5 billion the year before.[23] The projected deficit drew intense criticism, even from within the administration. Simon earned Ford's ire when he told the press that the deficit was "horrendous," and Ford told his aides that he wished that the treasury secretary would "shut up." But Ford had been as candid with the press as Simon. A few weeks earlier, Ford admitted that he had been horrified to submit a budget with a projected $30 billion deficit. Congress did not like the budget either. Senator Hubert Humphrey called it "completely unacceptable." Chairman of the House Ways and Means Committee Al Ullman said it would be "a disaster for the economy."[24]

Rockefeller continued to fight for control of domestic policy. He proposed that his aides James Cannon and Richard Dunham be appointed the executive director and director deputy of the Domestic Counsel, replacing Nixon holdovers James Cavanaugh and Michael Raoul-Duval. Rumsfeld opposed the appointments, but the vice president won this round. After several contentious meetings, Ford publicly announced his decisions at a dinner for Rockefeller at the Waldorf-Astoria on February 13. He declared that Rockefeller would be in charge of domestic policy, but the paper flow would go through Rumsfeld. He agreed to appoint Cannon the executive director of the Domestic Counsel and Dunham the deputy director, and he made the heads of the ERC and EPB members of the Domestic Counsel. His intention was to make those organizations subject to Rockefeller's oversight, but in the end they would eclipse the influence of the Domestic Counsel. Rockefeller knew that his victory was illusory because the paper flow would be controlled by Rumsfeld. "Right there, the whole thing was sunk. And I knew it, because Rumsfeld had maintained control of what he called the paperwork, which was the flow of daily business which is where policy is made."[25]

Rockefeller would also be disappointed by his lack of influence over his former protégés Cannon and Dunham. Dunham would leave to run the Federal Power Commission in September 1975, and Cannon proved to be his own man. He moved across to the White House from the vice presidential suite in the Executive Office Building, and he told Rockefeller that his primary allegiance would be to Ford:

> I said that I work for Ford. I came here to work through Ford for the country. I never made any question about it, my loyalty to Ford. When it came to a choice, though, I would give [Rockefeller] my best advice — but I worked for the president and not the vice president.[26]

Rockefeller told Cannon that he should get rid of all Nixon holdovers, including Cavanaugh, but Cannon kept him and learned to value his abilities. Duval remained, and he would become a trouble-shooter for Ford, given responsibility for specific issues that particularly interested the president.[27]

Congress was undaunted by the prediction that the deficit would grow to more than $50 billion. In March, it passed tax cuts that were 40 percent higher than Ford had proposed, totaling $22.8 billion, without any corresponding spending cuts. The tax cuts put Ford in a quandary. He was tempted by the economic stimulus they would provide, particularly because he knew that the recession would be deeper than expected. In March, administration economists predicted that the unemployment rate would average 8.8 percent for the year. At the same time, inflation was still going strong, giving Ford a reason to veto the tax cut. The economists predicted that the inflation rate would be 10.6 percent for the year. Based upon the new projections, the economists predicted that the budget deficit would be $51.9 billion in fiscal year 1975, up from the $34.7 prediction in January, and they predicted that the deficit would grow to $72.5 billion in 1976, up from the $52 billion projection in the budget he submitted a month before.[28]

Ford was concerned that if he signed the tax cuts without any corresponding spending reductions, the 1975 budget deficit would increase to $70 billion. Treasury Secretary Simon led the charge to convince Ford to veto the tax cuts, but he was opposed by Burns and Greenspan, who told Ford that the tax cut would give a boost to the economy during the recession. Greenspan said that he was "right in the middle," but he was convinced that a veto would be overturned. In the end, Ford decided that the economy needed the stimulus from the tax cuts, and he signed the bill on March 29. In his message accompanying the bill, Ford told Congress that he would continue to fight for spending reductions. "This is as far as we dare to go. I will resist every attempt by the Congress to add another dollar to the deficit. I will make no exceptions."[29]

The economy began to improve during the second quarter of 1975 — the recovery was given a boost by the drop in withholding rates to effectuate the tax cuts. On April 16, Greenspan told the Cabinet that although the recession was deeper than anticipated, it would not be as severe as some had feared. The unemployment rate fell to 8.6 percent in June from its peak of 9.2 percent in May, but it stayed at 8.4 percent through the summer. Inflation had abated. During the first quarter of 1975 the consumer price index rose by a seasonally-adjusted annual rate of 6.6 percent, compared with 12.2 percent in the previous six months.[30]

Faced with the recession, the Fed continued to allow the money supply to rapidly expand. On May 2, Greenspan told Ford that the rate of monetary growth "would not be consistent with stable prices once full employment is reached." But he told Ford that, in light of the recession, letting the money supply grow was the right thing to do. "Until the recovery is well underway, however, such a simulative economic policy is desirable."[31]

———— ~~~ ————

Congress passed parts of Ford's energy program, including the administration bills to set up an emergency storage program and to allow production in the Naval Reserves, but it refused to eliminate price controls on oil and gas. In frustration, Zarb asked Scoop Jackson what it would take to make Congress interested in passing energy legislation, and the Senator said that it would take another embargo.[32] On the evening of May 27, Ford vented his frustration in an address to the nation from the Oval Office. "Four months are already lost. The Congress has acted only negatively." He announced that he would impose the first $1 excise tax on imported oil on June 1, followed by the second $1 increase on July 1. Congress responded with the Petroleum Price Review Act, which rolled back the price increases and imposed an even more complex system of price regulation. Ford vetoed the bill, and the controls were set to lapse on August 15.[33]

Ford and Congress were getting conflicting estimates of the effect that lifting the price controls would have on the economy. The Congressional Budget Office predicted that decontrol would increase the inflation rate by 2 percent and concluded that it would be "a significant setback both for the nascent economic recovery and for the continuing battle against inflation." Ford was getting very different advice from his Counsel of Economic Advisors and the Federal Energy Administration. The CEA estimated that lifting the controls would have a "one-shot inflationary impact," resulting in an increase in the unemployment rate of less than 0.2 percent and an increase in the inflation rate of less than 0.4 percent. "It is clear that the major problems ... will be political as distinct from economic." The Federal Energy Administration agreed. "The economic recovery will continue strongly even with decontrol."[34]

Two weeks before Congress took its summer break, Ford submitted a compromise energy decontrol program. On July 16 he proposed elimination of price controls over a 30-month period, subject to a $13.50 ceiling price on domestic old oil, but the House rejected the bill within one week. On July 31 Congress passed a 6-month extension of price controls, along with the Staggers Amendment which rolled back the price of new oil to $7.50 per barrel. Ford knew that he had to veto such an extreme extension of the controls, but he asked Zarb to negotiate a simple extension of controls to October 31 in return for his commitment not to submit any new decontrol proposals until October 20. Zarb was able to reach a compromise with congressional leaders for a 45-day extension of controls. The Senate sustained the president's veto, but unless the administration could reach a compromise with Congress, another showdown on energy controls was inevitable when the 45-day extension lapsed.[35]

———— ~~~ ————

The economy perked up during the second half of 1975. In September, Ford's economists reported that the economy was growing at an annual rate of 9 percent, and they predicted that the unemployment rate would fall to 7½ by the end of 1976.[36] In November, the Counsel of Economic Advisors provided another upbeat update, reporting that the recovery was off to a "strong start" but that growth was "unsustainably high" and would probably slow down. Not all the news was good; the unemployment had risen to 8.6 percent.[37]

In light of the improved economy, Ford considered his next economic move. In a meeting in the Oval Office, Lynn and Greenspan convinced him to continue his freeze on new federal programs until the end of his first term. Rockefeller and his Domestic Council aides were upset that a decision with such import on domestic policy had been decided without their input, but the freeze was consistent with Ford's central beliefs, and it is unlikely that anyone could have swayed him on the issue. Ford's biggest concern was the growing deficit, and he considered letting the tax cuts lapse. Administration economists estimated that the deficit would grow to $79 billion in fiscal year 1976 and $68 billion in 1977, but they suggested that if the tax cut were allowed to expire, the deficit would be reduced by 9 percent to $73 billion in 1976 and by 25 percent to $51 billion in 1977.[38] But Ford had another idea; he wanted to propose a second round of tax cuts and demand corresponding spending cuts. The idea appealed to the president because it would have the same impact on the deficit as letting the controls lapse; but Ford was too confident in his ability to force Congress to cut spending. In the end, he would be forced to accept tax cuts alone, and the deficit would continue to grow.

On October 6, 1975, Ford gave a televised speech on the economy and proposed a $28 billion tax cut, conditioned on Congress passing corresponding spending cuts. The speech was written by David Gergen, who Cheney had hired as an alternative to Hartmann's speechwriters. The speech was much more coherent than Ford's earlier economic addresses, and it did a better job of exhibiting his intelligence. He tried to talk the country into choosing less government. "To put it simply, we must decide whether we shall continue in the direction of recent years — the path toward bigger government, higher taxes and higher inflation — or whether we shall now take a new direction, bringing to a halt the momentous growth of government, restoring our prosperity and allowing each of you a greater voice in your own future." He tied his proposals to that choice. "Tonight will set forth two proposals that, taken together as they must be, represent the answer I believe we must choose. First, I propose that we make a substantial and permanent reduction in our federal taxes, and second that we make a substantial reduction in the growth of federal spending." Ford stressed the importance of spending cuts, and he promised to veto any tax cut that did not include them. "I would not sign the tax reduction legislation unless Congress pledged to cut anticipated federal spending by an equivalent $28 billion."[39]

Congress moved quickly to pass tax cuts, but not the ones Ford proposed. Congress passed a $17 billion tax cut by extending the existing cuts by an additional year. That was a change that Ford could live with, but he could not accept the failure of Congress to reduce spending. In fact, it increased the limit for federal spending in fiscal 1977 to $413 billion. Ullman knew that Congress was asking for a veto, and he proposed a compromise in November in the form of a "strong statement" in favor of spending limitations. Ford rejected the proposal, and he announced that he would not accept less than a $395 billion limit for fiscal year 1976. But in the end, Ford would be forced to accept nothing more than a strong statement from Congress.[40]

Ford vetoed the tax cut on December 17 — two days before Congress was scheduled to adjourn — and he asked Congress to "send me a bill that ... takes the honest and responsible first step toward a balanced Federal budget, a stable economy, lower taxes and reduced rates of government spending."[41] Ford knew that the battle would continue, and he told his advisors that they could tell congressional leaders that the administration would work to forge a compromise if his veto was sustained; and he designated James Lynn to lead the negotiations. The House sustained the veto the next day by 17 votes, and Lynn hammered out a settlement with congressional leaders that night. It was hardly ideal — all Congress did was promise spending cuts the next year — but Ford considered the pledge important. "The important thing was that the lawmakers had committed themselves to trim spending simultaneously with any further extensions of the tax cut measure." The next week, Congress passed the Revenue Adjustment Act of 1975, which included a $9 billion tax cut. As usual, Simon lobbied Ford to veto the bill, but this time he stood alone. Ford's other aides convinced him that the bill was the best they could hope for.[42]

Inflation had abated, but it was still very real — the inflation rate for 1975 was 9.1 percent.[43] Burns admitted as much in testimony before the Senate Committee on Banking. "The long-range problem of inflation is unsolved." He explained that the current rate of monetary growth "cannot be maintained indefinitely without running a serious risk of releasing new inflationary pressures."[44]

Faced with continued inflation, Ford again embargoed Soviet grain purchases. In addition to his fear of increasing inflation, he was driven to his embargo by the concerted refusal of longshoremen to load grain on ships headed to the Soviet Union, which caused grain shipments to sit at dockside. The strike had been started by the International Longshoreman's Association in July, with the support of AFL-CIO president George Meany. The longshoremen were trying to force the Soviets to transport the grain on American ships. On August 3, Secretary of Agriculture Earl Butz announced a "hold" on sales to the Russians, and in September Ford embargoed sales of grain and beef to the USSR and Poland after the Agriculture Department projected that grain production would be hurt by dry weather.[45]

In October, Greenspan and Seidman sent memos to Ford explaining the economic reality of the situation, which was that the embargo had no impact on grain prices. Seidman explained that during the three months of the embargo the Soviets had "been buying from third countries, thereby displacing other customers who as a result have entered American markets." As Greenspan explained, "The ultimate price effect in the U.S. markets would be the same." Seidman estimated that lifting the ban on sales to the Soviets would increase the inflation rate by less than 0.2 percent. Greenspan noted that the problem with Soviet purchases had been that they were "sporadic and generally unanticipated," and he recommended that the United States scrap its embargo and negotiate a long-term agreement. "The solution to the volatility of grain prices is not to control exports but to induce the Soviets to even out the purchases from the world market."[46]

Ford sent Assistant Secretary of State Charles Robinson to Russia to negotiate a long-term trade deal, and, after a visit to the White House, Meany announced that the longshoremen would suspend the strike for a month. Several weeks later, Ford announced a long-term agreement in which the Soviets committed to purchasing six million metric tons a year for the next five years and to use American ships to transport one third of their purchases. Ford lifted the embargo, and the longshoremen stopped their strike.[47]

Ford's embargo had little impact on inflation, but it would affect his campaign for president. American farmers were furious that he had taken sales away from them, and their anger was aggravated when he vetoed a bill to boost prices for dairy products, grain, and cotton. As a result, Ford would be concerned in 1976 about his support in the farm states — which should have been solidly behind his candidacy — and he would choose his vice president to protect that base of support rather than playing to win. It may have cost him the election.

The energy battle was rejoined before the 45-day extension of price controls was due to expire on November 15. Not surprisingly, Congress did not pass an energy bill by that date, and Ford and congressional leaders agreed to an additional extension until December 15. Congress did not make that date either, but two days later it finally passed a compromise energy bill, the Energy Policy and Conservation Act of 1975. In the bill, Congress restored price controls on oil and even reduced the price of new domestic oil to $7.66 per barrel. On the plus side, the president could increase oil prices by 10 percent per year, leading to full decontrol over a 40-month period. The bill also adopted Ford's proposals for a strategic storage program, coal conversion, and emergency stand-by authorities.

Ford was faced with a tough choice — oil price controls had lapsed, and signing the bill would reinstate them. The bill gave Ford the power to gradually eliminate them, but only over a three-year period. If Ford vetoed the bill, the controls would be gone, but Congress could reinstate them without giving Ford the power to eliminate them. Ford's advisors were split. Zarb and Friedersdorf told Ford that Congress would probably override a veto, and Zarb concluded that the pricing provisions were the best that could be expected from the current Congress. Simon — who never saw a bill he wouldn't veto — recognized that Congress was unlikely to produce a better bill, but he did not think Congress would pass a worse bill if Ford vetoed this one. Ford chose the ability to gradually deregulate over an uncertain future battle with Congress, and he signed the Energy Policy and Conservation Act on December 27.[48]

The Federal Energy Agency immediately began implementing the deregulatory provisions of the Act. Zarb told Ford that his goal was "deregulation to the maximum extent possible, together with a price structure that will lead to more exploration and recovery of domestic oil."[49] The FEA lifted price and allocation controls from residential fuel oil, middle distillates, military jet fuel, and other products. Approximately half of refinery output had been decontrolled, but gasoline, natural gas liquids, commercial jet fuel, and aviation gasoline were still subject to controls.

By the time Ford left office, the FEA had completed hearings on decontrol of gasoline, and Zarb gave Ford three options: (1) lift controls in December 1976, so Congress would be forced to act before he left office, (2) lift controls in early January 1977, so the new administration would have 15 days to act once it took office if it disagreed with decontrol, and (3) allow the new administration to make the decision. Zarb agreed with congressional leaders who asked Ford to allow the incoming administration to decide.[50] Ford chose not to wait, but he gave Carter the ability to reverse his decision. On his second-to-last day in office, he eliminated controls on gasoline, but Carter rescinded the action after taking office.[51] Carter used the power granted by the law to finally eliminate price controls by executive action in April 1979, sounding very much like Ford when he justified his action. "We still face the basic reality about America's use of oil: We must use less, and we must pay more for what we use."[52]

Ford was unsuccessful in his efforts to deregulate natural gas. Congress took no action until the Senate finally voted on a proposal to temporarily lift controls to prevent shortages in the winter of 1975, but even then it turned down a proposed amendment for permanent deregulation. Deregulation languished in the House until February 1976, when the House passed legislation that lifted controls on small producers but imposed additional controls on large companies. With no hope of compromise in conference, decontrol legislation died. In 1978, Congress finally acted to change the form of regulation of natural gas, but the law created an even-more-complicated system of interim controls, which would finally be lifted during the administration of the first George Bush in 1989.[53]

After controls on oil and gas were finally lifted, the market was allowed to respond to changes in production. As new fields came into production, the price of oil fell; during times of conflict in the Middle East, oil prices jumped. But the Fed had learned not to overreact, and the oil price spikes did not lead to sustained inflation. After deregulation, the market was able to respond to supply declines, and the nation was never again subjected to the oil and gas shortages that plagued America in the '70s.

———∽∾∾———

The economic recovery continued through the end of Ford's presidency, with a "pause" just before the election that may have cost him a second term. The unemployment rate fell from over 8 percent at the start of 1976 to 7.3 percent in May. On April 16, Greenspan wrote a memo to Ford titled "Reasons for Better Than Expected Economic Improvement." His description of the economy was glowing. "Production and employment continues to rise, unemployment is trending downward, retail sales have strengthened further, business investment is just beginning to increase, inventories are low, and surprisingly inflation remains subdued, an indication that the long term unraveling of inflationary forces continues." And he predicted even better results. "The cumulative momentum that we are now beginning to see in the economy is typical of the early to middle stages of a business cycle recovery which still has a significant way to go on the upside."[54]

The recovery continued through summer and fall, continuing to grow at a 4-percent rate, which Ford's economists reported would "still be consistent with a strong continued recovery."[55] Despite a fall of leading economic indicators in September, Ford's economic advisors predicted a better economy during the fourth quarter. "Signs of an acceleration of real growth appear to be at hand."[56] Unfortunately for Ford's chances at reelection, the acceleration would slow in November.

The inflation rate fell to 5 percent, but that was deceptive because oil and food prices had stabilized, while the price of other goods continued to increase by an annual rate of more than 8 percent, and the Fed continued to let the money supply grow at a rapid rate. Ford's economists cautioned that "while the news on the price front has been good, we should guard against an overly-optimistic appraisal of our success against inflation."[57]

———∽∾∾———

At first blush, Ford's record of handling the economy is impressive. He inherited double-digit inflation and a deep recession, and by the time he left office inflation had been cut in half and the economy had recovered. But there are two significant blemishes on his record. The first is surprising considering Ford's commitment to fiscal responsibility. The federal deficit grew from $6.1 billion in fiscal year 1974 to $73.7 billion in 1976, partially as a result of Ford's tax cuts. But the deficit wasn't a systemic problem during his presidency. National debt remained at a low 33–36 percent of GDP through his administration. It wasn't until the massive deficits under Ford's republican successors that the growth of the debt began to outpace the growth of the economy.[58]

The second blemish on Ford's record was that he did not tackle the underlying problem of inflation. Although the inflation rate had dropped by half during his presidency, the core inflation rate (removing food and energy prices) fell by only a fifth, and the growth of the money supply actually accelerated. It would take until the end of the '70s for the government finally to take the difficult actions necessary to tame inflation. Burns continued to allow the money supply to grow at unprecedented rates until the end of his term in January 1978. Jimmy Carter misfired in choosing Burns' successor, William Miller, who continued Burns' expansive policies for his year in office. Carter finally forced the country to bite the bullet when he appointed Paul Volcker in August 1979. When Volcker clamped down on money growth, interest rates shot up and the recession was deep, but inflation would finally be tamed.[59]

9

CIA Scandal

When Ford boarded Air Force One for his trip to Vail on December 22, 1974, he was planning to use his holiday to focus on economic and energy policy, but the plan was frustrated even before he landed in Colorado. CIA director William Colby called Ford on the plane and told him that the *New York Times* was reporting that the CIA had been spying on American citizens. In a front-page article that morning Seymour Hersh claimed that the agency had conducted "a massive, illegal domestic intelligence operation during the Nixon administration against the antiwar movement and other dissident groups within the United States" by amassing files on more than 10,000 American citizens, surveilling antiwar demonstrators, and infiltrating agents into dissident groups.[1] Ford wasn't surprised by the article because Colby had already warned him that Hersh was working on a story about domestic spying, and Ford told the CIA director that he wouldn't tolerate any illegal activities by the agency while he was president. But Colby neglected to tell Ford that Hersh was basing his article on an internal CIA study that would become known as "the Family Jewels," which cataloged a host of illegal activities by the agency.[2]

The Family Jewels report was created at the order of Schlesinger during his short tenure as CIA director. Schlesinger had been shocked by reports that former CIA agents had been involved in Watergate, and he sent a memo to every current and former employee of the agency asking them to identify any illegal activities. Before the survey was complete, Schlesinger was named secretary of defense, and Colby replaced him. Just after taking office in September 1973, Colby's staff presented him with a 693-page report, most of which covered the agency's domestic spying operations, which violated the CIA's charter limiting it to foreign activities. According to the report, the agency had tailed columnist Jack Anderson, tapped the phones of two other reporters, and broke into several offices in the D.C. area. The report described CIA operations to open mail of U.S. citizens, monitor antiwar groups, and place operatives in dissident groups to create cover stories for foreign operations. Helms' story did not report on the most incendiary activities — apparently, his source did not have access to a more-secret addendum to the report, which revealed that the agency had unsuccessfully attempted to assassinate foreign leaders.[3] The agency had forsworn assassinations by the time Ford took office. Helms issued orders banning assassinations in 1972, and Colby followed with orders of his own the next year.[4]

When Colby received the report he briefed congressional leaders, including chairman of the House Armed Services Committee Lucien Nedzi. Nedzi suggested releasing the report, but Colby would not agree because he thought that "the skeletons should stay where they are, in the closet."[5] It was the height of Watergate, and Colby did not show the report to Nixon, and he did not show the report to Ford when he took office. The first time Ford learned about the report was when Colby called him on Air Force One. During the call the president asked for a summary of the report, and he said that he would meet with Colby as soon as he returned to Washington. Ford reiterated his order that the CIA stay within its charter, as he explained to the press when he landed in Vail. "I told him that under no circumstances would I tolerate any such activities under this administration."[6]

Two days after his phone call to Ford, Colby gave a summary of the Family Jewels to Kissinger to take to Vail. The summary contained no names or classified information, and in his cover note Colby suggested that Ford give it to the press. The summary explained that the CIA had kept files on 9,944 American citizens, but Colby concluded that "it is not accurate to characterize it as having engaged in 'massive domestic intelligence activity.'"

Colby cancelled his Christmas vacation and stayed in Washington waiting for a summons to Vail, which never came. "The silence from there was deafening." He concluded that the administration had decided to "draw the wagons around — and leave me isolated and exposed on the outside."[7] He was wrong; Ford had simply decided to address the issue when he returned, which is exactly what he had told Colby during his phone conversation from Air Force One. Colby's suspicions led the CIA director to a decision that would ultimately cost him his job — he decided that he would defend his agency as he saw fit, without coordinating with the administration. For the next ten months both Kissinger and Ford would be disappointed at Colby's refusal to work with them. Kissinger would also be dismayed at the director's willingness to give classified information to Congress, and he would accuse the devout Catholic of wanting to confess every time he went to Capitol Hill.[8]

—⁓—

Hersh's article found fertile ground in Congress, which was already investigating whether the agency had been involved in Augusto Pinochet's coup in Chile against the government of Salvador Allende. The story of the CIA's involvement in Chile broke a month after Ford took office, but it was based on testimony that was six months old. On April 22, Colby had given confidential testimony to the House Armed Services Subcommittee in which he admitted that the CIA had been involved in trying to destabilize the Allende government. Massachusetts Democrat Michael Harrington sent a letter to chairman of the House Foreign Affairs Committee Thomas Morgan summarizing the testimony and requesting an investigation. When he got no response, the letter appeared in the *New York Times* and the *Washington Post*. In a September 16 press conference, Ford admitted that the CIA had given money to the opposition to Allende's government, but he denied that the U.S. had any role in the coup.[9]

Both Ford's comments and Colby's testimony contradicted the testimony of former CIA director Richard Helms before the Senate Foreign Relations Committee. In November the *Progressive* published an article claiming that Helms had lied, and Idaho senator Frank Church announced that he would hold hearings about the allegations. Ford tried to talk Church out of the hearings, to no avail.[10] With Church already investigating the CIA role in Chile, it was almost certain that Congress would investigate the Family Jewels.

—⁓—

As promised, Ford met with Colby on the evening of January 3, the day he returned from Vail. The CIA director briefed the president about the Family Jewels report, and he tried to convince Ford to release his summary, to no avail. Ford told Colby that he intended to convene a blue-ribbon panel to investigate the agency and to forestall a congressional inquiry. "We don't want to destroy but to preserve the CIA. But we want to make sure that illegal operations and those outside the charter don't happen."[11] Ford's inclination to keep the report under wraps was reinforced during the next two days. When he described the report to

Kissinger the next day, the secretary of state voted against releasing the summary with his typical bluster. "What is happening is worse than in the days of McCarthy."[12] Ford also met with Helms, who was then ambassador to Iran, and the former CIA director told him that if there was an investigation, "a lot of dead cats will come out."[13]

On January 4, Ford issued an executive order establishing the commission, chaired by the vice president. Rockefeller was an easy choice because Ford trusted his judgment and because he had considerable experience in foreign intelligence. As a special assistant to President Eisenhower on Cold War strategies he had served on the 40 Committee, which approved all covert operations, and he had served on Nixon's Foreign Intelligence Advisory Board. In addition to Rockefeller, Ford appointed seven respected leaders of the political establishment, including Ronald Reagan, former dean of the Harvard Law School Erwin Griswold, AFL-CIO secretary Lane Kirkland, former University of Virginia president Edgar Shannon, former Joint Chiefs chairman Lyman Lemnitzer, former Treasury secretary Douglas Dillon, and former secretary of commerce John Connor. Ford asked the commission to report back in three months.[14]

Ford quickly learned that his strategy to forestall a congressional investigation would not work. On January 27 the Senate voted 82 to 4 to establish the "Senate Select Committee to Study Governmental Operations with Respect to Intelligence Activities" and gave it a 100-person staff. After weeks of pleading, majority leader Mike Mansfield acceded to Democrat Frank Church's requests for the chairmanship. Church, a former intelligence officer, was not a reflexive opponent of the CIA. When Senator James Abourezk and Representative Elizabeth Holtzman submitted a resolution to ban all covert operations, Church was a key figure in killing the proposal. But during the investigation Church became a sanctimonious moralizer, and he was given a lot to moralize about.

The administration was no more successful in forestalling an investigation in the House. The only restriction the House imposed on its investigation seemed routine, but it would be important in the end — it prohibited any unauthorized disclosure of confidential information. At first, Speaker Albert chose Nedzi to chair the committee, but his time overseeing the investigation was brief. He was forced to step down after the *New York Times* reported on June 5 that Colby had briefed him about the Family Jewels almost a year before Hersh's article.[15] Nedzi's fellow Democrats on the committee were outraged by his failure to take any action at the time he was first told about the report. They demanded that he resign his chairmanship, but he refused. The House leadership supported Nedzi, but the Democrats on the committee would not give up. The battle raged until the House created a new and expanded special committee on July 17, with a new chairman, Otis Pike, a silver-haired Democrat from Long Island with an acerbic tongue and a sharp sense of humor. He had no qualms about second-guessing others, and he never wavered in his zeal to root out what he saw as incompetence in the executive branch. Pike was considered to be a moderate, but he would not exercise the power of his chairmanship in moderation.[16]

The administration managed to keep the assassinations issue under wraps for two months, until Daniel Schorr broke the story on CBS News on February 28. Schorr reported that Ford had been "reportedly shocked" when Colby briefed him on the assassinations. He described a meeting in which Ford warned "associates" that the investigations could uncover assassination attempts on foreign leaders.[17]

The "associates" were actually seven *New York Times* executives and reporters who had dined at the White House on January 16. Puffing on his pipe, Ford said that he was "shocked" at the "horror stories" Colby told him. "If you knew what they were doing, it would curl your hair." Ford said that the investigation could uncover incidents which would "blacken the name of every American president back to Harry Truman." Abe Rosenthal asked, "Like what?" And Ford shot back, "Like assassinations." That evening, *Times* executives deliberated about whether to run the story. They decided to call Nessen and ask for permission, but the press secretary reiterated that Ford's comments were off the record. The paper decided not to run the story, but rumors about Ford's comments began to circulate among Washington journalists.[18]

When Schorr heard the rumors he started digging in the wrong area — he assumed that Ford was referring to assassinations in the United States of foreign agents from communist nations. He was steered in the right direction by Colby when Schorr interviewed the CIA director on February 27 and asked about the rumors. "Has the CIA ever killed anybody in this country?" Colby was not very deft in his response: "Not in this country." Schorr knew immediately that he had been on the wrong track, and he tried to guess who the foreign targets had been. He asked about Dag Hammarskjöld, the UN secretary general who had been killed in a plane accident, but Colby said, "Of course not." Schorr then asked about the leader of Zaire who had been killed after a CIA–supported coup. "Lumumba?" Colby was in a bind, because the African leader had been a target of an attempted assassination, and he answered that he couldn't talk about it. Schorr had the confirmation he needed, and he decided to run the story.[19]

Even though the story was no longer secret, Ford refused to affirm or deny that the country had tried to assassinate foreign leaders. All he was willing to say was that assassinations were not acceptable under his administration. "I am opposed to political assassination. This administration has not and will not use such means as instruments of national policy."[20] Ford tried to divert attention from the assassinations by asking the Rockefeller Commission to look into them, but he had no intention of making the commission's findings public. In his memorandum authorizing the assassination investigation, Buchen told the commission to "advise the president of the outcome" so Ford could decide whether the issue should be included in the commission's final report.[21]

—⁓⁓⁓—

The Rockefeller Commission conducted an exhaustive investigation, and it completed its work by early summer. Rockefeller told the press that the report would be released on June 5, but he had not cleared the date with Ford, which was a mistake. The president was in Europe, and he wanted to read the report before it was issued, so the release was delayed by five days. In the post–Watergate environment, the media was suspicious of the five-day delay, and reporters alleged that the president wanted to censor the report. In fact, the administration did tone down several conclusions of the commission, but no substantive information was censored or removed.

During the delay, Kissinger lobbied hard to keep the report on assassinations secret. The secretary of state thought that coming clean would harm the country's standing in the world, and Ford agreed. They both thought that the impact on America's foreign policy overcame the interest of the American people in the truth. In a June 9 press conference, Ford announced that the report would not cover assassinations, but he promised to turn over the evidence on the assassination attempts to the Church Committee. The announcement that the assassinations section would not be released caused another furor. In the press conference, reporters asked whether the administration was engaged in a cover-up and if the report would be seen as a whitewash.[22] Democrats accused Ford of skirting the assassinations issue. Scoop Jackson said, "He took a powder on it; he ducked it." Church promised that the Senate committee would not avoid the issue. "The buck stops with the Senate committee."[23]

The reporters at Ford's press conference weren't alone in predicting that the Rockefeller Commission report would be a whitewash. Tom Wicker wrote in the *New York Times* that having Rockefeller and other foreign policy insiders investigate the agency was like "a goat set to guard a cabbage patch" and "having the Mafia audited by its own accountants." After the report was released, he admitted that he was wrong. "The commission went much further than might have been expected in exposing illegal programs and procedures that the C.I.A. had undertaken, and it used much sharper language in condemning such actions."[24]

The Rockefeller Commission found that many CIA activities were "plainly unlawful and constituted improper invasions upon the rights of Americans," including: opening mail to and from the Soviet Union, administering LSD to people without their knowledge, and spying on antiwar groups in the United States. The domestic spying operation was colorfully named "Operation CHAOS," and the report explained that the agency reluctantly began the operation after intense pressure from Presidents Johnson and Nixon, both of whom were convinced that foreign agents had infiltrated the antiwar movement. The CIA reported several times to Johnson and Nixon that they could find no evidence of foreign infiltration of antiwar groups, but the presidents would not accept the conclusion — they kept sending the agency back to dig harder. The operation may have started as an investigation into foreign infiltration of the antiwar movement, but like many operations of its kind, it took on a life of its own. The agency opened files on 7,200 Americans and created a computerized index of 300,000 individuals and organizations.[25]

The Rockefeller Commission was thorough, but the Church Committee took the investigation a step further, conducting more than 800 interviews and holding more than 250 days of hearings. Colby thought the committee was fair, and Kissinger has admitted that it "acted, on the whole, responsibly."[26] The senior Republican, John Tower of Texas, was a staunch supporter of the CIA. Nevertheless, he was able to work efficiently with Church over the next year, making the committee proceedings relatively amicable and avoiding many of the excesses that would plague the House investigation. Church was willing to work with the CIA and the administration, and he told the committee staff to avoid "the needless pyrotechnics of the House committee."[27] In February 1975 the committee agreed with Ford that it would not to disclose any classified information without first consulting with the administration. The committee agreed to "carefully consider" the administration's reasons for secrecy, but it reserved the right to make the final determination. During its investigation the committee followed the procedure as agreed. Almost all issues were resolved by compromise, with one significant exception — the assassinations report.

Things were less amicable in the House. The disputes got heated in early September when the committee and the White House fought over four words. Pike had issued subpoenas for intelligence reports on recent crises, including the invasion of Israel by Egypt that started the 1973 Yom Kippur War. The administration turned over the documents, but only after obtaining the committee's agreement to keep them confidential. After reviewing the documents, the committee asked for declassification of a post-mortem report about the failure of the CIA to anticipate the Egyptian attack, and after hours of negotiations, Pike refused to concede on four words: "and greater communications security." He thought that the phrase was necessary to show that the CIA should have known about the attack, while the agency was concerned that the words could reveal that the U.S. was monitoring Egyptian communications. There was a fierce debate in the committee about whether to provoke a fight with the administration, but Pike would not back down, and the committee voted 6–3 to release the document on September 11, 1975.[28]

The dispute involved complex issues of the powers of each branch of government. Congress had the ability to decide what information to release, but if the administration did not trust it to make a responsible decision, it could refuse to comply with requests for information, forcing Congress to go to court, where the administration could make its case for confidentiality. For decades the legislative and executive branches usually avoided the court process because members of Congress acted responsibly. But this time Pike was intentionally picking a fight, and he wouldn't be happy with the result.

Faced with a deliberate confrontation, Ford overreacted. That night he convened a meeting to decide how to respond. Several aides suggested working with the committee to develop a process to resolve future disputes, but the prevailing opinion was that they needed to refuse to turn over any more confidential information until the committee agreed not to unilaterally declassify any more information. Ford did not need much prodding to fight.[29] The next day he sent Assistant Attorney General Rex Lee to deliver the news to the Pike Committee. Pike threatened to hold members of the administration in contempt, and he issued new subpoenas, but Ford refused to respond without a promise that classified information would be kept secret. The only accommodation the committee was willing to make was to give the administration one day's notice before it made any information public, but Pike was so obsessed with protecting his prerogatives that he refused to acknowledge that he was offering a compromise.[30]

Colby was frustrated with the unwillingness of the parties to work together, and he thought that the administration was paralyzed with dissention, so he met with Ford and asked him to name a point man to coordinate the administration responses to committee inquiries. Ford responded by creating the Intelligence Coordinating Group, and he gave Marsh and Michael Raoul-Duval the day-to-day responsibility for responding to document requests. Colby also begged Ford to work with the committee, and the president relented. On September 26, Speaker Albert, minority leader Rhodes, Pike, and Robert McClory, the ranking Republican member of the committee, went to the White House to meet with Ford, Colby, Rumsfeld, Kissinger, and Marsh. With the assistance of the congressional leaders, the administration and Pike worked out a procedure to handle disputes. The resolution was simple: if the administration and the committee could not agree on a classification issue, they would send it to the courts for resolution.[31]

Then Kissinger blew up the agreement when the Pike Committee subpoenaed a memorandum from Thomas Boyatt, the head of the State Department's Cyprus desk, which criticized the intelligence in the lead-up to the Cyprus civil war. Boyatt had submitted the memo through the State Department's "dissent" channel, which allowed its employees to try to convince the secretary of state to change the department's strategy on any issue. Kissinger thought that releasing the report would deter future use of the channel, and he refused to turn over the document. At the same time, he sent Lawrence Eagleburger to tell the committee that the State Department would not allow anyone to testify about advice they had provided to their superiors within the department.[32] Buchen and Attorney General Levi told Ford that the administration had a 50–50 chance of prevailing in court on the issue, and Levi suggested that Ford compromise with the committee "before Henry gets too intoxicated with the principle involved."[33]

The issue came to a head on October 31 when Kissinger appeared before the committee. The only compromise he was willing to offer was to provide a summary of the memo, mixed with summaries of other documents. The committee voted 8 to 5 to accept the offer and avoid a conflict with the administration. But a week later Kissinger refused to turn over a new batch of documents, and this time he refused to offer any compromise, so the committee voted 10 to 2 to hold him in contempt.[34] Levi told Ford that the administration would lose if the issue went to court, but Kissinger would not give up. "I persisted because the issue seemed to me a matter of principle over which I was prepared to resign and face a contempt citation."[35] As he did during so many conflicts during his administration, Ford supported his people — he wrote to the Pike Committee on November 19 that the administration would not comply with the subpoena. It took three weeks for cooler heads to prevail. In early December, Ford approved a face-saving, but strange, offer. The administration offered to send an official to the committee to read the document aloud, and the committee withdrew its contempt citations on December 11. That ended the battle, but not the war.[36]

———

In the Senate the major dispute came at the end of 1975 when the committee was ready to publish its report on assassinations. Ford wrote the committee warning that releasing the report would do "grievous damage" to the "reputation and the foreign policy of the United States." Church disagreed. "The national interest is better served by letting the American people know the truth and complete story. A basic tenet of our democracy is that the people must be told of the mistakes of their government so that they may have the opportunity to correct them." Church had the better side of the argument. Information should not be withheld from the people just because it will make the country look bad. The American people deserve to know what the government is doing, and public debate about activities like assassinations acts as a salutary check on the behavior of spies and presidents.

On November 3 the Church Committee voted to send the report to the Senate floor with a recommendation that it be made public. After meeting in secret session, the Senate declined to vote, sending the report back to the committee, which voted again to release it on November 20.[37] The committee explained its reasons in the report:

> We believe that the public is entitled to know what instrumentalities of their Government have done.... The Committee believes the truth about the assassination allegations should be told because democracy depends upon a well-informed electorate. We reject any contention that the facts disclosed in this report should be kept secret because they are embarrassing to the United States.[38]

The release of the assassinations report was an embarrassment to the country, and it was particularly embarrassing to several former presidents. It wasn't easy to identify who ordered the assassinations — Walter Mondale said that it was "like nailing Jello to a wall"[39] — but it was clear that most of the time the order came from the president or high-level administration officials. The revelations challenged the prejudices of partisan leaders in Washington. It was hard for Republicans to accept that Eisenhower had crossed the line, and it was nearly impossible for Democrats to accept that the Kennedys had. Nobody fought harder against that conclusion than Frank Church, who had been inspired to enter politics by John Kennedy. He clung to the idea that the CIA had acted on its own, and he even told the press that the agency "may have been behaving like a rogue elephant on a rampage."[40] At the end of its investigation, the committee disagreed with Church. "The Central Intelligence Agency in broad terms is not 'out of control.'"[41]

As Goldwater explained in his separate statement, no actual assassinations were committed by the United States. "Since World War II, no president or his agents ordered an assassination that was actually committed. Moreover, there is no evidence that any agency of the U.S. Government committed an assassination."[42] But it was not for want of trying. The first attempt was against Patrice Lumumba, the first democratically-elected prime minister of the Congo (called Zaire during the Ford administration). In late July 1960, less than a month after his country's independence, Lumumba visited Washington to ask for American support, but the visit proved to be his undoing. Lumumba appeared unhinged when he met with Secretary of State Christian Herter. "He was just not a rational being. The impression that was left was ... that this was an individual whom it was impossible to deal with." When Herter described Lumumba during a National Security Council meeting in August 1960, Eisenhower told the CIA to get rid of him by "very straightforward action." Many of the attendees, probably including CIA director Alan Dulles, interpreted the comment as an order to assassinate the Congolese leader. The committee found no conclusive evidence that Eisenhower ordered the assassination, but it concluded that there was a "reasonable inference" that he did.[43]

Dulles certainly acted like had been ordered to kill Lumumba. He sent a message to the CIA station in the Congo conveying orders from "high quarters here" that Lumumba's "removal must be an urgent and prime objective." Dulles ordered the continuation of attempts to foment a coup and authorized "even more aggressive action if it can remain covert." Richard Bissell told the committee that the cable was "a circumlocutious means of indicating that the President wanted Lumumba killed." A CIA scientist transported a toxin and hypodermic needles to the Congo, and the agency sent a European mercenary to carry out the assassination; but, for one reason or another, all of the CIA's attempts failed. Lumumba was ousted from office in a CIA–sponsored coup by Congolese president Joseph Kasavubu and Chief of Staff Joseph Mobutu. When Lumumba was captured by Mobutu's troops, he was delivered to his enemies in the province of Katanga, where he was killed. The Church Committee concluded that the CIA was not involved in his death. "It does not appear from the evidence that the United States was in any way involved in the killing."[44]

—◦◦◦—

The second assassination attempt detailed in the report was against Castro, and the project spanned the Eisenhower and Kennedy administrations. The particulars the committee uncovered were sensational, and the press had a field day with the outlandish plans developed by the CIA that were never implemented, including schemes to kill the Cuban leader with poison cigars, exploding seashells, and a contaminated diving suit. The CIA also dreamed up plots to sabotage Castro's speeches by spraying his broadcasting studio with a hallucinogenic drug, spiking his cigar with a similar drug, and dusting his shoes with a chemical that would cause his beard to fall out. The plans that *were* implemented were nearly as outrageous. The agency tried to kill Castro many times between 1960 and '65, even enlisting the Mafia to carry out the assassination.[45]

The agency was driven by intense pressure from both Eisenhower and Kennedy to topple the Cuban caudillo, but the committee found no direct evidence that either president approved the assassination attempts. "There was insufficient evidence from which the Committee could conclude that Presidents Eisenhower, Kennedy, or Johnson, their close advisors, or the Special Group authorized the assassination of Castro."[46] Nevertheless, Senator Baker concluded that it was likely that presidents knew about the assassination plots. "It is my personal view that on balance the likelihood that presidents knew of the assassination plots is greater than the likelihood that they did not."[47] The report chronicled clear evidence that CIA Director Allen Dulles ordered the assassination of Castro. It is not clear whether Eisenhower knew about the orders, but again he made some cryptic comments that Dulles may have interpreted as orders to kill the Cuban leader, including a May 1960 meeting when he said that he wanted to see Castro "sawed off."[48] Bissel testified that he assumed that Dulles told Eisenhower and Kennedy about the operation "in a circumlocutious fashion."[49]

Like Eisenhower, Kennedy gave ambiguous orders that were probably taken by senior CIA officials as approval to kill Castro, but the committee could find no evidence that he specifically ordered the assassination. After the Bay of Pigs fiasco, Kennedy told the CIA to "use all available assets ... to help Cuba overthrow the Communist regime." Attorney General Robert Kennedy told CIA officials that the removal of Castro was "the top priority in the U.S. Government — no time, money, effort or manpower is to be spared." Helms told the committee that the attorney general's words, and the intense pressure coming from the White House, led him to believe that he had implicit authorization to assassinate the Cuban leader. "I believe it was the policy at the time to get rid of Castro and if killing him was one of the things that was to be done in this connection, that was within what was expected."[50]

The report showed that the agency took the odious step of enlisting the Mafia in the assassination plot. In 1960, CIA agents approached gang leader Handsome Johnny Rosselli to deliver poisoned cigars to a worker in a restaurant where Castro dined, but the operation was unsuccessful. Toward the end of the Eisenhower administration the agency recruited Chicago mob boss Sam Giancana, and he brought Cuban Mafia don Santos Traficante into the operation. After Kennedy took office, the agency used Judith Campbell Exner, who was having affairs with both Kennedy and Giancana, to make contacts with the Mafia leaders. During the Kennedy administration, the CIA also recruited a highly-placed Cuban official, who asked for a high-powered rifle to use to assassinate Castro. At first, the official was told that the U.S. would have "no part of an attempt on Castro's life," but on the day Kennedy was shot a CIA agent met with the official and offered a pen armed with a hypodermic needle. The official "did not think much of the device," and he asked the agency to come up with something better.[51]

Several CIA officers testified that the agency first briefed Attorney General Kennedy on the assassination operation on May 7, 1962. They explained the use of the Mafia, but they told Kennedy that the operation had been terminated. Two days later, Kennedy met with FBI director J. Edgar Hoover and briefed him about the program, which he explained had been terminated. After the meeting, CIA officer Sheffield Edwards prepared a memo to the file explaining that the operations involving the Mafia were being terminated. In 1964, President Johnson discontinued the Cuban sabotage program and the policy of overthrowing Castro. There is no evidence that anyone told Johnson about the assassination attempts.[52]

—◦◦◦—

The assassinations report described another operation that spanned the Eisenhower and Kennedy administrations: the attempts to topple the dictator of the Dominican Republic, Rafael Trujillo. The CIA supported some of Trujillo's opponents, with the knowledge that they had plans to assassinate the dictator, but the agency never promoted the assassination. "Although there is no evidence that the United States instigated any assassination activity, certain evidence tends to link United States officials to the assassination plans." Both Eisenhower and Kennedy opposed the brutal dictator and provided encouragement to his opponents, who shot the dictator during a coup in 1961. The day before the coup, Kennedy cabled the State Department representative in the Dominican Republic that the United States "cannot condone assassination." But Kennedy added that if the coup succeeded, the U.S. would support the new government.[53]

The committee came to a similar conclusion about America's involvement in the murder of South Vietnamese president Ngo Dinh Diem. The committee concluded that the American government supported the 1963 coup that ousted the Vietnamese leader, but not his murder. "Indeed, it appears that the assassination of Diem was not part of the Generals' pre-coup planning but was instead a spontaneous act which occurred during the coup and was carried out without United States involvement or support." In fact, the United States actively discouraged the murder of Diem. When one of the coup plotters, General Duong Van Minh, told CIA agents that one of the options he was considering was assassination, the Vietnam station recommended that "we do not set ourselves irrevocably against the assassination plot." But when CIA director John McCone learned of the possible assassination, he ordered the Vietnam station to tell the coup leaders that the U.S. did not support assassinations, and those instructions were relayed to Minh.[54]

The assassinations report described one incident that occurred during Nixon's tenure in office: the assassination of the commander-in-chief of the Chilean Army, General Rene Schneider. In 1970 Salvador Allende won a plurality of the vote during a three-way race, and the election was sent to the Congress because no candidate had won a majority. It was not an extraordinary event in Chile — the Congress had voted many times in the past and had always reaffirmed the leading vote-getter. Nixon was determined to prevent that from happening, and his administration was trying to incite a coup to replace Allende with former president Eduardo Frei.

Schneider stood in the way of the plan because he believed that it was his duty to protect Chile's 200-year-old democratic process. On September 21 the ambassador to Chile sent a report to Kissinger explaining that, for the coup to succeed, General Schneider would have to be "neutralized, by displacement if necessary." The Church Committee concluded that the United States did not try to kill Schneider, but the CIA did participate in a plot to kidnap him. "We find that neither the President nor any other official in the United States Government authorized the assassination of General Rene Schneider. The CIA, and perhaps the White House, did know that coup leaders contemplated a kidnapping, which, as it turned out resulted in Schneider's death." The CIA provided three submachine guns to coup plotters who planned to use them to kidnap Schneider. The guns were never used because it was other plotters who tried to kidnap Schneider and shot and killed him in the process.[55]

———※※※———

While the CIA was inept at assassinations, it proved to be much better at toppling democratically-elected leaders. The Church Committee report showed that Lumumba was not the first democratically-elected leader to be toppled by the CIA — Eisenhower used the agency to incite coups against several foreign governments. In 1953 he sent CIA agent Kermit Roosevelt to Iran to oust democratically-elected premier Mohammed Mossadegh in favor of Shah Mohammad Reza Pahlavi. One year after the coup in Iran, the agency incited a coup against the democratically-elected leader of Guatemala, President Jacobo Arbenz Guzman, and the country was taken over by Colonel Castillo Armas, who became one of the most murderous dictators in the hemisphere.[56] Kennedy was not as afraid of leftist democratic leaders, and he did not use the agency for coups as frequently as his predecessor, but he did approve the overthrow of Diem in Vietnam, and he consistently pushed the CIA to overthrow Castro.[57] Continuing what can fairly be called America's "Bad Neighbor Policy" in Latin America, Johnson used the agency to support the coup against Brazilian president Joao Goulart in 1964, and Nixon pushed for a coup against Chile's Allende after his election in 1970.

The Church Committee issued a supplemental report on the CIA's involvement in

Allende's ouster, and it was a tragic story. Chile had been a democratic republic since 1932, and democracy was interrupted only three times before that during the country's history since independence in 1818. The CIA had been active in the country for years, funneling money to the democratic opposition to Allende, while the Soviets and Cubans funded Allende's campaigns. Once Allende was elected, Nixon authorized $10 million for a covert operation to undermine his government, and he told Helms to "make the economy scream."[58] Helms told the Church Committee that "If I ever carried a marshal's baton in my knapsack out of the Oval Office, it was that day." Kissinger testified that Nixon ordered the CIA to "do whatever he could to prevent Allende from being seated.... It is clear that President Nixon wanted him to encourage the Chilean military to cooperate or to take the initiative in preventing Allende from taking office."[59]

The operation progressed along two tracks. Track I included political, economic and propaganda activities, while Track II was designed to instigate a military coup. Kissinger testified that he and Haig "turned off" support of a coup in an October 15 meeting. He was right in a narrow sense. The White House conveyed orders to one potential coup leader, former general Roberto Viaux, to stop any coup planning. Viaux was a hothead extremist, and the CIA was convinced that any coup led by him would be a colossal failure. Kissinger and Haig told the CIA to "de-fuse the Viaux coup plot, at least temporarily." The CIA cabled orders the next day to its officers in Chile ordering them to tell Viaux to stand down because a "coup attempt carried out by him alone with the forces now at his disposal would fail." But if Kissinger and Haig intended to turn off coups by plotters other than Viaux, they did not deliver a clear message to the CIA, and the agency's orders made it clear that coup planning had not been turned off. "It is a firm and continuing policy that Allende be overthrown by a coup."[60]

The CIA remained in touch with potential plotters, and the agency had advance notice of Pinochet's coup, but the committee found no evidence that the Nixon administration had played a roll in the coup. "Was the United States directly involved, covertly, in the 1973 coup in Chile? The Committee has found no evidence that it was."[61] After the coup the CIA provided assistance to Pinochet's security forces, despite a United Nations report that the new regime was running at least eleven torture centers. The agency drew a line at participating in actual internal political repression, but it had no qualms about providing assistance to those doing the repressing.[62]

The Church Committee issued a special report on the FBI's attempts to discredit Martin Luther King, Jr. The report was spurred by a series of stories about the agency by Ronald Kessler in the *Washington Post*, including the revelation that J. Edgar Hoover had kept files on the private affairs of members of Congress. From 1963 until 1968 the FBI conducted a campaign to "neutralize" King. The ostensible purpose of the project was to investigate reports that two of King's advisors were members of the Communist Party, but in reality the operation was the result of Hoover's hatred of the civil rights leader. The FBI installed wiretaps on Kings phones, with the approval of Attorney General Robert Kennedy after the FBI convinced him that several of King's advisors could be communists. After Johnson took office he allowed the investigation to continue because he wanted to be sure that he would not be embarrassed by King's background after he embraced the civil rights movement. The FBI hid microphones in sixteen of Dr. King's hotel rooms, it examined his tax returns, and it investigated his financial affairs.

Kennedy and Johnson approved the wiretaps, but not how the FBI used the results. The agency taped King's conversations about an illicit affair, played the tapes for reporters, and sent him a copy to try to convince him to retire from public life. The agency also circulated libelous documents about the civil rights leader, and Hoover sent agents to slur Dr. King to members of Congress and to Cardinal Spellman when King was planning to visit the Pope. The agency even gave Marquette University officials libelous information about Dr. King when the university was considering giving the civil rights leader an honorary degree. Hoover had received an honorary degree from Marquette, and he was horrified at the thought that the same institution would give a degree to King.[63]

The Church Committee dedicated a large section of its report to an issue that was relatively unimportant: the fact that one CIA employee had ignored President Nixon's order to destroy certain toxic materials. In treaty negotiations, Nixon had renounced the use of biological weapons, and he ordered all such weapons to be destroyed. Helms passed on the president's orders to the rest of the agency, but one middle-level CIA scientist ignored the order because he had gone to great lengths to get his hands on eleven grams of shellfish toxin and eight milligrams of cobra venom. Colby learned about the remaining toxins in 1975, and he reported the incident to the Church Committee.[64]

Church decided to hold his first public hearing on the issue because it served two purposes. First, it provided evidence that the CIA was a rogue agency because it was the only incident the committee found in which the agency ignored an order from a president. Church also decided to open hearings with the issue because he wanted to brandish a dart gun the agency had developed to use the toxins to disable guard dogs. He told his staff, "We need to begin hearings with something dramatic.... I want that gun there!"[65]

The biological toxin issue was a rare exception to the Church Committee's focus on important matters, like assassinations, coups, and domestic spying. In most matters the committee acted responsibly, and it did a great public service by presenting in detail the illegal and immoral activities that the CIA had undertaken — usually at the direction of senior executive branch officials — in the name of the American people.

The Pike Committee did not comport itself with the same integrity. Daniel Schorr has written that the House committee was as leaky as any he ever covered — a shocking comment considering the confidential information the committee had been given.[66] Schorr reported Kissinger's confidential testimony about the American support of a Kurdish uprising in Iraq, and Hersh reported secret testimony that the CIA was planning to give $6 million to the communists' opponents in the upcoming election in Italy. To be fair, the Pike Committee was not the only source of leaks. Classified testimony before the Rockefeller Commission was leaked to the press, including testimony that the CIA had used Mafia members in a plot to assassinate Castro. And Kissinger blamed Colby for leaks from the CIA.[67]

Ford was infuriated by the leaks, and he used a tragic event to turn public opinion against the people who were revealing the nation's secrets. Since the end of the Vietnam War, several disgruntled former agents had published books revealing classified information. Some, like Frank Snepp, wrote illuminating histories of important events. Others, like Philip Agee, were simply irresponsible. In 1975 Agee published *Inside the Company*, the story of his life in the agency, and he included a list of all the agents he could remember as an appendix to his book. The magazine *Counterspy* also started publishing lists of CIA agents, and the magazine's winter 1975 issue included the name of Richard Welch, an agent in Peru who had since moved to Athens, Greece. The *Athens News* picked up the *Counterspy* report and identified Welch as a CIA operative. Welch was aware that he had been named as a CIA agent, but he was not concerned. He was also aware that it was well known that the agency head of station in Athens lived in a particular house, but he decided to live there anyway. He was assassinated as he and his wife were walking home from a Christmas party.

The administration played Welch's death for all it was worth. Colby, Buchen, Lieutenant General Vernon Walters, and Assistant Secretary of State Arthur Hartman were on hand to greet the plane carrying his body back to Washington. Welch was given the honors of a soldier killed in war, and he was one of the few non-military men to be buried in Arlington Cemetery. Ford and Kissinger attended the funeral, and the network news showed moving footage of Welch's family during the ceremony. The murder turned public opinion back to support of the CIA.[68]

The fight between the administration and Pike flared up again over the committee's final report. Pike thought the report contained no legitimate secrets, but the CIA disagreed. At the end of January the agency and committee staff held marathon negotiating sessions, but Pike cut the negotiations short by claiming that his agreement not to release confidential information without approval of the administration somehow did not apply to the final report. On January 21, 1976, the committee voted to include classified information in the report, and two days later the committee voted 9 to 4 to release it. But before the report was finished, the committee was scheduled to expire on January 31, and Pike asked the House Rules Committee for a few more weeks to develop the committee's recommendations. On January 28 the Rules Committee gave Pike the extension, but it also ordered Pike not to disclose confidential information without administration approval. The issue then went to the floor of the House, which voted 246 to 124 to keep the report confidential until the White House agreed that it contained no classified information or a court decided the issue.[69]

Before negotiations with the administration resumed, the report leaked. The *New York Times* began quoting portions of the report on January 19, and it described in detail the report's conclusions in subsequent stories.[70] Daniel Schorr followed by displaying his copy of the report on *CBS News*. After the House vote, Schorr decided to publish his copy, but CBS refused to air the report. Schorr turned to the press, and the *Village Voice* published the report with the headline "The Report President Ford Doesn't Want You to Read." Schorr was fired by CBS.[71]

It was not right that he took the heat. Schorr did not violate any laws, and there is nothing unethical about a journalist publishing a leaked report. The committee staff member who leaked the report was a different matter, as Kissinger later admitted to Schorr. "I think you got a bum rap. The blame should fall on whoever leaked the report, not the journalist who received it."[72] The House asked its Ethics Committee to conduct an investigation. The committee interviewed every member of the Pike Committee staff, but it could not determine who leaked the report. The committee subpoenaed Schorr, but he refused to name his source. The hearing was tense until Tennessee Republican James Quillen said, "I understand your sincerity, Mr. Schorr, and I respect it." Mississippi Republican Thad Cochran echoed the sentiment. "I support you a hundred percent ... in your refusal to name your source." The committee voted 6 to 5 not to hold Schorr in contempt.[73]

The report did not merit the fight. Like the Church Committee report, the Pike Committee Final Report took issue with the idea that the CIA was a rogue agency. "All the evidence at hand suggests that the CIA, far from being out of control, has been utterly responsive to the instructions of the President and the Assistant to the President for National Security Affairs."[74] But most of the report was not very thoughtful; it simply chastised the CIA for failing to anticipate events without considering whether it was reasonable to expect an intelligence agency to predict them.

The report criticized the CIA for failing to predict the coup in Portugal, despite the fact that coups are extremely difficult to predict by anyone who has not been brought into the confidence of the plotters. The section on Cyprus was curious. The committee was harsh in its criticism of the failure to predict when a coup would take place against Makarios, despite its acknowledgement that the CIA had predicted a coup in time for Kissinger to send a message to the Greek leadership objecting to any such action.[75]

The report had similar criticism of the CIA's intelligence reports before the Tet Offensive in Vietnam. As the report acknowledges, the agency had predicted a large offensive, but it was not able to identify the specific date it would start or just how big the attack would be. The inability of the agency to anticipate the strength of the offensive was an intelligence failure, but such failures are common in wars, and the Pike Committee made little effort to evaluate whether the failure was due to a systemic problem within the agency. The report's analysis of the failure to predict the Soviet invasion of Czechoslovakia was similarly lacking in substance, although it did include the disturbing news that NATO had lost the Soviet force during the two weeks leading up to the invasion.[76]

The report's analysis of the failure to predict the Egyptian attack that started the Yom Kippur War did not take into account Sadat's ruse of faking an invasion on a regular basis in the months before the attacks, causing the United States and Israel to falsely predict an invasion several times. When the real attack came, the CIA thought that the movement of the Egyptian army was a normal maneuver.[77] The analysis was further marred by its gratuitous speculation that Kissinger "presumably" learned of Egyptian intentions during discussions with the Soviets and Arabs:

> Kissinger had been in close contact with both the Soviets and the Arabs throughout the pre-war period. He, presumably, was in a unique position to pick up indications of Arab dissatisfaction with diplomatic talks, and signs of an ever-increasing Soviet belief that war would soon break out. When the Committee was denied its request for high-level reports, it was unable to learn whether Kissinger elicited this information in any usable form. It is clear, however, that the Secretary passed no such warning to the intelligence community.[78]

Kissinger was incensed when he read this baseless conjecture, and he was even more furious about the section on SALT, which said that the secretary of state had issued misleading statements to cover for Soviet violations.[79] In a stormy press conference, he threatened to resign.[80] Kissinger was also furious about the report's section on the Kurds, who were fighting for independence from Iraq. When Nixon and Kissinger visited Tehran in May 1972, the Shah of Iran, who considered Iraqi leader Saddam Hussein an enemy, asked for support of the Kurdish uprising against Hussein. The United States began a $16 million covert operation in an attempt to show Iraq that "being a friend of the Soviet Union didn't pay off,"[81] but the final lesson of the program was that being a friend of the U.S. did not always pay off either.

The Shah betrayed the Kurds, leaving the United States with no option but to cut off aid. During a meeting in Zurich in March 1975, the Iranian leader told Kissinger that he had promised Hussein to cut off support for the Kurds in return for concessions in the Shatt-al-Arab Waterway that separated the two countries. Kissinger tried to talk him into allowing continued American support, but the Shah refused to allow any aid through Iran, which left the United States with no alternative because Turkey was fighting its own battle against the Kurds. On March 9 Kissinger told the Syrians that the Iranians would allow their border with Iraq to remain open for two more weeks, and that the Kurdish leaders would be given a choice of moving to Iran or staying in Iraq.[82] The next day Kissinger told Rabin that he asked the Shah not to sell out the Kurds, "but he did it anyway." He was noticeably upset. "I was shaken too by the Iranian decision. Because we had participated in it too. The brutality of it."[83] Two hundred thousand Kurds used the two week grace period to flee to Iran, but the Shah forced 40,000 of them to return. At the same time, Hussein destroyed all Kurdish villages within 12 miles of the Iranian border, and he forcibly moved up to half a million Kurds to the south, many of them to the desert. Kurdish leader Mustafa Barzani wrote to Kissinger that his "people are being destroyed in an unbelievable way."[84] Kissinger and Ford regretted the tragedy, but the Shah had given them no option. Rather than explain the situation to the Pike Committee, Kissinger became petulant that anyone was questioning his judgment, and he disdainfully replied, "Covert action should not be confused with missionary work."[85]

———

Ford asked Buchen's Intelligence Coordinating Group to come up with proposals for structural changes to the intelligence community. On Saturday, January 10, Ford met with his team to consider the ICG's proposals. Kissinger and Scowcroft fought against reforms, but it was Rockefeller who dominated the meeting. He urged a joint oversight committee of both houses of Congress, and Ford accepted the suggestion.[86]

On February 17 Ford held a press conference to announce Executive Order 11905, his new plan for oversight of intelligence. In his order Ford banned political assassinations, drug experiments on humans without consent, domestic spying by the CIA, infiltration of dissident groups, and public disclosure of confidential information by government employees. Within the executive branch, oversight was given to the Committee on Foreign Intelligence, led by the director of the CIA. Ford proposed a joint congressional committee to oversee intelligence, but each house wanted its own body.[87] The House voted to establish a Select Committee on Intelligence on February 19, and the Senate voted to establish its own oversight committee in May 1976.

———

The structural changes weren't as important as the investigations themselves. During scandals, leaders in Washington reorganize to prevent further scandals, or to at least look like they are doing something. But usually it is the scandals themselves that have the most impact. In the case of the CIA, the scandals reminded the agency that its future actions might see the light of day, and hopefully acted as a check on its conduct. At the same time, the scandal was demoralizing to agency employees, and many administration officials, including Cheney and Rumsfeld, were convinced that the CIA's effectiveness had been meaningfully undermined.

Kissinger shared their concern, but he made an important distinction between the effect on intelligence gathering and covert operations. In one of the administration's last NSC meetings he declared that the scandal had not affected the quality of intelligence, but covert operations were another story. "We are unable to do it anymore."[88] The term "covert operations" can mean two things: undercover intelligence-gathering and secret military operations. To the extent the investigations damaged the CIA's ability to conduct the former — traditional undercover operations using human spies — the results have been unfortunate. Human intelligence is necessary, and since the scandal the agency has become too reliant on electronic eavesdropping. Scowcroft believes that the investigations of 1975 damaged the ability of the agency to conduct undercover operations, which he believes is a real loss. He also recognizes that it is not necessarily a bad thing that the CIA has had a harder time conducting the second type of covert operations, secret military activities.[89]

The agency's covert operations have usually been tragic for the countries involved and deleterious to the long-term interests of the United States. The coup in Iran is a good example. Kermit Roosevelt riding a tank through the streets of Tehran to install the Shah may have been a heroic act of derring-do, but its results were disastrous for Iran and the rest of the Middle East, and America would reap a bitter harvest. By deposing Mossadegh in favor of the Shah, the United States eliminated a moderate path to reform in Iran and an example of democracy for the rest of the Middle East. After the coup the only alternative to the autocratic Shah was the theocratic ayatollah, and Iran would become a destabilizing force in the region. Likewise, the effects of America's subversion of Lumumba were catastrophic for the Congo. After being robbed blind by Mobutu, the people of the Congo have suffered through the most destructive war anywhere since World War II. In Latin America the consequences of the agency's support of coups in countries like Guatemala, Brazil, and Chile were not as horrific as in the Congo, but they were tragic. For decades South and Central America were no longer home to democracy — other than in several small countries like Costa Rica, dictators ruled.

The intelligence investigations tarnished the reputation of the United States by exposing the CIA's illegal, immoral, and anti-democratic activities, but it was those actions themselves that were the true source of the damage to America's image. The real cause of the damage were the spies who engaged in the acts and the presidents who ordered them. In any event, the damage that the investigations did to the reputation of the agency and the United States was outweighed by the fact that the American people deserved to know what its government was doing in its name, the need for transparency in a democratic government, and the beneficial effects of not having unchecked agents acting for the government. The investigations did not eliminate all possibility that presidents would use the agency to subvert the law at home or abroad, but they made the possibility less likely, and they signaled that such acts would ultimately see the light of day. That is no small accomplishment for a democracy in a dangerous world.

10

Sinai II Agreement

When Ford took office the Middle East had been at peace for only a short time. Just nine months before, the very existence of Israel had been threatened for the third time in its twenty-five year history when the Arab nations launched surprise attacks on Yom Kippur. In short order the Egyptians took over virtually all of the Israeli defensive positions in the Sinai, and the Syrians captured half of the Golan Heights. After these initial losses the Israelis turned the tide, trapping the Egyptian Third Army in the Sinai Peninsula. During the war, Sadat sent messages to the U.S. that he was not intending to destroy Israel, just recover Egyptian territory in the Sinai.

With his army trapped in the desert, Sadat agreed to hold his country's first unilateral talks with Israel, and he asked Kissinger to negotiate a cease fire and relief for his Third Army. Kissinger brokered a tenuous disengagement agreement in a round of "shuttle diplomacy," in which he flew back and forth between the combatants. Under the Sinai I Agreement, the Israelis withdrew to a line in the Sinai east of the Suez Canal, with a UN force occupying the positions between the Israelis and the Egyptians. Sadat signed the agreement over the objections of his advisors.[1] Kissinger was with the Egyptian president in Aswan when he signed the agreement, and Sadat gave the American secretary of state a message to deliver to Israeli prime minister Golda Meir. "I am today taking off my military uniform. I never expect to wear it again except for ceremonial occasions.... When I threatened war, I meant it. When I talk of peace now, I mean it."[2]

Sadat wanted to follow up the disengagement agreement by negotiating a treaty for the return of the Sinai, but Kissinger explained that the Israelis needed to be led to the overall agreement, and he proposed that they try to negotiate a series of agreements leading to the final treaty. During the Ford administration Kissinger would try another round of shuttle diplomacy to negotiate the next agreement on the road to peace. It was Kissinger at his best, flying tirelessly between Egypt and Israel to further his vision for peace in the region. He would use his formidable intellect to understand the long-term interests of the parties, his sense of humor to defuse tense situations, and his force of personality to develop trusting relationships with the Israeli and Arab leaders. Ford and Kissinger would lay the groundwork for the greatest triumph of the Carter presidency, the Camp David Peace Accords.

Kissinger played a masterful role in the peace talks, but it was Sadat who was the true visionary. He had gained stature with the early victories in the Yom Kippur War, and it was to humanity's benefit that he used his new popularity to secure a lasting peace. Like Ford when he pardoned Nixon, Sadat was able to see more clearly than his contemporaries what was in the best interests of his country. When he was negotiating with the Israelis, Sadat would show remarkable patience because understood that the Israelis needed to learn how to trust him and that eliminating decades of suspicion would take time. He understood that it was the peace agreement itself that was important, and the details did not matter in the long run. His generals never saw the big picture, and they fought for every inch, as did the Israelis.

Kissinger embraced a step-by-step approach to peace because it would minimize the role of the Soviets in the region. Kissinger thought of the Middle East in Cold War terms — Under Secretary Alfred Atherton explained that he was always "preoccupied with the fact that behind the Egyptians and the Syrians were the Soviets; behind the Israelis stood the United States."[3] His overriding goal was to minimize Soviet influence in the Middle East, and he was trying to convince the Arab states that they could get more by allying with the United States than the Soviet Union.[4] That effort was given a boost in 1972 when Sadat kicked out his Soviet military advisors. At the time, it looked like he asked the Russians to leave to have a free hand to attack Israel, but later it became apparent that he did it to pursue an independent foreign policy; so Kissinger happily agreed to help Sadat's plan. He also believed that the step-by-step approach had a better chance of succeeding than an attempt to settle all issues with all countries in the region, which was the favorite approach of the Soviets. The Soviets knew that they would have little influence in bilateral talks, so they were pushing for a Geneva conference of all parties, including the PLO, and Kissinger's goal was to delay the conference.[5]

—◦∿∿◦—

After Ford's meeting with Egyptian foreign minister Fahmy during the first week of his administration, the next step was Israeli prime minister Yitzhak Rabin's visit to Washington a month later. Rabin had taken office three months earlier when Prime Minister Golda Meir and Defense Minister Moshe Dayan resigned under intense criticism for failing to anticipate the Yom Kippur War. Rabin was taking a risk by even considering talks with Egypt because the Israeli people had little tolerance for concessions to the Arab states after the surprise attacks that started the war.

In their September meeting, Kissinger suggested that the Israelis accept Sadat's plan of bilateral negotiations. Rabin agreed to the proposal, but he warned that Israel would not give up "a piece of land" without getting "a piece of peace." Rabin also pressed for approval of Israel's recent arms request because his government was committed to replenishing its arms supplies after the Yom Kippur War, and the Israeli armed forces wanted to upgrade their technology to address vulnerabilities exposed during the war. At dinner that night Ford approved the request for arms, and Rabin asked Kissinger to visit in October.[6]

At Rabin's request, Kissinger visited the Middle East between October 9 and 15, making stops in Egypt, Israel, Jordan, Saudi Arabia, and Morocco. He toured the Arab states first to get an understanding of their willingness to negotiate, and he was encouraged by what he heard, but it was apparent that they would not make any significant proposals until the Arab League meeting later in the month. Kissinger was less encouraged after his visit to Israel. Rabin told him that Israel would not give up an inch of territory to an Arab state that had not lifted its state of belligerency. In return for non-belligerency, Rabin said that Israel would withdraw thirty to fifty kilometers; but when Kissinger asked for a map, the Israeli leader said it was too early to draw lines. Kissinger told Rabin that he saw "no hope" of any Arab nation lifting its state of belligerency. After the meeting Kissinger grumbled to Joe Sisco that Rabin was "shivering in fear.... It's a lost cause."[7]

The Arab League meeting on October 28 confirmed that bilateral negotiations between Egypt and Israel were the only viable option. The League formally endorsed the PLO as "sole legitimate representative of the Palestinian people," which meant that a Geneva Conference was not practical because many hard-line Arab states, and the USSR, would not attend unless the PLO had a seat at the table, and Israel would not show up to any conference that included the PLO. The resolution also meant that negotiations with Jordan were out of the picture, because King Hussein could not claim to represent the Palestinians. The League rejected Syrian president Hafez al-Assad's proposal that no state could sign a separate agreement with Israel, leaving Sadat free to start negotiations.

———⁂———

When Kissinger returned to the Middle East in November he learned that two issues would impede his attempts to broker a Sinai II agreement: whether Egypt would lift its state of belligerency and which country would control the Mitla and Giddi passes in the Sinai. The passes were 30 miles east of the Suez Canal, and they were choke points for any Egyptian attack on Israel. Kissinger's first stop was in Egypt, where Sadat insisted that Israel withdraw from the passes and demanded that Israel give up the Abu Rudeis and Ras Sudr oil fields on the Gulf of Suez, which were the most economically important installations in the Sinai but not strategically significant. When Kissinger passed on Israel's demand that Egypt lift its state of belligerency, Sadat explained that doing so would be viewed as treason in the Arab world, so he proposed a pledge that disputes between the countries would not be solved by military means.

Kissinger's next stop was in Israel, where he delivered the news that, while Sadat would not agree to lift Egypt's state of belligerency, he would commit to a series of practical steps that would be the equivalent of non-belligerency. Rabin rejected the proposal out of hand, and he declared that Israel would not give up the passes and oil fields unless Egypt formally lifted its state of belligerency. Kissinger pleaded with the Israeli leaders to drop the demand, but without formal non-belligerency, Yigal Allon offered only to withdraw twenty miles — ten miles short of the passes. When Kissinger returned to Egypt and passed on the offer, Sadat was furious, but Kissinger convinced him to allow the Americans to try an "exploratory" shuttle. After the trip, Kissinger told Ford that the Israelis' refusal to make any accommodation was killing any chance of a deal.[8]

When Kissinger returned for the exploratory shuttle on February 13, the Israeli position had not changed. Nevertheless, Rabin asked the Americans to return in three weeks for a full shuttle. Kissinger was surprised when he arrived in Damascus, where Syrian president Hafez al-Assad said that he would consider lifting Syria's state of belligerency in return for the Golan Heights.[9] When he returned to the White House, Kissinger told Ford that a strong leader of Israel could seize the moment. "If we had a leader in Israel, this could be easy — five to eight kilometers on the Golan would do it."[10]

———⁂———

The full shuttle began on March 7. Kissinger was accompanied by his assistant Peter Rodman, his spokesman Robert McCloskey, Under Secretary Joe Sisco, Assistant Secretary Roy Atherton, and his deputy Hal Saunders. Like Kissinger's earlier trips, the shuttle was grueling — Winston Lord called them "rollercoasters of hope and despair."[11] The American team crisscrossed the region in an old Boeing 707 which had been Air Force One for President Johnson, making frequent stops in Jordan, Syria, and Saudi Arabia, trying to build support for the peace process.

The American team would arrive at all hours of day or night and start marathon meetings as soon as they landed. Kissinger insisted on verbatim transcripts of the negotiations, so Atherton, Saunders, and McCloskey took turns taking notes, and they spent each night transcribing them. The team had a strategy memorandum for each country, and they would update the memoranda and prepare checklists for the next day's meetings. In the days before computers, all of this was done by retyping the entire document. Often the work was done on the plane rides between meetings.[12] Rabin has described the process from the Israeli standpoint:

> No sooner had my own schedule been arranged than everything was disrupted by Kissinger's schedule. He would leave at abnormal hours, arrive at even more eccentric times, and often meet us for marathon talks that ignored the difference between day and night. No matter when he turned up, though, Kissinger always looked as if he just had ten hours of sound sleep.[13]

Shimon Peres recalls that the Israeli team prepared for "another sleepless night" every time Kissinger was scheduled to arrive, and they thought that he arrived several hours late on purpose. Kissinger would start with a long dissertation "describing, in dire terms, how the situation had deteriorated" interspersed with "whimsical accounts of his own virtuoso diplomacy."[14] Kissinger often launched into long explanations of his strategic vision for the region, which he called "seminars." He also spent a lot of time explaining to both the Israelis and the Egyptians the political problems the other side faced.[15] Joe Sisco has said that Kissinger's performance of the shuttles was "absolutely remarkable":

> The rapport he struck with all of the Middle Eastern leaders of consequence is unparalleled. King Hussein had great confidence in him.... King Fahd was taken with Kissinger. Sadat had full confidence in Kissinger.... And Assad just looked forward to seeing Kissinger on all of these occasions. I've never seen in my entire career a case of better rapport that was established by a Secretary of State with leaders in the area during the disengagement agreement negotiating period. It was a remarkable feat.[16]

⁓∾⁓

The first stop of the shuttle was on the morning of March 8 at Sadat's winter home in Aswan, Egypt, where the American negotiating team met at the Presidential Palace with Sadat, Foreign Minister Fahmy, and Chief of Staff Abdel Ghani el-Gamasy. On the Egyptian side, Sadat focused on the big picture, while Fahmy and Gamasy fought for each little issue because they were "very critical, and very doubtful" about Sadat's plan for peace.[17] Gamasy produced a map of the Sinai showing proposed Egyptian and Israeli lines, which gave Egypt control of the passes. When Kissinger explained that the proposal wouldn't fly with the Israelis, Sadat asked him to get the Israelis to agree to some forward movement in the Egyptian line, and he stressed that the Israeli line must be east of the passes. Sadat refused to formally lift Egypt's state of belligerency, but he promised to settle all future disputes by peaceful means, and he agreed to a series of practical concessions, including a limit on Egyptian forces in the Sinai, a UN–patrolled buffer zone between Israeli and Egyptian forces, free passage for Israel-bound ships through the Suez Canal, and easing the boycott on firms that did business with Israel.[18]

The next day Kissinger flew to Damascus, where he met Assad at the Presidential Palace. The Americans were well aware that the Syrian dictator was a brutal tyrant, but they found him engaging nonetheless. He flashed a sense of humor that matched Kissinger's, and they shared jokes at the expense of their respective staff members. Assad enjoyed Kissinger's discourses on foreign policy, and the American team found him to be perceptive when he discussed the situation in the Middle East.[19] Joe Sisco has called Assad "probably the most intelligent, the shrewdest, toughest — negotiated every tree in every yard in Syrian-Israeli disengagement agreement; was the tactician as well as the strategist; Byzantine, attractive, and strong. A realist. Not anti–American. Rather scathing about the Soviets."[20] Assad told Kissinger that he opposed a separate peace between Egypt and Israel — he would only support an agreement that "takes place on all the fronts."[21]

That night Kissinger flew to Jerusalem, where the Israelis were on edge because, just days before, Fatah terrorists had landed on a Tel Aviv beach, seized the Savoy Hotel, and killed nine civilians and two soldiers when Israeli troops attacked. The attack, along with the recent memory of the Yom Kippur War, made the Israelis even less willing to give up an inch of territory. At dinner that night Kissinger told Rabin that "Sadat is quite determined to come to an agreement" and would not fight over details if the Israelis made a reasonable counterproposal. Rabin was skeptical that Sadat would really go it alone in the end, and he didn't trust the Egyptian leader, who had a history of betraying the Soviets, Nasser, and Assad.[22] Rabin gave Kissinger a list of seven conditions, two of which would doom the shuttle (emphasis from the original):

- It has to be a *step towards peace*, its meaning to be interpreted in wording and in some practical measures that give evidence that it is not just wording.
- It has to be in terms of putting an end to the *use of force* in the context of an interim agreement. Whatever the legal formula is — nonaggression, non-belligerency, whatever — it must be a declared public commitment towards Israel, between Egypt and Israel.[23]

The next morning the Americans met with the Israeli negotiating team, which included Rabin, Foreign Minster Yigal Allon, Chief of Staff Mordechai Gur, and Defense Minister Shimon Peres. Rabin was serious and humorless; Peres was outgoing; and Allon was personable and often flashed his sense of humor. The public perception was that Peres was dead-set against giving up any land, and Kissinger shared that view. The reality was more complex — the government's intransigence was the result of its weak political position, and Peres' opposition to Rabin was caused by their mutual dislike. Like Peres, Ford never warmed to Rabin.[24]

Kissinger started the meeting by showing Gamasy's map, and he explained that Sadat understood that the lines would not be acceptable but insisted that the Israeli line be east of the passes. Kissinger asked the Israelis to respond with a real offer and not follow their usual negotiating strategy of fighting for every inch. "Surprise him by your moderation. Don't ask for three times what you want; ask for 1½ times of your final position." After the meeting ended with a promise to meet again the next evening, Kissinger sent an upbeat message to Ford reporting that the Israelis' attitude was "positive, and they seemed to be willing to discuss matters seriously."[25]

Kissinger wasn't as impressed by the Israeli attitude the next evening, when he reported to Ford that there was "no decisive change in the Israeli position." Rabin had no concrete proposal for a withdrawal from the passes or the oil fields. The Israelis were still demanding that Egypt lift its state of belligerency, but they indicated that they could accept a promise not to use force. The other major point was the term of the agreement — Sadat was proposing a one year agreement that could be renewed annually, while the Israelis wanted it to last until another agreement took its place.[26] When he met with Rabin and the negotiating team the next morning, Kissinger learned that they had hardened in their demand that Egypt lift its state of belligerency. Rabin explained that he had not yet asked for cabinet approval of any specific proposal for a withdrawal because he was not certain he would like the result.[27]

Disheartened but willing to keep trying, Kissinger flew to Aswan to meet with Sadat on March 12 and 13. Kissinger gave Sadat a personal letter from Rabin expressing his strong desire to reach a peace agreement, and he later told Ford that the letter "moved Sadat to tears." But the Egyptian president was disappointed by the Israelis' refusal to propose a specific line for withdrawal. He told Kissinger that, as a fall-back position, he would consider allowing the Israelis to hold the eastern edge of the passes as long as the Egyptians could move to the western edge. The Israeli demand for non-belligerency vexed Sadat. He was willing to give up just about everything else, and he suggested numerous alternatives, including declaring that the interim agreement was a step toward peace, promising to settle all issues by peaceful means as long as the peace process continued, and renouncing the use of force for the term of the agreement. He accepted Rabin's proposal that the agreement would last until it was superseded by another agreement, and he offered to open the Suez Canal to ships bound for Israel.[28]

When Kissinger flew back to Israel the next day, he relayed Sadat's offer along with a personal message to Rabin. "We will not use force whatever the problems." Rabin promised to give a response two days later.[29] While he was waiting, Kissinger flew to Damascus and promised Assad that the Americans would attempt to resolve the status of the Golan Heights once an agreement was reached on the Sinai.[30] That night Kissinger flew to Amman, Jordan, for dinner with King Hussein. Hussein told Kissinger that the Russian ambassador had been pushing for a Geneva Conference, but that he would not support one. Foreign Minister Rifai promised to "let Gromyko try for a year and a half."[31]

On the evening of the 16th the Israelis gave Kissinger their response, but they again refused to withdraw to a specific line. Rabin explained that the problem was that his cabinet would not accept anything less than non-belligerency. "If we can talk about non-belligerency, we can find a solution to the territorial issue…. We don't reject Gamasy's idea about the passes…. But we can't consider it unless we can hear a statement to the criminal world that there is an end to belligerency." Kissinger explained that non-belligerency was an impossible demand, and the meeting ended. The next day Rabin promised to try to convince the cabinet to accept a commitment "not to resort to the use of force and to resolve all disputes between them by negotiations and other peaceful means and they will refrain from all military or paramilitary actions." He authorized Kissinger to offer a withdrawal from the passes and oil fields in return for that language, but to make clear that any deal was subject to approval by the cabinet.[32]

That night Kissinger flew back to Aswan, where Sadat introduced his new vice president, Hosni Mubarak, whose blue air force uniform indicated that he was there to protect the interests of the military. Sadat was discouraged by the Israeli offer, and he complained that the Israelis "either cannot or do not want to settle." The next morning he tried one more time to address the Israeli demands. He agreed not to condition the pledge not to use force on progress in the peace talks, and to make the pledge both directly to the Israelis and in a letter to the American president.[33] Before he flew back to Israel the next day, Kissinger sent a message to Ford predicting that the shuttle would fail as a result of Israel's refusal to propose a specific line. He recommended that the president send a message to the Israelis warning that failure of the shuttle would "require an overall reassessment of the policies of the U.S. that has brought us to this point."[34]

When he got to Israel and relayed Sadat's offer, Kissinger waited two days for an Israeli response; but it was not worth the wait — the Israelis were still demanding a formal renunciation of belligerency. The Israelis said that they were willing to withdraw to the "middle" of the passes, but they refused to provide a map showing what that meant. After the meeting adjourned, Rabin met with his cabinet for ten hours.[35] The next morning Kissinger learned that the cabinet was still insisting on non-belligerency. The really disappointing news came when Rabin proposed the withdrawal line — the cabinet would agree only to withdraw to the middle of the passes, and Rabin said that the cabinet had no inclination to budge an inch further. Kissinger was blunt in his assessment of the offer. "There will not be an agreement." He said that President Ford had authorized him to say that the Israeli position would force the United States into an "overall reassessment of the policies of the U.S. that has brought us to this point."

At a meeting later that day the news was even worse. When Kissinger asked Rabin to show him the middle of the passes on a map, the prime minister pointed to a line that was closer to the western end than the middle. Rabin said that he told the cabinet that there was a 98 percent chance that the talks would break down. Allon, on the other hand, predicted that Sadat would take the offer. He told Kissinger, "You'll come back tomorrow with a smiling face."[36] In his report to Ford, Kissinger told Ford that the Israelis were "jeopardizing our entire position in the Middle East in the pursuit of entirely marginal points."[37] The report made Ford "mad as hell."[38]

When he got to Aswan late that night, Kissinger found nothing to smile about. Sadat was dejected — he did not consider the Israeli offer a serious attempt to settle.[39] When Kissinger returned to Israel on the 21st, he gave an emotional speech declaring the end of the shuttle. Rabin told Kissinger that the cabinet would meet that afternoon, but he would not recommend accepting Sadat's latest offer. Kissinger told the Israeli prime minister that the negotiations had reached an impasse, and the United States would not participate in any further negotiations.[40] During the cabinet meeting, Rabin received a letter from Ford warning that if the negotiations broke down, the United States would be forced to undertake a "reassessment" of its Middle Eastern policy. The letter alarmed the cabinet members, but it did not change the outcome — they refused to approve any new offers.[41]

The next day the State Department issued a statement that was carefully written to scare the living daylights out of the Israelis. "We, therefore, believe a period of reassessment is needed so that all concerned can consider how best to proceed toward a just and lasting peace."[42] The shuttle formally ended on March 23, and Kissinger broke into tears as he said goodbye from the Ben-Gurion Airport. As he watched Kissinger's plane flying away, Rabin thought to himself that he still "entertained a special regard and affection for that very unusual man."[43] Ford made a point to personally greet Kissinger when his helicopter landed at the White House that evening.

—◦◦◦—

Kissinger was furious because he thought that Israel's failure to provide a specific proposal doomed the shuttle, but he was expecting too much from the new leader of Israel's unwieldy democracy. Rabin could not command his cabinet, much less the Knesset, and after the recent terrorist attack and the surprise attacks that launched the Yom Kippur War, most Israelis were opposed to giving up any ground. There was little chance that any Israeli leader could have made a significant proposal at that point in time. In his frustration, Kissinger had convinced Ford to conduct a very public "reassessment" of America's relationship with Israel. There was no dissent within the administration to Kissinger's plan. Schlesinger proposed a policy of "dignified aloofness" from Israel. "We cannot allow Israel to continue its relationship with us as if there were no problems." Colby said that war was likely if negotiations did not resume, and Kissinger agreed.[44]

The administration took a few symbolic actions to turn up the heat. On May 15, Ford ordered suspension of some arms deliveries to Israel, but he clarified that "I have no apprehension about the vigor of our commitment to their security.... I reiterate my dedication to the survival of Israel, period."[45] Kissinger cut off the Israeli defense attaché's access to the Pentagon. He also replaced Ambassador to Israel Ken Keating with Malcolm Toon, who had developed a reputation for toughness when he was ambassador to Czechoslovakia and Yugoslavia. Kissinger told Toon to publicly explain that the United States was developing relations with moderate Arab states, and it might provide weapons to them.[46]

—◦◦◦—

The prospects for peace brightened when Ford met with Sadat in Austria at the start of June. The Egyptian leader started the conversation by declaring that he would never invite the Soviets back under any circumstances. He asked if the Americans had any new ideas, but Ford could offer none. Sadat silently puffed on his pipe, and then he came up with one of his own. He suggested that the Israelis might accept a buffer zone in the passes if it was guarded by Americans. He asked Ford and Kissinger to find out if the Israelis were interested. "We are willing to go as far as you think we should go. We trust you, and we trust the United States."[47] Kissinger was excited about the idea, and he told Ford that it might even be used to settle the Syrian problem. "The monitoring station will be a breakthrough. We could perhaps do the same on the Golan for the hills behind Quneitra. If we could do that by November we would have the Middle East defused and might never have to go to Geneva."[48]

At Ford's invitation, Rabin visited Washington on June 11. Before he talked to the president, Rabin met with Kissinger at Blair House to clear the air. After Kissinger vented about being misled during the shuttle, and Rabin railed at the "reassessment," they both calmed down and agreed to focus on the future. When they met with Ford in the White House the Israeli leader asked if the Americans had any ideas that could lead to a breakthrough. Ford responded that there was "one suggestion we have been considering," and he explained the idea of using American civilians to monitor the passes, without telling him that it was an Egyptian idea. Rabin liked it. The next night Kissinger, Sisco, and Rodman met with Rabin and Simcha Dinitz at Blair House. Rabin said that Israel was willing to return the oil fields and withdraw to the eastern edge of the passes, with a UN force between the armies for a four-year period. This time the Israelis had a map, which they rolled out to show the proposed line in the passes. Rabin claimed it was at the eastern end, but it was clearly in the middle of the pass, and Kissinger called it unacceptable.

That night the CIA noticed that the proposed Israeli line around the oil fields returned the wells in production to Egypt, but not the reserves. To make matters worse, Oakley and Saunders looked at the Israeli proposal for two roads to the oil fields, one for Israel and one for Egypt, and they noticed that the Egyptian road would be under water at high tide. When they explained the problems to Kissinger he "went up the wall" and demanded an explanation from Rabin and Allon. "I know that we Jews in the U.S. pull deals like this, but I didn't expect you Israelis to do anything like that!" It was apparent that Rabin and Allon had no idea that they had proposed a submerged road. After conferring with their experts, they proposed a joint road to be used by both the Egyptians and Israelis.[49] The next day Ford called Rabin and told him he was disappointed by the proposal, and Kissinger met with him and explained that the Egyptians would never accept the line as proposed by the Israelis.[50]

A few days later Rabin's military assistant, Ephraim Poran, delivered a new map to Kissinger. The line in the passes had not substantially changed, and Kissinger told Ambassador Dinitz that the Israeli position was an "outrage." Kissinger told Ford that the line would be unacceptable to Egypt, and he added his own paranoid interpretation. "I think they have decided to bring you down. That to me is clear."[51] As Kissinger predicted, Sadat was furious when he saw the line, and he accused the Americans of pampering Israel in a June 25 letter to Ford. Ford followed with a letter to Rabin on June 27 asking the Israelis to reconsider their decision by July 11, when Kissinger was scheduled to meet with Gromyko. If the Israelis refused to change the decision, Kissinger would agree to a Geneva conference.[52]

The Israelis got the point, and they sent Ambassador Dinitz to the Island of St. John to personally deliver a new proposal to a vacationing Kissinger. Dinitz brought a topographical map, again showing a line that Kissinger thought was unacceptable. But Dinitz had promising news — he reported that Defense Minister Peres proposed a series of four American monitoring stations on the roads to the passes. The proposal was an important signal that Peres, who at that time was considered to be the Israeli leader most opposed to the negotiations, was willing to support a deal with Egypt.[53] When Kissinger briefed Ford on July 8, Ford approved the idea of American warning stations, although he wanted to limit the number of Americans in harm's way.[54]

Kissinger asked Saunders to verify that the Israeli proposal put their line at the eastern edge of the passes. Experts from the National Photo Intelligence Center came to Saunders' office and spread photographs all over the floor. When they sketched out the Israeli proposal, it was apparent that the Egyptian line was nowhere near the passes, while the Israeli line was in the center of the passes. Kissinger told Sisco to meet with Dinitz and warn him that the proposal better be fixed before the shuttle. On July 18, Dinitz gave Kissinger a new map, which moved the Egyptian line to the edge of the passes, but the Israeli line was still well within the passes.[55]

Kissinger returned to the Middle East on August 20, and David Kennerly joined the trip, which he called "a brutal affair, physically as well as psychologically."[56] The first stop was Jerusalem, where the Americans met with the Israeli negotiating team in the Prime Minister's residence. The parties had agreed on the basic structure of an agreement in which they would each be just outside of the end of each pass, with American monitors in between, but they had not agreed on the number of monitoring stations, the line to the north of the passes, and the location of the Israeli line at the end of the Giddi pass. Kissinger tried to get the Israelis to agree to fewer than six warning stations, because Sadat and Ford wanted, at most, three. He suggested two manned stations and four remote unmanned stations, but the Israelis wanted all stations to be manned by Americans.

The American intelligence agencies had built a model of the passes, and Kissinger had his aides pull it out along with a large map. He related that Sadat was skeptical when he first saw the line, but he asked the administration to "send an American there and let the American tell whether it is in or out of the passes." Kissinger explained that the American survey team "came to the same conclusion that Sadat did. There is no other conclusion that you can come to." American and Israeli aides began crawling on the huge map on the floor and discussed the lines, foot by foot. Rabin finally leveled with Kissinger by explaining that in Israel's "overly-democratic state" they could not propose a different line because of political pressure. Kissinger relented, and he agreed to bring the proposal to Sadat.[57] Kissinger reported to Ford that the Israelis wanted to reach an interim agreement, but he said the desire was "grudging not generous."[58]

That afternoon Kissinger flew to Sadat's summer palace in Alexandria, where he met for four hours with Sadat, Mubarak, Fahmy, and Gamasy. The negotiating teams met at a long wooden table beside the ocean, wearing shorts and tropical shirts. According to Kissinger's report to Ford, the talks were "warm and cordial." Sadat accepted the Israeli proposal on the Mitla Pass because it could be considered outside of the pass, but he told Kissinger that if he accepted the line in the Giddi Pass he would become the laughing stock of the Arab world. Sadat said that six American warning stations were out of the question, but he agreed to two American warning stations and two more stations to be "managed" by the Americans but operated by each country.[59]

On Saturday, August 23, Kissinger flew to Damascus to "keep Assad calm."[60] Kissinger was not surprised when Assad rejected the Israeli proposal for the Golan Heights. The Syrian leader also admitted that, during the March shuttle, "We did our bit to make your mission fail."[61] The American team continued on to Tel Aviv and met with the Israeli negotiating team that night. Allon and Kissinger were good friends, and the Israeli foreign minister got a rise out of Kissinger by declaring that the Helsinki Accords confirmed Soviet control over Eastern Europe. After Kissinger fought back, Allon laughed. "I knew that would make you mad!" The meeting was unproductive, with only progress being made on the corridor to the oil fields. After the meeting ended at midnight, the Americans were taken to Jerusalem by helicopter.[62]

The next day, the Americans met with the Israeli negotiating team in the prime minister's office. The Israelis started by putting a large map on the wall, and Allon jokingly said, "Now you will see Israeli generosity." The Egyptians had asked for territory in northern Sinai that they had failed to take during the war. Rabin told Kissinger that the symbolic meaning of the territory precluded giving it back to the Egyptians, but he agreed to let the UN take the area. In the Giddi pass the Israelis offered to move their line 500 meters. Kissinger and the Israelis argued about whether the new line was out of the pass. It was the most that Israel was willing to move, and they gave Kissinger a map with the new proposal.[63]

Kissinger flew to Aswan and met with the Egyptians the next day. He later told the Israelis that Sadat greeted the map "with disdain," and the mood of the meeting remained ugly. Kissinger asked to see Sadat alone, and he explained that he understood his frustration, but someone had to stop the haggling. As usual, Sadat was able to see the bigger picture, and he asked Gamasy and Fahmy to come up with an alternative for the monitoring stations. Gamasy came back and talked through the new proposal with Kissinger. At the same time, Fahmy met with Sisco and hammered out a draft agreement. The next day Kissinger reported to Ford that the parties had "agreement on the map."[64]

The Americans flew to Jerusalem the next day, and they met with the Israeli negotiating team until midnight. Kissinger presented the draft agreement and Sadat's proposals. The Israelis thought they could concede on the monitoring stations, but they wanted to discuss the proposals by themselves.[65] The following day the Americans met with the Israelis for six hours, and the Israelis had a positive answer on the monitoring stations. The bad news was the Israelis' objections to the draft agreement — particularly the non-use-of-force language — and they gave the Americans a red-lined proposal with numerous changes. Kissinger told Rabin that the Egyptians were "on a ragged edge," and the changes could kill the shuttle.[66]

That afternoon the Americans flew back to Aswan. As expected, the Egyptians were irritated by the number of changes to the agreement, but they swallowed their frustration and accepted what they could. When Gamasy again pushed to move the Israeli line in the Giddi pass, Kissinger told him it wasn't possible, and Sadat put an end to the discussion. The Americans returned to Israel the next day, where the public debate was ominous. Moshe Dayan had spoken out against the agreement, and Peres appeared to be wavering in his support. The following day the Israelis gave Kissinger another red-lined version of the agreement. To work out the remaining few issues, Kissinger flew back and forth between Israel and Egypt over the next three days.[67]

On the evening of the 31st the American and Israeli negotiating teams met in a marathon session that began at 10:00 and ended at 5:30 the next morning. By the end of the meeting, most of the participants had fallen asleep, but Kissinger and Rabin continued to talk through the snoring. When Kissinger told Rabin that Fahmy was "carrying on like a Banshee" about the language promising not to use force, Peres finally consented to the latest Egyptian language. "In order to express our appreciation and affection for the Secretary, we won't go to war on this single issue."[68] That was it — the deal was done.

At the same time, the negotiating teams were finishing two side letters between the

United States and Israel. In the first the Americans agreed to sell arms to Israel, and in the second the U.S. promised not to negotiate with the PLO until it recognized Israel's right to exist. During the shuttle, Sisco had negotiated the letters with the Israeli staffers, and other members of the American team had objected to some of the terms, but Kissinger seemed to ignore the criticism. His plan became clear on that final night when he told the Israelis that the letters had to be renegotiated. He knew that the Israelis were committed, and they had no choice but to make concessions they would not have considered in the days before. It wasn't fair to Sisco, but it worked. Atherton spent the night renegotiating the letters with the Israelis, while Kissinger popped in to make decisions during breaks in his meeting with Rabin. In the final letters the United States guaranteed large amounts of sophisticated military supplies to Israel, promised not to negotiate with the PLO until they recognized Israel's right to exist, and committed to give "great weight" to Israel's need to occupy the Golan Heights in any future negotiations.[69]

When all the agreements were complete, the American team got only an hour of sleep before the signing ceremony with the Israelis. Immediately after the ceremony they boarded a plane for Alexandria, where a big table was set up on the lawn of Sadat's palace for the signing ceremony. After Fahmy signed the agreement, the exhausted Americans were looking forward to sleeping, when Sadat announced dinner. They barely stayed awake for the fresh shrimp, fish, and mangos.[70]

—⁓—

Sadat wasted little time before he pushed Israel to take the next step toward peace. When he visited Washington at the end of October 1975, he told Kissinger that he would consider a peace agreement in return for an Israeli withdrawal from the Sinai to within 25 kilometers of the Israeli border, and Kissinger promised to raise the idea with Rabin. It took the Israelis some time to respond, but in February 1976 Kissinger received word from Ambassador Simcha Dinitz that the Israeli cabinet had approved a plan to offer to withdraw to 25 kilometers within its 1967 borders. The problem was that the cabinet had redrawn the line so that Israel would keep a third of the Sinai Peninsula. Kissinger knew that Sadat would reject the line, but the concept was more important than the details at that point, and he passed the proposal to Sadat on March 11. As he expected, Sadat rejected the proposal, but he wanted to keep the process moving.[71]

On November 19, 1975, Ford met with Syrian ambassador Richard Murphy and offered to begin to mediate negotiations on the Golan Heights, and at the end of January Kissinger made the same offer to Rabin, who was visiting Washington. Rabin was favorably inclined, but he reiterated that a lifting of belligerency would be the prerequisite of any deal. Rabin also proposed a peace agreement with all states in which Israel would withdraw to 25 kilometers from its 1967 borders. If the other states did not agree — and neither Rabin nor Kissinger thought they would — Sadat would have a pretext to proceed with his own agreement.[72] The groundwork had been laid for renewed discussions between Israel and Egypt. But before any further progress could be made, the entire Middle East became consumed with a civil war in Lebanon.

—⁓—

The Lebanese civil war was a reflection of how the power relations in the Middle East could create strange allies, as Israel and Syria cooperated to support the Christians in Lebanon. Despite the fact that they were no longer the majority in the country, the Christian Maronites had the senior position in a power-sharing agreement with the Muslims in the country. The president was a Christian, who appointed a Sunni Muslim as prime minister, while the Speaker of the Parliament was a Shiite. Most of the officers in the armed forces were Christians, but the contending groups each fielded a militia that was more powerful than the army. The Israelis supported the Christian Maronites, who also had the support of Assad. This unstable arrangement could not survive when the PLO set up shop in southern Lebanon after they were kicked out of Jordan.

A civil war had been raging since the spring of 1975 when the Maronite militia boarded a bus filled with Palestinians and killed all 27 passengers; and the Israelis used the spreading war as an excuse to bomb PLO camps in the south of the country. The war flared up again in December 1975 when the Christian militias responded to the death of four Christians by setting up roadblocks, pulling Muslims out of cars and hacking them to death. The entire Middle East was almost dragged into the war when Saudi King Khalid declared that his country would support Syrian mediation of the conflict. Rabin responded by declaring that Israel would oppose any outside intervention in Lebanon, and Sadat declared that Egypt would not "stand by handcuffed" if Israel invaded. An uneasy truce was established on January 22, 1976, after Assad brought the parties together and strong-armed them into an agreement. Assad may have brokered the agreement, but he did not honor it. The Syrians created the Palestine Liberation Army, nominally as part of the PLO, but really as cover to begin infiltrating Syrian troops into Lebanon. On January 28, Rabin told Ford that if the Syrian army invaded, Israel would respond by sending its army into southern Lebanon.[73]

Full-scale fighting flared up again in early March when the Sunni leader in Beirut proclaimed himself the governor of Lebanon and demanded that Christian president Sulieman Frangieh step down. On March 14 the chief of the Syrian army told American ambassador Richard Murphy that the only way to solve the crisis was for the Syrian army to "enter and take up positions to ensure Lebanon's border remained calm."[74] The discussion put the administration in a difficult situation — the Americans were opposed to a Syrian invasion of Lebanon, but their greater concern was to prevent a war between Syria and Israel. As Kissinger later explained, if Israel moved into Lebanon in response to a Syrian invasion, Syria would attack Israel, and the entire region could go to war. Rather than forcefully opposing Syrian infiltration, the administration acted as a go-between between Syria and Israel in an attempt to prevent a larger war.[75]

Murphy met with Assad and passed on President Frangieh's request for Syrian military support, and the Syrian leader replied that "we would not be Arabs if we did not extend the helping hand to our brothers."[76] A few days later Assad sent the Americans a note asking them not to oppose a military intervention by his troops. When the administration briefed the Israelis, Rabin replied that if the Syrians intervened, Israel would occupy southern Lebanon "as quietly as they can." Rabin also sent a memorandum which tacitly recognized that Syrian troops were already in the country and declared that an Israeli response would be triggered by the entry of any Syrian force above a brigade. The memorandum also indicated that the Israelis would respond if Syrian forces moved below the line ten kilometers south of the axis between Damascus and Beirut. The line became known as the "Red Line," and it delineated the respective Israeli and Syrian spheres of influence for decades.

The results were not all positive for Israel. Faced with Syrian attacks in the north, the PLO forces fled south, where the Syrians could not follow. The effect of the Israeli policy was to protect the PLO from Syria, but Israel preferred having PLO terrorists on its borders to Syrian troops. The situation stayed the same for the next few months — Syria continued to infiltrate its forces into Lebanon, but they stayed above the Red Line, and Israel did not respond.[77]

As March came to a close, Kissinger recommended that Ford send a special emissary to Lebanon, and Ford agreed to name Dean Brown, a respected former State Department officer who was the president of the Middle East Institute. King Hussein was visiting Washington at the time, and Brown went to Andrews Air Force Base to meet Hussein's plane. When Kissinger saw Brown, he asked him to drive to Foggy Bottom after the reception. Brown arrived at the State Department building, and Kissinger came right to the point. "Why don't you go to Beirut? ... Why don't you see if you can go out there and talk to those people and see if you can have some influence." When Brown accepted, Kissinger proposed that he leave that afternoon, and Brown flew out as "special envoy and representative of the president."[78] It was a dangerous post. After two of his cars were shot at, Brown "always drove with a pistol aimed at the driver, and a bodyguard, whom I didn't trust at all." [79] Brown had signed on for only a short stint, and he suggested a colleague, Frank Meloy, for his replacement.[80]

Brown tried to convince the contending parties to obey the cease fire, but Syria was determined to enter its neighbor in force. Assad manipulated the Lebanese political process to gain approval for his intervention. On May 8 the Lebanese National Assembly named Syria's favorite candidate, Elias Sarkis, the new president, but President Frangieh refused to resign. With this political cover, the Syrians invaded Lebanon in late May.[81]

On June 16 the new American ambassador, Francis Meloy, and his economic counselor Robert Waring disappeared, along with their driver. They had been abducted by a Palestinian terrorist group, and they were later found dead on a Beirut beach. That day Ford met with his National Security Council, and he was told that the ambassador and Waring were apparently dead. Ford ordered naval ships to steam toward Beirut for a possible evacuation.[82] At 5:50 the next evening Ford met in the Cabinet Room with his foreign policy advisors, who told him that the murder of Meloy might be a start of targeting of other Americans, and the French, British, and UN were evacuating. Ford was given several options: a convoy to drive overland to Damascus; a short convoy to Jounieh Bay followed by a navy evacuation; an airlift to waiting ships from the Beirut airport; an airlift from the American University; or a navy evacuation from the Beirut beaches.[83]

Kissinger had asked Dean Brown, who had just returned from his stint as special ambassador to Lebanon, to attend the NSC meeting. The secretary of state presented the plan that the military had developed for an evacuation, which required five squadrons of fighters to escort a convoy to Damascus. Kissinger then said, "Mr. President, Dean looks very skeptical." Brown explained that battleships and planes would not add protection. "Beirut doesn't operate the way other places do. What happens is, some guy gets out of a taxi cab, opens the trunk, pulls out a mortar, fires five shots at you, puts the mortar back in the taxi cab, and leaves. So then your offshore ships and your bombers bomb where he was, and he's in somebody else's neighborhood." Brown proposed an alternative plan:

> Here's the embassy. See this beach right here? That's the old polo ground. That's under the control of Arafat's Fatah. Those are the people that guard the embassy area. Just take some barges, landing craft ships, announce in advance that you're coming in with the American flag flying with no arms on board. None. You're just coming in to take off the Americans right off the beach there. Run them right up on the beach. They'll all come there, they'll get there.

Ford looked at Deputy Secretary of Defense Clements and said, "Well, this is no time to be macho. Do what he says." After the meeting, Kissinger told Brown, "Good job. That's what I wanted you to do." Apparently, he had invited Brown to bring some reality to the military plan.[84]

When Ford decided to evacuate all Americans in Beirut, the plan required the administration to deviate from its stated policy by dealing with the PLO. At the request of the

Ford discusses the evacuation of Lebanon with the National Security Council — which includes
George H.W. Bush (at left, leaning across table) and Nelson Rockefeller (at Ford's right, also lean-
ing across table) — on June 17, 1976. (Photograph by David Hume Kennerly; courtesy Gerald R.
Ford Library.)

United States, the Egyptians contacted the PLO, who agreed not to obstruct the evacuation.
Nessen announced the evacuation on June 18, and the administration invited all 1,400 Amer-
icans in the country to leave. Just over 350 people chose to leave, including 116 Americans.
They were evacuated without incident.[85]

In June 1976 the civil war flared up again when Syrian troops assisted the Christian militias in attacking PLO camps in the north, while the Israelis attacked PLO camps in the south.
The PLO appealed to its supporters, Egypt and the Soviet Union, but they took no military
action. All the Soviets did was to tell Assad to stop the attacks and threaten to cut off military aid. The situation became far less dangerous in October when Egypt and Syria signed
the Riyadh accords, in which Egypt agreed not to become involved in Lebanon, and Syria
agreed to refrain from interfering in Yemen.[86] The civil war died down, but the country would
be torn apart over and over again during the following decades.

Ford's record on the Middle East was impressive. He and Kissinger worked diligently to
diffuse tensions in the area, and they were largely successful. Ford usually accepted Kissinger's
advice on strategy, but that was because they agreed on what needed to be done, not because
the president wasn't engaged. Ambassador to Israel Malcolm Toon was impressed with Ford's
grasp of strategy. "Not only was he a very fine guy, but a guy that showed very good understanding of the problems in the Middle East."[87] Kissinger has praised Ford's performance:

When he became President, Gerald Ford re-started the peace process in the Middle East. He was
also responsible for the second disengagement agreement between Egypt and Israel, which, for the

first time since the creation of the State of Israel in 1948, introduced political elements, and not simply military elements, in the relationship between Arab nations and Israel. This laid the basis for the peace agreement which was signed by President Carter in 1979.[88]

He was right to praise Ford's efforts, and Kissinger deserved praise as well. Kissinger saw the opportunity to start the peace process between Egypt and Israel, and the eventual result was the Camp David Peace Accords. The underlying issues in the Middle East remained. The Palestinians would continue fighting Israel for control over the country, and democracy would not come to the Arab nations, but Israel's existence would be more secure, and the danger of region-wide war would be greatly reduced. Without Egypt's support, Israel's neighbors would never again invade.

11

The Fall of South Vietnam and Cambodia

The country was at peace when Ford took office, thanks to the agreement Nixon and Kissinger brokered in January 1973 which allowed the country to disengage from Vietnam. The agreement gave peace to Southeast Asia in name only. The communists were allowed to maintain 150,000 troops in South Vietnam, and it was apparent that Hanoi was treating the peace as a cease fire to be broken when convenient. Across the border in Cambodia the communist Khmer Rouge had never agreed to stop fighting, and the government was barely hanging on. At the start of 1975 the communists abandoned all pretense of peace, launching major offenses in Vietnam and Cambodia. Ford could only sit by and watch as America's allies crumbled and fell in a matter of months. He was restrained by Congress from taking any military action and even from sending more aid to America's allies. America's failure to support its allies during the first few months of 1975 was not honorable, but by that point the United States was probably incapable of making a difference.

Ultimately, the governments of South Vietnam and Cambodia were responsible for their own undoing. In both countries the United States was allied with corrupt and antidemocratic leaders. The Kennedy administration had supported the coup that brought Nguyen Van Thieu to power in Vietnam, but American leaders never had much respect for him. At the time of the coup, Assistant Secretary of State William Bundy called him "the bottom of the barrel, absolutely the bottom of the barrel."[1] Thieu was a proud soldier with a thin smile, and he would dominate South Vietnamese politics until the very end, rigging elections and squelching all dissent. In Cambodia the United States had enthusiastically embraced Lon Nol when he ousted Prince Norodom Sihanouk in 1970, and American support never wavered for the thoroughly corrupt and completely incompetent Cambodian president.

Thieu may have been incompetent, but he was smart enough to understand that the Paris Peace Accords wouldn't bring peace. Nixon had to strong-arm him into signing the peace agreement, and he told the Americans that the provision allowing 150,000 communist troops to remain in the South doomed his country. His opponents in the North were convinced to sign the agreement by China. Zhou Enlai told a visiting Vietnamese delegation to "let the Americans leave. The situation will change in six months or one year."[2] North Vietnamese leader Le Duan accepted the recommendation. "You have advised us to solve the problem of US withdrawal first and solve the Saigon problem later. We think this is correct."[3]

Cambodia didn't receive even a temporary reprieve from the Paris Peace Accords. Kissinger claimed that the North Vietnamese had made commitments to restrain the Cambodian communists, but they denied making any such promises.[4] Whether they made such commitments was beside the point. The Khmer Rouge were not a party to the agreement, and the North

Vietnamese had virtually no influence over them. Despite the view in Washington that the Vietnamese and Cambodian communists worked in tandem, the reality was that the Khmer Rouge took orders from nobody, and they never agreed to stop fighting.

Nixon and Kissinger intended to respond to breaches of the accords with renewed bombing, and Nixon sent a letter to Thieu promising as much. "You have my absolute assurance that if Hanoi fails to abide by the terms of this agreement it is my intention to take swift and severe retaliatory action."[5] To the extent that Nixon intended to defy popular opinion and resume bombing, his ability to do so was eliminated when Congress banned further military action in Southeast Asia. In July 1973 Congress cut off funding for the bombing of Cambodia or the use of ground troops in that country, and at the end of the year Congress prohibited the use of funds for military actions "in or over or from off the shores of North Vietnam, South Vietnam, Laos, or Cambodia."[6]

———~~~———

Hamstrung by Congress and enmeshed in Watergate, Nixon took no action when the communists broke the letter and spirit of the accords. When the North Vietnamese refused to withdraw from Cambodia and Laos in the months after the peace, Nixon did not approve Kissinger's request to send B-52s against North Vietnamese bases in those countries, and Nixon did not respond when Hanoi continued to send troops and arms into the South.[7]

The violations were not limited to the communists. Thieu refused to cooperate in establishing the new National Council required by the agreement, and he was the first to resume military operations in the fall of 1973. The North Vietnamese responded by asking China and the USSR for massive amounts of aid, but they received less than they asked for. Without full backing of Moscow and Beijing, and afraid that Nixon would respond to a new offensive with B-52 bombings, the North Vietnamese decided to launch a series of raids instead of a full offensive. The raids were highly successful, and the communists were encouraged by Nixon's failure to respond. The lack of American response convinced the North Vietnamese Central Committee to switch from hit-and-run raids to attacks aimed at taking territory north of Saigon. When the communist leaders met in Hanoi during March 1974 they adopted the slogan "counterattack and attack"—the communist forces would attack the weaknesses in the South's positions and shift to conventional large-scale war if the opportunity arose.[8]

Their attacks in the Central Highlands north of Saigon during the summer of 1974 convinced the communist military leaders that their forces were superior to the South Vietnamese Army, and they urged their political leaders to shift to large-scale conventional warfare. The North Vietnamese believed that the armies of the South had become "passive," with low morale and rampant desertions. As North Vietnamese chief of staff General Van Tien Dung has explained, American aid cuts forced the South Vietnamese army to "change over from large-scale operations and deep-penetration helicopter and tank assaults to defense of their outposts, digging in and carrying out small search operations."[9]

———~~~———

When Ford took office, the communist forces in Southeast Asia were waiting for the right moment to launch a full-scale assault, and the Americans knew that a big offensive was coming. The intelligence agencies were reporting that the Soviets and Chinese had ramped up military aid to North Vietnam from the relatively low levels of 1973.[10] In reality, the Chinese had stepped up aid to the Khmer Rouge, and the Soviets had increased support for the North Vietnamese, but the Chinese support for the Vietnamese was nearing its end. The relations between China and Vietnam had been falling apart during 1974, as the countries began feuding over territory. The situation was exacerbated by the fact that the Khmer Rouge, allied with the Chinese, were becoming virulently anti–Vietnamese.[11]

The Americans knew that their allies would be in trouble when the communists attacked. In May a National Intelligence Estimate warned that the South would not survive without air and naval support from the United States.[12] Congress was more sanguine about the situation. In July 1974 the House Committee on Foreign Affairs issued a report on aid to Indochina, recognizing that South Vietnam could not survive without substantial military and economic aid, but at the same time concluding that the Vietnamese could get by with significantly less aid than the administration had requested. The report concluded that "it is unlikely that the North Vietnamese can win a military victory" in fiscal year 1975.[13]

With his intelligence agencies predicting a renewed offensive, Ford knew that further military action by the United States was out of the question.[14] It was apparent to everyone (except perhaps Kissinger) that the American public had no stomach for further military involvement in the region, and Congress had forbidden any use of force. All Ford could do was to fight for more aid for South Vietnam and Cambodia, and he took every opportunity possible to plead his case. When he met with congressional leaders a month after he took office, Wayne Hays told him that nothing could be done until after the November elections. "Try to hold the line and come back after the elections."[15]

The next day Ford received a rosy view of the situation in a meeting with Ambassador to Vietnam Graham Martin, an old-style anti-communist who would refuse to admit reality for the next few months. Philip Habib called Martin "a strange man. He was wrong about a lot of things, and he is very stubborn."[16] Martin told the president that it was "remarkable" how much the Vietnamese public had embraced Thieu, and he told Ford that $700 million was enough to "hold through the winter."[17] On September 18 the House/Senate Conference Committee authorized $700 million in military assistance for South Vietnam in fiscal year 1975. When the funds were appropriated in the Foreign Assistance Act of 1974, Ford thought he had no chance to sustain a veto, so he signed the bill in Vail on December 30, calling the funding levels "clearly inadequate."[18]

The communists launched offensives in both Cambodia and South Vietnam at the start of 1975. Contrary to the American belief at the time, the assaults were not coordinated because the Khmer Rough and the Vietnamese communists had become bitter enemies. The Khmer Rouge had cut off contacts in 1973 when the North Vietnamese severely cut back aid. The rift was a manifestation of the rampant paranoia among the Cambodian communists. The Khmer Rouge were even more secretive than most communist rebel organizations. Their leader, Saloth Sar (who would later be known as Pol Pot), was just a rumor — nobody knew if he really existed. Life was grim in the Khmer Rouge zone, which was filled with death camps they called "reeducation centers." The communists had begun mass movements of people, forcing people out of cities and moving thousands of people to the border areas with Vietnam.[19]

There was very little chance that Lon Nol's army could stop the upcoming Khmer Rouge offensive. Kissinger admits that only American air power could have restored the "balance" in Cambodia.[20] In reality, a new round of carpet bombing was unlikely to deter the Khmer Rouge, who controlled most of the countryside and nearly half of the population, leaving Phnom Penh and other cities as enclaves surrounded by Khmer Rouge forces. All roads to the capital were cut off, with supplies being sent up the Mekong River. Other cities were being supplied by air drops from a huge airlift that the U.S. Defense Department had organized using chartered private air companies.[21]

A House Committee on Foreign Affairs report concluded that the only hope for Cambodia was a "Laos-type" settlement for a national unity government.[22] Several members of the Ford administration were also thinking about a Laos-type settlement. The idea was to bring back Sihanouk, who had fled to China, and have him broker a peace agreement. But negotiations were just a pipe dream, because neither the Khmer Rouge nor the Lon Nol government had any interest in a settlement. The Chinese told the North Vietnamese that both Sihanouk and the Khmer Rouge opposed negotiations.[23] In his return trip from Vladivostok, Kissinger begged the Chinese to convince the Khmer Rouge to stop the fighting. When he met with Deng Xiaoping, Kissinger proposed negotiations to reinstall Sihanouk, but Deng's only response was, "That is your idea."[24]

The Khmer Rouge launched their final offensive on New Years Day 1975. They quickly secured the banks of the Mekong and mined the river, cutting off the supply route to Phnom Penh. The only remaining supplies coming into the city were brought in by the American airlift. Within three months the Khmer Rouge had cut Lon Nol's army nearly in half—he had only 60,000 troops remaining.[25] American ambassador to Cambodia John Gunther Dean pled in vain for the authority to try to broker an agreement to jettison the Lon Nol government and return Sihanouk to power, writing to Kissinger, "I am afraid that we have precious little time left in Cambodia."[26] He was right.

In Vietnam the communists had already scored a major victory in December when they attacked across the southern provinces of South Vietnam, trying to isolate Saigon. The victory was assured when one of Thieu's senior officials gave them a detailed report of a planning session of the top South Vietnamese military leaders. When they learned that the South Vietnamese decided to move reserves south and not reinforce the western highlands north of Saigon, the communists redirected their forces to where they knew the enemy was weak, and they took Phuoc Binh, capital of Phuoc Long Province, on January 7.[27]

On the day that Phuoc Binh fell, Colby told Kissinger's Special Action Group that a major offensive in North Vietnam was not likely for six months, and probably a year. It is not that the CIA was using faulty intelligence—the information it had on the inner workings of the North Vietnamese leadership was remarkably accurate. Colby was basing his prediction on a December 23 National Intelligence Estimate, which in turn was based on information from a highly-placed member of the communist Southern Command. The report recognized that there was a split in the North Vietnamese leadership between hardliners within the military who wanted to immediately launch a major offensive and the civilian leaders who wanted to wait until 1976. The analysis correctly predicted that if the current season yielded a few victories, the hardliners would try to convince the Politburo to launch a full-scale offensive.[28]

The capture of Phuoc Binh changed the balance of opinion in the Politburo, which had been meeting in Hanoi since December 18. The primary concern of the North was that the U.S. would send troops back in. At this point the communists were afraid only of a massive reintroduction of ground troops—they would not have been deterred by renewed bombing or increased military aid to the South. At the end of their meeting they got their answer. During the battle for Phuoc Binh, the United States Navy sent the aircraft carrier Enterprise on maneuvers to the area, and when the deployment turned out to be a bluff, the North Vietnamese leaders were convinced that the American participation in the war was over. Party leader Le Duan summed up the collective conclusion. "Now that the United States has pulled out of the South, it will be hard for them to jump back in. And no matter how they may intervene, they cannot rescue the Saigon administration from its disastrous collapse." On that basis, the leadership unanimously adopted a plan to attack the highlands of Tay Nguyen, a hundred miles northeast of Saigon, leading up to a general uprising in 1976. They also unanimously agreed that, if the opportunity presented itself, they would take the South in 1975.[29]

Moscow agreed to support the offensive, and it greatly increased arms shipments. Ford tried to convince Congress to follow suit, to no avail. On January 28 he asked Congress for a $300 million supplemental appropriation for Vietnam, but the House Foreign Affairs Committee turned down the request on March 13.[30]

Ford's request was based on a CIA estimate that, at the current rate of expenditure, Thieu's army had enough ammunition to last for nine months — well beyond the end of the fiscal year on June 30, 1975. But if the North launched a major offensive, the ammunition would only last until the end of April, and the additional $300 million would bridge the gap to the next fiscal year.[31] As it turned out, the North did launch a renewed offensive, and Saigon fell in April, before the CIA had estimated that supplies would run out. On that basis alone, the failure of Congress to appropriate more aid did not cause the fall of Vietnam, but things weren't that simple. The aid cuts caused the leaders of the South to change their tactics. There were reports of soldiers being given just a few grenades and a limited number of bullets, but those shortages appeared to be caused by arbitrary limits set by South Vietnam's leaders.[32] The fall of Saigon was ultimately the result of bad leadership in South Vietnam, but the cutoff of U.S. aid contributed to the catastrophe. If nothing else, it was a morale blow.

Ford also asked for $222 million more for Cambodia to "facilitate an early negotiated settlement."[33] Congress had authorized $200 million for military aid during fiscal year 1975, and Ford had the authority to draw down an additional $75 million in military stocks. By the end of February this money had been spent, and Philip Habib told Congress that without the additional funding, the Cambodians would run out of ammunition by the end of March (just after the government actually fell).[34] Schlesinger privately told Ford that the additional aid would increase Cambodia's chances of survival through the dry season from less than 10 percent to 50–50. "They have a severe psychological problem but no actual arms shortages."[35]

The North Vietnamese started their assault on the Central Highlands in March. The offensive was led by chief of staff General Van Tien Dung, and the first place he struck was Ban Me Thuot, the key defensive position in the Highlands. He ordered diversionary attacks which convinced the South Vietnamese generals that the attack would be north of Ban Me Thuot at Pleiku. Dung later explained that, when the South Vietnamese fell for his diversions, it "signaled the great defeat which was coming for them."[36] At two in the morning on March 10 the full offensive was opened with an artillery attack on the Ban Me Thuot air field, and the battle was over in a day.[37]

After the debacle at Ban Me Thuot, the CIA predicted that the communists would launch a major spring offensive "designed to achieve a fundamental change in the balance of power in the South."[38] The State Department staff thought that the South would fall quickly.[39] The North Vietnamese agreed with these assessments, and the Politburo and Central Military Committee were convinced that they could gain "tremendous victories" faster than they had anticipated.[40] Two of the South Vietnamese colonels captured in Ban Me Thuot told the communists that the coast cities of Cam Ranh and Nha Trang were ready for the taking. They said that the South Vietnamese army was stricken by low morale, and they predicted that the entire army would fall apart. Most importantly, they told the North Vietnamese that the South would abandon the Central Highlands.[41]

Thieu had decided to abandon the Highlands, which was consistent with earlier American advice to withdraw to a shorter, more defensible position. But there was no effort made to coordinate the movements of more than 25,000 soldiers and no provision made for the 300,000 refugees that moved with them. The withdrawal became a rout when the communists attacked the retreating columns. Roads became clogged with refugees; army forces lost contact with each other; and South Vietnamese soldiers left vast amounts of munitions behind as they ran south. At the end of the operation, Thieu's army was no longer an organized fighting force. The attacking North Vietnamese forces moved south and east, cutting off Da Nang, the major port on the north coast.[42]

Dung knew the South was doomed. "After this strategic mistake, defeat in the war was certain; it was only a matter of time."[43] After the withdrawal, the North Vietnamese Political Bureau and Central Military Committee met in Hanoi and decided that Saigon should be taken "sooner than had been foreseen."[44] They ordered Dung to attack the former capital of Hue, just north of Da Nang on the coast. Thieu made things worse by ordering his commanders to defend Hue, then changing his mind and ordering a withdrawal, and finally ordering his troops to stand their ground and fight. His troops were given no time to prepare a defense, and the battle was over in a few days. The 1st Infantry Division, one of Saigon's finest, was decimated in the attack.[45]

—⁓—

On the day Hue fell, March 25, Thieu wrote to Ford and asked for a "brief but intensive" campaign of B-52 strikes.[46] Ford was hardly in a position to grant the request, as Congress had prohibited any offensive military action in Southeast Asia. Still, he was tempted. "I regret I don't have authority to do some of the things President Nixon could do." Kissinger urged the president to give Thieu everything he asked for. "If we don't move fast we will be in big trouble."[47] Ford decided to send chief of staff General Frederick Weyand to Vietnam to get a real assessment of what Thieu needed. When Kennerly heard about the mission, he asked to go back to the place where he won his Pulitzer Prize, and Ford agreed to send him along.[48]

While Weyand was away, Ford received uniformly negative assessments from his advisors. In a private meeting on March 27, Kissinger was pessimistic about Vietnam's chances. "Subject to Weyand's views, it looks like they have lost virtually everything and North Vietnam has suffered very little.... I say this with a bleeding heart—but maybe you might put Vietnam behind you and not tear the country apart again."[49] The next day Colby told the NSC that South Vietnam was likely to fall in 1976. Colby predicted that Da Nang would fall within weeks, and General Brown agreed.[50] Weyand heard the same things when he arrived in Saigon—except from Ambassador Martin. Intelligence agents from the CIA and the Defense Attaché's Office explained that only B-52 strikes had any chance of averting a defeat, and even that probably wouldn't be enough. Martin objected to such "defeatism," and he predicted that an airlift of military supplies would be enough for the South to hold off defeat and reach a negotiated solution with the communists.[51]

The Weyand mission would arrive just in time to witness the tragic fall of the old American base of Da Nang. The result was a human catastrophe, as hundreds of thousands of people fled the city—before the attack Da Nang had swelled by a half million people as refugees fled the advancing North Vietnamese army. The United States sent Boeing 727 and 747 cargo planes to fly refugees to the south. Refugees tried to storm the last American planes, and some grabbed the landing gear, falling into the sea as the plane climbed into the air.[52] On the day Da Nang fell, the North Vietnamese Political Bureau reaffirmed the decision to take Saigon as soon as they could, in April if possible.[53] Thieu had no ability to stop them. The South Vietnamese army was decimated, and only 90,000 troops were left to defend Saigon against the 300,000 communist troops that were methodically moving south.[54]

American intelligence reports predicted disaster. On March 31 the CIA station in Saigon sent a message to Washington predicting that the war would be over within a few months, and two days later the station reported that "military aid ... would not repeat not change the prognosis."[55] On April 4 the CIA sent an alert reporting that "the only question over the defeat of South Vietnam is timing — whether it will collapse or be militarily overwhelmed in a period of weeks or months."[56]

On April 5, Weyand and the rest of the Vietnam mission landed in Palm Springs, California, where Ford was vacationing. When Weyand met with Ford, Kissinger, Ambassador Martin, and Scowcroft, he reported that defeat was guaranteed by the current level of American support, and that an additional $722 million was needed for "any real chance of success." He recommended U.S. air strikes as the most effective action the country could take, but he recognized the legal and political factors that prevented them. He concluded that "the US, alone, can not save South Vietnam but it can, however inadvertently, seal its doom."[57] Mulling over what he had heard, Ford was convinced that his only option was to ask Congress for more aid. He later explained why he rejected Weyand's proposal for airstrikes:

> One, I doubted if the American people would have understood and accepted it, the majority. There's no doubt the press would have violently reacted adversely. Secondly, I probably wasn't convinced that the military operation would necessarily have achieved success at that point. There's no doubt that worldwide opinion would have been very adverse. If my recollection is accurate, General Weyand didn't push that option very hard.[58]

Not everyone on the mission agreed with Weyand's assessment that more aid could make a difference. Kennerly showed his photographs to Ford the next day, including shots of ships and busses packed with refugees that shocked the president, and he finished his presentation with a bold statement. "Vietnam has no more than a month left, and anyone who tells you different is bullshitting."[59] NSC staff member Clinton Granger sent Scowcroft a memorandum expressing his dissent to the "can-do" attitude of Weyand and Martin, and he predicted that the South Vietnamese army would not last through May even with an airlift of military supplies. "There is little the United States can do to alter the course of future events in South Vietnam, short of reintroduction of U.S. airpower in considerably quantity — and even that probably would not turn the tide on the ground."[60]

On April 7, Martin sent a cable to Scowcroft dissenting from the general opinion that Hanoi would inevitably win. He said that the military situation was "grim," but not "hopeless." His greatest concern was not the advancing North Vietnamese army but "an unauthorized, uncoordinated action or statement from Washington that could tear the fragile fabric of confidence that is gradually being restored." He followed with five pages of rambling recommendations on how the administration should handle Congress, and he closed with condescending advice that "you keep the panic button firmly locked away."[61] Kissinger told Ford that the ambassador was too attached to Thieu. "Martin wants a new version of the Easter Rebellion."[62] Martin refused to begin evacuating people from Saigon, and he fought against Schlesinger's demands to evacuate all Americans. Martin convinced Ford and Kissinger to hold off, and by mid–April only 1,500 Americans had left the city, mostly on commercial flights.[63]

In Saigon, Thieu had lost all support. On April 2, General Nguyen Cao Ky sent a representative to ask the Americans if they would support a coup, but the CIA, at Colby's direction, unequivocally refused. Prime Minister Khiem began to lobby the rest of the cabinet to remove Thieu and replace him with General Duong Van Minh. Big Minh had been a prominent leader in opposition to Thieu, and many within Vietnam — and even more within the American anti-war community — saw him as someone who might be able to negotiate with the communists.[64] It had always been a pipe dream, and now that the North was on the verge of complete victory there was no chance of a settlement. Without any other option, the South Vietnamese leadership turned to Minh in desperation.

———— ∿∿∿ ————

Things were even worse in Cambodia, where the only remaining decision was when to order a final evacuation. Almost all other embassies had closed, and foreigners were leaving the country on every available flight. By the end of the month it was apparent to everyone that Cambodia was finished, and on March 28 Colby told the NSC that Lon Nol would leave for Indonesia on April 1. Kissinger explained that the French had been in contact with Sihanouk, who wanted to negotiate, but the Khmer Rouge refused to participate — they would accept only unconditional surrender. The military wanted to evacuate as soon as possible, but Kissinger suggested that the evacuation wait until after Ford's upcoming speech to Congress asking for more aid. Ford decided to hold off a little longer.[65]

In Cambodia on April 1, President Lon Nol boarded an American transport plane, claiming that he was going on a "goodwill tour" to Indonesia and Taiwan. Nobody expected him to return, and not many rued his departure. With Lon Nol gone, there was no reason to delay the evacuation, and on April 3 Ford gave Ambassador Dean the authority to start the operation at his discretion. The number of Americans was reduced to fifty in five days.[66] The final fifty would be withdrawn at the last moment, which looked like it could come any day.

———— ∿∿∿ ————

On April 9, Ford met with the National Security Council to prepare for his speech to Congress the next day. Colby explained that in Cambodia "an orderly surrender is the best that can be hoped for." He also predicted that South Vietnam would surrender. Weyand explained that "we all agree that the long-range prospects are just impossible for them." Schlesinger agreed. "We must recognize that it is gone." Schlesinger proposed a strategy designed only to buy time to get the remaining Americans out of Saigon, and he suggested that Ford openly explain that strategy to the American people. Deputy Secretary of Defense Clements agreed. "I think the time has come to be candid." But Ford was convinced otherwise by Deputy Secretary of State Robert Ingersoll, who predicted that it would cause "chaos in Saigon." Ford decided that he intended to "make a strong speech." He would ask Congress for the full $722 million recommended by Weyand, despite the fact that his congressional advisors told him that it had no chance.[67]

On April 10, Ford made his case for more aid before a joint session of Congress, starting with what had become his standard opening line. "Tonight is a time for straight talk among friends." He told the public that Weyand recommended that an additional $722 million was necessary for "any chance of success" in Vietnam. As for Cambodia, Ford read a letter from the new acting president of Cambodia, Saukham Khoy. "For a number of years now the Cambodian people have placed their trust in America. I cannot believe that this confidence was misplaced and that suddenly America will deny us the means which might give us a chance to find an acceptable solution to our conflict." But Ford admitted that "as of this evening, it may soon be too late." He closed by reminding Americans that "this moment of tragedy for Indochina is a time of trial for us. It is a time for national resolve."[68] There was no applause. In fact, two freshmen representatives, Toby Moffett of Connecticut and George Miller of California, turned their backs on the president and walked out of the chamber.[69]

The speech had no effect. The Senate Armed Services Committee rejected Ford's request on April 17, but it did appropriate $200 million and the use of troops for the evacuation.[70]

———∽∼∾———

The next day Ford approved the final evacuation from Phnom Penh, Operation Eagle Pull. "The Commander should be told that all Americans must be aboard the last chopper."[71] Thirty-six helicopters flew for three hours, evacuating 82 Americans, 35 citizens of other nations, and 159 Cambodians. No soldiers were killed or wounded, and the Americans didn't fire a shot. Just before noon on April 12, Dean boarded a helicopter and took off with the last flight. President Saukham Khoy accompanied Dean in the final helicopter, but his successor, Sirik Matak, refused to leave the country he loved, staying behind to be tortured and beheaded by the Khmer Rouge. Matak sent a note in response to Dean's offer of evacuation. "I cannot, alas, leave in such a cowardly fashion. As for you, and in particular your great country, I never believed for a moment that you would have this sentiment of abandoning a people which has chosen liberty. You have refused us your protection, and we can do nothing about it."[72]

Five days later, on April 17, Khmer Rouge soldiers marched single file into the capital, wearing black clothes and sandals made from old tires. Night fell on Cambodia.

———∽∼∾———

The administration was also trying to accelerate the evacuation of Vietnam, but Martin ignored his orders to do so because he was convinced that the communists would not attack Saigon. On April 10, Kissinger cabled Martin with instructions "personally from the president" to evacuate all but 1,250 Americans. "On this there is now no more flexibility."[73] But the next day Martin responded with a prediction that the North Vietnamese would negotiate rather than trying to take Saigon.[74]

Kissinger told Ford and Schlesinger that a million Vietnamese were "endangered," with an "irreducible list" of 174,000.[75] Ford was determined to get as many of the endangered Vietnamese out as possible, and he stood firm in face of criticism from the Defense Department and Congress. Schlesinger urged Ford to concentrate on evacuating Americans, leaving the Vietnamese behind, and Kissinger was the lone member of the Vietnam Working Group who supported evacuating a large number of Vietnamese.[76] On April 14, members of the Senate Foreign Relations Committee begged Ford to evacuate all Americans except for those that could be carried in a single helicopter lift. Several members, including Democrats Frank Church and Joseph Biden, objected to any large-scale evacuation of Vietnamese. Ford was firm — he would evacuate at a pace that would not cause panic, and he would save as many Vietnamese as possible.[77]

Kissinger kept telling Martin to step up the pace, but to no avail. On April 15 the secretary of state sent a short note demanding a plan to evacuate all but 1,500 Americans.[78] Martin responded with a bizarre assessment of the situation in Vietnam. "I am deliberately leaning over backward to keep myself a dispassionate observer viewing Vietnam as if from a seat on the moon." Martin did sound like he was observing Vietnam from the moon. He was remarkably upbeat about South Vietnam's chances, even claiming that there was "rough equivalency" in the number of troops on each side. He explained that there was no need to accelerate the pace of the evacuation because he could evacuate more than 200,000 people in less than one day. Again he closed by urging the secretary of state to "control the panic button in Washington."[79] Kissinger responded the next day with a cable ordering Martin to evacuate the dependants of the embassy staff and all American contractors by the end of the week, and he wanted a plan to get the total number of Americans down to 2,000.[80]

On the 17th a high-level informant told the CIA that Hanoi had decided to take Saigon regardless of what the United States did or whether Thieu stepped down.[81] The same day, Colby told the Vietnam Working Group that the final assault would begin in a matter of days, and that a communist victory was likely within "one to three weeks."[82] Yet Martin still did not believe that an attack was imminent. On April 18 he sent a cable to Kissinger predicting that the North Vietnamese would not invade Saigon. He was "reluctant" to carry out Kissinger's order to withdraw Vietnamese who had cooperated with the Americans.[83] The next day Martin sent another cable promising to "shave the time to be prepared for total evacuation as much as possible," but he claimed that there was "still no reason to precipitate the panic." He refused to put Vietnamese on ships in the harbor, but he did promise to "try to meet your goal of getting down to what can be moved in one helo lift."[84]

Ford was concerned that the North Vietnamese would try to block the evacuation, so he decided to approach the Soviets and see if they could help. At noon on April 19, Kissinger gave Dobrynin a note from Ford asking the Soviets to negotiate a two-week cease fire to allow an American evacuation. The note offered to discuss "the special political circumstances" that could make a cease-fire possible — a veiled reference to ousting Thieu — and Kissinger offered to restart the Paris peace process. When Dobrynin delivered a reply from Brezhnev five days later, it reported that the North Vietnamese would not put "obstacles" in the way of the evacuation of American citizens, and the North Vietnamese spokesman in Paris publicly announced the same thing that night. There was a significant omission in the note — it said nothing about whether the communists would oppose evacuation of the South Vietnamese. Kissinger's interpretation was that the communists were saying "get them out," without giving formal approval.[85]

The North Vietnamese didn't agree to a cease-fire, but they acted like one was in effect. The communists wanted to make sure all of their available forces were in place before attacking Saigon, so the assault was put off until the end of April. And they were serious about not wanting to obstruct the airlift — the last thing they wanted to do was to get in the way of the Americans leaving. They monitored the progress of the evacuation, and they held off the assault until it was almost complete.[86]

On the morning of the 18th, General Nguyen Van Toan flew to Saigon and told Thieu that the end would come within three days. Later that morning, leaders of the opposition asked him to step down. To his aides, Thieu appeared to be a broken man. On the morning of the 20th Martin drove to the Presidential Palace. During an hour-and-a-half discussion he told Thieu that the South could hold on only a month if the communists attacked Saigon, so the only answer was negotiation. Even at that late date Martin believed that the North Vietnamese would prefer to negotiate rather than take Saigon militarily. He knew that Thieu was an obstacle to an agreement, so he asked him to resign. The French ambassador had met with Thieu earlier that morning and delivered the same message. Thieu's only response was that he would do what he thought was best for the country.[87]

On the morning of April 21, Xuan Loc, the most important strategic location just north of the capital, fell to the communists, leaving nothing between the North Vietnamese Army and Saigon. Thieu announced his resignation at 7:30 that evening in a tearful, two-hour speech to the National Assembly and the Supreme Court. He railed at the United States. "You ran away and left us to do the job that you could not do."[88] The feeble 71-year-old vice president, Tran Van Huong, took over. Immediately after Thieu's resignation, the North Vietnamese announced that nothing had changed and that they would never negotiate with Huong. The next day Colby told the Vietnamese Working Group that the communists were unlikely to stop their assault on the capital, and he reconfirmed that assessment each day for the next few days.[89]

⁂

As Saigon began its death throes, Ford gave a speech about the war at the Tulane University Field House on the evening of April 23. The students cheered like mad when he announced that the war was "finished as far as America is concerned." Hartmann had inserted the clause into the speech without Kissinger's knowledge, and he convinced Ford that it was important to assure the nation that it would not be dragged back into the war. The president told the students that the United States was still strong. "We, of course, are saddened indeed by the events in Indochina. But these events, tragic as they are, portend neither the end of the world nor of America's leadership in the world."[90]

In Vietnam the communists rejected President Huong's offer of negotiations to form a government of national conciliation. On April 24, Huong offered Minh the office of prime minister with complete control over the government and the military, but Minh refused because he thought that accepting the office from one of Thieu's men would compromise his ability to negotiate with the communists. The only way he would accept the job was if Huong resigned first.[91]

That same day Ford met with the NSC. When Schlesinger reported that 1,700 Americans remained in Saigon, Ford was furious, and he demanded that all non-essential personnel be evacuated.[92] Kissinger again cabled Martin and told him to get the number of Americans in Vietnam down to 1,100, this time by Friday. He urged Martin to redouble his efforts to get Vietnamese out of the country. "We are amazed at the small number of Vietnamese being evacuated, considering the substantial amount of aircraft available."[93] Martin responded the next day with a cable refusing to reduce the number of Americans any further.[94] Kissinger protected Martin by telling Ford that the ambassador had reduced the number of Americans to 1,150, but "180 more Americans came out of the woodwork." Ford asked Kissinger to "keep the pressure on him."[95]

On the evening of April 24, President Huong asked Martin to come to the Presidential Palace. He told the American ambassador that he was concerned about Thieu's safety, and he asked the United States to fly him out of the country. Martin and a group of American Marines escorted Thieu to Tan Son Nhut airport the next night. Martin walked Thieu to the boarding ramp and "told him goodbye. Nothing historic. Just goodbye."[96]

Out of respect, Huong had been waiting for Thieu to leave before he asked the National Assembly to appoint Minh his successor. On the morning of April 26, Huong put the issue to the assembly, but several other candidates stepped forward for the doomed position. After meeting all day, the assembly could not decide whether to appoint Minh, Ky, or one of the other leaders jockeying to become number one on the communists' list for elimination. The assembly finally authorized Huong to make the choice. The next day he held a small ceremony with the leaders of the National Assembly and the Supreme Court, in which he was expected to name Minh president, but Huong surprised them all by simply stating that he could not bring himself to do it. That finally forced the National Assembly to act, and it passed a resolution authorizing Huong to transfer power to Minh. Minh was sworn in at the Presidential Palace at five in the evening of the 28th. One of his first acts was to send a note to Martin asking all American military personnel to leave within 24 hours.[97]

———〰〰———

On the day Thieu resigned, the United States began an around-the-clock evacuation from the Tan Son Nhut Airport in Saigon. On the morning of the 27th the North Vietnamese began to move toward the city from all directions, taking the suburbs but not the central city. Dung received his orders to move into central Saigon just after midnight on the morning of April 29 in Vietnam (just after noon on April 28 in Washington). As his troops advanced into the city, the Tan Son Nhut airport was hit with artillery fire, killing two American Marines and shooting down three South Vietnamese airplanes. Shelling the airfield was not part of the plan, so the North Vietnamese command ordered it to stop.[98] At 10:30 that evening Kissinger called Ford and explained that the North Vietnamese army was converging on the airport, and the military was recommending a switch to helicopters to complete the evacuation. Ford asked for Martin's views, and Kissinger called back within minutes to report that the ambassador agreed. It was 10:45 in the morning in Saigon when Ford ordered a switch to helicopters. At Ford's direction, Marsh and Friedersdorf called congressional leaders to notify them that the final phase of evacuation had begun.

It was early afternoon in Saigon on April 29 when Radio Saigon began playing "White Christmas," the signal to Americans that Operation Frequent Wind was underway. The U.S. Navy had forty ships off the coast of Vietnam, trying to deal with South Vietnamese pilots landing on their ships without approval — they had to push the South Vietnamese planes and helicopters over the side to make room for their own craft. The final evacuation began when thirty-six helicopters took off from the USS *Hancock* for the airport, and they spent the next few hours bravely ferrying people from the airfield as the North Vietnamese troops moved in.

At five in the morning Washington time the airport was deemed too dangerous, so the evacuation site was switched to the American embassy, which was filled with Americans and Vietnamese waiting to be evacuated. Outside the gates, thousands of Vietnamese were pushing to get in. Throughout the evacuation, Martin hovered about and oversaw the operation. He may have taken far too long starting the evacuation, but he was a hero on this day. He could barely stand upright because he was suffering from pneumonia, yet he stayed at his post, ashen and weak. Most importantly, he insisted that as many Vietnamese be flown out as possible, despite demands from the Defense Department that only Americans be evacuated. The Marines guarding the embassy and the pilots landing there persevered beyond ordinary human endurance. At one point one of the Marines on the roof fell asleep where he stood, falling off. He was put on the next helicopter. The helicopter pilots flew for hours, often landing on rooftops throughout Saigon to rescue stranded Americans and at-risk Vietnamese.

Ford went to sleep just before two on the morning on April 29. When he woke at 9:30, Kissinger told Ford that the airlift was going well, with more than 4,500 Vietnamese and 450 Americans evacuated. An hour later the secretary of state reported that the South Vietnamese had surrendered. At the Presidential Palace, Minh had been trying in vain to contact the communists to begin talks, but the North Vietnamese weren't interested in anything but total surrender. Minh announced unconditional surrender that evening in a radio address. "We are here to hand over to you the power in order to avoid bloodshed." He ordered the South Vietnamese soldiers to stop opposing the advance of the communists and put down their weapons.

Schlesinger was furious that the airlift was proceeding through the night, endangering

Kissinger (with back to camera) and Scowcroft brief Gerald and Betty Ford about the evacuation of Saigon late at night on April 28, 1975. (Photograph by David Hume Kennerly; courtesy Gerald R. Ford Library.)

American pilots. He demanded that it end within two hours, but Martin called Kissinger and asked for more time. Kissinger asked how many people remained to be evacuated, and Martin estimated the specific, but inaccurate, number of 726. Kissinger agreed to send helicopters to evacuate that number of people, but he demanded that the airlift be over by 3:45 Saigon time, and he told Martin to get on one of the helicopters. At three in the morning Martin begged for six more helicopters, which were immediately dispatched. As ordered, Martin gave his final order at 3:45. It was a heartbreaking order — the remaining flights were reserved for Americans. Once again Martin asked for six more helicopters, which were immediately dispatched. When they arrived at 4:20 a Marine relayed an order from the White House: Martin was to get on board. It was 5:24 in the morning when the helicopter took off, with Martin looking at the more than 400 Vietnamese left in the courtyard below. When the helicopter flew over the sea, he looked down on fishing boats carrying refugees "as far as you could see."[99]

Like most Americans, Ford watched the evacuation on television, feeling helpless as he watched helicopters leaving the embassy roof. "It was one of the saddest days in my life, to see the United States literally kicked out, beaten by the North Vietnamese."[100] At 5:30 that evening Ford gave a speech on national television announcing that all Americans had been evacuated from Saigon, and Nessen and Kissinger gave press conferences announcing the same thing. Kissinger had barely finished when his aides told him that there were still 129 Marines left in the embassy. Inexplicably, they had been forgotten — nobody had told them to leave, so they stayed at their posts. The telephones at the embassy still worked, and they called Washington for orders. The helicopters were sent back, and all of them were evacuated safely. They closed heavy wooden doors behind them as they ran up the stairs, while the abandoned

Vietnamese battered through the doors and ran after them. As the helicopters lifted off the roof, the desperate Vietnamese dove for their landing gears. With the president, secretary of state and press secretary all having declared that all Americans had been evacuated, Nessen proposed that he let the discrepancy pass, but Rumsfeld would not hear of it. "No. This war has been marked by so many lies and evasions that it is not right to have the war end with one last lie. We ought to be perfectly honest and say that at the time we said the evacuation was over it really wasn't over."[101]

In all, seventy helicopters flew 630 flights for 21 hours, with some pilots flying for more than 10 straight hours. Nearly 1,400 Americans were evacuated, along with more than 5,500 South Vietnamese. In addition to the two Marines killed at the airport, two Marine pilots were killed when their helicopter crashed into the sea. More than sixty thousand Vietnamese escaped by commercial airline, boat, and barge.[102]

At the break of dawn on August 30 the North Vietnamese entered Saigon, which they renamed Ho Chi Minh City. Big Minh was meeting with his cabinet as the communists took the Presidential Palace, and they were all arrested on the spot. Thus ended the first war the United States had lost since the War of 1812. More than 58,000 Americans lost their lives in Vietnam, which made it the fourth deadliest war in American history.[103] In the end, American involvement had only extended the struggle and increased the suffering — between 1.5 and 3 million Vietnamese died — without affecting the outcome. Despite the best intentions of the American leaders, their support for the South Vietnamese caused only pain. The question remains: was it inevitable?

After the fall of Saigon, Kissinger offered to return his Nobel Peace Prize, but the Nobel committee refused. In recent years he has written extensively defending the Paris Peace Accords, claiming that the South Vietnamese would have prevailed had Congress not cut off military aid, and, more importantly, had the Nixon and Ford administrations been able to respond with renewed bombing. Former defense secretary Laird agrees with Kissinger's assessment. "Without U.S. funding, South Vietnam was quickly overrun.... I believed then and still believe today that given enough outside resources, South Vietnam was capable of defending itself."[104] Kissinger admits that the final $722 million sought by Ford would not have changed the outcome. "On one level, it was preposterous. Vietnam was likely to collapse before any equipment could arrive there." He still thought the request was important to uphold the honor of the United States. "What mattered was how we ourselves would feel about our conduct afterward."[105]

It was the earlier cuts that hurt. The United States sent only $621 million in military assistance to South Vietnam in fiscal year 1975, down from $938 million in 1974.[106] The aid reductions did not cause the Vietnamese or Cambodian armies to run out of munitions — each country fell just at the time they would have begun to experience shortages — but the funding cuts did change the South Vietnamese operational plans. The South Vietnamese leaders set arbitrary limits on ammunitions for soldiers, and the insecurity of supply of tanks and planes caused them to switch from fluid to static operations. These changes weren't all necessary, and they were implemented incompetently. As a result, morale took a hit, largely because of the evaporation of U.S. support, but also because the soldiers were discouraged by their incompetent leaders.

As for renewed bombing raids, they may have prolonged the fall by a year, but they probably would not have changed the outcome. Over the years, the North Vietnamese had demonstrated the ability to continue offensive operations despite heavy bombing by American forces.

Nixon's bombing of the North may have contributed to the communists' willingness to sign the Paris Peace Accords, but the ultimate reason they signed was to get America out of the war. They had never wavered from their ultimate goal of conquering the entire country. In 1974–75 the North Vietnamese leadership had set a firm goal of victory in 1976, and renewed bombing was unlikely to divert them from that goal. Renewed bombing may have deterred them from advancing the time for final victory to 1975, but they were more concerned with reinsertion of American ground troops than with a new bombing campaign.

In the final analysis, it is hard to accept that the South Vietnamese could have prevailed after the United States pulled out, when they couldn't win with more than 500,000 American soldiers fighting at their side. It was unlikely, but still possible. Scowcroft's conclusion seems most apt. "Who knows? They lasted longer than we expected them to."[107] In his memoirs, Ford came to a similar conclusion. "Could we have won the war? There, I think, the answer is yes, although I'm not as sure of that today as I was in the late 1960s."[108] Who knows? Maybe more aid could have made the difference. Maybe an airlift of supplies would have given the South Vietnamese soldiers the confidence they needed to stop the communist advance. We will never know because Congress didn't try.

—ⁿⁿⁿ—

It was the futility of the war that made it the most divisive of America's foreign adventures. At the time, neither side was willing to admit that the war presented difficult moral and practical issues. Antiwar forces believed that America had supported the war simply to advance its interests, and not to help the Vietnamese people, while war supporters accused the antiwar protesters of embracing the communists and being blind to their oppressive regimes. There was a shard of truth to these accusations, and each side took the most extreme statements made by their opponents as proof of their prejudices. But each side missed the fundamental point made by their opponents. For the most part, war supporters believed antiwar protesters were naïve about the nature of the communist regimes. Antiwar Americans, on the other hand, thought that war supporters were being naïve about the ability of the United States to prevail. For the most part, they did not oppose the war because they supported the communists. Most of them had come to the painful conclusion that the communists would inevitably win, and supporting the South Vietnamese was just prolonging the war and the suffering it caused.

It is a difficult moral question. Is it right to support a government that is fighting a losing war against a murderous and tyrannical opponent? Supporting the government will most likely only prolong the suffering caused by the war, without changing the outcome. But isn't there a moral obligation to support anyone opposing tyranny, because they all have some chance, however slim, of winning? In the polarized atmosphere in America, neither side was willing to admit that the issues around the war were complicated, or that their opponents might be motivated by honorable beliefs. Although Ford had been an ardent war supporter, he was one of the few people who recognized that his opponents had good intentions. "The American people are smarter than politicians give them credit for. They saw that our military policy was not going to end the war."[109]

The fall of Saigon ended the intense domestic discord caused by Vietnam, but the war continued to be a source of division. The underlying cause of the rift was the apparent inability of Americans to retain more than one lesson of history. Before Vietnam, the nation generally agreed that the proper metaphor for every foreign crisis was Munich in 1938. After Vietnam, conservatives still viewed every foreign crisis as a repeat of Munich, while liberals saw every crisis as a repeat of Vietnam. Conservatives were driven by their one lesson of history to advocate intervention, while liberals thought that every intervention would result in a quagmire.

———≈≈≈———

War supporters were wrong when they predicted that the communists in Southeast Asia would form a unified, expansionist bloc. Communist Vietnam proved to be less expansionist than feared. On July 20, 1976, a CIA memorandum reported that it had been monitoring the situation to determine if Vietnam would try to export revolution to the rest of the region or whether it would concentrate on developing internally. The agency concluded that Vietnam had "opted for the later course."[110] If anything, the communist regimes in Vietnam and Cambodia proved to be more dangerous to each other than to other nations in the area. By the end of the war the two countries were already at odds, and they would soon be in open battle.

On the other hand, war supporters were proven right that the communists were worse than the regimes that the United States had supported. After the fall of Saigon, the Vietnamese communists immediately sent hundreds of thousands of people to concentration camps (they called them "reeducation camps"), where most of them spent years. In all, between 500,000 and 1 million people passed through the camps. More than a half million people were relocated from the cities to "new economic zones," and more than a million more fled the country, many risking their lives on rickety boats. After nationalization of industry and forced collectivization of agriculture, the economy went into a tailspin, resulting in widespread famine.[111]

Things in Cambodia were far worse, but at the time, the outside world had little insight into what was happening. Colby explained to Ford on April 24 that the Khmer Rouge were acting "behind a curtain of silence." All the administration knew was that the new government was "moving ruthlessly" against former officials, and that large numbers of city residents were being forced to the countryside.[112] The Ford administration didn't even know who was leading the country. The Khmer Rouge did not officially exist, and among the people it was just a rumor, called the "revolutionary organization." The Khmer Rouge leaders were referred to as if they were mythical creatures. Few in Cambodia knew who Pol Pot, Khieu Samphan, and Ieng Sary were. The CIA didn't realize that Pol Pot and party leader Saloth Sar were the same person until the last month of the Ford administration.[113]

In Cambodia things were worse than anyone imagined. The Khmer Rouge leaders had developed an extreme form of Maoism, and they promised to take Cambodia where "no country in history has ever gone before."[114] They wanted to eliminate all commerce, private property, cities, machinery, and technology. They set out to create a pre–Ur civilization — or, more accurately, they set out to eliminate civilization. The day Phnom Penh fell, the Khmer Rouge declared it day one of Year Zero. The influx of refugees had swollen Phnom Penh to more than two million residents, and every one of them was forced to leave the city. The Khmer Rouge forced hospital patients out of their beds, and the sick trudged down the streets in their hospital gowns, many wheeling IV bags. The Khmer Rouge went house to house, forcing everyone onto the street, no matter how old or young. In the process, they piled furniture, refrigerators and TV sets in the middle of the streets and turned them into giant bonfires.

Phnom Penh was not the first city the Khmer Rouge had emptied. For years they had been emptying the villages and cities in the areas they controlled. They burned down all buildings in the empty villages so no one could return. After they took Phnom Penh, the Khmer Rouge emptied cities across Cambodia, and within two weeks the cities of the country were ghost towns. With the cities emptied, two million people were on the move with no food or water. The weak fell by the roadside and were left to die, and anyone who caused trouble was killed on the spot. The people marching out of the cities found that the countryside was not ready to house or feed them. Anyone who dissented to their rule — and those who they mistrusted for any reason — were sent to prison camps where they were tortured and killed. As they cleared out the population, the Khmer Rouge executed between 50,000 and 100,000 army officers, government employees, and their families.[115]

The outside world saw little of what was happening. Most reporters left before the fall, but a few remained, along with 600 other foreigners huddled in the French Embassy in Phnom Penh. At the end of April the Khmer Rouge ordered them all to leave, and they were trucked out of the country during the first week of May. When they left, the reporters wrote about the evacuation of the cities, but after that, there were no longer any sources of information in the country. A handful of communist countries had embassies in Phnom Penh, but even they were forced to stay in a small area of the city and were accompanied at all times by Khmer Rouge agents. One of the rare visitors to Phnom Penh remembers it as a ghost town:

> The streets were deserted. We saw no one. Some of the doors of the houses were padlocked; others were swinging open. In the factories and at the Ministry, everyone wore black. They had sandals made from car-tyres, and a checkered scarf, a karma. We used to talk to them ... but all that came out was propaganda.[116]

The world got to see more of what was happening when Charles Twining was sent to the U.S. embassy in Thailand in June 1975. Twining went to the Cambodian border to interview refugees, and he found himself talking to emaciated people who told horrific stories of a hell on earth. They told him about a country where people were living on just a few teaspoons of rice a day, where people were not allowed to travel just a mile or two down the road, where all books were banned, where people were killed for speaking a foreign language, where children were separated from parents, where any physical contact between men and women was forbidden unless expressly approved by the state, where mass weddings were arranged and pairings were announced by Khmer Rouge cadres, where religion was forbidden, where all radios, telephones, televisions and cars were destroyed, where mail and money did not exist, and where all the people did was work the fields from the moment they got up to the moment they went to bed. It was a country without joy, thought, or diversion. Over and over he heard stories of executions — of people being strangled, beaten to death, or killed with a swing of a hoe to the back of the head.[117]

On May 10, 1976, Scowcroft sent Ford a memorandum summarizing Twining's interviews. He concluded that the Khmer Rouge were "radically reconstructing that country using extremely harsh and brutal methods to implement their policies."[118] The administration passed the information on to Amnesty International. In a study issued in the last month of the administration, the CIA concluded that the Khmer Rouge had instituted the "most extreme of the world's totalitarian regimes." The agency estimated that hundreds of thousands of people had died, "possibly over 10 percent of the entire population."[119]

―――――

The Khmer Rouge would spend the next three years killing indiscriminately. Every member of the government, from Pol Pot to the lowest guard, had the right to kill. The people were guarded by soldiers as young as twelve years old, who repeated the same slogan over and over. "To keep you is no gain; to kill you is no loss." Enemies of the regime included members of the former government, former members of the armed forces, ethnic Vietnamese, ethnic Chinese, Muslims, Buddhist monks, teachers, professionals, people with more than a seventh-grade education, people who spoke foreign languages, and people living in areas near the Vietnamese border. The Khmer Rouge tried to eliminate all "capitalists," meaning anyone who had engaged in business, including noodle vendors and taxi drivers.

Torture, rape, and murder were rampant. Former prisons and mass graves now dot the countryside of Cambodia. In the pre-industrial society built by the Khmer Rouge the favorite tools of torture were bare hands or simple wooden and metal tools. The most primitive forms of execution were routine — the guards beat prisoners to death with their bare hands, or they chained them up and left them to starve to death. The Khmer Rouge even turned on themselves, and purges within the communist ranks became common. Pol Pot became suspicious of leaders who showed any independence, and he would have them executed, along with anyone who had ever worked in their organizations and all citizens of the areas they controlled.[120]

In 1985 a UN report described the atrocities committed by the Khmer Rouge as "the most serious that had occurred anywhere in the world since Nazism."[121] The Cambodia Mass Grave Mapping Project has found more than 20,000 mass graves containing more than a million bodies.[122] The general consensus is that between 20 and 25 percent of the population died, or between 2 and 3 million people.[123] Maybe this horror and death would have happened even without American involvement in Cambodia. The Khmer Rouge leaders had mapped out their reign of terror years before when they were students in Paris. Then again, maybe they wouldn't have taken power if Nixon had not bombed and invaded the country. There are many possibilities, but one thing is certain: American involvement in Cambodia had produced the worst possible outcome.

———

Ford quickly learned how aggressive the shadowy new government in Cambodia could be. Two weeks after the fall of Saigon the Khmer Rouge captured the S.S. *Mayaguez*, an American merchant vessel. Urged by Kissinger to use the incident to restore American prestige, Ford swung into action and directed a rescue operation, saving the ship and crew.[124]

The crisis began at just after two in the afternoon on May 12 in the Gulf of Thailand. The S.S. *Mayaguez*, a container ship owned by J. R. Reynolds Industries, was steaming toward Thailand carrying a shipment for the Department of Defense. As the *Mayaguez* passed just south of the Poulo Wai Islands, which are sixty miles from the Cambodian shore, it was suddenly approached by several ships from the Cambodian navy. A torpedo boat fired in front of the merchant vessel, forcing it to stop. Captain Charles Miller radioed an emergency message to the Indonesian office of Delta Exploration, explaining that they were being towed to an unknown Cambodian port. When the company informed the U.S. embassy in Jakarta, the embassy sent a series of messages to Washington between 5 and 7 in the morning on May 12 (the time difference between Washington and the Gulf of Thailand was eleven hours). The Cambodians actually treated their captives well. Crew member Herbert McDonald said, "They were so nice, really kind. They fed us first and everything. I hope everybody gets hijacked by them."[125]

When word passed through the ship that they had been taken by the Cambodians, chief engineer Cliff Harrington was baffled. "Cambodians? We aren't even at war with Cambodia."[126] But the Khmer Rouge weren't trying to strike at America, they were making a point in a dispute with Vietnam and Thailand about who owned the tiny Poulo Wai Islands, and, more importantly, about which country would own oil that might be discovered in the Gulf of Thailand. The Thieu and Nol governments had quarreled over an oil rig that Cambodia had licensed near the islands, and the South Vietnamese navy had briefly blockaded the rig in September 1974. Now the Cambodians were trying to assert their sovereignty by seizing ships that strayed close to the islands. In the ten days before the *Mayaguez* was captured, the Khmer Rouge had fired on or detained seventeen vessels. On May 7 the Cambodians had detained a Panamanian ship, releasing it after thirty-five hours.[127]

———

At 7:40 on May 12, Scowcroft told Ford about the incident during his regular morning intelligence briefing, and Kissinger was told about the seizure during his staff meeting twenty minutes later.[128] Ford and Kissinger were worried that the lives of the crew were at risk from the radical new Cambodian regime. More importantly, they saw the seizure as an opportunity to regain some of the respect the country had lost with the fall of Vietnam. Kissinger has explained his thinking in his memoirs: "In the aftermath of Indochina's collapse, the United States needed to demonstrate that there were limits to what it would tolerate."[129] It is remarkable how many members of the administration shared this view, which Hartmann has recounted the most dramatically: "Did the United States of America, torn internally and with a novice, little-known leader, still have any guts? The world was waiting for the answer."[130]

The National Security Council met at just after noon to discuss the situation. CIA director Colby said that the agency's best information was that the ship was being taken to the mainland Cambodian port of Kompong Som. Schlesinger gave Ford his options, including seizing Cambodian assets, holding a small island hostage, and blockading Cambodia. Kissinger leaned over the table and made an impassioned plea for action. "As I see it, Mr. President, we have two problems. The first problem is how to get the ship back. The second problem is how the U.S. appears at this time.... I think what we need for the next 48 hours is a strong statement, a strong note and a show of force." Rockefeller agreed with Kissinger that "a violent response is in order. The world should know that we will act and that we will act quickly." Ford asked the military to prepare for a rescue mission, and he ordered the naval forces in the region to head for the Gulf of Thailand, including the aircraft carrier *Coral Sea*, the destroyers *Wilson* and *Holt*, and the helicopter carrier *Okinawa*.[131]

During the meeting, Rockefeller compared the crisis to the North Korean seizure of the USS *Pueblo* in 1968.[132] Hartmann also recalls that the president's advisors "were all haunted, of course, by the Pueblo affair."[133] After the *Pueblo* was seized, the United States did not respond before the North Koreans moved the crew to mainland prisons, where they could not be effectively rescued, and the crew remained in captivity for more than a year. Ford was determined not to repeat that mistake. "I was determined not to allow a repetition of that incident, so I told Schlesinger to make sure that no Cambodian vessels moved between Koh Tang and the mainland."[134]

Kissinger told Ford that using American bases in Thailand for a rescue mission could cause problems, but Ford later explained that offending Thailand was a risk he was willing to take. "Until Mayaguez and her crew were safe, I didn't give a damn about offending their sensibilities. "[135] That night the Thai premier informed the Americans that he would not allow the bases to be used for military action against Cambodia.

After the NSC meeting, Ford issued a statement calling the seizure of the *Mayaguez* an act of piracy, and he threatened the Khmer Rouge with "the most serious consequences" if they did not release the ship and crew. Ford wanted to officially demand the return of the ship and crew, but there was no one to give the demand to, because no foreign nation had an embassy in Phnom Penh. China was the only country that had any personnel in the city, and Ford asked Kissinger to contact the Chinese. Later that afternoon, Deputy Secretary Ingersoll met with Huang Zhen, the chief of the Chinese liaison office in Washington, but Zhen refused to take any message on behalf of Cambodia. The next day the U.S. Embassy in Beijing delivered copies to the Cambodian embassy and the Chinese foreign ministry. China again refused to take the note, and Cambodia returned it by mail.

For the rest of the day the administration received conflicting reports about the whereabouts of the ship and crew. At 1:30 the next morning, Scowcroft called Ford with the news that the ship was less than an hour out of the mainland port of Kompong Som, and Ford gave the approval for use of F-4 fighters to fire in front of the ship to prevent it from reaching the mainland. But at two in the morning Scowcroft called Ford with the news that the Cambodians had anchored the ship off of Koh Tang, halfway to the mainland, and American fighters had fired in the water in front of the ship as a warning to stay put. When Ford woke at six the next morning he talked by phone with Schlesinger for more than an hour. Schlesinger reported that reconnaissance planes had seen two smaller vessels tied up to the *Mayaguez*. A short time later the boats were seen moving toward the island, and one had "a lot of people on board," many of whom appeared to be Caucasian. Later reports indicated that the planes had seen the boats offloading people on the island. In fact, the crew was still on one of the fishing boats. Ford told Schlesinger not to allow any vessels to move from Koh Tang to the mainland.

When the NSC met again at 10:22 that morning, Colby reported that the *Mayaguez* was still anchored off Koh Tang, but the crew was believed to be on the island. Colby reported that the Cambodians "presumably have few troops or weapons" on Koh Tang, and Schlesinger added that a Cambodian defector estimated there were sixty soldiers on the island. Rockefeller repeated the administration mantra. "Many are watching us, in Korea and elsewhere," and he recommended sinking Cambodian boats in the area. It is a good thing that Ford did not accept Rockefeller's suggestion because the crew was still on one of the fishing boats. Schlesinger recommended taking the ship and then moving against the island, and he estimated that he could have troops in position in twelve hours. Ford decided on a three-step approach: 1) stop and, if necessary, sink all vessels moving to and from Koh Tang to prevent the crew from being taken to the mainland; 2) take the *Mayaguez* when forces were ready; and 3) rescue the crew from Koh Tang with the Marines from Okinawa.[136] That evening the administration contacted congressional leaders and informed them that force would probably be used to rescue the crew and ship.

⚬⚬⚬

At dawn in Cambodia on the 14th (still evening on the 13th in Washington), five Cambodian boats left Koh Tang for the mainland. Pursuant to Ford's orders, American fighters tried to turn them back. Three gunboats turned around, while another was sunk when fighters tried to disable the rudder, causing a fire. One fishing boat kept steaming toward the mainland—the *Mayaguez* crew was on the boat. Scowcroft asked Ford for instructions, and the president ordered the boat to be sunk if it could not be stopped any other way. But when a fighter got close enough to destroy the boat, the pilot saw 30 to 40 people on board who appeared to be Caucasian. Scowcroft relayed the new information to Ford, who ordered the fighters to try to stop the boat without sinking it.

When Ford convened the third NSC meeting at 10:40 in the evening, Scowcroft reported that the fishing vessel was six miles from the mainland and the pilots could not stop it without sinking it. Ford ordered the plane to continue to try to turn the boat around, but not to sink it, and he ordered the military to sink other boats around Koh Tang. Schlesinger estimated that there were 100 Khmer Rouge troops on Koh Tang, and Colby agreed. "There is not a large force on the island." Schlesinger recommended delaying any attempt to take the island until first light on the 15th in Cambodia, so the *Holt* would be in position to support the assault. Ideally, he wanted to wait one more day until the *Coral Sea* was in position. Ford was willing to consider waiting until the *Coral Sea* was in position, but told Schlesinger to be prepared to go earlier. "I think we should be ready to go in 24 hours. We may, however, want to wait." Kissinger recommended a bigger assault to "prove that others will be worse off if they tackle us.... I am thinking not of Cambodia, but of Korea and of the Soviet Union and of others." He recommended taking the ship, seizing the island, and bombing the mainland. Schlesinger's deputy, William Clements, was skeptical about bombing the mainland. "I think dropping a lot of bombs on the mainland will not help us with the release of the Americans."[137]

On the night of May 13, reporters asked Deng Xiaoping, who was visiting Paris, about the American threats to use force. He laughed. "If they intervene, there is nothing we can do."[138] The next morning a Chinese diplomat in Teheran approached his American counterpart and relayed that the Chinese government was "embarrassed" by the Cambodian seizure of the *Mayaguez* and was pressuring the Khmer Rouge to release the boat and crew, which he predicted would happen soon. It was an important message that China would not intervene in support of the Khmer Rouge, and the incident was no longer an international crisis; it was just an operation to retrieve the boat.

American planes harassed the fishing boat with riot control agents, but they could not force it to turn around, and the boat made it to the mainland port of Kompong Som. The U.S. planes harassing the boat lost sight of it when it reached port because they didn't have approval to fly over the mainland, so they did not see that the boat had anchored in the harbor without offloading anyone. During the afternoon in Cambodia, American F-111s observing Kompong Som harbor saw the fishing boat proceed a few miles to the island of Koh Rong Som Lem. The crew was taken ashore, but the Americans still thought that they were on Koh Tang. On the island the Khmer Rouge soldiers offered to take Captain Miller and his crew to the *Mayaguez*, where they could radio the American forces that the ship and crew would be allowed to leave if all American planes left Cambodian airspace. The Cambodians brought a gunboat to ferry Miller to the *Mayaguez*, but he refused to board because he was convinced that the American forces would sink any gunboat approaching the *Mayaguez*. He asked for a fishing boat, but none was available. The Cambodians finally agreed to put the crew on a fishing boat at daybreak the next morning and allow them to sail to the *Mayaguez*. The ship and crew would be allowed to leave the Gulf of Thailand as long as American planes did not attack Cambodian territory.

At 11:45 on the morning of May 14, Ford met with Kissinger and Scowcroft. Kissinger predicted that the Navy's proposed operation wouldn't be "ferocious" enough. Ford promised to agree not to use B-52s only if he was convinced that carrier strikes would be meaningful.[139] Ford convened his fourth NSC meeting at 3:52 that afternoon. Air Force General David Jones recommended that the assault begin first thing the next day. "We can do it with a high assurance of success." He said that the B-52s were ready, but he recommended not using them. "From a targeting standpoint, it represents overkill." Kissinger disagreed. "We should move massively and firmly." He made the same point later by slamming his fist on the table and urging that they "do it ferociously." Ford gave the green light to the operation, including bombing Kompong Som with carrier-based planes rather than B-52s. "They should not stop until we tell them to."[140]

The rescue operation began at 4:15 in the morning of May 15 when the first wave of helicopters took off from the Utapao base in Thailand. The available helicopter force only allowed

200 Marines to be taken to the Koh Tang Island every four hours, which turned out to be inadequate because there were more Cambodian troops on the island than anticipated. For some reason the local American forces expected only twenty Khmer Rouge troops on the island — they had not received later intelligence estimates of 100 troops. The helicopters began landing Marines on the island at just after 7:00, where they met heavier fire than they expected. The pre-attack reconnaissance flights were instructed to remain above 6,000 feet, and they missed an antiaircraft battery near the landing site. The antiaircraft guns were not identified until the Utapao base received photographs of reconnaissance flights just before the operation, and the order to take out the battery was botched as a result. Of the first eight helicopters, three crashed, two were disabled, and fifteen Marines were killed.

While the first helicopters were landing on Koh Tang, the Khmer Rouge were putting the crew on the fishing boat at Koh Rong Som Lem. The crew was set free, and Minister of Information Hu Nim announced that the ship was being released during a radio broadcast. An hour later the *Holt* pulled alongside the *Mayaguez*, which was empty, and the first wave of bombers left the *Coral Sea* for the mainland. As the *Mayaguez* was being boarded, Scowcroft brought Ford a translated version of the Cambodian broadcast. At first, Ford told Schlesinger to hold up the first round of bombing, but the broadcast said nothing about the crew, so he ordered the operation to proceed. The United States had no way to contact the Khmer Rouge to clarify the message, so Ford asked Nessen to tell the press that the military operations would cease as soon as the Cambodians announced that the crew was being released. When the first wave of planes from the *Coral Sea* reached the mainland they did not drop any bombs because they judged the situation to be too dangerous without first identifying targets, which they relayed to the following waves. The following waves hit the airfield and naval base at Kompong Son, destroying seventeen aircraft and a fuel depot.

Three hours into the operation a reconnaissance plane spotted the *Mayaguez* crew aboard the fishing boat, waving their white t-shirts on bamboo poles, and the USS *Wilson* was sent to pick up the crew. At 11:00 at night in Washington, Ford finished dinner with his son Daniel and returned to the Oval Office for a meeting with Kissinger, Scowcroft, Rumsfeld, Hartmann, Marsh, Nessen, and Friedersdorf. Just after Ford arrived, Schlesinger called with the news that a fishing boat had been spotted carrying Caucasians waving white flags, and he called again several minutes later to tell the president that the *Wilson* had rescued the crew. Ford hung up and let out a whoop. "They're all safe." The room erupted in shouts of joy. Scowcroft asked whether to stop the operation, but Kissinger convinced Ford the final bombing run should go ahead. "Let's look ferocious! Otherwise they will attack us as the ship leaves."[141] It was just after midnight when Ford appeared on television and announced that the crew and ship were safe.

The Marines on Koh Tang were still fighting. A group of twenty-two Marines was isolated from the main force because their helicopter had crashed on the other side of the island. The first helicopter sent to rescue the isolated group was hit by ground fire and had to return to the *Coral Sea*, and it took several more hours to evacuate the Marines. Eighteen Americans had been killed and fifty wounded during the operation. In addition, another twenty-three Americans were killed during the preparation for the operation when their helicopter crashed traveling to Utapao.

Ford was furious when he learned that all four bombing runs were not completed. At an NSC meeting to review the operation, General Jones reported that the first wave had not dropped its ordinance, and the fourth wave was stopped before it was complete because the crew had been rescued.[142] Ford described his pique in his memoirs:

The first strike never took place, although we were told it had been "completed." The Navy jets dropped their bombs into the sea. It's possible that communications problems may have contributed to the misunderstanding.... What is harder for me to understand is why the fourth air strike — and I had specifically ordered four — was never carried out. I hadn't told anyone to cancel that attack. Apparently, someone had, and I was anxious to find out who had contravened my authority. Perhaps I should have pursued my inquiry, but since we had achieved our objective, I let the matter drop.[143]

Ford and Kissinger thought that Schlesinger had ignored the order to complete the final bombing run. He may have, and he certainly had no respect for Kissinger's symbolic acts. "Henry was an incorrigible signal-sender, even when it might have been dangerous."[144] Either way, Ford had one more reason to dislike his secretary of defense.

At the meeting, Colby reported that the Thai government had decided to expel a senior member of the U.S. mission to Bangkok in protest over American use of military bases in Thailand. The government was facing leftist protests over the American actions, but the military was quietly supportive.[145] Thailand had already requested that the U.S. shut down its bases within a year, and after the operation the government demanded an immediate withdrawal. The U.S. responded with an apology for "misunderstandings," and the situation blew over. The American bases were closed on schedule.[146]

Ford's advisors were uniformly impressed by his performance during the crisis, and the American public agreed. His approval ratings increased from 39 to 51 percent in the Gallup Poll.[147] His performance was impressive, but the incident was not momentous. Kissinger offered the most apt description of the affair in his memoirs when he acknowledged "the reality that we had entered Indochina to save a country, and that we had ended by rescuing a ship."[148]

12

Helsinki

After Vladivostok, the focus of U.S.–Soviet relations shifted from SALT to the Conference on Security and Cooperation in Europe. The nations of Europe and the United States had been negotiating since early 1973 to end the state of war that had never been officially lifted after World War II. The conference's work would be completed in the summer of 1975 when the participating nations met in Helsinki to sign its Final Act. The Soviets had been clamoring for the treaty because they wanted the countries of Europe to recognize the boundaries that had been established after World War II. The United States and its NATO allies took advantage of the Soviet desire for a treaty to extract a commitment to respect human rights; and in return, they agreed that the existing boundaries of Europe could only be changed "by peaceful means and by agreement."

The Final Act was divided into four sections, which were labeled "baskets." In Basket One, the parties agreed that their borders were "inviolable," not to be changed except by peaceful means. Basket One also included "confidence building measures," requiring advance notice of large troop movements. The NATO nations had demanded these measures as a deterrent to a Warsaw Pact invasion of Western Europe. Basket Two contained general commitments to trade and technical exchanges. In Basket Three the parties committed to respect human rights and allow movement of people and information between countries. Basket Four set procedures to monitor compliance.[1]

The Soviets badly wanted the agreement to respect borders, but that did not mean the NATO countries were giving up anything by making the commitment. They had given similar assurances in the UN charter and other international agreements. Furthermore, there was little desire in the West — or among the people of Eastern Europe, for that matter — to reverse most of the border changes that followed the war. Areas of Poland had been incorporated into the USSR, and, in return, Poland received lands that had been part of Germany; and no one was pushing for those changes to be reversed. Nor did anyone propose undoing the arrangement under which the USSR and Bulgaria incorporated small parts of Romania, while Romania, Czechoslovakia, and the Soviet Union received parts of Hungary. And there was no groundswell to take Trieste from Italy and give it back to Yugoslavia. The only real disputes were over the NATO countries' objection to the Soviet Union's absorption of Lithuania, Latvia, and Estonia, and the desire of the German people to reunify. But West Germany had no intention of using force to achieve reunification, and West and East Germany had agreed in a 1971 treaty that their existing boundaries were "inviolable."

The NATO nations had no plans to forcibly wrest the countries of Eastern Europe from Soviet domination — they had not even used their military might to respond when the Soviets invaded East Germany in 1953, Hungry in 1956, and Czechoslovakia in 1968. Nevertheless, the Final Act would not prohibit a future military action by NATO to stop a Soviet invasion of a Warsaw Pact country, and by signing the Helsinki Accords the USSR was committing not to invade the nations within its orbit.[2] The promise did not mean much — the Soviets had violated similar promises in the past — but it was better than nothing, and nothing was what the United States and its NATO allies were giving up.

At the time, it seemed that the only hope for the elimination of Soviet dominance of Eastern Europe was for the Warsaw Pact nations to gradually move out of the Soviet orbit, and that possibility was enhanced by the Final Act. Privately, leaders in Eastern Europe told the administration that the Final Act would allow them more freedom to act independently.[3]

As innocuous as the Final Act was, it became a lighting rod for critics of détente. The cries against détente had been growing since the Vladivostok summit. As the date for the Helsinki meeting approached, a storm of protest rose against the accords. Critics claimed that the Final Act ceded control of Eastern Europe to the Soviet Union. The claim became a truism — no one explained how the accords actually ceded control of anything, nor did anyone explain how the people of the Warsaw Pact would be less free after the accords than they were before the Helsinki Conference.

As Ford was fending off criticism for giving in to the Soviets, Brezhnev was under fire from his country's hard-liners for agreeing to the human rights provisions of the Final Act. When Gromyko presented the draft treaty to the Politburo, the Soviet leaders were shocked by the human rights commitments. Gromyko quieted the Politburo critics by pointing out that the Final Act guaranteed each country its own laws, so the Soviets could interpret the human rights provisions in the way it saw fit. "We are masters in our own house."[4] The Soviet leaders were right to be concerned, and they would be the losers at Helsinki.

—⁓—

The cries against Helsinki reached a crescendo when Ford made the mistake of refusing to meet with Soviet dissident Aleksandr Solzhenitsyn. Solzhenitsyn was a true hero who had courageously brought the sufferings of his people to the attention of the world. He spent eight years in Soviet labor camps and several more in internal exile in Siberia, and he gave vivid life to the camps in *One Day in the Life of Ivan Denisovich* and *Cancer Ward*. In 1974 the Soviets expelled him after the publication of his multi-volume masterpiece, *The Gulag Archipelago*, which documented in detail the millions who had died in the Soviet prison camps.

AFL-CIO president George Meany invited Ford to a June 30 dinner for Solzhenitsyn, and Senators Strom Thurmond and Jesse Helms asked him to invite the Russian dissident to the White House on the day of the dinner. Kissinger asked members of the administration not to attend the dinner because he did not want to offend the Soviets, and he knew that Solzhenitsyn would criticize détente in his speech. Three officials attended anyway, Schlesinger, Secretary of Labor John Dunlop, and Daniel Patrick Moynihan, who had taken office as ambassador to the U.N. that day. Marsh suggested that Ford attend, but Kissinger and Scowcroft talked him out of it.

It is not that Ford and Kissinger had no respect for Solzhenitsyn. In the first days of the administration, Kissinger read the entirety of *The Gulag Archipelago* — no mean feat — and he gave a copy to Ford.[5] But Kissinger did not want to antagonize the Soviets in the weeks before Helsinki, and Ford was not looking forward to being excoriated by the Soviet dissident, who he called "a goddamn horse's ass." Like other visionaries, Solzhenitsyn was a difficult person, and Ford was right to fear that he would lecture him about his failure to stand up to the Soviets. Just two weeks before, Solzhenitsyn had written an article in the *New York Times* that repeated the canard that the Final Act would sanction Soviet domination of Eastern Europe.[6] And Ford was right that his political opponents were proposing the meeting to embarrass him, but that was not a reason to turn down the meeting. Solzhenitsyn was one of the great men of the 20th century, and Ford should have agreed to meet with him, even though the meeting was sure to be uncomfortable. Helms and Thurman were irate at Ford's snub, and they publicly asked Ford to meet with Solzhenitsyn on July 4. Ford rejected the invitation, but he asked Solzhenitsyn to visit after the Helsinki Conference.[7]

Kissinger was right when he predicted that Solzhenitsyn would condemn détente. At the June 30 dinner, Solzhenitsyn quoted Khrushchev's "we will bury you" taunt and said that the Soviets now just called it "détente."[8] Three weeks later he called the Final Act "a mass grave for all the countries of Eastern Europe."[9] Like many détente critics, Solzhenitsyn mistakenly believed that the Western democracies were becoming weaker while the Soviet Union was growing in power. He wrote in the *New York Times* that "the last thirty years are clearly a long, though tortuous, decline of the West.... Soon they will be twice as powerful as you, and then five times, and then ten times."[10] He would prove to be profoundly wrong on this point, but he had been courageously correct over the years in exposing the crimes of the Soviet regime.

———

As the Helsinki Conference neared, détente detractors thundered against the Final Act. The *Wall Street Journal* had terse advice for Ford: "Jerry, Don't Go."[11] Ronald Reagan said "I am against it, and I think all Americans should be against it."[12] William Safire wrote in the *New York Times* that the agreement favored the Soviets. "In case you hadn't heard, World War II will soon be coming to its official end. The Russians won."[13] The *National Review* claimed that the Helsinki Accords were telling the people of Eastern Europe: "Abandon hope, all ye who read our words."[14]

To address these concerns, Ford met with Americans of Eastern European descent on the morning of July 25, the day before he left for Helsinki. When they drafted Ford's comments, Hartmann's speechwriters, worried about the political fallout of Helsinki, included a sentence denouncing the conference. Fortunately, Scowcroft saw the speech and removed it.[15] But he left in a statement that the United States was not recognizing the incorporation of the Baltic nations into the Soviet Union:

> I can assure you as one who has long been interested in this question that the United States has never recognized the Soviet incorporation of Lithuania, Latvia, and Estonia and is not doing so now. Our official policy of nonrecognition is not affected by the results of the European Security Conference.[16]

Although Scowcroft had no problem with the statement, Kissinger hit the roof when he heard it — as usual, the secretary of state was far too sensitive about offending the Soviets. When Kissinger saw Scowcroft and Hartmann outside the Oval Office, he exploded. "You will pay for this! I tell you, heads will roll." Hartmann had included the same statement in Ford's speech at the airport when he left for Europe, and Kissinger made him take it out. But it was too late to take it out of the printed copy, and the statement got even more press when reporters noticed the omission.[17]

Ford tried to show that he was not abandoning the nations of Eastern Europe by visiting some of the more independent Eastern European countries on his trip. He visited Poland on his way to Helsinki, and Romania and Yugoslavia on the return trip. All three nations were every bit as totalitarian as their brethren, but their leaders had tried to implement foreign policies that were independent of the Soviet Union.[18]

———

Ford signing the Final Act of the Conference on Security and Cooperation in Europe in Helsinki, Finland, August 1, 1975. (Photograph by David Hume Kennerly; courtesy Gerald R. Ford Library.)

On July 30, representatives of thirty-five nations met in Helsinki for the largest meeting of European leaders since the Congress of Vienna in 1815. The negotiations of the Final Act had been completed before the conference, so the sole purpose of the meeting was to sign the document. The conference lasted two days, both of which were filled with tedious speeches from every head of state in attendance. When Ford spoke on the morning of August 1, he declared that the people of Europe and North America were tired of "empty words and unfulfilled pledges," and he concluded by putting the Soviets on the spot. He looked Brezhnev in the eye — in a gesture that no observer could miss — and told him that the Soviets better fulfill their commitments. "History will judge this Conference not by what we say here today, but by what we do tomorrow — not by the promises we make, but by the promises we keep."[19] At 5:00 that evening the thirty-five nations signed the Final Act.

━━━⟳⟳⟳━━━

Before the conference the *National Review* declared that the Final Act told the people of Eastern Europe to "abandon hope," but the people of Eastern Europe had long before abandoned all hope of being liberated by NATO armies — Berlin, Hungary and Czechoslovakia taught them that they were on their own. So the people of Eastern Europe took hope from the accords.

Ironically, the first time the accords were used to attack the Soviet regime happened at the same time Ford was being excoriated for signing them. During the 1976 presidential campaign, Ronald Reagan had been hammering Ford for Helsinki. In a nationally-televised speech on March 31, Reagan said that the Helsinki agreement gave approval to the Soviet enslavement of Eastern Europe. "Mr. Ford traveled halfway 'round the world to sign the Helsinki Pact, putting our stamp of approval on Russia's enslavement of the captive nations. We gave away the freedom of millions of people, freedom that was not ours to give."[20] Carter would later echo Reagan's statements in the debates. "We've virtually signed, in Helsinki, an agreement that the Russians have dominance in Eastern Europe."[21]

Reagan's attacks on Ford's foreign policy became particularly fierce before the primary in Texas on May 1. On the day before the primary a Russian physicist named Yuri Orlov began the process that proved the attacks on Helsinki to be misguided. On April 30, Orlov called Ludmilla Alexeyeva and asked her to go for a walk through the streets of Moscow. Alexeyeva was a prominent dissident, and as they were walking down the Moscow streets that night he asked her to help form the "Public Group of Assistance to Implementation of the Helsinki Agreements in the USSR." He explained that the group would document human rights abuses in the Soviet Union and send the documents to the nations that had signed the accords. Orlov recruited other members, including Anatoly Shcharansky, a noted refusnik, and Aleksandr Ginzburg, who had been working as a personal secretary for Andrei Sakharov and running the Moscow operations of Solzhenitsyn's foundation to provide money to families of political prisoners.

The dissidents had an important insight that would not have occurred to détente opponents in the West. They recognized that the Soviets valued the appearance of the law, and by demonstrating that the USSR was not complying with the terms of the accords, the Helsinki Watch Group could have a significant impact. The other key insight of the dissidents was that their safety did not lie in secrecy, but in openness. The Helsinki Group acted entirely in public. They signed every document, demonstrated in the open, and talked on the record to reporters. If the Soviet government took action against them, it would be buying bad publicity and proving that it ignored its own laws.

Orlov announced the new group on May 13 at the home of Sakharov, whose wife Yelena Bonner had joined the group. The group immediately began documenting human rights abuses, and within a year Helsinki groups had been formed in Ukraine, Lithuania, Georgia, and Armenia, and groups followed in Norway, the United States, Italy and other Western countries. The Helsinki groups proved effective at getting coverage in Western media, and their work helped lead to the downfall of communism in Eastern Europe and the Soviet Union. Orlov and his colleagues paid a dear price for their courage. Before the Helsinki Group was dissolved in 1982, twenty of its members went to prison, and five died in prison camps. Orlov spent nine years in prison.[22]

Orlov and the other dissidents in the Warsaw Pact nations were remarkably effective using the Final Act as a tool to crack the façade of the totalitarian regimes oppressing them. Vaclav Havel has acknowledged Helsinki's importance to the dissident movement:

> There, communist governments guaranteed certain rights and freedoms, even though those governments, of course, had no intention of respecting them.... And these movements were based on that they took them literally and they referred to these agreements. That was one source of the idea of resistance which was non-violent and even legalistic, I'd say. All we wanted was for the government to abide by these valid laws and international treaties.[23]

—◦◦◦—

At the same time that dissidents within Eastern European countries were using the Helsinki Accords to challenge the power of their communist governments, those same governments were using the accords to pull away from the Soviet Union. The countries of Eastern Europe used Basket Two to increase trade and communications with each other and with

Western Europe, and it was communication and trade more than anything that led to the fall of communism in Europe.[24] Wojciech Jaruzelski has explained that the Warsaw Pact nations also became less belligerent as a result of the Final Act. "The Helsinki meeting created a new climate, which was not favorable to excessively militaristic rhetoric."[25] William Hyland has identified the Accords as the beginning of the end of communism in Europe. "If it can be said that there was one point when the Soviet empire finally began to crack, it was at Helsinki."[26] Anatoly Dobrynin has come to the same conclusion:

> The Helsinki Final Act ... played a significant role in bringing about the long and difficult process of liberalization inside the Soviet Union and the nations of Eastern Europe. This in the end caused the fundamental changes in all these countries that helped end the Cold War.[27]

Even some of the virulent critics of détente have reconsidered their opposition to Helsinki. For example, Richard Perle has admitted that he and Jackson were mistaken when they attacked the accords:

> Looking back, I think we were wrong. We under-estimated the potential of basket three. We probably over-estimated the importance of basket one, it proved to be almost a non-event, it was pretty ephemeral. But basket three remained and it was a source of encouragement to the dissidents and at the end of the day, the dissidents more than anyone else, brought down the Soviet Union, so on reflection and looking back at it, I think on balance, Helsinki was a good thing.[28]

Kissinger may have been right about Helsinki, but his critics were on the mark when they accused him of not being willing to criticize the Soviets. He didn't understand the value of moral persuasion, which he demonstrated in his handling of Ambassador to the UN Daniel Patrick Moynihan. Moynihan had written an article titled "The United States in Opposition," urging that America speak up at the UN. When Kissinger read the article he suggested that Ford appoint Moynihan to a commission to implement his recommendations. Ford chose more direct action, and he appointed him ambassador to the UN.[29] When he appointed Moynihan, Ford told him he expected "strong statements and the guts to veto and vote against."[30]

When Moynihan took office he acted exactly as he said he would, fighting against the usual anti–American rhetoric in the General Assembly. It drove Kissinger crazy, and he told Ford that "Moynihan is a disaster."[31] Moynihan knew that Kissinger was trying to undermine him, and he couldn't handle the lack of support. The ambassador from the United Kingdom to the UN, Ivor Richards, gave a talk in November 1975 declaring that the General Assembly should not be a "confrontational arena.... Whatever else the place is, it is not the OK Corral and I am hardly Wyatt Earp."[32] When the speech was reported in the *Washington Post*, Moynihan thought that Kissinger was behind the criticism, and he resigned in February 1976.[33]

The Moynihan episode showed the unfortunate side of détente. It was important for the United States to continue to speak out for freedom and to condemn the human rights violations of the Soviet Union, China, and other communist nations. It wasn't necessary to détente for the country to tone down its rhetoric, but sometimes it made negotiations easier. Kissinger frequently took the easy route and told the administration to temper its criticism of the Soviets, because he didn't understand the value of the bully pulpit. He didn't understand the power of words, but neither did his critics, who failed to comprehend the power of the human rights commitments in the Helsinki Accords, which would bring down an empire.

While they were in Helsinki, the superpowers met to try to resolve final issues on SALT II. Before the trip, Ford met with the NSC to develop a negotiating position. Colby explained that the danger of the Soviets cheating on an agreement was not a concern. Schlesinger agreed that the possibility of the Soviets cheating on silo size "has eventually no significance militarily, but it is a political problem." In the meeting, there was agreement that the Backfire was designed for tactical, not strategic, missions. It could be refueled in flight and reach America, but that was true of all planes. Colby told Ford that "the Backfire is being deployed initially for use in peripheral operations; its use against the US is an open question." Despite the lack of concern about the plane, Ford's advisors could not come up with a practical alternative to solve the Backfire issue.

Things looked better for a resolution of the cruise missile issue because the administration could live with much of the current Soviet position. The U.S. had no objection to the Soviet proposal on land-based cruise missiles, which was that missiles with a range of more than 5,500 kilometers would be banned, because it would allow the U.S. to place cruise missiles in Europe which could reach most of the USSR, while the Soviets could not reach the U.S. with their cruise missiles. The administration didn't like the Soviet proposal on air- and submarine-launched cruise missiles, but a compromise appeared possible.[34]

In Helsinki, Ford and Kissinger met with Gromyko and Brezhnev on the day after the conference closed. Brezhnev was clearly not as mentally sharp as he was in Vladivostok. He had to take regular breaks for Gromyko to explain the discussions, and the Americans overheard several instances when, even after Gromyko explained the issue to him, Brezhnev said, "I don't understand." The talks went well at first, as the parties agreed on verification procedures and on a 600-kilometer limitation on the range of ship-launched cruise missiles. But the parties could not agree on the range of air-launched cruise missiles, and Ford and Brezhnev fought about the capabilities of the Backfire. When Ford claimed that it had the range to reach the U.S., Brezhnev disagreed. "You get your intelligence reports, and I get mine. But we sit here and don't believe each other." The meeting closed with Brezhnev asking Kissinger to visit Moscow in September.[35] As they were getting ready to leave Helsinki, Brezhnev pulled Ford aside and told him that he hoped he would be reelected in 1976.[36]

—◦◦◦—

The next week Ford told the NSC that there would be no deal unless the administration compromised. "If we continue with our position of a 3,000 kilometer limit on ALCMs and a 1,500 kilometer limit on SLCMs and if, in addition, we make no movement on how we want to handle Backfire, then I don't think there's going to be an agreement." Reading the transcript of the meeting, it is hard to understand why these issues would ultimately kill SALT II. Colby explained that there was no real danger of the Soviets developing first strike capability during the term of the agreement. "We see no technical developments that are likely to give them a strategic first strike against us." General Brown concurred with the CIA's assessment that the Backfire was not designed for strategic missions, like attacking the United States. "We agree that it is probably designed for peripheral missions.... The Backfire is not a first strike weapon." Schlesinger's comments provide the most insight into why the Backfire was a problem. "If Backfire can only attack by overflying the US on a one-way mission, it is less important substantively versus politically terms. Critics on the Hill will argue that if the aggregate is 2400 and the Backfire is free, they will be able to do more than us."[37] Two days earlier Rockefeller and Kissinger heard the same thing from Ford's Foreign Intelligence Advisory Board. Board member John Foster explained that the Backfire wasn't a big issue. "Backfire is part of the noise level. I would give it to them."[38]

In a meeting a month later Ford continued to press the NSC for a solution. "I think it is in the national interests to get a SALT II agreement — I mean the right kind — but a SALT

II agreement is in the country's interest." During the meeting Schlesinger admitted that the Backfire was built for peripheral missions. "All our studies agree that it was optimized that way." Again his concerns were political. "The biggest problem on Backfire is political — how it will be viewed on the Hill."[39] Despite the fact that there were no significant military concerns, Schlesinger and his successor, Rumsfeld — both of whom were motivated by political, not military concerns — would use the Backfire and cruise missile issues to foil Ford's efforts to reach an arms control agreement.

———

At the end of the year, Kissinger's aide Hal Sonnenfeldt gave détente critics an emotionally-charged issue when he made ill-considered remarks about the Helsinki Accords. Sonnenfeldt was Kissinger's right-hand man in negotiations with the Soviets. He accompanied Kissinger in all of his discussions with Brezhnev, and Kissinger used him as a foil for jokes. Détente critics would take Sonnenfeldt's obscure ramblings and declare that the administration had a new "doctrine" approving of Soviet domination of Eastern Europe. Sonnenfeldt certainly did not intend his comments to say that. Within the government he had long been an advocate for trying to free Eastern European countries from Soviet dominance.[40]

And Sonnenfeldt's comments certainly were not an administration "doctrine." They were off-the-cuff remarks in an informal discussion with other State Department officials. His aide prepared a summary of the discussion, which was included in a State Department newsletter. When Rowland Evans and Robert Novak obtained the newsletter, one paragraph caused a firestorm:

> The Soviets' inability to acquire loyalty in Eastern Europe is an unfortunate historical failure, because Eastern Europe is within their scope and area of natural interest. It is doubly tragic that in this area of vital interest and crucial importance it has not been possible for the Soviet Union to establish roots of interest that go beyond sheer power.... With regard to Eastern Europe, it must be in our long term interest to influence events in this area — because of the present unnatural relationship with the Soviet Union — so that they will not sooner or later explode, causing World War III.... So it must be our policy to strive for an evolution that makes the relationship between the Eastern Europeans and the Soviet Union an organic one.... So our policy must be a policy of responding to the clearly visible aspirations in Eastern Europe for a more autonomous existence within the context of a strong Soviet geopolitical influence. This has worked in Poland. The Poles have been able to overcome their romantic political inclinations which led to their disasters in the past.[41]

Sonnenfeldt's musings were abstruse. At first glance he appeared to be saying that the administration wished that the Soviets had more control over the Warsaw Pact nations. Read more closely, Sonnenfeldt was saying that the United States was encouraging the nations of Eastern Europe to act more independently of the Soviet Union, without provoking another Soviet invasion. To the extent that Sonnenfeldt was saying that the United States was not willing to risk a world war to defend the independence of Eastern European countries, he was simply stating reality. But his inference that it would be better if the Soviets had more power over its satellites was disturbing. Disturbing or not, Sonnenfeldt's remarks were not the declaration of a new doctrine, as Kissinger explained in typically egocentric fashion. "If it were truly a new doctrine of this administration, it would not be named after Hal Sonnenfeldt."[42]

Détente critics played the comments for all they were worth. When they broke the story, Evans and Novak said, "The Sonnenfeldt doctrine exposes the underpinnings of détente." In the *New York Times*, C. L. Sulzberger actually wrote that Sonnenfeldt's private comments were an invitation to the Soviets to exert sovereignty over Eastern Europe. "It would seem to be an invitation to the Kremlin to assert fuller control of Eastern Europe, perhaps even absorbing it into the U.S.S.R." Reagan took advantage of Sonnenfeldt's ill-considered remarks. He said that the administration was saying "slaves should accept their fate."[43] It was much ado about nothing, but the uproar over Sonnenfeldt's comments showed how deep opposition to détente had become.

13

Portugal and Spain

The congressional intelligence investigations may have saved Portugal. When Ford took office the Iberian nation was the subject of a fight between democratic and communist forces, and it looked like the communists were winning. In previous similar situations the CIA had supported right-wing extremists in coups that restored order, but those episodes were being aired in congressional hearings, so the administration could not try anything similar in Portugal. At the time, it was the widely-held belief of the foreign policy establishment that that once communists controlled certain positions of power they would be unstoppable by democratic forces, and the only alternative was a right-wing dictatorship. Kissinger shared this view. He believed that once the communists gained control of "levers of power," such as the army and the police, "it is almost inconceivable that in power they won't seek to bring about such political change that they couldn't be voted out."[1]

It was the lesson that foreign policy leaders took from the 1917 Russian Revolution, the fall of China and the Eastern European countries in the '40s, and the fall of Cuba in the '50s. It was a simplistic analysis — Eastern Europe went communist because it was occupied by the Soviet army, not because indigenous communist elements controlled levers of power, and the success of Lenin, Mao, and Castro had as much to do about the venality and incompetence of their opponents as anything else. That was the extent of the sample size, because every time the communists came near power in other countries, the CIA supported right wing military coups. As a result, countries like Indonesia, Zaire, Chile, and Guatemala were ruled for decades by despotic generals.

The battle for Portugal would be different. The country had thrown off its fascist dictators in the months before Ford took office, and for the next two years democratic factions fought with communist forces who were trying to take over the country. The American representatives in Portugal actively discouraged right-wing leaders from attempting a coup, and the democrats were able to prevail, leading to decades of peace and prosperity. The strategy wasn't Kissinger's first choice. Throughout 1975 he complained to Ford that he couldn't take real action because of the intelligence investigations. In February he complained about "what we are doing to ourselves — like Portugal. I don't dare do anything."[2]

Portugal had been ruled by right-wing dictators since 1926, most of that time by a former economics professor named Antonio de Oliveira Salazar. Salazar's view of a perfect society was one where everything and everyone was dedicated to the state, domestic peace was assured by stifling all dissent, and women were confined to their homes. His secret police had spies in every neighborhood, and they ran a concentration camp for dissenters on a barren Cape Verde island. Not surprisingly, Portugal remained undeveloped in this stifling environment — per-capita income was the lowest in Europe, and between 1960 and the revolution in 1974, more than 1.5 million people left the country, leaving just over 3 million people in the workforce.

Portugal was the last European country to let go of its empire. During the '60s serious insurrections broke out in Angola, Guinea-Bissau, and Mozambique, and the wars took a terrible toll on Portugal. One in four men of military age was in the military, despite rampant draft evasion, and almost half of the government's budget went to the wars. In 1968, Salazar became incapacitated after his deck chair collapsed. The new premier, Marcelo Caetano, relaxed censorship a little, but the totalitarian regime remained in place. Like Kerensky in Russia, Caetano's fate was sealed by his refusal to withdraw his country from an unpopular war. He refused to let go of Portugal's colonies, and the battles to keep them continued to bleed the country dry.[3]

The first cracks in the regime came in 1974 with the publication of *Portugal and Its Future,* by General Antonio de Spinola, a veteran of the wars in Guinea-Bissau and Angola. Spinola looked like an anachronism, sporting a monocle and carrying a riding crop, but his book was a huge hit because it was the first admission by a high government official that the wars could not be won. Spinola was adopted by a group of young officers who had formed the Movimento das Forças Armadas, or Armed Forces Movement (MFA). While Spinola was made the nominal leader, the group was really led by the moderate Ernesto Melo Antunes and leftists Colonel Vasco dos Santos Gonçalves and Captain Otelo Saraiva de Carvalho. The MFA overthrew the government on April 25, 1974. Not a shot was fired in defense of the fascist regime, and virtually all of Portugal flooded into the streets to celebrate. Caetano ceded power to Spinola, and he and his top officials were allowed to fly to Brazil. Both the United States and the Soviet Union were caught by surprise by the revolution.

At first the new government was dedicated to freedom and democracy, which would prove to be exactly what the vast majority of Portuguese wanted. The new government released political prisoners, abolished the secret police, declared its support for freedom of speech, and promised free elections. Political parties were allowed for the first time in decades, and Spinola promised to hold free elections within a year.

The two leading protagonists in the battle for the country returned to Portugal in the days after the revolution. The leader of the Socialist Party, Mario Soares, flew back from Paris, and he and two colleagues joined the new government. The chunky Soares was a riveting public speaker, and he would lead his country to freedom. His primary antagonist would be Communist Party general secretary Álvaro Cunhal, who flew back from Prague. Cunhal had spent ten years in Salazar's prisons, seven in solitary confinement. He was vain and imperious, with "thick white hair, a deep voice, bushy eyebrows."[4] When he landed in Lisbon, Cunhal was shocked when the conservative general Galvão de Melo told him that the official television station was ready to air his address that evening. Cunhal also joined the government.

The first government collapsed on July 9 (one month before Ford took office), and Spinola was forced to name a new prime minister, General Vasco Gonçalves. The new prime minister was a puritanical and aloof communist supporter. When he took office, Gonçalves spoke out against pornography being sold in magazine stands, and he called a German musical featuring naked women a "CIA plot." Spinola was also forced to accelerate the timeline for independence for the colonies, which he predicted would take a generation. On July 27 he announced that Portugal was beginning the transfer of power. "The moment has come for our overseas territories to take their destinies into their own hands."[5] Almost a million white colonists returned to Portugal.[6]

The country took a turn to the left two months after Ford took office when Spinola was forced to resign. He brought matters to a head three days earlier by calling Gonçalves and another leftist member of the government, Otelo Carvalho, to his palace, where he and other right-wing officers berated them and refused to let Otelo leave. The left wing was convinced that Spinola was masterminding a coup, and they set up barricades throughout Lisbon. The crisis was resolved when Chief of Staff Costa Gomes forced Spinola to release Otelo and resign. Costa Gomes became president.[7]

The Americans in Lisbon considered the new president a "communist Trojan horse."[8] Less than three weeks after Gomes took power, he and Soares visited Washington. Ford was respectful when he met them in the Oval Office at noon on October 18, and he urged the Portuguese to begin a democratic process.[9] Kissinger was less tactful when he met them the next day. The secretary of state predicted that Soares would be "another Kerensky." When Soares responded that he had no desire to be a Kerensky, Kissinger responded, "Neither did Kerensky."[10] It was a witty response but hardly a fair comparison. Kerensky was a preening dictator who had lost the support of his people because he cared only about maintaining his power. Soares was the exact opposite — he was a true democrat, and he would risk his life during the next year to bring freedom to his people.

———⌇∽∽∽⌇———

While he thought the democrats still had a chance, Kissinger was willing to take small steps to support them. He surprised everyone in December by supporting a proposal by Senator Kennedy to provide $55 million in aid to Portugal, declaring that the aid was a demonstration of support for Gomes because "we are fully conscious of the efforts he is making to guide Portugal toward democracy."[11] He had the administration give Portugal $25 million, which was the most he could pledge without congressional action. In February he convinced Ford to support a $1 million grant to send Portuguese abroad for education, and $750,000 in U.S. AID assistance. "A half-hearted program is better than none."[12]

Despite his public statements, Kissinger suspected that Portugal was falling into the communist camp. The Soviets were trying to create a communist takeover, led by Cunhal and Gonçalves, and they poured money into the country. Where Kissinger was mistaken was in his pessimistic view that the communists were certain to prevail. Kissinger's pessimistic assessment was contradicted by the affable but ineffective Ambassador Stuart Nash Scott, so the secretary of state summarily fired Scott and replaced him with Frank Carlucci, a no-nonsense career officer who had worked in the Congo during the elimination of Lumumba and in Chile during Pinochet's coup. Kissinger was sure that this was the perfect man to take a hard line in Portugal, but he was to be sorely disappointed. When Carlucci arrived in Lisbon he quickly realized that the situation was more promising than Kissinger believed.[13]

———⌇∽∽∽⌇———

Until Carlucci arrived in Lisbon in January 1975, the Portuguese embassy was considered a backwater. Under Secretary Laurence Eagleburger told him that "it was the worst embassy in the world."[14] Carlucci quickly upgraded the embassy staff, and he embarked on an energetic effort to understand the situation by meeting church and political leaders. When Soares came to the ambassador's residence just days after he arrived, Carlucci thought the socialist leader seemed defeated, but his mood improved during their regular meetings over the next two years. Carlucci spent hours arguing issues with Gonçalves, who always took a marxist line, as did Costa Gomes. Carlucci reached out to the Catholic Church to enlist its support, and he developed contacts in the MFA to demonstrate that America understood that it contained both communist and democratic elements. Carlucci's political affairs advisor, Richard Melton, also reached out to the younger members of the MFA, and he found them eager to make contact with the United States. Carlucci took a "firm stand" against Azorean separatism, and he told the CIA to refrain from supporting the extreme right. As a result, the CIA played only a minor role in the crisis, and there was no attempt to engineer a coup.[15]

Carlucci understood that Portugal was a conservative, religious country whose people would not naturally embrace communism. He told Kissinger that the situation wasn't hopeless, and he recommended working with democratic elements to promote a reasonable outcome. Carlucci recalls that Kissinger was "coolly critical of what he regarded as my willingness to bet on the democratic parties which he didn't regard as very strong at that point."[16] Back in Washington, Kissinger fumed. "Whoever sold me Carlucci as a tough guy?"[17] Carlucci told Kissinger that his bellicose statements were "pushing Portugal into the arms of the communists," and Kissinger responded, "If you are so goddamn smart, you make the statements."[18]

With covert operations impossible during the intelligence investigations, Kissinger wanted to write off and isolate the country as a lesson to the rest of Europe, but the rest of NATO disagreed. West Germany wanted to engage the government and help lead the country to democracy. Willy Brandt had helped Soares establish the Socialist Party in exile, and German organizations assisted other democratic parties. The French Socialist Party helped finance Soares, who had spent years in exile in Paris and had developed close ties with François Mitterrand and other socialist leaders. The European governments worked with the democratic parties and trade unions, but they also warned the Portuguese military and the Soviet Union that they would not accept a communist takeover in Portugal.[19]

A communist victory looked more likely after Spinola launched a coup on March 11, 1975. Virtually all of the military sided with the MFA, forcing Spinola to flee for exile in Spain. Radical elements took advantage of the coup to consolidate power. The third government fell, and the new government, under Vasco Gonçalves, was heavily influenced by the communists. Cunhal and Gonçalves began to lobby for a delay in the elections — polls were showing that they would get less than 15 percent of the vote — but moderate elements in the MFA refused to go along with the plan.[20]

After Spinola fled, General Otelo appeared on television and declared that Carlucci was behind the coup attempt, and he suggested that the American ambassador leave "because I cannot, at this time, guarantee his physical security." Carlucci immediately went to the television station and demanded to be put on the air. To his surprise, he was allowed to make a televised address, in which he said that he was entitled to protection as the ambassador of a NATO country, and reiterated America's support of democracy in Portugal. Carlucci also called Otelo to complain, and the general sent troops to protect the American ambassador's residence. Carlucci was telling the truth when he denied involvement in Spinola's attempt to take power. Contemporaneous CIA documents show that the agency was surprised by the coup and confused about what was happening. Nevertheless, many Portuguese continued to blame the United States, and for the rest of the year demonstrators marched on the American embassy. At one point Carlucci ordered his troops to tear gas them, and on another occasion they surrounded his car and rocked it back and forth.[21]

When the new government took power, Ford was terrified that the communists would leak NATO secrets to the Soviets, and he and Kissinger began to discuss whether to deny Portugal access to NATO information or to expel the country from the alliance altogether. Kissinger wanted to kick Portugal out of NATO, but the alliance had no established process for removing one of its members, and the other allies would not even consider the idea. Ford and Kissinger need not have worried because the Portuguese officers assigned to NATO voluntarily absented themselves from meetings where sensitive information was discussed, so they had nothing of import to send back to Lisbon where it could be leaked to the Soviets.[22]

———∽∾∾———

The elections were held as scheduled on April 25. The American embassy predicted that the Socialists would win, but the rosy assessment was greeted with skepticism at the State Department.[23] Soares campaigned with the slogan, "Socialism, yes! Dictatorship, no!" When 90 percent of the population turned out to vote, they gave him a sweeping mandate for democracy. The socialists received 38 percent of the vote, and the right wing party got 26 percent. The country had no interest in communism; the party received only 18 percent of the vote.[24] It was a historic victory for democracy and a crushing blow for communism, but Kissinger told Ford that the outcome didn't matter:

> The election was a popularity contest with no significance. There has been no change in direction because of the election. Algeria is their role model. The Europeans are ecstatic. But we could face in ten years a Socialist Europe whose cement is anti–Americanism.[25]

The communists didn't go quietly. Cunhal told journalist Oriana Fallaci that elections didn't matter. "We Communists don't accept the rules of the election game! ... I care nothing for elections. Nothing! Ha, ha!"[26] During a trip to Europe for a NATO summit meeting, Ford met with Prime Minister Gonçalves at Ambassador Firestone's residence in Brussels on the afternoon of May 29. Throughout the meeting Gonçalves tried to allay Ford's concerns by explaining that the military controlled foreign affairs, not the civilian government. Gonçalves promised that the Portuguese would "abide by our commitments and that we do not wish to weaken NATO." When Ford declared that the United States would not "tolerate a communist influence in NATO," Gonçalves promised, "There will be no such influence."[27] Two days later, Ford, Kissinger and Assistant Secretary Hartman met with Spanish dictator Francisco Franco in the generalissimo's office in Madrid. When they discussed Portugal, Franco told Ford that any outside interference in the country would do more harm than good. "Any foreign intervention would go against the moderate forces because it would unite the Portuguese against them."[28]

Gonçalves' promise that the communists would not dominate his government was proved worthless within two weeks. On July 9 the radical MFA members announced the transformation of Portugal into a "revolutionary workers' state," and a triumvirate of Gomes, Gonçalves, and Otelo took over. Soares resigned from the government, and he and his fellow socialists took to the streets. The counterrevolution began instantly, especially in the conservative north, where people attacked communist party headquarters. In July 1975, Soares led a massive rally in Lisbon against the junta. As he strode at the head of 10,000 protesters marching down the Avenida da Liberdade in Lisbon, the crowd yelled, "The people are no longer with the MFA," and, "Soldiers back to barracks." In another address, Soares asked the crowd, "Who chose these men? Little by little our revolution has been stolen from us."[29] After the demonstration in Lisbon, American embassy official Bill Kelly wrote a cable titled "Mario Soares: Standing Tall in a Deep Hole," which convinced Kissinger to support Carlucci. Kissinger told his ambassador that he had little faith that the socialists could prevail, but he reluctantly agreed to give his proposals a chance.[30]

Except for the communist strongholds in the south, Portugal was rising up against the communist takeover. In early August crowds in Oporto booed and spit on two top communist generals, and a crowd attacked Cunhal when he tried to give an address in the central town of Alcobada. Gonçalves was at the breaking point, and he was visibly agitated during his television appearances. By mid–August the CIA was upbeat about the changes in Portugal. "There are strong indications that a new leadership advocating a more moderate course will soon be in power." The agency noted that "a large body of moderate officers" had begun to speak out after the civilian protests.[31] The agency was referring to an anti-communist manifesto called the "Document of the Nine" which had been issued by nine prominent MFA moderates, led by Melo Antunes. It soon became apparent that the vast majority of the officers agreed with the manifesto, and Gonçalves was forced to resign on September 6. A new government took over, led by the moderate Admiral Pinheiro Azevedo.[32] By September 23, Ford thought things were going better, and he asked Italian minister of foreign affairs Mariano Rumor, "Are you as encouraged as I am about Portugal?"[33]

The communists tried to take power again on November 25 when radicals in the MFA launched a coup. They were disorganized and incompetent, and the revolt was quickly put down by the rest of the army. Although the communists in the government were not involved, they were forced out, as were the radicals in the military. That ended the crisis. On February 14, 1976, the military agreed to hand the government over to civilian leaders, and a new constitution was adopted in April.[34]

On April 25, more than 80 percent of voters went to the polls to elect a new National Assembly. The Socialists won again, this time with just under 35 percent of the vote. The moderate PPD came in second with just under 25 percent, and the right wing CDS came in third with 16 percent. The communists lost big again, collecting less than 15 percent of the vote. The presidential election was held at the end of June, and moderate General Ramalho Eanes swept the field. Eanes had become a national hero by leading the action to put down the communist coup in November. He was a leftist, but not a communist, and he was dedicated to democracy. Eanes asked the socialists to form a government, and Soares became prime minister on July 16.[35]

At the end of his presidency, Ford approved a large aid package to bolster the Soares government, which was in an economic crisis. In November, Kissinger told Ford that America was "Portugal's sole remaining hope," and he recommended contributing more then $500 million to a $2 billion package of loans with the Europeans. OMB recommended that a more-stringent austerity program be imposed on Portugal, but Simon and Scowcroft agreed with Kissinger that such a program was not politically possible, so Ford approved Kissinger's plan.[36]

The Soares government survived the economic crisis, but he would remain in office for just two more years. Nevertheless, Portugal has been a stable democracy ever since Soares took office. The Ford administration allowed the democratic forces to win, which was an accomplishment of restraint rather than action, and everyone was better off as a result. The Portuguese people were obviously better off under a democratic government rather than a dictatorship, and NATO was better off with a stable ally on the western coast of Europe rather than a military dictatorship beset by internal turmoil.

A similar scenario unfolded in Spain during the last year of Ford's presidency when Generalissimo Francisco Franco died at the end of 1975. Franco had brooked no opposition for four decades, but as his health began to fail, he finally gave up a bit of power in 1969 when he began to share power with vice president Carrero Blanco. At the same time, Franco named

Betty Ford (left) meets with Queen Sophia of Spain before dinner in the White House, June 2, 1976. (Photograph by David Hume Kennerly; courtesy Gerald R. Ford Library.)

as his successor Prince Juan Carlos, who had been groomed by Franco to take over as the ruling monarch, but who would reject the crown and lead his country to democracy. Prior to Franco's death, the Basque separatist group Euskadi Ta Askatasuna (ETA) was conducting a terror campaign against his regime. When the ETA assassinated Blanco, Franco replaced him with the hidebound Arias Navarro. Later that summer Franco extended martial law and increased censorship.[37]

According to Kissinger, the administration believed that the arrangements made by Franco would lead to democracy.[38] It is hard to see why. Ariasi was clearly opposed to democracy, and public perception of Juan Carlos was split between those who thought he was a die-hard Francoist and those who thought he was a lightweight playboy. At first, the new King appeared to be pandering to the military, releasing only a few political prisoners and keeping Arias as prime minister. The only glimmer of hope came when Juan Carlos appointed several reformers to the government on December 4. In February, Arias declared that he would staunchly defend Francoism, and one of his first acts was to send in troops and police to crush striking workers who were pushing for democracy.[39]

During the summer of 1976, Juan Carlos visited the United States, and he met with Ford in the Oval Office on June 2. The visit was cordial, and Juan Carlos left with assurances of American support.[40] When he returned to Spain, he asked Arias to resign and named Adolfo Suarez Gonzalez prime minister. The democratic opposition was appalled by the appointment of a long-time Francoist, but Juan Carlos knew his old friend. Suarez told his cabinet that he would make changes faster than the Francoists could respond. He announced a referendum on proposed political changes, followed by free elections, and Juan Carlos issued a royal pardon of political prisoners. Other than the Communist Party, political groups were allowed to operate, and the newly-free press flourished.

On September 8, Suarez submitted his reform program to the cabinet and senior military leaders. The military men approved it only out of loyalty to the King, and the plan passed legislature in October. The military leaders demanded that the Communist Party be excluded from reforms, and Suarez gave vague promises. He was not being completely above-board because he had been meeting with Communist Party general secretary Santiago Carrillo to work out the details of the party's legalization, which became official the next April. Carrillo would be a key actor. Unlike the communists in Portugal, he did not oppose democracy.

Despite a campaign of terror by the ETA and the ultra right, the populace turned out for the December 15 referendum, and the new political program passed with 94 percent of the vote. Spain held its first democratic elections on June 15, 1977. More than 80 percent of the populace turned out, and the Francoists received just 8 percent of the vote, while the communists received only 9 percent.[41] It was the beginning of democracy in Spain, but it would continue only because King Juan Carlos and Suarez would lead the country through the violence of the next few years.

With Spain's adoption of democracy, there were no more fascist governments in NATO. When Ford took office, fascist regimes bookended Western Europe, but with the rise of democracy in Greece, Portugal, and Spain during his administration, democratic regimes prevailed throughout NATO and Western Europe. The United States didn't play a major role in these developments, but it didn't stand in the way, and that was a historic change.

14

Cities in Crisis

When Ford took office, the great cities of the American north were in a bad way — a fact that was brought home by two events during his presidency: a busing crisis in Boston and a financial crisis in New York. On each occasion his first impulse was to keep the federal government out of the fray, partly because he shared the aversion the rest of America felt for the cities, but mainly because he deeply believed that it wasn't the proper job of the federal government to bail out local governments.

The cities had been changing for decades, as African Americans fled oppression in the South and sought a better life in the North. Between 1950 and 1970 the African American proportion of New York rose from 10 percent to 21 percent; in Los Angeles the change was from 9 percent to 18 percent; and in Chicago, 14 percent to 33 percent.[1] The cities became segregated, and segregation was compounded by political leaders who chose to locate large public housing projects in African American neighborhoods, which became ghettos of crime and despair. Those neighborhoods were further destroyed by race riots that struck many cities in the '60s. Use of illegal drugs had skyrocketed, and crime increased with drug use.[2]

While cities of the North declined, the suburbs were booming, and the South was being transformed. Until World War II, the South was the most rural, impoverished, and uneducated region of the United States, where only 25 percent of whites had a high school diploma and only 5 percent of African Americans had one. Southern whites — who had strenuously opposed the civil rights movement — benefited from the economic expansion that followed its elimination. No longer a moral pariah, the South integrated into the national economy. Affluent and ambitious African Americans no longer needed to move north, and educated whites were no longer unwilling to move south.

The affluent whites who had moved to the suburbs viewed the cities with disdain. Fixing the problems in the cities no longer seemed relevant to their lives, and the problems began to seem more intractable as the government turned from eliminating legally-mandated discrimination to addressing the poverty that had been created by three hundred years of denying opportunities to non-whites. So the first reaction that most Americans had to violence in Boston and bankruptcy in New York was to support Ford's choice to keep the federal government uninvolved. It was only when Ford's policy appeared to be spiteful that public opinion forced him to help New York.

———∿∿∿———

The first crisis began one month after Ford took office when Boston schools opened and students were bused for the first time to achieve racial balance. Busing was the next stage in the civil rights movement, and it was intensely unpopular across the country, with 80 to 90 percent of whites, and just over half of African Americans, opposed to the remedy.[3] In Boston, racist whites used the unpopularity of busing to attack the African American students who were being bused into their neighborhoods.

The fact that busing was unpopular did not make it different from the other major civil rights reforms, but the fact that it never gained acceptance did. When the Supreme Court struck down segregation in public education in 1954, the decision was opposed by half of American whites. By 1972, attitudes had changed — 84 percent of whites thought that African Americans and whites should attend the same schools. Support for housing integration followed a similar pattern. In 1942, two-thirds of whites said that they would object to African Americans with "the same income and education" moving to their block — 86 percent thought that African Americans should live in separate areas — but by the time Ford took office, fewer than 15 percent of whites said that they would object to African Americans with the same income and education moving to their block. Interracial marriage was the last taboo broken. Before the Supreme Court struck down laws prohibiting interracial marriages in 1967, if there was one thing that white Americans agreed on it was that marriage should be defined as a union between a man and a woman of the same race — only 17 percent of whites supported interracial marriage. Interracial marriage started gaining acceptance, but when Ford took office, 39 percent of whites still favored laws forbidding them.[4]

Busing was being used to attack a very real problem. The school systems in the north had not been legally segregated, but administrators had operated them to achieve *de facto* segregation. After they had integrated the legally-segregated systems of the South, federal courts began attacking the segregated systems in the north.[5] But busing faced stiff opposition, and the opposition never waned. The primary problem was that busing forced students to attend different schools, while earlier reforms had opened opportunities for African Americans who chose to attend different schools. While the other reforms were quickly accepted as an expansion of liberty, busing always seemed to be a step back from freedom.

In 1971 the Supreme Court first addressed the issue in *Swann v. Charlotte-Mecklenburg Board of Education*, holding that "busing was a permissible tool for desegregation purposes."[6] But the court undermined the effectiveness of busing just two weeks before Ford took office. In *Milliken v. Bradley* it took away courts' ability to order busing across city and suburban systems.[7] The ruling eliminated busing as an effective tool — whites could move to the suburbs to avoid busing — and the remaining effects would be almost exclusively negative, but busing advocates would not give up.

One of the busing supporters who persisted was Massachusetts federal judge W. Arthur Garrity. On July 21, 1974, Garrity imposed a busing plan after he found that the Boston School Committee had intentionally created a segregated school district. The order was a damning indictment of the school system, demonstrating that the committee built schools in certain locations and of a particular size to promote segregation, allowed white students to transfer out of black schools, and refused to transfer white students from overcrowded schools to underutilized black schools. Tensions ran high as the schools prepared to open on September 12. A crowd of 4,000 people hung Garrity in effigy, and jeered and threw tomatoes and eggs as Ted Kennedy tried to calm them. When the schools opened, the most restive section of town was the insular Irish neighborhood of South Boston known as "Southie." Whites in Southie stoned the buses carrying black students and yelled racial epithets. The conflict in South Boston continued for several weeks, but the rest of the city was relatively calm.

On October 8, Mayor Kevin White asked Garrity to order the federal government to deploy 125 federal marshals in South Boston to keep order, but the judge denied the motion and scolded the mayor for not doing enough to keep the peace.[8] The next day, Ford told the press that he had not received a request for marshals. "As far as I know, no specific request has come to me for any further federal involvement, and therefore, I am not in a position to act under those circumstances."[9] Mayor White continued to make petulant comments to the press about the need for federal troops, but he made no formal request. He declared that he could not comply with the second phase of the busing order unless the city received "federal assistance in guaranteeing the safety of school children."

Governor Francis Sargent sent additional police to the city, and he sent a message to Ford that he would call out the National Guard if the situation deteriorated.[10] Attorney General Levi told Ford that there was "no justification for federal involvement in Massachusetts because the Governor has not yet used all of the means at his disposal."[11] The governor's message confirmed Ford's decision not to deploy troops, and without a formal request from the governor, sending them would have been a breach of protocol and a violation of states' rights. Historically, presidents have deployed federal troops only after they received a formal request by the governor or state legislature. Ford put 1,500 troops on an increased state of readiness, but when no request came from the governor, he ordered them to stand down.[12]

Violence flared up again on December 11 after a black student stabbed a white classmate at the South Boston High School. A crowd of whites surrounded the school, trapping 135 black students inside. As the crowd threw rocks and bottles, police on horseback and motorcycles broke through to free the students. The school board closed the South Boston high school for a month, and Mayor White again displayed his talent for overreaction by asking the school board to shut down the school permanently.[13]

During the second year of busing, 1975–76, Ford sent a task force of 100 federal marshals and 50 FBI agents, who joined 1,000 city police officers and 550 state troopers. The governor also had 600 national guardsmen ready. The additional forces didn't stop the violence. Busing opponents had graduated from bottles to firebombs. The police confiscated more than a dozen before they could be used, but crowds threw several others, including one through the window at the NAACP headquarters. At night, bands of white youths battled police in Southie and Charlestown. Fights broke out between blacks and whites at South Boston High School until Judge Garrity put the school under federal control.[14]

While the racist history of the Boston school system was a good example of why many people supported busing, the city was also a prime example of the unintended negative effects of the remedy. After a year and a half, the school district lost almost 18,000 white students, a drop of nearly 20 percent of the total student population, shifting the school district from majority white to majority non-white.[15] The negative impact of busing convinced Ford that it was not an effective remedy. He had spoken out against busing ever since he voted for the Civil Rights Act of 1964, and he made his opposition clear in his confirmation hearings when he said that forced busing "has caused more trouble and more tension wherever it has happened than almost anything else in our society of late."[16]

When Ford took office, a busing bill was already on his desk. The bill was a compromise between the House, which had passed the Esch Amendment prohibiting courts or the federal government from ordering busing "to any but the school closest or next closest to the student's home," and the Senate, which had turned down the amendment by one vote. The conference committee bill prohibited busing "beyond the school next closest" to a student's home unless it was to "guarantee the student's civil rights." Ford's advisors told him the bill was the best he could get, and he signed it on August 21, accompanied by a statement that set forth his views on busing:

> In general, I am opposed to the forced busing of schoolchildren because it does not lead to better education and it infringes upon traditional freedoms in America.... I believe that all school districts, North and South, East and West, should be able to adopt reasonable and just plans for desegregation which will not result in children being bused from their neighborhoods.[17]

Ford's aides almost uniformly agreed with his position, with the vocal exception of Secretary of Transportation William Coleman, the only African American in the Cabinet. The minutes of a September 1975 Cabinet meeting record Coleman's impassioned plea for the president to look at busing in a new light:

> He stated emphatically that where communities had anticipated school busing as a necessary process, the communities established task forces to work on the problem, and have done very well. He cited Pasadena, California, as a good example. School busing has worked without violence; quality education has not suffered, and the community has embraced the concept. There is a feeling by many, that Federal judges are now involved in the management of schools.... History will show, believes Secretary Coleman, that the Federal judges acted with great restraint, judgment, and wisdom in assisting the court ordered busing.

Coleman pointed out that Ford was complaining about judges taking over the schools in Boston, yet that was exactly the solution he was proposing for New York, where he wanted bankruptcy judges to run the city.[18]

———— ❧ ————

Ford was doing exactly what Coleman said — he was encouraging New York City to submit to the control of federal bankruptcy judges. The city was on the verge of default, and the most he was willing to do to help was submit legislation to give a bankruptcy court the power to handle the situation. He shared the opinion of most Americans that the problem was the fault of the city's liberal leaders, and he allowed his disdain for city leaders to overshadow the fact that it was not in the country's best interest to have its leading city go bankrupt. He could have constructively engaged the city and state leaders to develop a plan to get the city back on a sound financial footing. He chose instead to publicly refuse help, making him look like an ogre and shifting sympathy to the city. In the end, he would work with the city to stave off bankruptcy, but he would get no credit for the effort — it just looked like he was caving to public pressure.

The reputation of the city's leaders as spendthrifts was grounded in reality. A series of liberal mayors, Republican and Democratic, had greatly expanded the city's social services programs and agreed to massive increases in wages and benefits for city workers — without doing anything to pay for them. New York spent ten times as much as any other city — more than $12 billion per year, compared to just over $1 billion by Chicago and Los Angeles. It spent 100 times more than Chicago and Los Angeles on education and public welfare. The city university enrolment was 265,000 — it accepted all graduates of New York high schools — and tuition was free. The city was $120 million in the red for fiscal year 1975, and its deficit was projected to hit $900 million in 1976. New York had less than 4 percent of the people in the country, yet it sold 18 percent of municipal bonds and a staggering 39 percent of short-term bonds.[19]

These problems were inherited by two newly-elected Democrats, Mayor Abraham Beame and Governor Hugh Carey. The crisis began in earnest in April 1975 when the city was unable to borrow additional funds — it found no takers for its bonds. To stave off bankruptcy, the city needed to borrow at least $1.4 billion by mid–June, but it had little hope of finding banks to loan more than a fraction of that. The city's bankers were not impressed by Beame's proposals to cut $250 million from the city's budget, believing most of the proposed cuts were "gimmickry."[20]

It was in this context that Treasury Secretary Simon and Fed Chairman Burns met with Mayor Beame on May 8 and told him not to expect a federal bailout.[21] Prior to the meeting, Simon told Ford that a default by New York would have some impact on the market for municipal securities, but that "the cataclysm predicted by some City officials and some bankers is unlikely."[22] Burns later told Congress the same thing. "The damage stemming from a prospective default by New York City is likely to be short-lived. Indeed, the possibility of such a default has already been discounted to an appreciable degree by the market."[23] The next day, Rockefeller spoke out against aid to the city, and on May 12 Simon issued, with Ford's approval, a press release stating that federal aid to New York "would not be appropriate."[24]

On May 13, Ford and Rockefeller met with Mayor Beame and Governor Carey, who had submitted a joint request for a $1 billion 90-day loan. Ford thought a loan would just delay the day of reckoning. "What New York had to do was to get its own house in order."[25] In the meeting the president had nothing to offer, and his refusal to help was supported by his vice president, who said that the federal government was not the city's last hope: "Mr. President, you ought to know the State of New York has the capacity to do exactly what the governor is asking you to do."[26] The next day, Ford sent a letter denying the city's request, suggesting that "the proper place for any request for backing and guarantee is to the State of New York."[27] Carey was furious, and he publicly accused Ford of a "level of arrogance and disregard for New York that rivals the worst days of Richard Nixon and his gang of cutthroats.... We didn't even get 30 pieces of silver."[28]

Later that month the city and state hammered out an agreement to stave off bankruptcy. The state advanced $800 million in aid, and it created the Municipal Assistance Corporation (Big MAC), with $3 billion of borrowing authority to oversee the city's finances.[29] The deal had been brokered by Felix Rohatyn, one of the shrewdest investment bankers on Wall Street, who became the head of Big MAC.

Beame intentionally created a new crisis later that summer. He wanted to show that cutting expenses would cause chaos, so he cut the things that would create the most pain. On July 1 he abruptly laid off a quarter of the city's workforce, including 5,000 policemen, 2,000 firemen, and 10,000 sanitation workers. The remaining sanitation workers responded by going on strike, leaving garbage piling up in the streets. During the night, garbage piles were set on fire, and the head of the firemen's union crowed to the press: "This is a burning city — a dying city."[30]

The cuts didn't solve the city's problems. On August 1 the Domestic Council told Ford that the city would go into default on August 7 if Big MAC could not sell $1 billion in additional securities, but even if it were successful, the new securities would only postpone the crisis.[31] But the August sale netted only half the amount it sought, and in mid-August the Treasury Department provided an update to Ford. "The outlook for New York City is poorer today than at any time in recent months." The report bemoaned the fact that the city had not made any significant progress in reducing expenditures or in increasing revenues, "instead, posturing and maneuvering seem to dominate day-to-day developments." Unless the city and state made significant changes, "default could only be avoided through the issuance of a Federal guarantee on Big MAC obligations."[32]

At the end of August, Carey submitted an aid package to the state legislature, including an additional $2 billion in borrowing authority for Big MAC and a plan to balance the city budget within three years. Carey agreed to the package when Beame gave up his staunch objections to a joint city/state board to control city finances, called the Emergency Financial Control Board. But the banks refused to provide more financing, and the mayor continued to fight against significant spending cuts.[33]

On September 2, Carey and Beame met with Ford and asked for a federal loan guarantee program. Ford refused to consider the idea, and he began to grill the two New York leaders on their plans to cut expenditures. "Are you going to cut down your retirement benefits and your overhead? Are you going to stop giving free tuition to students at the city university?" Beame and Carey predicted that a city default would cause a string of bank failures, but Fed Chairman Burns told Ford that that wouldn't happen. "Don't let them sell you a bill of goods."[34] Greenspan was more measured. He told Ford that a default would have an impact on smaller banks and a temporary market disruption, but he thought that the impact would be manageable.[35]

In September the New York legislature approved Carey's plan for additional borrowing authority for Big MAC and to establish the Emergency Financial Control Board. The legislation extended the state's credit to the limit, but it would get the city only through the end of November. The Teachers Union refused to aid the city during negotiations for a new contract. After negotiations broke down, Teachers Union president Albert Shanker addressed 20,000 teachers in Madison Square Garden. After a 20-minute tirade in which he lambasted the state of the school system, he called for a strike vote, and the teachers shouted "aye" in unison. The strike lasted only five days — a deal was reached to eliminate two 45-minute preparation periods each week in return for cutting the work week by two hours. This time the assembled teachers booed Shanker in Madison Square Garden, but the deal passed in a close vote. Shanker was humiliated when the Emergency Financial Control Board rejected the agreement.[36]

Ford continued to take a hard line against helping the city, urged on by William Simon, who warned that if legislation were passed for New York, other cities would demand help as well. "Structural deficits in countless municipalities would be the end result of this process."[37] Ford told his economic advisors that he would not consider any options that included providing assistance to the city, and he warned them that "New York State and City officials should be given no encouragement with regard to expecting future new Federal assistance."[38] Simon told the press that the federal government "will do nothing to help the city avoid default or lead it out of bankruptcy."[39]

Not everyone in the administration agreed with Ford's hard line. Seidman and Lynn thought that Ford had to do something, and Rockefeller started publicly urging him to act. He first made his position known privately in a June 3 meeting with Ford, and then at a Cabinet meeting on September 17. The vice president was convinced to go public on September 26 at his annual lunch for New York Republicans at his home in Pocantico Hills. Most of the guests told him that they didn't care what happened to the city, but they said that it would be politically expedient for the federal government to show that it cared. When Rockefeller met with Ford the next week, he urged action, and he asked whether he could go public with his recommendations. Ford gave him the go-ahead. At an October 11 Columbus Day dinner in New York City, Rockefeller declared that "time is of the essence and the resolution of this immediate New York City situation is crucial." He urged Congress to "act in time to avoid catastrophe."[40]

In October the state could sell only $150 million of the $250 million in bonds it floated.

A crisis was averted only when state comptroller Arthur Levitt agreed to use $250 million of state employee pension fund money to purchase some bonds that the state had not been able to sell. Big MAC chairman Felix Rohatyn told the press that time was running out. "The dikes are crumbling and we're running out of fingers."[41] At just after midnight on October 24, Mayor Beame called Ford to tell him that the city might default within 12 hours. The crisis was the result of Shanker's refusal to go along with a plan to use union pension funds to buy bonds. Seidman decided that there was no reason to wake the president. Later that day Ford met with Nessen, Rumsfeld, and Greenspan to discuss New York. When Ford asked whether any of them thought that the administration should do anything, Rumsfeld said, "Not just 'no,' but 'Hell, no.'"[42] The crisis was averted when Shanker relented at the last minute.

———

Most Americans had supported Ford's refusal to bail out New York, but that changed when he sounded like a scrooge in a speech on October 29. His plan was to ask Congress to amend the bankruptcy laws to allow the city to file for bankruptcy and give the federal government the power to guarantee funds to maintain essential public services. But Ford's speechwriters didn't emphasize the plan — they stressed his opposition to a bailout. He declared that he was "prepared to veto any bill that has as its purpose a Federal bailout of New York City to prevent a default." He implied that bondholders were all big banks. "Why, they ask, should all the working people of this country be forced to rescue those who bankrolled New York City's policies for so long — the large investors and big banks?" And he concluded by asking an irrelevant question. "Let me conclude with one question of my own: When that day of reckoning comes, who will bail out the United States of America?"[43]

After the speech his friend Jacob Javits told him that he made a "grave error in not coming to the aid of the city." [44] When the press asked Rockefeller about Ford's speech, he admitted that "there is some honest difference of opinion. But it just happens he is the President of the United States and I am Vice President of the United States."[45] Rohatyn probably had the best response. "I feel like somebody who tries to check into a hospital and keeps getting referred to the cemetery."[46] It was the *New York Daily News* headline the next day that everyone remembered: "FORD TO CITY: DROP DEAD."

Before the speech a Gallup poll showed that 42 percent of Americans favored helping the city, and 49 percent opposed assistance. After the speech a Harris poll showed that 69 percent of people supported federal loan guarantees, while only 18 percent were opposed. Louis Harris told Congress that Ford's "attitude of 'New York be damned' has changed the attitude of the American people."[47]

On ABC's *Issues and Answers*, Rockefeller said that the result of a default would be "chaotic."[48] But Ford wouldn't budge. On November 3 he told the press that the only legislation he would approve was amending the bankruptcy code "because I think that is the only fundamental solution."[49] On November 4, Governor Carey sent Ford another missive, explaining that the state had put its credit at risk on behalf of the city. "In effect, the contagion of New York City has now spread to agencies of New York State."[50] The next day, Ford's economic advisors predicted that the city would default in December unless the federal government stepped in, but the president reiterated that he would "accept no compromise."[51]

———

Things started to break in mid–November when the state and city met with the banks and reached a comprehensive deal. The state agreed to provide $6.8 billion in assistance to the city and pass legislation to allow the city to borrow $2.5 billion in loans from its pension funds. The city agreed to raise taxes by $200 million and balance its budget by fiscal year 1977-78. In return, the banks had agreed to refinance the city loans, and the state and city agreed to ask the federal government to provide "seasonal financing" of $1.3 billion, to be repaid by June 30, 1976. Similar financing would be required in 1976 and 1977, to be repaid by June 30 in those years.[52]

Ford recognized that the agreement was a serious attempt to get the city's finances in order, and he started to qualify his statements. On November 10 he met with Senate leaders, who asked whether he would veto any bill providing aid to New York. Ford avoided the question, but he did admit that he was "encouraged" by recent events.[53] Four days later Ford told the press in Atlanta that he was evaluating the situation, but he repeated that he was "encouraged."[54] On November 19 he issued a statement expressing that he was "gratified that the leaders of New York appear to have accepted primary responsibility for solving the financial problems of the city and are proceeding in the direction of a long-term solution in accordance with the State constitution and laws. I am impressed with the seriousness of their intentions." He held out hope for federal action. "If they continue to make progress, I will review the situation early next week to see if any legislation is appropriate at the Federal level."[55]

In November, Carey called the state legislature into special session, and the relief package was approved on November 25. Carey sent Ford a letter outlining the legislature's action the next day. "Now these commitments have been fulfilled and with the same trust we await the response of the Federal Government."[56] Ford responded with a statement that he would propose legislation for a loan program for the city. "I have, quite frankly, been surprised that they have come as far as they have.... This is a realistic program.... Therefore, I have decided to ask the Congress when it returns from recess for authority to provide a temporary line of credit to the State of New York to enable it to supply seasonal financing of essential services for the people of New York City."[57] Congress quickly passed Ford's proposal, and he signed the legislation on December 9.

The crisis was averted, and the city, state, and federal governments had joined to act responsibly. Ford's hard line had driven a reasonable solution, but he could have accomplished the same thing without the negative fallout. He could have explained his program in two ways. One was to sound tough and refuse to help the city because of its failure to fix its problems. The other was to sound accommodating and offer to help if the city fixed its problems. He chose to talk tough, and it would hurt significantly in the upcoming election.

15

Halloween Massacre and the End of SALT

After the dramatic reaction to the pardon, Ford should have learned to avoid making other abrupt announcements. But he hadn't learned, as he demonstrated on Halloween 1975 when he announced a major shake-up of his senior staff. In one fell swoop he asked Rockefeller not to run for a second term, took the National Security Advisor title from Kissinger, and fired Schlesinger, Colby, and Morton. He made the changes without consulting anyone, and he gave no thought to how the changes would be announced. The press dubbed the shake-up the "Halloween Massacre," and the public reaction was overwhelmingly negative. The most virulent criticism came from conservatives who believed that the dismissal of Schlesinger signaled that Kissinger would be given a free hand. The exact opposite happened because Ford replaced Schlesinger with Rumsfeld, who would use his influence with the president to effectively end any chance of a new arms control agreement during the Ford administration.

Ford was driven to fire Schlesinger by persistent press reports that the Defense Department opposed the administration's SALT efforts. On October 12, Oswald Johnston of the *L.A. Times* ran an article indicating that the Joint Chiefs objected to Kissinger's latest proposal to the Soviets, quoting a confidential Defense Intelligence Agency report that was critical of détente. According to the article, Defense Department officials had circulated the report among the Washington press corps. Ford met with Schlesinger and excoriated him for the leak, and he finally decided to do what he should have done when he took over: get a new secretary of defense.[1]

Ford was convinced to make the change four days later during a meeting of his kitchen cabinet, which was made up of several of his old friends, including Mel Laird, Bryce Harlow, John Byrnes, David Packard, Bill Whyte, and Bill Scranton. At least once a month they gave him unvarnished advice in meetings with the president in the Cabinet Room. In the October 16 meeting Ford asked why his approval ratings stayed below 50 percent despite the upturn in the economy, and Bryce Harlow gave an impassioned speech condemning the public rifts in the administration, and in particular the leaks about fights between Kissinger and Schlesinger. After Harlow's speech, Ford "decided to sever my relationship with him at the earliest opportunity."[2]

It didn't take much thought for Ford to conclude that Rumsfeld would be the man to replace Schlesinger. He had the president's confidence; he shared Ford's views on defense; and he would be easily confirmed by Congress. Furthermore, Ford had the perfect replacement for the chief of staff. "I knew that I could ask Cheney to step into Rumsfeld's shoes and that the White House would function just as efficiently."[3]

Having decided to replace Schlesinger, Ford thought it would be a good time to make other changes that were being urged on him. He was being bombarded with suggestions that he needed to appease Reagan and the right wing by getting rid of Rockefeller. The charge was led by Rumsfeld and Bo Calloway, a conservative from Georgia who had been brought in to run Ford's presidential campaign. Calloway was an uncompromising conservative with a loose tongue, and he had been telling the press for weeks that Rockefeller had to go. Ford's opinion of Rockefeller hadn't changed, but his political advisors were telling him that the only way to stop a Reagan challenge was to dump the vice president, so he made the painful decision to ask him to step down.

Ford had also decided to replace CIA director Colby. He was frustrated by Colby's failure to defend the agency during the congressional investigations, but Ford claims that he did not fire Colby for his disclosures to the intelligence committees. "I supported his decision to tell the truth about past agency misdeeds even though both of us recognized that his testimony would be embarrassing."[4] According to Ford, he wanted to appoint a new CIA director to embody his determination to reform the intelligence community. He asked Edward Bennett Williams to take the job, but the attorney turned down the offer because of pressing business commitments. Ambassador to China George Bush had asked to come home, and Ford decided that running the CIA was "the right spot for George. He was an able administrator, and in other posts he had held — member of Congress, ambassador to the United Nations and chairman of the Republican National Committee — he had succeeded splendidly."[5]

The kitchen cabinet had also been urging Ford to take the national security advisor title from Kissinger, and he had heard the same thing from the transition team when he first took office. Ford disagreed at first, but over time he thought that freeing Kissinger from more mundane tasks was a good idea. Ford knew that NSA deputy director Brent Scowcroft could seamlessly step into Kissinger's shoes. There was one other change that could not wait. Rogers Morton had become too sick to remain secretary of commerce, and Ford decided to replace him with Elliot Richardson.[6]

———∽∾∽———

Ford met with Rockefeller on October 28 and explained that the right wing was growing in strength. In response, Rockefeller offered to withdraw as his running mate. "I'll do anything you want me to do. I'll be on the ticket or I'll be off the ticket. You just say the word." Ford couldn't bring himself to ask Rockefeller to withdraw. "There are serious problems, and to be brutally frank, some of these difficulties might be eliminated if you were to indicate that you didn't want to be on the ticket in 1976. I'm not asking you to do that, I'm just stating the facts." Rockefeller took the hint. "I understand.... I'll give you a letter saying that I don't want to be considered as a Vice Presidential nominee."[7]

Ford planned to announce the staff changes on Monday, November 3, but on that Saturday he learned that Rockefeller's resignation had been leaked to *Newsweek*, so he was forced to set up the other meetings on a last-minute basis. On Sunday, November 2, he broke the news to Schlesinger and Colby in successive meetings. The meeting with Colby lasted fifteen minutes, and the CIA director responded like the professional he was. Ford offered to make him ambassador to NATO or Norway, but Colby declined the offer. At 8:25 Ford met with Schlesinger, and the hour-long meeting did not go well. The secretary of defense refused to resign. "I haven't resigned, sir. You're firing me." Ford offered to make him the director of the Export/Import Bank, but Schlesinger declined the offer out of hand. For most of the meeting he argued about the reasons he was being fired, further convincing Ford that he needed to go.[8]

On that Sunday afternoon Ford met with Rumsfeld and told him that he would replace Schlesinger, but Rumsfeld urged Ford to wait until his next term. "Hell, the cow is out of the barn. It's too late for something like this to help your image. Let's wait until after the election."[9] Rumsfeld recalls that Ford "was very stubborn. He would not be moved."[10] Later that afternoon Ford met with Kissinger and told him that he was no longer head of the NSA. That Monday Ford called Richardson, who agreed to become secretary of commerce. When Ford sent a cable to Bush in China offering to make him CIA director, Bush sent a cable back agreeing to take the job, despite reservations about what it would mean for his political future. "If this is what the President wants me to do, the answer is a firm 'yes.'"[11]

<hr/>

Ford announced the changes at 7:30 that Monday night. He hadn't worked with his staff to develop a strategy for the announcement, and his lack of preparation showed. He defended his right to make staff decisions in a way that made him look arbitrary and power-hungry. Over and over he stressed that as president he had the right to put together his own team, which was hardly the best way to explain why he was making the changes.[12] The changes were a public relations disaster. Ford had been leading Reagan by 22 points in the polls, but after the Halloween Massacre, Reagan pulled ahead.[13]

Ultimately, the decision Ford regretted was asking Rockefeller to step down. Kissinger calls forcing Rockefeller out "the single worst decision of Ford's presidency."[14] Ford's old friend Melvin Laird explained that Ford and his aides "panicked" about the Reagan challenge and got rid of Rockefeller to appease him.[15] Reagan declared that he was "certainly not appeased."[16] Ford later rued his failure to stand up to the right wing. "I was angry with myself for showing cowardice in not saying to the ultraconservatives, 'It's going to be Ford and Rockefeller, whatever the consequences.'"[17] As the convention neared, Rockefeller told Ford that he made a mistake by not demanding that Bo Callaway deliver the southern delegations before he agreed to resign. Ford responded gracefully. "You didn't make the mistake. We made the mistake."[18] Later, Ford called his firing of Rockefeller his "biggest professional regret. He was a good man. I should have gone to bat for him."[19]

Dumping Rockefeller was a mistake, both professionally and politically. The right wing was not mollified, and Reagan was more convinced that he could beat Ford because the move made the president look weak. Most importantly, dumping Rockefeller made Ford look like he trying to be something other than his true self. Everyone saw through the move, and Ford looked like he didn't have the courage of his convictions.

<hr/>

The atmosphere at the White House improved after the Halloween Massacre, and it was Rumsfeld's departure that made the most difference. Cheney ran a tight ship, but his personal style was much less confrontational than his predecessor's. His Secret Service codename was "Backseat" for his willingness to operate in the background.[20] A few weeks into the Cheney regime, Nessen noted that there had been "a real change at the White House since Rumsfeld left, a change of mood almost like a fresh breeze blowing through."[21] Cheney brought back David Gergen, who loved working in the Ford White House. "The fourteen months that followed were among my happiest in government. Jerry Ford's decency made everyone feel welcome on his team."[22]

Cheney took control of the campaign, and he proved to be an adept political advisor. His chief lieutenants, David Gergen, Jerry Jones, James Connor, Jim Cavanaugh, and Michael Raoul-Duval, met with Alan Greenspan in Jones' office each day to discuss the issues. The

Ford and Cheney meet in the weeks after Cheney became chief of staff, November–December 1975. (Photograph by David Hume Kennerly; courtesy Gerald R. Ford Library.)

meetings became the most important staff meetings in the White House. Cavanaugh gradually took charge of domestic issues; Duval and Marsh focused on foreign affairs; and Gergen had public relations and speechwriting. On economic issues Cheney often turned to Paul O'Neill, while Raoul-Duval became a key player in the presidential campaign, helping prepare Ford for the debates.[23]

The appointment of Gergen was an overt attempt by Cheney to create an alternative to Hartmann's speechwriting shop. Cheney also invaded Nessen's territory by expanding the White House Communications Office, which operated independently of the press secretary, although it was nominally under his control.[24] Hartmann continued to fight against the new leadership. When he learned that speechwriter Pat Butler was trying to work with Gergen and Cheney, Hartmann fired him "on two or three occasions," including once on a campaign flight. Cheney rescinded the order.[25]

⁓

The press concluded that Ford fired Schlesinger as a concession to Kissinger, but Kissinger was most concerned about the loss of his NSA title, which was a blow to his enormous ego. He came close to resigning, and Winston Lord and Lawrence Eagleburger even drafted statements explaining why he was resigning.[26] Two foreign leaders were instrumental in talking him out of it. British foreign minister Callaghan called him and said, "One does not resign on an issue of status. If you do, you will ruin what you stand for. Resignations can only be done for principle."[27] Sadat asked him not to go. "I know you are thinking of resigning. Don't do it. Ford is a good man. And we need you for a while longer in the Middle East."[28] Kissinger was convinced that he should stay as long as Ford remained committed to their shared foreign policy goals. He took an unsigned letter of resignation to the president and told him he would sign it if it would help politically. Ford would not hear of it. "Don't leave. I need you. I believe in what we are doing."[29] That convinced Kissinger that the president was dedicated to continue their work, and he decided to stay.

Kissinger later admitted that taking the NSA title away "made sense whatever the blow to my feelings."[30] He discovered that not much changed when Scowcroft took over as national security advisor because their views coincided. The loss of the title never hurt Kissinger's influence—he and Scowcroft continued to meet with Ford every morning for a briefing on intelligence and foreign issues.[31]

It was the firing of Schlesinger that cost Kissinger control over foreign policy. Rumsfeld proved to be an effective opponent, and the secretary of state found himself without the ability to operate as he saw fit. In particular, Kissinger lost his control of the SALT negotiations. While many of his advisors wanted to table SALT discussions until the election was over, Ford still wanted an agreement. "I felt confident that we would resolve all our differences and sign the accord soon."[32] Ford may have wanted a SALT agreement, but Rumsfeld effectively stymied the negotiations. According to Hyland, "The more Rumsfeld took hold, the more he turned hard right."[33] He wasn't driven solely by political motives. Rumsfeld believed that détente was enabling the Soviets to pull ahead of the United States militarily.[34]

—————

On November 8, Brezhnev sent a message to Ford suggesting that Kissinger visit Moscow in December to try to reach agreement on the remaining issues. Ford accepted the offer, and the trip was scheduled for December 18. But the administration could not resolve its internal disputes, and Ford was forced to ask Dobrynin to postpone Kissinger's trip by a month.[35]

The National Security Council meetings to prepare for Kissinger's trip again demonstrated that strategic issues were not standing in the way of an agreement. Colby explained that the CIA thought that it was "unlikely that Backfires will be specifically assigned to intercontinental missions." The CIA, the Joint Chiefs, and Kissinger all agreed that even if they agreed to Soviet demands on cruise missiles and the Backfire bomber, a Soviet first strike would still leave the U.S. with more than enough to respond with overwhelming force—50 Minuteman missiles, as well as the bulk of its submarine-launched missiles and its bombers, a total of more than 3,000 warheads. Colby summed up the CIA analysis. "During the next ten years, the Soviets almost certainly will not have a first-strike capability to prevent devastating retaliation by the United States." Ford was encouraged, and he asked for a new proposal by the first week in January.[36]

Scowcroft presented the new proposal in an NSC meeting on January 13. The Soviets would be allowed to introduce Backfires until the end of the current agreement without counting them in the aggregate limit, but Backfires introduced after October 3, 1977, would count. Cruise missiles with a range of more than 600 kilometers on surface ships would be included in the MIRV total. There was general agreement on the proposal, including from General Brown:

> My general and immediate reaction is that the number of Backfires excluded is not troublesome. This can be rationalized as an offset against the FB-111. What's new is counting bombers and surface ships in the MIRV limit. The Chiefs have agreed with counting bombers with ALCMs in the MIRV limit, but have not addressed including surface ships. My personal reaction is that this is a reasonable thing and I will try to be persuasive with the Chiefs.[37]

The agreement lasted less than a day. When he returned to the Department of Defense, Rumsfeld wrote Ford a memo proposing that the U.S. and USSR execute a SALT II treaty based on the agreements made in Vladivostok, and leave cruise missiles and the Backfire to a second agreement to be negotiated later. The problem was that the Soviets had been very clear in earlier meetings that they would not agree to table discussions on cruise missiles. Kissinger immediately asked for a meeting with Ford and Rumsfeld. When they met at 9:35 on January 14, Kissinger started the discussion melodramatically, declaring that he could not go to Moscow, but Ford mediated an agreement that Kissinger would lead by proposing that only the first 250 Backfires would not count. Rumsfeld would not agree to allow Kissinger to use a fallback if the Soviets rejected the proposal, which was a near certainty. He would only agree that Kissinger could cable back for further instructions, so that Ford could convene another NSC meeting.[38]

In the final NSC meeting before Kissinger's trip, Ford laid out the plan. When Kissinger got the Soviet reaction to the new proposal, he would send it back to Washington on Wednesday night, when Ford would be meeting with Colby and the Joint Chiefs. The group would decide whether to counter with Scowcroft's proposal, which allowed the Soviets to deploy 300–400 Backfires, and the U.S. an equal number of cruise missiles on surface ships, without counting them. Ford told Kissinger to get a good agreement, and the administration would sell it to the American people:

> If we can get an agreement that can be substantively defended, then we should do it. It will be a tough political atmosphere and some people will be inclined to play politics with it; but if we can defend the agreement substantively, then we can win. I want to emphasize the substance, not the political aspects. If we can get a good substantive agreement, then we should do it.[39]

—⁓—

When Kissinger arrived in Moscow on the evening of January 20 he was met by Gromyko, who told him that the Soviets would not under any circumstances agree to defer the issue of cruise missiles. Gromyko made the same point again when he pulled Kissinger aside before his first meeting with Brezhnev. In the meeting, Brezhnev rejected the U.S. proposal, as expected. He was frustrated that he might not get an agreement. At one point he started pacing back and forth and threw up his hands. "Backfire, Backfire, I wish I had never heard of it."[40] After the meeting that night, Kissinger sent a cable to Washington asking for authority to counter with Scowcroft's proposal, along with a demand to reduce overall launchers from 2,400 to 2,200.[41]

As planned, Ford met with the NSC to consider the Soviets' response and Kissinger's proposal. At the meeting the Joint Chiefs and the Defense Department were hostile to every idea. When they discussed Scowcroft's idea of tying cruise missiles and Backfire bombers, Clements called it "a very poor trade.... I don't know what kind of rationale we would use to explain the trade." Admiral Holloway agreed with Clements. "The fundamental problem is the question of 250 Backfire versus 25 surface ships with SLCMs. This is not an equitable solution." The Joint Chiefs were not basing their opposition on military factors; they simply did not think the offer was "a fair trade."

Scowcroft thought that Clements' objections did not hold water. "We are setting aside the Backfire and surface SLCMs not so much for an equal trade, but we are setting aside the gray area systems. We don't always have comparability in SALT." Colby also disagreed with the Chiefs. "In any event, we were projected to continue to have our retaliatory capability in the years ahead. We will have enough surviving warheads. Deterrence will still work." Ford was furious — Scowcroft says that it was the angriest that he had ever seen the president. Ford asked Admiral Holloway to study the issue, but he would not force the Joint Chiefs to adopt a proposal that they opposed.[42] Kissinger was given nothing to offer the next day, and all hope for a SALT II agreement was gone. In his message to Kissinger, Scowcroft called the meeting "surreal":

> I have just come from a two-hour NSC meeting which I can only describe as surreal.... After the meeting, the President was angrier than I have ever seen him. He ranted about the total inconsistency with previous Defense positions.[43]

The negotiating team had not received the summary of the NSC meeting by the first negotiating session the next day, so they outlined their ideas for Brezhnev, who seemed intrigued, and he hinted that the Soviets could agree to a reduction of launchers to 2,300, or an "even larger" reduction if the U.S. would agree to a 600 kilometer restriction on sea and land-based cruise missiles. The Soviets would not agree to count the Backfire in the 2,300 limit, but Brezhnev did agree not to upgrade the range and capability of the airplane. Brezhnev was offering a significant reduction in its nuclear forces, along with limits on throw-weight, silo size, and Backfire capability. In return, the United States would not have had to curtail its planned forces, but Ford was not willing to reach an agreement over the objection of the Defense Department in an election year. Kissinger was furious when he received Scowcroft's report of the meeting because he knew that it killed the chances for an agreement which was very much within reach.

At the next meeting, all the parties could say was that they would study the proposals on the table. Kissinger was clearly frustrated in his report to Ford. "I could probably have wrapped up the agreement under normal conditions.... I had no choice but to let the opportunity to exploit this breakthrough go by."[44] As he left Moscow on January 23, Kissinger was resigned to the fact that his dream of a SALT II treaty was dead.[45] When he returned, Kissinger vented his frustration in a meeting with Ford, Rumsfeld, Scowcroft, and Cheney. "We have a mad situation. Everything which the Soviets give up gets pocketed and we give nothing. We aren't negotiating with the Soviet Union, we are negotiating with Jackson."[46]

———

Knowing that he owed Brezhnev a new proposal, Ford convened a NSC meeting on February 11. Again Ford said that he wanted an agreement. "I want to reassert that a SALT agreement is in the best interests of this country! It is possible to do this. I reassert this with emphasis!" Kissinger gave three options. The first two options were revisions of how to treat the Backfire and cruise missiles. The third was deferring the Backfire and cruise missile issues. Kissinger explained that he had already "tried this three times and it has always been rejected." Nevertheless, Rumsfeld chose it. "I like the deferral option. It is honest and in the interest of long-term arms limitation. I believe it is negotiable."[47] If Rumsfeld honestly believed that the deferral option was "negotiable," he miscalculated. Not surprisingly, Kissinger — who is the person who had been negotiating with the Soviets — would prove to be a much better judge of what the Soviets would accept than the secretary of defense.

Ford wasn't happy, but he wasn't willing to go against the recommendation of the Joint Chiefs and the Defense Department, so he proposed the deferral option in a February 16 letter to Brezhnev.[48] The day he sent the letter, Ford told the director of the U.S. Arms Control and Disarmament Agency Fred Ilke that he knew it would be rejected. "I don't think it has much chance."[49] Ilke responded with a memo that showed that he shared Rumsfeld's delusion about what the Soviets would accept. "If you should decide to choose the deferral option, it seems to me that the chances of Soviet acceptance would be quite good.[50] Brezhnev took several weeks, but his response was what Ford expected:

In the course of the talks already after Vladivostok — and you, certainly know it well — the Soviet side took a number of important steps to meet the American side in attempts to find mutually acceptable resolutions to the remaining issues. Unfortunately, the same cannot be said about the position of the American side including the latest proposals which you call compromise ones in your letter.[51]

When he received Brezhnev's letter, Ford was finally resigned to the fact that he would not achieve a SALT agreement before the election. "Reluctantly, I concluded we would not be able to achieve a SALT agreement in 1976."[52] It was one of the few times he avoided doing what he thought was in the nation's interest for political reasons. It wasn't his first choice — his aides maneuvered him into the decision. If they did it for political reasons, they weren't doing Ford any favors. He had already publicly announced that he wanted to achieve a SALT II agreement, and distancing himself from the negotiations just made him look weak and indecisive. Strong détente opponents would vote for Reagan regardless of what Ford did, and he gave up his ability to appeal to centrist voters as a man of peace.

16

Deregulation

Richard Nixon had presided over the apogee of regulation in American history — his wage and price controls were the most extreme peace-time economic regulations since Jefferson embargoed all foreign trade, and his administration saw a new direction of regulatory growth designed to prevent negative effects of economic activity (called "externalities"), such as damage to the environment, injuries to workers, and harm to consumers. Nixon signed more than twenty laws to protect consumers, workers, and the environment; he created the Equal Employment Opportunity Commission, the Occupational Safety and Health Administration, and the Environmental Protection Agency; and he signed into law the Clean Air Act and the Endangered Species Act.[1]

When he took office, Ford reversed the trend. He did not try to roll back regulations to protect against economic externalities, which he understood were beneficial, but he did fight against expanding them. He made a concerted action to roll back economic regulations — that is, regulations designed to improve the performance of the market rather than regulations designed to prevent the negative impacts of economic activity. Deregulation was an esoteric issue that Ford "made a great hullabaloo about,"[2] but the media paid little attention. Although it got little press, Ford's deregulation program was visionary, and it changed the lives of ordinary Americans for the better.

Deregulation came naturally to Ford, and his deregulatory inclinations were reinforced by his economic advisors, most prominently Alan Greenspan.[3] Economists throughout the government had supported deregulation for years, and Ford gave them leadership and support that they had never experienced. "Under him, the loose, informal subcommunity of reformers inside the executive branch was converted into a more organized force, aided by White House leadership to settle internal differences, and inspired by the belief that a president was prepared to take political risks on behalf of their cause."[4]

Ford made deregulation a key element of his fight against inflation. In his Whip Inflation Now speech, Ford asked Congress to set up a commission on regulatory reform:

> To increase productivity and contain prices, we must end restrictive and costly practices whether instituted by Government, industry, labor, or others.... I ask the Congress to establish a National Commission on Regulatory Reform to undertake a long-overdue total reexamination of the independent regulatory agencies.[5]

When Congress ignored his request, Ford set up a staff organization to lead the charge, the Domestic Council Review Group on Regulatory Reform, and he put Roderick Hills in charge of the effort. A DCRG staffer explained that Ford supported the council's programs in spite of political opposition. "Political arguments didn't appeal to Ford at all. He was very solid."[6] In February 1976, DCRG Chairs Edward Schmults and Paul MacAvoy told Ford that regulated corporations and unions had been fierce in their opposition to his deregulatory proposals, and MacAvoy asked Ford if he wanted to push such an unpopular program in an election year, but Ford was not deterred.[7]

Nixon, on the other hand, had backed away from deregulation when he ran into opposition from regulated companies and their unions. The Teamsters were one of the few unions to support Nixon, and when they objected to legislation drafted by his Transportation Department to deregulate trucking, Nixon withdrew his support.[8] Almost uniformly, Nixon appointees to regulatory commissions favored more regulation, not deregulation. At the CAB, Chairman Secor Browne opposed deregulation, as did his successor Robert Timm. Under Browne and Timm, the commission followed an informal policy of denying all new route applications, and the CAB eliminated the little freedom airlines had to sell discount fares.

Ford was not cowed by opposition from politically-connected companies and unions. Hills explained that Ford pushed deregulation knowing that he would face strong opposition. "He was aware that his support for such reform would be strongly opposed by the industries affected, by labor unions and by strong congressional elements. He persisted, nonetheless."[9] Secretary of Transportation Coleman tells an illuminating story. When Coleman presented a draft trucking deregulation bill to Ford, the president took a puff on his pipe and asked about the political impact. When Coleman explained that both the Teamsters and the trucking companies would fight hard against it, Ford was pleased. "Well, if the Teamsters and truckers are against it, it must be a pretty good bill."[10]

Ford decided to focus his deregulatory efforts on transportation. "Few sectors of the American economy were more stifled by government regulation than the transportation industry, and I thought deregulation was urgently required."[11] He was following the advice of virtually every transportation expert. "Prominent economists who opposed deregulation could not be found; deregulation was, in effect, a recommendation of the economics profession as such."[12] Professor Mike Levine summed up expert opinion at the time. "If you poked an economist then and said 'airlines,' they'd say 'deregulate.'"[13]

Ford was right; by the 1970s regulation in the transportation industry was a complicated mess. Railroad regulations had been enacted at the end of the 19th century when the railroads had taken advantage of the lack of practical alternatives to monopolize the movement of people and goods.[14] During the 1920s the railroads' monopoly over the transport of goods was challenged by new semi-trailers, which enabled trucking companies to compete with very little capital. At the same time, the transport of people was revolutionized by the Ford Motor Company, which mass-produced automobiles and the first successful airliner. The sensible response to the erosion of the railroads' market power would have been to lift regulations, but eliminating regulation was not in vogue during the failure of *laissez-faire* capitalism that was the Great Depression. During the New Deal, Congress passed laws patterned on the 1887 railroad legislation to regulate trucking, airlines and communications.[15] The purpose of the regulatory scheme was no longer to protect consumers from monopolists; the regulations were designed to protect the regulated companies from competition.

The Interstate Commerce Commission was given jurisdiction over railroads and trucking companies, and it prevented competitive entry by rarely granting new trucking permits. Trucking companies were not allowed to flexibly schedule to meet demand. The ICC forced trucks to travel set routes at set prices. Over time, the regulations became absurd. Truckers petitioned for authority to "tack" two routes together, and the commission decided that, since two companies could transport a load by one company carrying the load on the first route and another on the second, it was only fair to allow one company to carry the load on both routes. The commission allowed a company that had two adjoining routes to transport goods, between the endpoints, as long as it traveled the entire route. For example, if a company had licenses to serve Chicago to Minneapolis and Minneapolis to St. Louis, the company could transport goods between Chicago and St. Louis, but only if it drove through Minneapolis.[16]

Air travel was also regulated during the New Deal when the Civil Aeronautics Board was given jurisdiction over airlines. For 40 years the CAB did not allow a single new major airline to start flying. Airlines rarely were allowed to fly new routes, and the CAB took years to decide applications. By limiting competition, the CAB kept prices high, and flying was unavailable to the masses. For the few who could afford to fly on a regular basis, flights were frequent and airports uncrowded. But everything was not better for the Jet Set. Passengers often had to change airlines to reach their destinations because the commission did not allow one airline to serve both legs of a trip. The CAB almost killed Federal Express in its infancy when it denied the company's petition to fly cargo in large aircraft. The company often had to fly two smaller planes when one larger plane would have been much more economical, and it almost folded.[17]

The regulatory edifice made the country more insular than it wanted to be. Each commission subsidized local service by keeping the price of long distance service artificially high. In effect, the federal government decided that it was more important that children be able to visit grandparents who lived in nearby towns than it was for children to visit grandparents who lived across the country. Despite the fact that costs were similar between long and short trips, the CAB required that airlines charge more for long trips than for short ones.[18] As a result, most Americans could not afford to fly to other areas of the country — the cheapest coast-to-coast round-trip flight in 1974 cost more than $1,400 in today's dollars. The poor also could not afford to take a bus to visit relatives and friends in other parts of the country because the ICC forced bus companies to charge artificially high prices for long trips to subsidize service between nearby towns. Most people could not afford to regularly phone friends and relatives in other parts of the country because the FCC and state regulators set long distance rates high to subsidize local service. Coast-to-coast calls cost $2 a minute in today's dollars.

The only way most Americans could keep in contact with other areas of the country was to get in a car and drive. The Eisenhower Highway Act of 1955–56 made driving across the country practical. It had also eliminated once and forever the possibility that the railroads could monopolize transportation. But the regulatory edifice for all other forms of transportation remained intact and kept the nation apart.

———⌘———

To some extent, Ford was forced to focus on transportation because Pan Am was on the verge of bankruptcy and the railroads were in even worse shape. Nationalization of the rails was a real possibility, and the first step was taken in 1971 when the federal government formed Amtrak to take over passenger traffic. Penn-Central filed bankruptcy at the same time — at that time the largest bankruptcy in U.S. history — and the federal government created Conrail to operate the Penn-Central tracks and other bankrupt routes in the northeast.[19] Ford made his railroad deregulation legislation more palatable by adding funding for Conrail, which key members of Congress dearly wanted. In May 1975 he submitted the Railroad Revitalization and Regulatory Reform Act, proposing to allow railroads to change rates within a range without ICC approval. He also promised to veto any bill that was stripped of its deregulatory provisions, and Congress passed the bill in its entirety in 1976.[20] Ford was less successful with legislation to deregulate trucking. Congress took no action on the legislation he submitted in November 1975.[21]

It took three years for the ICC to take advantage of its new flexibility under the railroad act because chairman George Stafford, a Nixon appointee, proved to be staunchly opposed to reform.[22] Part of the responsibility was Ford's. He started his administration choosing commissioners because of their overall qualifications, paying little attention to whether they shared his deregulatory agenda. After Ford appointed him to the ICC in 1975, Roger Corber called deregulation "a prescription for disaster," and he followed with a speech denouncing deregulation. Ford was surprised to read about the speech in the Grand Rapids paper, and he asked his aides, "Isn't this one of ours?"[23] Ford started to pay attention with later appointments. His other ICC appointees, Betty Jo Christian and Charles Clapp, were consistent supporters of competition and deregulation, but they did not form a deregulatory majority because Ford had misfired with his appointment of Corber.[24]

Ford was more successful forcing changes at the CAB. When Ford took office, chairman Robert Timm was being investigated for trips he took at the expense of regulated airlines. Ford wanted to fire Timm, but White House counsel Philip Buchen explained that he could only remove a member of an independent commission after a finding of malfeasance. But Ford did have the power to take away his chairmanship, and in December 1974, administration aides told him that the president would not reappoint him as chairman. They tried to convince Timm to resign, but he refused. Timm remained on the commission for another year, but Ford gave the chairmanship to commissioner Richard O'Melia.[25]

━━━∾∾∾━━━

Ford received formidable support for airline deregulation from Democratic senator Ted Kennedy, who had convinced one of the prominent proponents of deregulation, a young Harvard law professor named Stephen Breyer, to join his staff. Breyer knew that he wanted to attack regulation, but he was unsure where to begin until the morning of September 27 when he read in the *Washington Post* that Secretary of Transportation Claude Brinegar had called a meeting with the major airlines to discuss how to help Pan Am. He decided to attend the meeting, where he was shocked to hear Brinegar extort the airlines to fix prices. "Raise your prices! What's wrong with you airlines?" Brinegar then asked the visitors to leave so the airlines could reach an agreement in private. When he returned to Capitol Hill, Breyer told Kennedy that he had seen a classic case of price fixing. "It was a cartel, a simple cartel being organized by the government."[26] Breyer suggested that Kennedy's Subcommittee on Administrative Practice and Procedure hold hearings on airline regulations:

> I thought, well, maybe we could have a hearing on this very meeting. Why is the president on the one hand saying, "Keep prices down," and the secretary of transportation, on the other hand, is trying to raise the price? And we did have that hearing.[27]

Brinegar, a Nixon appointee, did not share Ford's deregulatory agenda. He sent Treasury Department lawyer Robert Binder to talk Breyer out of the hearings. Binder was neither successful nor tactful. He told Breyer that the hearings would cause Pan Am to fail because the publicity would spur the airline's bankers to cancel its lines of credit. When Breyer pointed out that the scenario was farfetched, Binder called him a "lunatic college professor."[28] Unlike Brinegar, the Ford administration as a whole supported the Kennedy hearings, and the Domestic Counsel staff worked closely with Breyer and the rest of Kennedy's staff.[29]

Kennedy held round one of the hearings in November 1974, focusing on the CAB rules for charter airlines. Charter airlines existed only because of a quirk in the regulatory system. While airlines were not allowed to discount their rates, charter airlines were able to offer low fares. The flights were supposed to be for legitimate organizations chartering planes for group events, but charter airlines began to offer low fares to people who would join clubs for the sole purpose of buying a cheap ticket. The CAB began to crack down on the charters, sending investigators to determine whether groups like the "Left Handed Club" were legitimate.

On the first day of the hearings, Deputy Attorney General Keith Clearwaters presented the administration's position. Clearwaters declared that the CAB had exceeded its authority in setting minimum charter rates, and he testified that the commission's effort to broker a deal to raise rates was illegal. "No justification whatever has been shown for government-sanctioned price fixing in the charter industry."[30] The star witness that day was Sir Freddy Laker, who was trying to get permission to fly cheap flights (approximately $500 in today's money for a one-way ticket) between London and the United States. In his testimony, Laker called the obsession for saving Pan Am "PanAmania." He told the committee that "people seem to have lost their senses out of a concern over what will happen to Pan American, TWA and British Airways."[31]

The hearings forced the CAB to begrudgingly ease a few rules. The commission announced that it was backing away from announced plans to force charter airlines to raise rates.[32]

—◦◦◦—

Kennedy began round two of the hearings in February 1975. This time the subject was the entire regulatory scheme for the airline industry. Kennedy opened the hearings by proclaiming that regulation harmed consumers. "The cost of this regulation is always passed on to the consumer. And that cost is astronomical."[33]

Brinegar had resigned, and the administration presented a uniform position in favor of deregulation. On the first day, Acting Secretary of Transportation John Barnum testified that the time was ripe for change. "I believe we are now at a regulatory watershed." He submitted the administration's proposal for reforming the CAB. The Justice Department sent Thomas Kauper, who told the committee that "the overall effect" of regulation "has been to produce an almost unprecedented substantial reduction in air travel — more empty seats on scheduled flights and fewer charter flights."[34]

It took a tragedy for the media to give the hearings prominent coverage. Breyer's investigators had convinced a staffer named William Gingery to provide copies of confidential CAB documents, but a few days before his scheduled testimony, Gingery was found dead in his apartment. He had shot himself, leaving a 20-page suicide note filled with invective about his superiors at the commission. According to Gingery's note, documents he found in a safe the Friday before his testimony pushed him over the edge. "Last Friday I learned that I am a fool." The documents showed that Timm had ordered O'Melia (then head of the enforcement bureau) to close an investigation into airlines slush funds for illegal contributions. In the days after the suicide, the hearing room was packed with reporters. Timm denied ever telling O'Melia to shut down the investigation, but his testimony was contradicted by O'Melia and several CAB investigators.[35]

The next dramatic event occurred when Kennedy and Breyer proved that CAB officials were lying when they testified that there was no moratorium on new route awards. Breyer's investigators unearthed a memorandum referring to "informal instructions of the chairman's office in connection with the unofficial moratorium on route cases." Timm continued to deny the existence of any moratorium, but his convoluted testimony was hardly credible, especially after O'Melia admitted the existence of the moratorium. "In fact, as far as I am concerned, there is no route moratorium as of now."[36] Breyer thought that O'Melia's admission was a seminal event. "Deregulation began at that moment."[37]

In his final report, Breyer was harsh in his indictment of the CAB, declaring that the hearings "reveal a strong likelihood of highly improper and possibly criminal behavior on the part of the Board members themselves." The report also referred to "improper and perhaps illegal board efforts aimed at protecting the industry at the expense of the consumer." He suggested that Congress take away the CAB's authority over prices, its ability to restrict entry, and its power to confer antitrust immunity. In response to Breyer's report, Kennedy and Ford exchanged letters promising to work together for deregulation.[38]

Timm's testimony was the last straw for Ford, who decided to remove him from the commission. When Timm again refused to resign, the White House sent him notice of a hearing to determine whether the president would remove him from office. Timm did not go quietly. He accused the White House of intervening in the affairs of the CAB, and leveled wild accusations against fellow board members. On December 5, Buchen sent him a letter setting forth the charge of obstructing the investigation of airline campaign contributions and making false statements to investigators and Congress. Timm finally resigned on December 10, 1975.[39]

—⁂—

Within a month of the end of the hearings, Ford appointed John Robson chairman of the CAB.[40] Before the appointment, administration officials never asked Robson for his views on deregulation. "Now, I can't tell you that somebody in the Ford administration didn't think that [deregulation] was what I would do, but they never talked to me about it."[41] Before he took office, Robson was "objective and agnostic" about deregulation, but he became a supporter.[42]

Robson quickly changed how things were done at the commission. On July 6 he announced that the CAB would begin an experiment allowing airlines to raise or lower prices within "zones of reasonableness," and to enter and exit certain specified routes without permission. At the end of July the CAB issued a staff report recommending deregulation within five years. In August the commission liberalized charter rules, and in September it finally granted several new routes to airlines. The commission continued to approve new routes throughout Robson's tenure.[43]

Under Robson's direction, the CAB began to allow airlines to discount prices. In March 1977 the CAB allowed Texas International to charge "Peanuts" fares and American to charge "Supersaver" fares, at discounts of 35 to 45 percent. The Supersaver prices seem high today — round-trip coast-to-coast tickets cost $750 to $900 in today's dollars — but at the time they were significantly lower than other available fares. United and TWA had opposed the application, but they followed American's lead when the commission approved the application. By 1978, discount fares were widely available, and the number of Americans traveling by plane shot up. Prices fell by 8 percent, adjusted for inflation, and air traffic jumped by 17 percent.[44]

—⁂—

Ford submitted legislation to deregulate the airline industry on October 8, 1975. The legislation included provisions to: (1) increase the opportunities for entry and liberalize charter service rules, (2) remove certificate restrictions and route regulation within five years, and (3) give airlines "a delayed and restricted but nonetheless revolutionary right" to change prices without CAB permission. The legislation was sent to the Aviation Subcommittee of the Senate Commerce, Science, and Transportation Committee, chaired by Nevada Democrat Howard Cannon, where it was considered along with a deregulatory bill submitted by Kennedy. Cannon's committee began hearings in April 1976.[45]

In April 1976, Robson testified that federal regulation hurt the airlines financially, and he warned that "the present regulatory system may have great difficulty in coping successfully with the future." Robson called for "gradual and controlled" deregulation.[46] Secretary of Transportation Coleman also told the committee that regulations were responsible for the sad financial shape of the airlines. "We believe the fault clearly lies in the regulatory system." On behalf of the administration, Coleman testified that the regulatory regime had to go:

> We feel that the present system or aviation regulation does not adequately or successfully serve the traveling public, the airlines' interests, or the public interest. There must be fundamental changes.[47]

The testimony of Robson and Coleman that regulation harmed the industry made a big impact on Cannon. He was a supporter of the charter airlines, and he was upset by the CAB's treatment of the charters. After consistent lobbying by Kennedy, Cannon announced that he supported reform.[48] The committee was still considering the deregulation bills when Ford left office.

The most lasting impact of Ford's deregulatory efforts was that they laid the groundwork for some of the most significant achievements of Carter's presidency. "Jimmy Carter seized on deregulation very early in his administration largely because Ford had prepared the issue for action."[49] In the presidential campaign, Carter promised to champion deregulation. "The reform of our regulatory agencies would be one of the highest priorities of a Carter Administration."[50] He was true to his word, and he scored a remarkable string of victories. He lifted most of the remaining regulations on oil and gas, and he revolutionized the transportation industry by eliminating controls on airlines, railroads, and trucking companies.

Air freight was deregulated by the Air Cargo Deregulation Act of 1977, and passenger traffic was deregulated by the Airline Deregulation Act of 1978.[51] The trucking industry was deregulated by the Motor Carrier Act of 1980. Although the act did not completely lift regulations, it did the most important thing by allowing entry into the market, and the ICC commissioners used the flexibility granted by the act to revolutionize the industry.[52] Railroads were freed from regulations by the Staggers Rail Act of 1980, which Carter called the "capstone" of his deregulatory efforts.[53]

Deregulation was an example of leaders who are accused of being unimaginative taking up dry issues and changing people's lives. Ford and Carter transformed American society. The most visible change was that air travel was brought to the people. "Airline deregulation democratized air travel in America."[54] Prices fell, and passenger travel tripled. Round-trip fares have declined by 40 percent since 1978, after adjusting for inflation — in today's dollars, the average round trip fare has fallen from $414 to $256.[55] Airlines have filled their planes with more passengers and switched to hub operations, a much more efficient way to operate. In the modern "hub and spoke" design, an airline sets up a designated hub airport in each region of the country, and nearly all flights in the region terminate at the hub, with passengers flying between hubs to reach other sections of the country. In the hub and spoke design, airlines schedule regional flights to arrive at approximately the same time at a hub, so that connecting flights can be coordinated to minimize delay. The hub design has allowed the airlines to offer one-stop flights between hundreds of cities.[56]

The changes in the transportation of goods were less visible than the changes in passenger travel, but they were every bit as important. Deregulation of trucking resulted in a profusion of new companies, services, and prices. Prior to the Motor Carrier Act of 1980, the ICC had granted only 18,000 trucking licenses, but in the next ten years the number of trucking licenses rose to 45,500. Inflation-adjusted prices fell more than 20 percent during the first five years of deregulation.[57] Railroads have performed more profitably since deregulation, reversing the inevitable slide to nationalization. "Thanks mostly to the Staggers Act, railroads have managed to reverse course over the last two decades."[58] At the same time, prices have fallen. In 1988 railroads charged 2.6 cents per ton-mile, down from 4.2 cents at the time the act was passed.[59]

All of the results were not positive, however. Employment has grown, but truckers make less. The Teamsters Union was hit hard; the percentage of truckers belonging to the union dropped from 60 to 28 percent in ten years. Since deregulation, truckers have experienced a 10 percent drop in pay relative to the wages of all workers.[60]

The biggest changes have resulted from the increased flexibility transportation companies received from deregulation. No longer tethered by governmentally-mandated routes and schedules, air freight companies, trucking companies, and railroads started to respond to spikes in demand and offer just-in-time delivery. Business expenses plummeted, overnight delivery became common, fresh fruits and vegetables were available in the winter, and warehouses were converted into lofts.

The deregulation of transportation has allowed businesses across the country to operate more efficiently. Before deregulation, companies produced goods in the expectation that there would be a demand for them. Deregulation of transportation joined with innovations in computing, production, and communications to cause a revolution in business, as entire industries adopted "just-in-time" production and delivery, producing goods to meet demand.

The deregulation battle brought out the best in Ford — Greenspan has called it the administration's "great unsung achievement."[61] The president saw what was best for the country, and he did not waiver in the face of entrenched opposition. He did not gain politically from his deregulation program — if anything, he lost political support. And he got very little credit at the time in the media for his ideas, as most reporters thought it was odd that he spent so much time talking about deregulation. But the American people are better off today because he persevered.

17

Angola

The summer of 1975 was hardly an opportune time for the Ford administration to embark on a covert military operation in the Third World. With the wounds of the Vietnam War still fresh, and with congressional committees investigating past CIA covert operations, the nation was skeptical of involvement in foreign conflicts. And the newly-assertive Congress was almost certain to shut down any covert operation. But the realists in the administration refused to recognize reality, and they blithely intervened in a civil war in the west–African nation of Angola without considering the impact that Congress shutting down the operation would have on America's reputation. To make matters worse, they failed to recognize the shortcomings of the groups they supported in Angola. In the north of the country the United States backed a losing effort, and in the south it allied with the racist regime in South Africa, doing serious damage to America's reputation throughout the continent.

The Angolan crisis was a by-product of the revolution in Portugal. Just a week before Ford took office, General Spinola announced that independence would be granted to the remaining Portuguese colonies, including Angola. Angola is on the west coast of Africa, approximately one-third of the way up from the southern tip. In 1974 it was bordered on the north by Zaire, to the west by Zambia, and to the south by Namibia, then a protectorate of the apartheid regime of South Africa. Until the Portuguese revolution, most of the countries in Africa's southern cone were ruled by their minority white populations. Portugal ruled Angola and Mozambique, white regimes presided over South Africa and Rhodesia (now called Zimbabwe), and South Africa administered Namibia as a protectorate. In southern Africa only Zambia and Botswana were ruled by blacks, while north of Angola virtually all states were ruled by blacks.

To the newly-independent countries of Africa, one thing was of primary importance — liberating the blacks of South Africa, Rhodesia, and Namibia, and making sure that the rest of Africa remained free of white rule. The racist regime of South Africa was a pariah, although Pretoria was pursuing its version of détente, trying to establish relations with the other nations of Africa. The primacy of racial concerns was something that the Ford administration never took into account during the Angolan crisis. They were preoccupied with keeping the Soviets and Cubans out of Angola, and they did not understand why the neighboring black nations were more concerned with keeping out the South Africans.[1]

In most of the Portuguese colonies the independence groups were unified — as well as marxist and totalitarian — and they took control of their countries without significant opposition. Things were different in Angola, where three independence groups had been warring against each other as much as fighting against the Portuguese.[2] There was not much to dis-

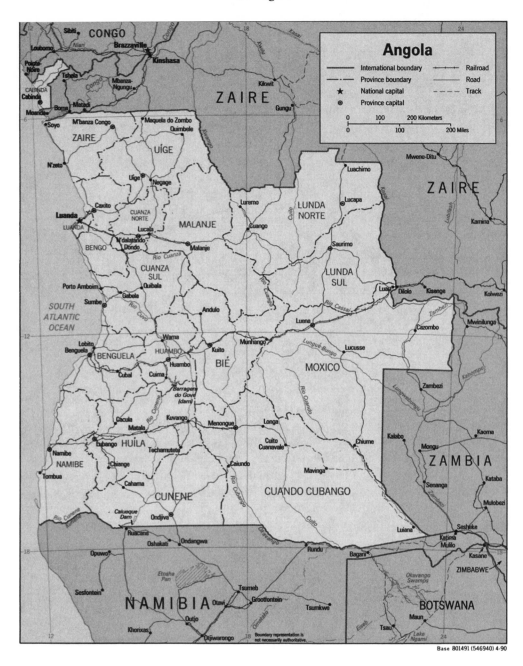

tinguish between the three revolutionary groups vying for power: the Frente Nacional de Libertação de Angola (FNLA), the Movimento Popular de Libertação de Angola (MPLA), and the União Nacional para a Independencia Total de Angola (UNITA).[3]

The MPLA was avowedly marxist. The organization drew its strength from the Mbundu people who lived around the capital of Luanda, and it had the most support among the few intellectuals in the country, the mixed-race *mesticos*, and the residents of other urban areas. The MPLA was led by a soft-spoken poet and doctor named Agostinho Neto. Neto's mild manner masked a cruel streak; he ruthlessly put down any challenges to his rule, often resorting to torture to maintain power.

Prior to the Portuguese revolution, the MPLA received more aid from Yugoslavia than any other country because Tito saw an opportunity to pry an independence movement out of the Soviet orbit. The Soviets gave assistance to the MPLA, but they were anything but steadfast in their support. They considered Neto to be "psychologically" unpredictable, and they were afraid that the MPLA would ally itself with the Chinese. Over the years the Soviets had intermittently stopped and restarted aid, and they made a tactical mistake by withdrawing their support just before the Portuguese revolution. The MPLA also received support from Cuba, Algeria, Guinea, the Republic of the Congo, East Germany, Czechoslovakia, Sweden, Norway, and Denmark. In 1965, Castro had sent several advisors to assist the MPLA in an invasion of the enclave of Cabinda, north of Angola, but the operation was a complete failure, and the Cubans soured on Neto. The MPLA was rent by dissention, and the organization was considered to be weaker than its main rival, the FNLA.[4]

The FNLA was the group that received most American support. The CIA sent money to the organization until 1969 when Nixon stopped the payments to appease Portugal. The organization was led by Holden Roberto, and Roberto took his orders from the dictator of Zaire, Mobutu Sese Seko. Mobutu had twice used Zairian troops to crush FNLA factions who had challenged Roberto's rule. The organization drew its support from the Bakongo people who lived in northern Angola. At the time of the Portuguese revolution, the FNLA's entire army was in Zaire, and for 17 years Roberto had never stepped foot in Angola. Nor had he seen battle; he preferred to remain in Zaire, surveying the troops he had conscripted from Angolan refugees.

Roberto wore army fatigues and dark glasses — the favorite uniform of many of Africa's worst tyrants — and he fit the bill. He maintained camps in which he imprisoned, tortured, and killed his opponents. When his troops crossed into Angola in 1961 they went on a killing spree, massacring and mutilating whites, educated blacks, and non–Bakongos. In response, the Portuguese went on a killing spree of their own, massacring more than 20,000 people, also targeting educated Angolans. More recently, Roberto had ordered his troops to massacre MPLA columns fighting the Portuguese in Angola. Roberto's language was the least marxist of the three rebel leaders, but that did not prevent him from obtaining support from communist countries. The Chinese had been supporting the FNLA since 1971, and Roberto also received support from Romania, North Korea, France, Israel, West Germany, Senegal, Zambia, Tanzania, South Africa, India, Algeria, Libya, and Uganda.

The third rebel group, UNITA, received some support from the United States, but most of its support came from South Africa. It was led by the charismatic Jonas Savimbi. UNITA drew its strength from the Ovimbundu people of southern Angola. Savimbi was the only rebel leader who fought within the country during Portuguese rule, and he was the only leader who offered any chance of being a democrat. Neto and Roberto were prototypical despots — Roberto the artless thug and Neto the paranoid control freak — while Savimbi was an ideological chameleon, saying what his patrons wanted to hear. He began as a radical marxist, inveigling against "American imperialism," and UNITA received support from North Vietnam, China, Iraq, Egypt, North Korea, and Zambia. By 1974 — when Savimbi was looking for support from the U.S. and South Africa — he sounded like an anti-communist freedom fighter. Later, it became clear that Savimbi's marxist roots were most indicative of his true nature, as he installed a Stalinist dictatorship in the areas of Angola he controlled. Savimbi's true beliefs were probably best reflected in his speeches to the Ovimbundu people, when he sounded like a racist railing against the *mesticos* of the MPLA.

After the Portuguese revolution the independence groups established home bases for the upcoming civil war, and foreign nations began to choose sides. In August 1974, Roberto's troops crossed into Angola and took control of the territory along the northern border with Zaire. Most of his support came from Zaire, although the CIA resumed sending small amounts of money, and China sent 100 military advisors.[5]

Neto fortified his base in Luanda by distributing AK-47 rifles throughout the slums of the capital, and in November 1974 his troops took control of Cabinda, an oil-rich enclave north of Angola on the African coast. In October 1974 the Soviets decided to resume support of the MPLA, but shipments did not begin until December. The MPLA also received the informal support of the Portuguese administration after the new regime in Lisbon appointed a new governor-general of Angola, Admiral Rosa Continuo, an avowed marxist who was known as the "Red Admiral."[6]

At the same time, the MPLA lost a key supporter. During a power struggle, Neto's henchmen had tortured several of his opponents, and Zambian president Kenneth Kaunda was shown photographs of MPLA troops using vises to crush prisoners' skulls. Kaunda was a devout Christian, a former pacifist, and a mild autocrat by African standards, and he was deeply affected by what he saw. He openly broke with the MPLA at a September conference in Brazzaville. At the end of the conference Neto was scheduled to fly with Kaunda back to Zambia, but Kaunda publicly refused to let him on the plane.[7]

For the time being, Cuba decided to sit on the sidelines. In early October, Neto sent an urgent message to Castro asking for military advisors. At first, Castro agreed, but he later decided instead to send representatives to determine what Neto really needed. In December two Cuban officials traveled with MPLA leaders through Angola for two weeks, and they left with positive views of Neto's prospects. Despite the encouraging report, the Cubans would not send aid for another six months.[8]

After establishing their bases, the parties agreed to a cease-fire on January 15, 1975, in the resort town of Alvor, Portugal. The three independence groups agreed to form a unity government to rule the country until elections on November 11. On January 31 a huge crowd of singing and dancing Angolans cheered as the Portuguese turned the country over to the unity government. A peace agreement had been signed, and a transitional government had taken power, but no one expected the peace to last.[9]

The United States didn't feel constrained by the peace agreement from increasing aid to the FNLA. From the first days of Ford's presidency, Mobutu had been pressing the administration to provide more assistance to Roberto. One week after the Alvor Accords the 40 Committee (which signed off on all covert operations) met to consider a plan the CIA had put together to appease the Zairian dictator. At the meeting there was little objection to increasing its assistance to Roberto by $300,000 per year. Most experts at the State Department wanted to cut ties with Roberto, but the department's representative, Joe Sisco, decided to stay silent when he saw that opposition would be futile — the need to placate Mobutu was too strong. The decision to increase aid to Roberto was sealed toward the end of the meeting when Colby said that the agency had received "disturbing intelligence" that the Soviets had begun shipping arms to the MPLA. The CIA had also suggested sending $100,000 to UNITA, but the request was turned down because Mobutu had no ties to Savimbi. After the meeting, Colby briefed John Sparkman and Clifford Chase of the Senate Foreign Relations Committee, as required by the new Hughes-Ryan Amendment.[10]

A lot has been made of the decision to increase aid to Roberto as the first breach of the peace, but it is difficult to understand why. The United States had already been sending aid to Roberto, and all the 40 Committee did was to increase the amount. The type of aid was not changed — the CIA continued to send only money, not arms or ammunition — and the additional $200,000 sent to Roberto was insignificant compared to the support he was receiving from Zaire and China, and compared to the support the Soviets were providing to the MPLA. And the 40 Committee meeting did not cause a Soviet reaction; they had already decided to provide munitions to the MPLA, and they never wavered from that plan. There is a better case that Soviet arms shipments led to the American decision to increase aid for Roberto, but that interpretation is probably not accurate either. The driving motivation for the decision was to placate Mobutu, and the 40 Committee almost certainly would have approved the aid increase without the reports of Soviet arms shipments.

Peace lasted less than a month, but identifying which party broke the truce first depends on how various incidents are viewed. The first violent acts occurred when Neto's troops intermittently fired on Roberto's forces in Luanda during the first two weeks of February. The attacks appeared to be unorganized, but the MPLA leadership made no attempt to restrain their men. On February 13 the MPLA attacked the Luanda offices of a former member of the organization, Daniel Chipenda, killing between 15 and 20 Chipenda supporters and driving the rest from the capital. Chipenda announced the next week that he was joining the FNLA. Through the end of March the MPLA and the FNLA were in a state of undeclared war within Luanda. The first major clash came on March 23 when Roberto's troops attacked Neto's Luanda headquarters and massacred 51 MPLA recruits at a training camp north of the capital. At the end of March, Roberto sent 500 troops into Luanda, where they were met with heavy fire from Neto's forces.

Sporadic fighting followed until late April when Roberto launched a full-scale attack on MPLA forces throughout the country. The Portuguese responded by declaring martial law on May 15, but they were unable to restrain the warring parties. At the end of May, fighting flared up again when Neto attacked FNLA troops in the north and UNITA troops in the south, and his soldiers massacred as many as 300 UNITA recruits on the outskirts of Luanda.[11]

In March and April, Neto's forces received a boost when the Soviets sent more than a hundred tons of arms, and 100 MPLA soldiers traveled to the Soviet Union for training. Neto scored a much bigger coup when he convinced 3,500 to 6,000 troops from Katanga, a province of Zaire that had rebelled against Mobutu, to join his army. The new troops made his forces approximately equal to the numbers Roberto could put in the field. Mobutu was furious when he learned that Neto had taken in the Katanganese, so he sent 1,200 Zairian soldiers into Angola to bolster Roberto. Savimbi had been left out of the largess from the U.S. and the USSR, so he turned to South Africa, risking his reputation — and any hope of international support — if the request became public. The South Africans were willing to provide aid, but they were convinced that the split with the FNLA doomed UNITA. The South Africans demanded that Savimbi reconcile with Roberto, and when he refused they denied his request.[12]

<hr />

Ford and Kissinger didn't pay much attention to events in Angola until Zambian president Kenneth Kaunda visited Washington on April 19 and 20. In a private meeting Kaunda asked them to support his plan for the Organization of African Unity (OAU) to negotiate an agreement to make Savimbi the president of Angola. He claimed to represent Zairian president Mobutu, Tanzanian president Julius Nyerere, and Portuguese foreign minister Melo Antunes.[13]

Kissinger claims that Kaunda "convinced President Ford and me that the Soviet Union was intervening in Angola with military advisers and weapons and that we should oppose this intrusion for the sake of Angola's neighbors."[14] While the Zambian leader did urge the Americans to take an interest in Angola and to support a negotiated resolution there, he did not ask them to start a covert operation, and he certainly did not suggest in any way that the United States provide military assistance to Roberto. During the meeting, Kaunda was dismissive of Neto and Roberto, and he talked up Savimbi, but only as a compromise candidate in a negotiated resolution of the crisis. Kaunda succeeded in convincing Ford and Kissinger to pay attention to Angola, but his request for support of a negotiated resolution fell on deaf ears.

After the meeting, Ford asked for an analysis of whether the administration should start supporting Savimbi. Kissinger turned to Assistant Secretary of State for African Affairs Nathanial Davis, who had been in office for just over two weeks. Kissinger had fired Davis' predecessor, Donald Easum. Easum had incurred Kissinger's wrath by telling him that the U.S. had no choice but to support majority rule in Rhodesia, take a harder line against South Africa, and develop relations with the Frelimo rebels in Mozambique. Davis had been ambassador to Chile at the time of Pinochet's coup, and Kissinger assumed that he would take a hard line on Angola.[15] To Kissinger's surprise, Davis warned against supporting Savimbi. The reason he gave was prescient — he predicted that Savimbi would ultimately be undone by his connections to South Africa.[16]

Ford wanted a more complete analysis of his options, so Davis led a task force that included the Department of Defense, the CIA, and the State Department to prepare one. In its June 13 report the task force provided three options: "hands off," diplomacy, and covert military intervention. The task force recommended the diplomatic option — pushing Portugal to take a more active role in resolving the conflict, pressuring the Soviets to stop arms shipments, and working with the OAU to mediate the conflict. The task force thought that the covert military option was a bad idea because they doubted that it would be successful, and American prestige should not be committed to a losing effort.[17]

It was an intelligent analysis but not enough to overcome the influence of Mobutu, who was proving to be an unreliable ally. The Eisenhower administration had supported the coup that brought Mobutu to power because they thought Patrice Lumumba was "just not a rational being."[18] But Mobutu was hardly a "rational being" either. He demonstrated his irrationality in June 1975 by expelling U.S. ambassador Deane Hinton, accusing him of trying to instigate a coup. The real problem was that Mobutu was angry about America's failure to adequately support Roberto and its refusal to bail Zaire out of an economic crisis. Mobutu had been sending messages that if the United States did not increase its support, he would consider switching to the other side. He visited China and North Korea, threw out his Israeli advisors, established relations with the PLO, and invited North Korean advisors to Kinshasa.

When Mobutu kicked out Hinton, Kissinger got the message that he wanted the U.S. to support Roberto. "We're not helping on Angola and that's what I figured was in his mind. It's important to him." But Kissinger was concerned with more than Mobutu — he did not want Angola to become a communist ally of the Soviet Union. "It simply cannot be in our interest to have Angola go communist. It is next to the largest country in Africa and it's next to South Africa."[19] Those were the factors that governed his actions during a meeting of the 40 Committee on June 19 — just days after Mobutu ordered Ambassador Hinton out of the country. Kissinger asked the CIA to develop a limited $6 million covert operation to support Roberto. He did not want an operation big enough to win the war, just enough to prevent the MPLA from winning before the election. When the 40 Committee approved the proposal, Kissinger sent former ambassador to Zaire Sheldon Vance to talk to Mobutu. In their first meeting on June 21, Mobutu said that he would let bygones be bygones. "Before you start, I want you to know I have already forgiven you Americans, but I will never forget."[20]

When the National Security Council briefed Ford on the results of the 40 Committee meeting, Schlesinger disagreed with the operation, accurately predicting that Roberto was too weak to win. "Mr. President, may I follow up — if we do something, we must have some confidence that we can win, or we should stay neutral. Roberto is not a strong horse. The fact that he stays in the Congo suggests that he doesn't have the tenacity to win." It was wise advice, but it fell on deaf ears, partially because Ford had little respect for his secretary of defense. Ford focused on the weaknesses of the task force's proposed diplomacy option, and he ignored the weaknesses of a possible covert operation. At his core, Ford preferred action. "It seems to me that doing nothing is unacceptable. As for diplomatic efforts, it is naïve to think that's going to happen."[21]

Ford was right; it was naïve to think that the diplomatic option would work. But it was also naïve to think that Roberto could win, and it was naïve to think that Savimbi wouldn't be undone by his support from South Africa. The task force report was actually a realistic assessment of the situation — they recommended the diplomatic option not because they naively thought it would work, but because they realistically recognized that the other options were worse.

<hr>

The fighting flared up again in July when Neto attacked FNLA forces in Luanda, driving Roberto's troops from the capital, along with thousands of Bakongo and Ovimbundu refugees. A week later he drove FNLA and UNITA troops from the area surrounding the capital. At the same time, Roberto's troops drove the MPLA from northern Angola. All hope for peace was gone.[22]

On July 14 — after Roberto's troops had been driven from the capital — the 40 Committee met to consider the CIA's plan for Angola. Prior to the meeting, CIA director Colby received a memorandum from his staff that indicated that Roberto's "military position has been seriously weakened since the sharp clashes of late May and early June."[23] The CIA proposal reflected that assessment — it said that the covert operation would not be enough to guarantee that Roberto and Savimbi would win, but it was enough to prevent a quick Neto victory.[24] State Department professionals did not support the plan. Two days before the meeting, Davis sent Kissinger a memorandum explaining that it was "virtually certain" that the covert program would quickly become public. He was dismissive of Roberto's leadership abilities and predicted that by supporting the FNLA and UNITA, the U.S. would be setting itself up for failure. "In world balance of power terms the worst possible outcome would be a test of will and strength which we lose. The CIA paper makes clear that in the best of circumstances we won't be able to win."[25]

Davis was objecting in vain because Ford had already decided to approve a covert operation. A week before the 40 Committee meeting he told Kissinger that he supported the operation and told him to "steer" the meeting to the right result.[26] Kissinger followed orders, and he steered the committee to the right result. Colby started the meeting by predicting that a $100 million program could win the war outright, but he said that a program of that size could not be kept secret, so the committee members rejected the option. They approved the smaller option on the assumption that it could be kept covert, without considering whether the assumption was valid in light of the ongoing CIA investigations. Kissinger recommended a $14 million program to support both Roberto and Savimbi, and the committee approved his recommendation.[27]

After the meeting, Davis tried once more to change Kissinger's mind. On July 16 he sent another memo repeating his earlier conclusion that the small $14 million program could not be "effective and covert."[28] In a meeting the next day Kissinger told Ford about Davis' objections, but the secretary of state urged him to approve the covert operation. "On Angola, I favor action. If the U.S. does nothing when the Soviet-supported group gains dominance, I think all the movements will draw the conclusion that they must accommodate to the Soviet Union and China. I think reluctantly we must do something."[29] The next day Ford gave Kissinger his decision. "I have decided on Angola. I think we should go." Kissinger agreed, but he recognized that victory was anything but certain. "It may be too late because Luanda is lost. Unless we can get it back, it is pretty hopeless."[30] When he learned that the operation would go ahead, Davis decided to resign. Kissinger asked Davis if he would stay at the State Department in another role, and when Davis agreed, Ford appointed him ambassador to Switzerland.[31]

Colby briefed key members of Congress, and he found little opposition. Only two senators objected, Joseph Biden of Delaware and Dick Clark of Iowa, the chairman of the Senate Subcommittee on Africa. The other senators raised only one concern — they told Colby that it was important that the United States not get into a joint operation with South Africa. Colby assured them that the South Africans would not be involved.[32] The promise was true for less than a week, when the South Africans began sending arms to Roberto.[33]

Davis was not alone in his dissent. Tom Killoran, the administration's counsel general in Luanda, thought that Neto would be a better leader than his rivals, and he believed that the MPLA wanted good relations with the United States. Many of the CIA agents running the covert operation would come to the same conclusion, including Bob Temmons and John Stockwell. Robert Hultslander, the Angola station chief, "came to share Killoran's assessment that the MPLA was the best qualified movement to govern Angola." Hultslander had no respect for Roberto. "I admit that I developed a bias against the FNLA and its leaders, which I never tried to hide. Its ties with Mobutu merely added to my assessment that this organization was lead by corrupt, unprincipled men who represented the very worst of radical black African racism." Fundamentally, Hultslander opposed the program because he "was convinced it would not succeed."[34]

The U.S. Embassy in Zaire sent a message to Kissinger setting forth its objections to the Angola program. "Baldly stated, then, the present policy offers only the slimmest hope of success."[35] Kissinger aide William Hyland sent his boss a memorandum in response, reminding the secretary of state that victory was not the only goal. He stressed that the program was intended to "demonstrate to Mobutu and Kaunda (and other Africans) that we are not paralyzed, that as a great power we will stand against the intrusion of Soviet power.... Mobutu is more likely to turn against the US if he thought we were passive observers and had no concern at all about his problems than if we make some effort to help him."[36]

───※───

As the United States was considering what to do, Neto's troops drove the FNLA out of the areas surrounding Luanda. The MPLA began pushing into Roberto's home turf in the north, and the FNLA finally counterattacked when Roberto returned to Angola on July 20 after 14 years of voluntary exile. Roberto's plan was to drive the MPLA back to Luanda and take the capital itself. With the assistance of Zairian troops, he was able to drive all the way to Caxito, 30 miles north of Luanda. He stopped there, waiting for the Portuguese troops to leave before he tried to take the capital.

UNITA finally joined the fighting when Savimbi's security forces discovered a MPLA plan to shoot down his plane. As Savimbi explained, "From that day onwards, we were in the war."[37] The Portuguese negotiated an evacuation of MPLA forces from Savimbi's stronghold in the Huambo region of central Angola, but as Neto's forces were being evacuated, Savimbi demonstrated the ruthless cruelty for which he would later become famous. UNITA troops boarded planes transporting several senior MPLA leaders, abducting and assassinating them.[38]

⸻

During the week after he approved the program Ford released $14 million in funding to the CIA, and he increased the program's budget to $24.7 million on August 20. The agency gave $2,750,000 to Mobutu to pay for the support he was giving to the FNLA, and it paid Roberto and Savimbi $1 million each over the next five months. The CIA operation, now named IAFEATURE, was assigned to John Stockwell, who used the remaining money to buy arms. In August, 83 American military advisors were sent to Angola, Zaire, Zambia, and South Africa. The first planeload of CIA arms arrived in Zaire on July 29, and over the next six months the agency delivered 622 mortars and machine guns, 4,210 antitank rockets, and 20,986 rifles. The quantity of guns was more than sufficient — two for each of the 10,000 fighters that UNITA and the FNLA had in the field — but the quality was not. Because the operation was covert, the CIA had to buy untraceable arms, which meant that most of the guns were more then twenty years old. The U.S. was not the only country sending aid. Zaire provided Roberto two more paratroop companies, the French chipped in by providing ammunition and antitank missiles, and the South Africans provided machine guns and mortars.[39]

Neto was begging Cuba for arms and money, claiming that the country was "being subjected to a silent invasion by soldiers from Zaire." On August 3, Castro sent seven military officers to Angola to determine what the MPLA really needed. When Neto asked for weapons, uniforms, food, and 100 military advisors to train his troops, Cuba gave him what he asked for, and more. When the delegation returned on August 8, Castro decided to send 480 advisors, along with arms, uniforms and food for 5,300 troops.[40] A senior Cuban military officer explained why they decided to send more advisors than asked. "If we were going to send our men, we had to send enough to fulfill the mission and to defend themselves, because too small a group would simply have been overwhelmed."[41] The first Cuban military advisors arrived in late August, and the bulk of the 480 military advisors arrived in early October aboard three Cuban ships — actually, modified merchant tubs — the *Vietnam Heroico*, the *Coral Island*, and the *La Plata*. The ships also carried 12,000 Czech rifles and 110 trucks. The Cubans had three training centers up and running in Angola by October 20.

Castro asked for Soviet advisors and assistance in transporting the troops to Angola, but Brezhnev was afraid that sending Soviet advisors before Angolan independence would hurt relations with the United States, so he turned down the request.[42] The Soviets did not expect civil war until after Independence Day on November 11, and they were planning to wait until then to increase their assistance. They moved up the timeline because they were disturbed by the Chinese assistance to Roberto and Savimbi, particularly because Romania and North Korea were also involved. In late August they sent the MPLA ten armored cars, along with mortars, 16mm guns, antiaircraft guns, and light weapons. But the Soviets were not willing to do more than send aid. In August the MPLA sent a representative to Moscow to ask for military advisors, but the Soviets again refused to send any until after independence.[43]

While the first 480 Cuban military advisors were arriving in Angola, Mobutu sent two of his elite paratroop battalions to help Roberto clear the area north of Luanda and pave the way for an assault on the capital on the eve of independence. At the same time, the South Africans sent their first military advisors to assist UNITA. But first they made a small incursion into Angola on August 9 when they crossed the border to protect a power plant on the Cunene River just inside the country, which they had helped fund. The South Africans were concerned that the plant would be targeted by the Namibian independence organization SWAPO, the South-West Africa People's Organization. At the time, they had no intention to invade any further, but the MPLA and the Cubans did not know that. South Africa followed by sending advisors to UNITA beginning on September 24 and established two training camps in southern Angola.[44]

—∽∾∾—

By late September Cuba and South Africa each had numerous military advisors in southern Angola, and when they came into contact, the conflict escalated beyond anyone's intentions. In the fog of war, when the South Africans met the Cubans they assumed that they were combat troops. On October 5, South African advisors accompanied Savimbi's troops north of his home base of Huambo to stop three MPLA columns converging on the city. The MPLA troops were led by Cuban advisors, and they scored some early successes before UNITA stopped their advance. The South Africans attributed the MPLA's effectiveness to Cuban participation, even though the Cuban troops did not engage in the fighting.

The commanding South African officer, Kaas van der Waals, reported that he had faced Cuban troops, and he requested a squadron of armored cars from Pretoria. The South African command assumed that Cuban troops would give the MPLA the ability to win the war quickly unless they responded. On October 14 they airlifted a squadron of armored cars, Task Force Foxbat, to Silva Porto, just east of Huambo. The South Africans also created a second task force, named Zulu, which crossed into Angola on October 14. Each task force had more than 100 armored cars, and by the end of the month they had 1,000 combat troops in Angola. The South African government tried to keep the presence of this invasion force a secret, and it ordered its press not to report on the operation.[45]

Foreign Minister Hilgard Muller later explained that Pretoria entered Angola with "a limited objective," but its four-stage battle plan provided Prime Minister John Vorster the ability to expand its goals if conditions looked favorable. The first two phases reflected the primary goal of the campaign, which was to make sure that the MPLA did not take over the southern areas of Angola. The South Africans correctly assumed that the MPLA would allow SWAPO rebels to operate freely in the areas they controlled, and Pretoria was trying to make sure that they were as far away from Namibia as possible. The third phase was designed to prevent a quick MPLA victory and force a negotiated solution after independence. These first three phases were all that the South Africans expected to achieve at the time they decided to invade. The task forces entered Angola with instructions not to push out of UNITA territory and to be prepared to evacuate on November 11. They never expected to get to phase four, which was to capture Luanda and install Savimbi. As it turned out, they had the opportunity to take the capital, but they pulled back at the last minute, faced with stiff Cuban opposition and dispirited by the U.S. Senate vote to cut off all aid to Angola.[46]

There is no evidence that the United States knew ahead of time that the South Africans would send the task forces into Angola. Kissinger and Scowcroft both deny knowing about the invasion.[47] Stockwell writes that he saw "no evidence that the United States formally encouraged them to join the conflict."[48] At the same time, it is clear that the United States had been encouraging the South Africans to support Roberto and Savimbi. As Joe Sisco explained, "while it cannot be demonstrated that the administration explicitly took steps to encourage South Africa's intervention, it certainly did not discourage it."[49] The South Africans claim they had American approval before they crossed the border. When he was asked whether the U.S. had "solicited" South African intervention, Prime Minister Vorster said that he would not call someone who said so a liar.[50] Defense Minister P. W. Botha told the South African Parliament that the U.S. encouraged them to intervene:

> I know of only one occasion in recent years when we crossed a border, and that was in the case of Angola when we did so with the approval and knowledge of the Americans. But they left us in the lurch. We are going to retell the story: the story must be told of how we, with their knowledge, went in there and operated in Angola with their knowledge, how they encouraged us to act and, when we had nearly reached the climax, we were ruthlessly left in the lurch.[51]

It is possible that the administration asked South Africa to invade, but it was more likely that they had been pushing Pretoria to get involved in Angola without proposing an invasion, and the South Africans assumed that the U.S. would support them crossing the border. It is also clear that the administration didn't understand the extent of the South African invasion. Internal CIA documents confirm Kissinger's claim that the agency reported throughout the conflict that there were 100 to 200 South African troops in Angola.[52]

The South African invasion convinced the Chinese to pull out, and the Soviets and Cubans to become more involved in Angola. The Chinese had become disillusioned with Roberto, and they knew that being associated with South Africa would destroy their reputation in the Third World, so they pulled out their advisors on October 27.[53] The Soviets had been engaged in an internal debate regarding whether to increase their support to the MPLA, and the news that the South Africans had crossed the border prompted them to plan a massive airlift of arms upon Angola achieving independence.[54]

The Cubans decided to escalate their involvement after their advisors got into a firefight with the South Africans. It was the second time that Cuban troops took part in the fighting. Their first involvement was on October 23, at the heights of Morro da Cal, twenty miles north of Luanda. Roberto was trying to take the heights to prepare for a final assault on the capital. His 3,500 troops in the area, which included 1,200 Zairian paratroopers, easily outnumbered the 1,100 MPLA troops and 40 Cuban advisors. When the FNLA troops attacked on October 23 the Cuban advisors joined in the fierce fighting. Roberto's troops were ultimately able to dislodge the MPLA, and Neto's forces retreated ten miles south to Quifangondo and dug in.[55]

On November 2 the Cubans took part in the fighting for the second time when they joined MPLA forces in a battle with Task Force Zulu at Catengue, a city on the road north to the port city of Benguela. After a short fight the Cuban/MPLA force had to withdraw when they realized that they were being outflanked by South African armored cars. The South Africans were able to take Benguela after a fierce fight on November 6, and they pushed 20 miles north the next day and took Lobito, Angola's primary port.[56]

The report that his troop had faced South African armored cars spurred Castro into action. The Cuban cauldillo had planned to wait until after independence to send troops, but the report of his advisors battling South Africans coincided with a new plea from Neto. On November 3 an MPLA envoy arrived in Cuba to ask for combat troops, not just advisors. Castro agreed to send troops the next day. As Castro explained, he decided to send "the men and the weapons necessary to win that struggle."[57] Castro named the mission "Operation Carlota" after a slave woman who had wielded a machete in a Cuban revolt on November 5, 1843. Operation Carlota began when two planes carrying a battalion of 652 troops left Cuba on November 7, landing in Angola the next day. At the same time, ships carrying an artillery regiment set sail for Africa.[58]

Castro did not consult with the Soviets before he sent in his troops. Karen Brutents, a Third World expert for the Soviet Central Committee, says that the Cubans acted on their own and pulled the USSR in after them:

> We didn't know that the Cubans were coming to rescue the Angolans.... But when the Cubans were already in Angola, we got involved step-by-step, because the Cubans needed food and weapons. And we found ourselves involved up to our ears in Angola, although we were not planning on it. The Cubans did all this completely independently from us.[59]

On November 12 the first of 60 Soviet advisors landed in Africa, but they were not given control of the Cuban troops. When Castro discussed Angola with the Soviets, he made it clear that he was calling the shots. He told Anatoly Dobrynin, "It is my command."[60] He personally directed the operation, spending 14 hours a day in his Havana command center and talking regularly to his troops in Angola. "His absorption in the war was so intense and meticulous that he could quote any statistic relating to Angola as if it were Cuba itself, and he spoke of its towns, customs and peoples as if he had lived there all his life."[61]

On November 8 the Cuban advisors took part in the fighting for the third time. This time the troops involved were the Cuban advisors in the enclave of Cabinda, on the coast north of Angola. Mobutu coveted the oil-rich territory, and he invaded with a battalion of his own troops and the Cabindian independence organization FLEC, along with a dozen French mercenaries. Mobutu's forces were checked by the 1,000 MPLA troops and 232 Cuban advisors in the enclave, and Mobutu's plan to take Cabinda failed. The French mercenaries proved to be worthless, and one later described their contribution to the battle. "We sent the guys from FLEC out in front of us to probe the area. It was a massacre. We stayed behind, chugging down beers, and when things went bad we got out of there."[62] The Zairian troops were cut to pieces when they marched "like a parade ground drill" through the N'to valley.[63] Sending troops in single-file through a valley showed the profound incompetence of the Zairian military leaders, and Roberto would lose the war when he did the same thing a week later during his attack on Luanda.

On the eve of independence, three foreign armies were actively engaged in Angola — three battalions of the Zairian army were within 20 miles of the capital; South Africa had two armored task forces 120 miles to the south of the Luanda; and a Cuban army was landing to hold the capital for Neto.

The South Africans didn't plan to stay long. On November 10, Savimbi flew to Pretoria to meet with Prime Minister Vorster, and he was disappointed to learn that the South Africans still planned to withdraw after independence. Savimbi begged Vorster to keep the troops in the country until the OAU summit on December 9 because, like many others, he was hoping that the OAU could force a settlement. Savimbi's disappointment turned into shock when Vorster predicted that Roberto would take Luanda with South Africa's help. He was talking about an attack that was planned for the next day north of the capital. To help Roberto take Luanda, South Africa sent four 140mm mortars with crews, while the CIA provided mortars and recoilless rifles. That assistance paled in comparison to what Roberto received from Zaire. Half of his 1,500 men were Zairian troops, and Mobutu provided a dozen armored cars, twenty jeeps, and two 130mm cannons he had received from North Korea.

Roberto had flown in to command the battle in person, and his presence would cause his army's defeat. He had very little experience in combat, and he proved to be an exceptionally inept military leader. His incompetence was exacerbated by his arrogance, as he refused to listen to his advisors. In the valley between his troops and the MPLA positions a narrow road cut through a swamp. Roberto's Portuguese advisors pushed for an attack through the swamps to flank the MPLA positions, and the South Africans suggested that he flank even wider to the east. But Roberto decided on a frontal assault in a single column down the road, even though his advisors told him that the plan was suicidal.

At the other end of the valley Neto's forces had just gotten a huge boost. The first 120 Cuban combat troops landed in Luanda on November 9, and they immediately headed north to join the battle. The newly-arrived Cuban troops manned the heavy guns, mortars, and Soviet-made Katyusha rockets behind the front line. Roberto also put his guns behind his line on the heights north of the valley, and the battle opened on the morning of November 10 when his artillery opened fire. Roberto watched the battle from the heights, along with his CIA and South African advisors, but the attack was delayed by 40 minutes because he tarried at breakfast, giving the defenders time to leave their bunkers and take position. Neto's troops held their fire as the FNLA troops made their way down the road. When the column was trapped in the valley, Neto's troops opened fire with mortars and rockets. At the same time, one of Roberto's North Korean cannons exploded, causing him to panic. He ordered his troops to retreat, causing a rout as the FNLA and Zairian troops turned and ran.

The battle was the end for Roberto, and his troops never stopped running until they reached the Zairian border, except for those that deserted, raping and pillaging the countryside. By the end of November, Roberto had lost half his troops, and the rest had no stomach for continuing the fight. The problem was not lack of munitions — Zairian C-130 transport planes continued to deliver arms and equipment to the troops as they retreated. By the end of November, Neto's northern front was secure. It was a dramatic reversal. Two days before Angolan independence it looked like Roberto might take over the country in one brash move, but as independence dawned, he was done.[64]

On the day before independence the Portuguese quietly left the country. Just after noon on November 10, High Commissioner Leonel Cardoso stood in front of the Presidential Palace in Luanda and addressed a handful of foreign reporters. "In the name of the President of the Portuguese Republic; I solemnly proclaim the independence of Angola and its full sovereignty. It is up to the Angolan people to decide in what manner they will exercise it." He followed with a cheer: "Viva Portugal! Viva Angola!" His troops lowered their flag, and the remaining Portuguese made their way to the harbor where ships were waiting to take them home.[65]

At midnight each rival group held an independence ceremony. In the city of Ambriz north of Luanda, Roberto declared the birth of the "Democratic People's Republic of Angola." In the south-central city Huambo, Savimbi held a ceremony in the sports stadium and raised the UNITA flag. In the capital, Neto announced the founding of the independent "People's Republic of Angola," and he declared that the MPLA was "the only representative of the Angolan people."[66]

On Angolan independence day Kissinger told Ford that "with a few arms and mercenaries, either side could win. We have done well with the weapons we sent. But it may turn with the new Soviet weapons going in."[67] The administration learned of Roberto's defeat soon enough, but the extent of his defeat never really sunk in. On November 13, Ed Mulcahy told Kissinger that the FNLA "took a real pasting."[68] Six days later Kissinger told Ford, "The trend is against us in Angola."[69] But he never acknowledged the reality that the only remaining chance of defeating the MPLA was for the South African task forces to drive north and take Luanda. And he never recognized that the rest of Africa would embrace Neto when they realized that he was fighting South African troops.

At this point Ford's best option would have been to end the covert operation. The operation had been planned to prevent a MPLA victory before independence, which had been achieved. The administration could have explained that the resulting MPLA victory was the result of Roberto's incompetence rather than Cuban troops or a Soviet airlift. No one expected Savimbi to win, and the administration could have considered supporting his guerilla operation as the South Africans withdrew. The decision would have maintained as much American credibility as possible; it would have avoided putting the administration in the embarrassing position of publicly begging the Soviets to end their airlift; and it would have prevented a losing showdown with Congress. It would have been an unpleasant decision, but it was the best, most-realistic alternative.

But Ford and Kissinger did not honestly assess their alternatives, despite being given an unvarnished view of the facts in a November 26 memo from the CIA, the State Department, and the Defense Department. The interagency analysis called the prospects for a settlement "remote," and it predicted that Roberto's current position would be overrun, "despite substantial Zairian backing with men and equipment." The memo provides further evidence that the administration was not aware of the extent of the South African invasion, which it called "several hundred South African and a few Portuguese professional soldiers." The agencies predicted that Moscow and Havana would continue to support the MPLA at whatever level necessary to prevail, while South Africa "has implied that it will withdraw its forces rather than risk them in heavy fighting so far north."[70]

The administration continued to act like nothing had changed in Angola. Kissinger asked for a plan to win the war, and the CIA's proposal was considered in a November 14 meeting of the 40 Committee. The agency provided three plans costing an additional $30, $60, or $100 million, but those amounts would require congressional approval, so the committee asked for a cheaper option that would keep the war going. The CIA proposed a new program of $28 million — a paltry amount compared to the sums that the Soviet Union, Cuba, Zaire, and South Africa were expending — but the administration did not have even that much. The CIA Contingency Reserve Fund had only $7 million remaining for fiscal year 1975. The administration decided to submit a request to Congress for the $28 million, to be considered in private session. The CIA recommended that the agency use the remaining $7 million in the Contingency Reserve Fund on arms and mercenaries, and Ford approved the release of the money on November 27.[71]

The decision to hire mercenaries was shameful — when mercenaries had been used in other African conflicts, such as the civil war in Zaire, they had ravaged the areas they controlled, stealing everything and killing at whim. As Stockwell explained, it was "a senseless gesture, but something, at least, to report to the 40 Committee."[72]

After independence, the Soviets began flying huge quantities of arms to Angola, including artillery, tanks, and helicopters. Cuba continued to send troops — by December 1, Castro had approximately 2,500 troops in the country.[73] At first the Soviet airlift was condemned by many African nations, including Nigeria and Tanzanian president Julius Nyerere. But African opposition to the airlift ended in late November when the South African role in the fighting became public. On November 23 the *Washington Post* reported that South African troops were fighting with UNITA.[74] Three days later Savimbi admitted to the *Daily News of*

Tanzania that a limited number of South African troops were fighting in his army. "I need people to fight with armored cars that we cannot operate ourselves. They are South African or Rhodesian, but there are more French." The reaction of black Africa was presaged by the headline of the article: "Savimbi Admits Betrayal." Nigeria immediately switched sides, recognizing Neto's government and giving $20 million to the MPLA, and Nyerere announced that Tanzania would begin training MPLA soldiers.[75]

Nyerere later sent a letter to Ford which succinctly explained the impact of the South African intervention on black African opinion. "America is concerned about Cuban troops and Russian weapons in support of the MPLA. Tanzania is much more concerned about the intervention of South African troops and weapons."[76] In an article a year later Nyerere stressed the central importance of race. "Within Rhodesia, Namibia, and South Africa, and within the nations immediately bordering them, the commitment to the struggle against minority or colonial rule overrides all other matters."[77]

The revelation of South African involvement reinforced the Chinese decision to stay out of Angola. When Ford and Kissinger were in Beijing in December they pleaded with the Chinese to become reengaged, but Deng declined because of the involvement of South Africa. "The relatively complex problem is the involvement of South Africa, and I believe you are aware of the feelings of the black Africans toward South Africa."[78]

In the second week of December the *New York Times* ran a series of stories that gave the details of the CIA program, including a December 14 article by Seymour Hersh which revealed that Davis had resigned to protest the Angola program and that the operation had been undertaken against the nearly-unanimous advice of African experts within the State Department.[79] The articles gave support to the small but growing congressional opposition to the operation. On December 5, chair of the Senate Subcommittee on Africa Dick Clark joined with Republican senator Clifford Case to submit a resolution to "prohibit any further military or related assistance to or for Angolan interests without specific authorization under the Foreign Assistance Act." The Clark Amendment would not have impacted the operation in Angola because the administration already needed congressional appropriations for any further operations.

Clark was upstaged by Democratic senator John Tunney from California who was looking for a high-profile issue to use to overcome his reputation as a lightweight. At first Angola did not look promising because Clark looked primed to grab the glory on that issue. But his aid Mark Moran mentioned that the Defense Appropriations Bill was up for a vote before the full Senate three days before the Subcommittee on Foreign Assistance would vote on the Clark Amendment. Tunney decided to submit a last-minute amendment to the bill to bar any further expenditure in Angola, and he convinced his old Yale roommate Ted Kennedy to support it.

The debate on the bill was expected to be short and uncontroversial, but Tunney disrupted the proceedings by demanding to know how much had been spent in Angola, and he spent the next three days fighting with administration representatives who refused to provide the information. After three days of debate, Tunney introduced his amendment to cut off funding for Angola. While the debate raged on the Senate floor, the administration slipped badly in hearings before the Subcommittee on Foreign Assistance. The CIA representative was Deputy Director of Operations Bill Nelson, and Ed Mulcahy testified for the State Department. Nelson testified before Mulcahy arrived, and he admitted that the CIA was sending arms to Angola. Mulcahy followed with the official administration position, which was that arms were not being sent directly into Angola. The senators were furious that Mulcahy had lied to them, and the committee overwhelmingly passed the Clark Amendment.

The amendment was taken up by the full Senate in closed session the next day, Wednesday, December 17. During the debate Kissinger landed in Washington from a trip to Europe. His aides met the plane and told him that things were going badly, so he went directly to Capitol Hill. Kissinger met with two dozen senators that afternoon in a futile attempt to reach a compromise. Tunney wouldn't budge, and Kissinger would not agree to anything that he thought would infringe on executive authority in foreign affairs.

The Tunney Amendment was set for a vote on Friday, December 19, the last day before Congress recessed. The night before the vote, Kissinger met with congressional leaders in the office of Senate majority leader Mike Mansfield, but his appeals were to no avail. The next day Senator Griffin tried to lead a filibuster, but Ford was concerned that the Senate would not pass the defense appropriation bill before the recess, and he asked Griffin to stop. The Senate passed the bill in a 54 to 22 vote. The revised appropriations bill was sent to the House, but Speaker Albert decided that the House did not have time to consider the Angola issue, so he tabled the bill until the next congressional session. The House passed the bill in January in a 325 to 99 vote. Ford considered vetoing the Defense Appropriations Act, but he was convinced by his aides that the veto would be overridden, and he signed the bill with the Tunney Amendment on February 9.[80]

When the Senate voted on December 19, Roberto had already been defeated. The Cuban troops had already been sent south to fight the South Africans, and the MPLA was methodically pushing Roberto's forces into Zaire. The only viable hope of defeating Neto and his Cuban allies was for the South African task forces to drive north and take Luanda. But the South Africans had become bogged down, and the leaders in Pretoria were coming to the conclusion that a drive to the capital would result in an unacceptable level of casualties.

When the South Africans began moving north after independence day they faced an MPLA force that had been reinforced with Cuban troops. The offensive stalled, and the task forces were stuck 120 miles south of Luanda by rains that turned the roads into mud. The South Africans tried to move north again on December 9, but the advance again stalled for a few days during a fierce battle when Cuban forces opened fire as the attacking column tried to cross a small wooden bridge. Although the South Africans won the battle, the fight convinced Pretoria that they would suffer unacceptable casualties if they tried to take Luanda — the military told Vorster's cabinet that they would suffer 40 percent casualties among the 1,500 troops in Angola. The South African command ordered the task forces to take as much territory as possible for UNITA and then gradually withdraw from the country.[81]

The decision to withdraw was reinforced by the realization that the United States would also pull out of Angola. As the Senate was considering the Clark Amendment, South African ambassador Pik Botha called Vorster and predicted that Congress would cut off aid. "If you rely on American assistance, then I want to warn you that assistance will either be terminated or will be withdrawn, and then you stand alone." Vorster was shocked. He told Botha that he had received assurances from "the highest level" in the United States government that aid would continue. (Botha is convinced that the assurances did not come from Ford or Kissinger.) Botha told Vorster that, despite any assurances he had received, Congress would cut off aid. "Sir, I do not know what your sources are, but I'm living close to Capitol Hill; I know the senators, I know quite a number of congressmen; I know the sentiments there, and they vote the budget, and they are going to withdraw Dr. Kissinger's funds."[82] After the Senate vote,

Vorster asked Botha to find out if the administration would send aid if the fighting escalated. The South African ambassador met with Scowcroft, who could make no promises.

In late December the South Africans debated whether to withdraw from Angola entirely. Ambassador Botha flew home for the meeting, carrying with him a request from the Ford administration to delay the withdrawal until the upcoming OAU meeting. Vorster decided to withdraw to 30 miles north of the border, but only after the OAU meeting. On December 25, South African Major General van Deventer met with Savimbi at his home base at Bie and confirmed that the South Africans would withdraw after the OAU conference. Savimbi made one more attempt to convince the South Africans to stay. He flew to Windhoek, Namibia, and asked Vorster to take Luanda, but the prime minister declined.[83]

Although they probably would have withdrawn from Angola even if Congress had not cut off funds, the South Africans felt a deep sense of betrayal at the failure of the U.S. to support them, and they used every opportunity to complain to the Americans. In early February a visiting congressional delegation was told that South Africa had invaded Angola believing that the U.S. "intended to put up strong resistance to Soviet and Cuban intervention."[84] In 1978, defense minister P. W. Botha rose in parliament and said that the United States "recklessly left us in the lurch."[85]

━━◦∿∿◦━━

Kissinger claims that the administration was on the verge of a breakthrough when the Senate vote killed any chance of success. He claims that the Soviets responded to American pleas by suspending their airlift between December 10 and 25.[86] Kissinger is probably overreaching. There is no contemporaneous evidence that the Soviets suspended the airlift, and there is certainly no evidence that they did so because the administration asked them to. Dobrynin does not mention any suspension in his memoirs, and he never told Ford or Kissinger that the Soviets were suspending the airlift. In fact, he refused Kissinger's request to stop the airlift during a December 9 meeting.[87] During the time the airlift was supposedly suspended, Kissinger and Ford continued to press Dobrynin to stop the Soviet involvement in Angola, and Dobrynin continued to refuse the requests. On December 23, Kissinger again asked the Soviets to stop all activities in Angola, and he proposed a compromise solution to refer the issue to the OAU. Dobrynin refused, pointing out that the OAU was already trying to mediate the conflict, without success.[88]

There is evidence of interruptions in the Cuban troop flights and the Soviet arms shipments, but they were the result of technical difficulties rather than a response to American pressure. Cuban Central Committee member Jorge Risquet remembers that the Soviets did halt their airlift. "Yes, it's true, there was a Soviet pause, for which we received no explanation."[89] Professor Odd Arne Westad, who has reviewed the Soviet archives, did not see any evidence that the Soviets halted the airlift in response to American pressure, but he did see evidence of technical problems that caused periodic delays.[90]

At the time, the administration was confused about how the Cuban troops were being carried to Angola, and the erroneous reports of a suspension appear to be a result of that confusion. Kissinger's aide, William Hyland, writes that the "Soviet airlift of Cuban troops was temporarily suspended."[91] But there was no "Soviet airlift of Cuban troops" to be suspended. Until January 1976 the Cubans flew their troops to Angola themselves, using Soviet-made IL-18 planes. There was a short suspension of the Cuban airlift, but the interruption was the result of technical problems, not American pressure on the Soviets. The IL-18s needed to stop to fuel on the way to Angola. At first, Barbados allowed the Cubans to refuel at their airport, but on December 17 the government acceded to U.S. pressure and refused to allow the Cubans to land. The flights were suspended until the Portuguese agreed to allow the Cubans to refuel in the Azores on December 20. Beginning January 9, the Soviets started transporting the Cuban troops in its larger IL-62s, which did not need to stop for fuel.[92]

--- ⚬⚬⚬ ---

In a meeting three days after the Senate vote, Ford called it "mildly deplorable," and he told the NSC to spend any money it legally could in Angola. "Every department should spend all it can legally — do all we can in that area."[93] The CIA still had $5 million of the $7 million authorized by Ford in November, and the Tunney Amendment had not taken effect, so the agency quickly spent the remaining money.[94]

Some of the money went to hire mercenaries, and it was a barbarous yet pitiful operation. At first the mercenaries were led by Costas Georgiou, who went by the name "Colonel Callan." Callan was brave to the point of recklessness, and he impressed Roberto when he jumped into a road and stood exposed as he shot his antitank weapon into an oncoming MPLA armored column. Roberto was so impressed that he gave him command of the motley mercenary army. Even Callan's fellow mercenaries called their new leader a "homicidal maniac." He terrorized the area around his base in Sao Salvador, 50 miles south of the border with Zaire. He randomly executed citizens for imagined complicity with the MPLA, and he treated his own troops with the same cruelty — he summarily executed any he thought were disloyal or ready to desert, at one point executing many while they were sleeping. One of Callan's soldiers later described the situation:

> All war is dirty, but in our particular context of the FNLA in northern Angola, with Europeans or British soldiers working under Callan, it was particularly dirty, in so much as we — and I use the word "we" collectively — committed what would be crimes, and in that respect the Angolan Government got the wording right: "war crimes." We did kill when we had no particular reason to. We tortured to achieve information that they probably didn't have, and this was not captured enemy soldiers: these were probably just local civilians. And that atmosphere permeated its way through the whole unit, where there was an air of lawlessness there.[95]

Callan was captured by the MPLA, and he was tried in June 1976 along with twelve other mercenaries. The court convicted the mercenaries, calling them "dogs of war with bloodstained muzzles." Callan and four other mercenaries were executed.[96]

Not all the mercenaries were homicidal maniacs, but all of them were inept. Most of the mercenaries were recruited in England, where recruiters trolled the taverns for unemployed workers with minimal military training. They were dropped off in northern Angola with no training, inadequate equipment, and no leadership. One observer called the mission "a hopeless farce."[97] The mercenaries had no chance, and most of them were killed in a pointless effort. On February 10 the remaining forty-five mercenaries, most of them wounded, returned to England.[98]

--- ⚬⚬⚬ ---

When the OAU summit opened on January 10, 1976, there was no real chance of a negotiated resolution, and the only real question was whether a majority of the OAU states would vote to recognize Neto's government. A resolution to recognize the MPLA had been submitted by Nigeria, and it was competing with a resolution in favor of a government of reconciliation in Angola. Ford sent letters to the leaders of the member states urging them to vote for a government of national reconciliation. After several days of debate, the vote was a tie, 22 to 22. But the vote did not really reflect the extent to which the African states had switched to support the MPLA. Within six weeks, 41 members of the OAU recognized the Neto regime.[99]

After the OAU meeting, South Africa had no reason to remain in Angola, and on January 14 Vorster ordered his troops out of the country. Two days later two South African generals met with Roberto, Chipenda, and Savimbi and announced that they would withdraw within the week. The South Africans kept a small force protecting the Cunene hydroelectric plant for two months, and the last troops left the country on March 27 after the Neto government committed to the safety of the plant. Defense Minister P. W. Botha stood at the border and saluted the troops as they passed by.[100]

Faced with the withdrawal of the South African troops, Savimbi traveled to Zaire to meet with CIA deputy director Vernon Walters and chief of the CIA Zaire station Stuart Methven. Savimbi asked whether he should continue to fight a conventional war or go into the bush and begin a guerilla campaign. Walters and Methven thought that UNITA would not be good guerilla fighters, so they demurred until they could get an official response from Washington. Savimbi began to send his men into the forests, but before he made a final decision — and the day after the United States gave its recommendation — he lost hundreds of troops. On February 8 the administration told Savimbi that it could not provide any more aid, and the next day the MPLA took Savimbi's main base in the city of Huambo, killing more than 600 UNITA soldiers defending the city. The MPLA discovered several sites where Savimbi's troops had massacred MPLA sympathizers during the last days of their rule.[101]

Kissinger kept trying in vain to convince the Soviets to stop supporting Neto. On January 20 he arrived in Moscow in his final effort to reach agreement on a SALT II treaty. As usual, Kissinger and Brezhnev fielded questions from the press before they met in private. When a reporter asked if Angola would be discussed, Brezhnev said no. "I have no questions about Angola. Angola is not my country." Kissinger disagreed. "It will certainly be discussed." But Brezhnev was dismissive. "You'll discuss it with Sonnenfeldt. That will insure complete agreement. I've never seen him have a disagreement with Sonnenfeldt." True to his word, Kissinger brought up the issue after the press was gone. Kissinger objected to "8,000 Cubans running around" in Angola, but Brezhnev refused to address the issue.[102] Two days later Kissinger brought up the issue again with Gromyko, but the Soviet foreign minister made it clear that the Cubans were acting independently. "I have no intention of discussing whatever actions Cuba is taking. We have not been authorized by the Cuban Government to speak on its behalf."[103]

It is hard to understand why Kissinger kept pushing the issue, because the war was over. On January 21 the CIA reported that the MPLA had "already destroyed" the FNLA, and with the withdrawal of South African forces, Neto "almost certainly" would win the conventional war within weeks.[104] Five days later the administration gave a different assessment to the House Committee on International Relations, which was considering the administration's request for $32 million for Angola. Assistant Secretary of State for African Affairs William Schaufele admitted that the MPLA had the military advantage, but he denied that an MPLA victory was inevitable. "The present situation, although it has deteriorated, is not conclusive."[105]

Cuba continued to pour troops into Angola. In late January, Castro decided, without being asked, to send more troops. Neto was assured that the Cuban troops "would remain in Angola for as long as it took and for as long as he considered necessary."[106] By February there were 12,000 Cuban troops in the country, outfitted with modern equipment, including trucks, armored cars, tanks, helicopters, and MIG jets. In February the CIA estimated that the Soviets had spent $400 million in Angola.[107]

At the end of February the last FNLA troops crossed the border into Zaire, never to return. The conventional war was over, but Savimbi's guerrilla war would continue for the next twenty-five years. The CIA spent the last of its money by sending $1 million worth of arms to Savimbi for his guerrilla campaign, but word leaked that the CIA continued to spend money in Angola. Congress was not pleased, even though the payments were technically legal. Tunney wrote a letter to Ford demanding that all CIA action in Angola be terminated, and George Bush, who had just taken over the agency, ordered a halt to all payments.[108]

The MPLA did not end up being the worst government in Africa (it had stiff competition), but it was hardly a model democracy. Neto set up a government patterned on the USSR, and he strictly restricted press activities. He proved his ruthlessness in 1977 when one of his lieutenants, Nito Alves, tried to stage a coup. Neto's forces arrested and executed thousands of suspected sympathizers, dropping some into the sea from helicopters. After Neto's death in 1979, Jose Eduardo dos Santos ran Angola for almost thirty years, submitting to an election only once. The regime was corrupt and inept, and famine swept the country in the '80s.[109]

As bad as the government was, the worst damage was caused by Savimbi's guerilla war. Savimbi had no chance of winning, but the MPLA could not defeat him, and he fought for twenty-five more years. More than a million people died during the conflict, and the rival parties planted millions of landmines throughout the country, killing and maiming ordinary citizens for decades. In 1999, UNICEF declared that Angola's children were more likely to die or suffer malnutrition, abuse, or development failure than any other country in the world. During the same period, the UN Food and Agricultural Organization called Angola the country in most need of aid. Even though he lost an election in 1992, Savimbi would keep on fighting until he died in 2002, twenty-seven years after independence. Peace finally came to Angola.[110]

———❦———

At first the Soviets and Cubans were elated at their victory in Angola, but for the Soviets the victory turned bittersweet as they continued to support the government in its twenty-seven-year war with Savimbi. They did not get much from their investment. The MPLA refused to allow a Soviet naval base along the African coast, and to the extent that the Soviet Union and Cuba thought that they would be rewarded with exclusive access to Angola's rich natural resources, they were disappointed. American oil companies continued to do business with the MPLA, and half of the oil produced by Angola went to the United States, while most of the rest went to other western nations.[111] Soviet Central Committee member Karen Bruents later lamented the results of the Soviet support. "They were very rich: gas, oil, diamonds — but we didn't get anything from them. We sat there, protecting them from the South Africans, and at the same time the Americans were pumping their oil in Cabinda."[112]

While the United States didn't lose access to resources after pulling out of Angola, that wasn't Kissinger's primary concern in the crisis. He wanted to send a message to the Soviets and the Cubans that they would be in a fight whenever they intervened in Third-World conflicts. Dobrynin has admitted that the failure of the U.S. to respond in Angola led to an escalation of Soviet activities in the Third World. "Having suffered no major ... international complications because of its interference in Angola, Moscow had no scruples about escalating its activities in other countries, first Ethiopia, then Yemen, a number of African and Middle Eastern states, and, to crown it all, in Afghanistan."[113] The fact that the U.S. withdrew from Angola may have given Brezhnev "no scruples" about entering other conflicts, but he had not been deterred by scruples in the past. Brezhnev had a history of wringing his hands about the American reaction to Soviet interventions — and then intervening anyway. A stronger

U.S. response in Angola may have changed Soviet behavior in Ethiopia and Yemen, but it is hard to believe that they would have made a different decision regarding Afghanistan, where they believed that an invasion was necessary to protect their vital interests. A more likely result is that Brezhnev would have wrung his hands worrying about the possible impact on relations with the U.S., and then invaded anyway, like he did in Czechoslovakia.

In a perverse way, if the U.S. failure to react in Angola did clear the way for the invasion of Afghanistan, it may have lead to the collapse of the Soviet Union. The Soviet invasion of Afghanistan was as important as any other factor in the fall of the USSR, as the nine-year struggle led to widespread dissatisfaction in the populace and disillusionment of Soviet leaders like Gorbachev. The failure of the Soviet Army in Afghanistan also emasculated Soviet hardliners, who in previous times would have been able to block Gorbachev's reforms.

It is equally unclear whether the failure of the U.S. to respond in Angola persuaded Castro to send troops to other countries. Kissinger is convinced that it did. "Cuban troops remained there for another fifteen years and spread into Ethiopia, Somalia, and South Yemen in the Carter Administration."[114] He is correct that the Cubans actively intervened in African conflicts after Angola, but they had intervened in just as many before the conflict. During the Algerian civil war in the early 1960s Castro sent more than 350 troops to the country, along with tanks and artillery. In 1965 the Cubans sent 400 military advisors to Zaire, where they fought in the ongoing civil war. Castro also sent more than 60 troops to Guinea-Bissau in 1965–67, where they participated in the fighting, and additional troops to Congo-Brazzaville in 1965, where they helped the government put down a revolt. At the time he sent troops to Angola, Castro had military advisors in Zanzibar, Sierra Leone, Equatorial Guinea, Syria, and South Yemen, and Cuba had trained rebels from Mozambique, Zimbabwe, Eritrea, South Africa, and Namibia.[115]

Castro's troop deployments after Angola were very much like his previous interventions. Cuba sent 800 troops to assist the government of Mozambique to defend against South African–backed rebels, and Castro sent military advisors to Zambia, Uganda, Tanzania, Benin, São Tomé e Príncipe, Libya, and Algeria.[116] The one incident that was appreciably different occurred in Ethiopia. In 1978, Cuba sent more than 16,000 troops to assist the genocidal government of that country in fighting off an invasion by Somalia. After the invasion was beaten back in 1979, Cuba withdrew the majority of its troops, but several hundred remained for the next few years.[117] Ethiopia was a special situation, a border war between two communist countries. As Cuban vice premier Carlos Rafael Rodriguez later explained, Castro himself had mediated a truce between Somalia and Ethiopia, and when Somalia broke the truce, Cuba felt obligated to defend Ethiopia:

> During his visit to Africa, Fidel Castro met first with Siad Barre and then in Ethiopia with Mengistu, and agreed with them to conduct a historic meeting in Aden.... While the meeting did not lead to an agreement, nevertheless Siad Barre promised not to attack Ethiopia. And then, when Siad Barre attacked Ethiopia, we considered ourselves obligated to Mengistu, whom we had persuaded to attend the peace conference which had taken place in Aden.[118]

The Cuban government has remained proud of its support of its revolutionary brethren in Angola, and in particular they are proud of forcing the South Africans out of the country. The South African presence has given Cuba a useful propaganda tool, as Castro claimed credit for the fact that "the swastika of the South African racists does not fly over the palace of Luanda."[119] The Cuban intervention in Angola also led to South Africa giving up Namibia when the Reagan administration brokered an agreement in which South Africa agreed to grant Namibia independence in return for Cuba withdrawing its troops.[120] But Cuba paid a heavy price in Angola. Over the years, Castro sent nearly 50,000 troops to Angola, and more than 2,000 Cubans lost their lives in the conflict. Over two decades, Cuba spent 11 percent of its budget on its African expeditions, straining an economy already failing under Castro's mismanagement.[121]

———

The failure of the American covert operation in Angola was entirely foreseeable — the African experts accurately predicted the outcome. Even though Ford was an expert on congressional politics, he failed to see that the new liberal Congress would not support a covert operation. Ford and Kissinger also ignored predictions that Roberto was unlikely to win, and failed to heed warnings that Savimbi's support from South Africa would make him anathema to all moderate African states.

Failure wasn't inevitable, but it was the most likely outcome. Kissinger now claims that he was on the verge of forcing a negotiated solution, but it is hard to imagine that Neto, Roberto, and Savimbi would have reached an agreement when all attempts to force a truce had failed in the past. Even if the Soviets had stopped their airlift of arms — a highly-questionable assumption — Castro was personally committed to the adventure, and he would not have stopped his troop deployment. Furthermore, Kissinger had consistently rejected the type of diplomatic solution he now claims was in reach. He treated Davis' suggestion of a diplomatic solution with disdain, and the U.S. stifled an attempt by Savimbi to negotiate a resolution with the MPLA just weeks before independence.

The result of the covert operation was exactly what the State Department Africa experts predicted — Angola offered a no-win situation, and it was foolish to put American prestige on the line. By not listening to the experts who warned them to stay out, Ford and Kissinger brought about the worst possible result: an MPLA victory as a result of massive Soviet and Cuban support; the perception that the United States was acting in concert with South Africa; and an embarrassing public repudiation of the covert operations by Congress.

18

China and East Timor

Ford and Kissinger traveled to China at the end of November 1975. The trip had been planned for some time, but the arrangements were changed at the last minute because Mao Tse Tung's health had taken a turn for the worse. Ford decided to cut his stay in China to just three days, and he used the extra days to make brief stops in the Philippines and Indonesia.[1] The China trip wasn't much more than a photo op because the upcoming elections in the U.S. and the declining health of Chinese leaders made any progress toward normal relations impossible. It was the stop in Jakarta that made the trip memorable. Ford explicitly told Indonesian president Suharto that the United States would not object to Indonesia invading the former Portuguese colony of East Timor, and the result was a horrible genocide that would last until the end of the century.

———

The purpose of the trip to China was to signal that both countries remained committed to improved relations. The natural next step would be to formally normalize relations, but that required a solution to the issue of Taiwan, which had to be put on hold for the time being. Taiwan was a hot button issue for Republican conservatives, and Ford was not willing to antagonize them before the election. Kissinger explained the situation to his staff. "For political reasons it's just impossible for the US to go for normalization before '76. If there's any one thing that will trigger a conservative reaction to Ford, that's it."[2] The Chinese were not willing to address the issue either, because Mao was gravely ill and two factions were posturing to take power when he died. The conservatives, led by Deng Xiaoping, were battling the radicals, led by Mao's wife Jiang Qing. The radicals opposed closer relations with America, and Deng was not willing to antagonize them.

It looked like Deng was ascendant, which was a remarkable resurgence. He had been allied with Mao since the early '30s, and Mao appreciated his loyalty but hated his pragmatism. Deng made a near-fatal mistake when he used an adage from his farming childhood to support his proposal to allow private farming during the famines caused by collectivization. "It doesn't matter if the cat is black or white; so long as it catches the mouse, it is a good cat."[3] That was exactly the type of pragmatic thinking that Mao tried to eradicate with the Cultural Revolution. Deng and his wife were beaten by the Red Guards, and he spent years under house arrest, working at a tractor-repair plant. Mao allowed Deng's arrest, but he restrained all plans to eliminate him. Deng's prospects began to brighten in the early '70s when Mao turned against Jiang Qing and her radical associates, calling them a "Gang of Four." Deng was finally rehabilitated in 1974 when he was promoted to vice premier and named as Mao's co-successor. He and Wang Hongwen were given day-to-day control of the government when Zhou Enlai was admitted to the hospital for cancer.[4]

Kissinger made a trip to China in October to prepare for Ford's visit, and he got a frosty reception. The Americans had very little insight into the workings of the Chinese leadership, and Kissinger attributed the cooling of relations to Watergate, Zhou Enlai's loss of power, and America's improving relations with Taiwan. Kissinger told Ford that Deng "is the key official now," and he thought that his cool reception was "linked to the Chinese perception of the US as a fading strategic power in the face of Soviet advance."[5] He had completely misread the situation. The Chinese were icy because of changes in their power structure, but not due to Zhou's loss of power. It was Deng who had lost power, and Jiang Qing and the radicals who were ascendant. In September 1975, Mao turned against Deng, and he named an unknown functionary, Hua Guofeng, as his successor. With the radicals again holding power, the Chinese showed no interest in improving relations.

When Mao met with Kissinger it was apparent that he was very sick. He was suffering from Lou Gehrig's disease, and he could no longer walk to the door without two nurses supporting him. He constantly needed oxygen; he drooled; and he spoke in grunts. His translator would repeat his words to verify that he heard them correctly before translating them, and for most of the conversation Mao wrote his comments on a note pad. Nevertheless, Winston Lord thought he "still seemed quite sharp." Mao urged the United States to get tougher with the Soviet Union. He told Kissinger, "The small issue is Taiwan, the big issue is the world."[6]

On November 29, 1975, Ford left Washington with Betty, their daughter Susan, and the usual foreign policy entourage. After an overnight stay in Alaska and a brief stop in Japan, the American delegation arrived in Beijing on December 1. Deng met them at the airport, and he continued to take the lead in discussions, meeting with Ford four times during the visit. He seemed nervous, afraid of what he might say in front of the other Chinese leaders. Jiang Qing showed up for only one photo session, treating Ford icily.

Gerald and Betty Ford meet with Deng Xiaoping in Beijing, December 2, 1975. (Photograph by David Hume Kennerly; White House photograph courtesy Gerald R. Ford Library.)

Deng was a diminutive man, and he sat perched on a short chair, with his white shocks showing and his feet barely touching the floor. The 71 year old had a hacking cough from chain-smoking, and he smoked cigarettes during his first meeting with Ford. During the first meeting Deng apologized for smoking, explaining, "I have tried for ten years to fight this habit, but I have always failed." Ford was relieved because it gave him a reason to take out his pipe.[7] In later meetings Deng chewed tobacco and spit into a spittoon by his side.

The primary impression Ford took from the trip was that the Chinese officials were deathly afraid of the Soviet Union, and he spent a lot of time reassuring them that the United States was still committed to stopping Soviet expansionism. The parties could make no headway on the Taiwan issue, but Deng was careful to say that, while bilateral issues like Taiwan were important, "the problems we consider most important are the international issues.... As Chairman Mao once said to the Doctor, our common task is that we face how to deal with that SOB." In the most disconcerting part of the meeting Deng explained that the Chinese believed that a new world war was a real possibility:

> In the contemporary world, there are only two countries qualified to fight such a war, the Soviet Union and the United States; and we believe at present the danger comes from the Soviet Union.... We also feel that the contemporary situation is very similar to the state of affairs prior to the outbreak of World War II. To put it plainly, we believe that to a very great degree the Soviet Union has taken the place of Hitler.[8]

At three in the afternoon on December 2 the Chinese announced that Mao would meet the American delegation an hour later. Ford quickly sent for his daughter Susan, who was visiting the Great Wall, and she and Betty accompanied the American delegates to the meeting in the Forbidden City. Ford met with Mao for nearly two hours. Mao talked about their joint interest in reining in the "Socialist Imperialists" to the north, and he expressed an interest in continued good relations with the United States, but he recognized that domestic factors for both countries would prevent normalizing relations for the time being. "Probably this year, next year, and the year after there will not be anything great happening between our two countries. Perhaps afterwards the situation might become a bit better." At the end of the meeting the 81-year-old Chinese supreme leader demonstrated his willpower by escorting Ford to the door.[9]

In the final meeting Deng also acknowledged that the Taiwan issue would wait for another time. "We have understood Mr. President's point; that is, that during the time of the election it will not be possible to make any new moves. As for our side, we have told the Doctor many times that we are very patient. And in our relations we have always put the international aspect first and the Taiwan issue second."[10] After the meeting, Ford, Kissinger and the rest of the American delegation left Beijing, to stop in the Philippines and Indonesia before heading back to Washington.

⸻

It was the last time the Americans would see the Chinese leaders. The first to go was Zhou Enlai, who died in January 1976. His death set off mass demonstrations by the Chinese people, who considered Zhou a moderate leader who had blunted Mao's most radical plans. A million people lined the route of his funeral procession, and marches in honor of Zhou continued into April. The crowds began to openly criticize Jiang Qing and the radicals.[11]

The Chinese were wrong about Zhou, who had never been a moderate, but that didn't really matter. The Chinese people were using his death to demonstrate how tired they were of Mao's policies. For decades China had been torn apart on a regular basis on the whim of the chairman. The country had just emerged from Mao's attempt at instilling uniformity of thought. During the Cultural Revolution, children were rounded up into Red Guard units and allowed to roam the country, rooting out any signs of intelligence, education, or independence. They beat people to death in every region, village, and neighborhood of the country. The entire country was forced to wear the same drab clothes and ride identical black bicycles. Millions were arrested, and more than a million were killed. At the end of the Cultural Revolution in 1968 Mao had the Red Army take control, and the military responded with mass repression that killed hundreds of thousands more.[12]

The Cultural Revolution was not the first of Mao's horrifying policies, and it certainly wasn't the first time he had targeted anyone who disagreed with him. He had been purging his enemies ever since the civil war, and during his rule the communists executed between 6 and 10 million people. Tens of millions of people passed through Mao's concentration camps, with 20 million not coming out. His economic policies would claim another 20 to 40 million lives. It was Mao's Great Leap Forward that caused the most misery. Half a billion people were forced into communes, and nearly 100 million were diverted from farm work to man makeshift steel furnaces. The steel they produced was worthless, and agricultural production plummeted. The result was the worst famine in world history — between 20 and 30 million people starved to death.[13]

As Mao became sicker, the Chinese longed for sanity and stability, but it looked like they would get more craziness under the Gang of Four. In April, Mao stripped Deng of his offices and forced him into hiding. It looked like Jiang Qing had won, but she sabotaged herself by trying to undermine Hua Guofeng, pushing him closer to her opponents.[14] When Mao died on September 9, 1976, he took his place with Hitler and Stalin as the three most murderous rulers in history — he was responsible for the deaths of more than 50 million people. There were no crowds of people who took to the streets to mourn his death. The Gang of Four kept power for a month, but when Jiang Qing demanded that the Politburo make her premier, Hua had the Gang of Four arrested on October 6. Deng was rehabilitated weeks later, and he would dominate the country until his death in 1997.[15] He would bring some much-needed stability and economic pragmatism to China, giving his people prosperity that they had never known under Mao. But he would prove to be an unreformed dictator, snuffing out all efforts to give his people political and intellectual freedom.

On the way home, Ford visited two of the dictators who had unconditional American support during the Cold War, Philippine president Ferdinand Marcos and Indonesian president Suharto. They were both fantastically corrupt, joining Mobutu as Transparency International's three biggest crooks of the twentieth century.[16] Of the two, Suharto was the tyrant. He didn't deserve to be ranked as one of the top three mass murders of the twentieth century, but he fit snugly in the second tier, which included Pol Pot of Cambodia, Saddam Hussein of Iraq, Jean Kambanda of Rwanda, Mengistu Haile Mariam of Ethiopia, the Young Turks of the Ottoman Empire, and Kim Il-Sung of North Korea. Suharto and the Indonesian military killed 500,000 suspected communist supporters after he took power in 1965; they killed more than 100,000 people after taking over West Papua in 1969; and they were about to launch a terror campaign in the small island of Timor that would kill hundreds of thousands more. To our country's eternal shame, Ford and Kissinger were about to explicitly approve Suharto's invasion of the tiny island.

The island of Timor is the easternmost of the Lesser Sunda Islands that make up the southern border of Indonesia. The island is just 400 miles north of Darwin, Australia. For hundreds of years the Dutch had ruled the western half of the island, while the eastern half was under Portuguese rule. Along with the other Dutch colonies in the area, the western half of Timor became part of Indonesia at the end of World War II, while the eastern half of the island remained a Portuguese colony. After the 1974 revolution the new Portuguese government could not decide whether to grant independence to the colony of 700,000 people or allow Indonesia to incorporate it. East Timor was predominantly Catholic, and the vast majority of its residents had no interest in becoming part of Moslem Indonesia.

Three parties emerged when the new Portuguese government allowed political activity for the first time. Only one party, Apodeti, was dedicated to integration with Indonesia. Apodeti had no popular support, and it was really a front for the Indonesian plan, Operation Komodo, to take over East Timor. The Timorese Democratic Union (UDT) was a moderate party pushing for democracy and independence. The Frente Revolucionária de Timor-Leste Independente (Fretilin) was a leftist party, also dedicated to independence. Like many independence movements at the time, Fretilin was an amalgam of marxist and democratic-socialist elements. Fretilin made the UDT nervous by claiming to be the "sole representative" of the East Timorese, but the best evidence is that the party was not predominantly communist. After extended review, the East Timor Truth and Reconciliation Commission concluded that "the mainstream of the Fretilin leadership was centre-left, although the party contained a spectrum of opinion that ranged from far-left to more conservative elements."[17] During East Timor's first elections in July 1975, Fretilin demonstrated its popularity by winning 55 percent of the vote.[18]

In early 1975, UDT, Fretilin, and Portugal agreed to a three-year plan to jointly rule the colony until elections in 1976. But the agreement was immediately undermined when Suharto refused to accept anything but incorporation. His intelligence services began a propaganda campaign claiming that East Timor were being taken over by communists, and the Indonesian army went on maneuvers to simulate an invasion of the island.

Even the threat of the hostile behemoth to the west could not stop the independence movements from fighting each other. In May 1975 the marxist factions in Fretilin gained prominence, causing the UDT to withdraw from the coalition. On August 10 the UDT attempted a coup, but Fretilin counterattacked, and by September they controlled most of the country and forced the remaining UDT members to cross into Indonesian territory. After they crossed the border, many of the UDT members signed a petition for incorporation into Indonesia. Some of them did it because they were desperate for Indonesian support, while others signed because the Indonesians were holding guns to their heads.[19] It was only a matter of time before Indonesia invaded.

———— ∿∿∿ ————

The first time Ford talked to Suharto about East Timor was July 5 when he met with the Indonesian president at Camp David. Suharto raised the issue by explaining that his country was committed to an "archipelago principle." He promised that "Indonesia will not use force against the territory of other countries," which sounded good, but he never said whether he considered East Timor to be the territory of another country. Suharto was clear that Indonesia did not consider independence an option for East Timor, "so the only way is to integrate into Indonesia." He also claimed that the majority of the East Timorese wanted integration into Indonesia.[20]

Ford appeared to accept Suharto's claim that the majority of the population wanted to be part of Indonesia, and Kissinger never disabused him of the idea. The State Department knew that Suharto's claim was false. Apodeti won only one delegate out of several hundred elected in July, and in March the American consulate on Java sent a cable explaining that there was "no potential reservoir of sympathy for Indonesian overlordship among the Timorese elite or the population at large."[21] The wishes of the people was not a factor that Kissinger and his aides found relevant — like many foreign policy experts, they took pride in being able to consider the big picture rather than issues like human rights and self determination. It's not that they didn't care about human rights; it's that they thought they were advancing those interests by only considering "reality." This attitude created a culture where the mere mention of human concerns was dismissed as naïve and unrealistic. East Timor was a classic example.

From early on, Kissinger assumed that Indonesia was going to invade East Timor. He was always loathe to confront American allies, and this time he genuinely believed that there was nothing the administration could do to stop Suharto. In an August 12 staff meeting Kissinger discussed the attempted UDT coup with Philip Habib, assistant secretary of state. Habib told him that it was "quite obvious that the Indonesians are not going to let any hostile element take over an island right in the midst of the Indonesian archipelago." Kissinger agreed. "It is quite clear that the Indonesians are going to take over the island sooner or later."[22] In October, Habib again told Kissinger that there was no chance that the Indonesians would allow East Timor to be independent. In a telling display of how foreign policy professionals took pride in not taking human suffering into account, they joked about how critics would raise "moral" issues.[23] The Australians also assumed that Suharto would invade. Australian ambassador to Jakarta Richard Woolcott, who understood the intensions of the Indonesians better than any other outsider, believed that they had made a decision to invade by the early summer.[24]

Neither the Americans nor the Australians made any effort to dissuade Suharto from invading. The most the U.S. embassy did was to warn him that if American arms were used, the administration might be obligated to cut off aid under the Foreign Assistance Act.[25] Australian prime minister Gough Whitlam told Suharto that his country would not object to an invasion, and Indonesian officials later said that Whitlam's comments helped convince them to invade.[26]

Indonesia's intentions were an open secret. In early September the CIA reported that Indonesia was infiltrating special forces into East Timor for the purpose of stirring up incidents to provide a pretext for an invasion. When Indonesia attacked a costal town in October it was reported in the *New York Times*. Five foreign journalists were executed in the town after the Indonesians took over, causing a brief international uproar. The attacks stepped up in November, with Indonesia even launching an amphibious attack on the coastal town of Atabae.[27]

On November 28, Fretilin proclaimed East Timor's independence to cheering crowds in the capital city of Dili. They thought they would have a better chance of gaining international support against an Indonesian invasion if East Timor was an independent nation. The next day Indonesia issued a "declaration of integration," drafted by the Indonesian security service and dutifully signed by Apodeti and UDT members in Indonesia.[28] Two days later the Indonesian foreign minister Adam Malik proclaimed, "Diplomacy is over. Now Timor-Leste issues shall be resolved on the battlefield."[29] Ford was due to arrive in Jakarta in less than a week, so the American embassy and the CIA asked the Indonesians to wait to invade until after he left, and Suharto agreed.

In his briefing materials Kissinger told Ford that Indonesia had been maneuvering to absorb the colony, but he claimed that Suharto was "showing considerable restraint." He concluded that a "merger with Indonesia is probably the best solution for the colony if the inhabitants agree." Kissinger reported that U.S. officials had been warning that use of American arms for an invasion would cause problems, which "appears to have been a restraining factor." He suggested that Ford address the issue only if Suharto raised it, and he proposed two talking points:

- We recognize the problem that Timor poses for Indonesia, and we appreciate the restraint that Indonesia has exercised to date.
- We note Indonesia has expressed willingness to see a merger of the territory with Indonesia take place with the assent of the inhabitants of Timor. This would appear to be a reasonable solution.[30]

When Ford arrived in Jakarta, Suharto raised the issue, claiming that "Indonesia has no territorial ambitions." Ford seemed to genuinely believe that the Timorese favored incorporation, and he asked whether "the other parties have asked for integration?" Suharto said they had, and he came to the point. "We want your understanding if we deem it necessary to take rapid or drastic action." Ford then made one the most regrettable statements of his career. "We will understand and will not press you on the issue. We understand the problem you have and the intentions you have." Both Ford and Kissinger told Suharto that the use of American arms could cause problems, and Kissinger encouraged the Indonesians to wrap up things quickly:

> It is important that whatever you do succeeds quickly. We would be able to influence the reaction in America if whatever happens after we return. This way there would be less chance of people talking in an unauthorized way. The president will be back on Monday at 2:00 P.M. Jakarta time. We understand your problem and the need to move quickly but I am only saying that it would be better if it were done after we returned.[31]

—◦◦◦—

Indonesia invaded at 4:30 the next morning, December 7, 1975 — a date which will live in infamy. The troops carried AK-47s and other arms purchased from non–Western countries, but many of their ships, planes, helicopters, and heavy weapons were American-made.[32] The Indonesians started the invasion with an attack on Dili. They cut of all access to the rest of the world by executing the only foreign reporter left in the country, Australian Roger East. The only report that got out that day was a broadcast from the Fretilin information minister: "A lot of people have been killed indiscriminately.... Women and children are going to be killed by Indonesian forces.... We are going to be killed."[33]

As the Indonesian troops took control of the capital, they randomly shot hundreds of people in the streets. They rolled grenades into houses of suspected Fretilin sympathizers; killed anyone in buildings with Fretilin flags; executed the remaining Apodeti and UDT leaders; and summarily shot the ethnic Chinese. Monsignor Martinho da Costa Lopez, later the Bishop of Dili, described the scene: "The soldiers who landed started killing everyone they could find. There were many dead bodies in the streets — all we could see were the soldiers killing, killing, killing."[34] The Indonesians ransacked the entire city, taking everything of value to ships in the harbor. They took cars from the streets, furniture from the homes, and artwork from the churches. Again, Costa Lopes described what he saw from his window: "They burned everything and everybody.... They ransacked the shops, looted the houses. They raped women ... sometimes even in front of their husbands. It was very bad. That day remained forever engraved in my memory."[35]

On the morning after the invasion Indonesian troops lined up a group of residents on the Dili wharf, many of them women with children. The soldiers forced people throughout the city to gather at the harbor and watch. One of the onlookers described the scene. "The Indonesians tore the crying children from their mothers and passed them back to the crowd. The women were then shot one by one, with the onlookers being ordered by the Indonesians to count."[36] They continued to execute groups all day and into the evening. Another spectator recalled the killings: "I was leaning against the wall, facing the sea, and saw ABRI killing people and throwing [their corpses] in the sea.... They were ordered to form lines and then were shot all at once. When one group was finished, another group would come forward. Each group was of around 20 people."[37]

As the troops swept out from Dili to more sparsely-populated areas, they killed entire villages of suspected Fretilin supporters. In 1976 visiting relief workers from Indonesia estimated that 10 percent of the population may have been killed. In 1977 a priest in East Timor managed to get a letter to two nuns in Lisbon. "Hundreds die every day. The bodies of the victims become food for carnivorous birds. Villages have been completely destroyed."[38] In case anyone was still unsure about their intentions, the Indonesians forced the puppet interim regime to sign an Act of Integration in Dili in May 1976, incorporating East Timor into Indonesia.[39]

After the invasion Portugal cut off relations with Indonesia, but the rest of the Western World remained mute. Australia took no action, and the British and French continued to sell arms to Indonesia. The Ford administration announced that it was suspending arms deliveries to Indonesia pending an evaluation of whether American arms were used.[40] But the transcript of Kissinger's December 18 staff meeting showed how disingenuous the review was. Kissinger was furious about a State Department memo concluding that the administration might be obligated to cut off aid. "I want to raise a little bit of hell about the Department's conduct in my absence.... Take this cable on East Timor. You know my attitude and anyone who knows my position as you do must know that I would not have approved it." Kissinger raged that the memo was "a disgrace" because its authors knew that he would disagree with it. "No one who has worked with me in the last two years could not know what my view would be on Timor." When legal advisor Monroe Leigh asked what they should tell Congress, Kissinger said, "We cut it off while we are studying it. We intend to start again in January."[41]

On December 23 the UN Security Council called for Indonesia to withdraw "without delay all its forces" from East Timor. The resolution was adopted unanimously, with even the U.S. voting to approve.[42] When the Security Council voted 12–0 in April 1976 that Indonesia withdraw its troops "without further delay," the United States abstained from the vote, although the Americans quietly lobbied against the resolution.[43] On June 17, Kissinger and his staff discussed a request by Indonesia to send a representative to accompany an Indonesian parliamentary delegation to East Timor. Habib explained that there was no need to comply with the request. "Let them go ahead and do what they've been doing. We have no objection. We've not objected in UN Security Council debates. They're quite happy with the position we've taken. We've resumed, as you know, all of our normal relations with them." Kissinger responded with a cryptic, and disturbing, comment. "Not very willingly. Illegally and beautifully."[44]

The first solid information about what was happening in East Timor came from an unlikely source. Former Australian counsel to East Timor James Dunn traveled to Portugal on his own initiative to meet with refugees from East Timor and collect their stories. The report he compiled was dramatic. Not only did he describe in detail the executions on the Dili wharf, he reported that the Indonesian troops had executed 2,000 people at a camp near the border, firing for hours at defenseless people. He reported that the Indonesian troops were forcing Timorese women to work naked in fields, like water buffalo, in retaliation for villages supporting Fretilin.[45]

Even though he had come into office touting his commitment to human rights, Jimmy Carter never questioned Indonesia's reports about what was happening in East Timor. His administration called the reports of atrocities "greatly overstated."[46] The 1977 State Department Human Rights Report parrots Suharto's claim that "most of the human losses in East Timor appear to have occurred prior to Indonesia's intervention."[47] Vice President Walter Mondale told Suharto that the Carter administration had "accepted the position of its predecessor and that it does not question the incorporation of East Timor into Indonesia."[48]

———◦◦◦———

While the American government intentionally looked away, Indonesia continued its slaughter in East Timor. The Indonesian government gave the military unlimited authority to arrest, detain, torture, rape, and kill. A journalist who managed to cross into East Timor reported that the Indonesians were "systematically wiping out the populations of villages known or suspected to be Fretilin supporters."[49] In one village the soldiers tied up every man, woman, and child in the street and ran over them with bulldozers. Indonesian troops burned down houses with people inside, executed hundreds of people at a time, and dropped suspected Fretilin members into the sea from helicopters. At the Dili beach, groups of people were killed and their bodies were left for the sea, which the people called the "sea of blood." The Indonesians killed off all educated Timorese, including public officials and teachers, along with their families. The Indonesians forcibly sterilized men and women, and issued birth control pills to Timorese women as "vitamins." People were not allowed to meet in the streets, and men and women were not allowed to hold hands or kiss in public.[50]

In 1977 the Indonesians began targeting the food supply of the Fretilin-controlled areas, and the result was a famine that Frank Carlin of the Catholic Relief Service called "the worst I have ever seen."[51] As the people left the devastated Fretilin-controlled areas for the Indonesian zones, the army turned the country into "one big prison" by herding the Timorese into camps, without any consideration about how to provide food and water. USAID estimated that 300,000 people — half of the population — were living in the camps, where famine was rampant.[52]

The American government continued to deny reality. In hearings before the House Foreign Affairs Subcommittee on Asian and Pacific Affairs in 1978, Carter administration officials blamed the starvation on the Portuguese.[53] The administration should have known better. Just after the hearings, the *New York Times* editorial page said that the "ruthless" Indonesian occupation had claimed between a tenth and a third of the population of East Timor.[54] In 1980 the *Times* noted that "like Cambodia, East Timor has become synonymous with starvation and refugees." It said that "Washington's role has not been glorious. Successive administrations have 'understood' without endorsing the Indonesian grab."[55]

Conservative journalists also spoke out against the slaughter. In 1986 the *National Review* called the Indonesian occupation "one of the grislier stories of human-rights violations, mass starvation, and wholesale slaughter. It is worthy of comparison with Pol Pot's bloody reign over Cambodia."[56] But the conservative Reagan administration followed the lead of its liberal predecessor. In 1992, Deputy Assistant Secretary for East Asian and Pacific Affairs Kenneth Quinn told the Senate Foreign Relations Committee that "the trend in East Timor in recent years had been positive." He actually called Suharto's Indonesia "a government that is seeking to be responsive to human rights concerns." He was more honest when he described the American response to the invasion:

> In 1976, U.S. policy-makers decided to accept Indonesia's incorporation of East Timor as an accomplished fact. They judged that nothing the United States or the world was prepared to do could change that fact. Thus, to oppose Indonesia's incorporation would have had little impact on the situation. With such reality in mind, previous Administrations fashioned a policy which has been followed consistently on a bipartisan basis: We accept Indonesia's incorporation of East Timor without maintaining that a valid act of self-determination has taken place. Clearly, a democratic process of self-determination would have been more consistent with our values, but the realities of 1975 did not include that alternative. Accepting the absorption of East Timor into Indonesia was the only realistic option.[57]

At the end of the century world opinion finally forced Indonesia to let go of East Timor, but not before the Indonesian army went on a final murder spree. During the occupation, more than 200,000 people died in East Timor. Between 21 and 26 percent of the population died — the same percentage as in Cambodia.[58] Many thousands more were tortured or raped, and half of the country was displaced.[59]

————— ⁓ —————

All this happened after the meeting between Ford, Kissinger, and Suharto where they "did not object to the invasion but did not encourage it," in the words of Ambassador David Newsom.[60] It is important to make clear what Ford and Kissinger did and did not do. Knowing that an invasion was imminent, Ford and Kissinger explicitly told Suharto that they would not object to his taking over East Timor, and they followed through on their commitment. The administration did not cut off aid to Indonesia, despite probably being obligated to by law. What they did not do was to approve of the resulting genocide. Indonesia did an effective job of shutting off access to East Timor, and it wasn't until the end of the Ford administration that detailed reports of the killings reached the outside world. Once the details were published, however, the Ford administration continued to maintain its dishonorable silence, as did the Carter, Reagan and Bush administrations. Time and again the American government accepted at face value the specious explanations of its ally, despite compelling evidence that Indonesia was engaged in mass murder.

Not surprisingly, Kissinger has never expressed doubts or concern about what he did. He has explained that East Timor "did not seem like a very significant event because the Indians had occupied the Portuguese colony of Goa ten years earlier and to us it looked like another process of decolonization." He also claims that the administration did not anticipate the genocide that would follow the invasion. "Nobody had the foggiest idea of what would happen afterwards."[61] Ford has been more thoughtful and self-critical. He later told Douglas Brinkley that he regretted not trying to talk Suharto out of the invasion:

> Our main goal was not to alienate Indonesia from us. So when Suharto raised the imminent invasion of Timor we didn't object.... I don't want to pass the blame. Given the brutality that Indonesia exhibited in East Timor, our support was wrong. Henry was not infallible. I didn't realize just how bad the situation would become. You've got to understand that, in the scope of things, Indonesia wasn't too much on my radar. Hindsight is easy. I should have questioned Henry more about the situation. My record shows, like Helsinki, that I personally cared about human rights. I listened to the experts on Indonesia. That was a mistake. At the time, though, it didn't seem like a mistake. We needed allies after Vietnam. Henry — and I'm not exonerating myself — goofed.... I truly, honestly feel for those families which suffered losses. I'm sorry for them. The whole thing

was tragic, but I only learned the extent of what happened there after I left Washington. Then it was too late.[62]

In their defense, Ford, Kissinger, and the rest of the foreign policy establishment firmly believed that there was nothing they could do to stop Suharto from invading. Ambassador Newsom shared that belief. "I don't think there was ever any doubt that that Indonesian government, and maybe any Indonesian government, would oppose an independence in one-half of an Indonesian island."[63] Maybe they were right. Maybe Suharto would have invaded even if Ford and Kissinger had told him they would cut off aid. Maybe the Indonesian army would have continued its butchery if later administrations had cut off aid in protest. It is very possible that they were right, but we will never know. And there is one reason why we will never know:

They didn't try.

19

Primary Campaign

When Ford looked forward to the 1976 elections, he thought he would have an easy time garnering the Republican nomination. Ronald Reagan was making noises about entering the race, but Ford thought he could stave off a challenge by moving to the right. He didn't realize that Reagan was not only driven by ideological passion — he really wanted to be president. As Elizabeth Drew noted at the time, Ford's efforts to appease Reagan only encouraged the right wing. "The Republican right, then, in a strong resemblance to the Democratic left, cannot accept compromises even by someone who is essentially sympathetic.... And so, like other Politicians who have tried to reach across some divisions in order to get elected, or to govern, Gerald Ford is being keelhauled."[1] His efforts to kowtow to the hardcore conservatives would make Ford look weak. Most importantly, he looked phony as he distanced himself from positions he had taken earlier in his presidency, and he wasn't able to energetically defend what he believed in.

Once he was nominated, Ford assumed that he would face one of the Democratic Party heavyweights — Ted Kennedy or Hubert Humphrey. As it turned out, neither candidate was willing to make the grueling run for the nomination, and new party rules gave a clear advantage to a candidate who was willing to run in all primaries and caucuses. That left an opening for the relatively-unknown governor of Georgia, Jimmy Carter. Almost alone among political professionals, Carter's advisors understood that the new rules would give the election to a candidate who ran early and everywhere, and they knew that Carter was the type of idealistic, overtly-honest candidate who could win in the post–Watergate environment.

The campaign was the first under the new federal campaign financing law, which limited individual contributions to $1,000 and restricted a candidate's spending to $10 million in the primaries. In the general election, each candidate would receive federal financing if they agreed to a spending limit of $13.1 million. No longer could an establishment candidate quickly amass a huge war chest from big donors and scare away dark-horse candidates who didn't have access to the same money.

On the Democratic side the old way of doing things was changed even further by new rules that banned winner-take-all primaries — delegates would be assigned to reflect the proportion of votes each candidate received in a state. In addition to Kennedy and Humphrey, the favorites were Washington senator Scoop Jackson, Minnesota senator Walter Mondale, Texas senator Lloyd Bentsen, and Arizona congressman Mo Udall. Two new possibilities were added in 1974 when Jerry Brown won the governorship in California and Hugh Carey won in New York. Brown would eventually run, but Carey was no longer a viable candidate after the New York City financial crisis.[2]

Georgia governor Jimmy Carter had been running since the day after the 1972 election, but very few people outside of his home state knew who he was. America had yet to notice the quirky politician who talked seriously about God's love and promised to never lie. When he appeared on the TV show *What's My Line?* in 1973, none of the contestants were able to identify him. To gain national exposure and develop a network of supporters he volunteered to be chair of the Democratic Campaign Committee. As chair of the DNC campaign operation, Carter "took off as if he were being chased."[3] He crossed the nation in 1974, campaigning for Democratic candidates — and for himself. He stayed in the homes of local Democrats, making his own bed and leaving thank-you notes. In his travels he was accompanied by two young aides, Hamilton Jordan and Jody Powell. At every stop, Jordan or Powell would write down the names of everyone Carter met, and he always followed up with a hand-written note or a phone call.[4]

He garnered a bit of national attention when he returned for the University of Georgia's Law Day on May 4, 1974. His job was to introduce the guest speaker, Ted Kennedy, but he stole the show with what Hunter Thompson called "a king hell bastard of a speech." His speech demonstrated the populist streak he had picked up from George Wallace and other southern politicians. He railed against the legal system for letting the rich go free while the poor went to jail.[5] The speech garnered good reviews, but nobody thought he could make a serious run for the presidency.

∽∾∽

The Democratic field began to take shape in late 1974. First, one of the big names dropped out when Kennedy announced that he would not run on September 23. Another possible frontrunner dropped out a month later when Walter Mondale announced that he would not run, admitting that he wasn't willing to be "on the road 18 hours a day and away from my family, the Senate and my state."[6]

The first candidate to formally announce that he was in the race was the liberal Arizona representative Mo Udall on November 23. Carter followed three weeks later when he announced his candidacy at the National Press Club in Washington and flew home to address a crowd of 2,000 Georgians in Atlanta that night. He brought on key advisors, including the soft-spoken Stuart Eizenstat as issues director and the fast-talking 25-year-old Pat Caddell as pollster. Major strategic decisions were made by Hamilton Jordan or Jody Powell, while Jerry Rafshoon controlled media issues. Jordan had been Carter's right-hand man for eight years. He was a chunky young man with a pink face and straight brown hair. Most importantly, he was brilliant, perceptive, and ruthless.[7]

Announcements continued throughout 1975. Scoop Jackson announced his candidacy on February 6 during a paid spot on CBS. Duke president James Terry Sanford, the former governor of North Carolina, announced his candidacy on May 29, but his would be an ill-starred campaign. He contracted the flu and was hospitalized for chest pains in January 1976, forcing him to drop out of the race. The campaign of Sargent Shriver lasted a little longer. He announced his campaign from the Mayflower Hotel on September 20, but after a lackluster campaign and a disappointing fundraising effort, he withdrew on March 22. Another short campaign was run by Texas senator Lloyd Bentsen. The common wisdom was that Bentsen was running only to be considered for the vice presidency. He visited thirty states in 1974 and announced his candidacy in February 1975. He quickly raised more than $1 million, but by October he realized that his lack of support meant that he should focus on Texas and neighboring states. When he found little support even there, he dropped out on February 10.[8]

The campaign of Pennsylvania governor Milton Shapp lasted only a few weeks longer than Bentsen's. Shapp announced his candidacy in September 1975, but he could not overcome the negative press from an investigation of campaign contributions to his 1970 campaign for governor, and he dropped out in March '76. His campaign would later be investigated by the FEC, which found that it had reported contributions made by people under assumed names, and he paid back $300,000 in matching funds.[9] Fred Harris ran a short but truly radical campaign, calling for wholesale redistribution of wealth and massive spending to guarantee employment. His campaign motto was "The Issue is Privilege," and he traveled the country in a camper throughout 1975, passing an empty ice cream bucket after his speeches for donations. He never had a chance, and he withdrew in April 1976.[10]

Indiana senator Birch Bayh got a late start, finally announcing his candidacy in October 1975.[11] He had already shown an inability to connect with his key supporters a month earlier when he had joined the other liberal candidates at a convention in Minneapolis, where they were trying to gain the support of liberal activists. Of the six candidates, Bayh made the worst impression during his remarks, and a *Washington Post* poll showed that Udall was the favorite of the delegates.[12]

Another candidate getting a later start was George Wallace, who declared his candidacy on November 12. He was paralyzed from the waist down from an assassination attempt in 1972. Wallace had given up the repulsive racism that had made him famous — he was now running against the Washington establishment and for "the survival and salvation of the middle class." The new campaign financing rules gave Wallace an advantage because he could collect small amounts from a large number of fervent supporters. Direct-mail guru Richard Viguerie joined the campaign and raised nearly $7 million. Other than Carter, no candidate would collect more in contributions.[13]

———⁓⁓⁓———

The two Republican candidates got off to late starts as well. Ford had eliminated all doubt about his candidacy in November 1974 when he told *U.S. News and World Report,* "I intend to run." But he waited too long to start his campaign because it took him a long time to realize that Reagan posed a real threat. For several months in the spring of 1975 his advisors urged him to set up a campaign committee and begin fundraising, but he did not set one up until June. Ford was forced into action by a *Newsweek* article reporting that he had made a secret decision not to run, and he announced his candidacy from the Rose Garden on July 8. Rumsfeld was named the White House liaison to the campaign, and he delegated the responsibility to Cheney.[14]

The administration put together an initial campaign staff which was not uniformly strong but included some very talented individuals. Unfortunately, one of them was not the campaign director. At Rumsfeld's urging, Ford asked Army Secretary Howard (Bo) Callaway to head up the campaign. The choice of the former Georgian congressman was an overt sop to the right wing. It wasn't an inspired choice, according to John Osborne. "The kindest thing to be said of him is that he is possessed of more good humor than intelligence."[15] There were two problems with the choice: Callaway had never run a national campaign, and he couldn't keep his mouth shut.

On the morning after Ford's official announcement Callaway repeatedly told reporters that the campaign was set up to nominate Ford, not Rockefeller. Ford told Callaway to refrain from making other negative comments about the vice president, but he kept at it. On July 24, Callaway told the press that Ford might choose a younger running mate. He called Rockefeller "the number one problem. You and I both know that if Rockefeller took himself out, it would help with the nomination." Again Ford told Callaway to knock it off, but he would not take responsibility. "I'm sorry. I really am. I got caught. The press was after me."[16]

The professionals brought in to assist Callaway were better choices. Robert Teeter came from Detroit to be the pollster; California newspaperman Peter Kaye joined as press secretary; and Stuart Spencer was hired as political director. Spencer had been a senior member of Reagan's runs for governor, and he gave organization to a directionless campaign. Cheney worked well with Spencer, but he never got along with Callaway.[17]

On a trip to California in September 1975, Ford decided to meet with Governor Jerry Brown to "size him up as a potential presidential candidate."[18] As he walked from the Senator Hotel to the Capitol Building, a woman in a bright red dress reached out, as if to shake the president's hand. Ford looked down and saw a pistol pointed at him. The woman was Annette "Squeaky" Fromme, a disciple of cult leader Charles Manson. She squeezed the trigger, but the gun did not fire. The Secret Service agents wrestled her to the ground. As they led her away, she said, "It didn't go off fellas."[19] Ford walked on to his meeting with Brown, where he didn't mention the incident.

Ford survived a second assassination attempt when he returned to the state three weeks later. As he left his San Francisco hotel for the trip to the airport, Ford waved at the crowd. Sara Jane Moore aimed a pistol back at him, but a man next to her saw the gun and knocked her arm as she fired. She missed the president by a few feet. Rumsfeld and the Secret Service agents shoved Ford in the waiting limousine and took off for the airport. When he got to the airport, Ford took the time to thank the security agents who had been protecting him. Kennerly was waiting at the top of the staircase to Air Force One. As Ford entered the plane, he asked, "Other than that, Mr. President, how'd you like San Francisco?"[20] For the rest of his administration, Ford continued to greet crowds the same way, reaching out and shaking hands, and he did not hesitate when meeting people on the campaign trail.

For most of 1975 the Ford campaign was waiting to see if they had a challenge for the nomination. In September, Jerry Jones reported that he had spoken to people close to Reagan who predicted that he wouldn't run and was holding the option open to force Ford to the right.[21] In reality, Reagan's main consideration was his future. After his term as governor ended he needed to run to maintain his status as the leading advocate for the right wing, and he genuinely believed that he would make a better president than Ford.[22]

While he delayed his announcement, Reagan's campaign was doing as much work as Ford's. In 1974, while Reagan was still governor, his aide Robert Walker had regular planning sessions in Washington with James Lake, the head of Reagan's D.C. office, and a young lawyer named John Sears. His aides Michael Deaver, Ed Meese, Jim Jenkins, Peter Hannaford, and Lyn Nofziger were doing the same thing in California. Reagan did not tell his aides his intentions until the spring of 1975, and he went public in July when he approved the formation of an exploratory committee chaired by Nevada senator Paul Laxalt. As soon as the committee was formed, Sears began to set up organizations in New Hampshire and Florida.[23]

On November 19, Reagan called Ford and told him he was entering the race. He said that he hoped the fight wouldn't be divisive, but a run against a sitting president of his own party was sure to be exactly that, and Ford told Reagan that his candidacy would hurt the party. The next day Reagan made his announcement from the National Press Club, promising to follow the Eleventh Commandment, "Thou shalt not speak ill of any fellow Republican."[24] For a brief time Reagan topped Ford in the polls, but the press considered him to be a lightweight. Reporters thought he didn't have a chance, and Ford didn't take him seriously either.[25]

Ford made a strategic mistake at the December 1975 Southern Republican Convention. Reagan made a personal appearance, but Ford's advisors convinced him that he would look more presidential if he stayed in Washington, so he sent Callaway. The southerners thought the president had snubbed them, and Callaway made things worse with a ham-handed personal attack on Reagan. Callaway claimed that "all the major people" in California were opposed to Reagan because his "rhetoric was great and his performance was poor."[26] Rockefeller also made a splash. He had been dumped just weeks before, and he told the Southern Republicans, "You got me out, you sons of bitches, now get off your ass."[27]

Ford's decision to send Callaway was part of the campaign's Rose Garden strategy. The primary goal was to remind the public about the good work he had done and how bad things were when he took office. According to Teeter's polls, 60 percent of Americans could not name anything that Ford had done that "particularly impressed" them. The polls also showed that, while the American people viewed the president as "honest, sincere, just, and friendly," they did not think of him as "competent, strong, intelligent, and a forceful leader." To make things worse, Teeter's polling showed that Republicans liked Reagan. "He is perceived as bold, decisive, strong, intelligent and competent and this perception is held with almost no negatives." Teeter and Spence thought that the remedy was for Ford to "appear more presidential." Like most of Ford's aides, they wanted him to limit his active campaigning, and they added an unfortunate suggestion to stop using the word "détente."[28]

———

While the other candidates spent 1975 setting up their organizations, Carter spent it campaigning — he visited 46 states, shaking people's hands and greeting them with the phrase: "I'm Jimmy Carter, and I'm running for president."[29] In November the campaign put on four concerts featuring the Marshall Tucker Band, Charlie Daniels, and the Allman Brothers. The concerts netted only $33,900, but they gave him some much-needed publicity.[30]

Carter's campaign strategy had been laid out in early memos from Hamilton Jordan. On the day before the 1972 election he gave Carter a memo explaining how to win the Democratic nomination in 1976. Jordan suggested that Carter take the mantle of southern populism from George Wallace — without the repugnant racism — by (in Jordan's words), "being a better qualified and more responsible alternative." The key would be to gain stature, money, and supporters with a win in New Hampshire, "a small state which is rural and independent and given to the kind of personal campaigning that you and your family are capable of waging." Then Carter could eliminate Wallace in Florida. After beating Wallace, he would be seen as the moderate alternative to the liberal candidates, because Scoop Jackson and Lloyd Bentsen were too conservative to win.[31] Jordan followed with a detailed plan on August 4, 1974, proposing that Carter run as an outsider, criticizing the federal government and the presidency for being out of touch with the people. He included detailed budgets for 1974, '75, and '76, with an extensive task list and a schedule for trips in 1975.[32]

Carter put in a lot of work on the Iowa caucuses — he traveled to the state 11 times during 1975. Iowa provided a good opportunity for the Carter campaign because it was a place where more effort and better organization could prevail. Caucuses are always more of a test of organization than popularity, and Iowa was even more appealing because of the small number of voters — only 35,000 Democrats had attended the caucuses in 1972. The campaign had been looking for a coordinator for its Iowa effort through the first half of 1975, and when no appropriate person could be found, campaign official Tim Kraft decided to lead the effort himself. Kraft moved to the state in September, and he proved to be adept at grass-roots organization. He visited 110 towns in the four months before the caucuses, convincing party leaders and ordinary Iowans to join the campaign.[33]

In October 1975 the Iowa Democratic Party held a dry run of the caucuses, and party leaders announced that they would hold a straw poll. Kraft saw it as an opportunity for publicity, so he worked hard to get his candidate's supporters to participate, and Carter won with 9.9 percent of the vote. Later in the month the party held a large fundraiser at Iowa State University in Ames, and this time it was the *Des Moines Register* that polled the participants. Again Kraft did his best to get committed supporters to attend, and Carter won the poll with 23 percent. News outlets across the country proclaimed him the frontrunner in Iowa. The next month, Carter's organizer in Florida pulled off a similar coup when Carter won 67 percent of the straw poll at a party convention. Suddenly, his campaign seemed real.[34]

The other candidates finally turned their attention to Iowa several weeks before the January 19 caucuses. Udall toured the state in a bus. Bayh didn't do much until the weekend before the caucuses, when he bussed in supporters from Indiana to go door to door. Carter knew that his biggest problem was that people didn't take his campaign seriously, and he earnestly told everyone he met, "I don't intend to lose." He was true to his word. Hard work and good organization won the day for Carter, who pulled in 28 percent of the votes. The second place candidate was Bayh with only 13 percent.[35]

After Iowa, the candidates headed to New Hampshire, where Udall expected to win. He put together a substantial organization in the state, but he couldn't out-campaign Carter. It was in New Hampshire that America got its first real look at Carter's extraordinary personal style. His wide grin became famous, but he was much more than that. He had genuine personal charisma and an extraordinary ability to connect with people in small groups, often converting them into ardent supporters. People believed it when he talked about the "close, personal, intimate relationship I have established with each and every one of you."[36] He was a born-again Christian who talked about "God's love." He spoke about a "deeply profound religious experience" that had changed his life.[37] He promised never to tell a lie, never to make a misleading statement, never to betray the peoples' trust, and never to avoid a controversial issue. He would stop making the promise after the primaries because his mother told him he would have a hard time living up to it.[38]

It was typically-blunt advice from his mother, known to all as "Miss Lilian," a firebrand liberal with a wonderful sense of humor. She was one of several eccentric Carters that the press found in his small home town of Plains, Georgia. His brother Billy ran a gas station, drank beer, and joked like a good old boy, while his sister Ruth Carter Stapleton was a fundamentalist preacher. They all had a strong sense of humor, a trait that seemed to have passed Jimmy by. Jimmy Carter was an earnest man who looked people in the eye and said, "I want to have a government as good and honest and decent and compassionate and filled with love as are the American people."[39] In the post–Watergate environment Carter's simple honesty was deeply appealing, and there were a legion of Georgians who were willing to attest that it was real. In the weeks before the New Hampshire primary the campaign went into high gear, flying in a planeload of Georgians to go door to door and vouch personally for his character and honesty.[40]

Udall was an appealing figure as well, with a self-depreciating sense of humor and an impeccable record of integrity. But his campaign, which was run jointly by his brother Stewart Udall and the political pro Jack Quinn, was disorganized and lacked direction. Quinn called it "the sloppiest campaign in memory. No one knows who is in charge, who can make a quick decision that will stick."[41] In New Hampshire the differences between the Carter and Udall campaigns would prove decisive. Carter came in first with 29 percent of the vote, to 24 percent for Udall and 16 percent for Bayh.

On the Republican side, New Hampshire was the first showdown between Ford and Reagan, and things looked bad for the president. During 1975, Ford had paid little attention to the state. Callaway had done nothing to put together an effective organization in the state, and the head of Ford's campaign, Representative James Cleveland, went on a three-week vacation during the campaign season. He faced an impressive Reagan team, which had the only computerized list of New Hampshire voters, and Reagan spent nineteen days campaigning in the state.[42]

Reagan's style drove Ford crazy, but it connected with voters. He gave his speeches from note cards that he carried at all times. On the plane he would pull them out and arrange the cards for the speech he wanted to give when he arrived. He told stories about government largess, most of which were apocryphal. He talked about the Chicago welfare queen who collected more than $50,000 (sometimes $150,000) a year using eighty different names. He told a story of a man who was told by the Social Security Agency that he was dead and who received a death benefit when he complained. The worst was his description of a housing project in New York. "If you are a slum dweller you can get an apartment with eleven-foot ceilings, a twenty-foot balcony, a swimming pool and gymnasium, laundry room and play room, and the rent begins at a hundred and thirteen dollars and twenty cents and that includes utilities."[43] To anyone who had ever been in one of the crime-infested, run-down projects in big cities, it was an appalling claim, and it was a prime example of why Ford thought he played fast and loose with the facts.

Reagan was still a novice in the national political scene, and he would make several mistakes because he did not understand local hot-button issues. His first mistake was in New Hampshire, where Ford took advantage of a proposal Reagan had made in September to cut the budget by $90 billion by transferring to the states the responsibility for "welfare, education, housing, food stamps, Medicaid, community and regional development, and revenue sharing."[44] On the ABC show *Issues and Answers* Reagan admitted that "you would have to have taxes increased at state and local levels to offset this, or to maintain some of these programs."[45] New Hampshire had no state income tax, and Ford's campaign ran ads claiming that Reagan's proposal would require one. Reagan also touched the political third rail, social security, which he suggested that it should be invested in private accounts. Again Ford's people pounced, accusing him of wanting to risk the trust fund in the market.[46]

Ford's time on the offensive didn't last because he could not avoid a reminder of Watergate and the pardon. On February 6 the Chinese government announced that Nixon had accepted an invitation to visit two days before the primary. Nixon accepted the offer because he mistakenly thought that Ford had New Hampshire sewn up, and he correctly concluded that it would be worse if he went later in the year. He had put off the trip the year before when Kissinger asked him to wait until after Ford's trip to China. The Chinese thought that Ford would react positively to the trip — they meant it as a signal that they still wanted good relations. The trip itself was inconsequential, but it provided some insight into the power struggle in China. Nixon was greeted by Hua Gofeng, in his first public appearance as Mao's heir-apparent, and Jiang Qing also made an appearance, demonstrating that the Gang of Four was ascendant.[47]

Reagan refused to comment on the trip. "Don't ask me ... ask the man who pardoned him."[48] Ford was not very adept when he tried to avoid the subject, and Fred Barnes of the *New Republic* called him on it. "Two or three times today you talked about your 'predecessor,' and you once referred to 'Lyndon Johnson's successor.' Are you trying to avoid saying the name Richard M. Nixon?" As usual, Ford's response was honest: "Yes."[49]

The vote was so close that Reagan probably lost the state by spending the final days campaigning in Illinois. When Ford went to bed at midnight on election night he was down by 1,500 votes, but gaining. In the end, Ford won by 1,317 votes (about 1 percent). He won 17 delegates to 4 for Reagan. Reagan was given the bad news by Sears the next morning. "We didn't quite make it last night. We're going to have to start talking about foreign policy."[50] Reagan handled the loss with aplomb. On the flight to Florida he broke out the champagne that his staff had purchased to celebrate the victory, and he raised a toast to his near-win with the reporters in the back of the plane.[51]

—◦◦◦—

Reagan would not contest the next primaries in Massachusetts and Vermont, and Ford won handily. Carter had not put much effort into Massachusetts, but on the night he won New Hampshire he met with his top aides to consider whether to make a push in the state. They were buoyed by their win, so they decided to step up advertising, and Carter drove down to Boston the next day. Udall was in a money crunch, and he cut off $15,000 earmarked for TV time.[52]

Both Scoop Jackson and George Wallace had skipped New Hampshire. Jackson's plan was to use his close ties to labor to win northern industrial states, starting with Massachusetts, and followed by New York and Pennsylvania. He was a conservative on foreign affairs but a liberal on economic issues. He proposed national health insurance, a massive public works program, and more aid for education, housing, and jobs. Jackson's campaign was run by Robert Keefe, who had close ties to labor. Keefe built the organization by tapping into labor and party leaders in the big primary states.[53]

Wallace hoped to do well in Boston, where busing was the big issue, but he coyly promised not to raise the topic. "I ain't gonna say a word about busing. Course, all them folks in Massachusetts know that if I'm President, there ain't gonna be any."[54] Jackson made no such promise, and he ran ads proclaiming his opposition to "forced busing."[55] Carter also opposed forced busing, but he refused to take advantage of the issue. "To run my campaign on an antibusing issue is contrary to my basic nature. If I have to win by appealing to a basically negative, emotional issue which has connotations of racism, I don't intend to do it, myself. I don't want to win that kind of race."[56]

In Massachusetts, Carter slipped on tax reform, which he had been touting for some time. In a televised issues forum on February 23 he proposed eliminating the deduction for home mortgages as part of his plan to lower tax rates and eliminate deductions.[57] It wasn't a bad idea because it would result in a more fair and efficient system, but the home mortgage deduction was a political sacred cow. But his tax comments didn't hurt as much as the snowstorm on election day. Jackson's supporters were well-organized labor unions who put 500 cars on the street to get voters to the polls, while Carter's support was soft. Jackson won with 23 percent of the vote, to Udall's 18, Wallace's 17, and Carter's 14. Carter had two pieces of good news that night. To his surprise, he won the African American vote in Massachusetts, and he won the Vermont primary on the same day. After disappointing finishes in Iowa, New Hampshire, and Massachusetts, Bayh announced that he was "suspending his campaign."[58]

—◦◦◦—

The second phase of Hamilton Jordan's plan was to wrest the mantle of southern leadership from Wallace by beating him in the March 9 Florida primary. Wallace had won the state handily in 1972, and a loss would be devastating for his campaign. Carter made no bones about what he was doing, and he sent a letter to supporters asking for "help now to end once and for all the threat Wallace represents to our country."[59] Again the Carter campaign bused in Georgians to go door to door, and they hit every part of the state. Carter beat Wallace by three points. Jackson, who tried to pick up delegates from the Jewish areas around Miami by touting his support for Israel, came in third.[60]

Reagan had enjoyed a three-point lead in Florida in December, but after winning New Hampshire Ford led by 51 to 34 percent. He needed the cushion, because his Florida campaign was in shambles. His state organization was led by Representative Louis Frey, who was more focused on running for governor than working for Ford. Frey publicly admitted that he preferred Reagan but joined the Ford campaign because he thought the president had a better chance of winning. At the end of January, Spencer's partner, Bill Roberts, went to Florida to take charge, and he quickly got things in order.

Ford clinched the state by campaigning in the pouring rain in West Palm Beach. The crowds cheered as the president waved from his car with the top down as he drove through 14 towns. The trip completely overshadowed Reagan's attack on his foreign policy. Reagan declared that the Helsinki Accords told the countries of Eastern Europe that they "should give up any claim of national sovereignty and simply become part of the Soviet Union."[61] And he hit another hot button — negotiations over the Panama Canal. The negotiations had begun under Johnson when rioting in the country demonstrated that the United States could not control the canal forever. Nixon continued the negotiations, and Kissinger went to Panama to sign a "Joint Statement of Principles" in February 1974. The principles were to form the basis of a new treaty, under which the United States would return jurisdiction of the canal to Panama, which would in turn grant the U.S. the right to use and defend the canal. The canal would be jointly operated, with an equitable split of proceeds, until the expiration of the treaty, with Panama taking over at that time.[62] Reagan lambasted Ford for continuing to negotiate with Panama. "When it comes to the canal, we built it, we paid for it, it's ours, and we should tell Torrijos and company that we are going to keep it!"[63]

The foreign policy attack would hurt Ford in upcoming states, but in Florida all the voters remembered was Ford's rain-soaked tour, and he won the primary with 53 percent, picking up 43 more delegates.

Carter had dealt a crushing blow to Wallace in Florida, and Jordan now told him that it was time to eliminate Udall in Wisconsin and Jackson in Pennsylvania. Jordan thought that those wins would sew up the nomination, but things would get complicated during the next two weeks.

First, California governor Jerry Brown entered the race. Without consulting anyone, he decided to run, and, again without telling anyone, he announced his candidacy in a March 12 discussion with reporters. "No one has captured the enthusiasm and the imagination of the Democratic party. I'm offering myself as an alternative."[64] Like Carter, Brown used rock concerts to raise money, starring his future girlfriend Linda Ronstadt, as well as Jackson Browne and the Eagles. The next week Idaho senator Frank Church announced that he was entering the race. His work overseeing the intelligence investigations was complete, and Church declared, "It's never too late — nor are the odds ever too great — to try."[65] But it was too late, and he really had no chance. The elimination of winner-take-all primaries made it virtually impossible for a late entrant to catch up to Carter, who continued to rack up delegates during the weeks before the new candidates participated in primaries.

-----~~~-----

Carter and Wallace were the only Democratic candidates participating in the March 16 Illinois primary. Udall and Jackson stayed out of the race for fear of offending Chicago mayor Richard Daley. Carter tried a different tack with Daley, going out of his way to woo the mayor and promising to let him lead the Illinois delegation at the convention. The primary was non-binding, and caucuses were held on the same day to select the delegates. Carter won the beauty contest with just under half of the votes, easily beating Wallace's 26 percent. Most surprisingly, Carter gained 55 delegates, second only to the 85 that went to the Daley slate led by Adlai Stevenson. Wallace was disappointed by winning only three delegates rather than the 25 he had expected.[66] Daley was impressed; he called the Carter effort "a campaign that some respect must be paid to."[67]

On the Republican side, Ford continued his string of victories. Despite a sharp foreign policy attack by Reagan, Ford won 59 percent of the vote. In the days before the primary, Ford had to weather news reports alleging that Callaway had used his influence as army secretary to gain approval for his family's plan to build a ski resort. When the reports hit the papers, Cheney met with Callaway and talked him into leaving the campaign. Peter Kaye was at the meeting, and he recalled that "Cheney played him like a guy landing a fish. Bo was flopping around, then lying there for a while, amid long, awkward silences, and then would start flopping around again. Finally, Bo asked, 'What should I do?' 'Better get a lawyer, Bo,' Cheney told him."[68] On March 13, Callaway announced that he was stepping down "temporarily." Ford asked Rogers Morton, who he had just removed as secretary of commerce, to take the job. Later investigations cleared Callaway of wrongdoing, but he never rejoined the campaign.[69]

After his win in Illinois, Ford had 166 delegates to Reagan's 54, and he assumed that "it would be just a matter of time" before Reagan dropped out.[70] Ford asked Senator John Tower, House Minority Leader John Rhodes, and House Republican Whip Robert Michel to meet with Reagan aides and push him to withdraw. In a meeting with Morton on March 20, Sears suggested that his candidate would drop out. Reagan knew nothing about the meeting, and when he learned that Ford was encouraging him to quit, he was convinced to stay in the race until the end. It was an overture that was doomed to fail because Reagan and Ford disliked each other. Ford liked affable people, while Reagan tended to be reserved in private discussions. During campaign flights Reagan stayed in the forward compartment, spending little time socializing with his staff or the press.[71] He wasn't Ford's kind of guy, and Reagan had little respect for Ford. When the press asked him about Ford's suggestions, Reagan said, "Tell him to quit."[72]

Reagan would revive his campaign in the March 23 North Carolina primary. Senator Jesse Helms suggested that the Panama Canal attack would play well in his home state, and Reagan hit the theme over and over. To his eternal credit, Reagan refused to raise race issues. When some of his North Carolina supporters began circulating flyers alleging that Ford had considered naming a black as vice president, Reagan ordered them to be destroyed immediately. Reagan won with 52 percent of the vote, and he picked up 28 delegates, to Ford's 26. After North Carolina, Ford knew that Reagan would fight all the way to the convention.[73]

The North Carolina primary was the end of George Wallace's presidential ambitions. He won only 35 percent of the vote, to 54 percent for Carter. Wallace knew he was done, but his supporters convinced him to stay in the race in case lightning struck. Wallace stayed on the ballot, but he was no longer a serious threat — the days of race-baiting segregationists in American politics were over.[74]

<hr />

The campaign was disrupted when the FEC's ability to disburse federal funds was cut off on March 22. When it overturned the campaign financing law, the Supreme Court had stayed its decision for thirty days to give Congress and the president time to reconstitute the commission.[75] Ford asked Congress to avoid unnecessary delay by passing a simple law reconstituting the FEC, and he offered to reappoint the six commissioners. But Congress did not choose the simple solution because proponents on either side of the campaign financing issue tried to use the new legislation to gain an advantage. Wayne Hays announced that he would push to strip the commission of its power to initiate civil or criminal actions to enforce its rules. Proponents of campaign financing laws responded by pushing for stricter rules. While Congress fought, the court extended the deadline to March 22. When Congress didn't act by that date, the court refused to grant another extension, and the FEC could no longer distribute funds.

Congress finally passed the Campaign Act Amendments of 1976 on May 4, and Ford signed them into law on May 10. Ford was unable to reappoint all six commissioners because chairman Thomas Curtis had submitted his resignation. Ford's first few choices to replace Curtis turned down the office, and Ford finally nominated William Springer on May 18. The Senate approved the Springer nomination three days later, and all six commissioners were sworn in later that afternoon. The FEC immediately issued $3.2 million in matching payments to the campaigns.[76]

New York and Wisconsin held their primaries on April 6, a week after funds were cut off. If Carter could beat Udall in Wisconsin, which was traditionally friendly to liberal candidates, the Arizonan's campaign would be all but over. Carter had not developed a solid organization in the state, but two hundred Georgians flew there at their own expense to campaign for him. He was able to weather the cut-off of funds because donations to his campaign had picked up after his early victories — from $400,000 in February to $1 million in May. To keep spending at the same level, Carter borrowed $775,000 from Georgia banks. The campaign was $1.5 million in debt when the payments resumed, but it would pay off the debts with fundraisers between the last primary and the convention.[77]

Udall had planned to spend $350,000 in Wisconsin, but his campaign had only $100,000 in its coffers when matching funds were cut off. He would be undone by his unwillingness to mortgage his personal life to win. At the start of the campaign he told his brother "to see he didn't wind up in debt the rest of his life."[78] Stewart Udall heeded his brother's warning, and he cancelled TV ads and a planned mass-mailing in Wisconsin. Udall had been gaining in the polls, and the state organization begged for $35,000 for a last-minute advertising blitz. Stewart Udall would not be swayed, so the Wisconsin campaign made a plea to the candidate. After wavering for a few days, Udall decided to spend the money, but it was too late because the TV time had been sold to others.

The delay cost Udall the primary, which was so close that the networks first declared him the winner. Udall crowed, "I've been rich and I've been poor, and, believe me, rich is better. I've been second and I've been first, and, believe me, first is better."[79] With the late rural votes coming in strong for Carter, Caddell screamed for someone to stop his candidate from conceding. Powell told Billy Carter to pass on the news to the campaign workers. "Jesus. I'm so nervous I feel like I've got a green plum up my ass. Listen, it's going to be close as hell, but we're going to do it. The rural areas haven't come in yet. Spread the word down here so everyone doesn't leave."[80] Carter won by fewer than 7,500 votes. The *Milwaukee Sentinel* printed its early edition before Carter's late surge, and he posed for the press while holding the paper above his head, with the headline "Carter Upset by Udall" clearly visible. It was a great bit of drama, and it took the focus off of Carter's loss in New York. Jackson won handily with 38 percent of the vote, Udall came in second with 25 percent, and Carter was in third with a disappointing 13 percent, but he still picked up 35 delegates.[81]

Reagan was also put in a bind when the FEC stopped paying matching funds, but he had an innovative solution. He had been telling his staff that he could raise a lot of money if he went on TV, and with money running out, Sears suggested that Reagan give up on Wisconsin and deliver a televised fundraising speech. Reagan tried to buy a half-hour time slot on all three networks, but only NBC decided to sell him the time. He raised $1.3 million when his speech aired on March 31, and he received 45 percent of the votes in Wisconsin without even campaigning.[82]

<hr />

The next primary in Pennsylvania was a must-win for Jackson, but he had little money left after spending an astonishing $890,000 in New York. With matching funds cut off, Jackson spent only $163,000 in the state he had always targeted as the key to his campaign. Jackson's chances still looked good because he was a favorite of labor unions, and he had Philadelphia mayor Frank Rizzo on his side. Rizzo was a machine politician who had backed Nixon in '72, and Carter turned Rizzo's support of Jackson into a badge of dishonor, calling Rizzo a "boss" who wouldn't have backed Jackson without a secret deal. The supposedly powerful union leaders failed Jackson, and Carter won with 37 percent of the vote to Jackson's 25 percent. The primary was a beauty contest, but Carter did equally well in the caucuses, gaining 64 delegates to 19 for Jackson.[83]

Jackson looked like he was finished, and another possible candidate announced that he wouldn't run after Carter's victory in Pennsylvania. Throughout the primaries the press had speculated about whether Hubert Humphrey would make one more try for the presidency. He wasn't willing to run for the nomination, but he made it clear that he would be happy to accept it at an open convention. "If that happened to me, I wouldn't say no. I'd say, 'Let's go, boys. Let's get this show on the road.'"[84] He was hesitant to run after he ended his 1972 primary campaign $925,000 in debt and spent two years raising money to pay it off. "I'm tired of it. I don't want to have to go around and ask people to help me. I don't want to go to people anymore."[85] Humphrey ended all speculation on April 29 in an address from the Senate Caucus Room. He broke down as he read his statement, wiping his tears with a handkerchief. "I shall not seek it; I shall not compete for it; I shall not search for it; I shall not scramble for it. But I'm around."[86]

Carter continued his victories on May 1 by winning 92 delegates in Texas, where his state coordinator, Bob Armstrong, told his staff, "We're riding a fast horse. All we have to do is hang on and wave our hats."[87] Three days later Carter swept Indiana, D.C., and Georgia, losing only to Wallace in Wallace's home state of Alabama. Carter had amassed more than 600 delegates.

<hr />

Reagan put little effort into Pennsylvania, and Ford continued his string of victories. The 103 delegates were officially uncommitted, but counting them and the 154 delegates from New York — who were uncommitted but controlled by Rockefeller — Ford had 305 delegates to Reagan's 84.[88] But the tide turned in Texas on May 1. Reagan received a boost when Wallace's

Ford addresses the crowd during the primary campaign, May 26, 1976. (Photograph by David Hume Kennerly; courtesy Gerald R. Ford Library.)

candidacy fizzled, because he appealed to southerners who had been Democrats until the civil rights movement. Now they called themselves "independents," and they voted for Reagan in states like Texas that allowed crossover voting. Reagan stepped up his attacks on the administration's foreign policy, and he appealed to the worst in Wallace voters by attacking a recent Kissinger speech in favor of majority rule in Africa. Reagan crushed Ford, winning every county and all 96 delegates. Things didn't get better for Ford in the May 4 Alabama, Georgia, and Indiana primaries. Reagan won 130 of the 139 delegates that day, pulling ahead of Ford in total delegates.[89]

After the loss in Texas, most of Ford's advisors told the candidate to distance himself from Kissinger. Their advice was echoed by House minority whip Robert Michel, who suggested that Kissinger be "muzzled."[90] Ford stuck by his secretary of state. "I would like Kissinger to be secretary as long as I am president."[91] The best advice came from Goldwater, who sent a letter urging him to play to the center rather than to the right wing:

> You are not going to get the Reagan vote. These are the same people who got me the nomination and they will never swerve, but ninety percent of them will vote for you for President, so get after middle America. They have never had it so good. They are making more money and they are not at war.[92]

Goldwater was alone in suggesting that Ford move to the center. After Texas, Ford met with Cheney, Marsh, and Morton, and they decided to emphasize his commitment to conservative positions on defense, the budget, and economic policy. They never seriously considered stressing the areas, like détente, where he was more to the middle of the road than Reagan.[93]

Ford and Reagan split the May 11 Nebraska and West Virginia primaries. It was the halfway point, and Reagan had 468 delegates to Ford's 318.[94]

—◦◦◦—

Nebraska was the first state where Carter faced his new rivals, Brown and Church. They would do well over the next few weeks, shattering Carter's aura of invincibility, but his 600-delegate lead would prove to be insurmountable. Church campaigned extensively in Nebraska, while Carter visited the state only once. Church won by only 1 percent, or less than 2,000 votes, and on the same night, Carter won Connecticut. Church had proven that Carter could be beaten, but Carter continued his string of winning at least one state every election night, and he picked up 25 more delegates that day.[95]

Carter suffered a worse loss the next week when Michigan and Maryland held their primaries. Maryland was the first state in which Brown campaigned, and the California governor showed surprising charisma. When he arrived in Maryland on April 28, Brown was greeted by bigger crowds than any other candidate had been able to generate. The son of a California governor, Brown was somehow able to pull off a regular Joe routine. "I'm just an ordinary guy who works hard and comes home late."[96] Carter bused in 120 Georgian volunteers, but it was not nearly enough, and Brown trounced Carter by 48 to 37 percent.

Michigan was touch-and-go. Udall's campaign gained new life as a result of direct-mail efforts and matching funds, and Carter was disadvantaged by Michigan's open primary because he lost voters who crossed over to vote for Ford. Carter was saved by his strength among African Americans, and he edged out Udall by 44 to 43 percent. Again, it was not a good night for Carter, and the news reports were all about his new vulnerability, but he picked up 100 more delegates.[97]

—◦◦◦—

On the Republican side, Reagan was trying to deal Ford a death blow in his home state of Michigan, but he was fooling himself, and the state would revitalize the president's campaign. Ford was universally liked, and he had been very attentive to the state during his years in the House. He was also a home-state hero. He was a star of the state university national champion football team, and the people of the state were justly proud of his rise to the presidency. The only rational choice for Reagan was to concede the state to Ford, but he and Sears weren't thinking rationally. Reagan was furious that Ford had presumed to suggest that he drop out, and his campaign was euphoric after the big win in Texas. So they decided to stick it to Ford, budgeting $80,000 for the state, with the American Conservative Union spending an additional $20,000 on advertising.

Ford was concerned about Michigan because it was a crossover state where Wallace had won the Democratic primary in 1972. On the weekend before the primary, Ford took a whistle-stop train across the state, generating great TV and radio coverage. He asked Democrats and independents to cross over and vote, and the turnout was twice as high as any previous Republican primary in the state. Ford won 65 percent of the vote, and he gained 55 delegates to Reagan's 29. Reagan had made little effort in Maryland, and Ford picked up all of the state's 43 delegates.[98]

The race was a dead heat, but Ford pulled ahead of Reagan a few days later. The New York delegation announced that most of its 154 members would vote for him, and Pennsylvania followed by announcing that 88 of its 103 delegates were for Ford. To top it off, he picked up Vermont's 18 delegates.

—◦◦◦—

The next primary date, May 25, was a split decision in both the Republican and Democratic primaries. Six states held primaries on that day: Oregon, Nevada, Idaho, Tennessee, Kentucky, and Arkansas.

On the Democratic side, only Oregon was really contested. Idaho was Church's home state; Carter had Tennessee, Kentucky, and Arkansas locked up; and Brown was a shoo-in in Nevada, next door to his home state of California. Brown was running a write-in campaign, with hundreds of Californians crossing into the state on behalf of their governor. Church won the state with 35 percent of the vote, to 27 percent for Carter and 23 percent for Brown. It looked like a big loss for Carter, except that he won more than 110 delegates that day.[99]

On the Republican side, the May 25 Republican primaries looked like a tie, but in reality Ford won the nomination that day. Reagan had Idaho, Nevada, and Arkansas sewn up, but Oregon, Kentucky, and Tennessee were at play. Ford was the favorite in Oregon, while Reagan looked like the favorite in Kentucky and Tennessee, and wins in those two states would put him ahead in the total delegate count. Reagan hadn't put enough effort into the border states, and he compounded his problems with a gaffe in Tennessee when he said that he would consider selling the Tennessee Valley Authority. The people of the state were fiercely proud of the New Deal project, and the Ford campaign responded by sending out local politicians to defend the agency. Ford won the state by 2,200 votes, and he won Kentucky by 51 to 47 percent. Reagan made a late charge in Oregon, but Ford won by 52 to 48 percent. Winning Kentucky and Tennessee resulted in an 80-delegate swing for Ford.[100]

———— ∾∾∾ ————

The final primary showdown was on June 8 in California, Ohio, and New Jersey. Reagan had his home state of California sewn up, and he hadn't entered New Jersey, so Ohio was the main battleground on the Republican side. The week before the primaries, Reagan learned the danger of loose language when he speculated about sending troops into Rhodesia: "Whether you would have to go in with occupation forces or not, I don't know."[101] Ford called the idea "irresponsible," and he ran commercials taking advantage of the gaffe. "Last Wednesday, Ronald Reagan said he would send American troops to Rhodesia. On Thursday he clarified that. He said they could be observers, or advisers. What does he think happened in Vietnam? When you vote Tuesday, remember: Governor Ronald Reagan couldn't start a war. President Ronald Reagan could."[102]

As expected, Reagan won handily in California, and he picked up 167 delegates from the winner-take-all primary. Ford swept New Jersey, picking up all 67 of its delegates, and he scored a major victory in Ohio, winning 88 delegates, while only 9 went to Reagan. For the day, Ford won 155 delegates, and Reagan picked up 176.[103] Ford had 950 of the 1,130 delegates he needed.

On the Democratic side, Brown was sure to win big in California, so Carter concentrated on New Jersey and Ohio. His opponents split their efforts — Brown campaigned in New Jersey and Church ran in Ohio. Church's campaign took a hit when the Teton River Dam broke in his home state of Idaho, forcing him to return for a few days before the vote. Carter swept Ohio, and he picked up 119 delegates in the state. Brown's uncommitted slate won in New Jersey — partly because of a complex and confusing ballot — but Carter picked up 25 delegates there. He did not do as well as he had expected in California, but he won another 67 delegates from the state.[104]

Jackson dropped out after Ohio, telling the press, "We can all add."[105] But Brown's campaign manager, Mickey Kantor, later explained that they had not bothered to add. "We were a little slow on the uptake — at least I was. Four or five days before the election I still thought that if we won in New Jersey and won big in California the same day, we'd be in okay shape and would have a chance at the nomination."[106] Brown still thought he had a chance. From Los Angeles he trumpeted the fact he had won every state he entered, and he promised to travel the country to woo every uncommitted delegate.[107]

Carter had 1260 delegates out of 1505 needed to win, and he collected the remaining delegates he needed the next day. At midnight, as he was talking to the crowd that had greeted him on the streets of Plains when he arrived from California, he was handed a note that Wallace wanted him to call the Governor's Mansion in Montgomery. When Carter returned the call at 2:15 A.M., Wallace said that Carter made him "proud to be a southerner," and he promised to announce his support the next morning. When Carter woke up at 5:30, he asked Charles Kirbo to call Jackson, and he called Mayor Daley himself. He told Daley that he did not want Wallace's to be the only endorsement he received that day. Daley said that he would pledge his delegates to Carter, which gave Carter Wallace's 171 delegates, Daley's 86 delegates, and Jackson's 248 delegates, erasing any doubt that he would win the nomination.[108]

Carter made the process of selecting his running mate very public. He asked his top three choices, senators Edmund Muskie, Walter Mondale, and John Glenn, to visit him in Plains. Muskie arrived first. When the senator and his wife arrived in Plains on July 4 they stayed the night at the Carter house, and Muskie's interview began first thing the next morning. Carter was impressed, but his aides were afraid of the senator's famous temper. Mondale arrived on the morning of July 8, and he spent three hours talking with Carter. Carter was prepared to dislike Mondale because he considered him too liberal, and he was put off by the senator not entering the primaries because he wasn't willing to do the work. To Carter's surprise, they hit it off. Glenn arrived that afternoon; Carter was not at all impressed. Carter met with four others candidates when he went to New York for the convention, but he had already made up his mind to nominate Mondale.[109]

———⟡⟡⟡———

The choice of the vice presidential nominee was the only open question at the Democratic Convention in New York between July 10 and 15. There were two keynote addresses, a dull and uninspired speech by John Glenn and a rousing one by Barbara Jordan. Peter Rodino officially submitted Carter's name for the nomination. Udall and Brown were also put forward, but Udall immediately freed his delegates to vote for Carter, and Brown announced that California was voting unanimously for Carter during the roll call of the states.

Carter kept his vice presidential decision from everyone, even his wife, until the morning after he was nominated. He told Rosalyn just minutes before he called Mondale to offer him the job. Mondale said that he was "deeply honored and thrilled," and accepted. At ten that morning Carter went to the convention hall and told the assembled delegates that he had chosen, "if the delegates will approve, Senator Walter Mondale." Mondale gladly accepted. "No one could be honored more at having been selected by this remarkable and good man."

On Thursday evening Carter gave his acceptance speech from the podium, which was flanked with banners that asked: "For America's Third Century, Why Not the Best?" He introduced himself with his signature line: "My name is Jimmy Carter and I'm running for president." He had completely rewritten the speech given to him by his staff, and he added a populist denunciation of "unholy and self-perpetuating alliances between money and politics." But most of the speech was a repetition of his promises to make the country better. "We want to have faith again! We want to be proud again! We just want the truth again! ... We can have an American government that's turned away from scandal and corruption and official cynicism and is once again as decent and competent as our people." And he showed what an extraordinary candidate he was by talking about love. "I have spoken a lot of times this year about love, but love must be aggressively translated into simple justice."[110]

———∿∿∿———

For the first time since 1964 the Democrats had finished their convention without a bruising and divisive fight; this time it was the Republicans who were still battling. In years past, a candidate who gained more than 40 percent of the delegates was considered a lock for a first-ballot nomination, but both Ford and Reagan were over the 40 percent mark. At the end of the primaries Ford had 48 percent, or 992 delegates, and Reagan had 45 percent, or 886. It sounded like a close race, but Ford had to win 36 percent of the remaining delegates to garner the nomination, while Reagan had to win 64 percent. Sears realized that his candidate was facing long odds.

Ford appointed Houston attorney James Baker to lead his delegate-collection effort, and he used his incumbency to influence the uncommitted delegates, flying them to the White House and delivering funds for projects in their home districts.[111] But Ford didn't have all the advantages. Baker recalled that the Reagan campaign was better organized to win the remaining 11 state conventions, which would choose 267 delegates. "We never thought we'd need the convention states, so we were woefully out-organized by the Reagan forces in them, most of which are the Western states, where their natural strength was anyway."[112] Ford agreed. "We had done a terrible job organizing in those states because we hadn't thought it necessary.[113]

The Reagan campaign would perform well, but it could not overcome Ford's 100-delegate lead. Over the next few weeks Reagan beat Ford in conventions in Missouri, Washington, New Mexico, Montana, Colorado, and Utah, while Ford won the majority of delegates in Delaware, Minnesota, North Dakota, and Connecticut. At the end of the process the *Washington Post* put the count at 1,093 for Ford and 1,030 for Reagan, while the *New York Times* gave Ford 1,102 and Reagan 1,063. In other words, Ford needed between 28 and 37 more delegates to win, while Reagan needed between 67 and 100. The largest uncommitted delegation was Mississippi, with 30 votes. If Ford received the Mississippi delegation, he would win. If Reagan took it, he would be just behind in the total count.[114]

———∿∿∿———

Sears knew that he needed to swing for the fences to win, so he convinced Reagan to name his vice president before the convention. And the choice was a sign of how desperate the Reagan team was. Reagan chose liberal Pennsylvania senator Richard Schweiker because, as David Keene later explained, he had "nothing to lose."[115] They hoped that Schweiker could swing the Pennsylvania delegation back to Reagan and possibly sway the New Jersey delegation as well. In mid–July, Sears and Paul Laxalt met with Schweiker to ensure that he would accept the nomination if Reagan offered it. They never mentioned that they wanted him to deliver Pennsylvania, which Schweiker considered very unlikely, so he agreed. Sears then flew to California to pitch the idea to Reagan. The candidate liked the idea, and Schweiker flew out the next day and met with Reagan for six hours. Halfway through the discussion Reagan offered the position on his ticket, and they spent the rest of the time discussing the campaign. Reagan announced his choice on July 26.[116]

Schweiker failed to sway the Pennsylvania delegation. Just before Reagan's press conference, Schweiker called Drew Lewis, an old friend who was the head of Ford's campaign in Pennsylvania. Lewis explained that he had made a commitment to Ford, and when he hung up, Lewis called Ford and told him that the ninety Pennsylvania delegates committed to him were safe. Ford called the head of the Pennsylvania Republican Party, Billy Meehan, who said the same thing. "When I give my word, it's good."[117]

The Schweiker nomination also clinched the Mississippi delegation for Ford. The head of the delegation was Clarke Reed, a conservative true-believer who talked like a beatnik, referring to everyone as "that cat." Reed had been an early supporter of Reagan, but he was also a consummate deal-maker who wanted to be on the winning side.[118] The rest of the delegation was more moderate, and the state party had long followed the practice of voting as a bloc. When Reed learned that his old friend Harry Dent was trying to convince the moderate delegates to vote for Ford against his wishes, he was furious, and he called a meeting of the delegation to put a stop to it. Dent convinced Reed to let a Ford campaign official address the delegation, and Cheney agreed to fly down to Jackson for the meeting. Reed also invited the Reagan campaign to send a representative, and Keene was chosen to go. Before the meeting, Keene let Reed in on the news that Reagan would pick Schweiker. At the meeting, Cheney and Keene both gave short addresses, and the delegation invited Ford to address it the following Friday.

In the interim, Reed stewed about the choice of Schweiker. He had always fought against conservatives choosing liberal running mates, and he felt betrayed by Reagan's choice. So when Ford called before his trip to Mississippi and asked for his endorsement, Reed agreed. In a press conference announcing his endorsement, he called the Schweiker nomination "wrong and dumb."[119] Ford addressed the delegation on July 30. Schweiker and Reagan followed on August 5, but with Reed firmly committed to the president, they could not prevent the delegation from choosing Ford.

∼∽∾

When the convention opened in Kansas City on August 11 the Ford campaign estimated that it had five more votes than it needed for a first-ballot victory. An estimated 35 of the delegates were soft votes, but 25 more uncommitted delegates were leaning to Ford. The Reagan campaign agreed that Ford had the delegates to win, but Sears tried one last gambit. He submitted a proposed rule requiring each candidate to name a running mate before the first vote. He was trying to force Ford to follow Reagan's lead and pick someone who offended a number of delegates. Before the convention opened, the rules committee rejected the proposal, and Sears demanded a vote on the convention floor. Again it was Mississippi which was the focus of the lobbying. Reed was inclined to vote for the rule because he hated the idea of Ford choosing a liberal running mate, but his delegation voted 31 to 28 to oppose the rule. With the entire Mississippi delegation voting as a bloc against the rule, it lost on the convention floor.[120]

Having lost the nomination, Reagan's supporters took a meaningless slap at Kissinger with a platform plank called "Morality in Foreign Policy." It referred to Solzhenitsyn's "human courage and morality"; claimed that the Helsinki Accords took "from those who do not have freedom the hope of one day getting it"; urged that "in pursuing détente we must not grant unilateral favors with only the hope of getting future favors in return"; and called for no more "secret agreements, hidden from our people." It was a simple-minded attack, and Ford was furious. At first he said "fight it," but his advisors explained that most of the delegates left on the floor were hard-core Reaganites, and it would pass regardless of the position Ford took. The president knew that the plank was meaningless, so he told his people not to oppose it.[121]

The roll-call vote was anticlimactic—Ford won by 1,187 to 1,070. After the vote, he arranged to meet with Reagan to smooth things over. When they set up the meeting, each campaign insisted that Ford not offer Reagan the vice presidency. Reagan had already taken himself out of the running in Mississippi before the convention when he said that there was "no way" he would agreed to be Ford's running mate.[122] Before the vote he sent a note to the California delegation that said there was "no circumstance whatsoever under which I would accept the nomination for Vice President. That is absolutely final."[123] Ford later admitted that he might have chosen Reagan had he been given the opportunity. "At that convention we considered picking Governor Reagan as our vice presidential nominee.... But the Reagan people were adamant that they wouldn't let him run as my running mate, so it didn't happen."[124]

At 1:30 that night Ford went to Reagan's hotel room and asked for his help on the campaign, and Reagan agreed without hesitation. Ford asked him to comment on the people he was considering for his running mate, and Reagan said that Dole would be "an excellent choice."[125]

───※───

At 3:15 that night Ford finally turned to his choice of a running mate. In a conference room in the Crown Center he conferred with Rockefeller, Cheney, Marsh, Spencer, Teeter, and his old friends Melvin Laird, Bryce Harlow, Michigan senator Robert Griffin, and Texas senator John Tower. As the discussion progressed, the list was narrowed down to four candidates: Anne Armstrong, who, in addition to being ambassador to Great Britain, had been co-chair of the Republican National Committee, the first female counselor to the president under Nixon, and a member of Ford's Council on Wage and Price Stability; Assistant Attorney General William Ruckelshaus, who had been the director of the EPA and acting director of the FBI; Tennessee senator Howard Baker, who became a star during the Watergate hearings; and Kansas senator Bob Dole, who was an old friend from the days when he convinced the rest of the Kansas House Republicans to vote for Ford as minority leader. Ford wanted to choose a running mate who was acceptable to the right wing, and Reagan's praise for Dole would figure heavily in his choice.

Teeter pushed hard for Ruckelshaus because he would attract moderate voters and blunt the pardon issue. The group reluctantly decided he wasn't the right pick because he would be opposed by many conservatives, and he had little campaign experience. Spencer suggested Armstrong, and she would have been an inspired choice. She was a capable campaigner, a charming former business executive, and untainted by Watergate. And the choice of a woman would have brought new life to the ticket. But the Ford-Armstrong ticket came in last when Teeter polled potential voters on a Ford ticket with the potential running mates. The result was probably more a reflection of Armstrong's lack of name recognition than of how the ticket would ultimately perform, but the poll helped convince Ford that she wasn't the right choice. Baker had mild support with the group. He was a moderate who did not offend conservatives, but Ford didn't think he could win the border states even with Baker on the ticket, and Teeter's polling showed that he had little appeal in the rest of the country.

That left Dole, and the group had nothing but praise for the Kansan. He was a war hero; his humor made him a media favorite; and he had stature. He would be the most acceptable candidate to the right wing, and he would appeal to the farm states, where Ford had lost support. During the last hour of the discussion it was apparent that the president favored Dole. When the meeting ended at 5:00, Ford hadn't made a final decision. Just before he went to bed he received a message from Clarke Reed that some delegates were considering a push from the floor to name Reagan as the running mate, but Reed promised to put an end to it if Ford picked Dole. As Ford went to bed he was thinking about the importance of Dole's appeal to the farm states.

When the group reconvened at 9:30 it was clear that Ford had chosen Dole. The factors that pushed Dole over the top were Reagan's endorsement and the fact that Dole was an old friend of Ford's, while the president had never warmed to Baker. Ford made the actual decision after a half-hour of discussion, and he called Dole and offered him the job. Dole had been waiting expectantly with his wife in the Muehlebach Hotel, and he immediately accepted. Ford announced his choice from the Century Ballroom in the Crown Center Hotel just before noon on August 19.[126]

Dole was a fine candidate and an honorable public servant, but Ford's wasn't playing to win. His political benefits were that he would not offend the right wing and he played well in the farm states, but the farm states were solidly Republican, and winning them would not put Ford over the top. To win, Ford needed to capture some big northern states or to peel some southern states away from Carter, and he needed to appeal to centrist voters. Dole didn't help any of those things.

While Ford was at the convention a crisis broke out that was every bit as dangerous as the *Mayaguez* incident and the Lebanon evacuation. On August 18, U.S. troops entered the demilitarized zone between North and South Korea to cut down a tree that was blocking their view. The North Koreans responded by beating two of the soldiers to death. The U.S. Army filmed the incident, and there was no question that it was unjustified murder.

Scowcroft was with Ford in Kansas City when the incident happened, and the remaining NSC staff in the White House met to develop recommendations for the president. They kicked around serious escalations, such as sinking a North Korean naval vessel, until the commanding officer in Korea, General Richard Stillwell, had an inspired suggestion — reenter the zone and chop down the tree. Kissinger approved the plan with one change. If the North Koreans did not allow the incursion, an army barracks in North Korea would be shelled. From Kansas City, Ford approved the plan, but he insisted that the artillery assault on the North Korean barracks could not begin until he expressly authorized it.

Kissinger contacted the Soviets and the Chinese, and neither country objected. Before they implemented the president's orders, Deputy Secretary of Defense William Clements and Admiral James Holloway met with William Hyland in the White House. Clements was nervous that the plan would lead to war. He wanted Hyland to convince Kissinger and Scowcroft to kill the plan, but Clements would not make a formal request to suspend the action. Holloway looked uncomfortable, and he told Hyland that the Joint Chiefs supported Stillwell's plan. Hyland called Scowcroft and relayed Clements' concerns. Scowcroft was irritated, and he refused to bother Ford, who had just finished his address to the convention. Scowcroft told Ford of Clements' concerns at breakfast the next morning, but Ford decided that the plan should go ahead.

That day, an American tank force was deployed along the demilitarized zone. When the troops entered the zone to chop down the tree, American bombers flew toward North Korea and turned back just before they entered the DMZ. The North Koreans did not retaliate, and they issued an apology that day.[127]

Ford's acceptance speech on the 19th was delayed. A demonstration on behalf of Reagan was scheduled to last fifteen minutes, but his floor manager, Lyn Nofziger, deliberately kept the Reagan supporters cheering and blowing air horns for an hour. Rhodes invited Reagan to the podium to say a few words, where he staked the conservative claim on the party. "I believe the Republican Party has a platform that is a banner of bold, unmistakable colors with no pale, pastel shades"[128] As Nofziger intended, the demonstration pushed Ford's speech past prime time on the East Coast.[129]

It was unfortunate that Nofziger had been so petty, because Ford gave the performance of his life. Hartmann had been working on the acceptance speech for months, collecting phrases and soliciting suggestions from the rest of the administration. He loosened his strict rules against flowery language and stylistic devices, and the speech allowed Ford to shine. Ford added one point as he prepared that afternoon, challenging Carter to a series of debates. At 5:30 he called Cheney and Marsh to his suite and showed them what he had written on his legal pad. "I am ready, I am eager to go before the American people and debate the issues face to face with Jimmy Carter." They both loved it, and it was put into the speech.

Ford had practiced for the speech before television cameras, and the combination of his preparation and Hartmann allowing actual eloquence was dynamic. Ford proudly declared that he was the first incumbent since Eisenhower "who can tell the American people America is at peace." He looked in the cameras and proclaimed himself a man of the people. "You at home, listening tonight, you are the people who pay the taxes and obey the laws. You are the people who make our system work. You are the people who make America what it is. It is from your ranks that I come, and on your side I stand."[130]

20

Kissinger For/Against Human Rights

The Morality in Foreign Policy plank demonstrated how unpopular Kissinger had become with the right wing. He was no longer Super K; he was a political liability, so he spent much of the year traveling overseas. His travels exhibited the best and the worst of the secretary of state. He changed American policy to embrace majority rule in southern Africa — the United States would no longer be fighting the tide of history by supporting minority white regimes. At the same time, he approved of, or at least acquiesced in, torture, murder, and other human rights abuses in South America.

The self-righteous tone of the Morality in Foreign Policy plank wears thin when it is juxtaposed with its proponents' attack on Kissinger for embracing majority rule in southern Africa. Not that Kissinger supported majority rule for humanitarian reasons — he was trying to save America's influence in Africa. The debacle in Angola convinced him that the Soviets would have the upper hand in Africa as long as the U.S. was allied with white regimes, so he decided to "identify with the aspiration of the black nations in Africa."[1] He wanted the African nations to understand that the only way they could achieve majority rule was with American assistance.[2]

When he embraced majority rule, Kissinger was reversing a decision made early in the Nixon administration to unequivocally support the white states. State Department aides dubbed the decision the "tar baby option" because they knew it would result in unending complications and problems. The Africa Bureau spent the next five years trying to change Kissinger's mind, and he finally relented after Congress cut off the Angolan operation. He told Ford that he had come to the decision reluctantly. "Basically I am with the whites in Southern Africa. I think it no better for the majority to oppress the minority than vice versa. But in my comments I will support majority rule in Rhodesia. I will say the same thing about South Africa, but softer."[3] It may have been made for practical reasons, but the decision made Kissinger, in the words of Winston Lord, "the catalyst for Rhodesian independence as well as more American emphasis for black aspirations."[4]

Kissinger decided to announce the new policy in Zambia in May 1976. As he prepared to leave on April 23, Kissinger told the press that the Untied States was committed to "majority rule in the black African countries."[5] Kissinger's first stops were in Kenya and Tanzania, where he received approval for the new policy from Jomo Kenyatta of Kenya and Julius Nyerere of Tanzania. When he arrived in Zambia, Kissinger also won approval from Kenneth Kaunda. In return for American support of majority rule, the three leaders promised not to invite Cuban troops into their countries or to allow the Soviet Union or Cuba to become directly involved in the insurgent movements in southern Africa.[6]

Kissinger announced the new policy in Lusaka on April 27, proclaiming America's "unequivocal" support for "self-determination, majority rule, equal rights and human dignity for all peoples of southern Africa — in the name of moral principle, international law and world peace." He declared that the U.S. would maintain a policy of "unrelenting opposition" to white rule in Rhodesia, and he demanded that South Africa announce a "definite timeline acceptable to the world community" for Namibian independence. For South Africa itself, he demanded an evolution to equality in a "reasonable" time.[7]

It was a long-overdue moment — the United States finally supporting majority rule and self determination — but the speech cost Ford dearly among southern conservatives, who had given up defending segregation in the U.S. but not in Africa. The speech contributed to Ford's loss in Texas a few days later, and when Kissinger got off the plane in the Ivory Coast the traveling reporters sang "The Eyes of Texas Are Upon You."[8] From San Clemente, Nixon sent a message to Ford's campaign (through Gulley) that "Kissinger's talking too much about black Africa. It's pissing off the rednecks. The Negro vote's lost; don't let it lose you white votes."[9] The political fall-out wasn't a surprise to Ford. When Kissinger proposed the trip, the president instantly knew that it would cause him problems on the right. "This may hurt me. However, you go ahead and do what is correct."[10] When Kissinger returned, Ford praised his efforts to the NSC and reiterated that he would not be swayed by political factors. "We will continue to do what is right regardless of the primaries. This will sometimes be tough but it is right."[11]

―――∽∾∿―――

Kissinger's second major trip during 1976 was to South America, which was filled with military dictatorships as a result of a wave of right-wing coups that had swept through the continent in the name of fighting communism, starting with Brazil in 1964. The most recent coup was in the Southern Cone country of Argentina. After Pinochet took over in Chile, many leftists took refuge in Argentina, which was already facing ultra-leftist guerilla campaigns. The Argentine generals used the resulting unrest as an excuse to overthrow the government of Isabel Perón on March 24, 1976. The new government embarked on a terror campaign against leftists and anyone who spoke out against their reign of terror. The Chilean and Argentine dictatorships engaged in similar activities. They both made any suspected leftists disappear; they regularly tortured the men and raped the women they had kidnapped; and most of the people who disappeared never were seen again. Like so many other murderous governments at the time, they killed many of their targets by dropping them out of helicopters into the ocean.[12]

Kissinger fought his staff when they suggested that the United States should complain about human rights violations in the Southern Cone. They disagreed over whether the human rights violations were worse than their political opponents. For example, in a December 1974 staff meeting, Kissinger claimed that the human rights situation in Chile was no worse under Pinochet than it was under Allende, but Deputy Secretary Rogers disagreed. The primary disagreement was over what would happen if the United States cut off aid. Rogers agreed that Pinochet's regime would fall, but he predicted that the Christian Democrats would take over.[13] In a meeting two weeks later Kissinger was much more pessimistic. "You know the only possible outcome of this can be an extreme left wing government in Chile or driving the Chilean Government sort of toward the Arabs."[14] Kissinger even made fun of his staff's concerns in a meeting with Chilean foreign minister Patricio Carvajal. "I read the Briefing Paper for this meeting and it was nothing but Human Rights. The State Department is made up of people who have a vocation for the ministry. Because there were not enough churches for them, they went into the Department of State."[15]

When he traveled to Chile and Argentina in 1976, Kissinger completely undermined the American embassies in Santiago and Buenos Aires who were trying to take the juntas to task for human rights violations. He gave a preview of his actions on June 3 when he called Assistant Secretary of State for Latin America William Rogers and complained about the embassies emphasizing human rights. "I am not on the same wave length with you guys on this business. I just am not eager to overthrow these guys."[16] When he arrived in Chile on June 8, Kissinger told Pinochet that the U.S. supported his regime. "In the United States, as you know, we are sympathetic with what you want to do here. I think the previous government was headed toward Communism. We wish your government well." He explained that he would speak about human rights in his address that afternoon, but he was almost apologetic, implying that the only reason he was raising the issue was pressure from Congress. "My evaluation is that you are a victim of all left-wing groups around the world, and your greatest sin was that you overthrew a government that was going Communist."[17]

The next day Kissinger flew to Buenos Aires, where American ambassador Robert Hill had been taking a strong stand against the escalating human rights abuses. In April and May the Argentines kidnapped and tortured several American citizens, and they joined with Uruguayan security forces to kill former legislators from Uruguay.[18] Hill met with foreign minister Admiral Cesar Augusto Guzzetti on May 28 and protested the use of death squads in the country, but he reported to Washington that "I did not have the impression he really got the point."[19] The Argentines certainly didn't temper their actions, and their agents killed the former president of Bolivia six days later.[20]

When Kissinger arrived in Buenos Aires he delivered a much different message. At his meeting with Admiral Guzzetti, the Argentine foreign minister asked the United States to "understand and support" his government's actions to stem terrorism. Kissinger agreed. "We are aware you are in a difficult period. It is a curious time, when political, criminal, and terrorist activities tend to merge without any clear separation. We understand you must establish authority." After more discussion, Kissinger came to the point. "If there are things that have to be done, you should do them quickly. But you must get back to normal procedures." Kissinger closed with a promise to try to divert human rights criticism. "In the United States, we have strong domestic pressures to do something on human rights.... We want you to succeed. We do not want to harass you. I will do what I can."[21]

The next day the Argentine security forces kidnapped and tortured twenty-four Chileans and Uruguayans. Maxwell Chaplin, a deputy in the American embassy, met with Argentine Director General of International Policy Pereyra to object to the kidnapping, but he reported that Pereyra's response was "an impassioned, almost fanatic defense" of his government, and he "expressed satisfaction over his conclusion that Secretary Kissinger was realistic and understood the GOA problems." Chaplin concluded that Pereyra was "not disposed to give one inch on the issue of human rights."[22]

By the end of the Ford administration, the Argentine junta had killed more than 10,000 people, and in the following years the total would climb to 30,000.[23] The question remains: would any of these lives have been saved if the U.S. had taken a stronger stand against the junta's murderous policies? The answer is not easy. Most likely, the junta would not have tempered its behavior during the first few years, but it may have stopped if it faced continued opposition.

The regime continued its terror even after the Carter administration cut aid to Argentina in half and Congress cut off arms shipments. Harry Schlaudeman, who was the deputy assistant secretary of state for Latin America under Ford and the ambassador to Argentina under Carter, has concluded that the U.S. had very little ability to change the junta's human rights policies. "We had very little leverage with these people." But he does think that international pressure eventually tempered the regime's actions because the Argentine military was concerned that they could be tried in an international tribunal. According to Schlaudeman, Argentine president Roberto Viola "kept talking about what he said was an effort to create a Nuremberg for the Argentine military — put them on trial. This, of course, was the major objective of the military — to avoid a Nuremberg."[24]

The military juntas were also banding together to export their brand of terror. Guzzetti made a vague reference to the project during Kissinger's visit. "The terrorist problem is general to the entire Southern Cone. To combat it, we are encouraging joint efforts to integrate with our neighbors.... Chile, Paraguay, Bolivia, Uruguay, Peru."[25] They called the program "Operation Condor," and they tracked down and killed opponents who had taken refuge in other countries. The CIA and the State Department regularly reported on the activities of Operation Condor. On August 3 the State Department reported that the purpose of the operation was to "find and kill" leftists "in their own countries and in Europe." The memo explains that the targets included "nearly anyone who opposes government policy."[26] In September the embassy in Argentina sent a cable reporting that Operation Condor was beginning to hunt down regime opponents anywhere in the world.[27]

The South American juntas even struck in the United States. On September 21, 1976, former Chilean foreign minister Orlando Letelier was killed by a car bomb in Washington, D.C. Two Cuban exiles and an operative of the Chilean intelligence services had placed a bomb under the driver's seat of Letelier's car. They detonated the bomb as Letelier was driving around Sheridan Circle near Embassy Row, and the bomb lifted the car off the ground, killing Letelier and Ronni Moffitt.[28] The anti–Castro Cuban exiles had been spreading terror throughout the Americas, and they didn't shy away from actions in the Untied States. In the last three months of 1975 they bombed several targets in the Miami area, including the FBI building, the Dominican consulate, the Broward County Courthouse, and the Dominican Airlines ticket office. During the next two years the Cuban groups would bomb an airline office in Miami, the Venezuelan tourist office in Puerto Rico, and a Venezuelan office in New York.[29]

Toward the end of the presidential campaign, Kissinger made a concerted effort to make good on America's support of majority rule in Africa. He decided to tackle the issue of Rhodesia first, followed by Namibia and then South Africa. Rhodesia needed to be resolved immediately because the country was being torn apart by civil war, and there was no realistic possibility that the tiny white minority could continue to rule the blacks, who comprised 97 percent of the population. Ford had indicated earlier in the year that he would support the effort in response to a request by Rhodesian independence leader Joshua Nkomo for the United States to support majority rule. "Well, first, we believe that there ought to be more progress in Rhodesia where there are, as I recall the figures, some 220,000 whites and 5 or 6 million blacks. There ought to be movement toward a majority government. That, I think, has to be, inevitably, the result."[30]

Kissinger learned that an agreement was possible at the end of his trip to Africa. He met with Vorster during a break at the United Nations Conference on Trade and Development in Nairobi, and the South African prime minister had a surprise announcement. "I've got Ian Smith to agree to majority rule as a method, and he's going to resign as Prime Minister of Rhodesia, and open the way for majority rule in the country. But he insists on one thing, and that is the opportunity to meet you directly." The U.S. had refused to recognize the Rhodesian government, and accepting the offer was a significant change in American policy, but Kissinger agreed without hesitating or checking with Ford.[31] Kissinger emphasized to Vorster that America's new support for majority rule also pertained to South Africa — "history is against you" — but he explained that the U.S. would deal with Rhodesia first.[32] At the end of June he met with Vorster again in Grafenau, Germany, and he proposed a meeting between South Africa and SWAPO in Geneva, to be overseen by the UN. Vorster agreed to the conference.

It was Vorster's second attempt to settle the conflict in Rhodesia. A year earlier he withdrew his country's unconditional support of the white government, and he asked the leaders of Tanzania, Botswana, and Zambia to arrange a meeting between Smith and the Rhodesian liberation groups. In August 1975, Vorster and Kaunda presided over the meeting in a railway car that was pulled to the center of a bridge over Victoria Falls, the border between Zambia and Rhodesia, so neither side had to cross into the territory of the other. Little progress was made at the meeting, as some of the insurgents became drunk and disputatious, and Smith refused to give the rebels immunity.[33]

Now Smith was showing more willingness to negotiate, and Kissinger and Vorster started working together to get a deal done. In August Kissinger met with British foreign minister Callaghan, who offered assistance, including troops to oversee the transition. Callaghan and Kissinger agreed that Joshua Nkomo, the head of the Zimbabwe African People's Union, was the most reasonable independence leader, but they also agreed that he had little military power. The most powerful leader was Robert Mugabe, who led a substantial military arm and whose Shona tribe made up the majority of Rhodesia. The problem was that Mugabe was more radical than Nkomo, and he proved to be difficult to deal with.

On September 4, Kissinger and Vorster met at the Dolder Grand Hotel overlooking Zurich and approved a plan, called Annex C, which their staffs had jointly developed for majority rule in Rhodesia. During the two-year transition the country would be ruled by a council of two blacks and two whites. Vorster agreed to cut off Rhodesia if it did not accept the plan. He also agreed to convene a Zurich conference on Namibia and set a target date for Namibian independence of December 31, 1978.[34]

Kissinger traveled to Africa in September for a round of shuttle negotiations. At the first meeting in Pretoria, Vorster and Kissinger met for four hours with Ian Smith and seven other Rhodesians. Vorster threatened to cut off Rhodesia if Smith didn't accept the plan for majority rule — he had made the same threat in a private meeting a week earlier — and Kissinger warned that whites could not win a civil war. Smith promised that the Rhodesians were prepared to do what "no one expected we would do." Kissinger gave the Rhodesians a five-point memorandum setting out the terms of Annex C, and they agreed to meet again at Vorster's house in the evening. When they reconvened, Smith refused to sign on to Annex C. "You want me to sign my suicide note." He demanded that the plan be changed to give whites the chair of the transition council and control of the police and military. Kissinger agreed to propose the changes to Kaunda and Nyerere and send their response in time for Smith to present the plan to his parliament.[35]

During Kissinger's visits to Zambia and Tanzania, both Kaunda and Nyerere objected to the military and police being in white hands, but they were satisfied with the overall plan. Kaunda was effusive, and he expressed "satisfaction for what you have done." Nyerere was also happy. "Frankly, I think you have done it.... I for one will give it a chance." Nyerere also set out a condition for a Zurich conference on Namibia: South Africa would have to recognize SWAPO as the sole representative of the Namibians.[36] In his message to Smith, Kissinger wasn't upfront about the objections raised by Kaunda and Nyerere to a white being in charge of the military and police—he said that he "believed" that the condition could be accomplished. After he received Kissinger's message, Smith announced that he had agreed to the plan under pressure.[37] The British presided over the next round of the negotiations, a conference in Geneva on October 28, five days before Ford lost the 1976 election. It was an historic event—Ian Smith sat at the same table as Robert Mugabe, Joshua Nkomo, and other independence leaders—but the conference broke up without a resolution.

The Carter administration would continue the work that Kissinger started, brokering a transition agreement for Rhodesia after three hard years of negotiations.[38] Winston Lord believes that Kissinger's efforts led to the peace agreement. "The breakthrough occurred during Kissinger's tenure, although actual independence was not achieved until after Ford and he left office."[39] In Namibia the resolution took much longer. The country would not become independent until 1988, when the Reagan administration brokered a deal for the South Africans to let go of the country in return for Cuba withdrawing its troops from Angola. South Africa took even longer, but the white government agreed to majority rule in 1994.

The results of the American support of majority rule were not all positive. Zimbabwe (the new name of Rhodesia) has been anything but a model democracy. Robert Mugabe has ruled the country with an iron fist for decades. South Africa and Namibia, on the other hand, have become democratic. Their politics are messy, but the countries have developed better than almost anyone had expected at the time. The American change in policy did not directly lead to majority rule—that probably would have happened even if the U.S. had not changed policy—but the change in policy put America on the right side of the issue, and the United States was able to play a positive role in the region.

21

General Election

With the conventions out of the way, the Ford and Carter teams planned their strategies for the general election. They didn't have to worry about fundraising because both campaigns accepted $21.8 million in federal financing and agreed not to accept private donations. Both campaigns agreed that the battle would be fought in eight states. They agreed on New York, New Jersey, Pennsylvania, Ohio, Illinois, Michigan, and California. The Carter campaign thought that Indiana was at play, while the Ford campaign thought it could win Texas. Both campaigns agreed that Ford had to win five of the eight states to win.[1]

———— ❧ ————

Ford reshuffled his campaign, and in the process he made it a more professional and efficient organization. He replaced campaign chairman Rogers Morton, who was in bad health, with James Baker, who had done an impressive job collecting delegates. Cheney continued to be the White House contact for the campaign, calling most of the shots. After Baker took over, there was no more conflict between the campaign and Cheney. To improve the advertising the campaign brought on Doug Bailey and John Deardourff, at the suggestion of Teeter and Spencer. It became a capable staff, and the campaign would make no significant errors.[2]

In a series of meetings at the White House and in Vail, Ford and his political advisors agreed on a strategy for the general election. To prepare for the meetings the campaign collected memos on campaign strategy from Mike Duval, Jerry Jones, Foster Chanock, and Bob Teeter. The memos pulled no punches, and Spencer summed up the general theme for Ford. "Mr. President, as a campaigner, you're no fucking good!"[3] Ford and his aides developed a three-phase plan. During the first phase Ford would remain at the White House and look presidential. The debates would be the focus of the second phase, and Ford would make a big road trip in the final phase. They also decided that Dole would take the lead in attacking Carter. Ford thought that his opponent was careless of the facts, and he knew that he could take advantage of his ego, testiness, and liberalism.[4]

When he joined the campaign, Bailey was amazed that it had no media strategy, but his team quickly put together a plan that he was happy with even after the election. "If I had to do it all over again, I don't think we would change anything except the placement of some of the money in terms of key states."[5] The Ford campaign allocated half of its $21.8 million to advertising, and they decided to hold on to most of it to the end. Ford would run no TV commercials until after the first debate, and the campaign finished with a $4 million media blitz, the largest in campaign history.[6]

———— ❧ ————

Unlike Ford, Carter did not reshuffle his leadership, despite unsolicited advice from party heavyweights who encouraged him to bring on traditional campaign professionals. Jordan remained the campaign manager, calling most of the shots, and Powell stayed on as press secretary. Rafshoon was still in charge of advertising, Kirbo remained Carter's senior advisor, and Caddell remained the top pollster.[7]

Carter had a 20-point lead in the polls — the Gallup Poll put the race at 56 to 33 percent, while the Harris Poll had 61 to 32 percent. Teeter's polls showed Carter winning in a landslide.[8] Most of Carter's campaign felt comfortable with his lead, but not Pat Caddell. He could not understand how Ford had a 55 percent favorability rating, yet as a candidate he was polling lower than McGovern ever did. Caddell thought Ford's low numbers "just didn't make sense."[9] He told his fellow campaign workers, "I just wish he'd get it over with and drop in the polls. I'm getting nervous. He can't stay up there forever."[10] Jordan also warned the campaign not to be comforted by Carter's big lead. "Our clear and whole goal must be to simply win 270 electoral votes. We must never forget that in 1968 in six weeks Hubert Humphrey closed 20 points on Richard Nixon and almost won the presidency."[11]

Carter convened a two-day strategy session in Hilton Head, South Carolina, at the end of July, and he held another session at Miss Lillian's Pond House in Plains. He had been off the campaign trail since the Democratic convention in what his aides called his "Presidential Period," meeting with experts on domestic and foreign policy. The candidate was clearly frustrated, and he fumed about wanting to get back to "the shopping centers and the factory shift lines."[12] Like the Ford campaign, Carter's team budgeted just over $10 million of its $21.8 million for advertising. Where their plans differed was timing. The Carter campaign started advertising right away by buying time simultaneously on all three networks in June. It continued advertising before the first debate, while the Ford campaign remained silent.[13]

—❧—

Carter kicked off his campaign on Labor Day from Franklin Roosevelt's porch in Warm Springs, Georgia, and he continued his populist theme. "I owe the special interests nothing. I owe the people everything."[14] Later that day Carter rode in the pace car of the Darlington 500 stock car race, waving from the backseat of the Cadillac convertible, and the crowd loved it. Dole was waving from his own convertible five cars back, to little applause. Carter followed with a week-long trip to 20 cities, focusing on Catholic areas of big cities because Caddell's polls showed him running weak in those traditional Democratic strongholds.[15]

During his trip Carter sounded shrill when he tried to take advantage of a minor scandal concerning FBI director Clarence Kelley. At the end of August Kelly admitted that the bureau's carpenters had constructed drapery valances for his apartment, and he agreed to pay the bureau $335 for the work. Carter blasted Ford for not firing Kelley. "The director of the FBI ought to be purer than Caesar's wife."[16] Carter learned from the incident, and he handled later scandals with more restraint.

Ford kicked off his campaign on September 15 before a cheering crowd of 15,000 at the University of Michigan's Chrysler Arena. He stressed his accomplishments as president. "My administration has restored trust in the White House. My administration has turned the economy around. We are in the midst of a growing prosperity. We have peace and the capability and will to keep it." And he belittled Carter's promise not to lie. "It's not enough for anyone to say, 'Trust me.' Trust must be earned."[17] After the speech Ford returned to Washington, and he stayed in the White House for most of September. The networks were forced by the FCC's equal time rules to cover him signing bills and shaking hands with foreign leaders if they wanted to give any coverage to the Carter campaign. He got all the coverage he needed without being forced to campaign.[18]

Dole was sent on the road to tail Carter. As soon as Carter left a campaign stop, Dole arrived to attack what the candidate said there. The Ford campaign did nothing to restrain its vice presidential candidate. Lyn Nofziger, who was assigned to the Dole campaign, called him "an unguided missile."[19] Dole played his part with relish. He said that Carter "will shade his discussions, he will tell you anything you want to hear." He asked how Carter could give an interview to *Playboy*. "What kind of a judgment a man has that would grant such an interview?" He predicted that as president, Carter would have two hotlines, one to Moscow and one to George Meany.[20]

During the first phase of the campaign before the debates both candidates suffered through bad publicity. Carter's was self-inflicted. At the end of an interview that was published in *Playboy* on September 20 he tried to explain that his strongly-held religious views did not make him judgmental. Some of his statements just sounded weird, like when he admitted that he looked at other women "with lust in my heart." His attempts to sound streetwise caused him to use language that was inappropriate for a national leader. "Christ says don't consider yourself better than someone else because one guy screws a whole bunch of women while the other guy is loyal to his wife." He also promised not to "take on the same frame of mind that Nixon and Johnson did, lying, cheating and distorting the truth."[21] Johnson friends and supporters were furious, and Carter would spend a lot of time in Texas explaining the comment away. Many people were offended that Carter agreed to be interviewed by *Playboy* at all. To others, his answers just seemed bizarre — as Jordan said, "It increased the weirdo factor."[22] He compounded the problem when he told Norman Mailer during a *New York Times Magazine* interview, "I don't care if people say 'fuck.'"[23] Carter fell 10 points in the polls, but it was a temporary decline, and he bounced back by the first debate.[24]

Ford had little time to enjoy Carter's discomfort. On the day after the *Playboy* article was published, UPI reported that Ford's friend William Whyte, a vice president of U.S. Steel, had paid for three golfing trips to a New Jersey country club when Ford was a House member. Ford admitted that he took the trips, as well as other golf outings and trips paid for by business executives.[25] Carter tried to take advantage of the story, but he had to back off when it was reported that he had flown on corporate planes of Lockheed and Coca-Cola, and stayed in vacation lodges owned by the Union Camp Corporation and the Brunswick Paper Company while he was governor of Georgia.[26]

On the same day, Ford was hit with allegations about illegal campaign contributions by the Marine Engineers Beneficial Association, which had supported his House campaigns. Union president Jesse Calhoon was furious that Ford had vetoed a cargo preference bill, so he circulated stories that Ford had accepted cash payments. FBI director Kelley talked to Attorney General Levi about the issue, and they decided to refer the matter to Special Prosecutor Charles Ruff. When Ruff sent subpoenas to Grand Rapids for records, the matter was reported in the press.[27] The allegations would prove to be baseless, but the issue lingered for some time while Ruff conducted his investigation.

The first debate was held at the Walnut Street Theater in Philadelphia at 9:30 in the evening on September 23. Approximately half of the households in America tuned in for the debate, and 90 percent watched part of one of the three debates.[28] Ford rehearsed for the debate

Ford and Carter during the first debate in Philadelphia, September 23, 1976. (Photograph by David Hume Kennerly; White House photograph courtesy Gerald R. Ford Library.)

by practicing at a podium, answering questions from his aides. Carter, on the other hand, just read the briefing books without practicing, and his lack of preparation showed.[29]

Ford went on the attack from the beginning, visibly flustering his opponent. Carter stressed his populist themes. He called the tax code "a disgrace to this country. It's just a welfare program for the rich." He railed against "the business deductions. Jet airplanes, first-class travel, the $50 martini lunch — the average working person can't take advantage of that, but the wealthier people can." While Carter railed against the rich, Ford stressed how much better the economy was than when he took office:

> We were faced with heavy inflation — over 12 percent; we were faced with substantial unemployment. But in the last 24 months we've turned the economy around, and we've brought inflation down to under 6 percent. And we have added employment of about 4 million in the last 17 months to the point where we have 88 million people working in America today, the most in the history of the country.[30]

Just before the final statements, the audio system failed, causing a 25-minute delay. Ford's aides advised him to stand during the debate, and he remained standing. He looked irritated, and Carter looked impatient.[31] When the power turned back on, Carter gave his final statement, which promised unity and honesty. "For a long time our American citizens have been excluded, sometimes misled, sometimes have been lied to.... We need to restore the faith and the trust of the American people in their own Government." Echoing the theme of his campaign, Carter called for "a Government as good as our people." Ford responded by laying out his vision of post–Bicentennial America. "Our third century should be the century of individual freedom for all our 215 million Americans today.... We must make this next century the century of the individual." It was a ringing statement, but he blunted it with a hollow statement of fear. "We should never forget that a government big enough to give us every-thing we want is a government big enough to take from us everything we have."[32]

The impression Carter left with viewers was nervousness. His voice was soft, and he didn't answer questions persuasively. Martin Schram wrote that he "looked like a south Georgia boy who had been asked to debate the President of the United States."[33] Ford, on the other hand, was forceful and assertive. A Roper poll showed that the viewers thought Ford won, by 39 to 30 percent. Carter's lead in the Harris poll fell from 12 to 8 percent; his lead in the Gallup poll dropped from 16 to 8 percent, and his lead in the AP fell to 2 percent. The next day Carter admitted that he was in awe of being on the same stage as the president.[34] It wouldn't happen again.

The morning after the first debate Carter flew to Texas where he had to answer for his comments to *Playboy* about Johnson. Lady Bird Johnson had reportedly been "distressed, hurt and perplexed" by the comments.[35] Carter made things worse by claiming that the *Playboy* article was "a distortion of his true feelings." He said that the magazine had improperly jux-taposed his references to Johnson and Nixon, "which grossly misrepresents the way I feel about him."[36] *Playboy* had taped the interview, and Carter was further embarrassed when the magazine proved that its quotes were accurate.

A week later Ford was faced with his own embarrassing predicament, which was the result of his decision to keep Earl Butz in the Cabinet despite his penchant for making offen-sive remarks. On September 30, Ford had to deal with the repercussions of that decision when the secretary of agriculture was quoted making an outlandish joke. The joke was reported by John Dean, who was covering the convention for *Rolling Stone*. Dean described his trip home to California on a plane with Pat Boone, Sonny Bono, and a "distinguished member of Ford's cabinet." When Boone asked why the Republican Party couldn't attract more black votes, the cabinet secretary responded with an abhorrent comment. "I'll tell you why you can't attract coloreds, because coloreds only want three things ... first, a tight pussy; second, loose shoes; and third, a warm place to shit. That's all."[37]

It wasn't hard to identify the unnamed secretary as Butz, and the *New York Times* was ready to name him on the day the *Rolling Stone* article was published. The paper called Butz first, and the secretary of agriculture called Cheney and said that he made a mistake. When Cheney relayed the story to Ford in an afternoon campaign strategy meeting, the president said that he would issue a strong statement condemning the comments. John Deardourff was at the meeting, and he urged the president to fire Butz, but Ford said that he would decide what to do after he talked to the secretary of agriculture. When Butz came to the Oval Office the next morning Ford read him out, but he did not fire him. Butz issued an apology, but he added a gratuitous comment that he was "merely repeating a comment made decades ago by a ward politician in a large Midwestern city."[38] The press ridiculed Butz's apology, and Carter said that he should have been fired "long ago."[39] Ford heard the same thing from Betty all weekend, and he asked for Butz's resignation on Monday October 4. When Ford broke the news to Butz, the secretary of agriculture showed the depths of his insensitivity. He claimed that he didn't mean the comment as a racial slur, and he seemed to think that his only real mistake was that he "should have known better than to trust a man like John Dean."[40]

At the same time that Ford was dealing with Butz, he was trying to put the allegations about illegal campaign contributions behind him. He was worried that Ruff was letting the matter drag on, and he asked his friend Edward Bennett Williams for help. At Williams' sug-gestion, Ford held a press conference in the Oval Office and asked the special prosecutor to move quickly. "There is a saying that's prevalent in the law that 'justice delayed is justice denied.'"[41] Carter told the press that he accepted Ford's denials and considered the matter closed. The issue was officially over on October 13 when Ruff wrote Buchen that "the evidence developed has disclosed no violation of law on the part of President Ford. The matter has therefore been closed."[42]

———

The scandals were just a distraction compared to Ford's performance during the second debate. The subject was foreign policy, and everyone expected Ford to outshine his opponent. But the opposite happened, as the president made a gaffe that probably cost him the election.

Carter had learned from the first debate — this time he rehearsed — while Ford might have rehearsed too much. During his practices with Kissinger and Scowcroft, he was concerned about how to address the Helsinki Accords and the Sonnenfeldt Doctrine. So they went through the issue over and over, stressing that the U.S. had never recognized Soviet domination of Eastern Europe, and Helsinki had not changed that policy.[43] Ford's briefing book for the debate explained that American policy was to "recognize the independence, the sovereignty, and the autonomy of all Eastern European Countries.... The President of the United States believes that those countries are independent and sovereign."[44] The point was that the U.S. officially "recognized" the sovereignty of the countries of Eastern Europe, not that the Soviets actually allowed them to act as sovereign nations, but that was a distinction that Ford failed to make during the debate.

When the debate began at 6:30 in the evening of October 6 from the Palace of Fine Arts overlooking San Francisco Bay, it was Carter who came out swinging, putting Ford on the defensive:

> The Ford administration has failed, and I hope tonight that I and Mr. Ford will have a chance to discuss the reasons for those failures. Our country is not strong anymore; we're not respected anymore.... We've lost, in our foreign policy, the character of the American people. We've ignored or excluded the American people and the Congress from participation in the shaping of our foreign policy. It's been one of secrecy and exclusion.... In addition to that, we've become fearful to compete with the Soviet Union on an equal basis. We talk about détente. The Soviet Union knows what they want in détente, and they've been getting it. We have not known what we've wanted, and we've been out-traded in almost every instance.... I might say this in closing, and that is, that as far as foreign policy goes, Mr. Kissinger has been the President of this country. Mr. Ford has shown an absence of leadership and an absence of a grasp of what this country is and what it ought to be.

In his next answer, Carter focused his attack on Kissinger's penchant for secrecy. "In the secrecy that has surrounded our foreign policy in the last few years, the American people and the Congress have been excluded.... Every time Mr. Ford speaks from a position of secrecy — in negotiations and secret treaties that have been pursued and achieved, in supporting dictatorships, in ignoring human rights — we are weak and the rest of the world knows it." In response, Ford touted his successes in the Middle East negotiations, in Portugal, and in supporting majority rule in South Africa. "I believe that our foreign policy must express the highest standards of morality, and the initiatives that we took in southern Africa are the best examples of what this administration is doing and will continue to do in the next 4 years." But the points were lost in the midst of Carter's attacks on secrecy. It was not a fair accusation against Ford because the secret negotiations did not continue under his administration. But it was fair to call Kissinger overly fond of secrecy — he did not understand how secrecy went against America's tradition of open government, and he had set up Carter's attack.

Ford's real problems started when he launched into a defense of the Helsinki Accords. He made the simple point that the accords did not cede control of Eastern Europe to the Soviets. He should have stopped there, but he continued and made the statement that might have cost him the election. "There is no Soviet domination of Eastern Europe and there never will be under a Ford administration." *New York Times* editor Max Frankel seemed stunned, and he gave Ford a chance to clarify his answer. "I'm sorry, could I just follow — did I understand you to say, sir, that the Russians are not using Eastern Europe as their own sphere of influence in occupying most of the countries there and making sure with their troops that it's a Communist zone?" Ford didn't take the hint, and he made things worse with his answer:

> I don't believe, Mr. Frankel, that the Yugoslavians consider themselves dominated by the Soviet Union. I don't believe that the Rumanians consider themselves dominated by the Soviet Union. I don't believe that the Poles consider themselves dominated by the Soviet Union. Each of those countries is independent, autonomous; it has its own territorial integrity. And the United States does not concede that those countries are under the domination of the Soviet Union. As a matter of fact, I visited Poland, Yugoslavia and Rumania to make certain that the people of those countries understood that the President of the United States and the people of the United States are dedicated to their independence, their autonomy and their freedom.

Carter was quick enough to switch from his talking points to take advantage of Ford's gaffe. "I would like to see Mr. Ford convince the Polish-Americans and the Czech-Americans and the Hungarian-Americans in this country that those countries don't live under the domination and supervision of the Soviet Union behind the Iron Curtain."

After that exchange, the closing statements were anticlimactic. Carter continued to hammer his secrecy theme, and he called for a new emphasis on human rights. "We ought to be a beacon for nations who search for peace and who search for freedom, who search for individual liberty, who search for basic human rights. We haven't been lately. We can be once again." In his closing, Ford touted his record. "America is strong, America is free, America is respected. Not a single young American today is fighting or dying on any foreign battlefield. America is at peace and with freedom."[45] But all anyone remembered was his claim that Eastern Europe was not dominated by the Soviet Union.

After the debate, Hamilton Jordan was euphoric. "He did it! Jimmy cleaned his clock! ... And that Eastern Europe thing — I can't believe Ford said it. The issue will haunt Ford in the days to come. You can depend on it!"[46] Carter went on the attack, claiming that Ford had "disgraced our country by claiming Eastern Europe is free of the domination of the Soviet Union."[47]

Ford initially thought he had won the debate, but Teeter's polls showed that viewers thought that Carter won by 11 points, and as the press hammered the Eastern Europe issue, Carter's lead grew to 45 percent.[48] The rest of Ford's team knew he had made a huge mistake — Scowcroft went white when Ford spoke about Eastern Europe.[49] They tried to mitigate the damage that night when Cheney and Scowcroft took questions from the press at the Holiday Inn. Scowcroft tried to explain that Ford was talking about whether the U.S. officially recognized Soviet control over Eastern Europe. "I think what the President was trying to say is that we do not recognize Soviet dominance of Europe." Cheney tried to make a similar point. "The President was focusing on the fact we want separate independent relationships with each of those nations, and that was the purpose of his travels."[50] A year later Ford had a similar explanation when Jules Witcover asked why he made the statement:

Subjectively, the East European countries still consider themselves as a people independent. Governmentally they are not, particularly those countries that are actually occupied in part by Soviet forces. In the momentum to answer the question, I thought of it in the first sense, and not in the latter, and I still believe individual Poles consider themselves independent of the Soviet Union. Now, they recognize as I do that governmentally they're not. It was just a little careless on my part in not being more definitive. But it certainly came out the wrong way.[51]

Ford refused to explain his statement after the debate. On Air Force One the next day Spencer and Cheney went to Ford's compartment and tried to convince him to clarify his comments, but the president was incensed that anyone questioned his anti–Soviet credentials. He had been a strong anti-communist throughout his career, and he even flew to Europe after the invasion of Hungary to greet refugees fleeing Soviet oppression.[52] Cheney sent Hartmann in to try to change his mind. As Hartmann opened the door, Ford yelled, "I know what you're going to say and the answer is 'no!'" Ford showed how hurt he was by the questioning of his anti–Soviet credentials. "I've been fighting for twenty-five years for those captive nations and everyone in the country knows it."[53]

Ford's old friend Bryce Harlow later explained that it was the president's stubbornness that made him refuse to explain his statements. "Once Ford had arrived at a decision he had a startling stubbornness.... This quality got him in trouble in the presidential debates. Once he had made that blunder on the status of Eastern Europe he refused to budge. It took us days and days to get him unscrewed from that post."[54]

Ford's explanation the next day should have clarified the issue:

Last night in the debate, I spoke of America's firm support for the aspiration for independence of the nations of Eastern Europe. The United States has never conceded — and never will concede — their domination by the Soviet Union.... It is our policy to use every peaceful means to assist countries in Eastern Europe in their efforts to become less dependent on the Soviet Union and to establish closer and closer ties with the West and, of course, the United States of America. I am every much aware of the present plight of the Eastern European nations, and as I declared in this year's Captive Nations proclamation, and I quote, "The United States supports the aspirations for freedom, independence and national self-determination of all peoples. We do not accept foreign domination over any nation," period.[55]

But he created more uncertainty the next day when he told a group of San Fernando businessmen that the Polish people "don't believe that they are going to be forever dominated — if they are — by the Soviet Union."[56] The unnecessary inclusion of "if they are" just made things more confusing.

Cheney and Spencer finally convinced Ford to make a clarifying statement the next day, but it didn't really help. In a press conference behind the Glendale City Hall he said, "Perhaps I could have been more precise in what I said concerning Soviet domination of Poland.... President Ford does not believe that the Polish people over the long run — whether they are in Poland or whether they are Polish Americans here — will ever condone domination by any foreign force."[57] It was five days after the debate when Ford finally gave a clear explanation. At the White House he told a group of ethnic leaders that "The original mistake was mine. I did not express myself clearly; I admit it." He admitted that the Soviet military did dominate Eastern Europe, but vowed to never "accept or acquiesce in this Soviet domination."[58]

According to poll results, Ford's gaffe did not cost him much support. In the week after the debate, Caddell again showed Carter's lead falling.[59] The next week the numbers looked worse, and Caddell called the race "a stable but close election."[60] But there was more to the story. As Bailey later explained, the issue may not have cost Ford votes, but it killed the campaign's momentum:

Our own polling data would suggest that really in the end we did not lose any people because of the Eastern European statement. That, by and large, people were shocked by it; dumbfounded by it, and some people close to that issue were offended by it. And a good many people felt that it brought back memories of the Jerry Ford that they had learned to moan and groan over in the summer. But over time, almost all of those people came back to us. What it did cost us was momentum because we were just caught dead in our tracks for a week to ten days. And the progress of closing those gaps with about a half point per day stopped, at the same rate, after that ten day gap where everything just stood still.[61]

Dole made things worse by showing no restraint in the vice presidential debate on October 15. Dole said that George Meany was "probably Senator Mondale's make-up man." He talked about "the Vietnam War ... World War One or World War Two or the Korean War — all Democrat wars, all in this century." In his closing statement, Mondale summed up his opponent's performance. "I think that Senator Dole has richly earned his reputation as a hatchet man tonight."[62]

The third debate was held on October 22 at the College of William and Mary in Williamsburg, Virginia. Neither candidate was in attack mode — they both played it safe. For example, when Ford gave a non-answer to a question about his role in shutting down the Patman investigation of Watergate, Carter didn't take the opportunity to attack. "I don't have a response." In closing, Ford reminded the American people how bad things were when he took office. "I became President at the time that the United States was in a very troubled time. We had inflation of over 12 percent; we were on the brink of the worst recession in the last 40 years; we were still deeply involved in the problems of Vietnam; the American people had lost faith and trust and confidence in the Presidency itself." He was able to list how things were better in almost every aspect of American life:

We have cut inflation by better than half. We have come out of the recession and we are well on the road to real prosperity in this country again. There has been a restoration of faith and confidence and trust in the Presidency because I've been open, candid and forthright.... We are at peace — not a single young American is fighting or dying on any foreign soil tonight. We have peace with freedom.

It was an impressive record, and Ford predicted that Americans would say, "Jerry Ford, you've done a good job, keep on doing it."

Carter praised Ford's decency, but not his record. "Mr. Ford is a good and decent man, but he's been in office now more than 800 days, approaching almost as long as John Kennedy was in office. I would like to ask the American people what has been accomplished." He declared that he would restore America's greatness:

I believe in the greatness of our country, and I believe the American people are ready for a change in Washington. We have been drifting too long. We have been dormant too long. We have been discouraged too long.... With inspiration and hard work we can achieve great things and let the world know — that's very important — but more importantly, let the people in our own country realize — that we still live in the greatest Nation on earth.[63]

The polls showed that the debate was a tie, but Ford pulled within range of Carter in the election.[64]

With the final debate over, the Ford campaign unleashed the money it had been holding to the end, buying 30-minute TV slots on the days Ford was visiting key states. The program began with edited tape of Ford's campaign appearances earlier in the day, followed by interviews of the candidate by baseball announcer Joe Garagiola. The campaign dubbed it "The Jerry and Joe Show." Garagiola proved to be a dynamic and enthusiastic host, and the shows were a hit, with close to a million viewers in each of the six battleground states.[65] Carter had already spent most of his advertising money, but he had enough left to run new ads. For the final push, Rafshoon turned to New York advertiser Tony Schwartz, who produced ads showing Carter in a suit and tie, looking right into the camera, speaking of his concerns for the problems faced by America.[66]

In the final two weeks both candidates crisscrossed the country, concentrating on the eight key states they identified before the election, plus a few states that were unexpectedly close. Ford made stops in nine states where Teeter's polls showed that he had a chance: Virginia, North Carolina, South Carolina, Washington, Oregon, Indiana, Kentucky, Wisconsin, and Missouri. Carter and Mondale made last-minute stops in Flint, Michigan, hoping to score a surprise victory in his opponent's home state, where Ford's lead was 1 percent.[67] Ford had a thee-point lead in California, so he met with Reagan and asked him to make a final push on his behalf, but the candidate was disappointed in the results. "His speech to the GOP dinner that night was disappointing. Once again he stressed the virtues of the platform, yet his comments about me came as an afterthought and were noticeably lukewarm. Worse, during the rest of the campaign he refused to work directly for my election."[68]

<hr />

Each candidate had last-minute problems, but Ford's was more serious than Carter's. During his final stretch, Carter hammered Ford's record on the economy, and his criticism hit home when the economy stalled just before the election. Ford knew the downturn was a possibility — Greenspan and others had warned him of a "pause" in the recovery — but the pause came at the worst possible time. On October 28 the Commerce Department issued its leading economic indicators, which had declined for two months in a row. Unemployment had increased from 7.3 percent in May to 7.9 percent.[69]

Carter's last-minute crisis concerned his home-town church. On the Sunday before the election the Reverend Clennon King and three other African Americans asked to attend services at the Plains Baptist Church, but the church deacons refused, citing a rule barring "all niggers and civil rights agitators." The Plains minister, the Reverend Bruce Edwards, told the press that in no way was Carter responsible for the actions of the deacons. In fact, the candidate had "worked to rescind that policy."[70] Rosalynn Carter told speechwriter Patrick Anderson that they had paid a dear price for her husband's attempts to integrate the church. "It was tough. People wouldn't speak to us in church. But we were willing to take the consequences. Here's the kind of thing that happened. We went on a vacation trip to Mexico in 1965. A rumor started that we were at an integration camp in Alabama. It was right in the peanut season — that's how we make our money. But when we came home we didn't have any customers."[71]

Carter called his friend Andrew Young for advice. Young, one of the only African Americans in the House, told him to speak out but not to turn his back on his church. Carter issued a statement condemning the deacons' decision and pointing out that he had voted against the rule ten years before. In a press conference the next morning Carter said, "I can't resign from the human race because there's discrimination ... and I don't intend to resign from my own church because there's discrimination." He promised to "stay with the church to try to change the attitude which I abhor."[72]

On election day the candidates voted in their home towns, then Ford returned to Washington and Carter went to his headquarters in Atlanta. As they sat down to watch the returns, both candidates knew it would be close — the final Gallup poll showed Ford in the lead by 47 to 46 percent, while the Harris poll had Carter ahead by 1 percent.[73]

As they waited for the results, each candidate could look back on a remarkably clean campaign. Both candidates were willing to attack each others positions, but they both passed up opportunities for personal attacks. Before the final debate Caddell wanted to criticize the pardon, calling it "our strongest option," but Carter refused. "If we can win without it, I don't want to do it. It will spill blood all over the place. It will rip our country apart."[74] Ford refused to raise issues about the finances of the Carter peanut business. His campaign had employed Martin Price, a freelance investigative reporter, but when Baker learned that Price was looking into the finances of Carter's peanut business, he booted him off the campaign. Price was furious. "This election was given away! I mean those Ford people wouldn't use the stuff I got. It was the cleanest campaign I'd ever seen. It was a debacle!"[75]

—◦◦◦—

In Washington, Ford watched the returns from the White House with his family, the Doles, and other friends and supporters. In Atlanta, Carter watched the returns from the Omni International Hotel. He sat in his room watching three TVs, each tuned to a different network. In addition to his family, he was joined by Kirbo, Jordan, Powell, Caddell, and Rafshoon.[76]

There were no big surprises early in the evening; the networks declared Carter the winner in six southern states, along with Massachusetts and Rhode Island. They gave Ford Indiana, Kansas, Nebraska, and Connecticut. Later in the evening Ford picked up the farming and mountain states as expected, along with New Hampshire and Vermont. Still to come were all eight of the big battleground states: New York, New Jersey, Pennsylvania, Ohio, Illinois, Michigan, California, and Texas. Caddell told Carter that he would loose New Jersey, and New York looked shaky. Ford got the same news about New Jersey. His aides thought that Ohio was too close to call, but New York was promising.[77]

Ford received his first bad news at 1:20 when NBC called New York for Carter — a late surge from New York City put him over the top. Then NBC declared Carter the winner in Texas. Ford's only consolation was that the network colored North Dakota blue, indicating a Republican win. It was expected, but Ford was elated, and he yelled, "Go Blue!"[78] After losing Texas and New York, Ford needed to win all but one of Pennsylvania, Ohio, Illinois, Michigan, and California. But a few minutes later the networks gave Pennsylvania to Carter, although Ford took his home state of Michigan. Ford's only remaining hope was to sweep Ohio, Illinois, and California.

At three in the morning Cheney and Teeter asked Ford to talk in private, and they went to a nearby small room, joined by the president's old friend Jacob Javits. Teeter told Ford that he was unlikely to win, but it was still possible. Wisconsin could be a surprise, even though the networks had given the state to Carter, and Ohio and Mississippi were still up in the air. At 3:30 Ford was tired and told the crowd that he was going to bed. Nessen had just walked in with a UPI bulletin declaring Carter the winner, but he decided not to show it to the president. The other networks quickly followed, but Ford did not know that he had lost when he went to bed.[79]

The state that put Carter over the top was Mississippi, and Governor Cliff Finch called Carter's headquarters with good news. After the networks declared him the winner in the state, Carter called Finch back and said, "Mississippi just put me over. I love every one of you."[80] Carter went downstairs and gave a short speech to the assembled crowd of supporters. He congratulated Ford, calling him "a good, a decent man," and he finished with a typical Carter touch. "I love everybody here. It's been a good campaign. It's going to be a good Administration."[81]

When Ford woke up just after 9 it was Kennerly who gave him the bad news. "I'm afraid we've had it. Ohio is still out, but even if you win its 25 votes there's no state that's going to give you the four more you need to hit 270."[82] At ten, Cheney, Spencer, Marsh, and Teeter met with the president in the Oval Office. They explained that a few of his aides wanted him to challenge the results in Ohio and Wisconsin, but most of them saw that they won more close states than they lost, so a challenge was not really an option. Ford agreed with the majority. "The election is over. We lost."[83] When Ford called Carter to concede, they were both spent from the campaign, so the conversation was short. Just after noon Ford and his family went to the press room. He had a short prepared statement, but he was too exhausted to read it. On his behalf, Betty read his statement of support of the newly-elected president. "I believe that we must now put the divisions of the campaign behind us and unite the country once again in the common pursuit of peace and prosperity."[84]

Carter won by 2 percent of the vote, 50.1 to 48.0 percent. In the electoral college, the result was the closest since 1916. Carter won 297 votes to Ford's 241. Of the eight battleground states, Ford won four — New Jersey, Michigan, Illinois, and California — but he needed five.

———◦◦◦◦———

Ford's people told him early on that he would have to run a mistake-free campaign to win, and he nearly did. But it wasn't enough because, as Bailey later explained, Carter did too. "He didn't make any mistakes, since September, he didn't make any."[85] Ford was hurt by not moving to the center early enough. He won almost 90 percent of Republican voters, but not enough Democrats and independents. Teeter's polls showed that Ford's resurgence coincided with the changing perception of where he stood ideologically. Toward the end of the campaign his poll ratings rose as the voters started viewing him as a centrist candidate, but it was too late.[86] A dramatic accomplishment also may have done the trick. During the general election the Carter campaign was terrified that Ford would make a surprise announcement of a SALT II agreement.[87]

Carter's victory was an anomaly — a temporary interruption of the rise of the Republican Party. The party lost the presidency, but Democrats did not make significant gains in Congress. The Senate was exactly the same, with 62 Democrats and 38 Republicans, while the Democrats gained one seat in the House, and they picked up only one governor's mansion, giving them a 37 to 12 advantage. Still, many people at the time thought that Ford's loss was a sign that the Republicans were sliding into oblivion. No writer was less perceptive than Robert Novak, who wrote: "The loss of the Presidency was accompanied by continued Republican atrophy at all levels. The party is dying throughout the South.... The fiasco of 1976 was not only the product of Mr. Ford's undeniable shortcomings as a presidential candidate but a continuation of the long descent of the Republican Party into irrelevance, defeat, and perhaps eventual disappearance."[88] In reality, the Republican Party had been on the rise since the mid-'60s, and Carter's win was just a blip caused by Watergate. The Democrats would not win another presidential election for sixteen more years, and they would continue to lose seats in Congress through the end of the century.

———◦◦◦◦———

The final six weeks of Ford's presidency were non-eventful, spent mostly preparing Carter and his people. The most significant event was Ford's final state of the union address on January 12, 1977. He spoke with pride when he reversed his blunt opening of the 1975 state of the union speech. "The state of the Union is good."[89] He was right — the country was in better shape than when he inherited it. The recession was over, despite the pause in the economic recovery that may have cost him the election. Inflation had not been tamed for good, but the inflation rate was less than half of what it was when he took office.

The country was at peace, and Ford could look back on a successful foreign policy. He had laid the groundwork for a new arms control agreement with the Soviets and a major peace agreement in the Middle East. He had signed the Helsinki Accords, reducing tensions in Europe and giving the dissidents in the Warsaw Pact countries new ammunition with which to attack the communist regimes. He had allowed Portugal to peacefully transition to democracy. It was an accomplishment by inaction, but it was an example of the difference between Ford and his immediate predecessors, who had been driven by obsessions into rash action. As William Rogers explains, Ford's even temper prevented him from obsessing about enemies, and he avoided making major mistakes as a result. "He was not ... obsessed the way LBJ was with certain ghosts and fears that had no real basis in the world."[90] He wasn't obsessed with Cuba, like Eisenhower, Kennedy, and Nixon, and he wasn't obsessed with Vietnam like Johnson. He made mistakes, but he avoided major blunders and embarrassments.

More than anything, he helped the country past the divisive domestic conflicts of the '60s and early '70s. When Vietnam and Cambodia fell without further American involvement, the country put its fights over the war in the past. The pardon cost Ford dearly, but it allowed the country to get beyond Watergate. Ford's integrity and honesty gave the American people a reason to believe in their government again, and he brought into the administration many people who shared his dedication to good government — his administration might be the only one in modern history that had no ethical scandals involving top officials. In his last days in office Ford invited congressional leaders to the White House, and his political opponents recognized his accomplishments. Tip O'Neill gave a moving speech about how much he admired Ford's work, including his importance as the man who restored dignity to the White House after Watergate.[91]

Jimmy Carter recognized it too, and he acknowledged Ford's accomplishment during the inauguration. After escorting his successor to the inaugural in the presidential limousine, Ford sat in the front row behind Carter in the 20-degree cold. After taking the oath of office, Carter started his address with a tribute to Ford. "For myself and for our nation I want to thank my predecessor for all he has done to heal our land." He turned around, shook Ford's hand, and said quietly, "God bless you, sir. I'm proud of you." Ford's old friend Hubert Humphrey stood up and led a long ovation as Ford waved to the crowd.[92]

Chapter Notes

Chapter 1

1. "The Perils of Spiro," *The Washington Post*, September 25, 1968, A20.

2. "I never aspired to be president. My political ambition was to be Speaker of the House." Transcript of Live Chat with Gerald Ford, scholastic.com, available at *http://content.scholastic.com/browse/article.jsp?id=4655*.

3. Nixon, *RN*, 491.

4. Gergen, *Eyewitness*, 100 and 108.

5. Statement of George H. W. Bush on the death of Gerald Ford, December 26, 2006.

6. Statement of James Earl Carter on the death of Gerald Ford, December 26, 2006.

7. Griffiths, "Introduction," xiii–xiv.

8. Interview of Brent Scowcroft, by the author, October 27, 2006.

9. Reeves, *A Ford*, 28.

10. Interview of Honorable Barber Conable, February 1, 1985, Syers Interview Collection, Box 1, 4.

11. "A Man for this Season," *Time Magazine*, August 12, 1974; Witcover, *Marathon*, 37.

12. TerHorst, *Gerald Ford*, 315.

13. Cannon, *Time and Chance*, 412.

14. Safire, *Before the Fall*, 665.

15. For percentages of Americans who tuned in to the hearings, *see* Ronald Garay, "Watergate," www.museum.tv/archives/etv/W/htmlW/watergate/watergate.htm.

16. Testimony by John D. Ehrlichman, July 24, 1973, Ervin Committee Transcript, 534.

17. Testimony by Gordon C. Strachan, July 20, 1973, Ervin Committee Transcript, 272.

18. Testimony by Jeb Stuart Magruder, June 14, 1973, Ervin Committee Transcript, 254.

19. Testimony of John W. Dean III, June 25, 1973, and testimony by L. Patrick Gray III, August 3, 1973, Ervin Committee Transcript, 272–76 and 625–25.

20. Testimony by Richard M. Helms and testimony by General Vernon A. Walters, August 2, 1973, Ervin Committee Transcript, 603 and 611.

21. Testimony by Herbert W. Kalmbach, July 16, 1973, testimony by James W. McCord Jr., May 21, 1973, testimony by Anthony T. Ulasewicz, July 18, 1973, testimony by Frederick C. LaRue, July 18, 1973, and testimony of Maurice H. Stans, June 12, 1973, Ervin Committee Transcript, 146, 241, 276, 283–84, 446–49, 465, and 471–75.

22. Testimony by Jeb Stuart Magruder, June 14, 1973, Ervin Committee Transcript, 254–56.

23. Testimony of James W. McCord Jr., May 21, 1973, Ervin Committee Transcript, 152 and 164; testimony of John J. Caulfield, May 22, 1973, Ervin Committee Transcript, 179 and 182.

24. Testimony of John W. Dean III, June 25, 1973, Ervin Committee Transcript, 274–288.

25. Testimony of John W. Dean III, June 25, 1973, Ervin Committee Transcript, 290.

26. Figures are from Harris and Gallup Polls. Drossman and Knappman, *Watergate and the White House*, Volume 2, 36–38 and 43; Amster, "Chronology," 96 and 124.

27. Testimony by Alexander Butterfield, July 16, 1973, Ervin Committee Transcript, 436–39; Amster, "Chronology of Watergate Related Events," 121.

28. Wills, *Nixon Agonistes*, 384.

29. Richard Homan "Agnew: His History on Civil Rights," *The Washington Post*, August 19, 1968, A1.

30. Safire, *Before the Fall*, 304; PBS Online Newshour, *Remembering Agnew*, September 18, 1996, transcript available at www.pbs.org/newshour/bb/remember/agnew_9-18.html.

31. Albert, *Little Giant*, 324.

32. "Agnew Hit for Stand on Slums," *The Washington Post*, October 20, 1968, A8; Vice President Spiro Agnew, Speech, Houston, Texas, May 22, 1970; Vice President Spiro Agnew, Speech, Springfield, Illinois, September 10, 1970.

33. The late edition of the *Wall Street Journal* broke the story on August 6, and other papers picked up the story the next morning.

34. Nixon, *RN*, 912; Haig, *Inner Circles*, 352.

35. Bill Sievert, "Spiro Agnew: He Sure Had a Way with Words," *Rolling Stone*, November 22, 1973.

36. In announcing Richardson's appointment, Nixon called him "a man of unimpeachable integrity and rigorously high principle." President Richard M. Nixon, "Address to the Nation About the Watergate Investigations," April 30, 1973. Richardson told Haig that "the prosecution's case was absolutely solid and that if it came to trial, Agnew would almost certainly be convicted and would probably be sentenced to a prison term and a large fine." Haig, *Inner Circles*, 362.

37. Haig, *Inner Circles*, 353.

38. Haig, *Inner Circles*, 364.

39. Agnew, *Go Quietly*, 162.

40. As early as 1833, Joseph Story described the principle as established law with regard to the president. "The President cannot, therefore, be liable to arrest, imprisonment or detention, while he is in the discharge of the duties of his office." Joseph Story, *Commentaries on the Constitution of the United States*, 1833, Volume 3, 418–19.

41. Albert, *Little Giant*, 359.

42. Farrell, *Tip O'Neill*, 350.

43. The solicitor general pointed out that Aaron Burr had been indicted twice while he was Thomas Jefferson's vice president. "Memorandum of the United States Concerning the Vice President's Claim of Constitutional Immunity," *In re Proceedings of the Grand Jury Impaneled December 5, 1972, Application of Spiro T. Agnew, Vice President of the United States*, October 5, 1973 (D. Md.).

44. Cohen and Witcover, *A Heartbeat Away*, 241–42 and 302–305.

45. Agnew, *Go Quietly*, 13.

46. Agnew, *Go Quietly*, 17; Cohen and Witcover, *A Heartbeat Away*, 343–48.

47. Hatfield, *Vice Presidents of the United States*, 493–500.

48. Kissinger, *Years of Renewal*, 27.

49. Connally was indicted on July 29, 1974, for allegedly offering milk producers favorable decisions on milk support prices in return for contributions to Nixon's campaign, but he was later acquitted of the charges. Amster, "Events," 271; Woodward and Bernstein, *The Final Days*, 301.

50. Cannon, *Time and Chance*, 197.

51. "A Good Lineman for the Quarterback," *Time Magazine*, October 22, 1973.

52. John Herbers, "G.O.P. Gives Ideas," *New York Times*, October 12, 1973, 89.

53. Cannon, *Time and Chance*, 197. In another interview, Laird said, "We told Nixon that Connally wouldn't do." Interview of Melvin R. Laird, June 6, 1985, Syers Interview Collection, Box 1, 3.

54. Interview of Melvin Laird, by the author, via telephone, August 29, 2007.

55. Ford, *Time to Heal*, 69 and 102–103.

56. Nixon, *RN*, 925; Albert, *Little Giant*, 361.

57. Farrell, *Tip O'Neill*, 352.

58. Alan J. Borsuk, "Gerald R. Ford: 1913–2006; Best Friends on the Path to Power," *Milwaukee Journal Sentinel*, December 28, 2006; Larry Beundorf, "Gerald Ford's Former Security Agent Says Ford Was Devoted Husband, Father," *USA Today*, December 28, 2006.

59. Haig, *Inner Circles*, 368; Nixon, *RN*, 925–26.

60. Nixon, *RN*, 926.

61. *Congressional Quarterly 1973 Almanac*, Volume XXIX, 1062.

62. Cannon, *Time and Chance*, 230.

63. Ford, *Time to Heal*, 66; *Congressional Quarterly 1973 Almanac*, 1070.

64. Cannon, *Time and Chance*, 419.

65. Ford, *Time to Heal*, 104. Ford and Nixon remember this meeting differently. In his memoirs, Nixon states that he did not tell Ford he was his choice at the meeting. Nixon, *RN*, 926. This version of the meeting is based upon Ford's memoirs. Ford's recollections are more detailed than Nixon's, which is to be expected; the meeting was one of the most critical events of Ford's life, while it was one of many important events Nixon was involved in during this period.

66. Once again, recollections differ. Nixon recalls that he had Haig call Ford. Nixon, *RN*, 927. Ford recalls that Haig set up the call and Nixon delivered the news. Ford, *Time to Heal*, 106. Hartmann, who probably talked to Ford the next day, asserts that Nixon and Haig were both on the line at the start of the call and that Nixon said, "General Haig has some good news to tell you," and left the call. Hartmann, *Palace Politics*, 26.

67. President Richard M. Nixon, "Remarks Announcing Intention to Nominate Gerald R. Ford to Be Vice President," October 12, 1973; Ford, *Time to Heal*, 106–107; terHorst, *Gerald Ford*, 142.

68. Anthony Lewis, "It Will Not Down," *New York Times*, October 15, 1973, 37; Theodore H. White, *Breach of Faith*, 258.

69. "A Good Lineman for the Quarterback," *Time Magazine*, October 22, 1973; Reeves, *A Ford, Not a Lincoln*, 40; Hartmann, *Palace Politics*, 27; Richard L. Madden, "Choice Is Praised by Both Parties," *New York Times*, October 13, 1973, 1; "Congratulations to Ford Offered by Rockefeller," *New York Times*, October 13, 1973, 18; Greene, *The Presidency of Gerald R. Ford*, 30.

70. Cannon, *Time and Chance*, 219.

71. Bella S. Abzug, *New York Times*, Op-Ed, October 18, 1973.

72. Farrell, *Tip O'Neill*, 354.

73. Albert, *Little Giant*, 361.

74. Interview of Philip Allen Lacovara, Legends in the Law.

75. Cannon, *Time and Chance*, 223. The details of the Saturday Night Massacre are from: Interview of Melvin Laird, by the author, August 29, 2007; Carroll Kilpatrick, "Nixon Forces Firing of Cox; Richardson, Ruckelshaus Quit: President Abolishes Prosecutor's Office; FBI Seals Records," *Washington Post*, October 21, 1973, Page A01; "A Conversation with Robert H. Bork," Legends in the Law.

76. Bart Barnes, "Archibald Cox, 1912–2004: Watergate Prosecutor Faced Down the President," *Washington Post*, May 30, 2004, A01; Drossman and Knappman, *Watergate and the White House*, Volume 2, 103 and 127.

77. "A Conversation with Robert H. Bork," Legends in the Law.

78. Cannon, *Time and Chance*, 226–27.

79. Hartmann, *Palace Politics*, 219; Hatfield, *Vice Presidents of the United States*, 493–500.

80. Farrell, *Tip O'Neill*, 358.

81. Letter from IRS Commissioner Donald C. Alexander to the Honorable Wilber D. Mills, November 13, 1973, Ford Library, Folder "Ford, Gerald R.— Vice Presidential Confirmation, General (1)," Benton Becker Files, Box 1. Other allegations were found to have no basis, including an allegation that Ford improperly profited from a ghost-written book and article regarding the Warren Commission, and an allegation that he had sent contributors to the Republican congressional committee and then received similar contributions from the committee. Jack Anderson printed several allegations by a lobbyist named Robert Winter-Berger, including an allegation that Winter-Berger loaned Ford $15,000 in cash that was never repaid. Jack Anderson and Les Whitten, 1973, "Ford: Charges, Denials," United Feature Syndicate. The Senate Rules Committee did not consider Winter-Berger a credible witness. Senate Confirmation Report, 47–48. Anderson later apologized to Ford aide Robert Hartmann for being taken in by Winter-Berger. Hartmann, *Palace Politics*, 54.

82. Senate Confirmation Hearings, 13–143.

83. Senate Confirmation Hearings, 128–35. There is considerable debate about whether Ford was telling the truth (or, more charitably, whether his recollection was accurate) when he testified that he was not working at the behest of the White House. The White House transcripts later showed that Nixon told Dean to instruct Ford to use his influence to end the Patman hearings. Gold, *White House Transcripts*, Appendix 1, "Meeting: The President, Haldeman and Dean, Oval Office, September 15, 1972 (5:27–6:17 P.M.)," 57–68. Hartmann claims that Ford had already met with the committee Republicans before Dean contacted him and told him to intervene. Hartmann, *Palace Politics*, 74. Colson later claimed that he had talked to Ford about shutting down the investigation. Hersh, "The Pardon." Professor Greene reports that a document Ford used to prepare for the meeting had a handwritten note from Ford asking, "Is this what they want?" Greene, *Presidency of Gerald R. Ford*, 21.

84. *Congressional Record*, Volume 119, Part 29, 38213–38225.

85. House Confirmation Hearings, 8–9.

86. House Confirmation Hearings, 618.

87. Cannon, *Time and Chance*, 256. Cannon states that Rodino voted against Ford in committee, but the record shows that he did not vote to oppose the nomination until the full vote of the House. *Congressional Quarterly 1973 Almanac*, 1068. In announcing his vote, Rodino gave a different reason for his vote. "During the weeks that I have spent studying Jerry's public and private life, I have only grown to respect his character and integrity more.... I vote not against Mr. Ford's worth as a man of great integrity, but in dissent with the present administration's indifference to the plight of so many Americans." *Congressional Record*, Volume 119, Part 30, 39807–39899.

88. *Congressional Record*, Volume 119, Part 30, 39807–39899.

89. "Remarks of Gerald R. Ford After Taking the Oath of Office as Vice President," December 6, 1973.

90. "Ford for Vice President," *New York Times*, October 13, 1973, 34; "The Choice of Mr. Ford," *The Washington Post*, October 14, 1973, C6; "Squandered Opportunity," *Wall Street Journal*, October 15, 1973, 14.

91. "Vice President Ford," *Wall Street Journal*, December 7, 1973, 12.

92. William Greider, "Integrity and Sincerity," *The Washington Post*, December 7, 1973, A1.

Chapter 2

1. Gergen, *Eyewitness,* 73; Interview of Melvin Laird, by the author, August 14, 2007.

2. Reeves, *A Ford, Not a Lincoln,* 47.

3. Interview of Michael Raoul-Duval, by Stephen J. Wayne, February 9, 1977, Hyde and Wayne Interview Collection, Box 1, Folder "Raoul-Duval — Michael, Interview 2/9/77," 3.

4. Haig, *Inner Circles,* 511.

5. Greene, *Presidency of Gerald R. Ford,* 13.

6. Reeves, *A Ford, Not a Lincoln,* 44. In his memoirs, Ford described his mindset at the time. "At the time, I still believed that Nixon was innocent." Ford, *Time to Heal,* 109.

7. Hartmann, *Palace Politics,* 105 and 118.

8. *Congressional Quarterly 1973 Almanac,* 1063.

9. Hartmann, *Palace Politics,* 104.

10. Philip Shabecoff, "Ford Says 'Extreme' Wing Extends Watergate Ordeal," *New York Times,* January 16, 1974, 113.

11. Gold, *White House Transcripts,* Appendix 1: "Meeting: The President, Haldeman and Dean, Oval Office, September 15, 1972 (5:27–6:17 P.M.)," 57–68; Appendix 5: Telephone Conversation: The President and Dean, March 20, 1973 (7:29–7:43 P.M.), 126–31; Appendix 6: Meeting: The President, Dean and Haldeman, Oval Office, March 21, 1973 (10:12–11:55 A.M.), 132–80; and Appendix 14: Meeting: The President, Haldeman and Ehrlichman, EOB Office, April 14, 1973 (8:55–11:31 A.M.), 283–340. For Nixon's role editing the transcripts, see Woodward and Bernstein, *The Final Days,* 125.

12. Gold, *White House Transcripts,* Appendix 6: Meeting: The President, Dean and Haldeman, Oval Office, March 21, 1973 (10:12–11:55 A.M.), 132–80.

13. A Harris poll released on May 11 showed 49 percent in favor of Nixon's impeachment and removal from office, while a May 26 Gallup poll showed that 48 percent were in favor of removing Nixon from office (37 percent said no). Drossman and Knappman, *Watergate and the White House,* Volume 3, 141.

14. *Chicago Tribune,* May 9, 1974.

15. "Ford Says Documents Prove Nixon Innocent," *New York Times,* May 1, 1974, 39.

16. Apple, "Introduction," 99.

17. Apple, "A Tragedy in Three Acts," 30; Drossman and Knappman, *Watergate and the White House,* Volume 2–3, 26–35, 109, 116 and 119, and Volume 3, 41–42, 78, 129–33 and 187–96. According to Haldeman, Nixon later admitted to him that Rebozo had at least $200,000 in the account. Haldeman, *Ends of Power,* 20–21.

18. Testimony of John W. Dean III, June 26, 1973, Ervin Committee Transcript, 307.

19. Judiciary Committee Final Report, 209 and 592.

20. Gold, *White House Transcripts,* Appendix 1, "Meeting: The President, Haldeman and Dean, Oval Office, September 15, 1972 (5:27–6: 17 P.M.)," 57–68.

21. Judiciary Committee Final Report, 206–207 and 593–600.

22. Drossman and Knappman, *Watergate and the White House,* Volume 2, 70–71 and 91.

23. Judiciary Committee Final Report, 51–52 and 214–25.

24. Judiciary Committee Final Report, 43, 53, and 184–87.

25. Amster, "Events Leading to the Resignation of Richard M. Nixon," 93, 100–102, and 247; Drossman and Knappman, *Watergate and the White House,* Volume 2, 94.

26. Marjorie Hunter, "Ford Says Nixon Has Been Cleared," *New York Times,* July 13, 1974, 10.

27. Marjorie Hunter, "Ford Says Tapes Lead to 'Honest Differences,'" *New York Times,* July 19, 1974, 19.

28. Judiciary Committee "Comparison of White House and Judiciary Committee Transcripts."

29. Judiciary Committee "Comparison of White House and Judiciary Committee Transcripts," 48.

30. Interview of Richard Nixon, by Frank Gannon, June 10, 1983, Brown Media Archives, 1050; Haig, *Inner Circles,* 470. For the details of the meeting, see Farrell, *Tip O'Neill,* 375–76; Woodward and Bernstein, *Final Days,* 256.

31. White, *Breach of Faith,* 303.

32. Drossman and Knappman, *Watergate and the White House,* Volume 3, 209.

33. Haig, *Inner Circles,* 474.

34. Richard Lyons and William Chapman, "Judiciary Committee Approves Article to Impeach President Nixon, 27 to 11: 6 Republicans Join Democrats to Pass Obstruction Charge," *Washington Post,* July 28, 1974, A01.

35. Woodward and Bernstein, *The Final Days,* 293–94; Theodore H. White, *Breach of Faith,* 321.

36. Richard Lyons and William Chapman, "Judiciary Committee Approves Article to Impeach President Nixon, 27 to 11: 6 Republicans Join Democrats to Pass Obstruction Charge," *Washington Post,* July 28, 1974, A01.

37. Richard Lyons and William Chapman, "Judiciary Committee Approves Article to Impeach President Nixon, 27 to 11: 6 Republicans Join Democrats to Pass Obstruction Charge," *Washington Post,* July 28, 1974, A01; Drossman and Knappman, *Watergate and the White House,* Volume 3, 231.

38. Graham, *Personal History,* 466–67; Laurence Stern and Haynes Johnson, "3 Top Nixon Aides, Kleindienst Out; President Accepts Full Responsibility; Richardson Will Conduct New Probe," *Washington Post,* May 1, 1973, A01; Woodward and Bernstein, *The Final Days,* 317.

39. Amster, "Events Leading to the Resignation of Richard M. Nixon," 93, 100, 102 and 247; Drossman and Knappman, *Watergate and the White House,* Volume 2, 34–35, and Volume 3, 41–42, 78, 94, 129, 188, 191, and 196; Apple, "A Tragedy in Three Acts," 33; Haig, *Inner Circles,* 441; Anson, *Exile,* 108–109; Woodward and Bernstein, *The Final Days,* 23–24.

40. President Richard M. Nixon, "Statement About the Watergate Investigations," August 15, 1973; Statement of Evidence on Article I, Judiciary Committee Final Report, 237; Judiciary Committee Final Report, 628.

41. President Richard M. Nixon, "Statements About the Watergate Investigations," May 22, 1973.

42. President Richard M. Nixon, News Conference, March 6, 1974.

43. President Richard M. Nixon, "Statements About the Watergate Investigations," May 22, 1973.

44. President Richard M. Nixon, "Statements About the Watergate Investigations," May 22, 1973.

45. *U.S. v. Nixon,* 418 U.S. 683 (1974).

46. Woodward and Bernstein, *The Final Days,* 263; Theodore H. White, *Breach of Faith,* 9; "Introduction," R. W. Apple, Jr., Judiciary Committee Final Report, xviii.

47. Transcript of Meeting between the President and H. R. Haldeman in the Oval Office, June 23, 1972, 10:04 to 11:39 A.M.

48. Gergen, *Eyewitness,* 74.

49. Summers, *Arrogance of Power,* 457.

50. Nixon, *RN,* 1057; Haig, *Inner Circles,* 480; Interview of Richard Nixon, by Frank Gannon, June 10, 1983, Brown Media Archives, 1050.

51. According to Haig, Buzhardt had prepared the list of alternatives without being asked. Haig, *Inner Circles,* 481. For other descriptions of the meeting, see Woodward, *Shadow,* 5; Woodward and Bernstein, *Final Days,* 325.

52. Walter Pincus, "Origin of Pardon Idea in Question," *Washington Post,* February 1, 1976, p. 2; Haig, *Inner Circles,* 481.

53. Interview of Melvin Laird, by Andrew Downer Crain, August 14, 2007.

54. Haig, *Inner Circles,* 480.

55. Ford, *Time to Heal,* 2; Haig, *Inner Circles,* 480.

56. Ford, *Time to Heal,* 3; Hartmann, *Palace Politics,* 128.

57. Ford, *Time to Heal,* 3–4; Haig, *Inner Circles,* 482–83.

58. Ford, *Time to Heal,* 6; Hartmann, *Palace Politics,* 131.

59. Haig described his meeting with Nixon in a November 6, 1997, interview with Bob Woodward. Bob Woodward, *Shadow,* 7 and notes on 518–19. As noted by Woodward, in his memoirs Haig said that he never discussed the six options with Nixon. Haig, *Inner Circles,* 481.

60. Kissinger, *Years of Renewal,* 19.

61. Haig, *Inner Circles,* 478.

62. Nixon, *RN*, 1058.

63. Hartmann, *Palace Politics*, 133.

64. Ford, *Time to Heal*, 9; Cannon, *Time and Chance*, 299.

65. Hartmann, *Palace Politics*, 135.

66. Ford, *Time to Heal*, 9–10; Haig, *Inner Circles*, 485. Hartmann recalls that when he described the call the next day, Ford said that he was the one who placed the call to Haig. Hartmann recalls that Ford was not willing to explain the details of the call, but that Ford explained that he and Haig had not discussed the issue of pardons. Hartmann, *Palace Politics*, 135. Robert Woodward indicates that both Haig and Hartmann told him that Ford called Haig, but the rest of his description of the call is the same as Ford's. Woodward, *Shadow*, 7 and notes 518–19.

67. Haig described his call with Buzhardt in interviews with Robert Woodward on November 6, 1997, and February 5, 1998. Bob Woodward, *Shadow*, 518–19.

68. Interview of Richard Nixon, by Frank Gannon, June 10, 1983, Brown Media Archives.

69. Ford, *Time to Heal*, 11.

70. Interview of Richard B. Cheney, by Stephen Wayne, February 8, 1977, Hyde and Wayne Interview Collection, Box 1, Folder "Cheney, Richard — Interview, 2/8/77," 15; Cannon, *Time and Chance*, 268.

71. Scott Shane, "For Ford, Pardon Decision Was Always Clear-Cut," *New York Times*, December 29, 2006.

72. Hartmann, *Palace Politics*, 136.

73. William Safire, "Who's What Around the White House," *New York Times*, November 11, 1973, 306.

74. Hartmann, *Palace Politics*, 136–37.

75. Ford, *Time to Heal*, 13; Haig, *Inner Circles*, 485; Hartmann, *Palace Politics*, 137.

76. Hartmann has written that "there was no deal." Hartmann, *Palace Politics*, 270. Later, Ford told Robert Woodward that Haig had asked for a deal, but that Ford had rejected it in his phone call to Haig. "It was a deal, but it never became a deal because I never accepted." Woodward, *Shadow*, 34–35.

77. Woodward and Bernstein, *Final Days*, 333–34; Greene, *Presidency of Gerald R. Ford*, 14.

78. Nixon, *RN*, 1061; Interview of Richard Nixon, by Frank Gannon, June 10, 1983, Brown Media Archives; Haig, *Inner Circles*, 487.

79. Hartmann, *Palace Politics*, 139–43.

80. Mollenhoff, *The Man Who Pardoned Nixon*, 112.

81. Gergen, *Eyewitness*, 74.

82. White, *Breach of Faith*, 21.

83. Bush, *All the Best*, 165, 167 and 186.

84. Drossman and Knappman, *Watergate and the White House*, Volume 3, 231; Haig, *Inner Circles*, 494.

85. Drossman and Knappman, *Watergate and the White House*, Volume 3, 149 and 230; Haig, *Inner Circles*, 484; White, *Breach of Faith*, 15.

86. Minority Views of Messrs. Hutchinson, Smith, Sandman, Wiggins, Dennis, Mayne, Lott, Moorhead, Maraziti and Latta, Judiciary Committee Final Report, 479–81.

87. Woodward and Bernstein, *Final Days*, 333.

88. White, *Breach of Faith*, 21.

89. Woodward and Bernstein, *Final Days*, 389.

90. Drossman and Knappman, *Watergate and the White House*, Volume 3, 231.

91. Ford, *Time to Heal*, 16; Hartmann, *Palace Politics*, 145.

92. Nixon, *RN*, 1065–66; Hartmann, *Palace Politics*, 148–49; White, *Breach of Faith*, 23–27.

93. "The Unmaking of a President," *Time Magazine*, August 19, 1974; White, *Breach of Faith*, 24; Woodward and Bernstein, *Final Days*, 390–92.

94. Nixon, *RN*, 1067; Haig, *Inner Circles*, 495.

95. Haig, *Inner Circles*, 497–98; Ford, *Time to Heal*, 25.

96. Haig, *Inner Circles*, 497–99; Carroll Kilpatrick, "Nixon Resigns," *Washington Post*, August 9, 1974, A01; Naughton, "Persuading the President to Resign," 71.

97. Nixon, *RN*, 1072.

98. Nixon, *RN*, 1078; Ford, *Time to Heal*, 27–30; Interview of Richard Nixon, by Frank Gannon, June 10, 1983, Brown Media Archives.

99. Kissinger, *Years of Renewal*, 21–24.

100. Interview of Ambassador Robert B. Oakley, by Charles Stuart Kennedy and Thomas Stern, July 7, 1992, Diplomatic Studies Interview Collection.

101. Interview of Ambassador Winston Lord, by Charles Stuart Kennedy and Nancy Bernkopf Tucker, April 28, 1998, Diplomatic Studies Interview Collection.

102. Haig, *Inner Circles*, 500–501; Woodward and Bernstein, *Final Days*, 431.

103. Nixon, *RN*, 1080; White, *Breach of Faith*, 30; Woodward and Bernstein, *The Final Days*, 434–35.

104. Carroll Kilpatrick, "Nixon Resigns," *Washington Post*, August 9, 1974, A01.

105. Carroll Kilpatrick, "Nixon Resigns," *Washington Post*, August 9, 1974, A01; Albert, *Little Giant*, 366.

106. President Richard M. Nixon, "Address to the Nation Announcing Decision to Resign the Office of President of the United States," August 8, 1974.

107. Carroll Kilpatrick, "Nixon Resigns," *Washington Post*, August 9, 1974, p. A01.

108. Nessen, *It Sure Looks Different*, 7.

109. President Richard M. Nixon, "Remarks on Departure from the White House," August 9, 1974; President Richard M. Nixon, "Final Remarks to the White House Staff," August 9, 1974.

110. Kissinger, *Years of Renewal*, 26.

111. Ford, *Time to Heal*, 39–40; Nixon, *RN*, 1089.

Chapter 3

1. "Enter Ford," *Time Magazine*, August 19, 1974. Ford describes this as a favorite passage in Feldman, "Gerald Ford at 90."

2. Gerald R. Ford's Remarks on Taking the Oath of Office as President, August 9, 1974.

3. The economy had positive growth in real terms in every year between 1960 and 1973, with the sole exception of 1970, when it declined by less than one-half of one percent. *Economic Report of the President, 2005*, Appendix B, Spreadsheet Tables, Table B-4.

4. Gallup Poll, "Trust in Government," www.galluppoll.com/content/default.aspx?ci=5392; Richard Morin and Claudia Deane, "Poll: Americans' Trust in Government Grows," *Washington Post*, September 28, 2001; Bill Schneider, "Cynicism Didn't Start with Watergate," *CNN All Politics*, June 17, 1997, www.cnn.com/ALLPOLITICS/1997/gen/resources/watergate/trust.schneider/.

5. Ford, *Time to Heal*, 306–307.

6. Greenspan, *Age of Turbulence*, 65.

7. Senate Confirmation Hearings, p. 36. For comments on Ford's emotional stability see Greenspan, *Age of Turbulence*, 65; Haig, *Inner Circles*, 484; Gergen, *Eyewitness to Power*, 100.

8. Journalist Helen Thomas said that Ford "without a doubt, had the best laugh of any president I've covered, and he wasn't afraid to use it." Thomas, *Thanks for the Memories*, 99.

9. Hartmann, *Palace Politics*, 59.

10. Reeves, *A Ford, Not a Lincoln*, 26.

11. Cannon, *Time and Chance*, 91.

12. Reeves, *A Ford, Not a Lincoln*, 26.

13. Reeves, *A Ford, Not a Lincoln*. Rockefeller later told Ford that the incident never happened. Witcover, *Marathon*, 37.

14. "A Good Lineman for the Quarterback," *Time Magazine*, October 22, 1973; "A Man for This Season," *Time Magazine*, August 12, 1974; Reeves, *A Ford, Not a Lincoln*.

15. Berman, *No Peace, No Honor*, 14.

16. Kissinger, *Years of Renewal*, 27.

17. "A Man for This Season," *Time Magazine*, August 12, 1974.

18. Kissinger, *Years of Renewal*, 30.

19. Cannon, *Time and Chance*, 71.

20. Gergen, *Eyewitness*, 108.

21. Cannon, *Time and Chance*, 266.

22. Greenspan, *Age of Turbulence*, 65.

23. Cannon, *Time and Chance*, 23.

24. Osborne, *White House Watch*, 53–54. Richard Reeves also called him "stubborn," and then gratuitously threw in "ignorant." Reeves, *A Ford, Not a Lincoln*, 117. Carl Albert mentioned that Ford was a "stubborn man." Albert, *Little Giant*, 367. Robert Hartmann commented on Ford's stubborn streak. Hartmann, *Palace Politics*, 72. Bryce Harlow did too. "Once Ford had arrived at a decision he had a startling stubbornness." Interview of Bryce Harlow, July 27, 1985, Syers Interview Collection.

25. Henry Adams, *John Randolph*, 158.

26. Cannon, *Time and Chance*, 323–24; Hartmann, *Palace Politics*, 165.

27. Ford, *Time to Heal*, 132. Laird has explained that the transition team realized that sooner or later Ford would appoint a chief of staff. "We were not operating under the illusion that the collegial system would be a lasting legacy. We all suspected that eventually the White House would need a chief of staff. We knew that some strong individual had to take charge for the president." Interview with Melvin R. Laird, June 6, 1985, Syers Interview Collection, 4.

28. Ford, *Time to Heal*, 147.

29. Interview of Gerald R. Ford, by Martha J. Kumar, Palm Springs, California, White House 2001 Project, Presidential Transition Project, James A. Baker III Institute & University of North Carolina at Chapel Hill.

30. Ford, *Time to Heal*, 130.

31. Osborne, *White House Watch*, xxxiii.

32. Interview of Richard B. Cheney, by Stephen J. Wayne, February 8, 1977, Hyde and Wayne Interview Collection, Box 1, Folder: "Cheney, Richard — Interview, 6/27/75," 23.

33. Reichley, *Conservatives in an Age of Change*, 295.

34. National Security Advisor, Memoranda of Conversations, 1973–1977, Ford Library, Box 4.

35. Greene, *Presidency of Gerald R. Ford*, 133.

36. President Richard M. Nixon, "Statement on Signing Department of Defense Appropriations Authorization Act, 1975"; Public Law 93-365, 93rd Congress, H.R. 14592, August 5, 1974; "Conference Report Authorizing Appropriations for Fiscal Year 1975 for Military Procurement, Research and Development, Active Duty Reserve and Civilian Personnel Strength Levels, Military Training Student Loads and Other Purposes."

37. Werth, *31 Days*, 266.

38. Gerald R. Ford Remarks Announcing Appointment of J. F. terHorst as Press Secretary to the President, August 9, 1974.

39. "Off to a Helluva Start" *Time Magazine*, August 26, 1974.

40. Hartmann, *Palace Politics*, 175–77 and 209.

41. Alan J. Borsuk, "Gerald R. Ford: 1913–2006; Best Friends on the Path to Power," *Milwaukee Journal Sentinel*, December 28, 2006.

42. Kennerly, *Shooter*, 127–32.

43. "Enter Ford," *Time Magazine*, August 19, 1974; Witcover, *Marathon*, 41; Kennerly, 130.

44. Haig, *Inner Circles*, 515. James Cannon reports that this conversation convinced Ford that "Haig must go." Cannon, *Time and Chance*, 357. Haig puts the meeting after the pardon was issued, but the timeframe does not fit. Haig, *Inner Circles*, 515.

45. Press Briefing Following Cabinet Meeting, August 10, 1974, Ford Library, Ron Nessen Files, Box 1; Ford, *Time to Heal*, 131.

46. Cannon, *Time and Chance*, 357–58.

47. Memorandum from Attorney General Saxbe to the President, September 6, 1974, Ford Library, Philip Buchen Files, Box 35, Folder: "Nixon Pardon and Papers — Press Conference 1974/09/08 (Buchen) (2);" Nixon v. Administrator of General Services, 433 U.S. 425 (1977).

48. Memorandum, "History and Background of Nixon Pardon," Benton Becker, September 9, 1974, and Deposition of Benton Becker, *Nixon v. Sampson, et al.*, Civil Action No. 74-1518, U.S.D.C. Dist. of Colombia, November 13, 1974, Ford Library, Benton Becker Files, Box 2, Folder: "Nixon Pardon, Becker's Memorandum"; Hartmann, *Palace Politics*, 160–61; Anson, *Exile*, 28.

49. Hartmann, *Palace Politics*, 195. Gulley claims that the trucks contained only Nixon's personal effects, but he admits that he had been sending documents to San Clemente at the time. Gulley, *Breaking Cover*, 228–32.

50. Interview with Ambassador Hermann Frederick Eilts, by William Brewer, August 12 and 13, 1988, and Interview of Alfred Leroy Atherton, Jr., by Dayton Mak, Summer 1990, Diplomatic Studies Interview Collection; Kissinger, *Years of Renewal*, 366–68.

51. Cannon, *Time and Chance*, 360.

52. Gerald R. Ford: First Address to Congress and the Nation, August 19, 1974; Ford, *Time to Heal*, 134; "Ford Confronts the Deadliest Danger," *Time Magazine*, August 26, 1974; Cannon, *Time and Chance*, 361.

53. President Gerald R. Ford, "Statement on a General Motors Price Increase for 1975 Automobiles and Trucks," August 12, 1974.

54. Memorandum for the President from Jack Marsh, August 16, 1974, Ford Library, Kenneth Rush Files, Box 1, Folder: "General Motors' Price Hike"; Ford, *Time to Heal*, 135; Reeves, *A Ford, Not a Lincoln*, 155; President Gerald R. Ford, "Statement on a General Motors Announcement of a Reduction in 1975 Price Increases," August 21, 1974.

55. Berman, *No Peace, No Honor*, 3.

56. "Report: Title VII, Military Assistance South Vietnamese Forces," Senate Committee on Appropriations, August 16, 1974; Congressional Record — Senate, August 21, 1974, S15498.

57. Snepp, *Decent Interval*, 114.

58. Kissinger professes in his memoirs to having accepted the junta's renunciation of enosis, but it is hard to imagine that he really believed it. Kissinger, *Years of Renewal*, 215. For the events in Cyprus before Ford took office, see Minutes of Meeting, "Cyprus Critique," Secretary's Conference Room, August 5, 1974, Transcripts of Secretary Kissinger's Staff Meetings, NARA, Record's Group 5, Box 4, Folder: "Cyprus Critique"; Kissinger, *Years of Renewal*, 196–221; "Bulent Ecevit," *Economist*, November 11, 2006, 97; Mehmet Ali Birand, *30 Hot Days*, 1985; and Makarios Letter to General Ghizikis, July 2, 1974, reprinted at www.cyprus-conflict.net/30percent20Hotpercent20Days.htm.

59. Interview of Ambassador James W. Spain, by Charles Stuart Kennedy, October 31, 1995, Diplomatic Studies Interview Collection.

60. Interview of Ambassador Jack B. Kubisch, by Henry E. Mattox, January 6, 1989, Diplomatic Studies Interview Collection.

61. Cannon, *Time and Chance*, 339–55; "Bitter Hatred on the Island of Love" *Time Magazine*, August 26, 1974; "On the Overseas Line," *Time Magazine*, August 26, 1974; Kissinger, *Years of Renewal*, 224–231; Interview of Ambassador Robert B. Oakley, by Charles Stuart Kennedy and Thomas Stern, July 7, 1992, Diplomatic Studies Interview Collection.

62. "Bitter Hatred on the Island of Love" *Time Magazine*, August 26, 1974.

63. Memorandum of Conversation, President Ford, Secretary Kissinger and Major General Brent Scowcroft, August 13, 1974, Ford Library, National Security Council Memoranda of Conversations, 1973–1977, Box 4, Folder: "August 13, 1974 — Ford, Kissinger"; Kissinger, *Years of Renewal*, 225–28.

64. Senate Report, "A Crisis on Cyprus."

65. Interview of Ambassador Jack B. Kubisch, by Henry E. Mattox, January 6, 1989, Diplomatic Studies Interview Collection.

66. "Death of an Ambassador," *Time Magazine*, September 2, 1974.

67. Kissinger, *Years of Renewal*, 225.

68. Hartmann, *Palace Politics*, 209 and 243–46; Werth, *31 Days*, 83; Cannon, *Time and Chance*, 360–66.

69. Cannon, *Time and Chance*, 360; Werth, *31 Days*, 73.

70. Depositions of Benton Becker and Philip W. Buchen,

Nixon v. Sampson, et al., Civil Action No. 74–1518, U.S.D.C. Dist. of Colombia, November 13, 1974, copies can be found in: Ford Library, Benton Becker Files, Box 2, Folder: "Nixon Pardon, Becker's Memorandum"; Drossman and Knappman, *Watergate and the White House*, Volume 3, 234–35.

71. Memorandum from Attorney General Saxbe to the President, September 6, 1974, Ford Library, Philip Buchen Files, Box 35, Folder: "Nixon Pardon and Papers — Press Conference 1974/09/08 (Buchen) (2)."

72. Interview with President Ford, July 1988, Larry King Interviews; Anson, *Exile*, 51; Cannon, *Time and Chance*, 365–66.

73. Dobrynin, *In Confidence*, 319–22.

74. Ford, *Time to Heal*, 139; Kissinger, *Years of Renewal*, 256; Dobrynin, *In Confidence*, 334–35.

75. Ford, *Time to Heal*, 140; "Gerald Ford: Off to a Fast, Clean Start," *Time Magazine*, August 26, 1974.

76. Ford, *Time to Heal*, 211.

77. Greene, *Presidency of Gerald R. Ford*, 38–39.

78. President Gerald R. Ford, "Remarks to the Veterans of Foreign Wars Annual Convention, Chicago, Illinois," August 19, 1974.

79. Hartmann, *Palace Politics*, 214–15.

80. Nixon, *RN*, 1078; Ford, *Time to Heal*, 27–30.

81. Ford, *Time to Heal*, 144.

82. Turner, *Vice President as Policy Maker*, 27.

83. Hartmann, *Palace Politics*, 226; Cannon, *Time and Chance*, 367.

84. Ford, *Time to Heal*, 142–43.

85. Hartmann, *Palace Politics*, 227–28.

86. Ford, *Time to Heal*, 144–45; Interview of Nelson A. Rockefeller, by Michael Turner, New York, December 21, 1977, cited in Turner, *Vice President as Policy Maker*, xv, 44, and 52; Haig, *Inner Circles*, 512.

87. Turner, *Vice President as Policy Maker*, 30. "Loved the guy" quote from Reichley, *Conservatives in an Age of Change*, 299.

88. Ford, *Time to Heal*, 146.

89. President Gerald R. Ford, "Remarks on Intention to Nominate Nelson A. Rockefeller to Be Vice President of the United States," August 20, 1974.

90. "A Natural Force on a National Stage," *Time Magazine*, September 2, 1974.

91. Hugh Sidey, "So Like the Rest of America," *Time Magazine*, September 2, 1974.

92. "A Natural Force on a National Stage," *Time Magazine*, September 2, 1974.

93. Gergen, *Eyewitness to Power*, 94.

94. Interview of Jerry Jones, by Stephen J. Wayne, December 17, 1976, Hyde and Wayne Interview Collection, 7.

95. Hugh Sidey, "So Like the Rest of America," *Time Magazine*, September 2, 1974.

96. Woodward and Bernstein, *All the President's Men*, 265. Nixon aide Mel Laird explained the attitude of Nixon's staff: "These guys behaved the way they did not because they didn't understand politics; they didn't understand the difference between right and wrong." White, *Breach of Faith*, 140.

97. Witcover, *Marathon*, 40.

98. O'Neill, *Man of the House*, 271.

99. Hugh Sidey, "So Like the Rest of America," *Time Magazine*, September 2, 1974.

100. Hyland, *Mortal Rivals*, 150.

101. Witcover, *Marathon*, 42.

102. Cannon, *Time and Chance*, 350.

103. Kissinger, *Years of Renewal*, 25.

104. Nessen, *It Sure Looks Different*, 162.

105. "Ford: Plain Words Before an Open Door," *Time Magazine*, September 9, 1974.

106. Gergen, *Eyewitness to Power*, 140.

107. Cannon, *Time and Chance*, 369.

108. Interview with Pat O'Donnell, September 27, 1985, Syers Interview Collection, Box 1, Folder: "O'Donnell, Pat," 2.

Chapter 4

1. "Citizen Nixon and the Law," *Time Magazine*, August 19, 1974.

2. Cannon, *Time and Chance*, 37.

3. R. W. Apple Jr., "Ford Says He's a Man of the People Making Sure He Leaves Out No One," *New York Times*, August 13, 1974, 21.

4. Cannon, *Time and Chance*, 362; Mollenhoff, *The Man Who Pardoned Nixon*, 86.

5. Hartmann, *Palace Politics*, 136.

6. Cannon, *Time and Chance*, 299.

7. "Citizen Nixon and the Law," *Time Magazine*, August 19, 1974.

8. Senate Confirmation Hearings, 13–143.

9. "A New Counsel for Nixon's Defense," *Time Magazine*, September 9, 1974.

10. Interview of Philip Allen Lacovara, Legends in the Law; Haig, *Inner Circles*, 454; Woodward and Bernstein, *The Final Days*, 250; Anson, 49; Cannon, *Time and Chance*, 363–64.

11. Ford, *Time to Heal*, 161; Haig, *Inner Circles*, 513; Kissinger, *Years of Renewal*, 39.

12. Ford, *Time to Heal*, 159.

13. Ford, *Time to Heal*, 157.

14. Transcript of President Gerald R. Ford's News Conference of August 28, 1974. For Ford's belief that he was inadequately prepared for the press conference, see James Cannon's comments in: Scott Shane, "For Ford, Pardon Decision Was Always Clear-Cut," *New York Times*, December 29, 2006.

15. Woodward, *Shadow*, 15.

16. Ford, *Time to Heal*, 159.

17. Transcript of Live Chat with Gerald Ford, scholastic.com, available at *http://content.scholastic.com/browse/article.jsp?id=4655*.

18. Ford, *Time to Heal*, 159–61; Haig, *Inner Circles*, 513.

19. Ford, *Time to Heal*, 162.

20. Deposition of Philip W. Buchen, *Nixon v. Sampson, et al.*, Civil Action No. 74-1518, U.S.D.C. Dist. of Colombia, November 11, 1974, copy available at Ford Library, Benton Becker Files, Box 2, Folder: "Nixon v. Sampson (1)"; Ford, *Time to Heal*, 162.

21. Ford, *Time to Heal*, 164–65.

22. Werth, *31 Days*, 223.

23. For a description of the negotiations over the Nixon administration documents in Washington and San Clemente, see the following documents in Box 2 of Benton Becker's Files at the Ford Library: Memorandum, "History and Background of Nixon Pardon," Benton Becker, September 9, 1974; Deposition of Philip W. Buchen, *Nixon v. Sampson, et al.*, Civil Action No. 74-1518, U.S.D.C. Dist. of Colombia, November 11, 1974; Memorandum from Professor Benton L. Becker to Trever Ambruster, "Annotated History of the Nixon-Sampson Agreement," May 3, 1978; "Memorandum re: Nixon v. Sampson; Interview of Benton Becker," Kenneth S. Geller of the Watergate Special Prosecution Task Force, November 1, 1974. See also Ford, *Time to Heal*, 164–75; Hersh, "The Pardon"; Cannon, *Time and Chance*, 365–66; "At First, Nixon Spurned Idea of a Pardon, Lawyer Says," *New York Times*, November 13, 1999, A10; Woodward, *Shadow*, 18; *Nixon v. Administrator of General Services*, 433 U.S. 425 (1977); 43 Op. Att'y Gen. 1 (1974).

24. Memorandum, "History and Background of Nixon Pardon," Benton Becker, September 9, 1974, Ford Library, Benton Becker Files, Box 2, Folder: "Nixon Pardon, Becker's Memorandum"; Werth, 292.

25. Becker claims that Zeigler had been briefed by Haig that a statement of contrition was not a condition of a pardon, but Haig has denied having discussions with Zeigler. Becker's statement makes clear that he did not hide that fact from Miller or Zeigler, so if Haig did tip Zeigler off about Ford's position, it had no impact on the negotiations. Memorandum, "History and Background of Nixon Pardon," Benton Becker, September 9, 1974, Ford Library, Benton Becker Files, Box 2, Folder: "Nixon Pardon, Becker's Memorandum."

26. Letter from Special Prosecutor to Philip W. Buchen,

September 4, 1974, Tab C to President Gerald R. Ford Statement and Responses to Questions from Members of the House Judiciary Committee Concerning the Pardon of Richard Nixon, October 17, 1974.

27. Memorandum to: Leon Jaworski, from: Henry Ruth, Subject: Mr. Nixon, Tab B to President Gerald R. Ford Statement and Responses to Questions from Members of the House Judiciary Committee Concerning the Pardon of Richard Nixon, October 17, 1974. See also Ford, *Time to Heal*, 168.

28. Ford, *Time to Heal*, 161.

29. Anson, *Exile*, 52; Deposition of Philip W. Buchen, *Nixon v. Sampson, et al.*, Civil Action No. 74-1518, U.S.D.C. Dist. of Colombia, November 11, 1974, copy available at Ford Library, Benton Becker Files, Box 2, Folder: "Nixon v. Sampson (1)."

30. Memorandum re: "Nixon v. Sampson, and Interview of Benton Becker," Kenneth S. Geller of the Watergate Special Prosecution Task Force, November 1, 1974, Ford Library, Benton Becker Files, Box 2, Folder: "Nixon v. Sampson (2)"; Deposition of Benton Becker, *Nixon v. Sampson, et al.*, Civil Action No. 74-1518, U.S.D.C. Dist. of Colombia, November 13, 1974, Ford Library, Benton Becker Files, Box No. 2, Folder: "Nixon Pardon, Becker's Memorandum."

31. Memorandum from Professor Benton L. Becker to Trever Ambruster, "Annotated History of the Nixon-Sampson Agreement," May 3, 1978, Ford Library, Benton Becker Files, Box No. 2, Folder: "Nixon-Sampson Agreement— History"; Ford, *Time to Heal*, 172.

32. Ford, *Time to Heal*, 173; Adam Clymer, "At First, Nixon Spurned Idea of a Pardon, Lawyer Says," *New York Times*, November 13, 1999, A10.

33. Letter from Richard M. Nixon to Arthur F. Sampson, September 6, 1974, Ford Library, Philip Buchen Files, Box 35, Folder: "Nixon Pardon and Papers— Press Conference 1974/ 09/08 (Buchen) (2)"; Nixon v. Administrator of General Services, 433 U.S. 425 (1977).

34. Anson, *Exile*, 56.

35. Witcover, *Marathon*, 240.

36. TerHorst, *Gerald Ford*, 229.

37. Letter from Jerald terHorst to President Gerald R. Ford, September 8, 1974, Ford Library.

38. Alan J. Borsuk, "Gerald R. Ford: 1913–2006; Best Friends on the Path to Power," *Milwaukee Journal Sentinel*, December 28, 2006.

39. Ford, *Time to Heal*, 175.

40. President Gerald R. Ford's Remarks on Signing a Proclamation Granting Pardon to Richard Nixon, September 8, 1974; President Gerald R. Ford's Proclamation 4311, Granting a Pardon to Richard Nixon, September 8, 1974.

41. Ford, *Time to Heal*, 179.

42. Transcript of Press Conference of Philip Buchen, September 8, 1974, Ford Library, Philip Buchen Files, Box 35, File: "Nixon Pardon and Papers— Press Conference, 1974/ 09/08 (Buchen) (1)." Ford thought that Buchen and terHorst had misstated the reason he had issued the pardon. Ford, *Time to Heal*, 179.

43. Gergen, *Eyewitness to Power*, 121.

44. Gergen, *Eyewitness to Power*, 123.

45. Ford, *Time to Heal*, 180; Drossman and Knappman, *Watergate and the White House*, Volume 3, 237.

46. Ford, *Time to Heal*, 178–79.

47. James Cannon has reconstructed the conversation from Ford's notes. Cannon, *Time and Chance*, 386.

48. President Gerald R. Ford, "Remarks to Reporters Following a Visit with Former President Nixon at Long Beach, California," November 1, 1974.

49. All three quotes are from Drossman and Knappman, *Watergate and the White House*, Volume 3, 240.

50. Southwick, *Presidential Also-Rans*, 679.

51. "Reaction: Is the Honeymoon Over?" *Time Magazine*, September 16, 1974.

52. Clymer, *Edward M. Kennedy*, 225.

53. Drossman and Knappman, *Watergate and the White House*, Volume 3, 240.

54. "Reaction: Is the Honeymoon Over?" *Time Magazine*, September 16, 1974.

55. Cannon, *Time and Chance*, 385.

56. *Winston-Salem Journal*, September, 9, 1974.

57. *Houston Chronicle*, September 10, 1974.

58. Cannon, *Time and Chance*, 384.

59. *New York Times*, September 9, 1974.

60. Ford, *Time to Heal*, 197–98.

61. Gergen, *Eyewitness to Power*, 111.

62. Reeves, *A Ford, Not a Lincoln*, 75.

63. Ford, *Time to Heal*, 185.

64. Ford, *Time to Heal*, 185; Hersh, "The Pardon"; Cannon, *Time and Chance*, 387.

65. Transcript of Press Conference of Philip Buchen, September 8, 1974, Ford Library, Philip Buchen Files, Box 35, File: "Nixon Pardon and Papers— Press Conference, 1974/09/ 08 (Buchen) (1)."

66. Transcript of President Gerald R. Ford's News Conference of September 16, 1974. Ford remembered the question years later. Ford, *Time to Heal*, 180.

67. Ford, *Time to Heal*, 196; Cannon, *Time and Chance*, 387–88.

68. Ford, *Time to Heal*, 197; Cannon, *Time and Chance*, 388–89.

69. Ford, *Time to Heal*, 197; Cannon, *Time and Chance*, 389–90.

70. Cannon, *Time and Chance*, 389–90. Ford formally offered to testify in a letter to Chairman Hungate on September 30, 1974. President Gerald R. Ford, Letter to the Chairman of the Subcommittee on Criminal Justice of the House Judiciary Committee Offering to Testify Concerning the Pardon of Richard Nixon, September 30, 1974.

71. Haig, *Inner Circles*, 518.

72. Haig, *Inner Circles*, 518–19; Woodward, *Shadow*, 26.

73. President Gerald R. Ford Statement and Responses to Questions from Members of the House Judiciary Committee Concerning the Pardon of Richard Nixon, October 17, 1974.

74. Ford, *Time to Heal*, 178.

75. "Statement on Signing the Presidential Recordings and Materials Preservation Act," December 19, 1974; Transcript of President Gerald R. Ford's News Conference of October 29, 1974; Pub. L. No. 93-526; 44 U.S.C. §2107 (Supp. v, 1975); *Nixon v. General Services Administration*, 97 S. Ct. 2777 (1977); Memorandum from Professor Benton L. Becker to Trever Ambruster, "Annotated History of the Nixon-Sampson Agreement," May 3, 1978, Ford Library, Folder "Nixon-Sampson Agreement— History," Benton Becker Files, Box No. 2; Reeves, *A Ford, Not a Lincoln*, 108.

76. Remarks delivered by Senator Edward M. Kennedy on presenting the 2001 Profile in Courage Award to President Gerald R. Ford, May 21, 2001, available at www.jfklibrary.org/Ed ucation+and+Public+Programs/Profile+in+Courage+Award/ Award+Recipients/Gerald+Ford/Remarks+by+Senator+Edward +M.+Kennedy.htm.

77. Interview of President Ford, July, 1988, Larry King Interviews.

78. Feldman, "Gerald Ford at 90."

79. Ford, *Time to Heal*, 186.

80. Isaacson, *Kissinger*, 605; Osborne, *White House Watch*, xxiv. Rockefeller was wary of Rumsfeld's ambition. Turner, *Vice President as Policy Maker*, 230. Nessen asserts that infighting was caused by Rumsfeld's "manner and ambitions." Nessen, *It Sure Looks Different*, xi.

81. Interview of William Seidman, June 12, 1985, Syers Interview Collection, Box 1, Folder "Seidman, L. William," 4. Nessen says the same thing: "Don Rumsfeld gradually took over the chief-of-staff duties, although without the title. So much for the spokes-of-the-wheel theory." Nessen, *It Sure Looks Different*, 74.

82. Interview of Richard B. Cheney, by Stephen J. Wayne, June 27, 1975, Hyde and Wayne Interview Collection, Box 1, Folder: "Cheney, Richard— Interview, 6/27/75," 9–10. See also Interview of Roy L. Ash, by Frederick J. Graboske, August 4, 1988, Ford Library, Composite Oral History Accessions, Box

1, Folder: "Nixon Presidential Materials Project Oral Histories, Ash Roy L., Oral History, 8/4/88, 93-NLF-035," 15; Hartmann, *Palace Politics*, 282–83.

83. Osborne, *White House Watch*, 50; Nessen, *It Sure Looks Different*, 84 and 149–51; Gergen, *Eyewitness*, 114.

84. Osborne, *White House Watch*, 15.

85. Ford, *Time to Heal*, 132, 136 and 322; Hartmann, *Palace Politics*, 116.

86. Gergen, *Eyewitness to Power*, 100 and 142. James Reichley came to a similar conclusion. Reichley, *Conservatives in an Age of Change*, 315.

87. O'Brien, "Filling Justice William O. Douglas's Seat."

88. Ford, *Time to Heal*, 232–41; Interview of Edward H. Levi, by Victor H. Kramer, May 24, 1989, Ford Library, Composite Oral History Accessions, Box 1, Folder: "Kramer, Victor H., Interview of Edward H. Levi, 95-NLF-032."

89. Hartmann, *Palace Politics*, 279; Gergen, *Eyewitness*, 30.

90. Gergen, *Eyewitness*, 104.

91. Nessen called Hartmann's operation "a lackluster speechwriting office." Nessen, *It Sure Looks Different*, 74.

92. Interview with Pat Butler, June 27, 1985, Syers Interview Collection, Box 1, Folder: "Butler, Pat," 1.

93. Interview of Allen W. Moore, by Stephen J. Wayne, November 30, 1976, Hyde and Wayne Interview Collection, Box 1, Folder: "Moore, Allen W.—11/30/76," Section 1, 15.

94. Interview of Robert Hartmann, by Stephen J. Wayne, December 9, 1976, Hyde and Wayne Interview Collection, Box 1, Folder: "Hartmann, Robert—12/9/76," 3.

95. Gergen, *Eyewitness*, 107–108.

Chapter 5

1. For details of the controls, see President Richard M. Nixon, "Address to the Nation Outlining a New Economic Policy," August 15, 1971; Exec. Order No. 11615, 36 Fed. Reg. 15727 (August 15, 1971); Exec. Order No. 11627, 36 Fed. Reg. 20139 (October 16, 1971); "Special Message to the Congress Announcing Phase III of the Economic Stabilization Program and Requesting Extension of Authorizing Legislation," January 11, 1973; Exec. Order No. 11695, 38 Fed. Reg. 1473 (January 12, 1973); "Address to the Nation Announcing Price Control Measures," June 13, 1973; Executive Order No. 11723, 38 (June 15, 1973); Exec. Order No. 11730, 38 Fed. Reg. 19345 (July 19, 1973).

2. Safire, *Before the Fall*, 10. For Burns' background and economic philosophy, see Hetzel, "Arthur Burns and Inflation"; Christopher Farrell, "This Fed Heeds No White House," *Business Week Online*, February 6, 2004.

3. Ford, *Time to Heal*, 153.

4. The *National Review* noted in 1977 that Burns' "words have not always been a reliable indicator of his actions." "Sticking with Burns," *National Review*, July 22, 1977, 817.

5. "Statement by Arthur F. Burns, Chairman, Board of Governors of the Federal Reserve System, Before the Subcommittee on Domestic Monetary Policy of the Committee on Banking, Currency and Housing, U.S. House of Representatives, February 6, 1975," *Federal Reserve Bulletin*, Number 2, Volume 61, February 1975, 73.

6. "Statement by Arthur F. Burns, Chairman, Board of Governors of the Federal Reserve System, Before the Joint Economic Committee, August 6, 1974," *Federal Reserve Bulletin*, Number 8, Volume 60, August 1974, 566.

7. "Statement by Arthur F. Burns, Chairman, Board of Governors of the Federal Reserve System, Before the Joint Economic Committee, August 6, 1974," *Federal Reserve Bulletin*, Number 8, Volume 60, August 1974, 566.

8. "Statement by Arthur F. Burns, Chairman, Board of Governors of the Federal Reserve System, Before the Committee on Banking and Currency, U.S. House of Representatives, July 30, 1974," *Federal Reserve Bulletin*, Number 8, Volume 60, August 1974, 558.

9. "One may therefore argue that relatively high rates of monetary expansion have been a permissive factor in the accelerated pace of inflation. I have no quarrel with this view. But

an effort to use harsh policies of monetary restraint to offset the exceptionally powerful inflationary forces of recent years would have caused serious financial disorder and economic dislocation." "Statement by Arthur F. Burns, Chairman, Board of Governors of the Federal Reserve System, Before the Committee on Banking and Currency, U.S. House of Representatives, July 30, 1974," *Federal Reserve Bulletin*, Number 8, Volume 60, August 1974, 558.

10. Arthur Burns, December 7, 1970, cited in Nelson, "The Great Inflation of the Seventies."

11. In 1973 only 26.7 percent of non-farm workers belonged to unions, down from 31.4 percent in 1960. *Statistical Abstract of the United States 1974*. John Kenneth Galbraith has explained that wage increases have not led inflation since the 1950s. Galbraith, "Inflation, Unemployment, and Monetary Policy," 69.

12. "Statement by Arthur F. Burns, Chairman, Board of Governors of the Federal Reserve System, Before the Committee on Banking and Currency, U.S. House of Representatives, July 30, 1974," *Federal Reserve Bulletin*, Number 8, Volume 60, August 1974, 555.

13. "Last year, about 60 percent of the rise in consumer prices was accounted for by food and fuel." "Statement by Arthur F. Burns, Chairman, Board of Governors of the Federal Reserve System, Before the Committee on Banking and Currency, U.S. House of Representatives, July 30, 1974," *Federal Reserve Bulletin*, Number 8, Volume 60, August 1974, 555. At most, special factors made up half of the inflation the country faced. Burns' mistake was to "confuse changes in relative prices with persistent increases in the general level of prices. While monetary policy could affect the latter, changes in relative prices were caused by market forces beyond the Fed's control." Hafer and Wheelock, "Darryl Francis and the Making of Monetary Policy."

14. Memorandum from Darwin L. Beck to Mr. Axilrod, July 19, 1974, "Special Factors Affecting Money Supply in Recent Months," Tab 6, Ford Library, Folder: "Money Supply 1974–Feb. 1977," Arthur Burns Files, Box B-81; "Briefing Notes: Interest Rates and Monetary Policy," August 20, 1974, Ford Library, Folder: "President Nixon, Meetings with June 11, 1974m and August 20, 1974," Arthur Burns Files, Box B-89; *Economic Report of the President, 2005*, Appendix B, Spreadsheet Tables, Table B-69; *Statistical Abstract of the United States 1976*, no. 790 and fig. 16-2. Burns' tenure at the Fed was the first and only time in post-war history that the Fed consistently kept the federal funds rate below the rate of inflation. Lee Hoskins, "Monetary Policy," Shadow Open Market Committee, Washington, D.C., May 2, 2005.

15. When Ford took office, the Fed had been setting targets designed to "moderate growth in monetary aggregates." Record of Policy Actions of the Federal Open Market Committee Meeting Held on April 15–16, 1974, *Federal Reserve Bulletin*, Number 7, Volume 60, July 1974, 496; Record of Policy Actions of the Federal Open Market Committee Meeting Held on May 21, 1974, *Federal Reserve Bulletin*, Number 8, Volume 60, August 1974, 566; Record of Meeting of Federal Reserve Board Open Market Committee Meeting, June 18, 1974, *Federal Reserve Bulletin*, Number 9, Volume 60, September 1974, 660.

16. "Statement by Arthur F. Burns, Chairman, Board of Governors of the Federal Reserve System, Before the Committee on Banking and Currency, U.S. House of Representatives, July 30, 1974," *Federal Reserve Bulletin*, Number 8, Volume 60, August 1974, 556.

17. Minutes of Senior Economic Advisors' Meeting, August 20, 1974, Ford Library, Arthur Burns Files, Box B-118, Folder: "White House Senior Economic Advisors, Aug.–Sept, 1974."

18. "Recent Price Developments," *Federal Reserve Bulletin*, Number 9, Volume 60, September 1974, 658; Record of Policy Actions of the Federal Open Market Committee Meeting Held on July 16, 1974, *Federal Reserve Bulletin*, Number 10, Volume 60, October 1974, 712; Memorandum for Troika One from T-2, Edgar R. Fielder and Jack Carlson, "Economic Forecast and Policy," August 14, 1974, Ford Library, Kenneth Rush

Files, Box 1, Folder: "Economic Forecasts, August 14, 1974"; Minutes of Senior Economic Advisors' Meeting, August 20, 1974, Ford Library, Arthur Burns Files, Box B-118, Folder: "White House Senior Economic Advisors, Aug.–Sept, 1974."

19. *Statistical Abstract of the United States 1976*; Memorandum to the President from Frank Zarb, April 25, 1975, "Oil Imports," Ford Library, Frank Zarb Files, Box 1, File: "Memoranda to the President 4/18/75 – 5/30/75.; *Statistical Abstract of the United States 1976*; *Statistical Abstract of the United States 1974*; Reichley, *Conservatives in an Age of Change*, 358–65; Ford, *Time to Heal*, 228; Farrell, *Tip O'Neill*, 464; Kissinger, *Years of Renewal*, 666.

20. Michael Raoul-Duval Notes of December 14, 1974, Meeting with President Ford, Ford Library, Michael Raoul-Duval Papers, Box 5, File: "Meeting with the President, 12/14/74, Morton, et al."

21. Proclamation 4210, 38 Fed. Reg. 10725 (1973); 10 C.F.R. § 212.73 (1973); 38 Fed. Reg. 22,536 (Aug. 22, 1973); 38 Fed. Reg. 34414 (December 13, 1973); 39 Fed. Reg. 744 (January 2, 1974); 39 Fed. Reg. 1924 (January 15, 1974); Herman Kahn, "Oil Prices and Energy in General," Corporate Environment Program, Research Memorandum #2, Croton-on-Hudson, New York, Hudson Institute, August 1974, copy contained in Ford Library, Richard Cheney Files, Box 9, File: "Kahn, Herman (1)."

22. Breyer, *Regulation and Its Reform*, 244–46 ("Once the shortage was created, it was necessary to develop another system of regulatory allocation."); Memorandum to Gary Seevers from Bob Dohner, "Cost of Crude Price Decontrol," August 12, 1974, Ford Library, Kenneth Rush Files, Box 1, Folder: "Crude Oil Price Equalization, August 23, 1974;" Memorandum to the President from Frank Zarb, "Natural Gas Shortages," August 6, 1975, included in Briefing Papers from Energy Review with the President, August 9, 1975, Ford Library, Presidential Handwriting Files, Box 50, Folder: "Utilities – Energy (3)"; Breyer, "Reforming Regulation."

23. Yergin and Stanislaw, *Commanding Heights*, 60–64; Reichley, *Conservatives in an Age of Change*, 361–64.

24. Memorandum to Kenneth Rush, et al. from John Sawhill, "Crude Oil Price Equalization," August 12, 1974, Ford Library, Kenneth Rush Files, Box 1, Folder: "Crude Oil Price Equalization, August 23, 1974."

25. Memorandum to Gary Seevers from Bob Dohner, "Cost of Crude Price Decontrol," August 12, 1974, Ford Library, Kenneth Rush Files, Box 1, Folder: "Crude Oil Price Equalization, August 23, 1974."

26. Michael Raoul-Duval Notes of August 28, 1974, Meeting with President Ford, and "Meeting with: The President, Secretary Simon, Secretary Morton, John Sawhill," Ford Library, Michael Raoul-Duval Papers, Box 4, File: "Meeting with the President, 8/28/74, Energy."

27. Ford, *Time to Heal*, at 228–29 and 241–44; President Gerald R. Ford, Transcript of the President's News Conference of October 29, 1974; President Gerald R. Ford, Letter Accepting the Resignation of John C. Sawhill as Administrator of the Federal Energy Administration, October 29, 1974.

28. Interview of Richard B. Cheney, by Stephen J. Wayne, June 27, 1975, and Interview of Allen W. Moore, by Stephen J. Wayne, November 30, 1976, Hyde and Wayne Interview Collection, Box 1; President Gerald R. Ford, Executive Order 11808, Establishing the President's Economic Policy Board, September 30, 1974; Ford, *Time to Heal*, 232–41; Interview with L. William Seidman, June 12, 1985, and Interview with Roger B. Porter, May 13, 1985, Syers Interview Collection, Box 1.

29. The following documents all can be found in Ford Library, Kenneth Rush Files, Box 1, Folder: "Economic Policy Recommendations (1975 Budget) August 12–13, 1974": Memorandum for the President from Herbert Stein, "Analysis for Submission on Economic Policy by Your Advisors," August 13, 1974; Memorandum for the President from Kenneth Rush, "Recommendations for Current Economic Policy," August 12, 1974; Memorandum for Herbert Stein from Alan Greenspan, August 12, 1974; Memorandum for the President from Herb Stein, "Recommendations for the Economy," August 12, 1974;

Memorandum for Herbert Stein from Roy L. Ash, "Inflation and the 1975 Budget," August 12, 1974; Memorandum for the President from William Simon, "The Economy," August 12, 1974; Memorandum for the President from Arthur Burns, "Agenda for an Immediate Economic Program," August 12, 1974.

30. Ford, *Time to Heal*, 154.

31. Ford, *Time to Heal*, 204.

32. Ford, *Time to Heal*, 154, 189 and 204.

33. Conference on Inflation Transcript, Ford Library.

34. Ford, *Time to Heal*, 190–91; Nessen, *It Sure Looks Different*, 22; Hartmann, *Palace Politics*, 294.

35. First Lady Betty Ford's Remarks to the American Cancer Society, November 1975, Ford Library, Frances Kaye Pullen files, Box 3.

36. Kennerly, *Shooter*, 156; President Gerald R. Ford's Remarks at a Republican Fundraising Dinner in Detroit, October 10, 1974.

37. Betty Ford, *A Glad Awakening*, 1–7 and 36–39.

38. The Conference on Inflation, Remarks by Arthur F. Bums, Chairman of the Board of Governors of the Federal Reserve System, at the Conference on Inflation, Washington, D.C., September 27, 1974, *Federal Reserve Bulletin*, Number 10, Volume 60, October 1974, 699.

39. Ford, *Time to Heal*, 194.

40. Greenspan, *Age of Turbulence*, 66.

41. Testimony of Arthur Burns, "The 1973 Economic Report of the President," Hearings before the Joint Economic Committee, Part 2, 93 Cong., 1 Sess., February 20, 1973, 409.

42. President Gerald R. Ford Remarks Opening the Summit Conference on Inflation, September 27, 1974; President Gerald R. Ford Remarks Concluding the Summit Conference on Inflation, September 28, 1974.

43. President Gerald R. Ford's Address to a Joint Session of Congress on the Economy, October 8, 1974.

44. Reeves, *A Ford, Not a Lincoln*, 161.

45. Gergen, *Eyewitness to Power*, 126.

46. President Gerald R. Ford, Remarks to the Annual Convention of the Future Farmers of America, Kansas City, Missouri, October 15, 1974.

47. President Gerald R. Ford, "Remarks on Signing the WIN Consumer Pledge," November 13, 1974; "President Gerald R. Ford's Remarks to the White House Conference on Domestic and Economic Affairs in Portland, Oregon," November 1, 1974; "President Gerald R. Ford's Remarks at a Meeting of the Business Council," December 11, 1974; Hartmann, *Palace Politics*, 299.

48. Ford, *Time to Heal*, 227.

49. Memorandum from William Baroody for the President, and "A Status Report on the Citizens' Action Committee, Inc.," February 21, 1975, Ford Library, Presidential Handwriting Files, Box 4, Folder: "Business and Economics – National Economy 2/21–28/75."

50. Memorandum from Rumsfeld to the President, February 28, 1975, attached to Memorandum from William Baroody for the President, February 21, 1975, Ford Library, Presidential Handwriting Files, Box 4, Folder: "Business and Economics – National Economy 2/21–28/75."

51. The Open Market Committee raised its targets to "4¾ to 7¼ and 5¾ to 8¼ per cent for the annual rates of growth in Ml and M2, respectively." Record of Policy Actions of the Federal Open Market Committee, October 14–15, 1974, *Federal Reserve Bulletin*, Number 1, Volume 61, January 1975, 24.

52. Statement by Arthur F. Burns, Chairman, Board of Governors of the Federal Reserve System, Before the Subcommittee on Domestic Monetary Policy of the Committee on Banking, Currency and Housing, U.S. House of Representatives, February 6, 1975, *Federal Reserve Bulletin*, Number 2, Volume 61, February 1975, 71.

53. The target rate fell from 11½–13 percent on the day Ford took office to 5¼–6¼ percent in February 1975. "FOMC Ranges for Federal Funds Rate," February 23, 1975, Ford Library, Folder: "FOMC Memoranda, 3/75–4/75," Arthur Burns Files, Box 2.

54. Memorandum from William J. Fellner for the President, "Weekly Memo on Financial Conditions," December 30, 1974, Ford Library, Presidential Handwriting Files, Box 20, Folder: "Monetary and Financial Conditions Report (1)."

55. Statement by Arthur F. Burns, Chairman, Board of Governors of the Federal Reserve System, Before the Committee on Banking, Housing and Urban Affairs, U.S. Senate, February 25, 1975, *Federal Reserve Bulletin*, Number 3, Volume 61, March 1975, 152.

56. Ford, *Time to Heal*, 200.

57. Philip Shabecoff, "2 Dealers Cancel Soviet Grain Sale at Ford's Behest," *New York Times*, October 6, 1974, 1; Ford, *Time to Heal*, 313; Bernard Gwertzman, "Soviet Grain Deal of Smaller Size Approved by U.S.," *New York Times*, October 20, 1974, 1; "Farm Bureau: Historical Highlights, 1919–1994," American Farm Bureau, www.fb.org/about/thisis/fb_history.html; Mollenhoff, *The Man Who Pardoned Nixon*, 142–47.

58. Ford, *Time to Heal*, 189.

59. President Gerald R. Ford, "Statement on Senate Action Disapproving Deferral of a Federal Pay Increase," September 19, 1974; President Gerald R. Ford, "Special Message to the Congress Transmitting Budget Deferrals and Proposed Rescissions," and "Memorandum on Budget Deferrals and Proposed Rescissions," September 20, 1974; Cabinet Meeting Minutes, 11/15/74, Ford Library, James E. Connor Files, Box 3; President Gerald R. Ford, "Special Message to the Congress on Budget Restraint," November 26, 1974; President Gerald R. Ford, "Statement on Signing Budget Rescission Legislation," December 23, 1974; President Gerald R. Ford, "Statement on Signing Emergency Jobs, Unemployment Assistance and Compensation Legislation," December 31, 1974; Ford, *Time to Heal*, 189, 220, 227.

60. Interview with L. William Seidman, June 12, 1985, Syers Interview Collection, Box 1, 4–5.

61. Interview with Joe Jenkes, August 8, 1985, Interview with William T. Kendall, June 16, 1985, and Interview with L. William Seidman, William A. Syers, June 12, 1985, Syers Interview Collection, Box 1; Reichley, *Conservatives in an Age of Change*, 323; Greene, *Presidency of Gerald R. Ford*, 77.

62. President Gerald R. Ford, "Veto of Legislation to Reclassify and Upgrade Deputy United States Marshals," August 13, 1974; President Gerald R. Ford, "Veto of Animal Health Research Legislation," August 15, 1974; *Congress and the Nation, Vol. IV, 1973–1976*, 6, 10, 15, and 118; Reichley, *Conservatives in an Age of Change*, 324–330; Ford, *Time to Heal*, 293.

63. President Gerald R. Ford, "Remarks on Signing the Emergency Home Purchase Assistance Act of 1974," October 18, 1974; President Gerald R. Ford, "Statement on the Emergency Home Purchase Assistance Act of 1974," October 18, 1974; Cabinet Meeting Minutes, 6/4/75, Ford Library, James E. Connor Files, Box 4; Cabinet Meeting Minutes, 6/25/75, Ford Library, James E. Connor Files, Box 4; Ford, *Time to Heal*, 84 and 293; *Congress and the Nation, Vol. IV, 1973–1976*, 11.

64. Reichley, *Conservatives in an Age of Change*, 331.

Chapter 6

1. www.commoncause.org/site/pp.asp?c=dkLNK1MQIwG&b=189955#history.

2. Alexander, *Financing the 1976 Election*, 37, 39 and 559; John W. Gardner, "Foreword," vi–vii; Alexander, *Campaign Money*, 4 and 12; Witcover, *Marathon*, 30.

3. Marion Clark and Rudy Maxa, "Closed-Session Romance on the Hill," *Washington Post*, May 23, 1976.

4. Brian T. Usher, "Ohio: A Tale of Two Parties," Gerard J. McCullough, "Pennsylvania: The Failure of Campaign Reform," William Mansfield, "Florida: The Power of Incumbency," Sam Roberts, "New York: Loopholes and Limits," Robert Healy, "Massachusetts: Corruption and Cleanup," and Al Polczinski, "Kansas: Reform and Reaction," in Alexander, *Campaign Money*, 42–43, 143–44, 162, 226–30, 256–58, 274 and 278.

5. Alexander, *Financing the 1976 Election*, 801–805.

6. Gardner, "Foreword," and Alexander, "Introduction," in Alexander, *Campaign Money*, vii and 1–12.

7. *Congress and the Nation, Vol. IV, 1973–1976*, 3; Clymer, *Edward M. Kennedy*, 203–11 and 221; Alexander, *Financing the 1976 Election*, 39.

8. "Major Campaign Reforms Take Effect," *New York Times*, January 2, 1975, 27.

9. President Gerald R. Ford, Remarks on Signing the Federal Election Campaign Act Amendments of 1974, October 15, 1974; President Gerald R. Ford, Statement on the Federal Election Campaign Act Amendments of 1974; October 15, 1974.

10. *Buckley v. Valeo*, 424 U.S. 1 (1976).

11. Bill Moyers, "In the Kingdom of the Half-Blind," address delivered on December 9, 2005, National Security Archive, George Washington University, Washington D.C., transcript available at www.gwu.edu/~nsarchiv/anniversary/moyers.htm.

12. H.R. 12471, 93rd Congress, 2nd Sess.; S. 2543, 93rd Congress, 2nd Sess.; *Report to Accompany H.R. 12471, Amending Section 552 of Title 5, United States Code, Known as the Freedom of Information Act*, House of Representatives Committee on Government Operations, 93rd Congress, 2nd Sess., Report No. 93-876; *Report to Accompany S. 2543*, Senate Judiciary Committee, 93rd Congress, 2nd Sess., Report No. 93-854.

13. Memorandum to Roy Ash, et al. from Jerry Jones, "Decision and Information Memoranda Dealing with Policy Issues before Congress," August 19, 1974, and Memorandum from Roy Ash to the President, "Freedom of Information Act Amendments (H.R. 12471)," August 12, 1974, Ford Library, Presidential Handwriting File, Box 24, Folder: "Legislation (1) 9/8/74"; Letter from President Gerald R. Ford to the Honorable Edward M. Kennedy, August 20, 1974.

14. *Conference Report to Accompany H.R. 12471*, Committee of Conference, House of Representatives, 93rd Cong., 2nd Sess., Report No. 93-1380; Letter from the Honorable Edward M. Kennedy and the Honorable William S. Moorhead to President Gerald R. Ford, September 23, 1974.

15. Letter from CIA Director Colby to President Ford, September 26, 1974; Memorandum for President Ford from Ken Cole, "H.R. 12471, Amendments to the Freedom of Information Act," October 9, 1974; Letter to Roy Ash and Budget from Assistant Attorney General W. Vincent Rakestraw, October 9, 1974; Letter for Roy Ash from Martin R. Hoffman, General Counsel's Office, Department of Defense, October 11, 1974; Letter for Roy Ash from Linwood Holton, Assistant Secretary for Congressional Relations, Department of State, October 15, 1974; Memorandum for President Ford from Ken Cole, "Freedom of Information Act Amendments," October 16, 1974.

16. Memorandum for President Ford from Ken Cole, "H.R. 12471, Amendments to the Freedom of Information Act," September 25, 1974, Ford Library.

17. President Gerald R. Ford, Veto Message to the House of Representatives, October 17, 1974.

18. Interview with Max L. Friedersdorf, William A. Syers, September 26, 1985, Ford Library, Folder: "Friedersdorf, Max," Box 1, William A. Syers Papers, 1–2.

19. Interview with Melvin R. Laird, William A. Syers, June 6, 1985, Ford Library, Folder: "Laird, Melvin R.," Box 1, William A. Syers Papers, 5.

20. Albert, *Little Giant*, 368.

21. *Congress and the Nation, Vol. IV, 1973–1976*, 1–16; White, *Breach of Faith*, 337.

22. Alexander, *Financing the 1976 Election*, 60–61 and 726.

23. Marion Clark and Rudy Maxa, "Closed-Session Romance on the Hill," *Washington Post*, May 23, 1976.

24. Jack Maskell, "Expulsion, Censure, Reprimand, and Fine: Legislative Discipline in the House of Representatives," Congressional Research Service, Library of Congress, April 16, 2002.

25. Albert, *Little Giant*, 368–69; Alexander, *Financing the 1976 Election*, 724–36.

26. The details of the foreign bribery scandal were reported in *New York Times* and *Wall Street Journal* articles between May

1975 and June 1976, including: Robert M. Smith, "S.E.C.'s Tough Guy," *New York Times*, October 5, 1975, 167; and Michael C. Jensen, "U.S. Company Payoffs Way of Life Overseas," *New York Times*, May 5, 1975, 65.

27. Scott Armstrong and Maxine Cheshire, "Korean Ties to Congress are Probed," *Washington Post*, October 15, 1976, A1; and "Seoul Gave Millions to U.S. Officials," *Washington Post*, October 24, 1976.

28. Stone, "The Genesis of the Independent Counsel Statute."

29. *Watergate Special Prosecution Force Report* (1975).

30. Stone, "The Genesis of the Independent Counsel Statute"; Drew, *American Journal*, 322.

31. Gerald M. Pomper, "The Nominating Contests and Conventions," in Pomper, et al., *Election of 1976*, 3.

32. David S. Broder, "Assessing Campaign Reform: Lessons for the Future," in Alexander, *Campaign Money*, 312.

Chapter 7

1. George F. Kennan (identified as "X"), "The Sources of Soviet Conduct," *Foreign Affairs*, July 1947.

2. Minutes of National Security Council Meeting, Saturday, September 14, 1974, Ford Library, National Security Adviser, National Security Council Meetings File, Box 1.

3. Dobrynin, *In Confidence*, 474.

4. Isaacson, *Kissinger*, 112–13 and 849.

5. Theodore Draper, "Appeasement Détente," *Commentary*, February 1976, 27.

6. Norman Podhoretz, "Making the World Safe for Communism," *Commentary*, April 1976, 35.

7. Midge Decter, "America Now: A Failure of Nerve?" *Commentary*, July 1975, 29.

8. Kissinger's aide William Hyland has explained that "dangerous contests in the Third World could not be settled." Hyland, *Mortal Rivals*, 10.

9. Dobrynin, *In Confidence*, 405. For Kissinger's description of linkage, see Kissinger, *Years of Renewal*, 101.

10. Minutes of National Security Council Meeting of March 5, 1975, Ford Library, National Security Adviser, National Security Council Meetings File, Box 1.

11. "Interim Agreement Between the United States of America and the Union of Soviet Socialist Republics on Certain Measures with Respect to the Limitation of Strategic Offensive Arms," signed on May 26, 1972, approved by Congress on September 30, 1972, and signed by President Nixon on September 30, 1972, available at www.state.gov/t/ac/trt/4795.htm; Kissinger, *Years of Renewal*, 119–22 and 300; Hyland, *Mortal Rivals*, 82–83 and 200.

12. Interview of General Brent Scowcroft, by the author, Washington, D.C., October 27, 2006; Minutes of National Security Council Meeting, September 14, 1974, Ford Library, National Security Adviser, National Security Council Meetings File, Box 1.

13. Kissinger, *Years of Renewal*, 122–24.

14. Minutes of National Security Council Meeting, September 14, 1974, Ford Library, National Security Adviser, National Security Council Meetings File, Box 1.

15. Minutes of National Security Council Meeting, Saturday, September 14, 1974, Ford Library, National Security Adviser, National Security Council Meetings File, Box 1.

16. Kissinger, *Years of Renewal*, 119–22; Hyland, *Mortal Rivals*, 200.

17. Interview with Zachariáš, by Karel Sieber and Vojtech Mastny, Warsaw Pact Generals Interviews, 7–8.

18. "Record of Investigator's Conversation with Jaruzelski," September 26, 2002, Warsaw Pact Generals Interviews, Appendix 5, SOU 2002:108.

19. Nünlist, "Cold War Generals" (citing minutes of the 1976 meeting of Warsaw Pact defense ministers).

20. Dobrynin, *In Confidence*, 51.

21. Dobrynin, *In Confidence*, 31.

22. Notes of meeting, reprinted in Cherniaev, "The Unknown Brezhnev."

23. "Record of Investigator's Conversation with Jaruzelski," September 26, 2002, Warsaw Pact Generals Interviews, Appendix 5, SOU 2002: 108.

24. Gorbachev, *Memoirs*, 113.

25. Dobrynin, *In Confidence*, 371.

26. Minutes of National Security Council Meeting, Saturday, September 14, 1974, Ford Library, National Security Adviser, National Security Council Meetings File, Box 1.

27. Dobrynin, *In Confidence*, 33, 51, 131, 404 and 574.

28. Dobrynin, *In Confidence*, 336.

29. Memorandum of Conversation, President Gerald Ford, et al. and Senators Henry Jackson, Jacob Javits and Abraham Ribicoff, August 15, 1974, Ford Library, NSA/Memoranda of Conversations, 1973–1977, Box 5, Folder: "August 15, 1974 Ford, Kissinger, Senators Jackson, Javits and Ribicoff."

30. Kissinger, *Years of Renewal*, 258–59.

31. *New York Times*, October 19, 1974. The letters were reprinted in "Text of Letters Exchanged by Kissinger and Jackson," *New York Times*, October 19, 1974, 10. See also Isaacson, *Kissinger*, 616–17; Dobrynin, *In Confidence*, 335.

32. Memorandum of Conversation, President Ford, et al and Senator Jackson et al., October 18, 1974, 10:00 A.M., Ford Library, National Security Decision Memoranda and Study Memoranda, Box 6, Folder: "October 18, 1974 — Ford, Kissinger, Senators Jackson and Javits, Representative Charles Vanik"; Kissinger, *Years of Renewal*, 259; Isaacson, *Kissinger*, 618.

33. Dobrynin, *In Confidence*, 335.

34. Memorandum of Conversation, General Secretary Leonid Brezhnev, et al. and Secretary Henry Kissinger, et al., October 24, 1974, 11:00 A.M., reprinted in *The Kissinger Transcripts*, 327–43.

35. Isaacson, *Kissinger*, 618; Dobrynin, *In Confidence*, 335–36; Kissinger, *Years of Renewal*, 284.

36. Memorandum from Brent Scowcroft for the President, October 27, 1974, Ford Library, NSA/Kissinger Reports, Box 1, Folder: "Oct 24–27, Kissinger/Brezhnev Talks in Moscow (3)."

37. Isaacson, *Kissinger*, 618–19.

38. Ford, *Time to Heal*, 183–84 and 214.

39. Minutes of National Security Council Meeting, October 7, 1974, Ford Library, National Security Adviser, National Security Council Meetings File, Box 1.

40. Minutes of National Security Council Meeting of October 18, 1974, Ford Library, National Security Adviser, National Security Council Meetings File, Box 1.

41. Hyland, *Mortal Rivals*, 86.

42. Memorandum of Conversation, General Secretary Leonid Brezhnev, et al., and Secretary Henry Kissinger, et al., October 26, 1974, 7:10 P.M., reprinted in Burr, *Kissinger Transcripts*, 345–53.

43. Memorandum from Brent Scowcroft for the President, October 27, 1974, Ford Library, NSA/Kissinger Reports, Box 1, Folder: "Oct 24–27, Kissinger/Brezhnev Talks in Moscow (3)."

44. Dobrynin, *In Confidence*, 328.

45. Hyland, *Mortal Rivals*, 76–78. For the discussion, see Memorandum of Conversation, President Gerald R. Ford, et al. and General Secretary Leonid Brezhnev, et al., November 23, 1974, 2:30 P.M., Ford Library, NSA/Kissinger Reports, Box 1, Folder: "November 23–24, 1974, Vladivostok Summit (1)."

46. Dobrynin, *In Confidence*, 329.

47. Memorandum of Conversation, President Gerald R. Ford, et al. and General Secretary Leonid Brezhnev, et al., November 23, 1974, 6:15 P.M., Ford Library, NSA/Kissinger Reports, Box 1, Folder: "November 23–24, 1974, Vladivostok Summit (1)"; Hyland, *Mortal Rivals*, 91–94.

48. Memorandum of Conversation, President Gerald R. Ford, et al. and General Secretary Leonid Brezhnev, et al., November 24, 1974, 10:10 A.M., Ford Library, NSA/Kissinger Reports, Box 1, Folder: "November 23–24, 1974, Vladivostok Summit (1)."

49. Bauer, *At Ease in the White House*, 187; Dobrynin, *In Confidence*, 329.

50. Isaacson, *Kissinger*, 627; Burr, *The Kissinger Transcripts*, 325

51. Greene, *Presidency of Gerald R. Ford*, 125; Burr, *Kissinger Transcripts*, 325; Isaacson, *Kissinger*, 627; Hyland, *Mortal Rivals*, 99–100.

52. Minutes of National Security Council Meeting of December 2, 1974, Ford Library, National Security Adviser, National Security Council Meetings File, Box 1.

53. "Senate to Take up Trade Bill Next Week; Eased Soviet Emigration Rules Are Seen," *Wall Street Journal*, December 4, 1974, 5.

54. Ford, *Time to Heal*, 225.

55. Dobrynin, *In Confidence*, 336; Kissinger, *Years of Renewal*, 305.

56. Dobrynin, *In Confidence*, 337–38.

57. Goldberg, *Final Act*, 278.

58. Minutes of National Security Council Meeting of January 29, 1975, Ford Library, National Security Adviser, National Security Council Meetings File, Box 1.

59. Dobrynin, *In Confidence*, 337.

60. Burr, *The Kissinger Transcripts*, 325–26.

61. Minutes of National Security Council Meeting of January 29, 1975, Ford Library, National Security Adviser, National Security Council Meetings File, Box 1.

Chapter 8

1. Ford, *Time to Heal*, 203.

2. "The Economy in 1974," *Federal Reserve Bulletin*, Number 1, Volume 61, January 1975, 1–9.

3. "President Gerald R. Ford's Remarks at a Meeting of the Business Council," December 11, 1974.

4. The meeting included Secretary of the Interior Rogers Morton, Frank Zarb, Eric Zausner, and John Hill of the FEA, Russell Train of the EPA, Bill Seidman and Roger Porter of the EPB, William Eberle and Tom Enders of the State Department, Secretary of the Treasury William Simon, Roy Ash and Jim Lynn of OMB, and Don Rumsfeld, Milton Friedman, Kenneth Cole, Ron Nessen, and Alan Greenspan from the White House staff. Interview with Roger B. Porter, May 13, 1985, Syers Interview Collection, Box 1, 1.

5. Cannon, "Gerald R. Ford and Nelson A. Rockefeller," 139–40; Turner, *Vice President as Policy Maker*, 44 and 53–56; Ford, *Time to Heal*, 232–41; Hartmann, *Palace Politics*, 306 and 309.

6. Memorandum from William Seidman to the President, "Economic Policy Review," December 24, 1974, Ford Library, Presidential Handwriting Files, Box 4, Folder: "Business and Economics — National Economy 12/74."

7. Memo from Jude Wanniski to Paul Gigot, *The Wall Street Journal*, "Watergate Political Fallout," August 3, 1998, available at www.polyconomics.com/searchbase/08-03-98.html.

8. Jude Wanniski, "Sketching the Laffer Curve: How It Happened," *Yorktown Patriot,* June 14, 2005, YorktownPatriot.com, www.yorktownpatriot.com/printer_78.shtml.

9. Arthur B. Laffer, "The Laffer Curve: Past, Present, and Future," The Heritage Foundation, Backgrounder #1765, June 1, 2004, available at www.heritage.org/Research/Taxes/bg1765.cfm.

10. *Economic Report of the President, 2006* (Washington: Government Printing Office, 1976), available at *http://a257.g.akamaitech.net/7/257/2422/17feb20051700/www.gpoaccess.gov/eop/download.html*, Appendix B, Spreadsheet Tables, Table B-79.

11. Memorandum from William Seidman to the President, "Economic Policy Review," December 24, 1974, and Minutes of Economic Review Meeting, December 28, 1974, Ford Library, Presidential Handwriting Files, Box 4, Folder: "Business and Economics — National Economy 12/74"; Ford, *Time to Heal*, 227; Greenspan, *The Age of Turbulence*, 68.

12. Budget Outlook, January 14, 1975, Ford Library, Presidential Handwriting Files, Box 4, Folder: "Business and Economics — National Economy 1/9–31/74."

13. Michael Raoul-Duval Notes of December 19, 1974, Meeting with President Ford and Others, Ford Library, Michael Raoul-Duval Papers, Box 5, File: "Meeting with the President, 12/19/74, Morton, et al."

14. John Osborne, "White House Watch," *New Republic*, September 6, 1975, reprinted in Osborne, at 180.

15. Interview of Richard B. Cheney, by Stephen J. Wayne, June 27, 1975, Hyde and Wayne Interview Collection, Box 1, Folder: "Cheney, Richard — Interview, 6/27/75," 8–9.

16. Memorandum to the President from Frank Zarb, "National Energy Policy," December 19, 1975, contained in Briefing Papers on Energy Policy, December 19, 1974, Ford Library, Presidential Handwriting Files, Box 50, Folder: "Utilities — Energy Policy Briefing 12/19/74 (1)."

17. Nessen, *It Sure Looks Different*, 80–84; Hartmann, *Palace Politics*, 301–302; Ford, *Time to Heal*, 231.

18. President Gerald R. Ford's Address to the Nation on Energy and Economic Programs, January 13, 1975.

19. President Gerald R. Ford's Address before a Joint Session of the Congress Reporting on the State of the Union, January 15, 1975.

20. John Herbers, "Drastic Reversal," *New York Times*, January 14, 1975, 69.

21. Greene, *The Presidency of Gerald R. Ford*, 75.

22. "President Gerald R. Ford's Remarks Announcing Establishment of Oil Import Fees," January 23, 1975; President Gerald R. Ford, Letter to the Speaker of the House and the President of the Senate Transmitting Proposed Energy Legislation, January 30, 1975; President Gerald R. Ford, President Gerald R. Ford's Statement on Senate Action to Delay Imposition of Oil Import Fees, February 19, 1975; Memorandum to the President from Frank Zarb, "Energy Legislative Strategy," February 6, 1975, Ford Library, Frank Zarb Files, Box 1, File: "Memoranda to the President 2/1/75–3/24/75"; Ford, *Time to Heal*, 241–44.

23. President Gerald R. Ford, Annual Budget Message to the Congress, Fiscal Year 1976, February 3, 1975; President Gerald R. Ford, Remarks at a News Briefing on the Fiscal Year 1976 Budget, February 1, 1975; President Gerald R. Ford, Annual Message to the Congress: The Economic Report of the President, February 4, 1975; President Gerald R. Ford, "Special Message to the Congress Reporting on Budget Rescissions and Deferrals," January 30, 1975; President Gerald R. Ford's Remarks Upon Signing the Economic Report for 1975, February 3, 1975; Memorandum from William J. Fellner for the President, "Employment Situation in January," February 7, 1975, Ford Library, Alan Greenspan Files, Box 1, Folder: "February 1975."

24. President Gerald R. Ford, Transcript of the President's News Conference of January 21, 1975; Hartmann, *Palace Politics*, 301; Ford, *Time to Heal*, 241–44.

25. Turner, *Vice President as Policy Maker*, 44 and 53–62.

26. Turner, *Vice President as Policy Maker*, 60.

27. Interview of Michael Raoul-Duval, by Stephen J. Wayne, Post-November 2, 1976, Hyde and Wayne Interview Collection, 1–2.

28. *Congress and the Nation, Vol. IV, 1973–1976*, 11; Minutes of the Economic Policy Board Executive Committee, March 17, 1975, Ford Library, File: "E.P.B. Meeting Minutes, March 12–18, 1975," L. William Seidman Files, Box 21; Ford, *Time to Heal*, 241–44.

29. Minutes of the Economic Policy Board Executive Committee, March 17, 1975, Ford Library, File: "E.P.B. Meeting Minutes, March 12–18, 1975," L. William Seidman Files, Box 21; Minutes of the Economic Policy Board, Executive Committee Meeting, March 26, 1975, Ford Library, File: "E.P.B. Meeting Minutes, March 19–31, 1975," L. William Seidman Files, Box 21; Ford, *Time to Heal*, 241–44 and 257–59; Nessen, *It Sure Looks Different*, 86–87; Memorandum for the Economic Policy Board, "Administration's Budget Strategy," Ford Library, Folder "E.P.B. Meeting Minutes, May 21–31, 1975," William Seidman Files, Box 21; John Osborne, "White House Watch," *New Republic*, March 22, 1975, reprinted in Osborne, *White House Watch: The Ford Years*, 101; Greene, *The*

Presidency of Gerald R. Ford, 76; Michael Raoul-Duval Notes of March 26, 1975 Meeting with President Ford and Others, Ford Library, Michael Raoul-Duval Papers, Box 5, File: "Meeting with the President, 3/26/75, Seidman, et al."

30. Minutes of April 16, 1974, Cabinet Meeting, Folder: Cabinet Meeting Minutes, 4/16/74, Ford Library, James E. Connor Files, Box 3; Ford, *Time to Heal,* 257–58.

31. Memorandum from Alan Greenspan for the President, "Monetary and Financial Conditions," May 2, 1975, Ford Library, Presidential Handwriting Files, Box 20, Folder: "Monetary and Financial Conditions Reports (2)."

32. Frank G. Zarb, "How to Win the Energy War: The Politics of Oil," *International Herald Tribune,* May 24, 2007.

33. President Gerald R. Ford, Address to the Nation on Energy Programs, May 27, 1975; President Gerald R. Ford, Proclamation No. 4377, 40 Fed. Reg. 23429 May 27, 1975; H.R. 4035; President Gerald R. Ford, "Veto of a Petroleum Price Review Bill," July 21, 1975.

34. Memorandum to the President from Alan Greenspan, August 1, 1975, "Economic Effects of Immediate Decontrol," Ford Library, Frank Zarb Files, Box 1, File: "Memoranda to the President 8/1/75–8/6/75"; Congressional Budget Office Preliminary Statement, "The Impact of Decontrol of Oil Prices," September 5, 1975, Ford Library, Alan Greenspan Files, Box 48, File: "Oil Decontrol (1)."

35. Memorandum to the President from Frank Zarb, August 2, 1975, "Strategy on Decontrol," Ford Library, Frank Zarb Files, Box 1, File: "Memoranda to the President 8/1/75–8/6/75"; President Gerald R. Ford, Veto of a Bill to Extend Domestic Oil Price Controls, September 9, 1975; Briefing Papers from Energy Review with the President, August 9, 1975, and Memorandum from James Connor to Frank Zarb, August 9, 1975, Ford Library, Presidential Handwriting Files, Box 50, Folder: "Utilities — Energy (3)"; *Congress and the Nation, Vol. IV, 1973–1976: A Review of Government and Politics* (Washington: Congressional Quarterly, 1977), 11; Greene, *The Presidency of Gerald R. Ford,* 78; Reichley, *Conservatives in an Age of Change,* 368–69; Status reports to the President from Frank Zarb, Ford Library, Frank Zarb Files, Box 1, Folders: "Memoranda to the President 6/1/75–6/31/75," "Memoranda to the President 7/1/75–7/31/75," and "Memoranda to the President 8/1/75–9/15/75."

36. Cabinet Meeting Minutes, 9/17/75, Ford Library, James E. Connor Files, Box 5; Memorandum From L. William Seidman to the President, "Extension of 1975 Tax Reductions," September 25, 1975, Ford Library, File: "Briefing Papers, October 1975," L. William Seidman Files, Box 42.

37. Memorandum from Alan Greenspan for the President, "Monthly Report on Economic Conditions," November 14, 1975, Ford Library, Alan Greenspan Files, Box 2, Folder: "November 1975."

38. Minutes of the Economic Policy Board, Executive Committee Meeting, September 11, 1975, Ford Library, File: "E.P.B. Meeting Minutes, September 1–16, 1975," L. William Seidman Files, Box 22; Memorandum From L. William Seidman to the President, "Extension of 1975 Tax Reductions," September 25, 1975, Ford Library, File: "Briefing Papers, October 1975," L. William Seidman Files, Box 42.

39. President Gerald R. Ford, Address to the Nation on Federal Tax and Spending Reductions, October 6, 1975.

40. *Congress and the Nation, Vol. IV, 1973–1976: A Review of Government and Politics,* 11 and 16; Greene, *The Presidency of Gerald R. Ford,* 80; Memorandum from William Seidman, "Memorandum of Decisions," November 5, 1975, and Memorandum from William Simon for the President, "Strategy re: Tax Cut and Spending Limitation," November 4, 1975, Ford Library, Presidential Handwriting Files, Box 29, Folder: "Local Gov't — New York (6)."

41. President Gerald R. Ford, Veto of a Tax Reduction Bill, December 17, 1975.

42. Ford, *Time to Heal,* 339; Minutes of the Economic Policy Board, Executive Committee Meeting, December 10, 1975, Ford Library, File: "E.P.B. Meeting Minutes, Dec. 1975," L. William Seidman Files, Box 23; *Congress and the Nation, Vol.*

IV, 1973–1976: A Review of Government and Politics, 10–11; "Long, Put Santa Claus Back in His Sleigh," Congressional Quarterly Weekly Report, December 20, 1975, 2763; Memorandum of Decisions, L. William Seidman, December 18, 1975, Ford Library, File: "Briefing Papers, December 1975," L. William Seidman Files, Box 42.

43. *Statistical Abstract of the United States 1976,* figs. 14-2 and 16-2 and 433; Memorandum from Burton Malkiel for the President, "Monthly Report on Monetary Conditions," January 26, 1976, Ford Library, Alan Greenspan Files Box 2, Folder: "January 1976."

44. Statement by Arthur F. Burns, Chairman, Board of Governors of the Federal Reserve 1 System, before the Committee on Banking, Housing, and Urban Affairs, U.S. Senate, November 4, 1975, reprinted at *Federal Reserve Bulletin,* Number 11, Volume 61, November 1975, 744.

45. Ford, *Time to Heal,* 312–13; Minutes of Economic and Energy Meeting, July 17, 1975, Ford Library, Folder "Briefing Papers July–August 1975," William Seidman Files, Box 42; Cabinet Meeting Minutes, 9/17/75, Ford Library, James E. Connor Files, Box 5; Memorandum From L. William Seidman to the President, "The Effect on Food Prices of Additional Grain Sales to the Soviet Union and Eastern Europe," October 2, 1975, Ford Library, File: "Briefing Papers, October 1975," L. William Seidman Files, Box 42.

46. Memorandum from Alan Greenspan for the President, October 10, 1975, Ford Library, Alan Greenspan Files Box 2, Folder: "October 1975"; Memorandum from William Seidman for the President, "Additional Sales of Grain to the Soviet Union," October 14, 1975, Ford Library, Alan Greenspan Files Box 2, Folder: "October 1975."

47. President Gerald R. Ford, Statement on the United States–Soviet Union Agreement on Grain Sales, October 20, 1975.

48. *Congress and the Nation, Vol. IV, 1973–1976: A Review of Government and Politics,* 11 and 16; Memorandum to the President from Frank Zarb, November 7, 1975, "Recommendations on Energy Bill," Memorandum to the President from Frank Zarb, November 10, 1975, "Conference Energy Bill," and Memorandum to the President from Frank Zarb, December 12, 1975, "H.R. 7104/S. 622: The Energy Policy and Conservation Act," Ford Library, Frank Zarb Files, Box 2, File: "Memoranda to the President 11/25/75–12/12/75"; Memorandum to the President from Frank Zarb, December 16, 1975, "The Energy Policy and Conservation Act: If You Decide to Veto," Ford Library, Alan Greenspan Files, Box 44, File: "Energy — Legislation" ; Ford, *Time to Heal,* 340–41.

49. Memorandum to the President from Frank Zarb, January 13, 1976, "Implementation of the Energy Policy and Conservation Act Amendment to the Allocation Act," Ford Library, Frank Zarb Files, Box 2, File: "Memoranda to the President 2/13/76–4/16/76."

50. Memorandum to the President from Frank Zarb, December 30, 1976, "Gasoline Decontrol," Ford Library, Frank Zarb Files, Box 2, File: "Memoranda to the President 12/1/76–1/20/77."

51. President James E. Carter, "Gasoline Decontrol Announcement of Modification of Federal Energy Administration Regulations," January 24, 1977; Reichley, at 371.

52. President James E. Carter, "Richmond, Virginia Remarks at the State Democratic Party's Jefferson-Jackson Day Dinner," April 7, 1979.

53. *Congress and the Nation, Vol. IV, 1973–1976,* 11; Natural Gas Policy Act of 1978, Pub. Law 95-621; President James E. Carter, "National Energy Bills Remarks on Signing H.R. 4018, H.R. 5263, H.R. 5037, H.R. 5146, and H.R. 5289 Into Law," November 9, 1978; President Ronald R. Reagan, "Statement on Transmitting to Congress Proposed Natural Gas Deregulation Legislation, February 26, 1983; Natural Gas Wellhead Decontrol Act of 1989, Public Law No. 101-60 (1989); President George H. W. Bush, "Remarks on Signing the Natural Gas Wellhead Decontrol Act of 1989," July 26, 1989.

54. Memorandum from Alan Greenspan for the President, "Reasons for Better Than Expected Economic Improvement,"

April 16, 1976, Ford Library, Alan Greenspan Files Box 2, Folder: "April 1976."

55. Memorandum from Burton Malkiel for the President, "Monthly Report on Economic Conditions," June 25, 1976, Ford Library, Alan Greenspan Files Box 2, Folder: "June 1976." Real GNP grew by 4.4 percent annual rate in the second quarter, down from 9.2 percent in the first quarter. CPI grew at an annual rate of 6.1 percent in the second quarter, compared with 2.9 percent in the first. Memorandum from Burton Malkiel for the President, "Monthly Report on Economic Conditions," July 22, 1976, Ford Library, Alan Greenspan Files Box 2, Folder: "July 1976"; Memorandum from Alan Greenspan for the President, "Employment Situation in June," July 2, 1976, Ford Library, Alan Greenspan Files, Box 2, Folder: "July 1976"; Memorandum from Burton Malkiel for the President, "Employment Situation in September," October 8, 1976, Ford Library, Alan Greenspan Files, Box 2, Folder: "October 1976."

56. Memorandum from Burton Malkiel for the President, "Monthly Report on Economic Conditions," October 1, 1976, Ford Library, Alan Greenspan Files Box 2, Folder: "October 1976."

57. Memorandum from Burton Malkiel for the President, "Monthly Report on Monetary Conditions," March 31, 1976, Ford Library, Alan Greenspan Files Box 2, Folder: "March 1976."

58. *Economic Report of the President, 2006* (Washington: Government Printing Office, 1976), available at *http://a257.g. akamaitech.net/7/257/2422/17feb20051700/www.gpoaccess.gov/e op/download.html*, Appendix B, Spreadsheet Tables, Table B-79.

59. Eric Nielsen, "Federal Reserve Today: The Road to Independence," Federal Reserve Bank of Richmond, *Region Focus,* Fall 2004; Christopher Farrell, "This Fed Heeds No White House," *Business Week Online*, February 6, 2004; John Judd and Glenn D. Rudebusch, "Describing Fed Behavior," FRBSF Economic Letter, Federal Reserve Bank of San Francisco, 98–38; December 25, 1998, www.frbsf.org/econrsrch/wklyltr/ wklyltr98/el98-38.html; "Monetary Policy Twenty-Five Years after October 1979," Remarks by Chairman Alan Greenspan to the Conference on Reflections on Monetary Policy 25 Years after October 1979, Federal Reserve Bank of St. Louis, St. Louis, Missouri, October 7, 2004, available at www.federalre serve.gov/boarddocs/Speeches/2004/200410073/default.htm.

Chapter 9

1. Seymour M. Hersh, "Huge C.I.A. Operation Reported in U.S. Against Antiwar Forces, Other Dissidents," *New York Times*, December 22, 1974, 1.

2. Ford, *Time to Heal*, 229.

3. Memorandum for Executive Secretary, "Family Jewels," May 16, 1973, Digital National Security Archive, CIA Documents, MORI DocID 1451843; Colby and Forbath, *Honorable Men*, 337–50.

4. Memorandum from Director Colby to Deputy Directors, August 29, 1973.

5. Colby and Forbath, *Honorable Men*, 345–46.

6. Nessen, *It Sure Looks Different*, 54.

7. Colby and Forbath, *Honorable Men*, 391–98.

8. Kissinger, *Years of Renewal*, 317–23.

9. Transcript of President Gerald R. Ford's News Conference of September 16, 1974.

10. Helms, *A Look Over My Shoulder*, 414; David F. Schmitz, "Senator Frank Church, the Ford Administration, and the Challenges of Post-Vietnam Foreign Policy," *Peace & Change*, Oct. '96, Vol. 21, Issue 4, 438. The Justice Department indicted Helms three years later; he pled guilty to a lesser charge and received a suspended sentence and a $2,000 fine, which was paid by CIA retirees.

11. Memorandum of Conversation, President Ford, et al. January 3, 1975, Ford Library, National Security Advisor, Box 8, Folder: "January 3, 1975 — Ford, Colby, Buchen, Marsh." Ford made the decision to appoint a blue ribbon panel in a meeting on December 27. Notes for Meeting with President

Ford, December 27, 1974, Ford Library, Richard Cheney Files, Box 5, Folder: "Intelligence — Colby Report."

12. Memorandum of Conversation, President Ford, et al. January 4, 1975, Ford Library, National Security Advisor, Box 8, Folder: "January 4, 1975 — Ford, Kissinger."

13. January 4, 1975 — Gerald Ford, Richard Helms (Topic: CIA Domestic Activities), National Security Adviser, Memoranda of Conversations, Box 8; Memorandum of Conversation, President Ford, William Colby, et al., January 3, 1975, Ford Library, National Security Advisor, Box 8, Folder: "January 3, 1975 — Ford, Colby, Buchen, Marsh."

14. President Gerald R. Ford, Executive Order 11828 — Establishing a Commission on CIA Activities within the United States, January 4, 1975; President Gerald R. Ford, Statement Announcing Establishment of a Commission on CIA Activities Within the United States, January 4, 1975.

15. Nicholas M. Horrock, "Nedzi Is Said to Have Kept House in Dark on C.I.A. Violations," *New York Times*, June 5, 1975, 26.

16. Nicholas M. Horrock, "Nedzi Compromises on Inquiry of C.I.A.," *New York Times*, June 10, 1975, 81; James M. Naughton, "Nedzi Quits C.I.A. Panel; House Inquiry Is Delayed," *New York Times*, June 13, 1975, 77; John M. Crewdson, "A New Spy Panel Is Voted by House," *New York Times*, July 18, 1975, 6; Richard L. Madden, "Investigator with Wit," *New York Times*, July 19, 1975, 37.

17. Daniel Schorr, CBS News, February 28, 1975, available at the Vanderbilt University Television News Archive, wttp:// openweb.tvnews.vanderbilt.edu/1975-2/1975-02-28-CBS-8. html.

18. Lunch with the President," *Time Magazine*, June 23, 1975; Nessen, *It Sure Looks Different*, 57–59.

19. Schorr, *Clearing the Air*, 144–47.

20. Transcript of President Gerald R. Ford's News Conference, June 9, 1975.

21. Jeffreys-Jones, *The CIA and American Democracy*, 202.

22. President Gerald R. Ford's News Conference of June 9, 1975.

23. Christopher Lydon, "Democrats Accuse President of Avoiding Major Questions in C.I.A. Investigation," *New York Times*, June 11, 1975, 21.

24. Tom Wicker, "A Blue Ribbon Goat," *New York Times*, January 7, 1975, 33; Tom Wicker, "The Rocky Report: Better Than Expected," *New York Times*, June 13, 1975, 37.

25. Rockefeller Commission Report, 101–31.

26. Kissinger, *Years of Renewal*, 328; Colby and Forbath, *Honorable Men*, 405–407.

27. Olmsted, *Challenging the Secret Government*, 105.

28. "House Spy Unit Gets Crisis Data with Order to Keep Them Secret," *New York Times*, September 11, 1975, 20; Nicholas M. Horrock, "President Bars House Unit From Seeing Secret Data," *New York Times*, September 13, 1975, 57; Olmsted, *Challenging the Secret Government*, 118–122.

29. Colby and Forbath, *Honorable Men*, 435–36; Olmsted, *Challenging the Secret Government*, 122–23.

30. Nicholas M. Horrock, "President Bars House Unit from Seeing Secret Data," *New York Times*, September 13, 1975, 57; Olmsted, *Challenging the Secret Government*, 123–25; Philip Shabecoff, "President Ready to Defy House Bid for Vietnam Data," *New York Times*, September 17, 1975, 3; John M. Crewdson, "Ford Is Rebuffed by a House Panel on Offer of Data," *New York Times*, September 18, 1975, 85; David Binder, "Pike to Request Contempt Action in C.I.A Inquiry," *New York Times*, September 26, 1975.

31. Colby and Forbath, *Honorable Men*, 437–38; Nessen, *It Sure Looks Different*, 62.

32. Olmsted, *Challenging the Secret Government*, 126.

33. Olmsted, *Challenging the Secret Government*, 126.

34. Ford, *Time to Heal*, 356; Jeffreys-Jones, *The CIA and American Democracy*, 210; *Congress and the Nation, Vol. IV*, 12; Olmsted, *Challenging the Secret Government*, 132–41.

35. Kissinger, *Years of Renewal*, 334.

36. Press Briefing on Cabinet Meeting, December 10, 1975; Ford, *Time to Heal*, 356–57.

37. John M. Crewdson, "Senator Church Rejects Request by Ford That Panel Keep Secret Its Report," *New York Times*, November 5, 1975, 19; *Church Committee Final Report*, Book I, 13–14; Nicholas M. Horrock, "Data Made Public," *New York Times*, November 21, 1975, 89; David E. Rosenbaum, "No Vote by Senate," *New York Times*, November 21, 1975, 89; David F. Schmitz, "Senator Frank Church, the Ford Administration, and the Challenges of Post-Vietnam Foreign Policy," *Peace & Change*, Oct. '96, Vol. 21, Issue 4, 438.

38. Church Committee Assassinations Report, 2.

39. Nicholas M. Horrock, "'Leads' Reported in Inquiry on C.I.A.'" *New York Times*, October 5, 1975, 25.

40. John M. Crewdson, "Church Doubts Plot Links to Presidents," *New York Times*, July 19, 1975, 53.

41. Kissinger, *Years of Renewal*, 330; Church Committee Final Report, Book I, 11 and 97.

42. "Separate Statement of Barry Goldwater," Church Committee Assassinations Report, 343.

43. Church Committee Assassinations Report, 13, 51–53 and 255.

44. Church Committee Assassinations Report, 4, 13–17 and 48–49.

45. Church Committee Assassinations Report, 4–5, 71–72 and 255–56.

46. Church Committee Assassinations Report, 263.

47. "Separate Statement of Howard Baker," Church Committee Assassinations Report, 302.

48. Jeffreys-Jones, *The CIA and American Democracy*, 97, quoting transcript set forth in Stephen G. Rabe, "Eisenhower and the Overthrow of Trujillo" (paper at conference of the Society for Historians of American Foreign Relations, June 28, 1985), 11.

49. Church Committee Final Report, Book I, 120; Church Committee Assassinations Report, 73–85, 104–18, and 132–42.

50. Church Committee Assassinations Report, 148–49.

51. Church Committee Assassinations Report, 72, 86–89, and 176–77.

52. Church Committee Assassinations Report, 72–89, 104, 117–18, 132–42, and 176–77.

53. Church Committee Assassinations Report, 5, 191–98, 256, and 262.

54. Church Committee Assassinations Report, 5–6, 217–21, and 256–62 (citing Cable, Saigon to Director, 10/5/63).

55. Church Committee Assassinations Report, 226–62; Church Committee Report on Chile, 2–7.

56. Church Committee Final Report, Book I, 111.

57. Church Committee Final Report, Book I, 120.

58. Church Committee Report on Chile, 1–20; Helms, *A Look Over My Shoulder*, 404.

59. Church Committee Assassinations Report, 228.

60. Seymour Hersh, "The Price of Power: Kissinger, Nixon and Chile," *The Atlantic Monthly*, December 1982; Church Committee Assassinations Report, 239–246.

61. Church Committee Report on Chile, 2 and 39.

62. Church Committee Report on Chile, 40.

63. Church Committee Martin Luther King Report.

64. Church Committee Final Report, Book I, 389; Olmsted, *Challenging the Secret Government*, 91.

65. Nicholas M. Horrock, "Colby Describes C.I.A. Poison Work," *New York Times*, September 17, 1975, 93.

66. Schorr, *Staying Tuned*, 277.

67. Olmsted, *Challenging the Secret Government*, 149; Nicholas M Horrock, "Files Said to Link Mafia to C.I.A. in Plot on Castro," *New York Times*, May 20, 1975, L77; Kissinger, *Years of Renewal*, 317–23.

68. Interview of Ambassador Jack B. Kubisch, by Henry E. Mattox, January 6, 1989, Diplomatic Studies Interview Collection; Steven V. Roberts, "C.I.A. Station Chief Slain Near Athens by Gunmen," *New York Times*, December 24, 1975, 45; "U.S. Journal Named Welch," *New York Times*, December 24, 1975, 10; James M. Naughton, "Ford at Funeral for C.I.A. Officer," *New York Times*, January 7, 1976, 8.

69. John M. Crewdson, "House Unit on Intelligence Votes, 9–4, to Issue Report," *New York Times*, January 24, 1976, 13;

"House Rules Unit Votes to Block Release of a Report on the C.I.A.," *New York Times*, January 29, 1976, 16; David E. Rosenbaum, "House Prevents Releasing Report on Intelligence," *New York Times*, January 30, 1976, 61.

70. "House Unit Seeking Release of 2 C.I.A. Reports," *New York Times*, December 20, 1975, 2; John M. Crewdson, "House Committee Report Finds C.I.A. Understated Prices of Angolan Arms," *New York Times*, January 20, 1976, 65; John M. Crewdson, "Secrecy Is Cited," *New York Times*, January 26, 1976, 49.

71. Schorr, *Staying Tuned*, 280–84.

72. Schorr, *Staying Tuned*, 293.

73. Schorr, *Staying Tuned*, 297–98; Schorr, *Clearing the Air*, 247–48.

74. Pike Report, Section II, Part C (Risks), Subpart 1 (Covert Action).

75. Pike Report, Section II, Part B (Performance), Subparts 4 (Portugal) and 6 (Cyprus).

76. Pike Report, Section II, Part B (Performance), Subparts 1 (Tet) and 2 (Czechoslovakia).

77. Interview of Dr. Harold H. Saunders, by Thomas Stern, November 24, 1993, Diplomatic Studies Interview Collection.

78. Pike Report, Section II, Part B (Performance), Subpart 3 (The Mid-East War).

79. Pike Report, Section II, Part C (Risks), Subpart 1 (Covert Action), Case 2 (Arms Support), and Part C (Risks), Subpart 2 (SALT).

80. Bernard Gwertzman, "Kissinger Assails Report by Pike as 'Malicious Lie,'" *New York Times*, February 13, 1976, 69.

81. Interview of Dr. Harold H. Saunders, by Thomas Stern, November 24, 1993, Diplomatic Studies Interview Collection.

82. Memorandum of Conversation, Deputy Prime Minister and Minister of Foreign Affairs Adb al-Halim Khaddam, et al. and Secretary Henry A. Kissinger, et al., March 9, 1975, Ford Library, National Security Agency, Kissinger Reports on USSR, China and Middle East Discussions, Box 3, Folder: "March 7–22, 1975, Kissinger's Trip — Vol. I (2)."

83. Memorandum of Conversation, Prime Minister Yitzhak Rabin, et al. and Secretary Henry A. Kissinger, et al., March 9, 1975, Ford Library, National Security Agency, Kissinger Reports on USSR, China and Middle East Discussions, Box 3, Folder: "March 7–22, 1975, Kissinger's Trip — Vol. I (3)."

84. Kissinger, *Years of Renewal*, 576–96; Power, *A Problem from Hell*, 175–77.

85. Pike Report.

86. Osborne, *White House Watch*, 283–84; Nessen, *It Sure Looks Different*, 68–69.

87. President Gerald R. Ford's Executive Order 11905: United States Foreign Intelligence Activities, February 18, 1976.

88. Minutes of National Security Council Meeting of January 13, 1977, Ford Library, National Security Adviser, National Security Council Meetings File, Box 2.

89. Interview with General Brent Scowcroft, by the author, October 27, 2006.

Chapter 10

1. Interview of Alfred Leroy Atherton, Jr., by Dayton Mak, Summer 1990, and Interview with Ambassador Hermann Frederick Eilts, by William Brewer, August 12 and 13, 1988, Diplomatic Studies Interview Collection.

2. Kissinger, *Years of Renewal*, 355.

3. Interview of Alfred Leroy Atherton, Jr., by Dayton Mak, Summer 1990, Diplomatic Studies Interview Collection.

4. Interview of Dr. Harold H. Saunders, by Thomas Stern, November 24, 1993, Diplomatic Studies Interview Collection.

5. Interview of Alfred Leroy Atherton, Jr., by Dayton Mak, Summer 1990, Diplomatic Studies Interview Collection; Kissinger, *Years of Renewal*, 101 and 358.

6. Rabin, *Memoirs*, 247.

7. Minutes of National Security Council Meeting of October 18, 1974, Ford Library, National Security Adviser, National Security Council Meetings, Box 1; Ford, *Time to Heal*, 183; Kissinger, *Years of Renewal*, 392; Rabin, *Memoirs*, 248–49.

8. Kissinger, *Years of Renewal*, 395–90; Ford, *Time to Heal*, 245–46.

9. Kissinger, *Years of Renewal*, 395–96.

10. Memorandum of Conversation, President Ford and Secretary Kissinger, February 27, 1975, Ford Library, National Security Agency, Memoranda of Conversations, 1973–1977, Box 9, Folder: "February 27, 1975, Ford, Kissinger."

11. Interview of Ambassador Winston Lord, by Charles Stuart Kennedy and Nancy Bernkopf Tucker, April 28, 1998, Diplomatic Studies Interview Collection.

12. Interview of Alfred Leroy Atherton, Jr., by Dayton Mak, Summer 1990, and Interview of Dr. Harold H. Saunders, by Thomas Stern, November 24, 1993, Diplomatic Studies Interview Collection.

13. Rabin, *Memoirs*, 245.

14. Peres, *Battling for Peace*, 141–42.

15. Interview of Alfred Leroy Atherton, Jr., by Dayton Mak, Summer 1990, Interview of Dr. Harold H. Saunders, by Thomas Stern, November 24, 1993, and Interview of Ambassador Robert B. Oakley, by Charles Stuart Kennedy and Thomas Stern, July 7, 1992, Diplomatic Studies Interview Collection.

16. Interview of Under Secretary Joseph J. Sisco, by Michael Sterner, Diplomatic Studies Interview Collection.

17. Interview of Under Secretary Joseph J. Sisco, by Michael Sterner, Diplomatic Studies Interview Collection.

18. Memorandum of Conversation, President Anwar Sadat, et al. and Secretary Henry A. Kissinger, et al., March 8, 1975, and Memorandum for the President from Brent Scowcroft, March 9, 1975, Ford Library, National Security Agency, Kissinger Reports on USSR, China and Middle East Discussions, Box 3, Folder: "March 7–22, 1975, Kissinger's Trip — Vol. I (1 and 2)"; Kissinger, *Years of Renewal*, 402.

19. Interview of Dr. Harold H. Saunders, by Thomas Stern, November 24, 1993, Interview of Alfred Leroy Atherton, Jr., by Dayton Mak, Summer 1990, and Interview of Ambassador Robert B. Oakley, by Charles Stuart Kennedy and Thomas Stern, July 7, 1992, Diplomatic Studies Interview Collection.

20. Interview of Under Secretary Joseph J. Sisco, by Michael Sterner, March 19, 1990, Diplomatic Studies Interview Collection.

21. Memorandum of Conversation, President Hafiz Al-Assad, et al. and Secretary Henry A. Kissinger, et al., March 9, 1975, Ford Library, National Security Agency, Kissinger Reports on USSR, China and Middle East Discussions, Box 3, Folder: "March 7–22, 1975, Kissinger's Trip — Vol. I (2)."

22. Rabin, *Memoirs*, 260.

23. Rabin's Seven Points," March 9, 1975, and Memorandum of Conversation, Prime Minister Yitzhak Rabin, et al. and Secretary Henry A. Kissinger, et al., March 9, 1975, Ford Library, National Security Agency, Kissinger Reports on USSR, China and Middle East Discussions, Box 3, Folder: "March 7–22, 1975, Kissinger's Trip — Vol. I (3)."

24. Interview of Ambassador Malcolm Toon, by Dr. Henry E. Mattox, June 9, 1989, Diplomatic Studies Interview Collection; Kissinger, *Years of Renewal*, 64, 374, 387 and 457–58; Isaacson, *Kissinger*, 541; Peres, *Battling for Peace*, 144.

25. Memorandum for the President from Brent Scowcroft, March 10, 1975, and Memorandum of Conversation, Prime Minister Yitzhak Rabin, et al. and Secretary Henry A. Kissinger, et al., March 10, 1975, Ford Library, National Security Agency, Kissinger Reports on USSR, China and Middle East Discussions, Box 3, Folder: "March 7–22, 1975, Kissinger's Trip — Vol. I (4)."

26. Memorandum of Conversation, Prime Minister Yitzhak Rabin, et al. and Secretary Henry A. Kissinger, et al., March 11, 1975, and Memorandum for the President from Brent Scowcroft, March 11, 1975, Ford Library, National Security Agency, Kissinger Reports on USSR, China and Middle East Discussions, Box 3, Folder: "March 7–22, 1975, Kissinger's Trip — Vol. I (5)."

27. Memorandum of Conversation, Prime Minister Yitzhak Rabin, et al. and Secretary Henry A. Kissinger, et al., March 12, 1975, and Memorandum for the President from Brent Scow-croft, March 11, 1975, Ford Library, National Security Agency, Kissinger Reports on USSR, China and Middle East Discussions, Box 3, Folder: "March 7–22, 1975, Kissinger's Trip — Vol. I (6)."

28. Memorandum of Conversation, President Sadat, et al. and Secretary Henry A. Kissinger, et al., March 12, 1975, and Memorandum for the President from Brent Scowcroft, March 12, 1975, Ford Library, National Security Agency, Kissinger Reports on USSR, China and Middle East Discussions, Box 3, Folder: "March 7–22, 1975, Kissinger's Trip — Vol. I (6)"; Memorandum of Conversation, President Sadat, et al. and Secretary Henry A. Kissinger, et al., March 13, 1975, and Memorandum for the President from Brent Scowcroft, March 14, 1975, Ford Library, National Security Agency, Kissinger Reports on USSR, China and Middle East Discussions, Box 3, Folder: "March 7–22, 1975, Kissinger's Trip — Vol. I (7)"; Kissinger, *Years of Renewal*, 410.

29. Memorandum of Conversation, Prime Minister Yitzhak Rabin, et al. and Secretary Henry A. Kissinger, et al., March 14, 1975, and Memorandum for the President from Brent Scowcroft, March 14, 1975, Ford Library, National Security Agency, Kissinger Reports on USSR, China and Middle East Discussions, Box 3, Folder: "March 7–22, 1975, Kissinger's Trip — Vol. I (8)."

30. Memorandum of Conversation, Abd al-Halim Khaddam, et al. and Secretary Henry A. Kissinger, et al., March 15, 1975, 12:02–12:45, Memorandum of Conversation, Abd al-Halim Khaddam, et al. and Secretary Henry A. Kissinger, et al., March 15, 1975, 2:00–2:35, Memorandum of Conversation, President Assad, et al. and Secretary Henry A. Kissinger, et al., March 15, 1975, and Memorandum of Conversation, Abd al-Halim Khaddam, et al. and Secretary Henry A. Kissinger, et al., March 15, 1975, 6:45–7:15, Ford Library, National Security Agency, Kissinger Reports on USSR, China and Middle East Discussions, Box 3, Folder: "March 7–22, 1975, Kissinger's Trip — Vol. I (9).

31. Memorandum of Conversation, King Hussein of Jordan, et al. and Secretary Henry A. Kissinger, et al., March 15, 1975, 8:30–8:45 P.M., Ford Library, National Security Agency, Kissinger Reports on USSR, China and Middle East Discussions, Box 3, Folder: "March 7–22, 1975, Kissinger's Trip — Vol. I (10); Memorandum of Conversation, King Hussein of Jordan, et al. and Secretary Henry A. Kissinger, et al., March 15, 1975, 9:15–11:15 P.M., Ford Library, National Security Agency, Kissinger Reports on USSR, China and Middle East Discussions, Box 3, Folder: "March 7–22, 1975, Kissinger's Trip — Vol. I (10); Memorandum of Conversation, King Hussein of Jordan, et al. and Secretary Henry A. Kissinger, et al., March 16, 1975, 10:00–11:55 A.M., Ford Library, National Security Agency, Kissinger Reports on USSR, China and Middle East Discussions, Box 3, Folder: "March 7–22, 1975, Kissinger's Trip — Vol. II (1).

32. Cable from Secretary Kissinger for the President, March 17, 1975, Ford Library, Richard Cheney Files, Box 9, Folder: "Middle East"; Kissinger, *Years of Renewal*, 413.

33. Memorandum of Conversation, President Sadat, et al. and Secretary Henry A. Kissinger, et al., March 17, 1975, Ford Library, National Security Agency, Kissinger Reports on USSR, China and Middle East Discussions, Box 3, Folder: "March 7–22, 1975, Kissinger's Trip — Vol. II (2)"; Memorandum for the President from Brent Scowcroft, March 18, 1975, Ford Library, National Security Agency, Kissinger Reports on USSR, China and Middle East Discussions, Box 3, Folder: "March 7–22, 1975, Kissinger's Trip — Vol. II (3)"; Kissinger, *Years of Renewal*, 415.

34. Memorandum for the President from Brent Scowcroft, March 18, 1975, Ford Library, National Security Agency, Kissinger Reports on USSR, China and Middle East Discussions, Box 3, Folder: "March 7–22, 1975, Kissinger's Trip — Vol. II (3)."

35. Memorandum of Conversation, Prime Minister Rabin, et al. and Secretary Henry A. Kissinger, et al., March 18, 1975, Ford Library, National Security Agency, Kissinger Reports on USSR, China and Middle East Discussions, Box 3, Folder:

"March 7–22, 1975, Kissinger's Trip — Vol. II (4)"; Memorandum of Conversation, Prime Minister Rabin, et al. and Secretary Henry A. Kissinger, et al., March 19, 1975, Ford Library, National Security Agency, Kissinger Reports on USSR, China and Middle East Discussions, Box 3, Folder: "March 7–22, 1975, Kissinger's Trip — Vol. II (5)"; Memorandum of Conversation, Minister of Petroleum Ahmed Zaki Yamani, et al. and Secretary Henry A. Kissinger, et al., March 19, 1975, 2:25–2:55 P.M., Ford Library, National Security Agency, Kissinger Reports on USSR, China and Middle East Discussions, Box 3, Folder: "March 7–22, 1975, Kissinger's Trip — Vol. II (5)"; Memorandum for the President from Brent Scowcroft, March 19, 1975, Ford Library, National Security Agency, Kissinger Reports on USSR, China and Middle East Discussions, Box 3, Folder: "March 7–22, 1975, Kissinger's Trip — Vol. II (5)"; Kissinger, *Years of Renewal*, 418.

36. Memorandum of Conversation, Prime Minister Rabin, et al. and Secretary Henry A. Kissinger, et al., March 20, 1975, Ford Library, National Security Agency, Kissinger Reports on USSR, China and Middle East Discussions, Box 3, Folder: "March 7–22, 1975, Kissinger's Trip — Vol. II (6)."

37. Memorandum for the President from Brent Scowcroft, March 20, 1975, and Memorandum for the President from Brent Scowcroft, March 21, 1975, Ford Library, National Security Agency, Kissinger Reports on USSR, China and Middle East Discussions, Box 3, Folder: "March 7–22, 1975, Kissinger's Trip — Vol. II (7)."

38. Ford, *Time to Heal*, 247.

39. Memorandum of Conversation, President Sadat, et al. and Secretary Henry A. Kissinger, et al., March 20, 1975, and Memorandum for the President from Brent Scowcroft, March 21, 1975, Ford Library, National Security Agency, Kissinger Reports on USSR, China and Middle East Discussions, Box 3, Folder: "March 7–22, 1975, Kissinger's Trip — Vol. II (7)."

40. Memorandum of Conversation, Prime Minister Rabin, et al. and Secretary Henry A. Kissinger, et al., March 21, 1975, Ford Library, National Security Agency, Kissinger Reports on USSR, China and Middle East Discussions, Box 3, Folder: "March 7–22, 1975, Kissinger's Trip — Vol. II (7)"; Kissinger, *Years of Renewal*, 419; Interview of Alfred Leroy Atherton, Jr., by Dayton Mak, Summer 1990, Diplomatic Studies Interview Collection.

41. Memorandum of Conversation, Prime Minister Rabin, et al. and Secretary Henry A. Kissinger, et al., March 21, 1975, 10:10 P.M., and Memorandum for the President from Brent Scowcroft, March 22, 1975, Ford Library, National Security Agency, Kissinger Reports on USSR, China and Middle East Discussions, Box 3, Folder: "March 7–22, 1975, Kissinger's Trip — Vol. II (8)"; Kissinger, *Years of Renewal*, 424.

42. Copy of Press Release, Ford Library, Max Friedersdorf Files, Box 3, File: "Bipartisan Leadership Meetings, Jan.–March 1975."

43. Rabin, *Memoirs*, 245–46.

44. Minutes of National Security Council Meeting of March 28, 1975, Ford Library, National Security Adviser, National Security Council Meetings, Box 1.

45. Minutes of National Security Council Meeting of May 15, 1975, Ford Library, National Security Adviser, National Security Council Meetings, Box 1.

46. Interview of Ambassador Malcolm Toon, by Dr. Henry E. Mattox, June 9, 1989, and Interview of Ambassador Robert B. Oakley, by Charles Stuart Kennedy and Thomas Stern, July 7, 1992, Diplomatic Studies Interview Collection.

47. Kissinger, *Years of Renewal*, 438; Ford, *Time to Heal*, 290.

48. Memorandum of Conversation, Ford, Kissinger and Scowcroft, June 6, 1975, Ford Library, National Security Advisor, Memoranda of Conversations, 1973–1977, Box 12, Folder: "June 6, 1975 — Ford, Kissinger."

49. Interview of Dr. Harold H. Saunders, by Thomas Stern, November 24, 1993, and Interview of Ambassador Robert B. Oakley, by Charles Stuart Kennedy and Thomas Stern, July 7, 1992, Diplomatic Studies Interview Collection.

50. Ford, *Time to Heal*, 291–92; Rabin, *Memoirs*, 261–67; Kissinger, *Years of Renewal*, 443–44.

51. Memorandum of Conversation, Ford, Kissinger, Scowcroft, June 20, 1975, Ford Library, National Security Advisor, Memoranda of Conversations, 1973–1977, Box 13, Folder: "June 20, 1975 — Ford, Kissinger."

52. Kissinger, *Years of Renewal*, pp. 445–46.

53. Kissinger, *Years of Renewal*, 448–49; Peres, *Battling for Peace*, 142–45; Rabin, *Memoirs*, 261–67.

54. Memorandum of Conversation, Ford, Kissinger, Scowcroft, June 20, 1975, Ford Library, National Security Advisor, Memoranda of Conversations, 1973–1977, Box 13, Folder: "June 20, 1975 — Ford, Kissinger."

55. Interview of Dr. Harold H. Saunders, by Thomas Stern, November 24, 1993, Diplomatic Studies Interview Collection; Kissinger, *Years of Renewal*, 449.

56. Kennerly, *Shooter*, 187.

57. Memorandum of Conversation, Prime Minister Rabin, et al. and Secretary Henry A. Kissinger, et al., August 22, 1975, Ford Library, National Security Agency, Kissinger Reports on USSR, China and Middle East Discussions, Box 4, Folder: "August 21–September 1, 1975, Sinai Disengagement Agreement — Vol. I (1)"; Interview of Ambassador Robert B. Oakley, by Charles Stuart Kennedy and Thomas Stern, July 7, 1992, Diplomatic Studies Interview Collection; Kennerly, 187–88.

58. Memorandum for the President from Brent Scowcroft, August 23, 1975, Ford Library, National Security Agency, Kissinger Reports on USSR, China and Middle East Discussions, Box 4, Folder: "August 21–September 1, 1975, Sinai Disengagement Agreement — Vol. I (1)."

59. Memorandum for the President from Brent Scowcroft, August 23, 1975, and Memorandum of Conversation, Prime Minister Rabin, et al. and Secretary Henry A. Kissinger, et al., August 23, 1975, Ford Library, National Security Agency, Kissinger Reports on USSR, China and Middle East Discussions, Box 4, Folder: "August 21–September 1, 1975, Sinai Disengagement Agreement — Vol. I (3 and 4)"; Interview of Alfred Leroy Atherton, Jr., by Dayton Mak, Summer 1990, Diplomatic Studies Interview Collection; Kennerly, *Shooter*, 187–88.

60. Memorandum for the President from Brent Scowcroft, August 23, 1975, Ford Library, National Security Agency, Kissinger Reports on USSR, China and Middle East Discussions, Box 4, Folder: "August 21–September 1, 1975, Sinai Disengagement Agreement — Vol. I (3)."

61. "Tete-a-tete Meeting Between President H. Assad and Secretary of State Dr. Henry Kissinger," August 23, 1975, Ford Library, National Security Agency, Kissinger Reports on USSR, China and Middle East Discussions, Box 4, Folder: "August 21–September 1, 1975, Sinai Disengagement Agreement — Vol. I (3)"

62. Memorandum of Conversation, Prime Minister Rabin, et al. and Secretary Henry A. Kissinger, et al., August 23, 1975, Ford Library, National Security Agency, Kissinger Reports on USSR, China and Middle East Discussions, Box 4, Folder: "August 21–September 1, 1975, Sinai Disengagement Agreement — Vol. I (4)."

63. Memorandum of Conversation, Prime Minister Rabin, et al. and Secretary Henry A. Kissinger, et al., August 24, 1975, Ford Library, National Security Agency, Kissinger Reports on USSR, China and Middle East Discussions, Box 4, Folder: "August 21–September 1, 1975, Sinai Disengagement Agreement — Vol. I (5)."

64. Memorandum for the President from Brent Scowcroft, August 26, 1975, Ford Library, National Security Agency, Kissinger Reports on USSR, China and Middle East Discussions, Box 4, Folder: "August 21–September 1, 1975, Sinai Disengagement Agreement — Vol. I (7)."

65. Memorandum of Conversation, Prime Minister Rabin, et al. and Secretary Henry A. Kissinger, et al., August 25, 1975, Ford Library, National Security Agency, Kissinger Reports on USSR, China and Middle East Discussions, Box 4, Folder: "August 21–September 1, 1975, Sinai Disengagement Agreement — Vol. I (6)."

66. Memorandum of Conversation, Prime Minister Rabin, et al. and Secretary Henry A. Kissinger, et al., August 26, 1975,

Ford Library, National Security Agency, Kissinger Reports on USSR, China and Middle East Discussions, Box 4, Folder: "August 21–September 1, 1975, Sinai Disengagement Agreement — Vol. II (1)."

67. Memorandum of Conversation, Prime Minister Rabin, et al. and Secretary Henry A. Kissinger, et al., August 27, 1975, Memorandum for the President from Brent Scowcroft, August 28, 1975, Memorandum of Conversation, Prime Minister Rabin, et al. and Secretary Henry A. Kissinger, et al., August 28, 1975, Memorandum of Conversation, Prime Minister Rabin, et al. and Secretary Henry A. Kissinger, et al., August 31, 1975, and Memorandum of Conversation, Prime Minister Rabin, et al. and Secretary Henry A. Kissinger, et al., August 30, 1975, Ford Library, National Security Agency, Kissinger Reports on USSR, China and Middle East Discussions, Box 5, Folder: "August 21–September 1, 1975, Sinai Disengagement Agreement — Vol. III (1, 5, 6 and 7)."

68. Memorandum of Conversation, Prime Minister Rabin, et al. and Secretary Henry A. Kissinger, et al., August 31–September 1, 1975, Ford Library, National Security Agency, Kissinger Reports on USSR, China and Middle East Discussions, Box 5, Folder: "August 21–September 1, 1975, Sinai Disengagement Agreement — Vol. III (8)"; Rabin, 274.

69. Interview with Ambassador Hermann Frederick Eilts, by William Brewer, August 12 and 13, 1988, Interview of Ambassador Robert B. Oakley, by Charles Stuart Kennedy and Thomas Stern, July 7, 1992, and Interview of Alfred Leroy Atherton, Jr., by Dayton Mak, Summer 1990, Diplomatic Studies Interview Collection; Kissinger, Years of Renewal, 456; Greene, The Presidency of Gerald R. Ford, 155.

70. "Agreement Between Egypt and Israel," September 1, 1975, Ford Library, National Security Agency, Kissinger Reports on USSR, China and Middle East Discussions, Box 4, Folder: "August 21–September 1, 1975, Sinai Disengagement Agreement — Documents (1)"; Ford, Time to Heal, 309; Kissinger, Years of Renewal, 454; Interview of Alfred Leroy Atherton, Jr., by Dayton Mak, Summer 1990, Diplomatic Studies Interview Collection.

71. Kissinger, Years of Renewal, 1035–38.

72. Memorandum of Conversation, Ford, Scowcroft, Kissinger, and Syrian Ambassador Richard W. Murphy, November 19, 1975, Ford Library, National Security Advisor, Memoranda of Conversations, 1973–1977, Box 16, Folder: "November 19, 1975 — Ford, Kissinger Ambassador Richard W. Murphy (Syria)"; Kissinger, Years of Renewal, 1036–37.

73. For details of the civil war, see Kissinger, Years of Renewal, 1019–40.

74. Kissinger, Years of Renewal, 1039.

75. Minutes of National Security Council Meeting of April 7, 1976, Ford Library, National Security Adviser, National Security Council Meetings, Box 2.

76. Kissinger, Years of Renewal, 1044.

77. Kissinger, Years of Renewal, 1045–46; Peres, Battling for Peace, 193–200; Rabin, Memoirs, 280–81.

78. Interview with L. Dean Brown, by Horace G. Torbert, May 17, 1989, Diplomatic Studies Interview Collection.

79. Interview with L. Dean Brown, by Horace G. Torbert, May 17, 1989, Diplomatic Studies Interview Collection.

80. Interview with L. Dean Brown, by Horace G. Torbert, May 17, 1989, Diplomatic Studies Interview Collection.

81. Minutes of National Security Council Meeting of April 7, 1976, Ford Library, National Security Adviser, National Security Council Meetings, Box 2; Kissinger, Years of Renewal, 1–41; Kissinger, Years of Renewal, 1022 and 1047.

82. Cheney Notes of Meeting, June 16, 1976, Ford Library, Richard Cheney Files, Box 9, File: "Lebanon Evacuation, 6/76"; State Department Press Release, June 16, 1976, Ford Library, Richard Cheney Files, Box 9, File: "Lebanon Evacuation, 6/76"; Kissinger, Years of Renewal, 1047–48.

83. Memorandum from Brent Scowcroft, "Meeting on Lebanon Situation," June 17, 1976, Ford Library, Richard Cheney Files, Box 9, Folder: "Lebanon Evacuation, 6/76."

84. Interview with L. Dean Brown, by Horace G. Torbert, May 17, 1989, Diplomatic Studies Interview Collection.

85. Memorandum of Conversation, 6/18/1976, Box 19, National Security Adviser, Memoranda of Conversations, Ford Library; Greene, Presidency of Gerald R. Ford, 169; Nessen, It Sure Looks Different, 221.

86. Peres, Battling for Peace, 193–200; Kissinger, Years of Renewal, 1048–49.

87. Interview of Ambassador Malcolm Toon, by Dr. Henry E. Mattox, June 9, 1989, Diplomatic Studies Interview Collection.

88. Feldman, "Gerald Ford at 90."

Chapter 11

1. Neu, After Vietnam, 16.

2. Transcript between Zhou Enlai and Le Duc Tho, Beijing, 5:30 P.M., January 3, 1973, reproduced in Westad, et al., "Working Paper #22."

3. Transcript of meeting between Zhou Enlai and Le Duan, Pham Van Dong and Le Thanh Nghi, Beijing, June 5, 1973, reproduced in Westad, et al., "Working Paper #22."

4. Snepp, Decent Interval, 63–64.

5. Greene, Presidency of Gerald R. Ford, 132; Kissinger, Years of Renewal, 470.

6. Military Procurement Authorization Act of 1973, P.L. 93–155; McGovern Amendment to Foreign Assistance Act of 1973, P.L. 93–189.

7. Snepp, Decent Interval, 51–55; Isaacson, Kissinger, 635; Kissinger, Years of Renewal, 471.

8. Dung, Our Great Spring Victory, 2 and 10–11; Snepp, Decent Interval, 91–93 and 107.

9. Dung, Our Great Spring Victory, 18.

10. Joint Memorandum by CIA and Defense Intelligence Agency, "Communist Military and Economic Aid to North Vietnam, 1970–1974," March 4, 1975, Ford Library (estimating that the Soviets provided $400 million in military aid in 1974, up from $330 million in 1973).

11. Westad, et al., "Working Paper #22."

12. Kissinger, Years of Renewal, 479.

13. House Committee on Foreign Affairs, "United States Aid to Indochina: Report of a Staff Survey Team to South Vietnam, Cambodia and Laos," July 1974, U.S. Government Printing Office, 1974, 36–879.

14. Hartmann, Palace Politics, 318.

15. Memorandum of Conversation Between Ford and Congressional Leadership, September 12, 1974, Ford Library, National Security Adviser Memoranda of Conversations, Box 5, Folder: "September 12, 1974 — Ford, Bipartisan Congressional Leadership."

16. Interview of Philip C. Habib, by Edward Mulcahy, May 24, 1984, Diplomatic Studies Interview Collection.

17. Memorandum of Conversation Between Ford, Kissinger and Martin, Ford Library, National Security Adviser Memoranda of Conversations, Box 5, Folder: "September 13, 1974 — Gerald Ford, Henry Kissinger, Ambassador to South Vietnam Graham Martin (Topic: Vietnam)."

18. President Gerald R. Ford Statement on Signing Foreign Assistance Act, December 30, 1974; Kissinger, Years of Renewal, 483; Ford, Time to Heal, 226; Conference Report, "Making Appropriations for the Department of Defense, Fiscal Year 1975," Report No. 93-1363, 93rd Congress, Second Session, September 18, 1974; Public Law 93-437, 93rd Congress, H.R. 16243, October 8, 1974; President Gerald R. Ford, "Statement on Signing the Department of Defense Appropriations Act, 1975," October 9, 1974.

19. Jean-Louis Margolin, "Cambodia: The Country of Disconcerting Crimes," 582–632; Power, Problem from Hell, 93; Isaacson, Kissinger, 636.

20. Kissinger, Years of Renewal, 506.

21. Margolin, "Cambodia: The Country of Disconcerting Crimes," 626; Snepp, Decent Interval, 123.

22. "United States Aid to Indochina: Report of a Staff Survey Team to South Vietnam, Cambodia and Laos," House Committee on Foreign Affairs, July 1974, U.S. Government Printing Office, 1974, 36–879.

23. Transcript of meeting between Zhou Enlai and Le Thanh Nghi, Beijing, October 8–10, 1973, reproduced in Westad, et al., "Working Paper #22."

24. Memorandum of Conversation Between Deng Xiaoping, et al. and Henry Kissinger, et al., November 26, 1974, Ford Library, National Security Advisor, Kissinger Reports on USSR, China and Middle East Discussions, Box 2, Folders: "November 25–29, 1974 — Kissinger's Trip (1) to (4)."

25. "National Intelligence Estimate: Prospects for Cambodia through August 1975," February 13, 1975; Isaacson, *Kissinger*, 637; Greene, *Presidency of Gerald R. Ford*, 134–135; Snepp, *Decent Interval*, 142; Short, *Pol Pot*, 4.

26. Ambassador John Dean's Cable on the Cambodia Settlement, February 6, 1975, Ford Library, Presidential Country Files for East Asia and the Pacific, Box 4, Folder: "Cambodia — State Department Telegrams: To SECSTATE — NODIS (2)."

27. Memoranda from the Director of the White House Situation Room, "The Military Situation in South Vietnam," September 20, 1974, November 8, 1974, November 12, 1974, and December 10, 1974, Digital National Security Archive; Kissinger, *Years of Renewal*, 483.

28. Intelligence Memorandum, "Effectiveness of U.S. Intelligence Analysis on Vietnam, December 1974–April 1975," October 22, 1975, Digital National Security Archive; CIA Staff Notes, "Development in Indochina," January 7, 1975, Digital National Security Archive.

29. Dung, *Our Great Spring Victory*, 18–25; Snepp, *Decent Interval*, 122 and 137; Isaacson, *Kissinger*, 640.

30. "Communication from the President of the United States Transmitting a Proposed Supplemental Appropriation for Military Assistance, South Vietnamese Forces, and a Budget Amendment for Military Assistance for Cambodia in Fiscal Year 1975," House of Representatives, Estimate No. 02, 94th Congress, 1st Sess., January 28, 1974; "Supplemental Appropriation for Military Assistance to South Vietnam — Message from the President," Congressional Record — Senate, January 28, 1975, S1207-8.

31. CIA Memorandum, "South Vietnamese Ammunition Expenditures, 1972–1974, January 28, 1975, Digital National Security Archive. On March 12 — after it was clear that the North would launch a major new offensive — Schlesinger told the Cabinet that if Congress did not approve funding, the Vietnamese ammunition would run out by April 15. Cabinet Meeting Minutes, 3/12/75, Box 4, James E. Connor Files, Ford Library.

32. Snepp, *Decent Interval*, 103, 116, 214 and 238.

33. "Supplemental Appropriation for Military Assistance to South Vietnam — Message from the President," Congressional Record — Senate, January 28, 1975, S1207-8; "Communication from the President of the United States Transmitting a Proposed Supplemental Appropriation for Military Assistance, South Vietnamese Forces, and a Budget Amendment for Military Assistance for Cambodia in Fiscal Year 1975," House of Representatives, Estimate No. 02, 94th Congress, 1st Sess., January 28, 1974.

34. Statement by Philip C. Habib, Assistant Secretary for East Asian and Pacific Affairs, before the Subcommittee on Foreign Assistance and Economic Policy of the Senate Committee on Foreign Relations, February 24, 1975.

35. Memorandum of Conversation, March 11, 1975, Ford Library, National Security Adviser. Memoranda of Conversations, 1973–1977, Box 5, Folder: "March 11, 1975 — Ford, Schlesinger." See also "National Intelligence Estimate: Prospects for Cambodia through August 1975," February 13, 1975.

36. Dung, *Our Great Spring Victory*, 26–38.

37. March 25, 1975, Memo re: Vietnam Situation by Saigon Staff; Dung, 63–70.

38. Memorandum from William L. Stearman to Secretary Kissinger, March 12, 1975, Ford Library, National Security Adviser, NSC Institutional Files, Folder: "7501509 — Ominous Developments in Vietnam."

39. Interview of Philip C. Habib, by Edward Mulcahy, May 24, 1984, Diplomatic Studies Interview Collection.

40. Dung, *Our Great Spring Victory*, 73–77.

41. Dung, *Our Great Spring Victory*, 70.

42. Cable from Ambassador Graham Martin to General Brent Scowcroft, March 17, 1975, Ford Library, NSA/Backchannel Messages 1974–1977, Box 3, Folder: "Martin Messages 3/75 Incoming"; March 25, 1975, Memo re: Vietnam Situation by Saigon Staff; Snepp, *Decent Interval*, 208–214; Ford, *Time to Heal*, 250; Kissinger, *Years of Renewal*, 520–21; Dung, 99–100; Minutes of National Security Council Meeting of March 28, 1975.

43. Dung, *Our Great Spring Victory*, 94 and 100.

44. Dung, *Our Great Spring Victory*, 119.

45. Dung, *Our Great Spring Victory*, 101–103 and 119; March 25, 1975, Memo re: Vietnam Situation by Saigon Staff; Minutes of National Security Council Meeting of March 28, 1975.

46. Letter from President Nguyen Van Thieu to President Gerald R. Ford, March 25, 1975, relayed in Cable from Ambassador Graham Martin to General Brent Scowcroft, March 26, 1975, Ford Library, NSA/Backchannel Messages 1974–1977, Box 3, Folder: "Martin Messages 3/75 Incoming."

47. March 25, 1975 — Gerald Ford, Henry Kissinger, General Frederick Weyand, Ambassador to South Vietnam Graham Martin (Topic: Vietnam), Box 10, National Security Adviser, Memoranda of Conversations, Ford Library.

48. Ford, *Time to Heal*, 251; Kennerly, *Shooter*, 168.

49. Memorandum of Conversation, March 27, 1975, Ford Library, National Security Adviser, Memoranda of Conversations, 1973–1977, Box 5, Folder: "March 27, 1975 — Ford, Kissinger."

50. Minutes of National Security Council Meeting of March 28, 1975.

51. Snepp, *Decent Interval*, 280.

52. Administration Evacuation and Mayaguez Report; "Statement of Hon. Monroe Leigh, Legal Advisor to the Department of State," *War Powers: A Test of Compliance Relative to the Danang Sealift, the Evacuation of Phnom Penh, the Evacuation of Saigon, and the Mayaguez Incident*, Hearings Before the Subcommittee on International Security and Scientific Affairs of the Committee on International Relations, House of Representatives, 94th Congress, 1st Session, May 7, 1975, 4; George J. Church, "The Final 10 Days," *Time Magazine*, reported by Bonnie Angelo, Hannah Bloch, William Dowell, and Frank Gibney, Jr., April 24, 1995, Vol. 145, Issue 17, 24.

53. Dung, *Our Great Spring Victory*, 132–33.

54. Snepp, *Decent Interval*, 276 and 285.

55. Cable from CIA Saigon Station to Priority Director, April 2, 1975, Digital National Security Archive; CIA Memorandum from Saigon Station to Immediate Director, March 31, 1975, Digital National Security Archive.

56. Interagency Memorandum quoted in CIA Memorandum to Immediate Saigon, April 4, 1975, Digital National Security Archive; CIA Memorandum Summarizing April 4, 1975 Interagency Memorandum, Annex to Intelligence Memorandum, "Effectiveness of U.S. Intelligence Analysis on Vietnam, December 1974–April 1975," October 22, 1975, Digital National Security Archive.

57. Vietnam Assessment Report by General Fred C. Weyand, April 9, 1975, cover memo, Ford Library, National Security Adviser, Presidential Country Files for East Asia and the Pacific, Box 19, Folder: "Vietnam (13)"; Ford, *Time to Heal*, 253.

58. Interview of President Gerald R. Ford, Jerrold L. Schecter, February 10, 1986, Ford Library, Folder: "Schecter, Jerrold L., Interview of President Ford, 86-NLF-027," Box 1, Composite Oral History Accessions, 7.

59. Kennerly, *Shooter*, 174; Ford, *Time to Heal*, 253.

60. Assessment of General Fred C. Weyand's Report on Vietnam, April 5, 1975, Folder: "Vietnam (14)," National Security Adviser, Presidential Country Files for East Asia and the Pacific, Ford Library.

61. Cable from Ambassador Martin to General Brent Scowcroft, April 7, 1975, Ford Library, NSA/Backchannel Messages, 1974–1977, Box 3, Folder: "Martin Channel 4/75 Incoming (1)."

62. Memorandum of Conversation, April 8, 1975, Ford Library, National Security Adviser. Memoranda of Conversations, 1973–1977, Box 10, Folder: "April 8, 1975 — Ford, Kissinger."

63. Berman, *No Peace, No Honor*, 4; Ford, *Time to Heal*, 252–53; Snepp, *Decent Interval*, 347.

64. Snepp, *Decent Interval*, 286–90, 319–21 and 379; Berman, *No Peace, No Honor*, 267.

65. Minutes of National Security Council Meeting of March 28, 1975, Ford Library, National Security Adviser. National Security Council Meetings File, Box 1. In his memoirs, Kissinger says that it was John Hotridge who had contacted Sihanouk the day before and made an offer to negotiate, but the prince refused to consider the option. Kissinger, *Years of Renewal*, 513.

66. Administration Evacuation and Mayaguez Report; Kissinger, *Years of Renewal*, 514; Snepp, *Decent Interval*, 279.

67. Minutes of National Security Council Meeting of April 9, 1975, Ford Library, National Security Adviser. National Security Council Meetings File, Box 1.

68. Address by President Gerald R. Ford Before a Joint Session of the Congress Reporting on United States Foreign Policy, April 10, 1975.

69. Ford, *Time to Heal*, 254.

70. David E. Rosenbaum, "Defeat for Ford," *New York Times*, April 18, 1975, 69.

71. Memorandum of Conversation, April 11, 1975, Ford Library, National Security Adviser, Memoranda of Conversations, 1973–1977, Box 10, Folder: "April 11, 1975 — Ford, Kissinger, Schlesinger, General Brown, Rumsfeld, Buchen, Marsh."

72. Secretary of State Henry Kissinger before Senate Committee on Appropriations, April 15, 1975, reprinted in Department of State Bulletin, "In Congress," May 5, 1975, 586; Administration Evacuation and Mayaguez Report, 5–6.

73. Cable from Secretary Kissinger to Ambassador Graham Martin, April 10, 1975, Ford Library, NSA/Backchannel Messages 1974–1977, Box 3, Folder: "Martin Messages 4/75 Outgoing (1)."

74. Cable from Ambassador Graham Martin to Secretary Kissinger, April 13, 1975, Ford Library, NSA/Backchannel Messages 1974–1977, Box 3, Folder: "Martin Messages 4/75 Incoming (1)."

75. April 14, 1975 — Gerald Ford, Henry Kissinger, Secretary of Defense James Schlesinger, Senate Foreign Relations Committee (Topic: Vietnam), Box 10, National Security Adviser. Memoranda of Conversations, Ford Library.

76. Cable from Secretary Kissinger to Ambassador Graham Martin, April 17, 1975, Ford Library, NSA/Backchannel Messages 1974–1977, Box 3, Folder: "Martin Messages 4/75 Outgoing (1)"; Interview of President Gerald R. Ford, Jerrold L. Schecter, February 10, 1986, Ford Library, Folder: "Schecter, Jerrold L., Interview of President Ford, 86-NLF-027," Box 1, Composite Oral History Accessions, 9.

77. April 14, 1975 — Gerald Ford, Henry Kissinger, Secretary of Defense James Schlesinger, Senate Foreign Relations Committee (Topic: Vietnam), Box 10, National Security Adviser, Memoranda of Conversations, Ford Library; Ford, *Time to Heal*, 255.

78. Cable from Secretary Kissinger to Ambassador Graham Martin, April 15, 1975, Ford Library, NSA/Backchannel Messages 1974–1977, Box 3, Folder: "Martin Messages 4/75 Outgoing (1)."

79. Cable from Ambassador Graham Martin to General Brent Scowcroft, April 25, 1975, Ford Library, NSA/Backchannel Messages 1974–1977, Box 3, Folder: "Martin Messages 4/75 Outgoing (1)." (The date on the memo appears to be a typo. The transmission information indicates that it was sent on the 15th.)

80. Cable from Secretary Kissinger to Ambassador Graham Martin, April 15, 1975, Ford Library, NSA/Backchannel Messages 1974–1977, Box 3, Folder: "Martin Messages 4/75 Outgoing (1)."

81. Snepp, *Decent Interval*, 367–68.

82. CIA Memorandum Summarizing "DCI Briefing for WSAG Meeting, 'The Situation in Vietnam,'" April 17, 1975, Annex to Intelligence Memorandum, "Effectiveness of U.S. Intelligence Analysis on Vietnam, December 1974–April 1975," October 22, 1975, Digital National Security Archive.

83. Cable from Ambassador Graham Martin to Secretary Kissinger, April 18, 1975, Ford Library, NSA/Backchannel Messages 1974–1977, Box 3, Folder: "Martin Messages 4/75 Incoming (2)"; Cable from Secretary Kissinger to Ambassador Graham Martin, April 18, 1975, Ford Library, NSA/Backchannel Messages 1974–1977, Box 3, Folder: "Martin Messages 4/75 Outgoing (2)."

84. Cable from Ambassador Graham Martin to Secretary Kissinger, April 19, 1975, Ford Library, NSA/Backchannel Messages 1974–1977, Box 3, Folder: "Martin Messages 4/75 Incoming (2)."

85. Memorandum for the Record of National Security Council Meeting of April 24, 1975; CIA Memorandum of DCI Briefing, "The Situation in Vietnam," April 24, 1975, Digital National Security Archive; Dobrynin, *In Confidence*, 343–44.

86. Dung, *Our Great Spring Victory*, 155 and 202.

87. Cable from Ambassador Graham Martin to Secretary Kissinger, April 20, 1975, Ford Library, NSA/Backchannel Messages 1974–1977, Box 3, Folder: "Martin Messages 4/75 Incoming (2)"; Snepp, *Decent Interval*, 377–78.

88. Snepp, *Decent Interval*, 385, 394–97 and 402; Kissinger, *Years of Renewal*, 534; Ford, *Time to Heal*, 256; Berman, *No Peace, No Honor*, 268–69.

89. CIA Memorandum Summarizing "DCI Briefing for WSAG Meeting, 'Vietnam,'" April 20, 1975, Annex to Intelligence Memorandum, "Effectiveness of U.S. Intelligence Analysis on Vietnam, December 1974–April 1975," October 22, 1975, Digital National Security Archive.

90. President Gerald R. Ford's Address at a Tulane University Convocation, April 23, 1975; Nessen, *It Sure Looks Different*, 108; Hartmann, *Palace Politics*, 322.

91. Cable from Ambassador Graham Martin to Secretary Kissinger, April 24, 1975, Ford Library, NSA/Backchannel Messages 1974–1977, Box 3, Folder: "Martin Messages 4/75 Incoming (3)."

92. Memorandum for the Record of National Security Council Meeting of April 24, 1975; CIA Memorandum of DCI Briefing, "The Situation in Vietnam," April 24, 1975, Digital National Security Archive.

93. Cable from Secretary Kissinger to Ambassador Graham Martin, April 24, 1975, Ford Library, NSA/Backchannel Messages 1974–1977, Box 3, Folder: "Martin Messages 4/75 Outgoing (3)."

94. Cable from Ambassador Graham Martin to Secretary Kissinger, April 25, 1975, Ford Library, NSA/Backchannel Messages 1974–1977, Box 3, Folder: "Martin Messages 4/75 Incoming (3)."

95. Memorandum of Conversation, April 25, 1975, Ford Library, National Security Adviser, Memoranda of Conversations, 1973–1977, Box 11, Folder: "April 25, 1975 — Ford, Kissinger."

96. Snepp, *Decent Interval*, 436; Evan Thomas with Ron Moreau and Andrew Mandel, "The Last Days of Saigon," *Newsweek*, May 1, 2000, Vol. 135, Issue 18, 34.

97. Cable from Ambassador Graham Martin to Secretary Kissinger, April 26, 1975, Three Cables from Ambassador Graham Martin to Secretary Kissinger, April 27, 1975, Two Cables from Ambassador Graham Martin to Secretary Kissinger, April 29, 1975, Ford Library, NSA/Backchannel Messages 1974–1977, Box 3, Folder: "Martin Messages 4/75 Incoming (3)"; CIA Memorandum, "DCI Briefing for 26 April WSAG Meeting, Vietnam," April 26, 1975, Digital National Security Archive; CIA Memorandum Summarizing April 29, 1975, Daily Intelligence Publication, Annex to Intelligence Memorandum, "Effectiveness of U.S. Intelligence Analysis on Vietnam, December 1974 — April 1975," October 22, 1975, Digital National Security Archive; Kissinger, *Years of Renewal*, 539–40; Snepp, *Decent Interval*, 415, 438–46, and 461.

98. Dung, *Our Great Spring Victory*, 215–31; CIA Memorandum, "DCI Briefing for 29 April WSAG Meeting, Viet-

nam," April 26, 1975, Digital National Security Archive; CIA Memorandum, "DCI Briefing for 26 April WSAG Meeting, Vietnam," April 26, 1975, Digital National Security Archive; Ford, *Time to Heal*, 256.

99. Snepp, *Decent Interval*, 561.

100. Evan Thomas with Ron Moreau and Andrew Mandel, "The Last Days of Saigon," *Newsweek*, May 1, 2000, Vol. 135, Issue 18, 34.

101. Nessen, *It Sure Looks Different*, 113.

102. For details of the evacuation, see Administration Evacuation and Mayaguez Report; "Testimony of Hon. Monroe Leigh, Legal Advisor to the Department of State," and "Testimony of Hon. Martin R. Hoffmann, General Counsel, Department of State," *War Powers: A Test of Compliance Relative to the Danang Sealift, the Evacuation of Phnom Penh, the Evacuation of Saigon, and the Mayaguez Incident*, Hearings Before the Subcommittee on International Security and Scientific Affairs of the Committee on International Relations, House of Representatives, 94th Congress, 1st Session, May 7, 1975, 7–22 and 118–20; Cable from Secretary of State Kissinger to Ambassador Martin on President's Decisions on the Saigon Evacuation, April 29, 1975, Transcript of Telephone Conference Between Secretary of State Henry Kissinger and Ken Fried, April 29, 1975, 10:35 A.M., Cable from Secretary Kissinger to Ambassador Graham Martin, April 28, 1975, Three Cables from Secretary Kissinger to Ambassador Graham Martin, April 29, 1975, Ford Library, NSA/Backchannel Messages 1974–1977, Box 3, Folder: "Martin Messages 4/75 Outgoing (3)"; Three Cables from Ambassador Graham Martin to Secretary Kissinger, April 29, 1975, Ford Library, NSA/Backchannel Messages 1974–1977, Box 3, Folder: "Martin Messages 4/75 Incoming (3)"; Kissinger, *Years of Renewal*, 537–45; Snepp, *Decent Interval*, 474–568; Minutes of National Security Council Meeting of April 28, 1975.

103. *Statistical Abstract of the United States 1976*; Balogh, "From Metaphor to Quagmire," xvi and 28–29; Dung, *Our Great Spring Victory*, 236 and 245.

104. Melvin Laird, "Iraq: Learning the Lessons of Vietnam," *Foreign Affairs*, November/December 2005.

105. Kissinger, *Years of Renewal*, 527.

106. *Statistical Abstract of the United States 1976*.

107. Interview with General Brent Scowcroft, Andrew Downer Crain.

108. Ford, *Time to Heal*, 248–49.

109. Cannon, *Time and Chance*, 396.

110. CIA Memorandum, "Hanoi, ASEAN, and the United States," July 20, 1976, Digital National Security Archive.

111. Balogh, "From Metaphor to Quagmire," 29; Brigham, "Revolutionary Heroism," 85–99; Snepp, *Decent Interval*, 569–70; Memorandum from Brent Scowcroft for President Ford, "Escape from South Vietnam," July 10, 1976, Ford Library, National Security Adviser, Presidential Country Files for East Asia and the Pacific, Box 20, Folder: "Vietnam (30)"; Memorandum from William Gleysteen to Brent Scowcroft, "Indochina Refugee 'Boat Cases,'" December 10, 1976, Ford Library, National Security Adviser, Presidential Subject File, Box 18, Folder: "Refugees — Indochina (5)."

112. CIA Memorandum, "Backup for 24 April NSC Meeting, Cambodia," April 24, 1975, Digital National Security Archive.

113. CIA Research Study, "Democratic Cambodia: An Experiment in Radicalism," December 1976, Digital National Security Archive.

114. Short, *Pol Pot*, 7.

115. 1999 UN Report on Cambodia; Power, *Problem from Hell*, 95–98.

116. Short, *Pol Pot*, 10; Sydney H. Schanberg, "Cambodia Reds are Uprooting Millions as They Impose a 'Peasant Revolution,'" *New York Times*, May 9, 1975, 73; Power, *Problem from Hell*, 102–107.

117. Power, *Problem from Hell*, 115–17.

118. "Life Inside Cambodia," May 10, 1976, Ford Library, National Security Adviser, Presidential Country Files for East Asia and the Pacific, Box 3, Folder: "Cambodia (23)."

119. CIA Research Study, "Democratic Cambodia: An Ex-periment in Radicalism," December 1976, Digital National Security Archive.

120. 1999 UN Report on Cambodia; Etcheson, "The Number"; "Kampuchea: A Demographic Catastrophe," National Foreign Assessment Center, Central Intelligence Agency, May 1980, available at www.mekong.net/cambodia/demcat.htm; Margolin, "Cambodia: The Country of Disconcerting Crimes," 571–620; Power, *Problem from Hell*, 87–88 and 109–19; CIA Research Study, "Democratic Cambodia: An Experiment in Radicalism," December 1976, Digital National Security Archive.

121. Power, *Problem from Hell*, 154. Fifteen years later the UN used similar language when it concluded that the Khmer Rouge had committed "some of the most horrific violations of human rights seen in the world since the end of the Second World War." 1999 UN Report on Cambodia.

122. Etcheson, "The Number."

123. 1999 UN Report on Cambodia; Kiernan, "The Demography of Genocide in Southeast Asia"; Margolin, "Cambodia: The Country of Disconcerting Crimes," 589–90; Power, *Problem from Hell*, 143; Etcheson, "The Number."

124. The following reports have complete chronologies of the events of the seizure and rescue of the *Mayaguez*: Comptroller General Mayaguez Report, Appendix 7, "Chronology of Mayaguez Incident," 116–26; Congressional Research Service, "Chronology of the Events in the Mayaguez Incident"; Department of Defense, "Narrative Summary of Mayaguez/Koh Song Island Operation"; Ford, *Time to Heal*, 277; Greene, *Presidency of Gerald R. Ford*, 145–147; Kissinger, *Years of Renewal*, 551–76.

125. "Comments of a Liberated Crew," *Time Magazine*, May 26, 1975.

126. Isaacson, *Kissinger*, 649.

127. Memorandum to Director Colby from Lt. General Samuel Wilson, "Coverage of Events in the Gulf of Thailand Prior to the Seizure of the Mayaguez," May 14, 1975, Digital National Security Archive; CIA Report, "Cambodian Claims in the Gulf of Thailand: More Trouble Brewing," May 1975, Digital National Security Archive.

128. Kissinger, *Years of Renewal*, 548; Memorandum of Conversation, May 12, 1975, Ford Library, National Security Adviser, Memoranda of Conversations, 1973–1977, Box 11, Folder: "May 12, 1975 — Ford, Kissinger."

129. Kissinger, *Years of Renewal*, 551.

130. Hartmann, *Palace Politics*, 325.

131. Minutes of May 12, 1975, National Security Council Meeting, Ford Library, National Security Adviser. National Security Council Meetings File, Box 1.

132. Minutes of May 12, 1975, National Security Council Meeting, Ford Library, National Security Adviser. National Security Council Meetings File, Box 1.

133. Hartmann, *Palace Politics*, 326.

134. Ford, *Time to Heal*, 277.

135. Ford, *Time to Heal*, 276.

136. Minutes of May 13, 1975, National Security Council Meeting, Ford Library, National Security Adviser, National Security Council Meetings File, Box 1.

137. Minutes of National Security Council Meeting of May 13, 1975, at 10:40 P.M., Ford Library, National Security Adviser, National Security Council Meetings File, Box 1.

138. Kissinger, *Years of Renewal*, 559.

139. Memorandum of Conversation between President Ford, Secretary Kissinger and Lt. General Scowcroft, May 14, 1975, 11:45 A.M., Ford Library, NSA Memoranda of Conversations 1973–1977, Box 11, Folder: "May 14, 1975 — Ford, Kissinger."

140. Minutes of National Security Council Meeting of May 14, 1975, Ford Library, National Security Adviser, National Security Council Meetings File, Box 1.

141. Ford, *Time to Heal*, 283; Hartmann, *Palace Politics*, 328; Nessen, *It Sure Looks Different*, 128–29.

142. Minutes of National Security Council Meeting of May 15, 1975, Ford Library, National Security Adviser, National Security Council Meetings File, Box 1.

143. Ford, *Time to Heal*, 284.

144. Isaacson, *Kissinger*.

145. Minutes of National Security Council Meeting of May 15, 1975, Ford Library, National Security Adviser, National Security Council Meetings File, Box 1.

146. Kissinger, *Years of Renewal*, 574.

147. Memorandum for Dick Cheney from Jerry Jones, "Poll Information," May 27, 1975, Ford Library, Presidential Handwriting Files, Box 33, Folder: "Nat. Sec. Wars — Cambodia (2).

148. Kissinger, *Years of Renewal*, 575.

Chapter 12

1. Conference on Security and Co-Operation in Europe, Final Act, Helsinki, August 1, 1975.

2. John Osborne noted at the time that this was Kissinger's interpretation of the agreement. John Osborne, "White House Watch," *New Republic*, August 16–23, 1975, reprinted in Osborne, *The Ford Years*, 174.

3. Kissinger, *Years of Renewal*, 644–45 and 662.

4. Dobrynin, *In Confidence*, 346.

5. William F. Buckley, Jr., "On the Right," *National Review,* October 15, 1976, 1141.

6. Aleksandr Solzhenitsyn, "The Big Losers in the Third World War," *New York Times*, June 22, 1975, 193.

7. Bernard Gwertzman, "Detente Scored by Solzhenitsyn," *New York Times*, July 1, 1975, 6; Ford, *Time to Heal,* 297–98; Hartmann, *Palace Politics*, 337–39; Kissinger, *Years of Renewal*, 649; Nessen, *It Sure Looks Different*, 345.

8. Bernard Gwertzman, "Detente Scored by Solzhenitsyn," *New York Times*, July 1, 1975, 6.

9. Aleksandr I. Solzhenitsyn, "Solzhenitsyn Replies to His Critics," *Wall Street Journal*, July 18, 1975, 8.

10. Aleksandr I. Solzhenitsyn, "The Big Losers in the Third World War," *New York Times*, June 22, 1975, 193; Hilton Kramer, "Solzhenitsyn in City, Warns of Soviet Danger," *New York Times*, July 10, 1975, 63.

11. "Jerry, Don't Go," *Wall Street Journal*, July 23, 1975, 14.

12. James M. Naughton," Ford Sees 35-Nation Charter as a Gauge on Rights in East Europe," *New York Times*, July 26, 1975, 2.

13. William Safire, "Ending World War II," *New York Times*, April 14, 1975, 31.

14. "Helsinki: What's in It for the West?" National Review, Volume 27, No. 26, July 11, 1975, 97.

15. Hyland, *Mortal Rivals*, 112.

16. "Text of Remarks at a Meeting with Representatives of Americans of Eastern European Background Concerning the Conference on Security and Cooperation in Europe," President Gerald R. Ford, July 25, 1975.

17. "Remarks on Departure for Europe," President Gerald R. Ford, July 26, 1975; "Statement by President," *New York Times*, July 27, 1975, 5; Isaacson, *Kissinger,* 661.

18. Ford, *Time to Heal*, 302; Kissinger, *Years of Renewal*, 654–57.

19. President Gerald R. Ford's Address in Helsinki Before the Conference on Security and Cooperation in Europe, August 1, 1975; Ford, *Time to Heal*, 298–305; Hyland, *Mortal Rivals*, 121.

20. Ronald Reagan, "To Restore America," March 31, 1976, reprinted at *www.medaloffreedom.com/RonaldReaganTo RestoreAmerica.htm.*

21. Presidential Campaign Debate Between Gerald R. Ford and Jimmy Carter, October 6, 1976, transcript available at *www.ford.utexas.edu/LIBRARY/SPEECHES/760854.htm.*

22. Goldberg, *Final Act*.

23. Interview with Vaclav Havel, "Cold War Experience," CNN, reprinted at *www.cnn.com/SPECIALS/cold.war/episodes/ 19/interviews/havel/.*

24. Hyland, *Mortal Rivals*, 127.

25. "Record of Investigator's Conversation with Jaruzelski," Swedish Ministry for Foreign Affairs, September 26, 2002, Ap-

pendix 5 SOU 2002:108, reprinted at "Conversation with Jaruzelski," National Security Archive Website.

26. Hyland, *Mortal Rivals*, 128.

27. Dobrynin, *In Confidence*, 346–47.

28. "Interview with Richard Perle — 30.3.1997," cnn.com, *Cold War,* available at *www.gwu.edu/-nsarchiv/coldwar/inter views/episode-19/perle3.html.*

29. Memorandum of Conversation, March 26, 1975, Ford Library, National Security Adviser. Memoranda of Conversations, 1973–1977, Box 10, Folder: "March 26, 1975 — Ford, Kissinger."

30. Memorandum of Conversation, April 12, 1975, Ford Library, National Security Adviser, Memoranda of Conversations, 1973–1977, Box 10, Folder: "April 12, 1975 — Ford, Kissinger, Ambassador Daniel Patrick Moynihan (UN)."

31. Memorandum of Conversation, Ford, Scowcroft, Kissinger, January 8, 1976, Ford Library, National Security Advisor, Memoranda of Conversations, 1973–1977, Box 17, Folder: "January 8, 1976 — Ford, Kissinger, Scowcroft."

32. Reichley, *Conservatives in an Age of Change*, 344.

33. Herzog, *Living History*, 206–207.

34. Minutes of National Security Council Meeting of July 25, 1975, Ford Library, National Security Adviser, National Security Council Meetings File, Box 2.

35. Memorandum of Conversation, President Gerald R. Ford, et al. and General Secretary Leonid Brezhnev, et al., August 2, 1975, 9:05 A.M., Ford Library, NSA/Kissinger Reports, Box 1, Folder: "July 30–August 2, 1975, Ford/Brezhnev Meetings in Helsinki"; Minutes of National Security Council Meeting of August 9, 1975, Ford Library, National Security Adviser, National Security Council Meetings File, Box 2; Ford, *Time to Heal*, 303–306.

36. Dobrynin, *In Confidence*, 347.

37. Minutes of National Security Council Meeting of August 9, 1975, Ford Library, National Security Adviser, National Security Council Meetings File, Box 2.

38. Memorandum of Conversation Between Vice President Rockefeller, Dr. Henry Kissinger, General Brent Scowcroft, and the President's Foreign Policy Advisory Board, August 7, 1975, Ford Library, NSA Memoranda of Conversations 1973–1977, Box 14, Folder: "August 7, 1975, Rockefeller, Kissinger/ President's Foreign Intelligence Advisory Board."

39. Minutes of National Security Council of September 17, 1975, Ford Library, National Security Adviser, National Security Council Meetings File, Box 2.

40. Hyland, *Mortal Rivals*, 120.

41. The *New York Times* printed a copy of the summary of Sonnenfeldt's speech on April 6, 1976. "State Dept. Summary of Remarks by Sonnenfeldt," *New York Times*, April 6, 1976, 14; Kissinger, *Years of Renewal*, 862–65; Isaacson, *Kissinger,* 664.

42. Isaacson, *Kissinger*, 665.

43. Isaacson, *Kissinger*, 664.

Chapter 13

1. Memorandum of Conversation between Secretary Kissinger, Secretary James Callaghan, Minister Jean Sauvagnargues, Minister Hans-Dietrich Genscher, et al., December 12, 1975, Ford Library. See also Interview of Ambassador Edward M. Rowell, by Charles Stuart Kennedy, September 19, 1995, Diplomatic Studies Interview Collection.

2. Memorandum of Conversation, President Ford and Secretary Kissinger, February 25, 1975, Ford Library, National Security Advisor, Memoranda of Conversations, 1973–1977, Box 9, Folder: "February 25, 1975 — Ford, Kissinger." On August 7, 1975, he complained that "If we had done in Portugal what we did in Chile we would come out the same way." Memorandum of Conversation Between Vice President Rockefeller, Dr. Henry Kissinger, General Brent Scowcroft, and the President's Foreign Policy Advisory Board, August 7, 1975, Ford Library, NSA Memoranda of Conversations 1973–1977, Box 14, Folder: "August 7, 1975, Rockefeller, Kissinger/President's Foreign Intelligence Advisory Board."

3. For a description of the history of the Portuguese fascist regime, see Gallagher, *Portugal*, 1–172; Riegelhaupt, "Introduction," 1–16; Interview of Ambassador Edward M. Rowell, by Charles Stuart Kennedy, September 19, 1995, Diplomatic Studies Interview Collection; Marcum, *Angolan Revolution*, 1, 179, and 236–37.

4. Interview of Ambassador Edward M. Rowell, by Charles Stuart Kennedy, September 19, 1995, Diplomatic Studies Interview Collection.

5. "End of Last Empire," *Time Magazine*, August 12, 1974; Gallagher, *Portugal*, 200–201.

6. For a description of the Portuguese revolution, see Gallagher, *Portugal*, 186–200; Riegelhaupt, "The Sequence of Events," Bruneau, "Popular Support for Democracy," Lomax, "Ideology and Illusion," Downs, "Residents' Commissions and Urban Struggles," Gallagher, "From Hegemony to Opposition," Logan, "Worker Mobilization and Party Politics," and Makler, "The Consequences of the Survival and Revival of the Industrial Bourgeoisie"; Spikes, *Angola and the Politics of Intervention*, 90–103; Kissinger, *Years of Renewal*, 629–30 and 673; Interview of Ambassador Edward M. Rowell, by Charles Stuart Kennedy, September 19, 1995, Diplomatic Studies Interview Collection; Maxwell, *Making of Portuguese Democracy*, 66–69. For America's surprise at the revolution, see Minutes of Secretary of State Kissinger's Staff Meeting, October 8, 1975, Digital National Security Archive, also available at http://www. gwu.edu/~nsarchiv/NSAEBB193/HAK-10-8-75. pdf. For the Soviet surprise, see George, *Cuban Intervention in Angola*, 50–51.

7. Gallagher, *Portugal*, 202–209; Spikes, *Angola and the Politics of Intervention*, 114–18.

8. Interview of Ambassador Edward M. Rowell, by Charles Stuart Kennedy, September 19, 1995, Diplomatic Studies Interview Collection.

9. Memorandum of Conversation, President Gomes, et al. and President Ford, et al., October 18, 1974, Ford Library, National Security Advisor, Memoranda of Conversations, 1973–1977, Box 6, Folder: "October 18, 1974 — Ford, Kissinger, Portuguese President Costa Gomes, Foreign Minister Mario Soares."

10. Spikes, *Angola and the Politics of Intervention*, 119; Tad Szulc, "Lisbon & Washington: Behind the Portuguese Revolution," *Foreign Policy*, No. 21 (Winter, 1975-1976), 3–62.

11. Clymer, *Edward M. Kennedy*, 231.

12. Memorandum of Conversation, President Ford and Secretary Kissinger, February 25, 1975, Ford Library, National Security Advisor, Memoranda of Conversations, 1973–1977, Box 9, Folder: "February 25, 1975 — Ford, Kissinger"; Interview of Ambassador Edward M. Rowell, by Charles Stuart Kennedy, September 19, 1995, Diplomatic Studies Interview Collection.

13. Szulc, "Lisbon & Washington," 3–62; Gaspar, "International Dimensions"; Interview of Ambassador Edward M. Rowell, by Charles Stuart Kennedy, September 19, 1995, Diplomatic Studies Interview Collection; Interview of Richard H. Melton, by, Charles Stuart Kennedy, January 27, 1997, Diplomatic Studies Interview Collection; Interview of Frank Charles Carlucci, III, by Charles Stuart Kennedy, December 30, 1996, Diplomatic Studies Interview Collection; Isaacson, *Kissinger*, 674; Interview of Ambassador Bruce Laingen, by Charles Stuart Kennedy, January 9, April 7, August 25, 1992, February 17, May 27, 1993, Diplomatic Studies Interview Collection.

14. Interview of Frank Charles Carlucci, III, by Charles Stuart Kennedy, December 30, 1996, Diplomatic Studies Interview Collection. For the condition of the embassy, see Interview of Ambassador Edward M. Rowell, by Charles Stuart Kennedy, September 19, 1995, Diplomatic Studies Interview Collection; Interview of Richard H. Melton, by, Charles Stuart Kennedy, January 27, 1997, Diplomatic Studies Interview Collection; Minutes of Secretary of State Kissinger's Staff Meeting, October 8, 1975, Digital National Security Archive, also available at http://www.gwu.edu/~nsarchiv/NSAEBB/NSAEBB193/HAK-10-8-75.pdf.

15. Interview of General Brent Scowcroft, by the author, October 27, 2006; Interview of Frank Charles Carlucci, III, by Charles Stuart Kennedy, December 30, 1996, Diplomatic Studies Interview Collection; Interview of Richard H. Melton, by Charles Stuart Kennedy, January 27, 1997, Diplomatic Studies Interview Collection.

16. Interview of Frank Charles Carlucci, III, by Charles Stuart Kennedy, December 30, 1996, Diplomatic Studies Interview Collection.

17. Szulc, "Lisbon & Washington," 3–62; Interview of Frank Charles Carlucci, III, by Charles Stuart Kennedy, December 30, 1996, Diplomatic Studies Interview Collection; Isaacson, *Kissinger*, 674; Interview of Ambassador Bruce Laingen, by Charles Stuart Kennedy, January 9, April 7, August 25, 1992, February 17, May 27, 1993, Diplomatic Studies Interview Collection.

18. Interview of Frank Charles Carlucci, III, by Charles Stuart Kennedy, December 30, 1996, Diplomatic Studies Interview Collection.

19. Interview of General Brent Scowcroft, by Andrew Downer Crain, October 27, 2006; Interview of Ambassador Edward M. Rowell, by Charles Stuart Kennedy, September 19, 1995, Diplomatic Studies Interview Collection; Interview of Richard H. Melton, by, Charles Stuart Kennedy, January 27, 1997, Diplomatic Studies Interview Collection; Interview of Richard H. Melton, by Charles Stuart Kennedy, January 27, 1997, Diplomatic Studies Interview Collection; Kissinger, *Years of Renewal*, 631; Gaspar, "International Dimensions."

20. Lomax, "Ideology and Illusion," 117; Gallagher, *Portugal*, 210–212.

21. Interview of Frank Charles Carlucci, III, by Charles Stuart Kennedy, December 30, 1996, Diplomatic Studies Interview Collection; Interview of Ambassador Edward M. Rowell, by Charles Stuart Kennedy, September 19, 1995, Diplomatic Studies Interview Collection; CIA Memorandum, March 11, 1975, "Coup Attempt in Portugal," National Security Digital Archive.

22. Interview of Ambassador Edward M. Rowell, by Charles Stuart Kennedy, September 19, 1995, Diplomatic Studies Interview Collection; Ford, *Time to Heal*, 285. On April 2, 1975, in a meeting with Schlesinger and Scowcroft, Kissinger recommended that Portugal be forced out of NATO. "We must force them out of NATO." Memorandum of Conversation, April 2, 1975, Ford Library, National Security Adviser, Memoranda of Conversations, 1973–1977, Box 5, Folder: "April 2, 1975 — Kissinger, Schlesinger."

23. Interview of Frank Charles Carlucci, III, by Charles Stuart Kennedy, December 30, 1996, Diplomatic Studies Interview Collection.

24. Gallagher, *Portugal*, 213–215.

25. Memorandum of Conversation, May 1, 1975, Ford Library, National Security Adviser, Memoranda of Conversations, 1973–1977, Box 11, Folder: "May 1, 1975 — Ford, Kissinger."

26. Oriana Fallaci, "A Talk with the Communist Leader," *New York Times*, July 13, 1975, 189.

27. Memorandum of Conversation, Prime Minister Gonçalves, et al. and President Ford, et al., May 29, 1975, Ford Library, National Security Advisor, Memoranda of Conversations, 1973–1977, Box 12, Folder: "May 29, 1975 — Ford, Kissinger, Portuguese Prime Minister Gonçalves." For Ford's later description of the meeting, see Cabinet Meeting Minutes, 6/4/75, Ford Library, James E. Connor Files, Box 4.

28. Memorandum of Conversation, President Franco, et al. and President Ford, et al., May 31, 1975, 1:30 P.M., Ford Library, National Security Advisor, Memoranda of Conversations, 1973–1977, Box 12, Folder: "May 31, 1975 — Ford, Kissinger, General Francisco Franco, Spanish Prime Minister Carlos Arias Navarro, Foreign Minister Pedro Cortina Mauri."

29. Spikes, 174–75; Gallagher, 217; Bill Lomax, "Ideology and Illusion in the Portuguese Revolution: The Role of the Left," in Graham and Wheeler, 118.

30. Interview of Frank Charles Carlucci, III, by Charles Stuart Kennedy, December 30, 1996, Diplomatic Studies Interview Collection; Interview of Ambassador Edward M. Rowell, by Charles Stuart Kennedy, September 19, 1995, Diplo-

matic Studies Interview Collection; Interview of Richard H. Melton, by Charles Stuart Kennedy, January 27, 1997, Diplomatic Studies Interview Collection.

31. CIA Memorandum, August 14, 1975, "An Assessment of the Role the Portuguese Armed Forces Might Play in the Current Political Crisis."

32. CIA Intelligence Alert Memorandum from General Vernon Walters to Secretary Kissinger, October 10, 1975, "Portugal: A New Crisis of Authority"; CIA Intelligence Alert Memorandum from General Vernon Walters to Secretary Kissinger, August 29, 1975, "Portugal: A Step Closer to Civil War"; Gallagher, *Portugal*, 217–23; Riegelhaupt, "The Sequence of Events"; Gallagher, "From Hegemony to Opposition"; Lomax, "Ideology and Illusion."

33. Memorandum of Conversation, Ford, Scowcroft, Italian Minister of Foreign Affairs Mariano Rumor, and Italian Ambassador Roberto Gaja, September 23, 1975, Ford Library, National Security Advisor, Memoranda of Conversations, 1973–1977, Box 15, Folder: "September 23, 1975 — Ford, Italian Minister of Foreign Affairs Mariano Rumor."

34. Gallagher, *Portugal*, 224–29; Makler, "The Consequences of the Survival," 258.

35. Gallagher, *Portugal*, 229–41; Bruneau, "Popular Support for Democracy in Post Revolutionary Portugal"; Makler, "The Consequences of the Survival and Revival of the Industrial Bourgeoisie"; Interview of Ambassador Edward M. Rowell, by Charles Stuart Kennedy, September 19, 1995, Diplomatic Studies Interview Collection.

36. Memorandum for the President from Henry Kissinger, "Emergency Balance of Payment Assistance for Portugal," November 1, 1976, "Portugal: Justification for Special Financial (Balance of Payments) Assistance and Review of Options," November 1, 1976, and Memorandum for the President from Brent Scowcroft, "Emergency Balance of Payment Assistance for Portugal," November 6, 1976, Ford Library, Presidential Handwriting Files, Box 52, Folder: "Foreign Aff.— Foreign Aid — Portugal."

37. Preston, *Triumph of Democracy in Spain*, 9–73.

38. Kissinger, *Years of Renewal*, 632–33.

39. CIA Memorandum, December 8, 1975, "European Brief," Digital National Security Archives; Preston, *Triumph of Democracy in Spain*, 76–82; Interview of Ambassador Edward M. Rowell, by Charles Stuart Kennedy, September 19, 1995, Diplomatic Studies Interview Collection.

40. Memorandum of Conversation, Ford, Kissinger, Spanish King Juan Carlos, Foreign Minister Areilza, April 21, 1976, Ford Library, National Security Advisor, Memoranda of Conversations, 1973–1977, Box 19, Folder: "June 2, 1976 — Ford, Kissinger, Spanish King Juan Carlos, Foreign Minister Areilza."

41. Preston, *Triumph of Democracy in Spain*, 70–120.

Chapter 14

1. Themstrom and Themstrom, *America in Black and White*, 54, 63 and 76; Theodore H. White, *Breach of Faith*, 45. In 1950 there were no large cities with African American majorities. By 1970, African Americans were the majorities in Newark, Gary, Atlanta, and Washington, D.C. Theodore H. White, *Breach of Faith*, 45.

2. Since 1960 the murder rate had doubled, but it was only ten percent higher than it had been during prohibition. Following the repeal of prohibition, the murder rate fell and remained low through the '60s, when a different prohibition was flaunted by a large segment of the populace. *Statistical Abstract of the United States 1976*. See also Harold J. Brumm and Dale O. Cloniger, "The Drug War and the Homicide Rate: A Direct Correlation?" *Cato Journal*, Vol. 14, No. 3, Winter 1995, 509–17.

3. McAndrews, "Missing the Bus"; Themstrom and Themstrom, *America in Black & White*, 330–31; "Desegregation: A Historic Reversal," *Time Magazine*, August 4, 1974.

4. Themstrom and Themstrom, *America in Black and White*, 13, 18, 61, 73, 102, 221, 430, and 523–524.

5. For summaries of busing cases, see McAndrews, "Miss-

ing the Bus"; Department of Justice Memorandum Summarizing Busing Cases, August 22, 1975, Ford Library, Bobbie Greene Kilberg Files, Box 13, Folder: "Busing — General 3/75–8/75 (1)"; Memorandum from Dick Parsons to Jim Cannon and Philip Buchen, "Busing," October 6, 1975, Ford Library, Richard Parsons Files, Box 2, File: "Busing — Alternatives to."

6. *Swann v Charlotte-Mecklenburg School District*, 402 U.S. 1 (1971).

7. *Milliken v Bradley*, 418 U.S. 717 (1974).

8. Department of Justice Memorandum for the Deputy Attorney General, "Boston School Case," October 10, 1974, Ford Library, Geoffrey Shepard Files, Box 2, File: "Civil Rights — Boston, Busing"; John Kifner, "Kennedy Jeered on Boston Busing," and "Violence Mars Busing in Boston," *New York Times*, September 10 and 13, 1974; Clymer, 222.

9. Transcript of President Gerald R. Ford's News Conference of October 9, 1974.

10. Memorandum for the President from Ken Cole, "Busing in Boston," October 11, 1974, and News Bulletin, October 10, 1974, Ford Library, Geoffrey Shepard Files, Box 3, Folder: "Civil Rights — Busing, Boston"; Wayne King, "425 Extra Policemen," *New York Times*, October 11, 1974, 81.

11. Cabinet Meeting Minutes, 10/11/74, Ford Library, James E. Connor Files, Box 3.

12. Memorandum for the President from Kenneth Cole, "Use of Federal Troops in Boston (Procedure)," October 11, 1974, Ford Library, Geoffrey Shepard Files, Box 2, File: "Civil Rights — Boston, Busing"; Memorandum from Ken Cole to the President, "Busing in Boston," October 11, 1974, and Memorandum from Ken Cole to the President, "Boston Situation," October 17, 1974, Ford Library, Presidential Handwriting File, Box 24, Folder: "Human Rights — Equality: Education."

13. Memorandum from Laurence H. Silberman, Deputy Attorney General, to Honorable Donald Rumsfeld, "School Unrest in Boston," October 17, 1974, Ford Library, Presidential Handwriting File, Box 24, Folder: "Human Rights — Equality: Education"; John Kifner, "South Boston Schools Shut in Clashes Over Stabbing," *New York Times*, December 12, 1974, 97.

14. Memorandum from Richard Parsons, "Boston Desegregation Cases — Status Report," September 3, 1975, Ford Library, Richard D. Parson Files, Box 2, Folder: "Busing — Miscellaneous Correspondence, March–Sept. 1975 (1)"; John Kifner, "Boston Prepares for More Busing," "Schools in Boston Open Under Guard," "Federal Aides Studying Violence in Boston Busing," "Tension Is High in South Boston," *New York Times*, September 7, 9, and 13, 1975.

15. John Kifner, "White Pupils' Rolls Drop a Third in Boston Busing," *New York Times*, December 15, 1975, 48 and 65; Farrell, *Tip O'Neill*, 525.

16. Senate Confirmation Hearings, 115.

17. President Gerald R. Ford, Remarks on Signing the Education Amendments of 1974, August 21, 1974; President Gerald R. Ford, Statement on the Education Amendments of 1974, August 21, 1974.

18. Cabinet Meeting Minutes, 9/17/75, Ford Library, James E. Connor Files, Box 5.

19. *Statistical Abstract of the United States 1976*, 97h Edition, Washington, U.S. Bureau of the Census, 1976, Table 48; "How to Save New York," and "How New York City Lurched to the Brink," *Time Magazine*, June 16 and October 20, 1975.

20. Memorandum from Robert A. Gerard to Jim Falk, "New York City Financial Situation," May 1, 1975, Ford Library, John G. Carlson Files, Box 4, Folder: "New York Financial Crisis (1)"; Steven R. Weisman, "How New York Became a Fiscal Junkie," *New York Times*, August 17, 1975, 191.

21. "Simon Advises New York Officials Not to Expect Federal Bailout," May 9, 1975, Ford Library, John G. Carlson Files, Box 4, Folder: "New York Financial Crisis (1)."

22. Memorandum from Robert A. Gerard to Jim Falk, "New York City Financial Situation," May 1, 1975, Ford Library, John G. Carlson Files, Box 4, Folder: "New York Financial Crisis (1)."

23. Statement by Arthur F. Burns, Chairman, Board of Governors of the Federal Reserve System, Before the Joint Economic Committee, October 8, 1975, reprinted in *Federal Reserve Bulletin*, Number 10, Volume 61, October 1975, 632.

24. Talking Points, May 12, 1975, "Simon Rejects City of New York's Request for Financial Aid," Ford Library, John G. Carlson Files, Box 2, File: "New York City Financial Crisis (1)"; Memorandum to the President from William Seidman, "New York City," May 8, 1975, Ford Library, Presidential Handwriting File, Box 24, Folder: "Legislation (1) 9/8/74"; Turner, *Vice President as Policy Maker*, 133.

25. Ford, *Time to Heal*, 315.

26. Osborne, *White House Watch*, 135–36; Memorandum from James Cannon for the President, "Meeting with Governor Hugh Carey and Mayor Abe Beame," May 13, 1975, Ford Library, Presidential Handwriting Files, Box 28, Folder: "Local Gov't — New York (1)."

27. President Gerald R. Ford, Letter to Mayor Abraham D. Beame Responding to New York City's Financial Assistance Request, May 14th, 1975.

28. "Saying No to New York," *Time Magazine*, May 26, 1975.

29. Turner, *Vice President as Policy Maker*, 136.

30. "Some Bites Out of the Big Apple," "Rescuing New York, and Other Tales," and "How New York City Lurched to the Brink," *Time Magazine*, July 14, and August 11 and 17, 1975; Steven R. Weisman, "How New York Became a Fiscal Junkie," *New York Times*, August 17, 1975, 191.

31. Memorandum from Dick Dunham to Jim Cannon, attached to Memorandum for the President from Jim Cannon, "New York City Financial Situation," August 1, 1975, Ford Library, James M. Cannon Files, Box 23, Folder: "New York City Finances, May–August 1975."

32. Memorandum from Edwin H. Yeo for the President, "Report on New York City," August 18, 1975, Ford Library, Presidential Handwriting Files, Box 28, Folder: "Local Gov't — New York (2)."

33. Memorandum from William Seidman for the President, "New York City Situation," September 2, 1975, Ford Library, Presidential Handwriting Files, Box 28, Folder: "Local Gov't — New York (3)"; "Fighting the Unthinkable," *Time Magazine*, September 8, 1975.

34. Ford, *Time to Heal*, 316.

35. Cabinet Meeting Minutes, 9/17/75, Ford Library, James E. Connor Files, Box 3.

36. Presentation to President Ford on New York City Financial Crisis, September 24, 1975, Ford Library, James M. Cannon Files, Box 23, Folder: "New York City Finances, September 1975"; "Assembly Backs Carey's Plan for City," *New York Times*, September 9, 1975, 85; "Teachers: In a Striking Mood," "Unhappy Ending," and "How to Save New York," *Time Magazine*, September 22 and 19, and October 20, 1975.

37. Memorandum from William Simon for the President, "New York City," September 8, 1975, Ford Library, Presidential Handwriting Files, Box 28, Folder: "Local Gov't — New York (3)."

38. Memorandum from William Seidman, "Memorandum of Decisions," September 9, 1975, Ford Library, Presidential Handwriting Files, Box 28, Folder: "Local Gov't — New York (4)."

39. "Last Chance for New York," *Time Magazine*, September 15, 1975; Memorandum from William Seidman for the President, "Financing Options for New York City," September 8, 1975, Ford Library, Presidential Handwriting Files, Box 28, Folder: "Local Gov't — New York (4)."

40. "Remarks of the Vice President at the Annual Columbus Day Dinner," October 11, 1975, Ford Library, John G. Carlson Files, Box 2, File: "New York City Financial Crisis (2)"; Osborne, *White House Watch*, 207–208; Turner, *Vice President as Policy Maker*, 135–39; Hartmann, *Palace Politics*, 356; Cabinet Meeting Minutes, 9/17/75, Ford Library, James E. Connor Files, Box 3.

41. "How to Save New York," *Time Magazine*, October 20, 1975.

42. Greene, *Presidency of Gerald R. Ford*, 93.

43. President Gerald R. Ford, Remarks and a Question-and-Answer Session at the National Press Club on the Subject of Financial Assistance to New York City, October 29, 1975. According to David Gergen, he wrote some of the strong phrases and expected to tone them down during redrafting. He was surprised when they made it into the final unedited. Gergen, *Eyewitness to Power*, 114–15.

44. Memorandum from William T. Kendall to Max L. Friedersdorf, "New York City Crisis," William T. Kendall Files, Box 4, File: "New York City Crisis (1)."

45. Turner, *Vice President as Policy Maker* 141.

46. "The Anguished City Gears for D-Day," *Time Magazine*, November 10, 1975.

47. "Some Cheers for an Underdog," *Time Magazine*, November 17, 1975; "Watching New York Writhe," *Time Magazine*, September 8, 1975.

48. Greene, *Presidency of Gerald R. Ford*, 94.

49. President Gerald R. Ford, Interview with Television Reporters in Jacksonville, November 3, 1975.

50. Letter from Governor Hugh Carey to the President, November 4, 1975, Ford Library, James M. Cannon Files, Box 23, Folder: "New York City Finances, November–December 1975."

51. Memorandum from William Seidman, "Memorandum of Decisions," November 5, 1975, and Memorandum from William Simon for the President, "New York City," November 3, 1975, Ford Library, Presidential Handwriting Files, Box 29, Folder: "Local Gov't — New York (6)."

52. Memorandum from Stephen S. Gardner for the President, "New York Plan," November 14, 1975, Ford Library, Richard Cheney Files, Box 9, Folder: "New York City Financial Crisis, 11/75."

53. Notes of Meeting Between President and Senators, November 11, 1975, John G. Carlson Files, Box 4, File: "New York City Financial Crisis (3)."

54. President Gerald R. Ford, the President's News Conference of November 14, 1975.

55. President Gerald R. Ford, Statement on New York City's Financial Situation, November 19, 1975.

56. Letter from Governor Hugh Carey to the President, November 26, 1975, Ford Library, James M. Cannon Files, Box 23, Folder: "New York City Finances, November–December 1975."

57. President Gerald R. Ford, the President's News Conference of November 26, 1975.

Chapter 15

1. Oswald Johnston, "Administration Badly Split on Arms Control," *Los Angeles Times*, October 12, 1975; Memorandum of Conversation, Ford, Scowcroft, and Kissinger, October 16, 1975, Ford Library, National Security Advisor, Memoranda of Conversations, 1973–1977, Box 16, Folder: "October 16, 1975 — Ford, Kissinger."

2. Ford, *Time to Heal*, 320–24.

3. Ford, *Time to Heal*, 324.

4. Ford, *Time to Heal*, 324–25.

5. Ford, *Time to Heal*, 325.

6. Ford, *Time to Heal*, 325–26.

7. Ford, *Time to Heal*, 328.

8. Ford, *Time to Heal*, 328–30.

9. Isaacson, *Kissinger*, 670.

10. Reichley, *Conservatives in an Age of Change*, 351.

11. Kissinger, *Years of Renewal*, 842–43.

12. President Gerald R. Ford's Press Conference of November 3, 1975.

13. Ford, *Time to Heal*, 331.

14. Kissinger, *Years of Renewal*, 837.

15. Turner, *Vice President as Policy Maker*, 179.

16. Christopher Lydon, "Reagan Shocked at Schlesinger Ouster," *New York Times*, November 4, 1975, 27.

17. Ford, *Time to Heal*, 328.

18. Osborne, *White House Watch*, xxiii

19. Brinkley, *Gerald R. Ford*, 118.
20. Greene, *Presidency of Gerald R. Ford*, 162.
21. Nessen, *It Sure Looks Different*, 161.
22. Gergen, *Eyewitness to Power*, 115.
23. Interview of Michael Raoul-Duval, by Stephen J. Wayne, February 9, 1977, Hyde and Wayne Interview Collection, Folder: "Raoul-Duval — Michael, Interview 2/9/77," Box 1, 3; Interview of Richard B. Cheney, by Stephen J. Wayne, February 8, 1977, Hyde and Wayne Interview Collection, Box 1, Folder: "Cheney, Richard — Interview, 2/8/77," 2; Osborne, *White House Watch*, 298 and 400; Nessen, *It Sure Looks Different*, 249; Gergen, *Eyewitness to Power*, 132; Press Briefing, 8/30/76, Ford Library, Cabinet Meeting Collected Items, Box 4.
24. Interview of Richard B. Cheney, by Stephen J. Wayne, February 8, 1977, Hyde and Wayne Interview Collection, Box 1, Folder: "Cheney, Richard — Interview, 2/8/77," 2; Interview of Michael Raoul-Duval, by Stephen J. Wayne, February 9, 1977, Hyde and Wayne Interview Collection, Folder: "Raoul-Duval — Michael, Interview 11/2/76," 15; Walcott, "Separating Rhetoric from Policy"; Interview with Pat Butler, June 27, 1985, Syers Interview Collection, Box 1, Folder: "Butler, Pat," 2.
25. Interview with Pat Butler, June 27, 1985, Syers Interview Collection, Box 1, Folder: "Butler, Pat," 4; Walcott, "Separating Rhetoric from Policy," 3.
26. Interview of Ambassador Winston Lord, by Charles Stuart Kennedy and Nancy Bernkopf Tucker, April 28, 1998, Diplomatic Studies Interview Collection; Kissinger, *Years of Renewal*, 843; Isaacson, *Kissinger*, 671.
27. Kissinger, *Years of Renewal*, 609.
28. Kissinger, *Years of Renewal*, 843.
29. Kissinger, *Years of Renewal*, 843; Ford, *Time to Heal*, 352–53.
30. Kissinger, *Years of Renewal*, 839.
31. Kissinger, *Years of Renewal*, 189.
32. Ford, *Time to Heal*, 331.
33. Hyland, *Mortal Rivals*, 156.
34. Mann, *Rise of the Vulcans*, 70–71.
35. Kissinger, *Years of Renewal*, 845–47; Memorandum of Conversation, Ford, Scowcroft, Kissinger, Dobrynin, December 9, 1975, Ford Library, National Security Advisor, Memoranda of Conversations, 1973–1977, Box 17, Folder: "December 9, 1975 — Ford, Kissinger, Soviet Ambassador Dobrynin"; Dobrynin, *In Confidence*, 352.
36. Minutes of National Security Council Meeting of December 22, 1975, Ford Library, National Security Adviser, National Security Council Meetings File, Box 2.
37. Minutes of National Security Council Meeting of January 13, 1976, Ford Library, National Security Adviser, National Security Council Meetings File, Box 2.
38. Memorandum of Conversation, Ford, Scowcroft, Kissinger, Rumsfeld, January 14, 1976, Ford Library, National Security Advisor, Memoranda of Conversations, 1973–1977, Box 17, Folder: "January 17, 1976 — Ford, Kissinger, Rumsfeld."
39. Minutes of National Security Council Meeting of January 19, 1976, Ford Library, National Security Adviser, National Security Council Meetings File, Box 2.
40. Hyland, *Mortal Rivals*, 158–59 (Brezhnev quote); Memorandum for the President from Brent Scowcroft, January 21, 1976, Ford Library, National Security Advisor, Kissinger Reports, Box 1, Folder: "January 21–22, 1976 — Kissinger Moscow Trip (1); Ford, *Time to Heal*, 357; Dobrynin, 363.
41. Memorandum for the President from Brent Scowcroft, January 21, 1976, Ford Library, National Security Advisor, Kissinger Reports, Box 1, Folder: "January 21–22, 1976 — Kissinger Moscow Trip (1)."
42. Minutes of National Security Council Meeting of January 21, 1976, Ford Library, National Security Adviser, National Security Council Meetings File, Box 2.
43. Kissinger, *Years of Renewal*, 856.
44. Memorandum for the President from Brent Scowcroft, January 22, 1976, Ford Library, National Security Advisor,

Kissinger Reports, Box 1, Folder: "January 21–22, 1976 — Kissinger Moscow Trip (1)"; Hyland, *Mortal Rivals*, 161.
45. Kissinger, *Years of Renewal*, 860.
46. Memorandum of Conversation, President Ford, Secretary Kissinger, Secretary of Defense Rumsfeld, Lt. General Scowcroft and Richard Cheney, February 5, 1976, Ford Library, NSA/Memoranda of Conversations 1973–1977, Box 17, Folder: "February 5, 1976, Ford, Kissinger, Rumsfeld."
47. Minutes of National Security Council Meeting of February 11, 1976, Ford Library, National Security Adviser, National Security Council Meetings File, Box 2.
48. *The Kissinger Transcripts*, 430 and 469; Ford, *Time to Heal*, 358.
49. Memorandum of Conversation, President Ford, Secretary Kissinger, Arms Control Director Fred Ilke, and Lt. General Scowcroft, February 16, 1976, Ford Library, NSA/Memoranda of Conversations 1973–1977, Box 17, Folder: "February 5, 1976, Ford, Kissinger, ACDA Director Fred Ilke."
50. Memorandum from Fred Ilke to President Ford, February 12, 1976, Ford Library, NSA/Memoranda of Conversations 1973–1977, Box 17, Folder: "February 5, 1976, Ford, Kissinger, ACDA Director Fred Ilke."
51. Letter from Brezhnev to Ford, March 17, 1976, Ford Library, NSA/Memoranda of Conversations 1973–1977, Box 18, Folder: "March 18, 1976, Ford, Kissinger, Bush, Ilke, Rockefeller"; *The Kissinger Transcripts*, 469; Kissinger, *Years of Renewal*, 860; Ford, *Time to Heal*, 358.
52. Ford, *Time to Heal*, 358.

Chapter 16

1. MacAvoy, *Industry Regulation*, vii and 11; Niskanen, "Retrospective," 4; Derthick and Quirk, *Politics of Deregulation*, 10; Yergin and Stanislaw, *Commanding Heights*, 60–64; Schullman, *The Seventies*, 25 and 91; White, *Breach of Faith*, 49, 139 and 334; Farrell, *Tip O'Neill*, 327; Safire, *Before the Fall*, 216–221.
2. Osborne, *White House Watch*, xv.
3. For example, Greenspan urged Ford to deregulate the trucking industry. Michael Raoul-Duval Notes of April 25, 1974, Meeting with President Ford and Others, Ford Library, Michael Raoul-Duval Papers, Box 6, File: "Meeting with the President, 4/25/75, Greenspan, et al. (energy, farm bill, railroads)."
4. Derthick and Quirk, *Politics of Deregulation*, 49.
5. President Gerald R. Ford, "Address to a Joint Session of Congress on the Economy," October 8, 1974.
6. Derthick and Quirk, *Politics of Deregulation*, 46.
7. Memorandum from Edward Schmults and Paul MacAvoy to President, December 24, 1915, and "Notes on Meeting with the President," February 4, 1976, Ford Library Leach papers, Box 21.
8. Derthick and Quirk, *Politics of Deregulation*, 38.
9. Feldman, "Gerald Ford at 90."
10. Interview with William Coleman, Washington, July 6, 2004. The same incident is reported in Derthick and Quirk, 46, and Paul H. Weaver, "Unlocking the Gilded Cage of Regulation," *Fortune*, February 1977, 182.
11. Ford, *Time to Heal*, New York, 271–74.
12. Derthick and Quirk, *Politics of Deregulation*, 121.
13. Peterson and Glab, *Rapid Descent*, 46.
14. Interstate Commerce Act, 24 Stat. 379 (1887).
15. Civil Aeronautics Act of 1938, Pub. L. No. 75-796, 52 Stat. 973 (1938); Motor Carrier Act of 1935, Pub. L. No. 74-255, 49 Stat. 543 (1935). The ICC was first given jurisdiction over telecommunications companies in 1910 when common carriage rules were applied to the industry. Mann-Elkins Act, 36 Stat. 539 (1910). The full panoply of regulations was imposed by the Telecommunications Act of 1934. 48 Stat. 1064 (1934).
16. Breyer, *Regulation and Its Reform*, 223; Derthick and Quirk, *Politics of Deregulation*, 23; Osborne, *White House Watch*, 195–96. Faced with the oil crisis, the ICC decided that it no longer made sense for companies to drive hundreds of

miles out of the way. But rather than allowing a company to drive directly from one end point to the other, the commission eliminated the ability of truckers to tack. *Motor Common Carriers of Property, Routes and Service,* Ex Parte No. 55 (February 25, 1974), *aff'd, Thompson Van Lines v. U.S.,* 399 F. Supp. 1131 (D.C. Dist. 1975).

17. Sinha, "Regulation and Deregulation of U.S. Airlines"; Poole and Butler, "Airline Deregulation: The Unfinished Revolution."

18. Daniel Kaplan and Mark R. Dayton, "Policies for the Deregulated Airline Industry," Congressional Budget Office, Washington, U.S. Government Printing Office, 1988.

19. *Regional Rail Reorganization Act of 1973,* H.R. 9142, Public Law 93-236 (87 Stat. 985); President Richard M. Nixon, "Statement on Signing the Regional Rail Reorganization Act of 1973," January 2, 1974.

20. Pub. Law 94-210, 90 Stat. 31 (1976); President Gerald R. Ford, "Special Message to the Congress Proposing Reform of Railroad Regulations," May 19, 1975; President Gerald R. Ford, "Statement on the Railroad Revitalization and Regulatory Reform Act of 1976," February 5, 1976.

21. President Gerald R. Ford, "Special Message to the Congress Proposing Reform of Motor Carrier Regulation," November 13, 1975.

22. Ford, *Time to Heal,* 366; John Osborne, *White House Watch,* 195; Derthick and Quirk, *Politics of Deregulation,* 15.

23. Memo from Jim Connor to Ed Schmults, with enclosure, April 1976, and Memo from Ed Schmults to Connor, April 27, 1976, Ford Library, Schmults papers, Box 39.

24. Derthick and Quirk, *Politics of Deregulation,* 71, 75 and 85; Moore, "Regulation: Trucking Deregulation."

25. Memorandum for Philip W. Buchen from Dean Burch, September 20, 1974, Letter from Robert Timm to Philip Buchen, September 9, 1974, and Memorandum for Philip W. Buchen from Dean Burch, September 5, 1974, "Robert Timm, Chairman, Civil Aeronautics Board," Ford Library, Dean Burch Files, Box 2, Folder: "Civil Aeronautics Board"; Letter from Robert Timm to Philip Buchen, December 19, 1975, Ford Library, John E. Robson Papers, Box 5, Folder: "C.A.B.— Timm, Robert (material relating to W.H. efforts to force Timm's resignation from Board, and Dept. of Justice investigation of Timm's conduct)"; Notes, Ford Library, John E. Robson Papers, Box 5, Folder: "C.A.B.— Timm, Robert (2)."

26. Peterson and Glab, *Rapid Descent,* 33–34.

27. Interview with Stephen Breyer, "Commanding Heights: Up for Debate: Deregulation," PBS, reprinted at www.pbs.org/wgbh/commandingheights/shared/minitext/ufd_deregulation_full.html.

28. Peterson and Glab, *Rapid Descent,* 38.

29. Clymer, *Edward M. Kennedy,* 238.

30. Testimony of Kenneth I. Clearwaters, Air Charter Fares Hearings, 210–28.

31. Testimony of Frederick Alfred Laker, Air Charter Fares Hearings, 190.

32. "C.A.B. Drops Bid to Lift Cut-Rate Charter Prices," Robert Lindsey, *New York Times,* February 12, 1975, 40; "CAB Scraps Plan to Use Minimum Prices for Air Charters as Means to Raise Fares," *Wall Street Journal,* February 12, 1975, 6.

33. Opening Statement of Senator Kennedy, CAB Hearings, 1.

34. Statement of John W. Barnum and Statement of Thomas E. Kauper, CAB Hearings, Volume 1, 4–22 and 34–56.

35. Testimony of Robert Timm, CAB Hearings, Volume 3, 2374–84; Testimony of Stephen Alterman, CAB Hearings, 2303–2323; Testimony of Robert F. Rickey, CAB Hearings, 2326–2329; David Burnham, "It Took a Suicide Note," *New York Times,* March 30, 1975, 142.

36. Statements of Richard J. O'Melia, CAB Hearings, Volume 1, 648–49 and Volume 2, 1358.

37. Peterson and Glab, *Rapid Descent;* See also Breyer, *Regulation and Its Reform,* 337–38.

38. David Burnham, "Ford Lauds Panel for C.A.B. Report," *New York Times,* 22.

39. Letter from Robert Timm to Philip Buchen, December 19, 1975, and Notes on "Meeting Ex Session 12/16/75," Ford Library, John E. Robson Papers, Box 5, Folder: "C.A.B.— Timm, Robert (material relating to W.H. efforts to force Timm's resignation from Board, and Dept. of Justice investigation of Timm's conduct)"; Letter from Roderick Hills to Robert D. Timm, October 17, 1975, Letter from Philip Buchen to Robert D. Timm, December 5, 1975, and Letter from Robert D. Timm to the President, December 10, 1975, Ford Library, John E. Robson Papers, Box 5, Folder: "C.A.B.— Timm, Robert (2)."

40. President Gerald R. Ford, "Remarks at the Swearing In of John E. Robson as Chairman of the Civil Aeronautics Board," April 21, 1975.

41. John Robson interview with Richard Smithey of the Yale School of Organization and Management, July 24, 1981, cited in Derthick and Quirk, *Politics of Deregulation,* 66.

42. Robson, "Airline Deregulation."

43. "CAB Suggests Experimental Program to Test Consequences of Deregulation," Civil Aeronautics Board, Press Release, July 7, 1975; Pulsifer, et al., "Report of the CAB Special Staff on Regulatory Reform"; "Charter-Flight Rule Revisions Adopted by CAB," *Wall Street Journal,* August 11, 1975, 8; "CAB Adds Carriers to Routes Serving Omaha, Des Moines," *Wall Street Journal,* September 10, 1975, 3; "CAB Official Favors Washington-Cincinnati Route for 2 Airlines," *Wall Street Journal,* March 16, 1977, 21.

44. "A Discount Air Fare to Coast Approved," *New York Times,* March 16, 1977, 14; "CAB to Let American Air Try Lower Fare on New York–California Runs for a Year," *Wall Street Journal,* March 16, 1977, 6.

45. President Gerald R. Ford, "Special Message to the Congress Proposing Reform of Airline Industry Regulation," October 8, 1975.

46. "Statement of Hon. John E. Robson," 1976 Cannon Committee Hearings, 346–55.

47. "Statement of Hon. William Coleman," 1976 Cannon Committee Hearings, 229–30.

48. Derthick and Quirk, *Politics of Deregulation,* 22 and 241; Clymer, *Edward M. Kennedy,* 229; Peterson and Glab, *Rapid Descent,* 38.

49. Derthick and Quirk, *Politics of Deregulation,* 241. See also MacAvoy, *Industry Regulation,* 4 ("The Reagan administration carried on an effort that had been initiated as early as the Ford administration but that had reached its zenith with deregulation of airline, trucking, and railroad services in the Carter administration."); Cohen and Dolan, "Debunking the Myth" ("Carter benefited from a process that was well underway when he was sworn in on January 20, 1977.").

50. Carter, *Presidential Campaign of 1976,* 855.

51. President James Earl Carter, "Airline Deregulation Act of 1978 Remarks on Signing S. 2493 into Law," October 24, 1978; "Bill Deregulating Airline Industry Clears Conferees," *Wall Street Journal,* October 9, 1978, 2; Air Cargo Deregulation Act, Pub. L. 95-163 (1977); President James E. Carter, "Federal Mine Safety and Health Amendments Act of 1977 and Air Cargo Deregulation Bill Remarks on Signing S. 717 and H.R. 6010 into Law," November 9, 1977.

52. Moore, "Regulation: Trucking Deregulation"; Derthick and Quirk, *Politics of Deregulation,* 6, 73, 97, and 149–50.

53. President James Earl Carter, "Staggers Rail Act of 1980 Remarks on Signing S. 1946 into Law," October 14, 1980.

54. Poole and Butler, "Airline Deregulation: The Unfinished Revolution." See also Robson, "Airline Deregulation."

55. "2006 GAO Report," 9–20.

56. Kahn, "Lessons from Deregulation"; Kahn, "Airline Deregulation."

57. Derthick and Quirk, *Politics of Deregulation,* 2; Moore, "Regulation: Trucking Deregulation."

58. David Page and Ronald A. Wirtz, "Wrong Side of the Tracks?," *Fedgazette,* November 2003.

59. Moore, "Moving Ahead."

60. Moore, "Regulation: Trucking Deregulation."

61. Greenspan, *Age of Turbulence,* 71.

Chapter 17

1. Interview of General Brent Scowcroft, by the author, October 27, 2006.

2. Gleijeses, *Conflicting Missions*, 233; Spikes, *Angola and the Politics of Intervention*, 10 and 36–37; Marcum, *Angolan Revolution*, 1–3; Stockwell, *In Search of Enemies*, 31; Hare, *Angola's Last Best Chance for Peace*, 4.

3. To avoid a confusing jumble of acronyms, I have used the terms "MPLA," "FNLA" and "UNITA" to designate the independence groups and their military forces throughout this chapter. At certain times the groups adopted different names, and they used different names for their military forces. For example, the FNLA had been named the UPA and the GRAE in the past; the military arm of the MPLA was named the FAPLA; the MPLA government after November 11, 1975, called itself the People's Republic of Angola (PRA); and after independence UNITA and the FNLA briefly formed a government called the Democratic People's Republic of Angola (DPRA). I have also tried to avoid confusion by using the modern name of Namibia, although the country was called South West Africa during the South African rule, and I have used the name Zaire throughout, although the country is now named the Democratic Republic of the Congo.

4. Quote of Soviets being concerned about Neto's stability is from Spikes, *Angola and the Politics of Intervention*, 81, quoting Soviet deputy foreign minister Vasily Kuznetsov. For descriptions of the independence movements, see Gleijeses, *Conflicting Missions*, 175–77 and 243–44; George, *Cuban Intervention in Angola*, 51; Wright, "Men at War"; Marcum, *Angolan Revolution*, 2, 36–84, and 120–247; Marcum, "Lessons of Angola"; Harsch and Thomas, *Angola*, 25–34; Gleijeses, "Havana's Policy in Africa"; Westad, "Moscow and the Angolan Crisis"; James, *Political History*, 42–50; "Jonas Savimbi," *The Economist*, February 28, 2002; Leslie H. Gelb, "U.S., Soviet, China Reported Aiding Portugal, Angola," *New York Times*, September 25, 1975, 89; Morris, "Proxy War in Angola," 19; Spikes, *Angola and the Politics of Intervention*, 36–43, 50–64, 84, and 101; Stockwell, *In Search of Enemies*, 146–47 and 191; Sikorski, "Mystique of Savimbi," 34–37; Marquez, "Opération Carlota"; Prendergast, "Angola's Deadly War."

5. Westad, "Moscow and the Angolan Crisis."

6. Gallagher, *Portugal*, 201; Marcum, *Angolan Revolution*, 243 and 260; Spikes, *In Search of Enemies*, 100.

7. Westad, "Moscow and the Angolan Crisis"; Stockwell, *In Search of Enemies*, 67; Spikes, *Angola and the Politics of Intervention*, 105–111; Marcum, *Angolan Revolution*, 245–49; Dobrynin, *In Confidence*, 362–63.

8. Gleijeses, *Conflicting Missions*, 245; Gleijeses, "Havana's Policy in Africa."

9. Spikes, *Angola and the Politics of Intervention*, 128–37; Marcum, *The Angolan Revolution*, 245 and 255–58; Gleijeses, *Conflicting Missions*, 246–53; James, *Political History*, 54–55.

10. Memorandum of Conversation, Secretary Kissinger and Zaire State Commissioner for Foreign Affairs Umba-di-Lutete, August 13, 1974, Digital National Security Archive, RG 59, Central Policy Files, 1974, P820097-1210; Davis, "A Personal Memoir," 120; Kissinger, *Years of Renewal*, 794–95; Stockwell, *In Search of Enemies*, 67.

11. Kevin Brown, "Report from Luanda: A New Angolan Society," *The Nation*, July 17, 1976, 42; Marcum, *The Angolan Revolution*, 258; Gleijeses, *Conflicting Missions*, 250; Bender, "Kissinger in Angola," 80; Spikes, 137–55; Kissinger, *Years of Renewal*, 676; Stockwell, *In Search of Enemies*, 67; Marcum, *The Angolan Revolution*, 257–59; Statement of the UNITA Standing Committee, "Year of Generalized Popular Resistance," *Kwacha UNITA Press*, February 23, 1999.

12. Robert Moss, "How South Africa Took on Castro's Invaders," *Sunday Telegraph*, February 6, 1977; Spikes, 144–48; Marcum, *The Angolan Revolution*, 259 and 440–41; Westad, "Moscow and the Angolan Crisis"; Stockwell, *In Search of Enemies*, 68; Kissinger, *Years of Renewal*, 795–98; Gleijeses, *Conflicting Missions*, 250 and 283.

13. Memorandum of Conversation, President Kenneth

Kaunda, et al. and President Ford, et al., April 19, 1975, Ford Library, National Security Agency, Memoranda of Conversations, 1973–1977, Box 11, Folder: "April 19, 1975 — Ford, Zambian President Kenneth D. Kaunda, Minister of Foreign Affairs Vernon Mwanga."

14. Kissinger, *Years of Renewal*, 791 and 797–98.

15. Interview with Donald Easum, by Arthur Day, January 17, 1990, Diplomatic Studies Interview Collection; Bender, "Kissinger in Angola," 69–72; Gleijeses, *Conflicting Missions*, 280–82; Stockwell, *In Search of Enemies*, 52; Davis, "A Personal Memoir," 110–11.

16. Davis, "A Personal Memoir," 111.

17. National Security Study Memorandum 224, Ford Library, National Security Decision Memoranda and Study Memoranda, Box 2; Davis, "A Personal Memoir," 111–13.

18. Church Committee Assassinations Report, 53.

19. Memorandum of Conversation, Secretary Kissinger and Staff, June 18, 1975, Digital National Security Archive, RG 59, Central Policy Files, 1975, P770089-0492.

20. Action Memorandum from Acting Assistant Secretary of State for African Affairs Edward Mulcahy to Secretary of State Kissinger, June 20, 1975, Library of Congress, Manuscript Division, Kissinger Papers, CL 257, Geopolitical Files, Zaire, August 74–June 75; Gleijeses, *Conflicting Missions*, 289; Kissinger, *Years of Renewal*, 808; Spikes, *Angola and the Politics of Intervention*, 158; Stockwell, *In Search of Enemies*, 43.

21. Minutes of National Security Council Meeting of June 27, 1975, Ford Library, National Security Adviser, National Security Council Meetings File, Box 2.

22. Spikes, *Angola and the Politics of Intervention*, 159–66; Marcum, *Angolan Revolution*, 260–63; Kissinger, *Years of Renewal*, 806.

23. CIA Memorandum, "DCI Briefing for 14 July SRG Meeting, 'Angola,'" July 14, 1975, Digital National Security Archive.

24. Stockwell, *In Search of Enemies*, 52–54.

25. Davis, "A Personal Memoir," 109–16.

26. Memorandum of Conversation, President Ford, Secretary Kissinger, General Scowcroft, July 7, 1975, Ford Library, National Security Advisor, Memoranda of Conversations, 1973–1977, Box 13, Folder: "July 7, 1975 — Ford, Kissinger."

27. Spikes, *Angola and the Politics of Intervention*, 170–71; Marcum, *Angolan Revolution*, 263.

28. Davis, "A Personal Memoir," 116.

29. Memorandum of Conversation, President Ford, Secretary Kissinger, General Scowcroft, July 17, 1975, Ford Library, National Security Advisor, Memoranda of Conversations, 1973–1977, Box 13, Folder: "July 17, 1975 — Ford, Kissinger."

30. Memorandum of Conversation, President Ford, Secretary Kissinger, General Scowcroft, July 18, 1975, Ford Library, National Security Advisor, Memoranda of Conversations, 1973–1977, Box 13, Folder: "July 18, 1975 — Ford, Kissinger."

31. Davis, "A Personal Memoir," 117.

32. Spikes, *Angola and the Politics of Intervention*, 171–72; Morris, "Proxy War in Angola," 19.

33. Spikes, *Angola and the Politics of Intervention*, 166; Robert Moss, "How South Africa Took on Castro's Invaders," *Sunday Telegraph*, February 6, 1977; Gleijeses, *Conflicting Missions*, 291.

34. Interview with Robert W. Hultslander, by Piero Gleijeses, National Security Archives, available at www.gwu.edu/~nsarchiv/NSAEBB/NSAEBB67/transcript.html.

35. Telegram 9078 from the Embassy in Zaire to the Department of State, October 11, 1975, 0955Z, Library of Congress, Manuscript Division, Kissinger Papers, Box CL 257, Geopolitical Files, Zaire, August–November 1975.

36. Memorandum from William G. Hyland to Secretary of State Kissinger, Washington, October 15, 1975, Department of State, INR/IL Historical Files, Box 11, Africa 1975, re: Pike Committee.

37. Spikes, *Angola and the Politics of Intervention*, 178–92; Isaacson, *Kissinger*, 676–77; Marcum, *Angolan Revolution*, 261.

38. Spikes, *Angola and the Politics of Intervention*, 198.

39. Kissinger, *Years of Renewal*, 809; Stockwell, *In Search of*

Enemies, 53–55, 78, 86–87, 162 and 206; Spikes, *Angola and the Politics of Intervention*, 159, 171 and 191–93; Davis, "A Personal Memoir," 121; Robert Moss, "How South Africa Took on Castro's Invaders," *Sunday Telegraph*, February 6, 1977.

40. Memorandum from Raul Diaz Argicelles to Raul Castro, August 11, 1975, reproduced in Gleijeses, "Havana's Policy in Africa"; Falk, "Cuba in Africa," 1082; Gleijeses, *Conflicting Missions*, 254.

41. Transcript of Meeting between U.S. Secretary of State Alexander M. Haig, Jr., and Cuban Vice Premier Carlos Rafael Rodriguez, Mexico City, November 23, 1981, Embassy of USSR to Republic of Cuba, translation by Bruce McDonald; document on file at National Security Archive.

42. Westad, "Moscow and the Angolan Crisis, 1974–1976," 24; Gleijeses, *Conflicting Missions*, 260–61. Westad found one document in the Soviet archives summarizing Castro's request for assistance in sending "special forces" to Angola. Gleijeses could find no documentation of the request in the Cuban archives. Gleijeses cites the document Westad found as the only basis for his conclusion that Castro considered sending combat troops in August 1975 and decided not to when the Soviets denied his request. Gleijeses, *Conflicting Missions*, 379. It seems more likely that Castro's request for help transporting "special forces" related to his decision to send 480 advisors to Angola.

43. Gleijeses, *Conflicting Missions*, 259–68; Gleijeses, "Havana's Policy in Africa"; Spikes, *Angola and the Politics of Intervention*, 202 and 230; Stockwell, *In Search of Enemies*, 87; Westad, "Moscow and the Angolan Crisis."

44. Stockwell, *In Search of Enemies*, 87, 162, and 186–87; John Stockwell, "The Secret Wars of the CIA: Part I: The Inner Workings of the National Security Council and the CIA's Covert Actions in Angola, Central America and Vietnam," Other Americas Radio, October, 1987, available at www.thirdworldtraveler.com/Stockwell/StockwellCIA87_1.html; Kornbluh, "Conflicting Positions"; Spikes, *Angola and the Politics of Intervention*, 196–221; Steenkamp, *South Africa's Border War*, 39–43; Robert Moss, "How South Africa Took on Castro's Invaders," *Sunday Telegraph*, February 6, 1977; Kissinger, *Years of Renewal*, 820; Marcum, *Angolan Revolution*, 268–69; Gleijeses, *Conflicting Missions*, 295–96.

45. "Interview with Pik Botha," May 20, 1997, CNN.com, Cold War, Episode 17, "Good Guys, Bad Guys," www2.gwu.edu/~nsarchiv/coldwar/interviews/episode-17/bothal.html; Steenkamp, *South Africa's Border War*, 45–46; Stockwell, *In Search of Enemies*, 164; Spikes, *Angola and the Politics of Intervention*, 233; Falk, "Cuba in Africa," 1082–83; Gleijeses, "Havana's Policy in Africa"; Marcum, *Angolan Revolution*, 269; Gleijeses, *Conflicting Missions*, 289–301; Robert Moss, "Battle of Death Road," *Sunday Telegraph*, February 13, 1977; Robert Moss, "How South Africa Took on Castro's Invaders," *Sunday Telegraph*, February 6, 1977; Robert Moss, "Castro's Secret War Exposed: How Washington Lost Its Nerve and How the Cubans Subdued Angola," *Sunday Telegraph*, January 30, 1977.

46. Robert Moss, "How South Africa Took on Castro's Invaders," *Sunday Telegraph*, February 6, 1977; Robert Moss, "Battle of Death Road," *Sunday Telegraph*, February 13, 1977; Spikes, *Angola and the Politics of Intervention*, 219–20; Marcum, *Angolan Revolution*, 443; Gleijeses, *Conflicting Missions*, 301.

47. Interview of General Brent Scowcroft, by the author, Washington, D.C., October 27, 2006; Kissinger: *Years of Renewal*.

48. Stockwell, *In Search of Enemies*, 186; John Stockwell, "The Secret Wars of the CIA: Part I: The Inner Workings of the National Security Council and the CIA's Covert Actions in Angola, Central America and Vietnam," Other Americas Radio, October, 1987, available at *www.thirdworldtraveler.com/Stockwell/StockwellCIA87_1.html*.

49. Gleijeses, *Conflicting Missions*, 299.

50. Marcum, *Angolan Revolution*, 271.

51. W. Botha, Republic of South Africa, *House of Assembly Debates*, April 17, 1978, col. 4852, cited in Gleijeses, "Moscow's Proxy?" Edward George has interviewed W. Botha, who claims that Kissinger and the CIA knew about the invasion in ad-

vance. George, *Cuban Intervention in Angola*, 315, fn. 3. Donald Easum believes that Kissinger gave approval to the South Africans through business contacts. Interview of Donald Easum, by Arthur Day, January 17, 1990, Diplomatic Studies Interview Collection.

52. Minutes of meeting, November 5, 1974, Transcripts of Secretary Kissinger's Staff Meetings, NARA, Record's Group 59, Box 9, Folder: "Secretary's Staff Meeting"; Kissinger, *Years of Renewal*, 820.

53. Stockwell, *In Search of Enemies*, 191; Spikes, *Angola and the Politics of Intervention*, 255; Marcum, *Angolan Revolution*, 265; Gleijeses, *Conflicting Missions*, 330.

54. Westad, "Moscow and the Angolan Crisis" (Westad interviewed several of the officials involved in the decision); Spikes, *Angola and the Politics of Intervention*, 243.

55. Gleijeses, *Conflicting Missions*, 268–69; Gleijeses, "Havana's Policy in Africa."

56. Gleijeses, *Conflicting Missions*, 303; Robert Moss, "How South Africa Took on Castro's Invaders," *Sunday Telegraph*, February 6, 1977; Gleijeses, "Havana's Policy in Africa"; Spikes, *Angola and the Politics of Intervention*, 242–49; Steenkamp, *South Africa's Border War*, 46–47.

57. Fidel Castro Speech, "Angola: African Giron," April 19, 1976, Havana.

58. Marcum, *Angolan Revolution*, 273–75; Gleijeses, *Conflicting Missions*, 305; Marquez, "Operation Carlotta"; Spikes, *Angola and the Politics of Intervention*, 244–49. Robert Hultslander, former CIA Station Chief in Luanda, agrees that this was the first deployment of Cuban combat troops in Angola: "I agree with the history as you present it, and with your conclusions regarding the assistance provided by Cuban forces, which I believe did not arrive in any numbers until after we departed.... Although we desperately wanted to find Cubans under every bush, during my tenure their presence was invisible, and undoubtedly limited to a few advisors. We knew they were on the way, however, and I believe we knew about the Britannia flights through Brazzaville in early November." Interview with Robert W. Hultslander, Gleijeses, "Havana's Policy in Africa."

59. Interview of Karen Brutents, Central Committee of the Communist Party of the Soviet Union, August 1997, CNN Interactive, Cold War, Episode 17, "Good Guys, Bad Guys," www.cnn.com/SPECIALS/cold.war/episodes/17/interviews/brutents.

60. Dobrynin, *In Confidence*, 362–63.

61. Marquez, "Operation Carlotta." See also Gleijeses, "Havana's Policy in Africa" ("Cables from Fidel Castro to the Cuban commanders in Angola ... demonstrate the extraordinary degree of control that Castro exerted over the conduct of the war. In February 1996 I was allowed to read these cables, but, unfortunately, they may never be released.").

62. Francois Soudan, "Guerre Secret au Cabinda," *Jeune Afrique*, February 14, 1979, cited in Van Meter, "Cabinda: A Joint Operation," 246; Stockwell, *In Search of Enemies*, 164; Spikes, *Angola and the Politics of Intervention*, 251; Davis, "A Personal Memoir," 121–22; Gleijeses, *Conflicting Missions*, 312.

63. George, *Cuban Intervention in Angola*, 85, quoting the leader of the Cuban forces in Cabinda, Ramon Espinosa Martin.

64. The details of the battle are contained in: Robert Moss, "Battle of Death Road," *Sunday Telegraph*, February 13, 1977; Stockwell, *In Search of Enemies*, 165 and 214–15; Spikes, *Angola and the Politics of Intervention*, 250–75; Gleijeses, "Havana's Policy in Africa"; Gleijeses, *Conflicting Missions*, 308–11; Marcum, *The Angolan Revolution*, 269, 274 and 441–43; George, *Cuban Intervention in Angola*, 90–91.

65. Robert Moss, "Battle of Death Road," *Sunday Telegraph*, February 13, 1977; Spikes, *Angola and the Politics of Intervention*, xiii, 253, and 261–62; Marcum, *The Angolan Revolution*, 271; Stockwell, *In Search of Enemies*, 214.

66. Agostinho Neto, "Long Live the People's Republic of Angola," Independence Day Speech, November 11, 1975, and "Constitution of the People's Republic of Angola," reprinted in *Road to Liberation: MPLA Documents on the Founding of the*

People's Republic of Angola, 1–51; Spikes, *Angola and the Politics of Intervention*, 262–64; Marcum, *The Angolan Revolution*, 271 and 276; Stockwell, *In Search of Enemies*, 214.

67. Memorandum of Conversation, Ford, Scowcroft, and Kissinger, November 11, 1975, Ford Library, National Security Advisor, Memoranda of Conversations, 1973–1977, Box 16, Folder: "November 11, 1975 — Ford, Kissinger."

68. Minutes of meeting, November 13, 1974, Transcripts of Secretary Kissinger's Staff Meetings, NARA, Record's Group 59, Box 9, Folder: "Secretary's Staff Meeting."

69. Memorandum of Conversation, Ford, Scowcroft, Kissinger, November 19, 1975, Ford Library, National Security Advisor, Memoranda of Conversations, 1973–1977, Box 16, Folder: "November 19, 1975 — Ford, Kissinger."

70. Interagency Intelligence Memorandum, "Angola: Short-Term Military and Political Prospects," November 26, 1975, Digital National Security Archive.

71. Stockwell, *In Search of Enemies*, 21 and 206–207; Spikes, *Angola and the Politics of Intervention*, 258 and 271–73; Kissinger, *Years of Renewal*, 818; Isaacson, *Kissinger*, 678.

72. Stockwell, *In Search of Enemies*, 216.

73. Spikes, *Angola and the Politics of Intervention*, 229 and 269–70; Kissinger, *Years of Renewal*, 815; Stockwell, *In Search of Enemies*, 68; Marquez, "Operation Carlotta"; Gleijeses, *Conflicting Missions*, 317–20.

74. Fred Bridgland, "S. African Regulars Fight Inside Angola," *Washington Post*, November 23, 1975, 18.

75. Marcum, "Lessons of Angola," 419–20; Message from Slipchenko to Moscow, November 3, 1975, "Conversation with J. Nyerere," cited in Westad, "Moscow and the Angolan Crisis"; Spikes, *Angola and the Politics of Intervention*, 228–29, 268 and 276; Marcum, *The Angolan Revolution*, 272 and 442–43; Stockwell, *In Search of Enemies*, 192–93 and 202.

76. Memorandum from Brent Scowcroft to the President, "Information Items," January 27, 1976, Ford Library, Richard Cheney Files, Box 9, Folder: "Panama Canal — General."

77. Julius K. Nyerere, "America and Southern Africa," *Foreign Affairs*, Volume 55, Number 4, July 1977.

78. Gleijeses, *Conflicting Missions*, 331–32.

79. Seymour M. Hersh, "Angola-Aid Issue Opening Rifts in State Department," *New York Times*, December 14, 1975, 1.

80. Spikes, *Angola and the Politics of Intervention*, 275–87; Bender, "Kissinger in Angola," 101–103; Stockwell, *In Search of Enemies*, 230–31; *Congress and the Nation*, Vol. IV, 10–12; Ford, *Time to Heal*, 345; Kissinger, *Years of Renewal*, 832; "The Battle Over Angola," *Time Magazine*, December 29, 1975; Isaacson, *Kissinger*, 679–83; Reichley, *Conservatives in an Age of Change*, 352; Davis, "A Personal Memoir," 119.

81. Robert Moss, "Battle of Death Road," *Sunday Telegraph*, February 13, 1977; Richard Allport, "The Battle of Bridge 14: Operation Savannah — Angola 1975," www.rhodesia.nl/samil his.htm; Spikes, *Angola and the Politics of Intervention*, 266–81; Gleijeses, "Havana's Policy in Africa"; Gleijeses, *Conflicting Missions*, 313–21; Stockwell, *In Search of Enemies*, 214; Marcum, *The Angolan Revolution*, 272. Sorting through the South Africans' intentions is not easy. Willem Steenkamp asserts that the South Africans decided not to take Luanda and to gradually withdraw in November. Steenkamp, *South Africa's Border War*, 54. The South Africans have given several excuses for why they stopped before taking Luanda. In March 1976, Defense Minister Botha told the South African Parliament that "the Americans told him to stop," and in February 1977 the South Africans claimed that they stopped their advance at the request of Savimbi, who wanted to reach a settlement with Neto. Gleijeses, *Conflicting Missions*, 321. Either way, it is clear that the South Africans had decided to withdraw by the second week of December, before the Senate voted to cut off aid.

82. "Interview with Pik Botha," May 20, 1997, CNN.com, Cold War, Episode 17, "Good Guys, Bad Guys," www2.gwu.edu/~nsarchiv/coldwar/interviews/episode-17/botha1.html.

83. Gleijeses, *Conflicting Missions*, 340–41; Hyland, *Mortal Rivals*, 146; Spikes, *Angola and the Politics of Intervention*, 288–90.

84. Stockwell, *In Search of Enemies*, 232.

85. Ray, et al., *Dirty Work 2*, 271.

86. Kissinger, *Years of Renewal*, 822–32.

87. Memorandum of Conversation, Ford, Scowcroft, Kissinger, Dobrynin, December 9, 1975, Ford Library, National Security Advisor, Memoranda of Conversations, 1973–1977, Box 17, Folder: "December 9, 1975 — Ford, Kissinger, Soviet Ambassador Dobrynin"; Dobrynin, *In Confidence*, 360.

88. Dobrynin, *In Confidence*, 360.

89. Gleijeses, *Conflicting Missions*, 333.

90. E-mail from Odd Arne Westad to Andrew Downer Crain, December 11, 2006.

91. Hyland, *Mortal Rivals*, 145.

92. Gleijeses, "Havana's Policy in Africa"; Gleijeses, *Conflicting Missions*, 367–68; Memorandum from Secretary of State Kissinger to Diplomatic Posts, "Cuban Intervention in Angola," January 15, 1976; Robert Moss, "Castro's Secret War Exposed: How Washington Lost Its Nerve and How the Cubans Subdued Angola," *Sunday Telegraph*, January 30, 1977; Marquez, "Operation Carlotta."

93. Minutes of National Security Council Meeting, December 22, 1975, Ford Library, National Security Adviser, National Security Council Meetings File, Box 2.

94. Stockwell, *In Search of Enemies*, 233–34; Spikes, *Angola and the Politics of Intervention*, 288.

95. "Interview with Dave Tomkins," CNN.com, Cold War, Episode 17, "Good Guys, Bad Guys," www2.gwu.edu/~nsarchiv/coldwar/interviews/episode-17/tomkins1.html.

96. Bruce Kennedy, "Soldiers of Misfortune," CNN Interactive, Cold War, Episode 17, "Good Guys, Bad Guys," www.cnn.com/SPECIALS/cold.war/episodes/17/spotlight; "Interview with Dave Tomkins," CNN.com, Cold War, Episode 17, "Good Guys, Bad Guys," www2.gwu.edu/~nsarchiv/coldwar/interviews/episode-17/tomkins1.html; Spikes, *Angola and the Politics of Intervention*, 292, 297–305; "Mercenaries: 'A Bloody Shambles,'" *Time Magazine*, February 23, 1976.

97. Wright, "Angola's Dogs of War."

98. Wright, "Angola's Dogs of War"; Gleijeses, *Conflicting Missions*, 333–37.

99. Spikes, *Angola and the Politics of Intervention*, 289–96; Stockwell, *In Search of Enemies*, 233.

100. Robert Moss, "Battle of Death Road," *Sunday Telegraph*, February 13, 1977; Marcum, *Angolan Revolution*, 277; Spikes, *Angola and the Politics of Intervention*, 299–313; Gleijeses, *Conflicting Missions*, 341–45.

101. Stockwell, *In Search of Enemies*, 234–241; Drew, 33; Marcum, *Angolan Revolution*, 277; Spikes, *Angola and the Politics of Intervention*, 300–310.

102. Memorandum of Conversation, General Secretary Leonid I. Brezhnev, et al., and Secretary of State Henry A. Kissinger, et al., January 21, 1976, 11:00 A.M.–1:50 P.M., Brezhnev's Office, the Kremlin, Moscow, reprinted in Burr, *The Kissinger Transcripts*, 443–45.

103. Memorandum of Conversation, Andrei A. Gromyko, et al., and Secretary of State Henry A. Kissinger, et al., January 23, 1976, 9:34–11:45 A.M., Tolstoi House, Moscow, reprinted in Burr, *The Kissinger Transcripts*, 473.

104. CIA Intelligence Memorandum, "The Present Situation in Angola," January 26, 1976, Digital National Security Archive.

105. Spikes, *Angola and the Politics of Intervention*, 301.

106. Memorandum from Cuban Commander Risquet to Fidel Castro, January 29, 1976, reproduced in Gleijeses, "Havana's Policy in Africa."

107. Stockwell, *In Search of Enemies*, 231–32.

108. Stockwell, *In Search of Enemies*, 234, 242 and 245; Spikes, *Angola and the Politics of Intervention*, 308 and 310.

109. Maier, *Angola: Promises and Lies*, 21 and 36; Spikes, *Angola and the Politics of Intervention*, 318; Courtois, et al, *Black Book of Communism*, 697–700; Prendergast, "Angola's Deadly War"; "Angola: The Long Slow Walk to Normality," *The Economist*, September 4, 2004, 49.

110. Prendergast, "Angola's Deadly War"; Cleary, "Angola — A Case Study"; "Jonas Sahib," *The Economist*, February 28, 2002; "Angola: The Long Slow Walk to Normality," *The Econ-*

omist, September 4, 2004, 49; Danna Harman, "The Displaced Fight to Survive," *Christian Science Monitor* 163, vol. 93 (July 18, 2001), 6; Hare, *Angola's Last Best Chance,* xvi and 10–11; Spikes, *Angola and the Politics of Intervention,* 324.

111. "Constitution of the People's Republic of Angola," reprinted in *Road to Liberation: MPLA Documents on the Founding of the People's Republic of Angola,* 49–51; Spikes, *Angola and the Politics of Intervention,* 215–16; Stockwell, *In Search of Enemies,* 202–204; Gleijeses, *Conflicting Missions,* 343; Marcum, *Angolan Revolution,* 278–79; Robert Moss, "Moscow's Next Target in Africa: Paying the Price for Angola," *Sunday Telegraph,* February 20, 1977; Isaacson, *Kissinger,* 683; Falk, "Cuba in Africa," 1081–95.

112. Interview of Karen Brutents, Central Committee of the Communist Party of the Soviet Union, August 1997, CNN Interactive, Cold War, Episode 17, "Good Guys, Bad Guys," *www.cnn.com/SPECIALS/cold.war/episodes/17/interviews/brutents.*

113. Dobrynin, *In Confidence,* 403.

114. Kissinger, *Years of Renewal,* 833. See also Ford, *Time to Heal,* 359.

115. Gleijeses, *Conflicting Missions,* 377; George, 20–48.

116. Gleijeses, "Moscow's Proxy?" 3–51; Falk, 1087–88; Robert Moss, "Moscow's Next Target in Africa: Paying the Price for Angola," *Sunday Telegraph,* February 20, 1977.

117. Gleijeses, "Moscow's Proxy?" 3–51; Gleijeses, *Conflicting Missions,* 392.

118. Transcript of Meeting Between U.S. Secretary of State Alexander M. Haig, Jr., and Cuban Vice Premier Carlos Rafael Rodriguez, Mexico City, November 23, 1981, Embassy of USSR to Republic of Cuba, translation by Bruce McDonald; document on file at National Security Archive. See also Gleijeses, "Moscow's Proxy?" 3–51.

119. Fidel Castro Speech, "Angola: African Giron," April 19, 1976, Havana.

120. Falk, 1089–90; Spikes, *Angola and the Politics of Intervention,* 321–23.

121. Hare, *Angola's Last Best Chance*; Pascal Fontaine, "Communism in Latin America," in Courtois, et al., *Black Book of Communism,* 664; Gleijeses, "Moscow's Proxy?" 3–51; Falk, "Cuba in Africa," 1078.

Chapter 18

1. Interview of Ambassador Winston Lord, by Charles Stuart Kennedy and Nancy Bernkopf Tucker, April 28, 1998, Diplomatic Studies Interview Collection.

2. Memorandum of Conversation between Henry Kissinger, et al., July 6, 1975, available in: Burr, *Kissinger Transcripts,* 377.

3. Short, *Mao: A Life,* 513.

4. Short, *Mao: A Life,* pp. 2–3, 299–316, 443–44, 579–85 and 609–11; Fairbank, *China: A New History,* 302–303.

5. Memorandum from Henry Kissinger, "Analysis/Highlights of Secretary Kissinger's Meeting with Chairman Mao, October 21, 1975," handed to President Ford on October 24, 1975, and Memorandum for the President from Henry A. Kissinger, October 24, 1975, Ford Library, NSA/Kissinger Reports, Box 2, Folder: "October 19–23, 1975, Kissinger Trip (1)."

6. Memorandum from Henry Kissinger, "Analysis/Highlights of Secretary Kissinger's Meeting with Chairman Mao, October 21, 1975," handed to President Ford on October 24, 1975, Ford Library, NSA/Kissinger Reports, Box 2, Folder: "October 19–23, 1975, Kissinger Trip (1)"; Memorandum for the President from Brent Scowcroft, October 21, 1975, Ford Library, NSA/Kissinger Reports, Box 2, Folder: "October 19–23, 1975, Kissinger Trip (2)"; Memorandum of Conversation between Mao Zedong, et al. and Henry Kissinger, et al., October 21, 1975, available in: Burr, *Kissinger Transcripts,* 388–91; Interview of Ambassador Winston Lord, by Charles Stuart Kennedy and Nancy Bernkopf Tucker, April 28, 1998, Diplomatic Studies Interview Collection; Kissinger, *Years of Renewal,* 871–881; Short, *Mao: A Life,* 614–21.

7. Memorandum of Conversation between Teng Hsiao-p'ing, et al. and Gerald Ford, et al., December 2, 1975, 10:10 A.M., Ford Library, NSA/Kissinger Reports, Box 2, Folder: "December 1–5, 1975, President Ford's Visit to Peking," 2.

8. Memorandum of Conversation between Teng Hsiao-p'ing, et al. and Gerald Ford, et al., December 2, 1975, 10:10 A.M., Ford Library, NSA/Kissinger Reports, Box 2, Folder: "December 1–5, 1975, President Ford's Visit to Peking," 6 and 9; Ford, *Time to Heal,* 335–37; Kissinger, *Years of Renewal,* 887–93; Kennerly, 183.

9. Memorandum of Conversation between Chairman Mao Tse Tung, et al. and President Gerald Ford, et al., December 2, 1975, 4:10 P.M., Ford Library, NSA/Kissinger Reports, Box 2, Folder: "December 1–5, 1975, President Ford's Visit to Peking," 6 and 9.

10. Memorandum of Conversation between Teng Hsiao-p'ing, et al. and Gerald Ford, et al., December 4, 1975, 10:05 A.M., Ford Library, NSA/Kissinger Reports, Box 2, Folder: "December 1–5, 1975, President Ford's Visit to Peking," 3.

11. Short, *Mao: A Life,* 620–23; Kissinger, *Years of Renewal,* 895.

12. Short, *Mao: A Life,* 514–86; Margolin, "China: A Long March Into Night," 513.

13. Short, *Mao: A Life,* 483–509; Margolin, "China: A Long March Into Night," 463–98.

14. Short, *Mao: A Life,* 594–625; Kissinger, *Years of Renewal,* 895–96.

15. Short, *Mao: A Life,* 268–81, 382–88, 436–48, 460–70, and 627; Kissinger, *Years of Renewal,* 897; Burr, *Kissinger Transcripts,* 376 and 409; Margolin, "China: A Long March Into Night," 472–513.

16. Charlotte Denny, "Suharto, Marcos and Mobutu Head Corruption Table with $50bn Scams" *Guardian,* March 26, 2004.

17. Timor Commission of Truth and Reconciliation Final Report, Section 2, para. 91.

18. Burr and Evans, "East Timor Revisited"; Ramos-Horta, *Funu,* 49–50.

19. Memorandum from Jakarta Embassy to Secretary of State, "Propaganda Campaign re: Portuguese Timor," February 27, 1975; Timor Commission of Truth and Reconciliation Final Report, Section 3, paras. 139–63; Taylor, *East Timor,* 30–58; Kiernan, "War, Genocide, and Resistance"; Kiernan, "Cover-Up and Denial of Genocide"; Ramos-Horta, *Funu,* 36 and 46–55; Burr and Evans, "East Timor Revisited."

20. Memorandum of Conversation between President Suharto, President Ford, Kissinger, and Scowcroft, July 5, 1975, Ford Library, NSA/Memoranda of Conversations 1973–1977, Box 13, Folder: "July 5, 1975 — Ford, Kissinger, Indonesian President Suharto."

21. Cable from American Consulate Surabaya to American Embassy in Jakarta, "Estimate of Indonesian Military Capabilities," March 3, 1975.

22. Memorandum of the Secretary's Principal's and Regional Staff Meeting, August 12, 1975, Department of State.

23. Minutes of Secretary of State Kissinger's Staff Meeting, October 8, 1975, National Archives, Office of Secretary of State, Transcripts of HAK Staff Meetings 1972–1977, Box 8, also available at www.gwu.edu/~nsarchiv/NSAEBB/NSAEBB193/HAK-10-8-75.pdf.

24. Timor Commission of Truth and Reconciliation Final Report, Section 3, para. 143.

25. Taylor, *East Timor,* 52.

26. Timor Commission of Truth and Reconciliation Final Report, Section 3, para. 126; Ramos-Horta, *Funu,* 79.

27. Taylor, *East Timor,* 58–63; "Big Indonesia Attack in Timor Reported," *New York Times,* October 8, 1975; Timor Commission of Truth and Reconciliation Final Report; Ben Kiernan, "War, Genocide, and Resistance"; Burr and Evans, "East Timor Revisited."

28. Timor Commission of Truth and Reconciliation Final Report; Taylor, *East Timor,* 63–64; Burr and Evans, "East Timor Revisited"; Ben Kiernan, "War, Genocide, and Resistance."

29. Timor Commission of Truth and Reconciliation Final Report, Section 3, para. 217.

30. Memorandum for the President from Henry A. Kissinger, "Your Visit to Indonesia," National Archives, Record Group 59, Department of State Records, Executive Secretariat Briefing Books, 1958–1976, Box 227, President Ford's Visit to the Far East — Indonesia Nov–Dec. 1975, reprinted in Burr and Evans, "East Timor Revisited."

31. Department of State Telegram from American Embassy Jakarta to the Secretary of State, December 1975, Ford Library, Kissinger-Scowcroft Temporary Parallel File, Box A3, Country File, Far East-Indonesia, State Department Telegrams 4/1/75–9/22/76, reprinted in Burr and Evans, "East Timor Revisited."

32. Memorandum to Brent Scowcroft from Clinton Granger, "Indonesian Use of MAP Equipment in Timor," December 12, 1975, Ford Library, NSA Files.

33. Taylor, East Timor, 64.

34. Taylor, East Timor, 68.

35. Ramos-Horta, Funu, 17. For a description of the activities after the invasion, see Timor Commission of Truth and Reconciliation Final Report, Section 7.2.3.2; Ben Kiernan, "War, Genocide, and Resistance"; Taylor, East Timor, 69–70; Henry Kamm, "War-Ravaged Timor Struggles Back from Abyss," New York Times, January 28, 1980, A1.

36. Taylor, East Timor, 68.

37. Timor Commission of Truth and Reconciliation Final Report, Section 7, para. 152.

38. Pilger, Distant Voices, 243. See also Taylor, East Timor, 70–71.

39. David A. Andelman, "Indonesia Completes Takeover of Portuguese Colony of Timor," New York Times, May 3, 1976; Timor Commission of Truth and Reconciliation Final Report.

40. Burr and Evans, "East Timor Revisited"; Kiernan, "Cover-Up and Denial of Genocide"; Pilger, Distant Voices, 253.

41. Memorandum of Conversation, Secretary Kissinger, et al., December 18, 1975, Subject: Department Policy, available at: http://www.etan.org/news/kissinger/secret.htm.

42. S/RES/384 (1975), adopted by the Security Council on December 22, 1975.

43. S/RES/389 (1976), adopted by the Security Council on April 22, 1976; "U.N. Bids Indonesia Leave East Timor," New York Times, April 23, 1976.

44. Memorandum of Conversation, Secretary Kissinger, et al., June 17, 1976, Digital National Security Archive.

45. Taylor, East Timor, 79–81; Ben Kiernan, "War, Genocide, and Resistance in East Timor."

46. "Indonesia Charged with Atrocities, New York Times, March 13, 1977, 10.

47. "Excerpts from State Department Reports on the Status of Human Rights Abroad," New York Times, February 10, 1978, A14.

48. Cable from Jakarta Embassy to Secretary of State, May 10, 1978, "Summary of Vice President's Meeting with Suharto."

49. Taylor, East Timor, 85.

50. "Message to Suharto," National Review, May 9, 1986; Taylor, East Timor, 101–60.

51. "East Timor Getting Urgent Aid to Combat Famine," New York Times, October 31, 1979, A3.

52. Timor Commission of Truth and Reconciliation Final Report; East Timor-Indonesia, Displaced Persons, USAID, Situation Report No. 1, October 9, 1979; "East Timor Under the Indonesian Jackboot: An Analysis of Indonesian Army Documents," TAPOL, Occasional Report No. 26, October 1998, available at http://tapol.gn.apc.org/reports/REast.htm; Taylor, East Timor, 88–100; Burr and Evans, "East Timor Revisited."

53. Graham Hovey, "House Panel Hears of Starvation in East Asian Area of East Timor," New York Times, December 5, 1979, A3.

54. "An Unjust War in East Timor," New York Times, December 24, 1979, A14.

55. "The Shaming of Indonesia," New York Times, December 8, 1980, A26.

56. "Message to Suharto," National Review, May 9, 1986.

57. "Statement of Kenneth M. Quinn, Deputy Assistant Secretary for East Asian and Pacific Affairs," Senate Foreign Relations Committee, March 6, 1992.

58. Professor Kiernan estimates that between 116,000 and 174,000 people died during the first five years of the occupation. By the end of 1985, more than 200,000 had died. Kiernan, "The Demography of Genocide in Southeast Asia"; Kiernan, "War, Genocide, and Resistance." The Truth and Reconciliation Commission put the minimum number of deaths at between 102,000 and 189,000. Timor Commission of Truth and Reconciliation Final Report, Section 6, para. 8.

59. Timor Commission of Truth and Reconciliation Final Report, Section 6, para. 11.

60. Dana Milbank, "1975 East Timor Invasion Got U.S. Go-Ahead," Washington Post, December 7, 2001.

61. Transcript of Henry Kissinger's response to questions at the Park Central Hotel in New York City on July 11, 1995, available at www.etan.org/news/kissinger/ask.htm.

62. Brinkley, Gerald R. Ford, 131–32.

63. Interview of Ambassador David D. Newsom, by Charles Stuart Kennedy, June 17, 1991, Diplomatic Studies Interview Collection.

Chapter 19

1. Drew, American Journal, 55.

2. Witcover, Marathon, 120–27.

3. Glad, Jimmy Carter, 212.

4. Pomper, "Nominating Contests and Conventions," 10; Drew, American Journal, 143–44; Witcover, Marathon, 118.

5. Governor Jimmy Carter, "A Message on Justice," May 4, 1974, reprinted in Carter, Presidential Campaign 1976, vol. 1, pt. 1, 23; Hunter Thompson, "Jimmy Carter," Rolling Stone, 1976, reprinted in Dolan and Quinn, Sense of the Seventies, 215.

6. Witcover, Marathon, 126.

7. Anderson, Electing Jimmy Carter, 51 and 284–87; Woodward, Shadow, 42; Alexander, Financing the 1976 Election, 234; Schram, Running for President, 111; Drew, American Journal, 141.

8. Witcover, Marathon, 151–63 and 214; Alexander, Financing the 1976 Election, 259–61 and 270–82.

9. Witcover, Marathon, 149–50; Alexander, Financing the 1976 Election, 275–79.

10. Alexander, Financing the 1976 Election, 253–55; Witcover, Marathon, 145; Drew, American Journal, 46–47.

11. Witcover, Marathon, 153–54; Schram, Running for President, 15.

12. Schram, Running for President, 67–68; Drew, American Journal, 5–8.

13. Schram, Running for President, 78; Pomper, "The Nominating Contests and Conventions," 8; Witcover, Marathon, 165–72; Polsby and Wildavsky, Presidential Elections, 62; Alexander, Financing the 1976 Election, 292–98 and 717–19.

14. Briefing Paper, April 1975, Ford Library, Richard Cheney Files, Box 18, Folder: "President Ford Committee — Establishment (3)"; Memorandum from Jerry Jones to Don Rumsfeld, 7/1/75, Ford Library, Presidential Handwriting File, Box 71, Folder: "7/1/75"; Hartmann, Palace Politics, 322 and 333–34; Cannon, "Gerald R. Ford and Nelson A. Rockefeller," 142.

15. Osborne, White House Watch, 299.

16. Ford, Time to Heal, 296–97; Witcover, Marathon, 53–54.

17. Ford, Time to Heal, 295–96 and 347–48; Hartmann, Palace Politics, 334; Witcover, Marathon, 52 and 78–79; Greene, Presidency of Gerald R. Ford, 158; Osborne, White House Watch, 299.

18. Ford, Time to Heal, 309–10.

19. Witcover, Marathon, 59.

20. Kennerly, Shooter, 190; Ford, Time to Heal, 311.

21. Memo, Jerry Jones to Don Rumsfeld and Dick Cheney, 9/26/75, Ford Library, Jerry Jones Files, Box 25, Folder: "Reagan, Ronald (1)."

22. Witcover, *Marathon*, 46; Alexander, *Financing the 1976 Election*, 318.

23. Witcover, *Marathon*, 65–69 and 77; Drew, *American Journal*, 55–56.

24. Witcover, *Marathon*, 92–93; Ford, *Time to Heal*, 332–33; Drew, *American Journal*, 26.

25. Ford, *Time to Heal*, 294, 344, and 347.

26. Witcover, *Marathon*, 101; Ford, *Time to Heal*, 345.

27. Witcover, *Marathon*, 84; Ford, *Time to Heal*, 345.

28. Memorandum from Robert Teeter and Stu Spencer to Richard Cheney, November 12, 1975, Ford Library, James Reichley Files, Box 5, Folder: "Theme Speeches"; Memo, Robert Teeter to Richard Cheney, 12/24/75, Ford Library, Foster Chanock Files, Box 4, Folder: "Memoranda and Polling Data — Teeter (3)."

29. Schram, *Running for President*, 64; Witcover, *Marathon*, 197–98.

30. Alexander, *Financing the 1976 Election*, 234.

31. Memorandum from Hamilton Jordan to Jimmy Carter, November 4, 1972, available at www.c-span.org/presidential libraries/Content/Carter/CarterStrategy.pdf.

32. Memorandum from Hamilton Jordan to Jimmy Carter, August 4, 1974, Jimmy Carter Presidential Library, Records of the Office of Peter Bourne, Special Assistant to the President for Health Issues, 1976–1979, Collection JC-1032, copy also available at http://arcweb.archives.gov/arc/action/External Search?hitLimit=2000&searchExpression=1976+campaign+stra tegy+paper.

33. Memorandum from Tim Kraft to Hamilton Jordan, August 28, 1975, available at www.c-span.org/presidentialli braries/Content/Carter/CarterIowa.pdf; Witcover, *Marathon*, 197–99; Schram, *Running for President*, 6–7, 17, and 64.

34. Witcover, *Marathon*, 199–201 and 254–55; Schram, *Running for President*, 16.

35. Witcover, *Marathon*, 212–14 and 353; Schram, *Running for President*, 6–18; Drew, *American Journal*, 16 and 39; Anderson, *Electing Jimmy Carter*, 5.

36. Schram, *Running for President*, 98.

37. Schram, *Running for President*, 93–94.

38. Woodward, *Shadow*, 41; Drew, *American Journal*, 43 and 316.

39. Drew, *American Journal*, 43; Anderson, *Electing Jimmy Carter*, 10 and 16; Witcover, *Marathon*, 198.

40. Schram, *Running for President*, 19–24; Drew, *American Journal*, 43–63; Witcover, *Marathon*, 224–37.

41. Memorandum to Mo and Stewart Udall from Jack Quinn, "Areas of Immediate Concern," December 9, 1975, reprinted in Schram, *Running for President*, 13.

42. Ford, *Time to Heal*, 334 and 361; Schram, *Running for President*, 228; Drew, *American Journal*, 48.

43. Witcover, *Marathon*, 98–99 and 388–89; Ford, *Time to Heal*, 346; Osborne, *White House Watch*, 337.

44. Osborne, *White House Watch*, 288–89.

45. Witcover, *Marathon*, 378–79.

46. Ford, *Time to Heal*, 348–49 and 361–65; Witcover, *Marathon*, 380–87; Osborne, *White House Watch*, 289–93; Greene, *Presidency of Gerald R. Ford*, 163.

47. Anson, *Exile*, 122–30; Ford, *Time to Heal*, 360; Kissinger, *Years of Renewal*, 895; Burr, *Kissinger Transcripts*, 405 and 420.

48. Mollenhoff, *The Man Who Pardoned Nixon*, 264.

49. Thomas, *Thanks for the Memories*, 108.

50. Witcover, *Marathon*, 398.

51. Greene, *Presidency of Gerald R. Ford*, 163; Witcover, *Marathon*, 393–99; Ford, *Time to Heal*, 367.

52. Witcover, *Marathon*, 277.

53. Alexander, *Financing the 1976 Election*, 261; Witcover, *Marathon*, 157–60 and 191; Drew, *American Journal*, 35 and 136; Pomper, "The Nominating Contests and Conventions," 8; Schram, *Running for President*, 108.

54. Witcover, *Marathon*, 243.

55. Drew, *American Journal*, 67; Witcover, *Marathon*, 244.

56. Witcover, *Marathon*, 257.

57. Schram, *Running for President*, 30–31; Witcover, *Marathon*, 245–46.

58. Schram, *Running for President*, 27–34 and 77; Witcover, *Marathon*, 240–51; Alexander, *Financing the 1976 Election*, 265; Drew, *American Journal*, 35–37.

59. Witcover, *Marathon*, 255.

60. Witcover, *Marathon*, 253–60; Schram, *Running for President*, 77–84; Anderson, *Electing Jimmy Carter*, 6.

61. Burr, *Kissinger Transcripts*, 470.

62. Department of State News Release, "Panama Canal Treaty Negotiations: Background and Current Status," January 1975, Gerald R. Ford Presidential Library, Richard Cheney Files, Box 9, Folder: "Panama Canal — General."

63. Drew, *American Journal*, 239.

64. Witcover, *Marathon*, 263 and 332; Alexander, *Financing the 1976 Election*, 224; Schram, *Running for President*, 144.

65. Alexander, *Financing the 1976 Election*, 247.

66. Schram, *Running for President*, 86–91 and 99; Witcover, *Marathon*, 262; Drew, *American Journal*, 109.

67. Schram, *Running for President*, 91.

68. Witcover, *Marathon*, 406.

69. Ford, *Time to Heal*, 347 and 371–72; Witcover, *Marathon*, 406 and 413.

70. Ford, *Time to Heal*, 368.

71. Witcover, *Marathon*, 408–13; Ford, *Time to Heal*, 294 and 374–75; Hartmann, *Palace Politics*, 336; Drew, *American Journal*, 49.

72. Drew, *American Journal*, 116.

73. Ford, *Time to Heal*, 375; Drew, *American Journal*, 405; Alexander, *Financing the 1976 Election*, 325; Greene, *The Presidency of Gerald R. Ford*, 164–66; Witcover, *Marathon*, 411–15; Schram, *Running for President*, 228.

74. Schram, *Running for President*, 99–100; Witcover, *Marathon*, 264–72.

75. *Buckley v. Valeo*, 424 U.S. 1 (1976).

76. President Gerald R. Ford's Remarks on Transmitting Proposed Legislation to the Congress to Reconstitute the Federal Election Commission, February 16, 1976; President Gerald R. Ford's Special Message to the Congress Proposing Legislation to Reconstitute the Federal Election Commission, February 16, 1976; Witcover, *Marathon*, 220; Alexander, *Financing the 1976 Election*, 3, 31–37, and 811–14.

77. Alexander, *Financing the 1976 Election*, 236–40.

78. Witcover, *Marathon*, 276.

79. Drew, *American Journal*, 152.

80. Stroud, *How Jimmy Won*, 213.

81. Schram, *Running for President*, 105–19; Witcover, *Marathon*, 274–95; Drew, *American Journal*, 138; Alexander, *Financing the 1976 Election*, 287–88; Polsby and Wildavsky, *Presidential Elections*, 50.

82. Ford, *Time to Heal*, 375–79; Alexander, *Financing the 1976 Election*, 321–25; Witcover, *Marathon*, 413–417 and 426.

83. Witcover, *Marathon*, 295–308 and 17; Schram, *Running for President*, 125–28; Drew, *American Journal*, 166; Alexander, *Financing the 1976 Election*, 621.

84. Witcover, *Marathon*, 176; Gerald M. Pomper, "The Nominating Contests and Conventions," *The Election of 1976: Reports and Interpretations*, 8.

85. Schram, *Running for President*, 131; Witcover, *Marathon*, 176.

86. Drew, *American Journal*, 170; Schram, *Running for President*, 133–34.

87. Schram, *Running for President*, 137.

88. Ford, *Time to Heal*, 375–79; Witcover, *Marathon*, 416 and 26.

89. Witcover, *Marathon*, 419–20; Ford, *Time to Heal*, 379–81; Drew, *American Journal*, 173; Osborne, *White House Watch*, 323–24; Schram, *Running for President*, 228; Pomper, "Nominating Contests and Conventions," 21–22.

90. Osborne, *White House Watch*, 326; Kissinger, *Years of Renewal*, 941; Isaacson, *Kissinger*, 688.

91. Isaacson, *Kissinger*, 694.

92. Letter from Barry Goldwater to Gerald Ford, May 7, 1976, Ford Library, James Connor Files, Box 30, Folder: "Marsh, 1976–77 (2)."

93. John Osborne, *White House Watch*, 321.

94. Witcover, *Marathon*, 420–21; Ford, *Time to Heal*, 382–84.

95. Schram, *Running for President*, 137–42; Witcover, *Marathon*, 329–30; Alexander, *Financing the 1976 Election*, 228, 249, and 291.

96. Schram, *Running for President*, 145.

97. Schram, *Running for President*, 146–50; Witcover, *Marathon*, 337–39.

98. Ford, *Time to Heal*, 38–87; Witcover, *Marathon*, 421–25; Nessen, *It Sure Looks Different*, 215.

99. Schram, *Running for President*, 160–65; Witcover, *Marathon*, 339–41.

100. Witcover, *Marathon*, 426–28; Ford, *Time to Heal*, 387; Osborne, *White House Watch*, 334.

101. Witcover, *Marathon*, 430.

102. Witcover, *Marathon*, 431; Osborne, *White House Watch*, 334; Ford, *Time to Heal*, 388.

103. Witcover, *Marathon*, 429–31; Drew, *American Journal*, 218; Ford, *Time to Heal*, 388–89.

104. Schram, *Running for President*, 175–98; Witcover, *Marathon*, 342–50.

105. Alexander, *Financing the 1976 Election*, 267; Schram, *Running for President*, 130.

106. Schram, *Running for President*, 197.

107. Witcover, *Marathon*, 351–53.

108. Schram, *Running for President*, 1–5 and 198; Witcover, *Marathon*, 351–52; Anderson, *Electing Jimmy Carter*, 37.

109. Witcover, *Marathon*, 359–68; Schram, *Running for President*, 201–10; Gerald M. Pomper, "The Nominating Contests and Conventions," *The Election of 1976: Reports and Interpretations*, 27.

110. Polsby and Wildavsky, *Presidential Elections*, 116; Witcover, *Marathon*, 357–68; Drew, *American Journal*, 290–316; Gerald M. Pomper, "The Nominating Contests and Conventions," *The Election of 1976: Reports and Interpretations*, 11–31; Schram, *Running for President*, 213–16; Anderson, *Electing Jimmy Carter*, 42–64.

111. Ford, *Time to Heal*, 347–48 and 389–93; Witcover, *Marathon*, 431–34; Schram, *Running for President*, 228–29; Gerald M. Pomper, "The Nominating Contests and Conventions," *The Election of 1976: Reports and Interpretations*, 23–25.

112. Witcover, *Marathon*, 434.

113. Ford, *Time to Heal*, 389.

114. Ford, *Time to Heal*, 390–93; Drew, *American Journal*, 259, 289, and 318; Witcover, *Marathon*, 434–38.

115. Schram, *Running for President*, 230.

116. Osborne, *White House Watch*, 366; Schram, *Running for President*, 230; Greene, *Presidency of Gerald R. Ford*, 170–71; Witcover, *Marathon*, 456–63; Drew, *American Journal*, 333; Ford, *Time to Heal*, 394.

117. Witcover, *Marathon*, 464.

118. Witcover, *Marathon*, 443.

119. Ford, *Time to Heal*, 395–96.

120. Ford, *Time to Heal*, 397–99; Drew, *American Journal*, 352, 356, 369, 383, and 391; Osborne, *White House Watch*, 365 and 386; Witcover, *Marathon*, 479–83; Nessen, *It Sure Looks Different*, 231–33.

121. Witcover, *Marathon*, 484–86; Osborne, *White House Watch*, 375; Isaacson, *Kissinger*, 699; Ford, *Time to Heal*, 398; Nessen, *It Sure Looks Different*, 229 and 234.

122. Drew, *American Journal*, 275.

123. Witcover, *Marathon*, 503.

124. Caruso and Cannon, "Then We Were Off and Running."

125. Ford, *Time to Heal*, 399–400; Witcover, *Marathon*, 505; Schram, *Running for President*, 232–33; Osborne, *White House Watch*, 380; Pomper, "The Nominating Contests and Conventions," 26–27.

126. Ford, *Time to Heal*, 78 and 401–404; Cannon, *Time and Chance*, 83; Pomper, "The Nominating Contests and Conventions," 29; Nessen, *It Sure Looks Different*, 238–40; Schram, *Running for President*, 233–35; Witcover, *Marathon*, 505–509; Drew, *American Journal*, 398.

127. Hyland, *Mortal Rivals*, 169–70.

128. Drew, *American Journal*, 410.

129. Ford, *Time to Heal*, 406; Schram, *Running for President*, 230–32; Gerald M. Pomper, "The Nominating Contests and Conventions," 26–32; Nessen, *It Sure Looks Different*, 242.

130. Ford, *Time to Heal*, 405–406; Smith, "Speechwriting in the Nixon and Ford White Houses"; Schram, *Running for President*, 237; Nessen, *It Sure Looks Different*, 243; Drew, *American Journal*, 409; Witcover, *Marathon*, 509; Greene, *Presidency of Gerald R. Ford*, 173.

Chapter 20

1. Minutes of National Security Council Meeting of April 7, 1976, Ford Library, National Security Adviser, Box 2, National Security Council Meetings File.

2. Ford, *Time to Heal*, 380; Isaacson, *Kissinger*, 686; Kissinger, *Years of Renewal*, 925.

3. Memorandum of Conversation, Ford, Scowcroft, Kissinger, April 21, 1976, Ford Library, National Security Advisor, Memoranda of Conversations, 1973–1977, Box 19, Folder: "April 21, 1976 — Ford, Kissinger."

4. Interview of Ambassador Winston Lord, by Charles Stuart Kennedy and Nancy Bernkopf Tucker, April 28, 1998, Diplomatic Studies Interview Collection.

5. Isaacson, *Kissinger*, 687.

6. Kissinger, *Years of Renewal*, 928; Interview of Ambassador James W. Spain, by Charles Stuart Kennedy, October 31, 1995, Diplomatic Studies Interview Collection; Minutes of National Security Council Meeting of May 11, 1976, Ford Library, National Security Adviser, Box 2, National Security Council Meetings File.

7. "Text of Kissinger's Address in Zambia on U.S. Policy Toward Southern Africa," *New York Times*, April 28, 1976, 16.

8. Interview of Ambassador Winston Lord, by Charles Stuart Kennedy and Nancy Bernkopf Tucker, April 28, 1998, Diplomatic Studies Interview Collection.

9. Gulley, *Breaking Cover*, 264.

10. Interview of Ambassador Winston Lord, by Charles Stuart Kennedy and Nancy Bernkopf Tucker, April 28, 1998, Diplomatic Studies Interview Collection.

11. Minutes of National Security Council Meeting of May 11, 1976, Ford Library, National Security Adviser, Box 2, National Security Council Meetings File.

12. Chile Commission Report.

13. Transcript of "The Secretary's 8:00 A.M. Regional Staff Meeting," December 3, 1974, reprinted in Nixon on Chile Intervention.

14. Transcript of "The Secretary's Principals and Regional Staff Meeting," December 20, 1974, reprinted in Nixon on Chile Intervention.

15. Memorandum of Conversation Between Secretary Kissinger, et al. and Foreign Minister Carvajal, September 29, 1975, reprinted in Nixon on Chile Intervention.

16. Transcript of Telephone Conversation Between William Rogers and Secretary of State Henry Kissinger, June 3, 1976.

17. Memorandum of Conversation between Henry Kissinger, et al. and Augusto Pinochet, et al., June 8, 1976, reprinted in Kornbluh and White, "Pinochet: A Declassified Documentary Obit."

18. Osorio and Costar, "Kissinger to the Argentine Generals."

19. May 28, 1976 Telegram from United States Embassy in Buenos Aires to Secretary of State Henry Kissinger, reprinted in Osorio and Costar, "Kissinger to the Argentine Generals."

20. Osorio and Costar, "Kissinger to the Argentine Generals."

21. Memorandum of Conversation Between Secretary of State Henry Kissinger, Under Secretary of State Rogers, Under Secretary Maw, Luigi R. Einaudi, Anthony Hervas, and Argentinean Foreign Minister Guzzetti, Ambassador Carasales, Ambassador Pereyra and Mr. Estrada, June 6, 1976.

22. June 16, 1976, Telegram from United States Embassy

in Buenos Aires to Secretary of State Henry Kissinger, reprinted in Osorio and Costar, "Kissinger to the Argentine Generals."

23. Nunca Mas, Comision Nacional Sobre la Desaparicion de Personas, 1994; Osorio and Costar, "Kissinger to the Argentine Generals"; Osorio and Costar, "Kissinger to Argentines on Dirty War."

24. Interview of Harry W. Schlaudeman, by William E. Knight, May 24, 1993, Diplomatic Studies Interview Collection.

25. Memorandum of Conversation Between Secretary of State Henry Kissinger, Under Secretary of State Rogers, Under Secretary Maw, Luigi R. Einaudi, Anthony Hervas, and Argentinean Foreign Minister Guzzetti, Ambassador Carasales, Ambassador Pereyra and Mr. Estrada, June 6, 1976.

26. "State Dept. Memo to Kissinger on Operation Condor, August 3, 1976," "CIA Weekly Summary," and Memorandum for the Record of State Dept./CIA Weekly Meeting, August 3, 1976, reprinted in Kornbluh and Dinges, "Lifting of Pinochet's Immunity." See, also July 23, 1976, Telegram from United States Embassy in Buenos Aires to Secretary of State Henry Kissinger.

27. Memorandum from Buenos Aires to Director, Foreign Political Matters — Argentina, Foreign Political Matters — Chile, September 30, 1976.

28. *Isabel Morel De Letelier, et al, v. the Republic of Chile, et al*, 502 F. Supp. 259 (November 5, 1980 D.D.C.); Chile Commission Report, 610–32.

29. CIA Memo from Miami to Director, "Bombing of Cubana DC-8," November 2, 1976, and FBI Memo, Miami, Florida, "Coodinacion de Organizaciones Revolucionarias Unidas," August 16, 1978, reproduced in "Luis Posada Carriles: The Declassified Record."

30. President Gerald R. Ford, "Remarks and a Question-and-Answer Session at Wheaton College in Wheaton, Illinois," March 12, 1976.

31. Interview of William D. Rogers, by Stanley I. Grand, July 8, 1992, Diplomatic Studies Interview Collection.

32. Kissinger, *Years of Renewal*, 959.

33. Kissinger, *Years of Renewal*, 909–37 and 971–73; Spikes, *Angola*, 206–207.

34. Kissinger, *Years of Renewal*, 962–86.

35. Kissinger, *Years of Renewal*, 995–1000; Isaacson, *Kissinger*, 690–91.

36. Kissinger, *Years of Renewal*, 1003–1005.

37. Press Briefing, 9/28/76, Ford Library, Cabinet Meeting Collected Items, Box 4; Kissinger, *Years of Renewal*, 1011; Isaacson, *Kissinger*, 691.

38. Isaacson, *Kissinger*, 691–92.

39. Interview of Ambassador Winston Lord, by Charles Stuart Kennedy and Nancy Bernkopf Tucker, April 28, 1998, Diplomatic Studies Interview Collection.

Chapter 21

1. Schram, *Running for President*, 292 and 268; Nessen, *It Sure Looks Different*, 246; Witcover, *Marathon*, 594.

2. Ford, *Time to Heal*, 410; Nessen, *It Sure Looks Different*, 247; Greene, *Presidency of Gerald R. Ford*, 177; Alexander, *Financing the 1976 Election*, 412; Witcover, *Marathon*, 533 and 536–38; Osborne, *White House Watch*, 401.

3. Witcover, *Marathon*, 530.

4. Ford, *Time to Heal*, 409–14; Nessen, *It Sure Looks Different*, 247–54; Witcover, *Marathon*, 530–40; Schram, *Running for President*, 252 and 263–67; Greene, *Presidency of Gerald R. Ford*, 177–78.

5. Interview with Douglass Bailey, January 7, 1977, Ford Library, L. Patrick Devlin Interview Transcripts, 1976–77, Box 1, Folder: "Bailey, Douglas, 1/7/77," 14.

6. Devlin, "President Ford's Ad Man"; Interview with Douglass Bailey, January 7, 1977, Ford Library, L. Patrick Devlin Interview Transcripts, 1976–77, Box 1, Folder: "Bailey, Douglas, 1/7/77," 14; Ford, *Time to Heal*, 411; Nessen, *It Sure Looks Different*, 246; Witcover, *Marathon*, 552; Alexander, *Financing the 1976 Election*, 414 and 463.

7. Witcover, *Marathon*, 517–18 and 523.

8. Ford, *Time to Heal*, 409; Greene, *Presidency of Gerald R. Ford*, 175.

9. Schram, *Running for President*, 221.

10. Stroud, *How Jimmy Won*, 190.

11. Witcover, *Marathon*, 529.

12. Schram, *Running for President*, 218 and 271; Anderson, *Electing Jimmy Carter*, 76 and 99.

13. Witcover, *Marathon*, 522; Drew, *American Journal*, 473; Alexander, *Financing the 1976 Election*, 462–63.

14. Witcover, *Marathon*, 545–46; Anderson, *Electing Jimmy Carter*, 101; Schram, *Running for President*, 273–75.

15. Witcover, *Marathon*, 546; Schram, *Running for President*, 274–79.

16. Witcover, *Marathon*, 546–48; Greene, *Presidency of Gerald R. Ford*, 179–80; Nessen, *It Sure Looks Different*, 250; Drew, *American Journal*, 417.

17. Ford, *Time to Heal*, 413.

18. Nessen, *It Sure Looks Different*, 256; Schram, *Running for President*, 309; Polsby and Wildavsky, *Presidential Elections*, 196.

19. Witcover, *Marathon*, 613.

20. Drew, *American Journal*, 449–50.

21. Ford, *Time to Heal*, 416–17; Schram, *Running for President*, 300–301; Greene, *Presidency of Gerald R. Ford*, 179; Nessen, *It Sure Looks Different*, 299–300; Witcover, *Marathon*, 110–13, 562–67; Drew, *American Journal*, 430.

22. Witcover, *Marathon*, 570.

23. Anderson, *Electing Jimmy Carter*, 115; Witcover, *Marathon*, 579.

24. Schram, *Running for President*, 304–305.

25. Witcover, *Marathon*, 584; Drew, *American Journal*, 431; Greene, *Presidency of Gerald R. Ford*, 180; Nessen, *It Sure Looks Different*, 279 and 284–86.

26. Nessen, *It Sure Looks Different*, 286.

27. Ford, *Time to Heal*, 417–27; Drew, *American Journal*, 431; Greene, *Presidency of Gerald R. Ford*, 180–81; John Osborne, *White House Watch*, 405–10; Witcover, *Marathon*, 584.

28. Alexander, *Financing the 1976 Election*, 489.

29. Schram, *Running for President*, 295; Greene, *Presidency of Gerald R. Ford*, 181; Anderson, *Electing Jimmy Carter*, 114–15.

30. Presidential Campaign Debate Between Gerald R. Ford and Jimmy Carter, September 23, 1976, available at www.ford.utexas.edu/library/speeches/760803.htm.

31. Drew, *American Journal*, 439.

32. Presidential Campaign Debate Between Gerald R. Ford and Jimmy Carter, September 23, 1976, available at www.ford.utexas.edu/library/speeches/760803.htm.

33. Schram, *Running for President*, 296.

34. Ford, *Time to Heal*, 416; Witcover, *Marathon*, 579; Greene, *Presidency of Gerald R. Ford*, 182; Drew, *American Journal*, 437–38 and 444; Schram, *Running for President*, 314.

35. Schram, *Running for President*, 305.

36. Schram, *Running for President*, 306; Anderson, *Electing Jimmy Carter*, 115–16; Drew, *American Journal*, 444.

37. Nessen, *It Sure Looks Different*, 280.

38. Witcover, *Marathon*, 591; Ford, *Time to Heal*, 419–20; Nessen, *It Sure Looks Different*, 280.

39. Witcover, *Marathon*, 592.

40. Ford, *Time to Heal*, 420; Nessen, *It Sure Looks Different*, 283; Witcover, *Marathon*, 592.

41. Ford, *Time to Heal*, 419; Witcover, *Marathon*, 588–89; Woodward, *Shadow*, 32; Greene, *Presidency of Gerald R. Ford*, 182.

42. Nessen, *It Sure Looks Different*, 291; Ford, *Time to Heal*, 426; Greene, *Presidency of Gerald R. Ford*, 182; Osborne, *White House Watch*, 412 and 421; Witcover, *Marathon*, 589.

43. Memorandum of Conversation, Ford, Scowcroft, and Kissinger, October 3, 1976, Ford Library, National Security Advisor, Memoranda of Conversations, 1973–1977, Box 20, Folder: "October 3, 1976 — Ford, Kissinger"; Kissinger, *Years of Renewal*, 866.

44. Greene, *Presidency of Gerald R. Ford*, 184.

45. Presidential Campaign Debate Between Gerald R. Ford

and Jimmy Carter, October 6, 1976, available at www.ford.utexas.edu/library/speeches/760854.htm.

46. Schram, *Running for President*, 319.

47. Witcover, *Marathon*, 603; Drew, *American Journal*, 466.

48. Memo, Mike Duval to President, 10/18/76; folder "Debate Preparation," Ford Library, Michael Raoul-Duval Papers, Box 25.

49. Witcover, *Marathon*, 598; Ford, *Time to Heal*, 423.

50. Transcript of Press Conference by Brent Scowcroft and Richard Cheney, October 6, 1976, reprinted in Schram, *Running for President*, 320.

51. Witcover, *Marathon*, 599.

52. Ford, *Time to Heal*, 423–24; Schram, *Running for President*, 321; Greene, *Presidency of Gerald R. Ford*, 186; Nessen, *It Sure Looks Different*, 272; Osborne, *White House Watch*, 416–17.

53. Hartmann, *Palace Politics*, 413.

54. Interview with Bryce Harlow, July 27, 1985, Ford Library, Syers Interview Collection, Box 1, Folder: "Harlow, Bryce," 6.

55. President Gerald R. Ford, Remarks at the University of Southern California in Los Angeles, October 7, 1976.

56. President Gerald R. Ford, Remarks and a Question-and-Answer Session in Los Angeles with Members of the San Fernando Valley Business and Professional Association, October 8, 1976.

57. President Gerald R. Ford, Remarks and a Question-and-Answer Session with Reporters in Glendale, California, October 8, 1976.

58. President Gerald R. Ford, Remarks at a Meeting with American Leaders of Eastern European Ancestry, October 12, 1976.

59. Memorandum to Carter Campaign from Pat Caddell, October 16, 1976, reprinted in Schram, *Running for President*, 329–30.

60. Memorandum to Carter Campaign from Pat Caddell, October 20, 1976, reprinted in Schram, *Running for President*, 334–35.

61. Interview with Douglass Bailey, January 7, 1977, Ford Library, L. Patrick Devlin Interview Transcripts, 1976–77, Box 1, Folder: "Bailey, Douglas, 1/7/77," 23.

62. Witcover, *Marathon*, 614.

63. Presidential Campaign Debate Between Gerald R. Ford and Jimmy Carter, October 22, 1976, available at www.ford.utexas.edu/library/speeches/760947.htm.

64. Nessen, *It Sure Looks Different*, 277–78; Greene, *Presidency of Gerald R. Ford*, 186.

65. Osborne, *White House Watch*, 423–24; Nessen, *It Sure Looks Different*, 304 and 307; Schram, *Running for President*,
343; Witcover, *Marathon*, 538 and 625; Alexander, *Financing the 1976 Election*, 413.

66. Alexander, *Financing the 1976 Election*, 374–75.

67. Ford, *Time to Heal*, 429; Schram, *Running for President*, 349.

68. Ford, *Time to Heal*, 136 and 424.

69. Cannon, *Time and Chance*, 408; Greene, *Presidency of Gerald R. Ford*, 187; Witcover, *Marathon*, 619; Ford, *Time to Heal*, 428–29.

70. Schram, *Running for President*, 347; Nessen, *It Sure Looks Different*, 309.

71. Anderson, *Electing Jimmy Carter*, 13.

72. Witcover, *Marathon*, 634.

73. Ford, *Time to Heal*, 431; Nessen, *It Sure Looks Different*, 310; Schram, *Running for President*, 350.

74. Schram, *Running for President*, 332; Polsby and Wildavsky, *Presidential Elections*, 220.

75. Schram, *Running for President*, 326–28; Polsby and Wildavsky, *Presidential Elections*, 220.

76. Witcover, *Marathon*, 3–4.

77. Witcover, *Marathon*, 8–9; Ford, *Time to Heal*, 433.

78. Ford, *Time to Heal*, 434.

79. Ford, *Time to Heal*, 434; Witcover, *Marathon*, 10–13; Schram, *Running for President*, 355.

80. Witcover, *Marathon*, 11–12.

81. Schram, *Running for President*, 356; Drew, *American Journal*, 533.

82. Ford, *Time to Heal*, 434–35.

83. Ford, *Time to Heal*, 434–35; Schram, *Running for President*, 358; Witcover, *Marathon*, 13.

84. Ford, *Time to Heal*, 435; Drew, *American Journal*, 534; Schram, *Running for President*, 358–59.

85. Interview with Douglass Bailey, January 7, 1977, Ford Library, L. Patrick Devlin Interview Transcripts, 1976–77, Box 1, Folder: "Bailey, Douglas, 1/7/77," 18.

86. Pomper, "The Presidential Election," 73; Schram, *Running for President*, 367.

87. Burr, *Kissinger Transcripts*, 470.

88. Robert Novak, "Fiasco of '76," *National Review*, December 12, 1976.

89. Ford, *Time to Heal*, 438–39.

90. Interview of William D. Rogers, by Stanley I. Grand, July 8, 1992, Diplomatic Studies Interview Collection.

91. Interview with Phillip W. Buchen, March 13, 1985, Syers Interview Collection, Box 1, Folder: "Buchen, Phillip," 7–8; Farrell, *Tip O'Neill*, 437–37.

92. Nessen, *It Sure Looks Different*, 336; Schram, *Running for President*, 368–71; Ford, *Time to Heal*, 441; Witcover, *Marathon*, 654.

Bibliography

Administration Documents

All presidential statements, speeches, press conferences, proclamations, and executive orders are available at the American Presidency Project, www.presidency.ucsb.edu. The papers of the administration are held at the Gerald R. Ford Presidential Library in Ann Arbor, Michigan ("Ford Library" in the notes). The library had a limited number of documents available at www.ford.utexas.edu/library. Formerly-classified documents can be found in the Digital National Security Archive, available from Proquest at http://nsarchive.chadwyck.com/marketing/index.jsp.

Books and Articles

Agnew, Spiro T. *Go Quietly ... Or Else*. New York: William Morrow, 1980.

Albert, Carl, with Danney Goble. *Little Giant: The Life and Times of Speaker Carl Albert*. Norman: University of Oklahoma Press, 1990.

Alexander, Herbert E. *Campaign Money*. New York: Free Press, 1976.

_____. *Financing the 1976 Election*. Washington: Congressional Quarterly Press, 1979.

Ambrose, Stephen E., with Richard H. Immerman. *Ike's Spies: Eisenhower and the Espionage Establishment*. Jackson: University Press of Mississippi, 1981.

Amster, Linda. "Chronology of Watergate Related Events." In Staff of the New York Times, *Watergate Hearings*.

_____. "Events Leading to the Resignation of Richard M. Nixon." In Staff of the New York Times, *The End of a Presidency*.

Anderson, Patrick. *Electing Jimmy Carter*. Baton Rouge: Louisiana State University Press, 1994.

Anson, Robert Sam. *Exile*. New York: Simon and Schuster, 1984.

Apple, Jr., R. W. "Introduction." In Drossman and Knappman, *Watergate and the White House*, Volume 3.

_____. "A Tragedy in Three Acts." In Staff of the New York Times, *The End of a Presidency*.

Ashby, LeRoy, and Rod Gramer. *Fighting the Odds: The Life of Senator Frank Church*. Pullman: Washington State University Press, 1994.

Balogh, Brian. "From Metaphor to Quagmire: The Domestic Legacy of the Vietnam War." In Neu, *After Vietnam*.

Bauer, Stephen, with Frances Spatz Leighton. *At Ease in the White House*. New York: Carol Publishing Group, 1991.

Bender, Gerald J. "Kissinger in Angola: Anatomy of Failure." In Lemarchand, *American Policy in Southern Africa*.

Berman, Larry. *No Peace, No Honor: Nixon, Kissinger, and Betrayal in Vietnam*. New York: Touchstone, 2001.

Bernstein, Carl, and Bob Woodward. *All the President's Men*. New York: Simon and Schuster, 1974.

Breyer, Stephen. *Regulation and Its Reform*. Cambridge, Massachusetts: Harvard University Press, 1982.

_____. "Reforming Regulation." 59 Tul. L. Rev. 4 (October 1984).

Brigham, Robert. "Revolutionary Heroism and Politics in Postwar Vietnam." In Neu, *After Vietnam*.

Brinkley, Douglas. *Gerald R. Ford*. New York: Times Books, 2007.

Bruneau, Thomas C. "Popular Support for Democracy in Post Revolutionary Portugal: Results from a Survey." In Graham and Wheeler, *In Search of Modern Portugal*.

Burr, William, ed. *The Kissinger Transcripts: The Top Secret Talks with Beijing and Moscow*. New York: New Press, 1998.

Burr, William, and Michael L. Evans, eds. "East Timor Revisited: Ford, Kissinger and the Indonesian Invasion, 1975–76." National Security Archive Electronic Briefing Book No. 62, December 6, 2001. Available at www.gwu.edu/~nsarchiv/NSAEBB/NSAEBB62/.

Bush, George. *All the Best, George Bush: My Life in Letters and Other Writings*. New York: Scribner, 1999.

Cannon, James. *Time and Chance: Gerald Ford's Appointment with History*. New York, HarperCollins, 1994.

_____. "Gerald R. Ford and Nelson A. Rockefeller: A Vice Presidential Memoir." In Walch, *At the President's Side*.

Carter, James Earl. *The Presidential Campaign of 1976: Jimmy Carter*. Washington: U.S. Government Printing Office, 1978.

Caruso, Lisa, and Carl M Cannon. "Then We Were Off and Running." *National Journal* 36 (September 4, 2004): 2660.

Cherniaev, Anatolii. "The Unknown Brezhnev." *Russian Politics and Law* 42, no. 3 (May–June 2004): 34–66.

Cilliers, Jakkie, and Peggy Mason, eds. *Peace, Profit or Plunder: The Privatization of Security in War-torn African Societies*. Pretoria: Institute for Security Studies, 1999.

Cleary, Sean. "Angola — A Case Study of Private Military Involvement." In Cilliers, et al., *Peace, Profit or Plunder*.

Clymer, Adam. *Edward M. Kennedy: A Biography*. New York: William Morrow, 1999.

Cohen, David B., and Chris J. Dolan. "Debunking the Myth: Carter, Congress, and the Politics of Airline Deregulation." *White House Studies*, Spring 2001.

Cohen, Richard M., and Jules Witcover. *A Heartbeat Away: The Investigation and Resignation of Vice President Spiro T. Agnew*. New York: Viking Press, 1974.

Colby, William, and Peter Forbath. *Honorable Men: My Life in the CIA*. New York: Simon and Schuster, 1978.

Courtois, Stephane, Nicolas Werth, Jean-Louis Panne, Andrzej Paczkowski, Karel Bartose, and Jean-Louis Margolin. *The Black Book of Communism: Crimes, Terror, Repression*, Translated by Jonathan Murphy and Mark Kramer. Cambridge, Massachusetts: Harvard University Press, 1999.

Davis, Nathaniel. "The Angola Decision of 1975: A Personal Memoir." *Foreign Affairs* 57, no. 1 (Fall 1978).

Derthick, Martha, and Paul J. Quirk. *The Politics of Deregulation*. Washington: The Brookings Institution.

Devlin, Patrick. "President Ford's Ad Man Reviews the 1976 Media Campaign." *Indiana Speech Journal* 8, no. 2 (April 1978).

Dobrynin, Anatoly. *In Confidence*. New York: Random House, Times Books, 1995.

Dolan, Edward, and Paul Quinn. *The Sense of the 70s: A Rhetorical Reader*. Oxford University Press, 1978.

Downs, Charles. "Residents' Commissions and Urban Struggles in Revolutionary Portugal." In Graham and Wheeler, *In Search of Modern Portugal*.

Drew, Elizabeth. *American Journal: The Events of 1976*. New York: Random House, 1977.

Drossman, Evan, and Edward W. Knappman, eds. *Watergate and the White House: July–December 1973*, Volume 2. New York: Facts on File, 1973.

_____. *Watergate and the White House*, Volume 3. New York: Facts on File, 1974.

Dung, General Van Tien. *Our Great Spring Victory*. Translated by John Spragens, Jr. New York: Monthly Review Press, 1977.

Etcheson, Craig. "'The Number'— Quantifying Crimes Against Humanity in Cambodia." Mass Grave Mapping Project. Phnom Penh, Cambodia: Documentation Center of Cambodia, 1999. Available at www.mekong.net/cambodia/toll.htm.

Fairbank, John King. *China: A New History*. Cambridge, Massachusetts: Belknap Press, 1994.

Falk, Pamela S. "Cuba in Africa." *Foreign Affairs* 65, no. 5 (Summer 1987): 177–96.

Farrell, John Aloysius. *Tip O'Neill and the Democratic Century*. Boston: Little, Brown, 2001.

Feldman, Trude B. "Gerald Ford at 90 Reflects on His Presidency, Prays for Bush." World Tribune. com, August 9, 2003, http://216.26.163.62/2003/ss_ford_07_20.html.

Ford, Betty, with Chris Chase. *Betty: A Glad Awakening*. Garden City, New York: Doubleday, 1987.

Ford, Gerald R. *A Time to Heal*. New York: Harper & Row, 1979.

Frum, David. *How We Got Here: The 70s: The Decade That Brought You Modern Life (for Better or Worse)*. New York: Perseus, 2000.

Galbraith, John Kenneth. "Inflation, Unemployment, and Monetary Policy." In Benjamin M. Friedman, ed. *The Alvin Hansen Symposium on Public Policy, Harvard University*. Cambridge: MIT Press, 1999.

Gallagher, Tom. *Portugal: A Twentieth-Century Interpretation*. Manchester: Manchester University Press, 1983.

_____. "From Hegemony to Opposition: The Ultra Right Before and after 1974." In Graham and Wheeler, *In Search of Modern Portugal*.

Gardner, John W. "Foreword." In Alexander, *Campaign Money*.

Gaspar, Carlos. "International Dimensions of the Portuguese Transition." IPRI. Available at www.ipri.pt/investigadores/artigo.php?idi=3&ida=130#_ftnref32.

George, Edward. *The Cuban Intervention in Angola, 1965–1991*. London: Frank Cass, 2005.

Gergen, David. *Eyewitness to Power*. New York: Simon and Schuster, 2000.

Glad, Betty. *Jimmy Carter: In Search of the Great White House*. New York: W. W. Norton, 1980.

Gleijeses, Piero. "Havana's Policy in Africa, 1959–76: New Evidence from Cuban Archives." *Cold War International History Project Bulletin* 8/9 (Winter 1996). Available at www.wilsoncenter.org/index.

cfm?topic_id=1409&fuseaction=topics.publications&group_id=14051.

_____. *Conflicting Missions: Havana, Washington, and Africa, 1959–1976.* Chapel Hill: University of North Carolina Press, 2002.

_____. "Moscow's Proxy? Cuba and Africa 1975–1988." *Journal of Cold War Studies* 8, no. 2 (Spring 2006): 3–51.

Gold, Gerald, ed. *The White House Transcripts.* Toronto: Bantam Books, 1974.

Goldberg, Paul. *The Final Act: The Dramatic, Revealing Story of the Moscow Helsinki Watch Group.* New York: William Morrow, 1988.

Gorbachev, Mikhail. *Memoirs.* New York: Doubleday, 1995.

_____. *On My Country and the World.* New York: Columbia University Press, 2000.

Graham, Katharine. *Personal History.* New York: First Vintage Books, 1998.

Graham, Lawrence S., and Douglas L. Wheeler, eds. *In Search of Modern Portugal: The Revolution & Its Consequences.* London: University of Wisconsin Press, 1983.

Greene, John Robert. *The Presidency of Gerald R. Ford.* Lawrence: University Press of Kansas, 1995.

_____. "'I'll Continue to Speak Out': Spiro T. Agnew as Vice President." In Walch, *At the President's Side.*

Greenspan, Alan. *The Age of Turbulence: Adventures in a New World.* New York: Penguin Press, 2007.

Griffiths, Martha W. "Introduction." In Jerald F. ter-Horst, *Gerald Ford and the Future of the Presidency.* New York: Third Press, 1974.

Gulley, Bill, with Mary Ellen Reese. *Breaking Cover.* New York: Simon and Schuster, 1980.

Hafer, R. W., and David C. Wheelock. "Darryl Francis and the Making of Monetary Policy, 1966–1975." *The Federal Reserve Bank of St. Louis Review,* March/April 2003.

Haig, Alexander Meigs, with Charles McCarry. *Inner Circles: How America Changed the World: a Memoir.* New York: Warner Books, 1992.

Haldeman, H. R., and Joseph DiMona. *The Ends of Power.* New York: New York Times Book, 1978.

Hare, Paul J. *Angola's Last Best Chance for Peace: An Insider's Account of the Peace Process.* Washington: United States Institute of Peace Press, 1998.

Harsch, Ernest, and Tony Thomas. *Angola: The Hidden History of Washington's War.* New York: Pathfinder Press, 1976.

Hartmann, Robert T. *Palace Politics.* New York: McGraw-Hill, 1980.

Hatfield, Mark O., with the Senate Historical Office. *Vice Presidents of the United States, 1789–1993.* Washington: U.S. Government Printing Office, 1997.

Helms, Richard, with William Hood. *A Look Over My Shoulder: A Life in the Central Intelligence Agency.* New York: Random House, 2003.

Hersh, Seymour. "The Pardon: Nixon, Ford, Haig, and the Transfer of Power." *Atlantic Monthly,* August 1983.

Herzog, Chaim. *Living History.* New York: Pantheon, 1996.

Hetzel, Robert L. "Arthur Burns and Inflation." *Federal Reserve Bank of Richmond Economic Quarterly* 84/1 (Winter 1998).

Hyland, William G. *Mortal Rivals: Superpower Relations from Nixon to Reagan.* New York: Random House, 1987.

Isaacson, Walter. *Kissinger: A Biography.* New York: Simon and Schuster, 1992.

James, W. Martin, III. *A Political History of the Civil War in Angola, 1974–1990.* New Brunswick: Transaction Publishers, 1992.

Jeffreys-Jones, Rhodri. *The CIA and American Democracy,* Second Edition. New Haven: Yale University Press, 1989.

Kahn, Alfred E. "Lessons from Deregulation: Telecommunications and Airlines After the Crunch." Washington: AEI-Brookings Joint Center for Regulatory Studies, 2004.

_____. "Airline Deregulation." *The Concise Encyclopedia of Economics.* The Library of Economics and Liberty. Available at www.econlib.org/library/Enc/AirlineDeregulation.html.

Kennerly, David Hume. *Shooter.* New York: Newsweek Books, 1979.

_____. *Extraordinary Circumstances: The Presidency of Gerald R. Ford.* Austin, Texas: Center for American History, 2007.

Kiernan, Ben. "Cover-Up and Denial of Genocide: Australia, the USA, East Timor and the Aborigines." *Critical Asian Studies,* 34:2.

_____. "The Demography of Genocide in Southeast Asia: The Death Tolls in Cambodia, 1975–79, and East Timor, 1975–80." *Critical Asian Studies* 35:4 (2003).

_____. "War, Genocide, and Resistance in East Timor, 1975–99: Comparative Reflections on Cambodia," July 15, 2003.

Kissinger, Henry. *Years of Renewal.* New York: Simon and Schuster, 1999.

Kornbluh, Peter, ed. "Conflicting Positions: Secret Cuban Documents on History of Africa Involvement." National Security Archive Electronic Briefing Book No. 67.

Kornbluh, Peter, and John Dinges. "Lifting of Pinochet's Immunity Renews Focus on Operation Condor." June 10, 2004. Available at www.gwu.edu/~nsarchiv/NSAEBB/NSAEBB125/index.htm.

Kornbluh, Peter, and Yvette White, eds. "Pinochet: A Declassified Documentary Obit." National Security Archive Electronic Briefing Book No. 212

(December 12, 2006). Available at www.gwu. edu/~nsarchiv/NSAEBB/NSAEBB212/index.htm.

Lemarchand, Rene, ed. *American Policy in Southern Africa*. Washington: University Press of America, 1978.

Logan, John R. "Worker Mobilization and Party Politics: Revolutionary Portugal in Perspective." In Graham and Wheeler, *In Search of Modern Portugal*.

Lomax, Bill. "Ideology and Illusion in the Portuguese Revolution: The Role of the Left." In Graham and Wheeler, *In Search of Modern Portugal*.

MacAvoy, Paul W. *Industry Regulation and the Performance of the American Economy*. New York: W. W. Norton, 1992.

Maier, Karl. *Angola: Promises and Lies*. William Waterman Publications, 1996.

Makler, Harry M. "The Consequences of the Survival and Revival of the Industrial Bourgeoisie." In Graham and Wheeler, *In Search of Modern Portugal*.

Mann, James. *Rise of the Vulcans*. New York: Viking Press, 2004.

Marcum, John A. "Lessons of Angola." *Foreign Affairs* 54, no. 3 (April 1976).

_____. *The Angolan Revolution: Exile Politics and Guerrilla Warfare (1962–1976)*. Cambridge: MIT Press, 1978.

Margolin, Jean-Louis. "Cambodia: The Country of Disconcerting Crimes." In Courtois, et al., *The Black Book of Communism*.

_____. "China: A Long March into Night." In Courtois, et al., *The Black Book of Communism*.

Maxwell, Kenneth. *The Making of Portuguese Democracy*. Cambridge University Press, 1996.

McAndrews, Lawrence J. "Missing the Bus: Gerald Ford and School Desegregation: Rules of the Game: How to Play the Presidency." *Presidential Studies Quarterly*, September 22, 1997.

Mollenhoff, Clark R. *The Man Who Pardoned Nixon*. New York: St. Martin's Press, 1976.

Moore, Thomas Gale. "Regulation: Trucking Deregulation." *The Concise Encyclopedia of Economics*. The Library of Economics and Liberty. Available at www.econlib.org/library/Enc/TruckingDeregulation.html.

Morris, Roger. "The Proxy War in Angola: Pathology of a Blunder." *The New Republic*, January 31, 1976.

National Security Archive. "Luis Posada Carriles: The Declassified Record." Electronic Briefing Book No. 153 (May 10, 2005). Available at: www.gwu.edu/~nsarchiv/NSAEBB/NSAEBB153/index.htm.

_____. "Nixon on Chile Intervention: Declassified Kissinger Transcripts." Electronic Briefing Book No. 110 (February 3, 2004). Available at www.

gwu.edu/~nsarchiv/NSAEBB/NSAEBB110/index. htm ("Nixon on Chile Intervention").

Naughton, James M. "Persuading the President to Resign." In Staff of the New York Times, *End of a Presidency*.

Nelson, Edward. "The Great Inflation of the Seventies: What Really Happened?" Federal Reserve Bank of St. Louis, January 2004.

Nessen, Ron. *It Sure Looks Different from the Inside*. Chicago: Playboy Press, 1978.

Neu, Charles E., ed. *After Vietnam: Legacies of a Lost War*. Baltimore: Johns Hopkins University Press, 2000.

Neustadt, Richard E., and Ernest R. May. *Thinking in Time*. New York: Free Press, 1986.

Niskanen, William A. "A Retrospective." *Regulation* 25, no. 2 (Summer 2002).

Nixon, Richard. *RN: The Memoirs of Richard Nixon*. New York: Simon and Schuster, 1978.

Nünlist, Christian. "Cold War Generals: The Warsaw Pact Committee of Defense Ministers, 1969–90." Parallel History Project on Collective Security. Available at www.php.isn.ethz.ch/collections/coll_cmd/introduction.cfm?navinfo=14565.

O'Brien, David M. "Filling Justice William O. Douglas's Seat: President Gerald R. Ford's Appointment of Justice John Paul Stevens." *Supreme Court Historical Society 1989 Yearbook*. Supreme Court Historical Society Publications, available at www.supremecourthistory.org/04_library/subs_volumes/04_c11_f.html.

Olmsted, Kathryn S. *Challenging the Secret Government: The Post-Watergate Investigations of the CIA and FBI*. Chapel Hill: University of North Carolina Press, 1996.

O'Neill, Tip, with William Novak. *Man of the House: The Life and Political Memoirs of Speaker Tip O'Neill*. New York: Random House, 1987.

Osborne, John. *White House Watch: The Ford Years*. Washington: New Republic Books, 1977.

Osorio, Carlos, and Kathleen Costar, eds. "Kissinger to the Argentine Generals in 1976: 'If There Are Things That Have to Be Done, You Should Do Them Quickly.'" National Security Archive. Electronic Briefing Book No. 133 (August 27, 2004). Available at www.gwu.edu/~nsarchiv/NSAEBB/NSAEBB133/index.htm.

_____. "Kissinger to Argentines on Dirty War: 'The Quicker You Succeed the Better.'" National Security Archive. Electronic Briefing Book No. 104 (December 4, 2003). Available at www.gwu.edu/~nsarchiv/NSAEBB/NSAEBB104/index.htm.

Peres, Shimon. *Battling for Peace*. New York: Random House, 1995.

Peterson, Barbara Sturken, and James Glab. *Rapid Descent*. New York: Simon and Schuster, 1994.

Pilger, John. *Distant Voices*. Vintage Books, 1993.

Polsby, Nelson W., and Aaron Wildavsky. *Presidential Elections*. New York: Free Press, 1984.

Pomper, Gerald M. "The Nominating Contests and Conventions." In Pomper, et al., *The Election of 1976*.

_____. "The Presidential Election." In Pomper, et al., *Election of 1976*.

Pomper, Marlene M., Gerald M. Pomper, Ross K. Baker, Charles E. Jacob, Wilson Carey Mc-Williams, and Henry A. Plotkin. *The Election of 1976: Reports and Interpretations*. New York: David McKay, 1977.

Poole, Robert W. Jr., and Viggo Butler. "Airline Deregulation: The Unfinished Revolution." Competitive Enterprise Institute, December 1998. An updated version is available at Reason.org, Policy Study No. 255, March 1999.

Power, Samantha. *A Problem from Hell: America and the Age of Genocide*. New York: Basic Books, 2002.

Prados, John. *Lost Crusader: The Secret Wars of CIA Director William Colby*. Oxford: Oxford University Press, 2003.

Prendergast, John. "Angola's Deadly War: Dealing with Savimbi's Hell on Earth." Special Report. Washington: United States Institute of Peace, October 12, 1999.

Preston, Paul. *The Triumph of Democracy in Spain*. London: Methuen Publishing, 1986.

Rabin, Yitzhak. *The Rabin Memoirs*. Boston: Little, Brown, 1979.

Ramos-Horta, Jose. *Funu: The Unfinished Saga of East Timor*. Trenton: Red Sea Press, 1987.

Ray, Ellen, William Schaap, Karl Van Meter, and Louis Wolf, eds. *Dirty Work 2*. Secaucus, New Jersey: Lyle Stuart, 1979.

Reeves, Richard. *A Ford, Not a Lincoln*. New York: Harcourt Brace Jovanovich, 1975.

Reichley, James. *Conservatives in an Age of Change: The Nixon and Ford Administrations*. Washington: Brookings Institution, 1981.

Riegelhaupt, Joyce Firstenberg. "Introduction." In Graham and Wheeler, *In Search of Modern Portugal*.

_____. "The Sequence of Events: The Temporal Setting." In Graham and Wheeler, *In Search of Modern Portugal*.

Robson, John. "Airline Deregulation: Twenty Years of Success and Counting." *Regulation*, Spring 1998.

Safire, William. *Before the Fall: An Inside View of the Pre-Watergate White House*. Garden City, New York: Doubleday, 1975.

Schorr, Daniel. *Clearing the Air*. Boston: Houghton Mifflin, 1978.

_____. *Staying Tuned: A Life in Journalism*. New York: Pocket Books, 2005.

Schram, Martin. *Running for President 1976: The Carter Campaign*. Briarcliff Manor, New York: Scarborough House, 1977.

Schullman, Bruce J. *The Seventies*. Cambridge, Massachusetts: Da Capo Press, 2001.

Shenker, Israel. "Gerald R. Ford, the Sixty-Minute Man." In Staff of the New York Times, *End of a Presidency*.

Short, Philip. *Mao: A Life*. New York: Henry Holt, 1999.

_____. *Pol Pot: Anatomy of a Nightmare*. New York: Henry Holt, 2004.

Sikorski, Radek. "The Mystique of Savimbi." *National Review,* August 1989.

Sinha, Dipendra. "Regulation and Deregulation of US Airlines." *Journal of Transport History*, March 1999.

Smith, Craig R. "Speechwriting in the Nixon and Ford White Houses." California State University, Long Beach. Available at www.csulb.edu/~cr smith/nixford.html.

Snepp, Frank. *Decent Interval: An Insider's Account of Saigon's Indecent End*. New York: Random House, 1977.

Southwick, Leslie H. *Presidential Also-Rans and Running Mates, 1788–1980*. Jefferson, North Carolina: McFarland, 1984.

Spikes, Daniel. *Angola and the Politics of Intervention: From Local Bush War to Chronic Crisis in Southern Africa*. Jefferson, North Carolina: McFarland, 1993.

Staff of the New York Times. *The End of a Presidency*. New York: Holt, Rinehart and Winston, 1974.

_____. "Events Leading to the Resignation of Richard M. Nixon," *The End of a Presidency*. New York: Holt, Rinehart and Winston, 1974.

Steenkamp, Willem. *South Africa's Border War, 1966–1989*. Gibraltar: Ashanti Publishing, 1989.

Stockwell, John. *In Search of Enemies: A CIA Story*. New York: W.W. Norton, 1978.

Stone, Elaine W. "The Genesis of the Independent Counsel Statute." Brookings Institution, 1999, www.brookings.edu/gs/research/projects/ic/gen esis.htm.

Stroud, Kandy. *How Jimmy Won*. New York: William Morrow, 1977.

Summers, Anthony, with Robbyn Swan. *The Arrogance of Power*. New York: Penguin Books, 2000.

Szulc, Tad. "Lisbon & Washington: Behind the Portuguese Revolution." *Foreign Policy*, No. 21, Winter, 1975–1976.

Taylor, John G. *East Timor: The Price of Freedom*. London: Zed Books, 1999.

terHorst, Jerald F. *Gerald Ford and the Future of the Presidency*. New York: Third Press, 1974.

Themstrom, Stephan and Abigail. *America in Black and White: One Nation, Indivisible*. New York: Simon and Schuster, 1998.

Thomas, Helen. *Thanks for the Memories, Mr. President*. New York: Scribner, 2002.

Turner, Michael. *The Vice President as Policy Maker: Rockefeller in the Ford White House.* Westport, Connecticut: Greenwood Press, 1982.

Van Meter, Karl. "Cabinda: A Joint Operation." In Ray, et al., *Dirty Work 2.*

Walch, Timothy, ed. *At the President's Side: The Vice Presidency in the Twentieth Century.* Columbia: University of Missouri Press, 1997.

Walcott, Charles E. "Separating Rhetoric from Policy: Speechwriting under Gerald Ford and Jimmy Carter." *White House Studies,* September 22, 2001.

Weber, Ralph E., ed. *Spymasters: Ten CIA Officers in Their Own Words.* Wilmington, Delaware: Scholarly Resources, 1999.

Werth, Barry. *31 Days: The Crisis That Brought Us the Government We Have Today.* New York: Doubleday, 2006.

Westad, Odd Arne. "Moscow and the Angolan Crisis, 1974–1976: A New Pattern of Intervention." *Cold War International History Project Bulletin* 8/9 (Winter 1996). Available at www.wilsoncenter.org/index.cfm?topic_id=1409&fuseaction=topics.publications&group_id=14051.

Westad, Odd Arne, Chen Jian, Stein Tonnesson, Nguyen Vu Tung, and James G. Hershberg. "Working Paper #22: 77 Conversations Between Chinese and Foreign Leaders on the Wars in Indochina, 1964–1977." Cold War International History Project, Virtual Archive. Available at wics.si.edu/index.cfm?topic_id=1409&fuseaction=library.document&id=951.

White, Theodore H. *Breach of Faith: The Fall of Richard Nixon.* New York: Atheneum, 1975.

Wills, Garry. *Nixon Agonistes.* Boston: Houghton Mifflin, 1969.

Witcover, Jules. *Marathon: The Pursuit of the Presidency, 1972–1976.* New York: Viking Press, 1977.

Woodward, Bob. *Shadow: Five Presidents and the Legacy of Watergate.* New York: Simon and Schuster, 1999.

Woodward, Bob, and Carl Bernstein. *The Final Days.* New York: Simon and Schuster, 1976.

Wright, Robin. "Men at War: Angola's Liberation Leaders." *Christian Science Monitor,* December 12, 1975. Available at the Alicia Patterson Foundation, www.aliciapatterson.org/APF_Reporter/Index.html#W.

_____. "Angola's Dogs of War." *Christian Science Monitor,* May 17, 1976. Available at the Alicia Patterson Foundation, www.aliciapatterson.org/APF_Reporter/Index.html#W.

Yergin, Daniel, and Joseph Stanislaw. *The Commanding Heights.* New York: Simon and Schuster, 1997.

Government Documents

Chilean National Commission on Truth and Reconciliation. *Report of the Chilean National Commission on Truth and Reconciliation.* Translated by Phillip E. Berryman. ("Chile Commission Report").

Comision Nacional Sobre la Desaparicion de Personas. *Nunca Mas.* 1984. Available at www.justiceinperspective.org.za/index.php?option=com_content&task=view&id=74&Itemid=119.

Commission for Reception, Truth and Reconciliation in East Timor. *Final Report.* January 30, 2006 ("Timor Commission of Truth and Reconciliation Final Report"). Available at www.ictj.org/en/news/features/846.html.

Commission on CIA Activities Within the United States. *Report to the President.* Washington: U.S. Government Printing Office, June, 1975 ("Rockefeller Commission Report").

Comptroller General of the United States. *Seizure of the Mayaguez.* U.S. Government Printing Office, October 4, 1976 ("Comptroller General Mayaguez Report").

Congress and the Nation, Vol. IV, 1973–1976: A Review of Government and Politics. Washington: Congressional Quarterly, 1977.

Congressional Quarterly 1973 Almanac, Volume XXIX. Washington: Congressional Quarterly, 1974.

Congressional Record, Volume 119, Parts 29 and 30. Washington: U.S. Government Printing Office, 1973.

Economic Report of the President, 2005. Washington: Government Printing Office, 2005, available at http://a257.g.akamaitech.net/7/257/2422/17feb20051700/www.gpoaccess.gov/eop/tables05.html.

Government Accountability Office. "Airline Deregulation: Reregulating the Airline Industry Would Likely Reverse Consumer Benefits and Not Save Airline Pensions." Report to Congressional Committees, June 9, 2006. GAO-06-630 Airline Deregulation ("2006 GAO Report").

House of Representatives Judiciary Committee. *Comparison of White House and Judiciary Committee Transcripts of Eight Recorded Presidential Conversations.* 93rd Cong. Washington: U.S. Government Printing Office, May-June 1974.

_____. *Hearings on Confirmation of Gerald R. Ford as Vice President of the United States.* 93rd Cong., 1st sess., 1973, Serial 16 ("House Confirmation Hearings").

_____. *Impeachment of Richard M. Nixon, President of the United States: The Final Report.* New York: Viking Press, 1975 ("Judiciary Committee Final Report").

_____. *Report on the Confirmation of Gerald R. Ford as Vice President of the United States.* 93rd Cong., 1st sess., 1973, H. Rept. 93-695 ("House Confirmation Report").

House Select Committee on Intelligence. *Final Report.* Reprinted in *Village Voice,* February 16, 1976 ("Pike Report").

House Subcommittee on International Security and Scientific Affairs. "Chronology of the Events in the Mayaguez Incident," Prepared by the Congressional Research Service. *War Powers: A Test of Compliance Relative to the Danang Sealift, the Evacuation of Phnom Penh, the Evacuation of Saigon, and the Mayaguez Incident.* 94th Congress, 1st Session, June 4, 1975.

_____. "Narrative Summary of Mayaguez/Koh Song Island Operation." Prepared by the Department of Defense. *War Powers: A Test of Compliance Relative to the Danang Sealift, the Evacuation of Phnom Penh, the Evacuation of Saigon, and the Mayaguez Incident.* 94th Congress, 1st Session, June 4, 1975.

_____. "Report Dated April 12, 1975 from President Gerald R. Ford to Hon. Carl Albert, Speaker of the House of Representatives, in Compliance with Section 4(a)(2) of the War Powers Resolution." *War Powers: A Test of Compliance Relative to the Danang Sealift, the Evacuation of Phnom Penh, the Evacuation of Saigon, and the Mayaguez Incident.* 94th Cong., 1st Sess ("Administration Evacuation and Mayaguez Report").

Pulsifer, Roy, et al. "Report of the CAB Special Staff on Regulatory Reform." Washington: Civil Aeronautics Board, 1975.

Senate Committee on Rules and Administration. *Hearings on Confirmation of Gerald R. Ford as Vice President of the United States.* 93rd Cong., 1st sess., 1973 ("Senate Confirmation Hearings").

_____. *Report on the Confirmation of Gerald R. Ford as Vice President of the United States.* 93rd Cong., 1st sess., 1973, S. Report 93-26 ("Senate Confirmation Report").

Senate Committee on the Judiciary, Subcommittee to Investigate Problems Connected with Refugees and Escapees. *A Crisis on Cyprus: A Study Mission Report.* 93rd Congress, 2nd Session, October 14, 1974, reprinted at www.cyprus-conflict.net/consequencespercent20-percent2074percent20-senate.htm.

Senate Select Committee on Presidential Campaign Activities. *The Watergate Hearings — Break-In and Cover-Up, Proceedings.* Edited by the staff of the *New York Times.* New York: Viking Press, 1973 ("Ervin Committee Transcript").

Senate Select Committee to Study Governmental Operations with Respect to Intelligence Activities. *Alleged Assassination Plots Involving Foreign Leaders.* Washington: U.S. Government Printing Office, November 20, 1975 ("Church Committee Assassinations Report").

_____. *Covert Action in Chile 1963–1973.* December 18, 1975 ("Church Committee Report on Chile").

_____. *Dr. Martin Luther King, Jr., Case Study.* Supplementary Detailed Staff Reports on Intelligence Activities and the Rights of Americans. April 23, 1976 ("Church Committee Martin Luther King Report").

_____. *Final Report.* 94th Cong., 1st Sess ("Church Committee Final Report").

Senate Subcommittee on Administrative Practice and Procedure of the Committee on the Judiciary. *Airline Charter Fares.* 93rd Cong., 2nd Sess., November 7 and 8, 1974. Washington: U.S. Government Printing Office, 1975 ("Air Charter Fares Hearings").

_____. *Oversight of Civil Aeronautics Board Practices and Procedures.* 94th Cong., 1st Sess., Volume 1, February 6 — March 21, 1975. Washington: U.S. Government Printing Office, 1975 ("CAB Hearings").

Senate Subcommittee on Aviation of the Committee on Commerce. *Regulatory Reform in Air Transportation.* 94th Cong., 2nd Sess., April 6–13 and June 14–17, 1976. Washington: U.S. Government Printing Office, 1976 ("1976 Cannon Committee Hearings").

Statistical Abstract of the United States 1976, 97th Edition. Washington: U.S. Bureau of the Census, 1976.

United Nations. "Report of the Group of Experts for Cambodia Established Pursuant to General Assembly Resolution 52/135." 53rd Sess., 54th Year, Agenda Item 110 (B), March 15, 1999. Available at www1.umn.edu/humanrts/cambodia-1999.html ("1999 UN Report on Cambodia").

Interviews

Interview of William Coleman, Washington, D.C., July 6, 2007.

Interview of Melvin Laird, Ft. Myers, FL, August 14, 2007.

Interview of Melvin Laird, via telephone, August 29, 2007.

Interview of Robert Michel, Washington, D.C., December 12, 2007.

Interview of General Brent Scowcroft, Washington, D.C., October 27, 2006.

Interview Collections

Brown Interview Collection. Walter J. Brown Media Archives. University of Georgia. Available at www.libs.uga.edu/media/collections.

Diplomatic Studies Interview Collection. Association for Diplomatic Studies and Training Foreign Affairs Oral History Project. Available at wttp://memory.loc.gov/ammem/collections/diplomacy/about.html.

Hyde and Wayne Interview Collection. Ford Library. James F. C. Hyde and Stephen J. Wayne Oral History Collection, 1975–1977.

Larry King Interviews. "The Best of Interviews with Gerald Ford," *Larry King Live* Weekend, aired

February 3, 2001, 9:00 P.M. ET. Available at, cnn.com, http://cnnstudentnews.cnn.com/TRANSCRIPTS/0102/03/lklw.00.html.

"Legends in the Law." *Washington Lawyer*, December/January 1998 and January 2005.

Warsaw Pact Generals Interviews. Parallel History Project on Cooperative Security. Available at www.php.isn.ethz.ch/collections/colltopic.cfm?lng=en&id=15304&nav1=1&nav2=5.

Syers Interview Collection. William A. Syers Papers. Ford Library.

Index

ABC 192, 249
Abourezk, James 117
Abrams, Creighton 64
Abu Rudeis and Ras Sudr oil fields, Egypt 133, 135–36, 138, 140
Abzug, Bella 12, 13
ACLU 64
Adams, Henry 39
Afghanistan 101, 229–30
Africa 210–31, 264–65; majority rule 255, 264–65
Agee, Philip 126; *Inside the Company* 126
Agnew, Spiro 3–4, 6–7, 11, 38, 51; bribery scandal 7–8; resignation 8–9
Air Cargo Deregulation Act of 1977 208
Air travel deregulation 203–9
Airline Deregulation Act of 1978 208
Albert, Carl 7, 8, 10, 12–14, 32, 45, 65–66, 86–87, 117, 120, 225
Alexandria, Egypt 139–41
Alexeyeva, Ludmilla 173
Algeria 183, 212, 230
Alia al-Hussein, Queen of Jordan 50
Allende, Salvador 116, 124–25, 265
Allman Brothers Band 247
Allon, Yigal 133, 135, 137–40
Alves, Nito 229
Alvor Accords 213–14
American Airlines 19, 87, 207
American Bar Association 55, 89
American Cancer Society 77
American Conservative Union 256
American Economics Association 72
Amnesty International 162
Amtrak 204
Anderson, Jack 20, 115
Angola 92, 179, 210–31, 264
Antunes, Ernesto Melo 179, 183, 214
Apodeti 236, 238
Arab League 132–33
Arab oil embargo 37, 74
Arafat, Yasser 143
Arbenz, Jacobo Guzman 124
Arends, Les 65
Argentina 265–67
Armas, Castillo 124
Armenia 173
Armstrong, Anne 261
Armstrong, Bob 254
Ash, Roy 85
Ashland Oil 19, 87

Assad, Hafez al- 133–36, 139–40, 142–44
Assassination attempts on Ford 246
Associated Press 65
Associated Press Poll 274
Aswan, Egypt 131, 134–37, 140
Athens, Greece 47, 127
Athens News 127
Atherton, Alfred Leroy 132–33, 141
Australia 235, 237, 239
Austria 137
Azevedo, Pinheiro 183
Azores 181, 227

Bailey, Doug 270, 277, 281
Baker, Howard 13, 122, 261
Baker, James 259, 270, 280
Bakongo 212, 216
Ban Me Thuot, South Vietnam 150
Barbados 226
Barnes, Fred 250
Barnum, John 206
Baroody, William 80
Barre, Siad 230
Barrett, Bob 56
Barzani, Mustafa 129
Bay of Pigs 123
Bayh, Birch 245, 247, 249–50
Beall, George 7
Beame, Abraham 186–92
Becker, Benton 44, 49–50, 58–61
Beecher, William 5
Beijing, China 91, 165, 224, 233–34
Beirut, Lebanon 142–44
Benin 230
Bensten, Lloyd 55, 243–44, 247
Berlin, West Germany 172
Bernhard, Prince of the Netherlands 88
Bernstein, Carl 53
Best, Judah 8
Betty Ford Center 78
Biden, Joseph 154, 217
Big MAC *see* Mutual Assistance Corporation
Binder, Robert 205
Bissell, Richard 122
Blanco, Carrero 183, 185
Blech, Arthur 20
Bolivia 266–67
Bonner, Yelena 173
Bono, Sonny 274
Boone, Pat 274
Bork, Robert 8, 13, 14
Boston, Massachusetts 186–89, 250
Botha, P.W. 220, 226, 228

Botha, Pik 225–26
Botswana 210, 268
Boyatt, Thomas 120
Brandon, Henry 5
Brandt, Willy 91, 181
Braniff Airways 19, 87
Brazil 124, 130, 179, 265
Breyer, Stephen 205–7
Brezhnev, Leonid 50, 92, 94–95, 97–102, 155, 170, 172, 175–76, 198–201, 228–30
Brinegar, Claude 205–6
Brinkley, Douglas 241
British Airways 206
Broder, David 90
Brooke, Edward 30, 64
Brown, Dean 143
Brown, George 93
Brown, Jackson 251
Brown, Jerry 243, 246, 251, 256–58
Brown, Strachley 97–98, 151, 175, 198
Browne, Secor 203
Bruents, Karen 220, 229
Brunswick Paper Company 272
Buchanan, Patrick 7, 26
Buchen, Phillip 39, 42, 51, 127; informal transition team 39–41; Nixon pardon and presidential papers 44, 49–50, 57–61, 63, 65–67; White House counsel 49, 85, 103, 118, 120, 129, 205, 207, 275
Buckley v. Valeo 84, 253
Bulgaria 169
Bundy, William 146
Burdick v. U.S. 57
Burger, Warren 16, 36
Burns, Arthur 31, 39, 41, 46, 72–74, 76–78, 80, 112, 114, 190–91
Burton, Phillip 82
Bush, George H.W. 3, 10, 29, 30, 51–52, 113, 195–96, 229, 241
Busing 186–89, 250
Butler, Caldwell 21
Butler, Pat 70, 197
Butterfield, Alexander 6
Butz, Earl 80, 112, 274
Buzhardt, Fred 17, 23, 24, 27, 32, 49, 66
Byrd, Robert 9
Byrnes, John 39–41, 194

CAB *see* Civil Aeronautics Board
Cabinda, Angola 212–13, 221, 229
Cabinet 40, 42, 70

Caddell, Pat 244, 253, 271, 277, 280
Caetano, Marcelo 179
Calhoon, Jesse 272
Callaghan, James 46, 47, 197, 268
Callaway, Howard (Bo) 195–96, 245–47, 249, 252
Cambodia 31, 45, 146–50, 153–54, 159–67, 235
Cambodia Mass Grave Mapping Project 163
Cambodian genocide 161–67, 240–41
Camp David Accords 131, 145
Campaign Act Amendments of 1976 253
Campaign financing: Nixon campaign violations 19, 22–23, 87, 206; reform 82–87, 90, 243, 253, 270
Cannon, Howard 207–8
Cannon, James 108–9
Cardoso, Leonel 222
Carey, Hugh 186–93, 243
Carlin, Frank 240
Carlucci, Frank 40, 180–82
Carrillo, Santiago 185
Carter, Billy 248, 234
Carter, Jimmy 3, 8; general election campaign 173, 208, 262–63, 270–81; inauguration 282; presidency 74, 89, 92, 100–1, 113, 114, 131, 145, 208, 230, 240–41, 266, 269; primary campaign 243–44, 247–54, 256–59
Carter, Lilian 248
Carter, Rosalyn 258, 279
Carvajal, Patricio 265
Carvalho, Otelo Saraiva de 179–82
Casselman, William 44
Castro, Fidel 122–23, 126, 178, 212–13, 218, 220–21, 223, 228, 230–31
Catholic Relief Service 240
Caulfield, John 6
Cavanaugh, James 108–9, 196–97
CBS 5, 41, 117, 127, 244
Central Intelligence Agency: Angola 210, 212–18, 221–24, 227–29; assassination attempts 115, 117–19, 121–24; Bush replacing Colby 195–96; church committee 117–19, 121–26; coup attempts 116, 122–23, 178; domestic spying 115–16, 119; drug experiments 119; East Timor 237; family jewels report 115–17; Freedom of Information Act 85; Operation Condor 267; oil production, evaluation of 74; Pike Committee 117, 119–21, 126–29; Portugal 178–79, 181, 183; Rockefeller Commission 116–19, 126; scandal of 1975 115–30; Soviet Union, evaluations of 94, 102, 174–75, 198–99; Vietnam and Cambodia 149–53, 155–56, 161–62; Watergate 5, 23
Chanock, Foster 270
Chaplin, Maxwell 266
Charlie Daniels Band 247
Chase, Clifford 213, 224
Cheney, Richard 1–2, 129; assistant to Rumsfeld 40, 104–6; Ford's chief of staff 194, 196–97, 200; Ford's reelection campaign 245–

46, 252, 255, 260–61, 263, 270, 274, 276–77, 280–81
Chicago, Illinois 186, 189
Chicago Tribune 19
Chile 116, 124–25, 130, 178, 180, 215, 265, 267
China 174, 178; Angola, aid to insurgency groups 212–15, 217–18, 224; Cultural Revolution and Great Leap Forward 232, 234–35; Ford's trip to 232–35; Nixon and Kissinger reestablish relations 32, 41, 91, 92; Nixon's trip to 249–50; North Korea 262; power struggle following Mao's death 235; Soviet Union, relations with 233–34; Vietnam and Cambodia 146–49, 164–66
Chipenda, Daniel 214, 228
Christian, Betty Jo 205
Church, Frank: foreign bribery investigation 88; intelligence investigation 116–17, 119, 121, 126; primary campaign 251, 256–57; Vietnam 154
Church Committee 117–19, 121–26
Churchill, Winston 92
Citizen Action Committee 80
Civil Aeronautics Board (CAB) 203–8
Civil Rights Act of 1964 188
Civil Service Commission 85
Clapp, Charles 205
Clark, Dick 217, 224
Clark Amendment 224–25
Clean Air Act 202
Clearwaters, Kenneth 206
Clements, William 93, 143, 153, 166, 199, 262
Cleveland, James 249
Coca-Cola 272
Cochran, Thad 127
Cohen, William 21
Colby, William: Angola 213, 216–17; CIA scandal and investigations 115–20, 127; dismissal 194–95; Mayaguez 164–65, 168; Middle East issues 137; Soviet capabilities, estimates of 94, 102, 174–75, 198–99; Vietnam and Cambodia 149, 151, 153, 155–56, 161
Cole, Kenneth 85
Coleman, William 189, 203, 208
Colonel Callan (Georgiou, Costas) 227
Colson, Charles 5
Committee on Foreign Intelligence 129
Common Cause 82–83
Conable, Barber 4
Conference on Inflation 45, 77–78
Conference on Security and Cooperation in Europe (Helsinki Conference) 140, 169–74, 176, 260, 275
Congress: Angola 210, 217, 223, 224–56, 229, 231; choice of Ford, role in 4, 9–12; confirmation of Ford 12–16; deregulation 202, 204–8; energy 75–76, 105, 108, 110, 112–14; intelligence oversight 115–17, 119–21, 126–27, 129; New York crisis 191–93; 1974 freshman class 82, 86; reform 83–90, 253;

Soviet Union 94–97, 100–1; taxes and spending 77, 81, 108–9, 111–12; Turkey 49–50; Vietnam and Cambodia 41, 146–54, 159
Congress of Vienna 172
Congressional Budget Office 110
Congressional Budget Reform Act 81
Congressional Conference Committee 83, 85, 101, 148, 188
Congressional election of 1974 86, 244
Congressional Joint Committee on Internal Revenue Taxation 20
Connally, John 9, 10, 11, 14, 38
Connor, James 196
Connor, John 117
Conrail 204
Conte, Silvio 9
Continuo, Rosa 213
Conyers, John 12–13
Cooper, John Sherman 10
Coral Island 218
USS Coral Sea 164, 166–67
Corber, Roger 205
Cormier, Eric 65
Cost of Living Council 75, 77
Costa Rica 130
Cotton, Norris 30
Council of Economic Advisors 41, 75–77, 110
Counterspy 126–27
Cox, Archibald 13
Cox, Edward 31
Cranston, Alan 89
Cuba: Angolan intervention 210, 212–13, 218–31, 264–65, 269; CIA activities in 122–23, 125, 282
Cunhal, Álvaro 179–83
Curtis, Thomas 253
Cyprus crisis 46–49, 121, 128
Czechoslovakia 128, 169, 172, 212, 218, 276

Daily News of Tanzania 223–24
Daley, Richard 251, 258
Damascus, Syria 133–34, 136, 139, 142–43
Da Nang, South Vietnam 151–52
Davies, Roger 48
Davis, Nathanial 215–17, 224, 231
Dayan, Moshe 132, 140
Dean, John 5, 6, 18–19, 274
Dean, John Gunther 149, 153–54
Deardourff, Dan 270, 274
Deaver, Michael 246
Decter, Midge 92
Defense Appropriations Bill 224–25
Delta Exploration 163
DeMarco, Frank 21
Democratic Campaign Committee 244
Democratic convention 258–59
Democratic National Committee 4, 244
Democratic primary of 1976 243–59; break in federal funding 84, 253; California, Ohio and New Jersey primaries 258; convention 258–59; Florida primary 251; Illinois primary 252; Indiana, DC, Alabama and Georgia primaries 254; Iowa caucuses 247–48; Massachusetts and Vermont primaries 250; Michigan and Maryland pri-

maries 256; Nebraska and Connecticut primaries 256; New Hampshire primary 248–49; New York and Wisconsin primaries 251, 253–54; North Carolina primary 252; Oregon, Nevada, Idaho, Tennessee, Kentucky, and Arkansas primaries 257; Pennsylvania primary 251, 254; Republican convention 260–63; Texas primary 254

Deng Xiaoping 149, 166, 224, 232–35

Denmark 212

Dennis, David 22

Dent, Harry 260

Department of Agriculture 80, 112

Department of Commerce 85, 279

Department of Defense: Angola 215, 223; FOIA 85; SALT issues 93–94, 98, 194, 198–200; Vietnam 148, 154, 157, 163

Department of Justice 85, 89, 206; Ford's staffing of 70; Nixon's papers 49–50, 57; Watergate 13, 20

Department of Labor 74

Department of State: Angola 213, 215–17, 223–25, 231; FOIA 85; human rights 236, 239–40, 264–67; intelligence investigations 120–21, 123; Portugal 180–82; Sinai II negotiations 233, 236; Soviet Union 176; Vietnam 150

Department of the Treasury 85, 190

Department of Transportation 203, 205–6

Deregulation 75, 105, 110, 202–9

Deschler, Lew 65

Des Moines Register 248

Détente 45, 91–93, 173–74, 176–77, 201, 275

Diem, Ngo Dinh 124

Dili, East Timor 237–40

Dillon, Douglas 117

Dinitz, Simcha 138–39, 141

Dobrynin, Anatoly 50, 92, 94–98, 100–1, 155, 174, 198, 221, 226, 229

Dole, Robert: Vice presidential candidate 261–62, 270–72, 278, 280; Watergate and pardon 22, 30, 64

Domestic Council 52, 103, 108–10, 190, 205

Domestic Council Review Group on Regulatory Reform 202

Dominican Republic 123, 267

Dominick, Peter 30

Donohue, Harold 21

Dos Santos, Jose Eduardo 229

Douglas, William O. 15

Doyle, James 64

Draft evader clemency program 51, 61

Draper, Theodore 92

Drew, Elizabeth 243

Drinan, Robert 6, 13

Duan, Le 146, 149

Dulles, Alan 122–23

Dung, Van Tien 147, 150, 157

Dunham, Richard 108–9

Dunlop, John 170

Dunn, James 239

Duval, Michael Raoul 108–9, 120, 196–97, 270

Eagleburger, Lawrence 120, 180, 197

Eagles 251

Eanes, Ramalho 183

East, Roger 238

East Germany 94, 169, 212

East Timor 232, 235–42

East Timor Truth and Reconciliation Commission 236

Eastern Europe 91, 92, 140, 169–74, 176, 178, 275–78

Eastland, James 32

Easum, Donald 215

Ecevit, Bulent 46, 47

Economic policy 31, 37, 41, 45–46, 72–81, 103–14

Economic Policy Board 76, 103, 108, 112

Edwards, Bruce 279

Edwards, Sheffield 123

Egypt: Angola 212; Lebanon 142, 144; negotiations with Israel 44, 131–41, 144–45; Yom Kippur War 119–20, 128

Ehrlichman, John 5, 6, 20, 22, 23, 103

Eisenhower, Dwight 31, 117, 121–24, 215, 282

Eisenhower Highway Act 204

Eizenstat, Stuart 244

Election of 1976 270–81; Carter organization and strategy 270–71, 279–80; debate 1, domestic issues 272–74; debate 2, foreign policy 39, 173, 275–76; debate 3, general 278; Ford Eastern Europe gaffe 275–78; Ford organization and strategy 270, 278–80; results 280–81

Ellsberg, Daniel 5, 23

Emergency Employment Appropriations Act 81

Emergency Financial Control Board 191

Emergency Housing Act 81

Endangered Species Act 202

Energy policy 37, 72, 74–76, 103–8, 110, 112–14

Energy Policy and Conservation Act of 1975 113–14

Energy Resources Council 70, 103, 106, 108

Environmental Protection Agency 202

Equal Employment Opportunity Commission 202

Equal Rights Amendment 38

Equatorial Guinea 230

Eritrea 230

Ervin, Sam 5, 13, 20, 89

Ervin Committee 5–6, 13, 15, 19–21, 89

Esch Amendment 188

Estonia 169, 171

ETA *see* Euskadi Ta Askatasuna

Ethiopia 92, 229–30

Euskadi Ta Askatasuna (ETA) 185

Evacuation of Phnom Pehn 154

Evacuation of Saigon 157–59

Evans, Rowland 176

Evergreen Magazine 15

Exner, Judith Campbell 123

Export-Import Bank 95, 101, 195

Exxon Oil 87

Fahd bin Abdul Aziz Al Saud, King of Saudi Arabia 134

Fahmy, Ishmael 44–45, 132, 134, 139–41

Fallaci, Oriana 182

Family Jewels, CIA report 115–17

Fatah 134, 143

Federal Bureau of Investigation 5, 14, 20, 52, 125–26, 188, 271

Federal deficit 76–77, 81, 104–5, 108–11, 114

Federal Communications Commission 203–4, 271

Federal Election Campaign Act and amendments 83–84

Federal Election Commission 83–84, 86, 245, 253

Federal Energy Administration 75, 110, 113

Federal Express 204

Federal Power Commission 109

Federal Reserve Board 72–74, 78, 80, 109, 112–14

Federal Revenue Act 83

Federal spending 31, 41, 72, 76–77, 81, 105–12

Fellner, William 80

Finch, Cliff 280

Firestone 87

Fish, Hamilton 21

FLEC 221

Florida 82

Flowers, Walter 21, 22

Flynt, John 87

FNLA *see* Frente Nacional de Libertação de Angola

FOIA *see* Freedom of Information Act

Ford, Betty 3, 10–11, 16, 26, 31, 33–34, 36, 37–38, 43, 55, 77–78, 80, 184, 233–34, 274, 281; breast cancer 77–78

Ford, Gayle 38

Ford, Gerald: Africa, majority rule 264–65, 267–69, 275; Agnew scandal 8–10; Angola 210, 213–19, 222–27, 231; assassination attempts 246; Boston busing 183–86; campaign finance reform 84, 253; character 3–4, 10–11, 38–39, 53–54; China, trip to 232–34; Congress, relations with 85, 88–89; Cyprus crisis 46–49; decision to run for reelection 42–44, 52–53; deregulation 202–9; Dole, choice of 261–62; draft evader clemency 51; East Timor 232, 235–39, 241–42; economic policy 31, 37, 41, 45–46, 72–81, 103–14, 278–79; energy policy 74–76, 105–8, 110, 112–14; Freedom of Information Act 84–86; general election campaign 243, 270–81; Halloween Massacre 194–97; Helsinki Accords 140, 169–74, 176, 241, 275–76, 282; House career 3, 11, 14; inflation fight 72–81, 103, 106, 108, 109, 112, 114, 202, 205, 278; intelligence investigations 115–21, 126–27, 129; last days of Nixon presidency 24–35; Lebanon 143–44, 262; *Mayaguez* 163–68, 262; Middle East policy 44–45, 50, 131–32, 135–45, 275; New

York crisis 186–89; Nixon's papers and tapes 49–50, 57; North Korea 262; Panama Canal 251; pardon of Nixon 55–71, 131, 280, 282; Portugal and Spain 178, 181–85, 275, 282; primary campaign 243–47, 249–57, 259–63, 265; Rockefeller, choice of as vice president 31, 51–53; Soviet Union, relations with 50, 91, 93–102, 169–77, 198–201, 277, 281–82; speeches 45–46, 78–81, 106–8, 110, 111, 153–54, 156; testimony before Congress re: pardon 65–67; transition 36–44, 49, 53–54; vetoes 81, 84–86, 110–12, 204; vice president 17–18; vice presidential confirmation 12–16, 56; vice presidential nomination 9–12; Vietnam and Cambodia, fall of 146–60, 162, 278, 282; Watergate comments 18, 21, 28–29
Ford, John 38
Ford, Michael 38, 55
Ford, Steven 38
Ford, Susan 37, 38, 78, 233–34
Foreign Assistance Act 148, 224, 237
Foreign Corrupt Practices Act 87–89
Foreign Intelligence Advisory Board 117, 175
40 Committee 117, 213–17, 223
Foster, John 175
Foxe, Fanne 86
France 47, 143, 153, 155, 181, 212, 221, 223, 239
Franco, Francisco 98, 182–85
Frangieh, Sulieman 142–43
Frankel, Max 276
Freedom of Information Act (FOIA) 84–86
Freeze on governmental programs 110–11
Frei, Eduardo 124
Frelimo 215
Frente Nacional de Libertação de Angola (FNLA) 211–18, 220–23, 227–29
Frente Revolucionária de Timor-Leste Independente (Fretilin) 236–40
Frey, Louis 251
Friedersdorf, Max 81, 86, 114, 157, 167
Friedman, Milton 77, 81, 103
Fromme, Annette (Squeaky) 246
Fulbright, William 38
Future Farmers of America 79

Gallup Poll 63, 168, 192, 271, 274, 280
Gamasy, Abdel Ghani el- 134–35, 139–40
Garagiola, Joe 279
Gardner, John 82
Garment, Leonard 17, 24
Garrity, W. Arthur 187–88
Gas tax 76
General Motors 45, 46
General Services Administration 58, 61, 67–68
Geneva Cyprus peace conference 47
Geneva Middle East peace conference 132, 136, 138

Geneva Rhodesian peace conference 269
Georgia (country) 173
Georgiou, Costas (Colonel Callan) 227
Gergen, David 3, 17, 24, 38, 53, 63, 64, 70–71, 78, 111, 196–97
Germany 92, 169
Germond, Jack 4
Gerstenberg, Dick 45
Giancana, Sam 123
Giddi Pass 133–40
Gingery, William 206
Ginzburg, Aleksandr 173
Glendale, California 277
Glenn, John 258
Goa, India 241
Golan Heights 131, 136, 138–41
Goldwater, Barry 13–14, 29–30, 31, 32, 52, 64, 121–22, 255
Gomes, Costa 180, 182
Gonçalves, Vasco dos Santos 179–83
Goodell, Charles 38
Goodyear Tire 19
Gorbachev, Mikhail 92, 95, 101, 230
Gorman, Joseph 11
Goulart, Joao 124
Grafenau, West Germany 268
Grain sales 80–81, 112
Granger, Clinton 152
Gray, L. Patrick 5
Great Britain 46, 47, 143, 227, 239, 268–69
Grechko, Andrei 94
Greece: Cyprus crisis 46–49, 128; return of democracy 47, 185; Welsh assassination 127
Greenspan, Alan 38–39, 41, 74, 76–78, 80—81, 103, 105–6, 109–10, 112, 114, 191–92, 196, 202, 209, 279
Grenthko, Andrei 100
Griffin, Robert 4, 39, 41, 66, 224, 261
Griffiths, Martha 3
Griswold, Erwin 117
Gromyko, Andrei 94–97, 99–101, 136, 170, 175, 199, 228
Gross Domestic Product 104, 110
GTE 88
Guatemala 124, 130, 178
Guinea 212
Guinea-Bissau 179, 230
Gulf of Suez 133
Gulf of Thailand 163–67
Gulf Oil 19, 87
Gulley, William 44, 265
Günes, Turan 47
Gur, Mordechai 135
Guzzetti, Cesar Augusto 266–67

Habib, Philip 148, 150, 237, 239
Haig, Alexander: Chile 125; Ford chief of staff 42, 49, 51, 52, 56–60, 64–65, 68; last days of Nixon presidency 24–32, 55, 66, 67; Nixon chief of staff 7, 9, 11, 24–32
Haldeman, Robert 5, 6, 19, 20, 22, 23, 24
Halloween Massacre 39, 194
Halperin, Morton 5
Hammarskjöld, Dag 118
USS Hancock 157
Hannaford, Peter 246

Hanoi, North Vietnam 147, 149
Harlow, Bryce 9, 17, 27–28, 39, 41, 51–52, 66, 194, 261, 277
Harrington, Cliff 163
Harrington, Michael 116
Harris, Fred 245
Harris Poll 80, 192, 271, 274, 280
Hartman, Arthur 47, 127, 182
Hartmann, Robert: comments on Ford 38; counselor to the president 42, 49, 51, 55–57, 59, 61–62, 64–66, 77, 164, 167, 277; Ford's vice presidential chief of staff 17–18, 25–28; speechwriting 36, 70–71, 106, 156, 171, 197, 262
Hatfield, Mark 50
Havana, Cuba 221
Havel, Vaclav 173
Hays, Wayne 82–84, 87, 148, 253
Helms, Jesse 170–71, 252
Helms, Richard 5, 115–17, 123, 125
Helsinki, Finland 169–75
Helsinki Accords 140, 169–74, 176, 241, 260, 275
Helsinki Watch Group 173
Herbert, F. Edward 86
Hersh, Seymour 115–17, 126, 224
Hill, Robert 266
Hills, Roderick 202–3
Hilton Head, South Carolina 271
Hinton, Dean 215
Hitler, Adolph 92, 235
Hoffman, Walter 8–9
Hogan, Lawrence 21
Holloway, James 199, 262
USS Holt 164–67
Holtzman, Elizabeth 67, 117
Honduras 88
Honeywell 88
Hoover, J. Edgar 123, 125–26
House Administration Committee 82, 87
House Agriculture Committee 86
House Appropriations Committee 46
House Armed Services Committee 86, 115–16
House Banking, Currency and Housing Committee 15, 86
House Commission on Administrative Review 87
House Committee on Foreign Affairs 148–49
House Committee on International Relations 228
House Democratic Caucus, Steering and Policy Committee 86
House Ethics Committee 87, 127
House Foreign Affairs Subcommittee on Asian and Pacific Affairs 240
House Judiciary Committee: Ford confirmation proceedings 12, 15–16; Nixon impeachment proceedings 14, 15, 19–22, 29; pardon hearings 65–67
House Military Construction Subcommittee 87
House of Representatives: Agnew scandal 16; Angola 225; economic and energy issues 110–11, 114; election results 281; intelligence investigations 127, 129; reform issues 84–89
House Rules Committee 127

House Select Committee on Intelligence (Pike Committee) 117, 119–21, 126–29
House Subcommittee on Multinational Corporations 88
House Ways and Means Committee 86
Houston Chronicle 64
Hua Guofeng 233, 235, 249
Huambo, Angola 219, 222, 228
Hue, South Vietnam 151
Hughes, Howard 19, 22
Hughes-Ryan Amendment 213
Hultslander, Robert 217
Humphrey, Hubert 3, 12, 20, 64, 108, 243, 254, 271, 282
Hungary 169, 172, 276–77
Hungate, William 65–66
Hunt, E. Howard 5
Huong, Tran Van 156
Hurter, Christian 122
Hushen, John 63
Hussein, Saddam 128–29, 235
Hussein bin Talal, King of Jordan 50, 133–34, 136, 143
Hyland, William 53, 99, 174, 198, 217, 226, 262

ICC *see* Interstate Commerce Commission
Ieng Sary 161
Ilke, Fred 200
India 70, 97, 212, 241
Indiana 82–83
Indonesia 153, 163, 178, 232, 234–42
Inflation 37, 41, 45–46, 72–74, 76–81, 103, 106, 108, 110–12, 114, 202, 205
Ingersoll, Robert 153, 164
Intelligence Coordinating Group 120, 129
Internal Revenue Service 14, 19–21
International Longshoremen's Association 112
Interstate Commerce Commission (ICC) 203–5, 208–9
Ioannides, Dimitrios 46, 47
Iowa Democratic Party 248
Iran 97, 116, 124, 128–30
Iraq 126, 128–29, 212, 235
Israel: aid to Angolan groups 212, 215; Cabinet and Knesset 135–37, 141; Egypt, negotiations with 44–45, 131–41, 144–45; Lebanon civil war 142–44
Issues and Answers 192, 249
Italy 88, 126, 169, 173
ITT 19, 88
Ivory Coast 265

Jackson, Henry ("Scoop"): energy issues 108, 110; intelligence investigations 119; primary campaign 243–44, 247, 250–52, 254, 258; Soviet Union 50, 92, 94–98, 100–1, 200; Watergate 20
Jackson, Mississippi 260
Jackson-Vanik Amendment 50, 95–96, 101
Jakarta, Indonesia 163, 232, 237–38
Japan 80, 88, 97, 233
Jaruzelski, Wojciech 94–95, 174
Javits, Jacob 50, 96, 192, 280

Jaworski, Leon 14, 19, 32, 33, 49, 56–59, 64, 67, 68
Jefferson, Thomas 202
Jenkins, Jim 246
Jerusalem 134, 140
Jiang Qing 232–33, 235, 249
John F. Kennedy Library Foundation 68
Johnson, Lady Bird 274
Johnson, Lyndon 38, 119, 122–25, 133, 251, 272, 274, 282
Johnson, Oswald 194
Johnson & Johnson 88
Joint Chiefs of Staff 36, 93, 194, 198–200, 262
Jones, David 166–67
Jones, Jerry 49, 53, 196, 246, 270
Jones, Phil 41
Jonkman, Barney 11
Jordan 45, 50, 132–33, 136, 142
Jordan, Barbara 22, 258
Jordan, Hamilton 244, 247, 251, 271–72, 276, 280
J.R. Reynolds Industries 163
Juan Carlos I, King of Spain 98, 185

Kalb, Marvin 5
Kalmbach, Herbert 5, 6, 19, 22
Kambanda, Jean 235
Kansas City, Missouri 79–80, 260–63
Kantor, Mickey 257–58
Karamanlis, Constantine 47, 48
Kasavubu, Joseph 122
Katanga, Congo 122, 214
Kaunda, Kenneth 213–15, 217, 264, 268–69
Kauper, Thomas 206
Kaye, Peter 246, 252
Keating, Ken 137
Keefe, Robert 250
Keene, David 7, 259–60
Kelley, Clarence 52, 271–72
Kelly, Bill 182
Kennan, George 91–92
Kennedy, Edward 15, 64, 67, 85, 108, 180, 187, 205–8, 224, 243–44
Kennedy, John 121–24, 146, 282
Kennedy, Robert 121, 123, 125
Kennerly, David 42, 78, 139, 151–52, 246, 281
Kenya 264
Kenyatta, Jomo 264
Kerensky, Alexander 179–80
Kessler, Ronald 125
Khalid bin Abdul Aziz, King of Saudi Arabia 142
Khiem, Tran Thien 153
Khmer Rouge 146–49, 153–54, 161–67
Khoy, Saukham 153–54
Khrushchev, Nikita 171
Killoran, Tom 217
Kim Il-Sung 235
King, Clennon 279
King, Larry 67
King, Martin Luther 125
Kinshasa, Zaire 215
Kirbo, Charles 258, 271, 280
Kirkland, Lane 117
Kissinger, Henry: Africa, majority rule 255, 264–65, 267–69; Angola 214–17, 219–20, 222–26, 228–31, 264; China, Ford's trip to 232–34;

comments on Ford 38–39, 53; Cyprus crisis 46–49; East Timor 232, 235–39, 241–42; in Ford White House 1, 41–44, 56, 58; Ford's decision to keep 31–32, 40; Ford's decision to take away NSA title 194–98; hostility from the right 196, 260; intelligence and other investigations 88, 116–21, 126–29; Lebanon civil war 142–44; negotiations between Egypt and Israel 44–45, 131–41, 144–45; in Nixon White House 5, 8, 9, 24, 25, 30–33, 91, 125, 128, 275; North Korea 262, 264; Panama Canal 251; Portugal and Spain 178, 180–83, 185; South America, trip to 264, 265–67; Soviet Union, relations with 50, 92–102, 170–71, 174–76, 198–201; Vietnam and Cambodia 146–49, 151–59, 164, 166–68
Kleindienst, Richard 5
Koh Rong Som Lem, Cambodia 166–67
Koh Tang, Cambodia 164–67
Kompong Som, Cambodia 164–67
Kosygin, Alexey 94
Kotchain, Carl 88
Kozlov, Mikhail 99
Kraft, Tim 248
Kristol, Irving 92
Kubisch, Jack 47, 48
Kurdistan 126, 128–29
Kuykendall, Dan 56
Ky, Nguyen Cao 153, 156

Lacovara, Phillip 67
Laffer, Arthur 104–5
Laffer Curve 104–5
Laird, Melvin 1, 9, 10, 17, 25, 38, 42, 51, 61, 86, 159, 194, 196, 261
Lake, James 246
Laker, Freddy 206
Laos 147, 149
Latin America 41, 124, 130
Latvia 169, 171
Laxalt, Paul 246, 259
Lebanon 141–44, 262
Lee, Rex 120
Leigh, Monroe 239
Lemnitzer, Lyman 117
Lenin, Vladimir 178
Letelier, Orlando 267
Levi, Edward 70, 120–21, 188, 272
Levine, Mike 203
Levitt, Arthur 192
Lewis, Anthony 12
Lewis, Drew 259
Liberty (the Fords' dog) 78
Libya 212, 230
Liddy, G. Gordon 5
Lincoln, Abraham 16, 51, 65
Lisbon, Portugal 179–82, 239
Lithuania 169, 171, 173
Lockheed 88, 272
London Sunday Times 5
Lopez, Martinho da Costa 238
Lopez, Oswaldo 88
Lord, Winston 32, 133, 197, 233, 264, 269
Los Angeles, California 186, 189, 258
Los Angeles Times 194

Luanda, Angola 211, 213–14, 216–23, 225–26, 230
Lukash, William 76
Lumumba, Patrice 118, 122, 124, 130, 180, 215
Lusaka, Zambia 265
Lynn, James 76, 110–11, 191
Lynn, Larry 39

MacAvoy, Paul 202–3
Macomber, William 46
Magruder, Jeb 6
Mahn, James 21
Mailer, Norman 272
Makarios III 46, 128
Malik, Adam 237
Mansfield, Mike 10, 13, 28, 32, 64, 65, 117, 224
Manson, Charles 246
Mao Zedong 178, 232–35, 249
Marcos, Ferdinand 235
Marine Engineer Beneficial Association 272
Marquette University 126
Marsh, Jack 17, 25, 27–28, 40–42, 55, 57, 59, 65–66, 120, 157, 167, 170, 197, 255, 261, 263, 281
Marshall Tucker Band 247
Martin, Graham 148, 151–52, 154–58
Matak, Sirik 154
Mayaguez 163–68, 262
Mbundu 212
McClory, Robert 21, 120
McCloskey, Pete 3–4
McCloskey, Robert 133
McCone, John 124
McCord, James 5, 6
McDonald, Herbert 163
McGovern, George 64, 271
McNamara, Robert 50
Meany, George 112, 170, 271, 278
Meehan, Billy 259
Meese, Edward 246
Meir, Golda 131–32
Mekong River, Cambodia 148–49
Melo, Galvao de 179
Meloy, Frank 143
Melton, Richard 181
Mengistu Haile Mariam 230
Mercenaries, American use in Angola 223, 227
Merck 88
Methaven, Stuart 228
Meyer, William 78
MFA *see* Movimento das Forças Armadas
Michel, Robert 252, 255
Middle East 44–45, 130–45
Miller, Charles 163, 166
Miller, George 154
Miller, Herbert 58–61, 67
Miller, William 114
Milliken v. Bradley 187
Mills, Wilber 86
Miltich, Paul 56
Milwaukee Sentinal 254
Minh, Duong Van 124, 153, 156–57, 159
Minneapolis, Minnesota 245
Mitchell, John 5, 6, 21
Mitla Pass 133–40
Mitterrand, François 181
Mobutu Sese Seko (né Joseph) 122, 130, 212–18, 221, 235

Moffett, Toby 154
Moffitt, Ronnie 267
Mondale, Walter 12, 121, 240, 243–44, 258, 278, 279
Monetary Policy 46, 72–74, 76–78, 80, 109–10, 112, 114
Monroe, James 39
Moore, Alan 70
Moore, Jonathan 39
Moore, Sarah Jane 246
Moorhead, William 85
Morality in Foreign Policy platform plank 260–64
Moran, Mark 224
Morgan, Thomas 116
Morocco 132
Morro da Cal, Angola 220
Morton, Rogers 39, 40, 41, 76, 194–95, 252, 255, 270
Moscow, Soviet Union 97, 173, 175, 198–200, 218, 228
Mossadegh, Mohammed 124, 130
Most-favored nation status for the USSR 50, 95, 101
Motor Carrier Act of 1980 208–9
Movimento das Forças Armadas (MFA) 179–83
Movimento Popular de Libertação de Angola (MPLA) 211–25, 227–29, 231
Moynihan, Daniel Patrick 70, 170, 174
Mozambique 179, 210, 215, 230
MPLA *see* Movimento Popular de Libertação de Angola
Mubarak, Hosni 136, 139
Mugabe, Robert 268–69
Mulcahy, Ed 222, 224–25
Muller, Hilgard 219
Munich 160–61
Murphy, Richard 141–42
Murray, John 46
Muskie, Edmund 20, 258
Mutual Assistance Corporation (Big MAC) 190–92

NAACP *see* National Association for the Advancement of Colored People
Nairobi, Kenya 268
Namibia 210, 218, 224, 226, 230, 265, 267–68
Namibian peace conference 268–69
Nassar, Gamal Abdul 135
National Archives 20, 44, 68
National Association for the Advancement of Colored People (NAACP) 188
National Bureau of Economic Research 72
National debt 104, 114
National Photo Intelligence Center 139
National Review 171–72, 240
National Security Agency 20
National Security Council 52, 91, 97, 98, 101, 122, 129, 143, 151, 153, 156, 164–65, 167, 174–76, 198–200, 216, 227, 262, 265
NATO 40, 41, 48, 65, 91–92, 94, 128, 169–70, 172, 181–83, 185, 195
Natural gas price controls 37, 75, 105, 113–14
Natural gas shortages 37

Naval Petroleum Reserves 106
Navarro, Arias 185
NBC 61, 254, 280
Nedze, Lucien 115, 117
Nelson, Bill 224
Neoconservatives 91–92
Nessen, Ron 53, 61, 78, 80, 106, 118, 158–59, 167, 192, 196–97, 280
Netherlands 88, 235–36
Neto, Agostinho 211–18, 220–25, 227–29, 231
New Republic 250
New York City 82, 186, 189–93, 258–59
New York Daily News 192
New York Post 78
New York State 189–93
New York Teachers Union 191
New York Times 5, 12, 16, 64, 108, 115–19, 127, 170–71, 176, 224, 237, 240, 259, 274, 276
New York Times Magazine 272
Newsom, David 241–42
Newsweek 195, 245
Nha Trang, South Vietnam 150
Nicosia, Cyprus 47
Nigeria 223–24, 227
Nim, Hu 167
Nixon, Pat 28, 31, 33–34, 60
Nixon, Richard: China, trip to 249–50; choice of Ford 9–12, 16, 51; economic policy 103, 202–3, 205; Ford visit in hospital 64; foreign policy 44–47, 91–95, 119, 124–26, 212, 264–65, 282; last days of presidency 24–35; pardon 55–71, 131, 280, 282; resignation 33–34; Vietnam and Cambodia 146–47, 151, 160, 163; Watergate 3–6, 13–14, 17–23, 38–39, 53, 115, 271–72, 274; White House tapes and papers 6, 18–21, 23, 29–31, 32, 44, 49–50, 57–61, 67
Nixon, Tricia 27, 31
Nkomo, Joshua 267–69
Nobel Peace Prize 32, 159
Nofziger, Lyn 246, 262–63, 271
Nol, Lon 146, 148–49, 153
North Dakota 83
North Korea 164, 166, 212, 215, 218, 221, 235, 262
North Vietnam (including Central Committee and Politburo) 45, 146–57, 159–60
Northrop Corporation 19, 87–88
Norway 173, 195, 212
Novak, Robert 176, 281
Nyerere, Julius 214, 223–24, 264, 268–69

Oakley, Robert 47, 138
OAU *see* Organization of African Unity
Obey, David 16, 87
O'Brien, David 70
Occidental Petroleum 87
Office of Management and Budget 85, 183
Ohio 83
Oil and gas price controls 37, 72, 74, 105–8, 110, 112–14, 208
Oil and gas shortages 37, 75, 114
O'Melia, Richard 205–6
O'Neill, Paul 53, 76, 197

O'Neill, Thomas ("Tip") 9, 10, 12, 13, 22, 53, 61, 282
OPEC *see* Organization of Petroleum Exporting Countries
Operation Carlotta 220–31
Operation CHAOS 119
Operation Condor 267
Operation Eagle Pull (Evacuation of Phnom Pehn) 154
Operation Frequent Wind (Evacuation of Saigon) 157–59
Operation Komodo 236
Organization of African Unity (OAU) 214–15, 221, 226–28
Organization of Petroleum Exporting Countries (OPEC) 37, 74–75
Orlov, Yuri 173
Osborne, John 39, 40, 69, 245
Ostpolitik 91
Ottoman Empire 48, 235
Ovimbundu 212, 216

Packard, David 194
Pahlavi, Shah Mohammed Reza 124, 128–30
Pakistan 97
Palestinian Liberation Organization 45, 132–33, 141–44, 215
Palm Springs, California 152
Panama Canal 251–52
Pan American Airlines 204–6
Paraguay 267
Pardon of Nixon: announcement 62–63; campaign issue 280, 282; discussion of during last days of Nixon presidency 24–28, 55, 57; Ford's decision 39, 55–71; Ford's testimony before Congress 65–67
Paris Peace Accords 146–47, 159–60
Park, Tongsun 89
Park Chung He 89
Parma, Leon 42
Pasadena, California 189
Patman, John Wright 15, 86
Penn-Central Railroad 203
Pennsylvania 82
Peres, Shimon 134–35, 138–40
Pereyra, Argentine Director of International Policy 266
Perle, Richard 92, 96, 174
Perón, Isabel 265
Peru 126, 267
Petroleum Price Review Act 110
Philippines 232, 234–35
Phillips Petroleum 19
Phnom Penh, Cambodia 148–49, 154, 161–62
Pike, Otis 117, 119–21, 126–29
Pike Committee 117, 119–21, 126–29
Pinochet, Augusto 116, 125, 180, 215, 265–66
Plains, Georgia 248, 258, 271, 279
Plains Baptist Church 279
La Plata 218
Playboy Magazine 271, 274
Poage, W. R. 86
Podhoretz, Norman 92
Poland 169, 171, 176, 276–77
Pol Pot 148, 161–63, 235, 240
Poran, Ephraim 138
Porter, Sylvia 78
Portugal 128, 178–83, 185, 210, 212–15, 217, 222–23, 227, 236, 239–41
Portuguese Communist Party 179–83

Portuguese Socialist Party 179, 181–83
Poulo Wei Islands 163
Powell, Jody 244, 253, 271, 280
Presidential Libraries Act 44, 67
Pretoria, South Africa 221, 225, 268
Price, Martin 280
Progressive 116
Proxmire, William 39, 88
Public Group of Assistance to Implementation of the Helsinki Agreements in the USSR (Helsinki Watch Group) 173
USS *Pueblo* 164

Quifangondo, Angola 220
Quillen, James 127
Quinn, Jack 249
Quinn, Patrick 240–41

Rabin, Yitzhak 129, 132–42
Race relations 37, 186–89, 252, 279
Rafshoon, Jerry 240, 271, 279–80
Railroad Revitalization and Regulatory Reform Act 204–5
Railroads 203–4, 208–9
Railsback, Thomas 21, 22
Raoul-Duval, Michael 108–9, 120, 196–97, 270
Ray, Elizabeth 87
Reagan, Ronald: choice of Schweiker 259–60; comments on Ford's tax proposals 108; criticisms of détente 91–92, 171, 176; 1976 primary campaign 195, 172–73, 196, 201, 243, 246–47, 249–57, 259–63, 279; Nixon's consideration as VP 10–12; presidency 114, 230, 240–41, 269; Rockefeller Commission 117
Rebozo, Bebe 19, 22, 27
Recession and recovery 81, 103–6, 109–10, 114, 279, 281
Reed, Clarke 260–61
Reeves, Richard 38
Republic of the Congo 212
Republican convention 260–63
Republican primary of 1976 243–63; break in federal funding 84, 253; California, Ohio and New Jersey primaries 257; Florida primary 251; Illinois primary 252; Indiana, Alabama and Georgia primaries 255; Massachusetts and Vermont primaries 250; Michigan and Maryland primaries 256; Mississippi delegation, battle for 259–60; Nebraska and West Virginia primaries 256; New Hampshire primary 249–50; North Carolina primary 252; Oregon, Nevada, Idaho, Tennessee, Kentucky, and Arkansas primaries 257; Pennsylvania primary 254; Reagan foreign policy attack 172–73, 251–52; Texas primary 173, 244, 254–55, 265; Wisconsin primary 254
Revenue Adjustment Act of 1975 112
Rhodes, John 22, 29, 31, 32, 51, 64, 120, 252, 262
Rhodesia (Zimbabwe) 210, 215, 224, 230, 257, 264–65, 267–69
Ribicoff, Abraham 50, 96
Richards, Ivor 174

Richardson, Elliot 7–8, 13, 39, 88–89, 195–96
Richey, Charles 67
Rifai, Zaid al- 136
Risquet, Jorge 226
Riyadh Accords 144
Rizzo, Frank 254
Roberto, Holden 212–17, 220–23, 225, 227–28, 231
Roberts, Bill 251
Robinson, Charles 112
Robson, John 207–8
Roche, James 46
Rockefeller, Happy 12
Rockefeller, Nelson: domestic policy battles 103–4, 108–10; Ford's choice as vice president 31, 51–53; Ford's reelection campaign 254, 261; Ford's request to not run 194–96, 245–47; intelligence investigation 116–17, 129; *Mayaguez* 164–65; New York crisis 190–92; Nixon's consideration as VP 10–12; pardon discussions 55; SALT discussions 175
Rockefeller Commission 116–19, 126
Rockwell 88
Rodino, Peter 13, 14, 16, 21, 22, 64, 66, 258
Rodman, Peter 133, 138
Rodriguez, Rafael 230
Roe v. Wade 38
Rogers, William 10, 265–66, 282
Rohatyn, Felix 190, 192
Rolling Stone 274
Romania 169, 171, 212, 218, 276
Ronstadt, Linda 251
Roosevelt, Franklin 78
Roosevelt, Kermit 124, 130
Roosevelt, Theodore 33
Roper Poll 274
Rosenthal, Abe 118
Rosselli, Johnny 123
Rostow, Eugene 92
Rota, Spain 98–99
Ruckelshaus, William 13, 261
Ruff, Charles 272, 274–75
Rumor, Mariano 183
Rumsfeld, Donald: Ford's chief of staff 68–70, 103–5, 106, 108–9, 120, 167, 192, 196; Ford's consideration as VP 51–52; Ford's reelection campaign 244; lessons learned from Ford's presidency 1–2, 129; secretary of defense 81, 102, 176, 194–96, 198–200; transition team 40–41
Rush, Kenneth 45, 46
Ruth, Henry 59, 67

Sadat, Anwar 44, 128, 131–42, 197
Safer, Morley 37
Safire, William 4, 5, 7, 20, 27, 171
Saigon, South Vietnam 147, 149–59, 161, 163
St. Clair, James 17, 24, 25, 27, 49
Sakharov, Andrei 173
Salazar, Antonio de Oliveria 178–79
Saloth Sar (Pol Pot) 148, 161
Samphan, Khieu 161
Sampson, Arthur 61
Sampson, Nikos 46
San Clemente, California 32, 44, 50, 56, 58–61, 67, 265

Sandman, Charles 21
San Fernando, California 277
Sanford, Terry 244
San Francisco, California 246, 274
São Tomé e Príncipe 230
Sargent, Francis 188
Sarkis, Elias 143
Saudi Arabia 132–33
Saunders, Hal 133, 138–39
Savimbi, Jonas 212, 214–19, 221–24, 226, 228–29, 231
Sawhill, John 75
Saxbe, William 30, 49, 57–58, 70
SBC 87
Scalia, Antonin 49
Schaufele, William 228
Schlaudeman, Harry 266
Schlesinger, James: Angola 216; Cyprus 46; dismissal 69–70, 194–97; draft clemency 50; intelligence investigations 115; *Mayaguez* 164–68; SALT and Soviet Union issues 93, 97, 98, 100, 170, 175–76; Sinai II 137; Vietnam and Cambodia 150–54, 156–58
Schmults, Edward 202
Schneider, Rene 124
Schorr, Daniel 117–18, 126–27
Schram, Martin 274
Schwartz, Tony 279
Schweiker, Richard 259–60
Scott, Hugh 10, 11, 28, 29–30, 31, 32, 51, 55, 64
Scott, Stuart Nash 180
Scowcroft, Brent: Angola 219, 226; comments on Ford 3; intelligence investigations 129–30; *Mayaguez* 164–65, 167; national security advisor 195; North Korea 262; Portugal 183; SALT and Soviet Union issues 94, 170–71, 198–200, 275–76; Vietnam and Cambodia 152, 160, 162
Scranton, William 39, 40, 41, 194
Sears, John 5, 246, 250, 252, 254, 256, 259–60
Secret Service 44, 49, 196, 246
Security and Exchange Commission 87–88
Segretti, Donald 20
Seidman, William 17, 42, 69, 76, 103–6, 112, 191–92
Senate: Angola 218, 224–27; economic and energy issues 110, 113; election results 281; Ford confirmation 15; intelligence investigations 121, 129; reform issues 84–89, 253
Senate Armed Services Committee 154
Senate Commerce, Science, and Transportation Committee, Aviation Subcommittee 207
Senate Committee on Appropriations 46
Senate Committee on Banking 112
Senate Committee on Governmental Operations 89
Senate Finance Committee 101
Senate Foreign Relations Committee 154, 213, 241
Senate Rules Committee 14–15
Senate Select Committee on Presidential Campaign Activities (Ervin Committee) 5–6, 13, 15, 19–21, 89
Senate Select Committee to Study Governmental Operations with Respect to Intelligence Activities (Church Committee) 117–19, 121–26
Senate Subcommittee on Administrative Practice and Procedure 205–7
Senate Subcommittee on Africa 217, 224
Senate Subcommittee on Foreign Assistance 224–25
Senate Subcommittee on Separation of Powers 89
Senegal 212
Sequoia, Presidential Yacht 27, 30
Shanker, Albert 191–92
Shannon, Edgar 117
Shapp, Milton 245
Shcharansky, Anatoly 173
Shona 268
Shriver, Sargent 244
Siberia 98, 170
Sidey, Hugh 53
Sierra Leon 230
Sihanouk, Norodom 146, 149, 153
Sikes, Robert 87
Silva Porto, Angola 219
Simon, William 41, 74, 76, 103, 105, 108–9, 112, 114, 183, 190–91
Sinai I Agreement 131
Sinai II Agreement 131–41, 144–45
Sirica, John 20, 58
Sisco, Joe 132–34, 138–40, 213, 219
60 Minutes 37–38
Smith, Ian 268–69
Smith, Kendrick 5
Snepp, Frank 126
Soares, Mario 179–83
Solzhenitsyn, Aleksandr 170–71, 173, 260; *Cancer Ward* 170; *Gulag Archipelago* 170; *One Day in the Life of Ivan Denisovich* 170
Somalia 92, 230
Sonnenfeldt, Helmut 5, 98, 176–77, 228
Sonnenfeldt Doctrine 176–77, 275
Sophia, Queen of Spain 184
South Africa 210, 212, 214–26, 228, 230–31, 265, 267–69
South Boston (Southie) 187–88
South Korea 87, 89, 97, 262
South Vietnam 41, 46, 124, 146–60, 163
South Vietnamese National Assembly 156–57
South-West Africa People's Organization (SWAPO) 218, 268–69
Southern Republican Convention 247
Soviet Union: Angola, intervention in 210, 212–15, 217–18, 220–21, 223–24, 226, 228–31, 265; China, relations with 91, 233–34; détente 45, 91–95; Eastern Europe, relations with 91, 170–74, 176, 178, 275–78; grain purchases 80–81, 112; Helsinki Accords 140, 169–74, 176; Jewish emigration 50, 93, 95–97, 101; most-favored nation status 95, 101; Middle East, relations with 132, 135–36, 144; North Korea 262; Politburo 95, 98, 99, 170; Portugal and Spain 178–82; SALT I 91, 93–94, 128; SALT II 92–93, 97–102, 174–76, 198–201; Third World, relations with 92, 95, 125; Vietnam and Cambodia 147, 150, 155, 166
Spain 98, 181–85
Spain, James 46
Spanish Communist Party 185
Sparkman, John 213
Special Action Group 149
Special Prosecutor Law 89–90
Special Prosecutor's Office 49, 56, 58, 67, 89
Speechwriting 36, 70–71
Spellman, Cardinal Francis 126
Spencer, Stuart 246, 251, 261, 270, 277–81
Spinola, Antonio de 179–81, 210; *Portugal and Its Future* 179
Spokes-and-wheel White House staff structure 40
Sporkin, Stanley 87–88
Springer, William 253
Stafford, George 205
Staggers Amendment 110
Staggers Rail Act of 1980 208–9
Stalin, Joseph 94, 235
Standard Oil of California 87
Standard Oil of Indiana 87
Stanislaw, Joseph 75
Stapleton, Ruth Carter 248
State of the Union Address, 1975 106–8
State of the Union Address, 1977 281–282
Stein, Herbert 45, 76
Stennis, John 13
Stevenson, Adlai 252
Stillwell, Richard 262
Stockwell, John 217–9, 223
Strachan, Gordon 5
Strategic Arms Limitations Talks: backfire bomber 102, 175–76, 198–200; bombers 93–94, 97–98, 102, 198; cruise missiles 94, 102, 175–76, 198–200; intercontinental ballistic missiles (ICBMs) 93–94, 97–100, 198; multiple warheads (MIRVs) 93–94, 97–100, 198; SALT I 32, 91, 93–94, 128; SALT II negotiations 91–93, 97–102, 174–76, 194, 198–201, 281; submarines 93–94, 98, 198
Suarez, Adolfo Gonzalez 185
Suez Canal 133–34, 136
Suharto 232, 235–38, 240–42
Sulzberger, C. J. 176
Summit on Inflation 45, 77–78
Supreme Court, U.S. 23, 24, 36, 57, 84, 184, 253
Swann v. Charlotte-Mecklenburg 187
SWAPO *see* South-West Africa People's Organization
Sweden 88, 212
Switzerland 217
Symington, J. Fife 23
Syria 129, 132–33, 138–44, 230

Taiwan 153, 232–34
Tanaka, Kakuei 88
Tanzania 212, 214, 223–24, 230, 264, 268–69
Tasca, Henry 47

TASS 101
Tax cut and surcharge proposals 78, 81, 104–12
Teamsters Union 202, 209
Teeter, Robert 246–47, 261, 270–71, 276, 280–81
Tel Aviv, Israel 135, 140
Temmons, Bob 217
Tenneco 87
Tennessee Valley Authority 257
terHorst, Jerald 41, 49, 52–53, 56, 61, 63
Teton River Dam 257
Texas International 207
Thailand 162–63, 166, 168
Theis, Paul 70, 78
Thieu, Nguyen Van 41, 146–49, 151–53, 155–56
Thomas, Helen 56
Thompson, Hunter S. 244
Thornton, Raymond 21
3M 19, 87
Thrower, Ralph 20
Thurmond, Strom 12, 170–71
Time Magazine 38, 42
Timm, Robert 203, 205–7
Timorese Democratic Union (UDT) 236–38
Tito, Josip Broz 212
Toan, Nguyen Van 155
Toon, Malcom 137, 144
Tower, John 30, 119, 252, 261
Traficante, Santos 123
Transition teams 40–42, 39–41
Transportation 202–9
Trucking 203–4, 208–9
Trujillo, Rafael 123
Truman, Harry 39, 51, 91, 118
Tulane University 156
Tunney, John 224–25, 229
Tunney Amendment 224–25, 227
Turkey 46–49, 129
TWA 206–7
Twenty-Fifth Amendment 9, 12
Twining, Charles 162

Udall, Mo 243–45, 247–54, 256, 258
Udall, Stewart 249, 253
UDT *see* Timorese Democratic Union
Uganda 212, 230
Ukraine 173
Ullman, Al 108, 111
Unemployment 76, 109, 110, 114, 279
União Nacional para a Independencia Total de Angola (UNITA) 211–19, 222–25, 228
UNICEF 229
Union Camp Corporation 272
UNITA *see* União Nacional para a Independencia Total de Angola
United Airlines 207
United Brands 88
United Nations 125, 134, 163, 169, 174, 239, 269
United Nations Conference on Trade and Development 268
United Nations Food and Agriculture Organization 229

United Press International 56, 272, 280
United States Agency for International Development (USAID) 180, 240
United States Air Force 44, 49, 58, 94
United States Army 262
United States Court of Appeals for the District of Columbia Circuit 90
United States Marines 157–59, 165, 167
United States National Guard 188
United States Navy 149, 157, 166–68
University of Chicago 70
University of Georgia Law Day 244
University of Michigan 271
Uruguay 266–67
USAID *see* United States Agency for International Development
U.S. News and World Report 245
U.S. Steel 272
U.S. v. Nixon 23

Vail, Colorado 103–6, 115–16, 148, 270
Vance, Sheldon 215–16
Van der Waals, Kaas 219
Van Deventer 226
Vanik, Charles 95–96
Venezuela 87, 267
Veterans Administration 85
Veterans of Foreign Wars 51
Veto, Ford's use of 81, 84–86, 110–12, 204
Viaux, Roberto 125
Vietnam (post-war) 161, 163
Vietnam Heroico 218
Vietnam War 31, 32, 37, 45, 46, 51, 124, 126, 146–61, 163, 168, 210, 241, 282
Vietnam Working Group 154–56
Viguerie, Richard 245
Village Voice 127
Viola, Roberto 267
Vladivostok, USSR 50, 97–100, 149
Vladivostok summit 98–100, 169–70, 198, 201
Volcker, Paul 114
Vorster, John 219, 219, 221, 225–26, 228, 267

Wage and price controls 31, 45, 72
Waldie, Jerome 15
Waldorf-Astoria Hotel 108
Walker, Robert 246
Wall Street Journal 16, 104, 171
Wallace, George 20, 21, 244–45, 247, 250–55, 258
Walters, Johnnie 20
Walters, Vernon 5, 127, 228
Wang Hongwen 232
Wanniski, Jude 104
War of 1812 159
Waring, Robert 143
Warren Commission 38, 58
Warsaw Pact 91–92, 94–95, 169–70, 173–74
Washington, state of 83

Washington, George 44, 65
Washington Post 3, 16, 22, 50, 87, 116, 125, 174, 205, 223, 245, 259
Watergate 5, 17–23; bribing witnesses 5–6, 18–19, 23; campaign contributions 19, 22–23; campaign dirty tricks 20, 23; destruction of evidence 5, 20–21; effect on public mood 4, 37, 56; election issue 243, 248–49, 278, 281–82; enemies list 19–20; plumbers 5, 23; reforms 82, 87, 90; Saturday Night Massacre 13–14, 89; smoking gun tape 23, 29–31; tax returns 20–21, 22; use of federal agencies against opponents 19–20, 23; White House tape transcripts 18–19, 21; White House tapes 6, 18–21, 23; wiretaps 5, 23
Watergate Special Prosecution Task Force 49, 56, 58, 67, 89
Weicker, Lowell 64
Welch, Richard 126–27
West Germany 88, 169, 181, 212
West Papau 235
Westad, Odd Arne 226
Western Europe 95, 169–85
Weyand, Frederick 151–53
What's My Line 244
Whip Inflation Now 72, 78–81, 202
White, Kevin 187–88
White, Theodore H. 12, 29
Whitehead, Clay 39, 41
Whitlam, Gough 237
Whyte, William 39, 41, 272
Wicker, Tom 119
Wiggins, Charles 29
Williams, Edgar Bennett 195, 274
USS *Wilson* 164, 167
Winston-Salem Journal 64
Witcover, Jules 53, 276
Woods, Rose Mary 19, 20, 23
Woodward, Robert 53
Woolcott, Richard 237
World War II 169, 171

Xuan Loc, South Vietnam 155–56

Yemen 144, 229–30
Yergin, Daniel 75
Yom Kippur War 37, 44, 119–20, 128, 131–32, 135, 137
Young, Andrew 16, 279
Yugoslavia 169, 171, 212, 276

Zacharías, Mojmir 94
Zaire 118, 122, 130, 178, 180, 210, 212–18, 220–23, 225, 227–30
Zambia 210, 212–15, 218, 230, 264–65, 268–69
Zanzibar 230
Zarb, Frank 76, 103–4, 106, 110, 114
Zhen, Huang 164
Zhou Enlai 146, 232–34
Ziegler, Ron 11, 17, 26, 30, 32, 41, 58–61
Zimbabwe African People's Union 268